OS/2 WARP PRESENTATION MANAGER FOR POWER PROGRAMMERS

Uri Joseph Stern
James Stan Morrow

John Wiley & Sons, Inc.

New York • Chichester • Brisbane • Toronto • Singapore

Publisher: Katherine Schowalter
Editor: Theresa Hudson
Managing Editor: Micheline Frederick
Text Design & Composition: Integre Technical Publishing Co., Inc.

Designations used by companies to distinguish their products are often claimed as trademarks. In all instances where John Wiley & Sons, Inc. is aware of a claim, the product names appear in initial capital or all capital letters. Readers, however, should contact the appropriate companies for more complete information regarding trademarks and registration.

This text is printed on acid-free paper.

Library of Congress Cataloging in Publication Data:

ISBN 0-471-05839-4 (pbk)

Printed in the United States of America

10 9 8 7 6 5 4 3 2 1

DEDICATION

This book is dedicated to all of our loved ones:

Uri Stern:

*To Dori, for your love and understanding. You are the greatest.
And to my Mom, Dad, and Brother Irv.*

Stan Morrow:

*To my loving family:
Linda, Chantell, Joey, Jesse, and Jared.*

CONTENTS

PREFACE

For those of us who have been involved in OS/2 in one way or the other as users, developers, or just curious computer geeks, it has been a long, tiresome journey to get our beloved operating system to where it is today. The OS/2 operating system has one of the most dedicated group of devotees espousing the benefits of the operating system. Thanks to the effort of all the OS/2 fanatics, the operating system has matured into the most stable 32-bit operating system available for the personal computer today. This book will concentrate on programming the OS/2 Presentation Manager subsystem.

The first version of the OS/2 operating system resembled the command line interface that was popularized by the DOS operating system. The graphical user interface revolution that eventually conquered the computer industry was just beginning to emerge through efforts like those of the group at the Xerox Palo Alto Research Center (PARC). The Presentation Manager was a cooperative effort of the development teams of IBM and Microsoft. The IBM development originated from the programming labs in Boca Raton, Florida and Hursley, England.

The Presentation Manager GUI interface was first introduced with version 1.1 of OS/2 in late October 1988, and, like the operating system itself, it has grown and matured with each release. Versions 1.2 and 1.3 of the operating system introduced the Help Manager and an enhanced controls library, including items such as the combobox and the spin button. Version 2.0 introduced a radical new graphical user interface on top of the Presentation Manager, known as the Workplace Shell; and new advanced controls, including the container, the notebook, the value set, and the linear slider.

The multimedia presentation manager (MMPM), which had been available separately, began shipping as a part of OS/2 with the release of version 2.1. This provided programmers with powerful new multimedia controls, such as the graphical button and circular slider, as well as secondary windows and message boxes. Version 3.0, or OS/2 WARP, is primarily a performance release. The main body of the Presentation Manager has been converted to 32-bit code and a number of enhancements have been added to the existing library set. New features include pickup-and-drop direct manipulation support and distributed SOM technology.

OS/2 itself is a complete, 32-bit multitasking operating system for personal computers. The system supports multiple threads of execution in each application and provides preemptive multitasking on a thread basis. Various forms of interprocess and interthread communication are available, including shared memory, queues, and semaphores. Utilization of the memory management features of the Intel 386/486 processor family prevents processes from inadvertently corrupting the memory of other processes, and the operating system's I/O architecture prevents corruption when multiple processes attempt to communicate with the same device simultaneously.

OS/2 is gaining acceptance, and more software developers are realizing the potential for writing OS/2 PM-based applications. IBM is thoroughly committed to the OS/2 platform, and the recent merger with the Lotus development organization provides a wealth of possibility for OS/2 applications.

The Presentation Manager Graphical User Interface, or PM, provides advanced mechanisms for user interaction and allows multiple processes to share the video display, keyboard, and pointing device that comprise the system console. In addition to managing the user interface, PM provides facilities for displaying and manipulating graphical information and supplies the programmer with a rich set of predefined controls for interacting with the user. But PM is not a rigid system, it provides facilities that allow the programmer to modify the function of the existing controls, create new controls, and extend the functionality of the user interface.

While the basic concepts and programming techniques have remained the same, many new features have been added with each new release of Presentation Manager. Applications that take advantage of these new features typically provide an interface that is easier to understand and use than applications that are programmed exclusively with the early features. This book, written with the assumption that the reader is already familiar with the basics of Presentation Manager programming, provides an in-depth study of the features available with the Warp release of OS/2. This release provides a powerful, fast user interface that is essential for good graphical programming; it is one of the best in the industry. Quite simply, OS/2 Warp is the "Elvis" of operating systems.

This book and the source code on Wiley's FTP site are designed to provide the reader with a thorough understanding of the powerful features of the Presentation Manager and, where necessary, expand upon these features to help produce state-of-the-art power PM-based applications. The source code is not provided in the book itself because of the size of the samples. A listing of the sample programs from Chapters 2–17 found on the site can be found in Appendix A. Each source file contains well-documented code that explains the practicality of the concepts taught in the corresponding chapter. The code is meant to be used as a reference for the concepts discussed in the book. We sincerely hope that you find this book useful. Application development is the key to the success of OS/2 or any other operating system. Thanks for your commitment, and let's begin the journey.

ACKNOWLEDGMENTS

We have always said that if we ever get this book finished, we would pay homage to all those who have contributed to our efforts or offered their help. So here goes....

We would like to express our thanks and appreciation to the greatest development team on the planet, as well as, those who make OS/2 development and support possible.

- Glenn Brew   Thanks for all your help debugging those funky memory problems.
- Scott Jones   Thanks for all your help and patience!
- Dave Proctor   You are sorely missed at IBM. Thanks for realizing the need to satisfy customers.
- Joseph Correnti
- Albert Kuhn
- Lee Reiswig
- Laura Sanders
- The entire OS/2 Project Office—it's a tough job.
- The entire IBM PSP SWAT team for travelling the globe to debug and resolve OS/2-related issues.

We also would like to thank those individuals who have forged a new frontier for OS/2 through their efforts in promoting OS/2 through exceptional computer publications:

- Will Zachmann
- John C. Dvorak
- Dick Conklin
- Charles Petzold

We would also like to thank our families and friends without whose patience, understanding, and assistance this book would not have been possible.

We would also like to extend special thanks to all of the folks at John Wiley & Sons for helping to make this book a reality and offering their tireless patience and cooperation:

- Terri Hudson
- Terry Canela
- Micheline Frederick

Finally to all those who preach the gospel of OS/2, thanks.

INTRODUCTION

Chapter 1 is a review of the basics and provides an overview of the OS/2 operating system and the tools used to develop applications. The chapter goes on to discuss the basic concepts of PM programming, including anchor blocks, classes, message queues, and window concepts. The chapter also reviews several common PM pitfalls and how to avoid them.

Chapter 2 provides a general discussion of window controls and an in-depth study of the standard PM controls included with OS/2, including the pushbutton, listbox, combobox, spin button, entry field, and multiline entry field controls. The corresponding sample program uses most of the standard controls and shows how to maximize their usage.

Chapters 3 and 4 focus on the Presentation Manager input mechanisms. Chapter 3 deals primarily with keyboard input and describes the application programming required to receive and process user input. The scroll bar control, and the mechanisms required for manipulating the display in response to scrolling requests from the controls and the keyboard are also discussed. Chapter 4 discusses application handling of input from the pointing device, or mouse, and how to control the mouse pointer on the display. The chapter also delves into other pointer concepts and shows how the mouse pointer can be used to create a simple drawing utility. The clipboard and GPI concepts are also discussed.

Chapter 5 describes the OS/2 Information Presentation Facility (IPF). Though primarily concerned with how on-line help is implemented in application programs, the chapter also provides an outline for organizing the help text in a manner that supports the needs of users with different capabilities.

Chapter 6 details the programming required to add power to a PM application by taking advantage of OS/2's superior multithreading environment. As programs become more complex, the multithreading considerations discussed in this chapter become important. It describes how the use of threads can overcome one of the most prevalent problems in PM programming: restriction of the user's ability to interact with the system during the execution of lengthy procedures.

Chapter 7 delves into some of the features of the Workplace Shell interface introduced with OS/2 version 2.0. The direct manipulation interface and protocols that allow the user to manipulate files and other objects with the pointing device are described in detail along with the initialization file APIs that allow an application to restore itself to a previous operating state. The chapter goes on to provide a brief introduction to Workplace Shell and SOM programming.

Chapter 8 describes the use and customization of standard PM resources: menus, keyboard accelerator tables, bitmaps, icons, and string tables. The chapter also discusses the dialog template and the creation and use of dialog and message boxes. The standard file dialog is also described.

Chapter 9 discusses the PM mechanisms for transferring data between applications, including communication between PM and WINOS2-based applications. The clipboard provides a basically static transfer in which one application saves data to the clipboard and another application then reads the data. Dynamic Data Exchange, or DDE, allows dynamic transfer of data by establishing "conversations" between applications.

Chapter 10 describes subclassing, a method for modifying and enhancing the behavior of the system-defined control classes and other existing classes. The chapter also describes how a new control may be created by building on an existing class.

Chapter 11 discusses the advanced controls that were introduced with OS/2 version 2.0. The notebook control, the value set control, and the slider controls are examined.

Chapter 12 is devoted to the container control. This control, which is the basis for the Workplace Shell folder object, is finding wide acceptance in applications that perform operations on sets of data.

Chapter 13 describes the features that were once a part of the Multimedia Presentation Manager but are now included as part of the Presentation Manager family. These features include the graphic button control, secondary windows, and secondary message boxes.

Chapter 14 provides the framework for creating powerful application controls. When the controls provided with PM just do not meet an application's requirements, a new control can be created. Chapter 14 describes how this is accomplished.

Chapter 15 describes the format, creation, and manipulation of bitmaps. All graphics drawn by PM applications are ultimately converted into bitmaps for display on the video monitor. A thorough understanding of bitmaps is thus essential to efficient PM programming.

Chapter 16 describes the manipulation of fonts and explains how an application sends output to a hard copy device. Both of these functions seem relatively complex initially, but are manageable when viewed as a series of small, simple tasks.

Chapter 17 describes hooks, a mechanism that allows applications to modify the internal processing of PM at selected points. Several of the less documented hooks are demonstrated in the chapter's sample program, a simple screen capture utility called **PMSCREEN**.

Appendix A provides an easy reference for the sample source code located on Wiley's FTP site.

Most of the chapters are accompanied by a practical sample program that demonstrates the concepts and techniques discussed in the chapter. These programs were written and compiled using the headers, libraries, and basic tools provided in the IBM OS/2 Developer's Toolkit, now shipped as part of the IBM Developer Connection for OS/2 CD-ROM. The programs are written in C and were compiled with the IBM C Set++ Compiler. Minor changes may be required if another compiler is used.

CHAPTER 1

Welcome to the Presentation Manager for Power Programmers

In the beginning, computers were designed for the technical elite, computer scientists and mathematicians who used the power of the computer to make their jobs easier. Today, the benefits derived from the computer extend to all professions and walks of life, making almost everyone's job easier. Fortunately, while today's power-hungry processors get faster and more complex, the overall usability of the computer has been made easier, thus extending the benefits of the computer to all computer users.

The desire and need for personal computers to be more user friendly has created a whole new genre of computer programs based on the graphical user interface. These applications are designed to be intuitive, fast, and powerful and provide the user with a method of navigating through the complexities of the operating system without the pain of learning how to master the various program interfaces.

Today, it is essential that the native operating system provide close integration to a graphical user interface. The early Apple Macintosh machines were the first to combine the power of the operating system with an intuitive graphical interface. Although the early Macs had some techical shortcomings, the success of the machines demonstrated that there was a market for an object-driven operating system interface. The success of the Macintosh was due in large part to the simplicity of the graphical user interface, when compared with its DOS-based command line interface.

IBM, in conjunction with Microsoft, was in the forefront of the GUI vision, when they jointly introduced the Presentation Manager with version 1.1 of

OS/2. Although this version of PM was really nothing more than a graphical program starter, which seems quite lethargic and primitive by today's standards, it was an innovation for its time. It was one of the first fully integrated graphical programming interfaces inherent to an operating system. The design and feel of OS/2's Presentation Manager would be greatly improved with subsequent versions of the operating system. Despite the shortcomings of earlier versions of the operating system, the Presentation Manager component has been a successful part of the strategy of OS/2.

The current version of Microsoft Windows 3.1, unquestionably one of the most popular GUIs designed for the PC, is very similar in form and functionality to earlier versions of PM, and relies on much of the same design. The popularity of Windows and other GUIs is due to the growing base of computer users who demand the operating system functionality to be transparent, and allow the user the ability to perform complex tasks with simplicity.

The earlier attempts to construct a common graphical user interface that would provide simplicity and ease of use to the end user revolved around common utility programs to perform operating system tasks. For example, a File Manager was used to handle file manipulation and replace the command line by allowing the user to invoke programs directly from the file manager while working with groups of other files. A Print Manager provided the interface to the print subsystem, and a Control Panel guided the user through configuring system resources. Unfortunately, because of the multiple ways a user could accomplish these tasks and the lack of uniformity among these programs, they soon became inefficient and complex for the inexperienced GUI user.

The OS/2 Presentation Manager has evolved into a complete graphical programming environment; and with the addition of the Workplace Shell, an object-oriented environment that is based on the Presentation Manager subsystem, the object paradigm has finally been realized for OS/2. The shell now gives users the capability to think of operating system tasks as objects that interact with one another. Object orientation is the future of computer programming, and a wide array of computer programming languages based on the object technology are beginning to come of age. IBM offers the System Object Model, better known as SOM, which is the foundation for the Workplace Shell.

GOODBYE HELLO WORLD

Since this book is designed for developers with prior PM experience, this chapter will not insult your intelligence with a simple Hello World sample program. Many computer programming books use a simple sample program that usually does nothing but print a simple Hello World greeting to the user, to introduce the programming environment and concepts. Instead, this chapter will review some basic PM programming techniques and focus on the elements required to create sound Presentation Manager applications.

OS/2 COMPILERS AND LINKERS

There are several 32-bit C and C++ language compilers designed for the OS/2 platform. IBM, Borland, and Watcom each offer a comparable compiler; and believe it or not, even Microsoft has a 32-bit OS/2 compiler and although it has never been formally released, it is the compiler that was used to build several of the OS/2 components, including the OS/2 kernel (OS2KRNL). The IBM CSET/2 compiler was not available when the original development of the OS/2 2.x kernel began. Each compiler offers a wide array of features. The choice of compilers is really up to the application developer. All of the source code and sample programs written for this book are built using the IBM CSET/2 compiler. If you are building the sample applications with a different compiler and linker, please consult the programming references shipped with the compiler and linker environment for specific options.

PM INITIALIZATION

As an experienced PM developer, you already know that the first thread of any PM process is used to service the Presentation Manager. In order for any individual thread to call Presentation Manager functions, it must first initialize itself by calling the *WinInitialize* API. The *WinInitialize* API must be the first PM API called by any PM application or PM-based thread. The function returns an anchor block handle, indicating that the initialization was successful. The anchor block handle is used as a parameter to many other PM functions, although functionally the anchor block has very little value, and in most cases, a NULLHANDLE may be passed rather than a valid anchor block handle, and the functions will still succeed.

The intent of the anchor block handle was to provide a unique numbering scheme to identify the particular thread, thereby using this unique handle to initialize an application thread to enable the thread to call the PM API. The contents of the anchor block consist of the process identifier (PID) stored in the high word and the thread identifier (TID) stored in the low word. Although this handle currently serves no functional purpose, you should use caution when specifying a NULLHANDLE for the anchor block handle, since future versions of PM may actually use the anchor block handle for a purpose. For instance, if multiple desktops were implemented, the anchor block handle could be used to differentiate the desktop for a particular thread. Therefore, it is important to always try to use a valid anchor block handle for the APIs that use the anchor block handle as a parameter, rather than passing a NULLHANDLE.

```
HAB APIENTRY WinQueryAnchorBlock(HWND hwnd);
```

Figure 1.1   The WinQueryAnchorBlock prototype.

If you know the window handle use the code shown in Figure 1.1. If you do not know the window handle, you should specify HWND_DESKTOP as the window handle to obtain the anchor block handle. The HWND_DESK-TOP constant represents the desktop window handle, which may be used to represent the thread of the current desktop in use.

MESSAGE-BASED ARCHITECTURE

The Presentation Manager is based on a message-driven I/O design. Each user event is translated into a message and passed on to the application, through its window procedure message processing. The user input mechanisms are represented by the keyboard and mouse, and, in some cases, the pen. As a result of the user interacting with the input device, messages are generated in something called the system input queue based on the order of the occurrence. The system input queue is essentially a routing mechanism that is used to facilitate the delivery of both synchronous and asynchronous messages to the appropriate application message queue.

Sending versus Posting Messages

There are two API's used for getting a message delivered to a window. The *WinSendMsg* API is used to directly send a message to the specified window to be processed by the given window procedure. The code for **WinSendMsg** does not return to its caller until the window procedure completes the processing of the message. The *WinPostMsg* function is a little bit different since it is essentially for asynchronous processing, and it is used to place a message into the appropriate application message queue for the specified window. Basically, **WinPostMsg** places the message in the queue and then returns immediately. One of the most used metaphors to represent the process of sending versus posting says that sending the message is like sending your package via overnight mail—you hope it gets there immediately, while posting your message is more like sending your package for regular mail, it will get there, but other packages will arrive before it and who knows what the post office will do with it.

Using the WinPostQueueMsg API

There may be times that your application code may need to post a message to a particular message queue, but the window handle that represents the window to which the message is to be posted, is unavailable. PM provides a method of placing the message on the appropriate message queue through the use of the **WinPostQueueMsg** API. The prototype for the API is shown in Figure 1.2.

You will notice that the function prototype resembles **WinPostMsg**, with the exception of the first parameter, which is a message queue handle rather than a window handle. Functionally, the **WinPostQueueMsg** API works the same way that **WinPostMsg** does. The **WinPostQueueMsg** API works by building a QMSG structure on the fly and placing the structure on the appropriate message queue, specified by the hmq parameter. The *hwnd* element of the QMSG structure is set to NULL, while the *time* and *ptl* elements of the structure are set to the current system time and pointer position at the time the function is called. The remaining elements of the structure correspond to the passed message and message parameters. The API will return TRUE if the message is placed successfully on the message queue, or FALSE if an error occurred or the specified message queue is full.

Obtaining Information about a Particular Message Queue

A particular function may occasionally need to know information about the calling thread. For example, there may be times when you will have to write a specific API that can be called by multiple application interfaces. If you are writing a communications function that will be accessible by multiple applications, it may become necessary to determine whether the calling thread is actually a PM-based thread. A PM-based thread is any thread that calls **WinInitialize** and creates a message queue via **WinCreateMsgQueue**.

The API *WinQueryQueueInfo*, can be used to obtain information about a particular message queue and also determine whether the thread associated with a particular message queue has access to calling the Presentation Manager API. The message queue information obtained from the **WinQueryQueue-Info** API is in the form of a message queue information structure (MQINFO). The structure contains valuable information about the thread associated with the message queue. The **WinQueryQueueInfo** API will return TRUE if the call is a success or FALSE if the thread does not have an associated message queue.

Figure 1.3 shows the prototype for the **WinQueryQueueInfo** API.

- The **hmq** parameter is the handle of the message queue for which the information structure is being requested for. The message queue handle corre-

```
BOOL APIENTRY WinPostQueueMsg(HMQ    hmq,
                              ULONG  msg,
                              MPARAM mp1,
                              MPARAM mp2);
```

Figure 1.2 The WinPostQueueMsg prototype.

```
BOOL APIENTRY WinQueryQueueInfo(HMQ      hmq,
                                PMQINFO pmqi,
                                ULONG    cbCopy);
```

Figure 1.3   Obtaining current queue information.

sponds to the handle obtained through the **WinCreateMsgQueue** function or the HMQ_CURRENT constant can be used to obtain information about the current message queue.
- The **pmqi** parameter represents a pointer to a message queue information structure. A valid MQINFO structure is returned if the API is successful.
- The **cbCopy** parameter is simply the size of the message queue information structure in bytes. This value is used to determine the maximum number of bytes that should be copied into the **pmqi** parameter. This parameter should typically be set to the size of a MQINFO structure.

The message queue information structure contains valuable information shown in Figure 1.4.

- The *cb* element represents the size of the structure.
- The *pid* element represents the process identifier that the message queue's thread is within.
- The *tid* element is the thread identifier of the thread associated with the particular message queue.
- The *cmsgs* element represents the number of messages within the message queue.

The routine in Figure 1.5 will obtain the process ID and thread ID of the calling thread and display its contents within a message box.

```
typedef struct _MQINFO     // mqinfo
 {
  ULONG   cb;
  PID     pid;
  TID     tid;
  ULONG   cmsgs;
  PVOID   pReserved;
 } MQINFO;
typedef MQINFO *PMQINFO;
```

Figure 1.4   The MQINFO structure.

```
USHORT GetQueueInformation(VOID)
{
 MQINFO  mqinfo;
 PID     pid;
 TID     tid;
 BOOL    rc;

 CHAR    szBuffer[100];

 rc = WinQueryQueueInfo(HMQ_CURRENT,
                        &mqinfo,
                        sizeof(MQINFO));

 if (rc = FALSE)                 // If WinQueryQueueInfo returns FALSE,
  {                              // then the calling thread is not a PM
   return ERROR_NON_PM_THREAD;   // based thread so return ERROR
  }

 else
  {
    pid = mqinfo.pid;
    tid = mqinfo.tid;

    sprintf (szBuffer, "PID = %d TID = %d", pid, tid);
    DisplayMessages(NULLHANDLE, szBuffer, MSG_INFO);
  }
 return FALSE;
}
```

Figure 1.5   **Obtaining current queue information.**

Using WinCancelShutdown

All PM-based applications that do not create additional threads of execution, translate the input from the user by processing messages within the context of the application message queue. However, additional PM-based threads may have no need to process messages if there is no interaction from the user handled within the thread. The additional PM-based threads that do not communicate with the user via message processing should use the API **Win-CancelShutdown** to prevent the application message queue from receiving a WM_QUIT message. The application can call the API with the fCancelAlways flag set to TRUE, right after the message queue is created.

The format of the API is shown in Figure 1.6.

```
BOOL APIENTRY WinCancelShutdown (HMQ    hmg,
                                 BOOL   fCancelAlways);
```

Figure 1.6   **The WinCancelShutdown prototype.**

- The **hmq** parameter is the handle of the message queue.
- The fCancelAlways flag is used to control the processing of the WM_QUIT message. If this flag is set to TRUE, no quit messages are placed on the application message queue during shutdown.

COMMUNICATING WITH MULTIPLE WINDOWS OR QUEUES

There may be times that an application needs to communicate a particular message to multiple windows or message queues concurrently. The API **WinBroadcastMsg** can be used to post or send a message to all application message queues or all descendents of a particular window. For example, the **WinBroadcastMsg** API can be used to get a particular message to every window of an application.

The format of the **WinBroadcastMsg** appears in Figure 1.7.

- The **hwnd** parameter is the window handle representing the parent window.
- The next three parameters are the msg to be delivered along with its message parameters.
- The **rqf** parameter is a flag used to indicate how the message is to be delivered to the window. These flags are known as the broadcast message flags and are defined in PMWIN.H as:

BMSG_POST	0x0000	Indicates that the message is to be posted.
BMSG_SEND	0x0001	Indicates that the message is to be sent.
BMSG_POSTQUEUE	0x0002	Indicates that the message should be posted to all PM threads that have an application message queue.
BMSG_DESCENDANTS	0x0004	Indicates that the message should be broadcast to all of the descendents of the window specified by the **hwnd** parameter.
BMSG_FRAMEONLY	0x0008	Indicates that the message should only be broadcast to frame windows (which is identified as all windows using the CS_FRAME class style).

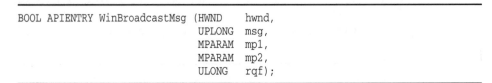

```
BOOL APIENTRY WinBroadcastMsg (HWND     hwnd,
                               UPLONG   msg,
                               MPARAM   mp1,
                               MPARAM   mp2,
                               ULONG    rqf);
```

Figure 1.7   The WinBroadcastMsg prototype.

SEMAPHORE HANDLING

PMWIN provides a set of API functions designed to allow 32-bit PM applications to wait on the 32-bit system semaphores. These semaphore API's are a necessary evil, since they are required to prevent hang situations that are caused by the inability of an application to process input while blocked. The **WinWaitEventSem** and **WinWaitMuxWaitSem** API's are essentially wrapper functions that call their control program API (DOS) equivalents, but these functions differ slightly, since they use a loop to peek the message queue about once every fifth of a second. This essentially allows PM to wait on the semaphore for the thread, so that the thread can continue to process the messages. PM-based applications that do not use the PMWIN semaphore wait calls could potentially hang the system because the application thread cannot process any sent messages due to the fact that it is blocked.

UNDERSTANDING OS/2 MEMORY

For any software developer planning to write successful OS/2 PM-based applications, it is critical that they understand how the OS/2 memory subsystem works. The 1.x versions of OS/2 used a segmented memory architecture, designed around the Intel 286 processor. Unfortunately due to the 64K segment size, there are many limitations that exist in PMWIN based on the 64K size. Fortunately, the OS/2 2.x versions and above are designed around a 32-bit flat memory model that removes the segment boundaries. However, it was not until OS/2 Warp that PMWIN was converted to 32-bit code. Although the 32-bit PMWIN removes a lot of the restrictions caused by the 16-bit PMWIN code, there are still limitations due to the need to provide backwards compatibility with the 16-bit code. For example, the 32K item restriction on the listbox control, still exists because the scrollbar controls used by the listbox use a 16-bit integer value as an index. Any changes made to correct this could cause applications that subclass the controls or hook the messages sent to the controls to break.

It is very important for experienced PM developers to fully understand how memory works in the OS/2 operating system. Since PM is a graphical based interface, it relies heavily on system resources to maintain its appearance. Poorly designed PM applications that do not take advantage of OS/2's superior memory architecture can cause system performance to degrade.

Resource Considerations

In an effort to provide portability across different platforms, developers have become accustomed to relying on the language run-time interface provided by their compiler, and as a result sometimes choose the equivalent language function call over the actual OS/2 API to which the runtime will eventually resolve. One scenario where this can be detrimental to the functionlity of the entire system is in the area of session management.

If you are an application developer who will start different sessions from within your program, be aware that when you are in the PM screen group, you should not use the ***DosExecPgm*** API or the C run-time calls such as *system* or *spawnl* to invoke a non-PM session type. You must use the ***DosStartSession*** API if you are going to start non-PM sessions such as OS/2 fullscreen, OS/2 windowed or DOS sessions from within a PM application. The reason is that **DosStartSession** properly maintains session origination, while the other calls do not. Without a method of determining how and where the session was invoked, the resources are not cleaned up when the session is ended. The result is that overuse of these calls can cause the application to exhaust the heap reserved for session management, and once the heap is gone, the user will be unable to start any other applications. The system may eventually respond by posting an error message like SYS0008 telling the operator that some resource on the machine has been exhausted.

Using the run-time function instead of the equivalent OS/2 API may not necessarily be bad, and in some cases may actually be the best call to use. For instance, care needs to be taken when dispatching individual threads using **DosCreateThread**. Although **DosCreateThread** is the individual API that any run-time **beginthread** function will call, **DosCreateThread** does not set up the run-time environment, and your thread may have problems calling some run-time functions. If this is the case, you should use your compiler's version of **beginthread** to create the separate thread of execution. In any case, using the run-time equivalent of a function allows for portability while, using the API provides greater flexibility since some options may not be available via the run-time library function.

MEMORY-RELATED ERRORS

There are several critical heaps maintained for OS/2, when any one heap is low on memory and unavailable to perform a given task, the application or shell may post an error message, like SYS0008 or PMV2001 or some other, indicating a memory or resource error has occurred. It is also possible that strange visual behavior may occur, such as windows not being updated properly depending on the heap; and in some cases, the system may eventually hang.

It is common that users assume no memory error has occurred since the size of the SWAPPER.DAT file has not grown to the full extent of the fixed disk where it resides. There is no correlation between swapper growth and memory usage to private heap usage. These heaps are a small portion of local storage used for specific memory management, so you can get the dreaded error message regardless of the amount of memory or disk usage on your system.

PMWIN CONSIDERATIONS

Under the OS/2 2.x versions of the Presentation Manager, the window manager (PMWIN) component is still 16-bit code. The largest code change within the OS/2 WARP operating system was to migrate the PMWIN code to 32-bit. There have been significant enhancements made to the design of PMWIN within the WARP release of OS/2. The code for PMWIN is now contained within the PMMERGE library. The move to 32-bit code for the most part provided a complete redesign of the underlying window manager architecture. Most notably, there were several enhancements made internal to PMWIN with regard to memory usage. The PMWIN heap management has been optimized to provide better performance.

Windows Galore

Sometimes, even experienced PM developers tend to lose sight of the fact that every control window is just that, a window; therefore, it requires a window handle or HWND as well. It is easy to forget the fact that static text windows require window handles. Under the OS/2 version 2.x release of the Presentation Manager, there were approximately 12,000 window handles available for use, but this limit is also based on the type of window class associated with the window, since different window classes can theoretically consume a different amount of heap required; consequently, the actual limit on available window handles is reduced. The 32-bit OS/2 WARP PM window manager, allows for approximately 11 times the number of window handles available in a 2.x system, but more important, the only limiting factor is the amount of virtual memory available. Of course, using that many window handles is extremely unrealistic in today's application environment. But then, someone also once said that 640K was enough memory, so who knows what may or may not be a realistic limit in the near future.

AVOIDING THE DREADED BAD-APPLICATION DIALOG

Any experienced OS/2 user has occasionally run into a situation at one time or another where the workplace shell enters a hung state. After patiently hitting the Ctrl-Esc key several times, the user is prompted with what is known as the *bad-app* dialog box, indicating that the program is not responding to system requests; it then prompts the user to end the offending process. OS/2 offers probably the best crash protection system available for PC operating systems, although poorly designed and poorly written applications can still cause problems for the operating environment.

Fortunately, the design of OS/2 and the Presentation Manager allow most hang situations to recover. There have been several changes made to the design of the OS/2 WARP 32-bit PMWIN that aid in preventing bad application code from compromising the integrity of the system. In any case, application developers must share the responsibility of ensuring that the user environment is safe for the user.

There has long been an unwritten rule for PM developers called the 1/10 rule. This rule applies to the processing of messages within the PM environment. Basically, if any message takes longer than 1/10th of a second to process, it's probably way too long, and the application should execute this code outside of the message processing, within a separate thread. In the software world of user interfaces, implementation is everything, and if the user has to see the busy mouse pointer too long, it can be extremely frustrating, let alone potentially causing a hang situation. The 1/10 rule is not written in stone, and almost every application, even the best-written ones, will more than likely violate this rule at one time or another.

The point is that application developers should be mindful of the application user interface, and understand that the user, no matter how uneducated an OS/2 user he or she may be, still desires the ability to multitask by performing different tasks concurrently. We were once told by a developer of a large computerized OS/2 banking system that it was okay for the end users to wait 20 seconds longer, while the single threaded application was processing a transaction, since the application was only designed for bank tellers and they have nothing else to do. Although this may or may not be true, the attitude, that any application can monopolize the user interface can be extremely damaging and is the wrong method of application design. Whether you are developing a simple file management utility or a complex plant floor scheduling application, the design of your application should be taken seriously and special consideration made to designing your application for end users. One of the biggest advantages of programming in OS/2 and the Presentation Manager environment specifically, is the availability of the superior multitasking and multithreading capabilities inherent to the operating system. After all, this is what separates OS/2 and PM from DOS/Windows. Unfortunately, a lack of well written 32-bit consumer applications exist in the software market today, and this can be attributed partially to some application vendors writing lackluster OS/2 applications when compared to their Windows-equivalent products. Fortunately, there are a few exceptions to the rule.

The PM Input Mechanism

In the OS/2 2.x versions of PM, the PM input mechanism was disabled until the application got around to creating its primary message queue. After the first message queue was created, the input mechanism was reenabled, although input was not tied to a particular window until the first window was created, then made visible and finally the recipient of the input focus. At this point, the input was tied to that window and the appropriate application message queue. Applications that attempt to do too much initialization code prior to arriving at the message processing loop can hang the system.

Since implementation is everything, it is important to get the main window of the application drawn as quickly as possible to allow the user to continue to interact with the rest of the system while maintaining the responsiveness of the system. Therefore, if you are designing an application that requires a lot of initialization prior to drawing your frame window, you should call **WinInitialize** and **WinCreateMsgQueue** to create a message queue as soon as possible, then dispatch a worker thread to do the rest of your application initialization. If the user needs to be kept away from the application functionality until the real initialization completes, then you can create a "please wait..." window to indicate that the application initialization is not complete. The goal is to get the first thread to the message processing loop as soon as possible.

DEBUGGING PM

Application developers who desire a powerful low-level debugger, can obtain a debug version of the OS2KRNL along with symbol files for all of the major OS/2 components from IBM. The kernel debugger provides the developer with unparalleled access to the OS/2 API layer, since it allows the developer to set breakpoints on the API functions and step through the code at an instruction level. The OS/2 toolkit ships with an INF reference file for the OS/2 kernel debugger. There are two different versions of the debug OS2KRNL: the all-strict debug kernel contains all of the debug code, while a scaled-down debug kernel known as the half-strict kernel more closely resembles the retail OS2KRNL that ships with the operating system. For the most part, the all-strict debug kernel will be adequate. The half-strict kernel is designed to offer slightly better performance than the full all-strict debug kernel and avoids any timing oddities introduced by the all-strict kernel that may impede the debug process.

There are also debug-specific versions of several OS/2 modules that can be used to assist with debugging. These debug modules are much slower and larger than the retail versions of the modules, because the modules will dump information to the debug terminal to indicate what the current function is up to. To enable the debug output to dump to the debug terminal, the developer must modify the PMDD statement in the CONFIG.SYS file to indicate the appropriate COM port to which to dump the debug information.

If errors occur within the code contained in the debug module, an error message is typically dumped immediately to the debug terminal, although sometimes an error may be recoverable, and the error output may not neces-

```
ERRORID APIENTRY WinGetLastError(HAB hab);
```

Figure 1.8   The WinGetLastError prototype.

sarily be significant. There are debug versions of PMWIN, PMGRE, and PMWP available, as well as PMMERGE for OS/2 WARP.

If you do not require the low-level power provided by the OS/2 kernel debugger, there are several good high-level debuggers that can be used to debug your application. The IPMD compiler that ships with the IBM CSET/2 product is one example of a high-level debugger that can be used by application developers to debug their applications.

The ability to debug your application to resolve code defects is critical to the success of the application. Let's face it, nobody writes perfect code, and the ability to resolve problems in your application quickly, can make a big difference. The application debug stage is an extremely important part of the application software development life cycle, yet often the most overlooked. Good debug tools are an important part of any development effort. There are a variety of good debug tools available for OS/2, such as the kernel debugger, dump formatter, and trace formatter, that can help developers and technical support personnel identify and resolve problems quickly.

ERROR HANDLING

The **WinGetLastError** API is designed to return error information if an error has occurred in one of the previous Win API function calls. The function should only be called if an error occurred to obtain the error, or if the error buffer needs to be cleared which will occur any time the function is called. The prototype for the API is found in Figure 1.8.

The return information from the **WinGetLastError** API consists of two words stored in the returned ERRORID, which is simply a ULONG value. The high word contains the severity of the error while the low word contains the actual error code. The error severity describes the type of error, and can be used to determine how an application should react to the error conditions, while the actual error code indicates the type of failure that occurred. The severities are defined in the header file, OS2DEF.H, shown in Figure 1.9.

```
SEVERITY_NOERROR              0x0000
SEVERITY_WARNING              0x0004
SEVERITY_ERROR                0x0008
SEVERITY_SEVERE               0x000C
SEVERITY_UNRECOVERABLE        0x0010
```

Figure 1.9   The severity definitions.

```
bp _WinSetErrorInfo "dw ss:sp 14;g"
```

Figure 1.10   Tracing errors using WinSetErrorInfo.

The errors are stored through the use of a internal function **_WinSetError-Info**. Application developers can set a breakpoint on this function with the OS/2 kernel debugger to find the occurrence of an error.

The breakpoint in Figure 1.10 is used to dump all of the errors recorded with **WinSetErrorInfo**. It effectively dumps the same information that **WinGet-LastError** would return, except it does it every single time an error is recorded. The breakpoint will display in words the stack represented by SS:SP for a length of four words and continue execution, so it will not halt your system at the breakpoint. Using this information can be helpful in determining where an error occurred.

Figure 1.11 shows a sample debug output.

The actual error codes are defined in the PMERR.H header file, and all begin with the prefix PMERR. Here, the error represented by 1001 corresponds to the error indicating an invalid window handle has been used.

```
PMERR_INVALID_HWND              0x1001
```

```
##bp _winseterrorinfo "dw ss:sp 14;g"

##g
0036:00003f56   04d9 d10e 205b 0008
001f:0000e796   ee49 d0df 1003 0008
001f:0000e79e   ee49 d0df 1003 0008
001f:0000f1aa   d051 d0df 1001 0008
0036:00003f7e   04d9 d10e 2044 0008
001f:0000f0a2   d051 d0df 1001 0008
001f:0000f534   d051 d0df 1001 0008

##ln d0df:d051
d0df:0000ede0 pmwin:_TEXT:TOTALLYBOGUSPMWINCODE + 69
d0df:0000ee57 WINSETWINDOWBITS - e

The first two words on the stack correspond to the return address where the
error was set with WinSetErrorInfo.  If the error originated from your
application code, you will have to walk the stack back to your application
code to find the appropriate routine containing the failure.

The third and fourth word correspond to the error and severity respectively.
In the bold lines above, the routine TotallyBogusPMWINCode within PMWIN
reported an invalid window handle.
```

Figure 1.11   Viewing PM errors via the debugger.

SUMMARY

Many of the subjects covered throughout this chapter and throughout the book may be old hat for experienced PM developers, but it is important to understand the concepts involved in the design of the Presentation Manager before embarking on a long and prosperous PM development path. Therefore, we will provide relevent background information and design considerations along with reviewing requisite subjects occasionally, so that you can thoroughly grasp the subject before viewing the sample source code.

The Presentation Manager and OS/2 have certainly come a long way since their inception. The Presentation Manager API offers application developers a rich set of programming functionality that allows developers to create powerful graphical programs that conform to the Systems Application Architecture (SAA) guidelines for application design. The future of PM development is exciting. Changes made to PM in OS/2 Warp, as well as the enhancements that are currently being designed and developed for the Presentation Manager in future OS/2 family products holds promise for the future of OS/2 and the popularity of native OS/2 PM based applications.

OS/2 has always had exceptional development tools available for application developers. Unfortunately the lack of native OS/2 applications has been the worst thorn in the side of OS/2 users. Although great progress has been made since OS/2 1.x, the road ahead is still long and bumpy. The battle at this time is neither won, nor is it lost. Radical new PM development tools continue to redefine the standards of graphical application design. The intent of this book is to teach valuable PM programming techniques while simultaneously providing insight into the design and development of the Presentation Manager. Now let's begin.

CHAPTER 2

Gaining Control: Mastering the Standard PM Control Windows

A *control* is a child window that can be used to solicit input from a user or provide information to a user. The proper use of control windows can make a susbtantial difference in the usability of the application. Several new controls have been added to the Presentation Manager code throughout the years to allow developers to provide a consistent interface to the user for communication with the application. Version 2.0 of OS/2 introduced several new control windows into the vocabulary of PM developers, including the notebook control, the value set control, and the powerful container control which is an integral part of the Workplace Shell's object-oriented implementation. With the release of OS/2 WARP, most of the basic controls have been enhanced thanks to the conversion of the window manager code to 32-bit. The release of the multimedia Presentation Manager that ships with the OS/2 product lines provides more powerful controls that can be used to enhance the application interface.

But, if the standard PM controls do not offer the functionality that you are looking for, PM provides the ability to modify the control through subclassing, or you can just create your own control. This chapter will focus on the basics of control windows and provide insight into mastering the standard PM controls that are often taken for granted, but critical to providing and obtaining input from the user.

Controls typically process user input and then provide a notification to the control's owner window. Like any other window, the input received from the user takes the form of messages that are processed by the controls window procedure. The code for the basic PM controls reside within the window manager code itself, which in the previous versions of PM was called PMWIN. In the 32-bit OS/2 WARP PM release, the PMWIN code is actually contained in the PMMERGE.DLL library. As part of the optimization required to improve performance for OS/2 WARP, the window manager (PMWIN), graphics engine (PMGRE), and shell API (PMSHAPI) components were combined into a single dynamic link library. Although the individual modules still physically exist in the \OS2\DLL directory, they are now much smaller in size. These modules are still required to support applications that dynamically link to them at load time. The purpose of these modules in OS/2 WARP is to simply forward the request for a given function to the proper location in PMMERGE to satisfy the application.

The standard PM controls are defined by a set of predefined window classes. The basic control windows that we are about to examine are derived from the following window classes. With the exception of the MLE control, the code for all of these controls resides within PMWIN in OS/2 2.x. The MLE code is contained in the PMMLE dynamic link library. Although you should already be familiar with all of the controls derived from the window classes listed here, a simple explanation of the control is provided.

These are the basic PM controls:

WC_STATIC   This window class represents the static window control. It is the most primitive control window. Its only purpose is to display information to the user, thus it is not used to obtain input from the user.

WC_BUTTON   The button window class actually provides three distinct controls: the pushbutton, the checkbox, and the radiobutton. Button windows are used to derive some action from the user.

WC_ENTRYFIELD   This window class represents the entryfield control, the entryfield is an editable rectangle that is typically used to solicit input from the user.

WC_MLE   This is the window class for the multiline entry field. It is used in the Chapter 8 sample program.

WC_SCROLLBAR   This window class represents the scrollbar control. The scrollbar window has very little significance on its own. It is primarily used to scroll the contents of another window, like in a listbox for example. The only input it receives from the user is the movement of the scrollbar slider.

WC_LISTBOX   This window class is used to create the listbox control. The listbox is a scrollable window that allows the user to make a selection from a list of items.

WC_COMBOBOX   This window class represents the combobox control. A combobox combines the functionality of the entryfield and the listbox controls to allow the user the ability to make a selection.

WC_SPINBUTTON This is the window class for the spinbutton control. The spinbutton control is used to allow the user to make a selection from a list of numeric values.

These are the advanced PM controls that are contained within PMCTLS:

WC_SLIDER This window class is for the slider control. This control is used to illustrate some kind of progression to the user. It is discussed in Chapter 11.

WC_VALUESET This window class is for the value set control. The value set allows the user to make a visual selection from a group of objects. This control is also discussed in Chapter 11.

WC_NOTEBOOK The notebook window class. The notebook control is a metaphor for a paper notebook. It provides information to users by allowing them to navigate through different pages of information. This is also discussed in Chapter 11.

WC_CONTAINER This is the most powerful and complex of all the standard PM controls. It allows for multiple views of the same information. It is discussed thoroughly in Chapter 12.

THE PURPOSE OF THE SAMPLE PROGRAM

The OS/2 WARP release of OS/2 contains a handy little utility called the Launchpad. The Launchpad is something that the user community has requested throughout the years. The purpose of the Launchpad is to provide immediate access to frequently used objects and the ability to start applications with a single press of a button. This chapter's sample program is simply called BUTTONS, and its purpose is similar to that of the Launchpad, except that BUTTONS is purely a program starter and does not deal with the manipulation of workplace objects. The BUTTONS program does provide an extremely intuitive interface that allows applications to be started at the touch of a pushbutton. BUTTONS offers a customizable user interface and allows applications to be configured with relative ease.

BUTTONS also provides graphical pushbuttons for lockup and shutdown. Figure 2.1 illustrates the sample program.

The sample program demonstrates most of the remaining basic PM controls. The comfortable button interface is created through the use of graphical pushbuttons. The BUTTONS control panel features the other remaining basic PM controls to configure and maintain the interface of the application.

Figure 2.1   The BUTTONS interface.

CONTROLS IN DIALOGS

The dialog box functionality allows the basic PM controls to be created and maintained more easily. The control window is created from the window keyword in the resource script file specifying the type of control that is to be created. It is far more efficient to create the basic controls in dialog boxes since the dialog box logic makes it easier to handle the sizing and positioning of the control within the dialog along with the simplicity of moving the keyboard input focus between controls.

Types of Controls

There are three basic types of PM controls that all controls, even those not provided as part of the Presentation Manager fall into. The basic categories are the *output only control*, the *input only control*, and the *combination input and output control*. The purpose of the output only control is simply to allow the application to display something to the user. The output only control type is the simplest since the user cannot interact in any way with the control, and the control does not need to provide communication to its owner window. Examples of this control type include the static text window and the groupbox.

The input only control type is a little more complex. The purpose of this control type is to allow the user to make a selection based on what the control displays to the user. This control type allows the user to manipulate the control to provide information (input) back to the application based on the user's selection or movement of the control. The pushbutton, radiobutton, checkbox, and scroll bar controls are classic examples of the input only control type.

Finally, the most complex control type combines both input and output communication methods between the control and the application. These types of controls provide information to the user while simultaneously allowing the user to make selections based on the information provided. The listbox, combobox, and spinbutton are all examples of the input/output control type. The entryfield and multiline entryfield controls are also derived from this control type since they can provide either input or output information, thus acting as a communication mechanism between the user and the application.

It is important to remember that a control is nothing more than a window based on a defined window class that is developed to be used by independent applications. Controls are usually designed to act as independent paradigms so that they can function without any specific application code. A properly designed control is a window that has no relation to any other window within your application. In other words, although a scroll bar may be used to scroll the contents of a window in your application, can the same scroll bar control window be used with any application? When designing a control window try to imagine it as the only window other than the desktop window. The design of the control window will be thoroughly discussed in Chapter 14.

CREATING THE CONTROL WINDOW

When a control window is created outside of a dialog window, the developer is responsible for creating the control through the use of the *WinCreateWindow* API. Although you should already be familiar with creating windows by using this function, there are several parameters that are specific to control window creation, so it is a good idea to review this API. The prototype for the function is given in Figure 2.2.

- The **hwndParent** parameter is the handle of the parent window. This parameter can be set to the desktop window, HWND_DESKTOP, to create a

```
HWND APIENTRY WinCreateWindow(HWND    hwndParent,
                              PSZ     pszClass,
                              PSZ     pszName,
                              ULONG   flStyle,
                              LONG    x,
                              LONG    y,
                              LONG    cx,
                              LONG    cy,
                              HWND    hwndOwner,
                              HWND    hwndInsertBehind,
                              ULONG   id,
                              PVOID   pCtlData,
                              PVOID   pPresParams);
```

Figure 2.2   WinCreateWindow.

top-level frame window. This parameter can also be set to HWND_OBJECT
to create an object window.

- The **pszClass** parameter is the window class name field. All window classes
  must either be registered through the use of **WinRegisterClass** or be a
  predefined public window class. The predefined public window classes are
  identified by the WC_ constants in PMWIN.H.
- The **pszName** parameter is a null-terminated string that represents the
  window text for the window being defined. Whether the window text is
  visible in the window is based on the type of window class for the window
  being created. For example, some control windows display text as part of
  the control, like a pushbutton. Other control windows, like the scrollbar,
  have no need for the text. Keep in mind that the window text represented
  by this string is an initial value and can be changed through the use of the
  WinSetWindowText API.
- The **flStyle** parameter specifies the window styles that are to be used for
  the window being created. The style flags are combined to create the appearance of the window. The window style identifier WS_VISIBLE can be
  used if the window is designed to be visible immediately after its creation.
  If the window is not initially visible, it will be created but not shown. The
  APIs **WinShowWindow** or **WinSetWindowPos** with the SWP_SHOW flag
  can then be used to ultimately show the window. Other than the visibility
  style, this value can be used to represent window styles that are dependent
  on the type of window class being created. For example, when you create
  a control window based on the WC_BUTTON window class, this parameter is used to identify whether the button is a pushbutton, radiobutton, or
  checkbox, and is also used to define the behavior of the button.
- The **x** parameter is simply the initial horizontal coordinate for the window.
  The value represents a window coordinate that is based on the origin of
  the parent window.
- The **y** parameter is simply the initial vertical coordinate for the window.
  The value represents a window coordinate that is based on the origin of
  the parent window.
- The **cx** parameter is the horizontal width of the window in window coordinates.
- The **cy** parameter is the vertical length of the window in window coordinates.
- The **hwndOwner** parameter represents the owner window. The owner window is the window to which messages are typically sent for controls. When
  the window represented by the **hwndOwner** window handle is destroyed,
  all windows that it owns are also destroyed.
- The **hwndInsertBehind** parameter is used to identify the placement of the
  window. This parameter represents the sibling window behind which the
  created window will be placed. This parameter can be set to the values
  of HWND_TOP or HWND_BOTTOM. If this value is HWND_TOP, the win-

dow that is created is placed on top of all its sibling windows. If this value is HWND_BOTTOM, it is placed on the bottom of all its sibling windows in the ZORDER. This value must either be the constant HWND_TOP, HWND_BOTTOM, or a window handle that is a child of the parent window.

- The **id** parameter is used to specify a window identifier. Typically, the window identifier is a unique number that is used to represent the relationship of the window to other windows. For example, if an application creates multiple control windows, each control window gets a unique ID that identifies the window, so that the owner window can determine which of the control windows initiated the notification. An application can obtain the associated window handle from the window identifier by calling the **WinWindowFromID** API.

- The **pCtlData** parameter is a pointer to a data structure that is specific for the control window being created. Therefore, the structure that is represented by this pointer is based on the window class of the window being created. The structure is automatically passed as part of the WM_CREATE message processing. Since the data of the structure can vary based on the control window being created, the first two bytes of the structure referenced by this pointer should contain the total size of the structure to be passed. This structure is very important since it contains control data for the type of control. For example, button class windows use the BTNCDATA structure while scroll bars use the SBCDATA structure.

- The **pPresParams** parameter is a pointer to presentation parameter information based on the window class of the window being created.

UNDERSTANDING THE OWNER AND PARENT WINDOW RELATIONSHIPS

The owner window and parent window both have a distinct relationship to the control window that is created. Unfortunately, these windows are often confused for one another. Understanding their differences is critical to mastering the philosophy of the control window. Although it is common for a control window to use the same window for the owner and parent, it is important to understand the difference in case it becomes necessary to have a window other than the window where the control is drawn on to process notification messages for the control. When a control window is created through the use of **WinCreateWindow**, the parent and owner window handles are specified through the use of the **hwndParent** and **hwndOwner** parameters.

The purpose of the parent window is to determine the positioning for the control window. The window coordinates of the control window specified by x, y, cx, and cy represent the coordinates of the control window relative to the lower left corner of the parent window. Therefore, the control window is relative to the position of its parent window, so that when the parent window is moved, the control window is also moved and repositioned based on the coordinates. As with any child window, a control window cannot be viewed outside the boundaries of its parent, meaning that the control will be clipped on the basis of its parent.

The purpose of the owner window is to process the notification messages that are sent by the control. In other words, the window procedure for the window represented by **hwndOwner** will get the notification messages for the control window that is created. For example, the iconic pushbuttons created by the BUTTONS program are drawn within the client window of the application. Therefore, it makes sense that the individual pushbutton control windows use the client window as the owner of the pushbuttons, which means that the client window procedure represented by **ClientWndProc** will be responsible for handling the button notification messages.

Control Window Communication Messages

For the application to communicate with the control, several messages are defined that are specific to the control. The messages are sent to the control window through the use of the **WinSendMsg** API function. The purpose of the control window communication messages is to allow the application to query or set the state of the control.

Control Window Notification Messages

Notification messages are messages that are sent to the owner window from the control based on input from the user. The input is triggered by the user manipulating the control, usually by clicking on it or pressing a key that corresponds to the control while the control has input focus. The notification messages let the application control the functionality of the individual control by allowing the developer to determine the action for the control to take. The notification messages received by the owner window are usually in the form of WM_COMMAND or WM_CONTROL messages, which are used to determine the visual impact that the control will take once the input from the user is completed.

Using Control Data

The function **WinCreateWindow** allows you to pass a pointer to a control data structure. The pointer is used to point to a structure containing the control data for the particular window. The first element of the structure must be a USHORT value that contains the size of the structure. The element containing the size of the structure is extremely important since it is used internally to determine the size of the available control data. Determining the size is extremely important because the control data may overlap a segment boundary. Knowing the size of the structure allows the Presentation Manager to ensure that the entire structure fits within a single segment.

The Button Window Class

The button window class is one of the simplest class types, yet it offers powerful functionality because the appearance of the button can be altered to create several different control windows derived from the same WC_BUTTON window class. The button styles are used to determine the appearance that the button control will take. The primary button styles that are used to determine the control's appearance are shown in Figure 2.3.

- The BS_PUSHBUTTON style is used to create a standard pushbutton control window. The pushbutton is a window that generally contains text, but may also contain a graphical image, like a bitmap or icon.
- The BS_CHECKBOX style is used to create the checkbox control window. As its name denotes, a checkbox is a small square pushbutton with a specified text string to its right. Checkboxes are used to allow the user to select an option via the selection. Checkbox controls are usually independent of each other.
- The BS_AUTOCHECKBOX style is similar to the BS_CHECKBOX style except that this control type will automically toggle its check state after the user has interacted with it by selecting it with the mouse pointer or by pressing the Spacebar.
- The BS_RADIOBUTTON style is used to create the radiobutton control. Unlike the checkbox control, radiobuttons are not independent of one another. They allow the user to select an individual option from a series of choices represented by the radiobuttons.
- The BS_AUTORADIOBUTTON style is used to create an automatic radiobutton. When this button style is used for a group of radiobuttons, and the button is clicked, it highlights the selected button while unhighlighting all other radiobuttons within the group. The group of radiobuttons is specified through the use of the WS_GROUP window style.

```
BS_PUSHBUTTON            0L
BS_CHECKBOX              1L
BS_AUTOCHECKBOX          2L
BS_RADIOBUTTON          3L
BS_AUTORADIOBUTTON      4L
BS_3STATE               5L
BS_AUTO3STATE           6L
BS_USERBUTTON           7L
```

Figure 2.3   Primary button window styles.

- The BS_3STATE style is used to create a checkbox control window that visually contains three display states. In addition to the checkbox button being checked or unchecked, it can also be halftoned to provide an additional button state to the user.
- The BS_AUTO3STATE style—you guessed it—is exactly like the BS_3STATE style except that the state of the checkbox is automatically toggled when the user selects it.

```
DLGTEMPLATE IDD_SETUP LOADONCALL MOVEABLE DISCARDABLE
{
 DIALOG "BUTTONS - Configure Program Buttons", IDD_SETUP, 32, 32, 330, 200,, FCF_DLGBORDER | FCF_SYSMENU | FCF_TITLEBAR |
                                                                              FCF_TASKLIST | FCF_MINBUTTON
 {
  CONTROL        ID_MAINWND,                   ID_MAINWND,      25, 120,  21, 21, WC_STATIC, SS_ICON |
                                                                                  WS_GROUP | WS_VISIBLE
  GROUPBOX       "Program Icon"                -1                3, 115,  70, 30
  PUSHBUTTON "~Find..."                        DID_FIND,       250, 170,  40, 16,
  LTEXT "Program File"                         ID_TEXT,         10, 180,  70,  8
  ENTRYFIELD      ""                           IDE_EXECUTABLE,  90, 180, 130,  8, ES_MARGIN

  LTEXT "Parameters"                           ID_TEXT,         10, 165,  70,  8

  ENTRYFIELD      ""                           IDE_PARAMETERS,  90, 165, 130,  8, ES_MARGIN
  PUSHBUTTON "#605"                            DID_LEFT,       110, 120,  32, 16, WS_GROUP | BS_ICON

  PUSHBUTTON "#606"                            DID_RIGHT,      150, 120,  32, 16, BS_ICON

  GROUPBOX    "Change Program Icon"            -1              220, 115, 100, 30
  PUSHBUTTON "~Icon..."                        DID_ICON,       230, 120,  40, 16,
  PUSHBUTTON "~Default"                        DID_DEFAULT,    270, 120,  40, 16,

  GROUPBOX           "Program Type"            ID_TEXT,         15,  30, 300, 70
  AUTORADIOBUTTON    "Default",                IDR_DEFAULT,     30,  70, 140, 10, WS_GROUP
  AUTORADIOBUTTON    "Presentation Manager",   IDR_PM,          30,  60, 140, 10,
  AUTORADIOBUTTON    "OS/2 Windowed Session",  IDR_OS2WINDOW,   30,  50, 140, 10,
  AUTORADIOBUTTON    "OS/2 Fullscreen Session", IDR_OS2FSCREEN, 30,  40, 140, 10,
  AUTORADIOBUTTON    "DOS Windowed Session",   IDR_DOSWINDOW,  170,  70, 140, 10,
  AUTORADIOBUTTON    "DOS Fullscreen Session", IDR_DOSFSCREEN, 170,  60, 140, 10,
  AUTORADIOBUTTON    "Seamless Win-OS/2 Session", IDR_WINWINDOW, 170, 50, 140, 10,
  AUTORADIOBUTTON    "Fullscreen Win-OS/2 Session", IDR_WINFSCREEN, 170, 40, 140, 10,

  DEFPUSHBUTTON      "~Apply"                  DID_OK,          30,   8,  45, 15, WS_GROUP
  PUSHBUTTON         "~Save"                   DID_SAVE,       100,   8,  45, 15,
  PUSHBUTTON         "~Close"                  DID_CANCEL,     170,   8,  45, 15,
  PUSHBUTTON         "~Help"                   DID_HELP,       240,   8,  45, 15,
 }
}
```

Figure 2.4   Sample dialog template using controls.

- The BS_USERBUTTON style is designed to allow the PM developer to create alternative buttons. It is up to the application to paint and maintain the button when the owner window receives a BN_PAINT notification message.

With the exception of the BS_3STATE and BS_AUTO3STATE styles, all of the other primary button styles can be specified in a dialog template simply by removing the BS_ header from the style. For example, the **ConfigureDlgProc** dialog procedure uses the dialog template in Figure 2.4, which contains most of the primary button styles.

There are several other secondary button window styles that control the appearance and functionality of the button that is created. These styles are designed to be ORed with the primary button styles to change the button function or appearance. Some of these button styles are exclusive to a specific type of primary button style.

The button styles in Figure 2.5 are specific to the BS_PUSHBUTTON primary button style and control the appearance of the border around the button window.

- The BS_DEFAULT style does not alter the default functionality of the pushbutton, but it does highlight the button by drawing a border around it, and also allows the user to use the Enter key to depress the button. This button style is used through the DEFPUSHBUTTON keyword in a dialog template. Only one button in a group can have this style set. This style can also be used by the BS_USERBUTTON primary style, but it is up to the application to define the appearance of the default button; for example, like drawing a border or changing the color.
- The BS_NOBORDER style is exactly as it sounds. The pushbutton is drawn without the border around it. The functionality of the button is not changed, only its appearance.

In addition, there are two button styles that control the message functionality of the button. When a pushbutton is depressed, the default button behavior is to generate a WM_COMMAND message to the owner window. Using either of the styles given in Figure 2.6 will cause a different message to be sent to the owner window.

```
BS_DEFAULT      0x0400L
BS_NOBORDER     0x1000L
```

Figure 2.5   Button border styles.

```
BS_HELP          0x0100L
BS_SYSCOMMAND    0x0200L
```

Figure 2.6   Button message styles.

- The BS_HELP style, when used in conjunction with the BS_PUSH-BUTTON primary style, will cause the button to generate a WM_HELP message instead of a WM_COMMAND message.
- The BS_SYSCOMMAND style, when used in conjunction with the BS_PUSHBUTTON primary style, will cause the button to generate a WM_SYSCOMMAND message instead of a WM_COMMAND message.

These button styles are useful in defining what the button is to accomplish when clicked. The BS_HELP and BS_SYSCOMMAND button styles are not designed to be used with one another, but if for some reason they are both set, the BS_HELP style will override the BS_SYSCOMMAND style causing the WM_HELP message to be generated in lieu of the WM_SYSCOMMAND message.

There are a few other button styles that can be used to alter the appearance of a pushbutton, listed in Figure 2.7.

- The BS_BITMAP style is used to substitute a bitmap image in the pushbutton window instead of the standard window text.
- The BS_ICON style is used to substitute an icon image in the pushbutton window instead of the standard window text.
- The BS_MINIICON style is the same except it uses a miniature icon.

The BS_ICON button style is the basis for the BUTTONS program, and each of the buttons drawn within the client area of the main window use this style to represent a function or program. When the button is pressed, the function is performed or the program is started. The buttons are created through a for loop that will call the **WinCreateWindow** function. All of the buttons use a combination of the WS_VISIBLE, BS_PUSHBUTTON, and BS_ICON window styles to create the buttons. The third parameter to the **WinCreateWindow** call specifies the window text of the button; and buttons that use BS_ICON have no need for window text. This parameter will change based on whether the icon is preloaded as a resource or needs to be loaded from the executable program.

```
BS_MINIICON    0x0020L
BS_BITMAP      0x0040L
BS_ICON        0x0080L
```

Figure 2.7   Button image styles.

The function buttons, which occupy the bottom row of buttons cannot change so we have no need to use different icons. Therefore, these icons are loaded as resources into the executable through the ICON statement in the resource script file. Here is an example of how the shutdown icon is declared in the BUTTONS.RC resource script file.

```
ICON IDI_SHUTDOWN PRELOAD shutdown.ico
```

The IDI_SHUTDOWN resource identifier is used to represent the actual icon shutdown.ico which will be built into the executable as a resource. The IDI_SHUTDOWN identifier is defined as a unique number that represents the icon. Here is how it is defined within BUTTONS.H.

```
#define IDI_SHUTDOWN  602
```

Note that the actual icon is now represented by the number 602. In order to load this icon in the button you can specify the number as the window text, preceded by the pound sign. For example, the code in Figure 2.8 will load the shutdown.ico icon within a pushbutton.

That is all there is to loading icons into the button from a resource. But what about the rest of the buttons necessary for the rest of the application interface? Since the purpose of the program is to allow the user to launch programs, the user must be responsible for configuring the applications that will be started. Therefore, since the applications will be different for each user, we do not have the ability to detect which icons to load as resources, so we have to extract the icon from the actual executable and then use that icon within the button. Unlike the manner that we used to load the icons for the function buttons, this time there will be no window text at all. Instead, the

```
WinCreateWindow (hwndClient,                          // Parent Window
          WC_BUTTON,                                  // Window Class
          "#602",                                     // Resource Identifier
          WS_VISIBLE | BS_PUSHBUTTON | BS_ICON,       // Window Styles
          50,                                         // Initial x
          0,                                          // Initial y
          50,                                         // Length of button
          50,                                         // Width of button
          NULLHANDLE,                                 // Owner is Client
          HWND_BOTTOM,                                // Sibling Window
          IDM_SHUTDOWN,                               // WM_COMMAND identifier
          NULL,                                       // Control Data
          NULL ) ;                                    // Presentation Parameters
```

Figure 2.8   Loading the icon button.

icon will be loaded from the control data that will be passed to the call to **WinCreateWindow**.

The format of the control data structure for the button window class is given in Figure 2.9.

- The **cb** parameter is the length in bytes of the control data structure.
- The **fsCheckState** parameter is the button check state that is used to determine whether the button is currently checked. It is the same value that is returned by the BM_QUERYCHECK message or the same value that is passed to the BM_SETCHECK message.
- The **fsHiliteState** parameter is the button highlight state that is used to determine whether the button is currently highlighted. It is the same value that is returned by the BM_QUERYHILITE message or the value that is passed to the BM_SETHILITE message.
- The **hImage** parameter represents a handle to an image file. The image file can either be in the form of an icon or a bitmap.

The BUTTONS program uses the **WinLoadFileIcon** API to obtain the handle to the icon from the application's executable. The configuration dialog box allows the user to enter the applications that they wish to create buttons for. The path and file names of the executables are then stored in an array called the program list, that will be written to a text configuration file called BUTTONS.PRO. When you are storing large data structures or arrays, it is good programming practice to create your own profile instead of using the OS2.INI file, since the size of the OS2.INI profile should be as small as possible for both performance and maintenance reasons. Alternatively, an application can create its own binary INI file using the Profile (Prf) library functions, to store the program information. The Prf API's are discussed later in the book. For the purposes of this sample program, it is easier to maintain a simple text based configuration file since it can be easily edited by the user. Since the beginning of the OS/2 Presentation Manager, a debate has raged among programmers as to whether or not the binary INI file format used by OS/2 or the text based INI files used by Microsoft Windows is superior. In any case that debate is irrelevant here.

```
typedef struct _BTNCDATA     // btncd
{
  USHORT  cb;
  USHORT  fsCheckState;
  USHORT  fsHiliteState;
  LHANDLE hImage;
} BTNCDATA;
typedef BTNCDATA *PBTNCDATA;
```

Figure 2.9   The button control data structure.

```
HPOINTER WinLoadFileIcon(PSZ   pszFileName,
                         BOOL  fPrivate);
```

Figure 2.10   The WinLoadFileIcon API.

For each of the program path and filenames stored in the BUTTONS.PRO file, the **WinLoadFileIcon** API is called to obtain its associated icon. Its prototype is in Figure 2.10.

- The **pszFileName** parameter is the path and file name of the executable that contains the icon.
- The **fPrivate** parameter is a BOOL flag that is used to determine whether a private copy of the icon is needed. If your application needs to modify the icon once it is determined, you can request a private copy solely for your application's use by setting this parameter to TRUE. Once you are done modifying the icon, free your private copy by calling the **WinFreeFileIcon** function. Otherwise, if the application only intends to display the icon, set this parameter to FALSE indicating that a single shared pointer to the icon is all that is needed. This will save on memory since a private copy of the icon will not have to be loaded.

Unlike most of the PM APIs, the code for the **WinLoadFileIcon** function is stored within the actual Workplace Shell library, PMWP.DLL, which means that this function was already 32-bit code before OS/2 WARP. The function returns a handle to a pointer that contains the icon. The icon that is returned is derived from the executable based on a series of precedence rules. Figure 2.11 contains the rules that **WinLoadFileIcon** uses to determine the order in which the icon will be loaded.

Once the icon is no longer needed, the application should call the **Win-FreeFileIcon** API to unload the graphics engine resources required for the icon. Figure 2.12 contains the prototype for the **WinFreeFileIcon** API. The **WinFreeFileIcon** API takes a single parameter, the pointer handle. The function will return TRUE if successful. The function works by first checking if the

- Use the ICON stored in the executables extended attributes.
- Use the .ICO file stored in the same directory with the same prefix as the executable.
- Use the ICON that is bound into the executable for PM and WINDOWS applications.
- Use the default ICON based on the actual program type.

Figure 2.11   The logic used to load an icon via WinLoadFileIcon.

```
BOOL APIENTRY WinFreeFileIcon(HPOINTER hptr);
```

Figure 2.12 **The WinFreeFileIcon prototype.**

icon specified is still resident and, if it is, the function returns FALSE. If the function is not resident, it will call **WinDestroyPointer** to destroy the pointer handle.

The code fragment shown in Figure 2.13 shows how the BUTTONS program creates the button windows and loads the program icons on the buttons.

```
// Fill in most of the Buttons Control Data Structure
btncd.cb             = sizeof(BTNCDATA);
btncd.fsCheckState   = NULLHANDLE;
btncd.fsHiliteState  = NULLHANDLE;

// Parse the BUTTONS profile(BUTTONS.PRO) looking for the executables to be
// started, along with the session types and any command line parameters.
ReadExecutablesFromProfile(BUTTONSPRO);

// The function buttons(first/bottom row of four buttons) correspond
// to Product-Information/Lockup/Shutdown/Command Prompt.  These icons
// are going to be loaded as resources from our executable.  To load
// these icons using the BS_ICON button style we will need to specify
// the resource number preceeded by a pound sign as the window text
// on the call to WinCreateWindow.  The remaining eight buttons are
// known as the program buttons, and need no window text.
for (usCounter = BID_ABOUT; usCounter < BID_END; usCounter++)
 {
   strcpy(szWinTitle, szResourceNumber[usCounter]);

   // For our program buttons (all buttons greater than the first row)
   // get the icon from the executable via WinLoadFileIcon().  If
   // the pointer handle returned by WinLoadFileIcon is NULL, we were
   // unable to get a valid icon from the various methods used by
   // WinLoadFileIcon, which probably implies that the path and
   // filename of the executable is bogus.  In which case, we will
   // load the SPTR_ICONQUESTION default pointer (a simple question mark)
   // to alert the user that something is wrong.
   if (usCounter > BID_VIOCMD)
    {
     hptrTemp[usCounter] = WinLoadFileIcon(pszAppName[usCounter], FALSE);
     if (hptrTemp[usCounter] == NULLHANDLE)
      {
       hptrTemp[usCounter] = WinQuerySysPointer(HWND_DESKTOP, SPTR_ICONQUESTION, FALSE);
      }
```

Figure 2.13 **Drawing the BUTTONS control panel.**   **continued**

```
    btncd.hImage = (LHANDLE)hptrTemp[usCounter];
 }

// Ok, so here we are about to create the BUTTONS control panel which consists of
// twelve pushbuttons.  The function buttons(first row) are non-configurable unlike
// the remaining eight buttons(known as the program buttons).  The buttons are a
// fixed size 50 x 50, beginning at the origin that is referenced from the
// usXPosition and usYPosition arrays.  This is where we pass the button control
// data structure which contains the icon information for the program buttons.
WinCreateWindow (hwndClient,                          // Parent Window Handle
                 WC_BUTTON,                           // Class Name
                 szWinTitle,                          // Window Text
                 WS_VISIBLE | BS_PUSHBUTTON | BS_ICON, // Window Styles
                 usXPosition[usCounter],              // Initial X coordinate
                 usYPosition[usCounter],              // Initial Y coordinate
                 50,                                  // Horizontal Length of Button
                 50,                                  // Vertical Length of Button
                 NULLHANDLE,                          // Owner Window Handle
                 HWND_BOTTOM,                         // Sibling Window
                 usCounter,                           // Resource Identifier
                 (PVOID)&btncd,                       // Button Control Data
                 NULL);                               // Presentation Parameters
}
```

Figure 2.13 Drawing the BUTTONS control panel.

THE BUTTON CONTROL MESSAGES

Button control messages signal the button actions (see Figure 2.14).

BM_CLICK

This message is used to send the button control a WM_BUTTON1DOWN and WM_BUTTON1UP message so that the behavior and appearance of the button indicate that it has been clicked by the user.

```
BM_CLICK           0x0120
BM_QUERYCHECKINDEX 0x0121
BM_QUERYHILITE     0x0122
BM_SETHILITE       0x0123
BM_QUERYCHECK      0x0124
BM_SETCHECK        0x0125
BM_SETDEFAULT      0x0126
```

Figure 2.14 The Button control messages.

BM_QUERYCHECKINDEX   This message is used to return the index (zero-based) of the button that is selected within a group of buttons. If no button in the group is selected, it will return a −1. This message is used for radiobuttons.

BM_QUERYHILITE   This message is used to determine whether the button is highlighted. The highlight status is returned.

BM_SETHILITE   This message is used to highlight a button.

BM_QUERYCHECK   This message is used to determine whether the specified button is checked. If the button is checked, the message will return TRUE; if the button is unchecked, the message will return FALSE. PMWIN.H contains a macro that resembles an API called **WinQueryButtonCheckState**, which simply sends the BM_QUERYCHECK message on to the button control to determine whether the button is checked. The macro works by using the API **WinSendDlgItemMsg** to send the message. Therefore, this macro is only used for dialog checkboxes and radiobuttons.

The **WinQueryButtonCheckState** macro is defined as shown in Figure 2.15.

BM_SETCHECK   This message is used to set the check appearance of the button. The first message parameter is used to set the check state. If **mp1** is set to 0, the button will be unchecked. If **mp1** is set to 1, the button will be checked. **mp1** can also be set to 2 for buttons that use the BS_3STATE or BS_AUTO3STATE button style. Setting **mp1** to 2 indicates that the button will be set to the intermediate state of the three state buttons. This message and the check functionality correspond to the radiobutton and checkbox buttons styles only. This message will return the previous check appearance of the button control. This message also corresponds to the **WinCheckButton** macro defined in PMWIN.H.

The WinCheckButton macro is defined as shown in Figure 2.16.

BM_SETDEFAULT   This message is used to set the appearance of a pushbutton to the default state. This message can be used by any button with

```
#define WinQueryButtonCheckstate(hwndDlg, id) \
((ULONG)WinSendDlgItemMsg(hwndDlg, id, BM_QUERYCHECK, \
(MPARAM)NULL, (MPARAM)NULL))
```

Figure 2.15   The WinQueryButtonCheckState macro.

```
#define WinCheckButton(hwndDlg, id, usCheckState) \
((ULONG)WinSendDlgItemMsg(hwndDlg, id, BM_SETCHECK, \
MPFROMSHORT(usCheckState), (MPARAM)NULL))
```

Figure 2.16   The WinCheckButton macro.

```
BN_CLICKED                 1
BN_DBLCLICKED              2
BN_PAINT                   3
```

Figure 2.17   The Button notification messages.

the BS_PUSHBUTTON or BS_USERBUTTON button style. The message essentially sets the BS_DEFAULT style for the button to indicate that the button is a default selection. The first message parameter is used to control the default button appearance. If **mp1** is set to TRUE, then the button control is set to the default button. If **mp1** is set to FALSE, then the default state is removed from the button.

The button notification codes are shown in Figure 2.17.

BN_CLICKED   This message is used to provide notification that the user has actually clicked a button.

BN_DBLCLICKED   This message is used to provide notification that the user has actually double-clicked a button.

BN_PAINT   This message is used to provide notification to the owner window to paint the button control. This notification message is only used for user-drawn buttons that use the BS_USERBUTTON button style. In this case, the second message parameter, **mp2**, will point to a USERBUTTON structure that contains all of the information required for painting the button. This structure is shown in Figure 2.18.

```
typedef struct _USERBUTTON    // userbutton
 {
  HWND    hwnd;
  HPS     hps;
  ULONG   fsState;
  ULONG   fsStateOld;
 } USERBUTTON;
typedef USERBUTTON *PUSERBUTTON;
```

Figure 2.18   The USERBUTTON structure.

Both pushbuttons and user-defined pushbuttons post a WM_COMMAND message to its owner window when the user clicks on the pushbutton. If the button code uses another style other than the BS_PUSHBUTTON or BS_USERBUTTON button style, like BS_SYSCOMMAND or BS_HELP, the message posted will be different. The BS_SYSCOMMAND button style posts a WM_SYSCOMMAND message, while the BS_HELP style causes a WM_HELP message to be posted to the owner window. If a window procedure uses duplicate window identifiers for different types of windows, it can differentiate the window type by looking for the command source value, which is passed in the low word of the second message parameter, **mp2**. Figure 2.19 contains the command source values defined in PMWIN.H.

The values contained in this figure can be used to determine which control generated the WM_COMMAND message. These values can be useful in determining what the user did to generate the command message if your window procedure needs to handle the command differently depending on the origin or if the application uses duplicate window identifiers for menu items, accelerators, and pushbuttons. For example, if you have a menuitem, pushbutton, and accelerator key that are all defined as 100 but are supposed to do different things, they won't, because the WM_COMMAND message will be the same for that value. Therefore, the window procedure can have code that validates the origin of the command message to appropriately interpret the correct command message code.

Button control windows that are not pushbuttons generate WM_CONTROL messages that are posted to the owner window. The message parameters contain the window identifier for the button and the notification message.

mp1 = button identifier

mp2 = notification message

For example, the code fragment in Figure 2.20 handles the WM_CONTROL message for a group of radiobuttons used to change colors.

The BUTTONS Control Panel can be configured by the user through the use of the Configure Program Buttons dialog box. The Program File entryfield

```
CMDSRC_PUSHBUTTON      1
CMDSRC_MENU            2
CMDSRC_ACCELERATOR     3
CMDSRC_FONTDLG         4
CMDSRC_FILEDLG         5
CMDSRC_PRINTDLG        6
CMDSRC_COLORDLG        7
CMDSRC_OTHER           0
```

Figure 2.19   Determining the source of WM_COMMAND messages.

```
case WM_CONTROL:
    switch (SHORT1FROMMP (mp1))
    {
     case CLR_BLUE:
         sColor = CLR_BLUE;
         return FALSE;

     case CLR_RED:
         sColor = CLR_RED;
         return FALSE;

     case CLR_PINK:
         sColor = CLR_PINK;
         return FALSE;

     case CLR_GREEN:
         sColor = CLR_GREEN;
         return FALSE;

    }
```

Figure 2.20   Processing the WM_CONTROL message.

is used to specify the program path and filenames for the executable programs. The Parameters entryfield is used to enter any command line parameters that can be passed to the program. The *Find* pushbutton will use the standard file dialog box to allow the user to select the executable. Two direction buttons, centered in the middle of the dialog box are used to navigate through the program list. As the user presses the forward button, the next executable program is displayed. If a program exists in the program list or is entered by the user, it is displayed in the static Program Icon. Figure 2.21 shows what the dialog box looks like, while Figure 2.22 shows the code that updates the Program File icon. The source code for the **UpdateIcon** routine updates the icon in the Configure Program Buttons dialog whenever the user selects one of the direction pushbuttons.

The **UpdateIcon** function takes three parameters. The first parameter is the dialog window handle. The second parameter represents the static icon window identifier. The last parameter, **pszIcon** represents the path and filename for the executable program whose icon is to be displayed. If this parameter is set to NULLHANDLE, the function will call **WinQuerySysPointer** to obtain the pointer handle for the question mark icon. This can be used to indicate to the user that the program path and filename could not be resolved, therefore, the icon could not be loaded. Otherwise, if **pszIcon** contains a valid path and filename, the program icon will be loaded via the **WinLoadFileIcon** API. The program file icon itself is finally updated by sending a SM_SETHANDLE mes-

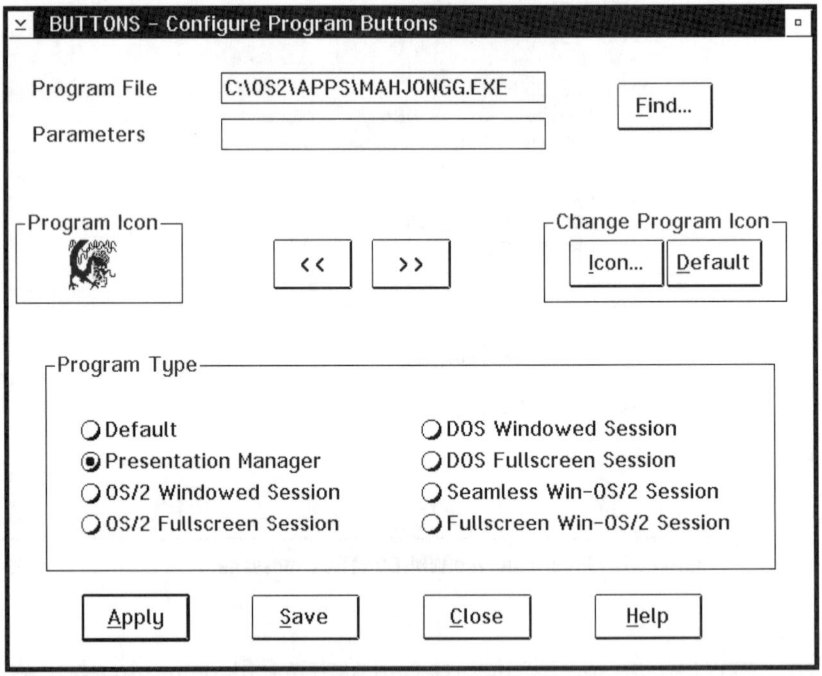

Figure 2.21   Configuring the BUTTONS control panel.

sage to the static icon window. The **mp1** parameter for the message contains the pointer handle.

When the end of the program list is reached, the buttons are disabled. The code fragment shown in Figure 2.23 handles the processing of the DID_LEFT and DID_RIGHT pushbuttons.

THE STATIC WINDOW CLASS

The static window class represents the simplest of all of the PM controls. The sole purpose of the static control is to provide information to the user. Typically, applications use static controls to display meaningful text, but there are several static window styles that can also be used to create graphical static controls. Since static controls just display information, no user input is required for a static control.

Processing static controls is very simple, since static controls do not send notification messages back to their owner window. Also, static controls do not comprehend input focus. When a static control gets a focus message via

```
BOOL UpdateIcon(HWND hwndDlg, ULONG ulIconID, PSZ pszIcon)
{
   HWND       hwndButton
   HPOINTER   hptr;
   BOOL       rc;

   hwndButton = WinWindowFromID(hwndDlg, ulIconID);
   WinShowWindow(hwndButton, FALSE);

   // If no executable is passed in pszIcon
   // then let's punt and just use the system pointer
   // that resembles a question mark???
   if (pszIcon == NULLHANDLE)
     {
      hptr = WinQuerySysPointer(HWND_DESKTOP, SPTR_ICONQUESTION, FALSE);
      if (!hptr)
        {
         DisplayMessages(ERROR_GETTING_SYSPTR, NULLHANDLE, MSG_INFO);
        }
     }

   else
     {
      hptr = WinLoadFileIcon(pszIcon, FALSE);
      if (hptr == NULLHANDLE)
        {
         // If WinLoadFileIcon failed return FALSE
         return FALSE;
        }
     }

   // Update our static icon and return TRUE
   WinSendMsg(hwndButton, SM_SETHANDLE, (MPARAM)hptr, NULL);
   WinShowWindow(hwndButton, TRUE);
   return TRUE;
}
```

Figure 2.22 The UpdateIcon function.

WM_SETFOCUS, the default static window procedure forwards the focus to the next possible child window that can have input focus. If there is no child window available that can possibly accept the input focus, then the focus is passed on to the owner of the static control window.

The BUTTONS sample program uses several forms of the static window control (see Figure 2.24), including the static text window and the GROUPBOX; and the Program File icon in the Configure Program Buttons dialog uses the SS_ICON static style.

```
case DID_RIGHT:
     if (!WinIsControlEnabled(hwnd, DID_LEFT))
       WinEnableControl(hwnd, DID_LEFT, TRUE);

     if (sCounter < LAST_BUTTON)
      {
       sCounter++;
       UpdateIcon(hwnd, ID_MAINWND, pszAppName[sCounter]);
       WinSetDlgItemText (hwnd, IDE_EXECUTABLE, pszAppName[sCounter]);
      }

     else
      {
       WinEnableControl(hwnd, DID_RIGHT, FALSE);
      }
     return FALSE;
```

Figure 2.23   The processing of the direction pushbuttons.

```
SS_TEXT              0x0001L
SS_GROUPBOX          0x0002L
SS_ICON              0x0003L
SS_BITMAP            0x0004L
SS_FGNDRECT          0x0005L
SS_HALFTONERECT      0x0006L
SS_BKGNDRECT         0x0007L
SS_FGNDFRAME         0x0008L
SS_HALFTONEFRAME     0x0009L
SS_BKGNDFRAME        0x000aL
SS_SYSICON           0x000bL
SS_AUTOSIZE          0x0040L
```

Figure 2.24   The static control styles.

ADDING MULTIPLE ITEMS TO A LISTBOX

One of the most significant improvements made to the standard PM controls in OS/2 Warp was in updates to the listbox control. A new control message was added that simplifies the process of adding multiple items to a listbox. The LM_INSERTMULTITEMS message allows an application to insert multiple items into a listbox within the context of a single message. Previously, adding items to a listbox required that the application send multiple LM_INSERTITEM messages; one for each individual item to be added to the listbox. The purpose of the LM_INSERTMULTITEMS message is to reduce the overhead required

```
typedef struct _LBOXINFO        //lboxinfo
 {
  LONG  lItemIndex;
  ULONG ulItemCount;
  ULONG reserved;
  ULONG reserved2;
 } LBOXINFO;
```

Figure 2.25   The LBOXINFO structure.

when adding items to the listbox; thereby, improving the time required to populate the listbox.

The message uses a structure called LBOXINFO. The structure is passed as the first message parameter. The second message parameter contains an array of pointers to NULL terminated strings, that contain the text to be inserted. The LBOXINFO structure is shown in Figure 2.25.

The LBOXINFO structure contains two significant elements that control how the items in the array will be displayed. The *lItemIndex* element specifies how the items are to be indexed and sorted within the listbox. The LIT_ constants defined in PMWIN.H, control the indexing. The *ulItemCount* element is used to specify the total number of items in the array of strings to be inserted. The source code in Figure 2.26 is used to insert the program list array into a listbox.

The **PopulateListBox** function uses the LIT_NONE constant to indicate that the inserted strings are not to be sorted. The BID_END value is used to indicate that there are 12 items in the program list array. However, the first four elements of the array are not used since they correspond to the function buttons rather than the program buttons. Therefore the second message parameter for the LM_INSERTMULTITEMS message, indicates that the start of the array will begin with the fourth element of the array. The current design of the

```
VOID PopulateListBox(HWND hwndListBox)
{
 LBOXINFO lboxinfo;

 // Populate LBOXINFO structure
 lboxinfo.lItemIndex  = LIT_NONE;      // don't sort
 lboxinfo.ulItemCount = BID_END;       //Number of items in array

 WinSendMsg(hwndListBox, LM_INSERTMULTITEMS, &lboxinfo, &pszAppName[4];
 WinSendMsg(hwndListBox, LM_SELECTITEM, MPFROMSHORZT(FALSE), MPFROMSHORT(TRUE));
 return;
}
```

Figure 2.26   Using the LM_INSERTMULTITEMS message.

worker routine for this message will stop inserting items at the first NULL. An application needs to ensure that all of the elements of the array to be inserted contain valid pointers to the text strings that will be inserted.

STARTING THE APPLICATIONS

The main purpose of the sample program is to allow the user to configure a series of graphical pushbuttons that, when depressed, will start a specific application. The user defines all of the programs that they wish to add to the BUTTONS control panel. The path and file names of the executables to be started are stored in a program list along with the application configuration information. The program list information is written to a file. The default profile containing the program list is called BUTTONS.PRO. Every time the BUTTONS program is started, the program list profile is read from disk, and the values are parsed. The program information derived from the list is used to configure each of the BUTTONS. Figure 2.27 contains a sample BUTTONS profile.

The most important part of the sample program is the program starter component itself. The BUTTONS sample program uses the API *WinStartApp* to launch the applications from the program list. The **WinStartApp** API is a quick and convenient method for starting different programs of multiple session types. Further, the required PROGDETAILS structure is a little bit less intimidating than the STARTDATA structure provided by **DosStartSession**, and **WinStartApp** provides a much better interface to maintain the environment. The format of the **WinStartApp** API is shown in Figure 2.28.

- The **hwndNotify** parameter is the handle of the window that is to receive notification when the program is terminated. The notification comes in the form of a WM_APPTERMINATENOTIFY message that is posted. The notification message can be used by an application to perform some task when the application is terminated. For example, an application may need to update the contents of another window based on an application terminating. A NULLHANDLE can be used in lieu of a valid window handle, if the posting of the notification message is not required.
- The **pDetails** parameter points to a PROGDETAILS structure. This structure contains the information required to start the session and is populated prior to calling **WinStartApp**. The structure contains valuable information about the type of session to be started, the path and file name of the executable, and the environment required by the application.
- The **pszParams** parameter is used to specify command line parameters that will be passed along to the application when it is launched.

```
;  """"""""""""""""""""""""""""""""""""""""""""""""""""""""""""""""""""""""""""""""""""""»
;  "  FILENAME:      BUTTONS.PRO                                                         "
;  "                                                                                     "
;  "  DESCRIPTION:   BUTTONS profile information                                         "
;  "                                                                                     "
;  "  NOTES:         This file contains the BUTTONS program list.  The BUTTONS           "
;  "                 control panel contains eight configurable pushbuttons.              "
;  "                 The program list contains nine entries.                             "
;  "                                                                                     "
;  "  RULES:         - The first entry is a dummy entry used to validate                 "
;  "                   if this file is indeed in the correct format.  The dummy          "
;  "                   entry must read BUTTONS.                                          "
;  "                                                                                     "
;  "                 - Comment lines begin with a semicolon and blank lines              "
;  "                   are ignored.                                                      "
;  "                                                                                     "
;  "                 - An asterisk is used to mark the end of the program list.          "
;  "                                                                                     "
;  "  COPYRIGHTS:    Uri J. Stern and James S. Morrow                                    "
;  "                 OS/2 WARP Presentation Manager for the Power Programmer             "
;  "                                                                                     "
;  "  PARAMETERS:    /F        = OS/2 Fullscreen session                                 "
;  "                 /f        = OS/2 Windowed session                                   "
;  "                 /D        = DOS  Fullscreen session                                 "
;  "                 /d        = DOS  Windowed session                                   "
;  "                 /W        = WinOS/2 Fullscreen session                              "
;  "                 /w        = WinOS/2 Seamless session                                "
;  "                 /%        = Specify Command line parameters to application          "
;  "                                                                                     "
;  """"""""""""""""""""""""""""""""""""""""""""""""""""""""""""""""""""""""""""""""""""""
;                                                                                       ...
BUTTONS
G:\DESCRIBE\DESCRIBE.EXE
E:\SMMATH\SMMATH.EXE /%
E:\KDEBUG\KE.EXE
E:\TOOLS\cdexpl.exe /p /%
F:\PCOMOS2\PCSWS.EXE /p /%F:\PCOMOS2\PRIVATE\uri.WS
E:\RELISH\RELISH.EXE /p /%
E:\TVFS\tvctl.exe /%-dorf
D:\CMVC\CMVC.EXE /%
```

Figure 2.27   **A sample BUTTONS profile.**

```
HAPP APIENTRY WinStartApp(HWND          hwndNotify,
                          PPROGDETAILS  pDetails,
                          PSZ           pszParams,
                          PVOID         Reserved,
                          ULONG         fbOptions);
```

Figure 2.28   **The WinStrtApp prototype.**

- The **Reserved** parameter is just that—reserved—and must be set to NULL.
- The **fbOptions** parameter contains the start application flags that are used to control the appearance and behavior of the session to be started. Some of these flags can be combined.

Figure 2.29 contains the start application flags for **WinStartApp**, which are defined in the PMSHL.H header file.

SAF_INSTALLEDCMDLINE	This flag is used to indicate that the command line parameters contained in the program details structure are to be used to pass parameters on to the application. If this flag is used, the **pszParams** parameter is ignored.
SAF_STARTCHILDAPP	This flag is used to indicate that the started application is to be a child of the session that calls the **WinStartApp** function.
SAF_MAXIMIZED	This flag is used to start the specified application in a maximized state.
SAF_MINIMIZED	This flag is used to start the specified application in a minimized state.
SAF_BACKGROUND	This flag is used to indicate that the session should be started in the background.

The **WinStartApp** API is the routine used by the Workplace Shell to start program objects. The **WinStartApp** API will return a handle that represents the application. The data type for the handle is a HAPP, which is actually the session identifier for the started session.

The code fragment in Figure 2.30 uses the **WinStartApp** API to start all of the programs in the program list profile.

The code to resolve the **WinStartApp** API is contained in the PMSHAPI dynamic link library. The code for **WinStartApp** is actually a wrapper function for the **DosStartSession** API; thus, **WinStartApp** will take the information passed in the PROGDETAILS structure and populate a STARTDATA structure that will be passed on to **DosStartSession**, to eventually invoke the session manager to start the program.

```
SAF_INSTALLEDCMDLINE   0x0001
SAF_STARTCHILDAPP      0x0002
SAF_MAXIMIZED          0x0004
SAF_MINIMIZED          0x0008
SAF_BACKGROUND         0x0010
```

Figure 2.29   The Start application flags.

```
HAPP StartApplication(PCH szPgmName, PCH szComLine, PCH szProgTitle)
{
 APIRET      rc;
 HWND        hwndNotify;
 CHAR        szDir[CCHMAXPATH];
 CHAR        szFile[CCHMAXPATH];
 ULONG       ulAppType;
 HAPP        happ;
 CHAR        szBuffer[250];
 PROGDETAILS progdetails;


 // Take the full program path and filename
 // and parse it so that the string X:\DIRECTORY\FILE.TXT
 // becomes two strings X:\DIRECTORY and FILE.TXT
 ParsePathFromFileName(szPgmName, szDir, szFile);


 // NOTE: Determine the application default type
 //       if the application is a Windows based
 //       application change the default for BUTTONS
 //       to be Enhanced Seamless as oppossed to a
 //       yucky WinOS/2 Fullscreen session, since
 //       seamless is groovy!
 rc = DosQueryAppType(szPgmName, &ulAppType);

 if ((ulAppType == 4096) || (ulAppType == 1024))
  {
   ulAppType  = PROG_31_ENHSEAMLESSVDM;
  }

 progdetails.Length                      = sizeof(PROGDETAILS); // Length of structure
 progdetails.progt.progc                 = ulAppType;           // Application Program Type
 progdetails.progt.fbVisible             = SHE_VISIBLE;         // Visibility Indicator
 progdetails.pszTitle                    = szProgTitle;         // Program Title
 progdetails.pszExecutable               = szPgmName;           // Executable Path and Filename
 progdetails.pszParameters               = szComLine;           // Command Line Parameters
 progdetails.pszStartupDir               = szDir;               // Working Directory
 progdetails.pszIcon                     = NULL;                // Program Icon
 progdetails.pszEnvironment              = NULL;                // Environment String
 progdetails.swpInitial.x                = 0;                   // Initial x Window Position
 progdetails.swpInitial.y                = 0;                   // Initial y Window Position
 progdetails.swpInitial.cx               = 0;                   // Initial cx Window Size
 progdetails.swpInitial.cy               = 0;                   // Initial cy Window Size
 progdetails.swpInitial.hwndInsertBehind = HWND_TOP;           // Window Placement
 progdetails.swpInitial.fl               = SWP_SHOW;           // Initial Window Flags

 happ = WinStartApp(NULLHANDLE,               // Notification window handle
                    &progdetails,             // Program Details Structure
                    NULL,                     // Command Line Parameters for the started program
                    NULL,                     // Reserved
                    SAF_INSTALLEDCMDLINE);    // Start Application Flags

 return happ;
}
```

Figure 2.30   The StartApplication function.

TERMINATING A STARTED APPLICATION

When the user starts a program by pressing one of the program pushbuttons, the client window procedure receives a WM_COMMAND message with a command identifier between BID_PROGRAM1 and BID_PROGRAM8, corresponding to the element of the program list array containing the program to be started. The **StartApplications** function will return a valid application handle (HAPP), if the program was successfully started. The application handle is stored in the window words of the corresponding program button window. This allows the View Program List dialog box to use the **WinTerminateApp** API to stop the execution of the program at the user request. The View Program List dialog box is shown in Figure 2.31.

The code fragment shown in Figure 2.32, shows how the programs are started, and how the application handle is stored in the window words of the program button window, whenever the user presses one of the program buttons.

When the user clicks the **Kill** pushbutton, the application handle is retrieved from the window words of the button window, and the **WinTerminateApp** API is called to stop the running program. The code fragment shown in Figure 2.33 handles the processing of the Kill pushbutton.

THE ES_UNREADABLE ENTRYFIELD CONTROL STYLE

The entryfield control is one of the most useful standard controls provided by the Presentation Manager. It provides a powerful mechanism to obtain input from the user. The entryfield can be customized by subclassing the default behavior of the control, to provide additional functionality. For example, an application can create customized numeric entryfields for obtaining phone numbers or social security numbers. One very important use of this control is to create a password entryfield. The Presentation Manager code provides an entryfield style called ES_UNREADABLE that is designed to automate the masking of the entryfield text as it is typed. Several commercial applications use this entryfield style to create a password entryfield.

As the name of the entryfield style denotes, the ES_UNREADABLE style causes the text in the entryfield control to be nonreadable, by replacing each character entered with an asterisk. An application cannot remove the ES_UNREADABLE style bit. Although this style has a practical use for creating a password entryfield, it does not provide a complete security mechanism for mission critical applications. Programmers with an application that has strict security requirements should rethink the design of their application and

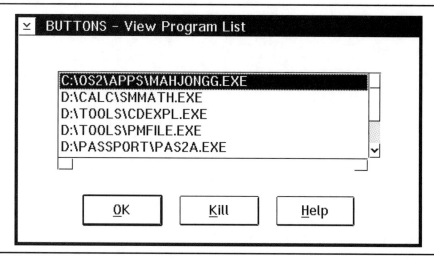

Figure 2.31   Viewing the Program List array.

```
// These are the program buttons, indicating that the user wants to start
// a program, so let's oblige!
case BID_PROGRAM1:
case BID_PROGRAM2:
case BID_PROGRAM3:
case BID_PROGRAM4:
case BID_PROGRAM5:
case BID_PROGRAM6:
case BID_PROGRAM7:
case BID_PROGRAM8:
    if (pszAppName[CMD_MSG])
     {
      ulSID = StartApplication(pszAppName[CMD_MSG], pszParams[CMD_MSG], 0, ulPgmType[CMD_MSG]);
     }

    if (!ulSID)
     {
      DisplayMessages(ERROR_STARTING_PROGRAM, NULLHANDLE, MSG_EXCLAMATION);
      return FALSE;
     }

    // The StartApplications routine returns a HAPP which is actually the
    // session identifier.  We will store the HAPP in the window words of
    // button window, that way we can call WinTerminateApp if the user
    // wants to kill a program they started from BUTTONS.
    hwndProgram = WinWindowFromID(hwnd, CMD_MSG);
    WinSetWindowULong(hwndProgram, QWL_USER, ulSID);
    return FALSE;
```

Figure 2.32   Starting the application and storing the HAPP in the window words.

```
case DID_KILL:
    usIndex = (USHORT) WinSendDlgItemMsg(hwnd, IDL_PROGLIST, LM_QUERYSELECTION, MPFROM2SHORT(4, 0), 0);
    usIndex += 4;

    hwndButton = WinWindowFromID(hwndClient, usIndex);
    ulSID = WinQueryWindowULong(hwndButton, QWL_USER);

    if (ulSID)
     {
      // User has asked to kill the application
      WinTerminateApp(ulSID);

      // Reset window words so that the next time the user
      // asks to kill the program and it is not started, they
      // get the error message indicating that the program is
      // not currently running.
      WinSetWindowULong(hwndButton, QWL_USER, NULLHANDLE);
     }

    else
     {
      DisplayMessages(ERROR_PROGRAM_NOT_RUNNING, NULLHANDLE, MSG_EXCLAMATION);
     }

    return FALSE;
```

Figure 2.33   Terminating the application.

implement additional security functionality. Getting at the actual text entered by the user can still be quite simple as shown in Figure 2.34.

Figure 2.34 shows how simple it can be to obtain the entryfield text even with the ES_UNREADABLE style by setting a breakpoint on the **WinQueryWindowText** function that will be used to extract the entryfield text.

Using the Delete Key with the Entryfield Control

The Delete key will delete either the current selection or the next character if there is no text selected within the entryfield. The Shift+Del key combination corresponds to the cut clipboard operation, only if there is selected text within the entryfield. If no text is selected, the key combination merely deletes the next character as if only the delete key was pressed, no text is cut to the clipboard. The Ctrl+Del key combination works by deleting from the cursor insertion point to the end of the entryfield.

```
##g
eax=00000009 ebx=0000db0e ecx=00000000 edx=92e0014f esi=00000004 edi=00003c54
eip=0000be79 esp=00009f26 ebp=00009f4e iopl=2 -- -- -- nv up ei pl nz na pe nc
cs=bdbf ss=001f ds=9077 es=014f fs=150b gs=07cb  cr2=00030000  cr3=001d6000
pmwin:_FRAMEMGR:WINQUERYWINDOWTEXT:
bdbf:0000be79 b827be         mov      ax,DGROUP (be27) ;br0

##p
eax=0000be27 ebx=0000db0e ecx=00000000 edx=92e0014f esi=00000004 edi=00003c54
eip=0000be7c esp=00009f26 ebp=00009f4e iopl=2 -- -- -- nv up ei pl nz na pe nc
cs=bdbf ss=001f ds=9077 es=014f fs=150b gs=07cb  cr2=00030000  cr3=001d6000
bdbf:0000be7c 55            push     bp

##p
eax=0000be27 ebx=0000db0e ecx=00000000 edx=92e0014f esi=00000004 edi=00003c54
eip=0000be7d esp=00009f24 ebp=00009f4e iopl=2 -- -- -- nv up ei pl nz na pe nc
cs=bdbf ss=001f ds=9077 es=014f fs=150b gs=07cb  cr2=00038804  cr3=001d6000
bdbf:0000be7d 8bec          mov      bp,sp

##p
eax=0000be27 ebx=0000db0e ecx=00000000 edx=92e0014f esi=00000004 edi=00003c54
eip=0000be7f esp=00009f24 ebp=00009f24 iopl=2 -- -- -- nv up ei pl nz na pe nc
cs=bdbf ss=001f ds=9077 es=014f fs=150b gs=07cb  cr2=00038804  cr3=001d6000
bdbf:0000be7f 1e            push     ds

##dw ss:bp
001f:00009f24  9f4e d158 908f db44 014f 0009 8de8 39d0
001f:00009f34  90b7 db0e 014f 0000 b167 9f50 d1c0 bdb7
001f:00009f44  9f6a 001f 000a 0000 0000 9f7a 30a1 90bf
001f:00009f54  0008 0009 1fd6 017f 8de8 39d0 90b7 3523
001f:00009f64  0000 0400 9f00 3623 0000 1f5c 0004 00ac
001f:00009f74  aa2f 8de8 39d0 9f92 2f09 90bf a922 001f
001f:00009f84  8023 1fd6 017f 0008 0009 7f27 0001 9faa
001f:00009f94  08cc 7f57 0009 1fd6 017f 8023 a922 001f

##db 14f:db44
014f:0000db44 4d 55 52 50 48 59 00 00-00 59 22 00 ae 1e 7f 01  MURPHY...Y".....

// The user's password was MURPHY.  Wonder if it's the same guy with the law???
```

Figure 2.34   Getting at the password.

Validating the Entryfield

There may be times that an application will need to validate the contents of an entryfield before the user interacts with another control window that would normally handle the processing of the entryfield. The code fragment shown in Figure 2.35 is used to validate the contents of the program file entryfield whenever the focus is switched away from this entryfield.

```
case WM_CONTROL:
    if (SHORT1FROMMP(mp1) == IDE_EXECUTABLE)
     {
      switch (SHORT2FROMMP(mp1))
        {
          // Now check to see if the user has changed the focus
          // away from the Program File entryfield by handling the
          // EN_KILLFOCUS notification message.
          case EN_KILLFOCUS:
                // Since focus is switching away from the entryfield
                // check to see if the actual text has been modified
                // by the user.  The new text is stored in szBuffer
                // and will be compared to the original text
                // that is stored in szEntryField.
                hwndEntryField = WinWindowFromID(hwnd, IDE_EXECUTABLE);
                WinQueryWindowText(hwndEntryField, sizeof(szBuffer), szBuffer);

                rc = strcmp(szEntryField, szBuffer)
                if (rc)
                 {
                   // If the text of the entryfield after the entryfield focus switch
                   // does not match the original program file, this means the
                   // user has modified the text in the entryfield, so we want
                   // to reset the Program Type radiobuttons to indicate that the
                   // program type is the default.  Of course, all of this will be
                   // lost if the user does not select the Apply/Save pushbuttons to
                   // record the changes.
                   WinSendDlgItemMsg(hwnd, IDR_DEFAULT, BM_SETCHECK, MPFROMSHORT(1), MPFROMLONG(0L));

                   // A little recursion here.  We first call UpdateIcon to try and
                   // set the icon based on the text in the entryfield.  If all goes
                   // well the entryfield contains a valid path and filename for an
                   // executable program.  However, if no icon can be pulled from the
                   // executable, it probably means our EXE program is totally bogus
                   // so we will call UpdateIcon again, only this time with a NULLHANDLE
                   // as the last parameter.  A NULLHANDLE indicates that the static icon
                   // should be changed to the system pointer for a question mark???
                   // This little hack is much faster than actually validating the
                   // executable...  The question mark icon provides a visual clue to
                   // the user that the path and filename for the executable is probably
                   // not valid and therefore, they should not Apply/Save the changes.
                   rc = UpdateIcon(hwnd, ID_MAINWND, szBuffer);
                   if (!rc)
                    {
                      UpdateIcon(hwnd, ID_MAINWND, NULLHANDLE);
                    }
                 }
                return FALSE;
        }
      break;
```

Figure 2.35   Validating the program file entryfield.

Typically, the text entered by a user within an entryfield is processed when the user interacts with some other control window, like a pushbutton, or when a window is closed. For example, when a button is pressed a WM_COMMAND message is generated and sent to the owner window. Within the context of this message the text of the entryfield can be queried and the appropriate processing of the user input can occur. However, there are times that an application may need to process the entryfield text immediately after it is changed by the user.

The Configure Program Buttons dialog box uses the code fragment shown in Figure 2.35 to ensure that the user has entered a valid executable path and filename in the Program File entryfield. The Program File entryfield corresponds to the IDE_EXECUTABLE identifier. The code handles the EN_KILLFOCUS notification control message. The EN_KILLFOCUS notification code is received whenever the specified entryfield control is about to lose the cursor input focus. Since this message will only be received when focus is switched away from the entryfield, it will not occur unless the user has changed the contents of the entryfield, since the entryfield is not the initial control that receives focus within this dialog.

The **szEntryField** string contains the initial text representing the specified executable path and filename. As the user shifts the input focus away from the Program File entryfield, for example by pressing the tab key, the current text in the entryfield is compared against the text in the **szEntryField** string. If the strings do not match a BM_SETCHECK message is sent to the default program type radiobutton. Finally, the **UpdateIcon** routine is called to update the static icon with the new program icon. If the icon cannot be obtained, the path and filename for the specified program is assumed to be invalid, so the **UpdateIcon** routine is called again to change the static icon to a question mark.

UPDATING THE PROGRAM BUTTONS

The **UpdateIcon** routine handles the updating of the static icon shown in the Configure Program Buttons dialog, but what about updating the actual program buttons once the user makes a change to the program list array? The answer is the **UpdateBtnIcon** function. This routine is similar in concept to the **UpdateIcon** routine, except the code works by updating the icon drawn on the button control, rather than an icon drawn on a static control.

The source code listing in Figure 2.36 shows how the program buttons are updated whenever the user selects the Apply button. The **UpdateBtnIcon** routine, is used to change the icon that is drawn on the program buttons to correspond to the new executable program that was specified by the user.

The code works by sending a WM_SETWINDOWPARAMS message to the pushbutton window. The **mp1** parameter of the message contains the address of a WNDPARAMS structure containing a pointer to a button control data

```
VOID UpdateBtnIcon(HWND hwndDlg, ULONG ulIconID, PSZ pszIcon)
{
    HWND        hwndButton;
    HPOINTER    hptr;
    BOOL        rc;
    WNDPARAMS   wp
    BTNCDATA    bcd;

    bcd.cb      = sizeof(BTNCDATA);
    wp.fsStatus = WPM_CTLDATA;
    wp.pCtlData = &bcd;

    hwndButton = WinWindowFromID(hwndDlg, ulIconID);
    WinShowWindow(hwndButton, FALSE);
    WinSendMsg(hwndButton, WM_QUERYWINDOWPARAMS, (MPARAM)&wp, NULL);
    bcd.hImage = WinLoadFileIcon(pszIcon, FALSE);
    WinSendMsg(hwndButton, WM_SETWINDOWPARAMS, (MPARAM)&wp, NULL);
    WinShowWindow(hwndButton, TRUE);

    return;
}
```

Figure 2.36 Changing the program buttons on the control panel.

structure, BTNCDATA. The *hImage* element of the BTNCDATA structure contains the handle of the icon for the new executable program. The icon is loaded from the executable by calling the **WinLoadFileIcon** API.

CHANGING THE ICON ASSOCIATED WITH AN EXECUTABLE

The Configure Program Buttons dialog box contain two pushbuttons that allow the user to change the icon that is associated with an executable. The pushbutton labeled *Icon* will use the standard file dialog to allow the user to specify the icon file that **ChangeIcon** function will use to change a program's icon. The *Default* pushbutton will reset the icon back to the original program icon. The **ChangeIcon** function is shown in Figure 2.37.

The **ChangeIcon** function allows the user to specify a different icon for a program in much the same way as the workplace shell does. The function uses the **WinSetFileIcon** API to store the icon file in the executable's extended attribute information. The **WinSetFileIcon** API uses an ICONINFO structure to set the icon information. The *fFormat* element of the structure is used to determine whether the function should store new icon data in the extended attribute information, or clear the icon data thus restoring the icon back to the default icon for the executable. If the *fFormat* element is set to ICON_FILE,

```
BOOL ChangeIcon(HWND hwndDlg, ULONG ulIconID, PSZ pszExecutable, PSZ pszIcon)
{
  BOOL       rc;
  ICONINFO   iconinfo;

  if (!pszIcon)
    {
     iconinfo.fFormat     = ICON_CLEAR;
    }

  else
    {
     iconinfo.fFormat     = ICON_FILE;
    }

  iconinfo.cb            = sizeof(ICONINFO);
  iconinfo.pszFileName   = pszIcon;
  iconinfo.hmod          = (HMODULE)NULL;
  iconinfo.resid         = NULLHANDLE;
  iconinfo.cbIconData    = NULLHANDLE;
  iconinfo.pIconData     = (PVOID)NULL;

  rc = WinSetFileIcon(pszExecutable, &iconinfo);
  if (rc != TRUE)
    {
     DisplayMessages(ERROR_CHANGING_ICON, NULLHANDLE, MSG_ERROR);
     return FALSE;
    }

  UpdateIcon(hwndDlg, ulIconID, pszExecutable);
  return TRUE;
}
```

Figure 2.37   The ChangeIcon function.

the new icon will be stored. If the *fFormat* element is set to ICON_CLEAR, the default icon information is restored. The ICON_CLEAR value is used whenever the user clicks the *Default* pushbutton. The last two parameters of the **Change-Icon** function, *pszExecutable* and *pszIcon*, correspond to the executable file and the icon file.

The function will return TRUE if successful and FALSE if an error occurs. If the function is successful, it will call the **UpdateIcon** routine to update the static icon, to reflect the new icon stored for the executable program. It is important to note that the **WinSetFileIcon** function will fail if the program is already running when the user attempts to change the icon. If this is the case, the **DisplayMessages** function will be called to give the user a meaningful error message.

DISPLAYING MESSAGES

It is important for PM applications to reuse code whenever possible. The SHCOMMON code located on Wiley's FTP* site provides a common set of functions that are used throughout several of the sample programs. The **DisplayMessages** function is used by every sample program. The purpose of this function is to provide a message to the user, indicating that the user may have to take an appropriate action based on the type of message. There are essentially four types of messages that this function can display.

- A message indicating a fatal error has occurred.
- A cautionary warning message.
- A warning messages that requires a Yes or No response.
- A message that is used to display information.

The **DisplayMessages** function uses the **WinMessageBox** API to display the message box containing the message information. The text to be displayed in the message box can either be loaded from a stringtable, or specified directly by the caller. The first parameter, **ulMessageID**, corresponds to the string resource identifier. If the caller of the function wishes to bypass the stringtable and simply pass a text string, then the caller must set the **ulMessageID** parameter to zero and the **pchText** parameter to the text string. The function uses the **WinLoadString** API to load the text string from the stringtable resource. The function will return the value returned by the **WinMessageBox** API. The source code for the **DisplayMessages** function is shown in Figure 2.38.

```
USHORT DisplayMessages(ULONG ulMessageID, PCH pchText, USHORT usMsgType)
{
   CHAR    szTempString[CCHMAXPATH];
   PSZ     pszMessageString;
   APIRET  rc;
   HAB     hab;

   // If a valid ulMessageID (a non-zero value) was passed, then we need to
   // load the appropriate message from the message/string table.  Otherwise
   // if ulMessageID is NULLHANDLE, then pchText contains the text to be displayed.
   hab = WinQueryAnchorBlock(HWND_DESKTOP);

   if (ulMessageID)
     {
       rc = WinLoadString(hab, (HMODULE)0, ulMessageID, sizeof(szTempString), szTempString);
       if (rc == FALSE)
         {
           DosBeep(1000, 1000);
```

Figure 2.38   The DisplayMessages function. **continued**

*Information regarding Wiley's FTP site can be found in the Appendix on page 537.

```
        }
      else
       {
        pszMessageString = szTempString;
       }
   }

  else
   {
    pszMessageString = pchText;
   }

  switch(usMsgType)
  {
   case MSG_ERROR:
        rc = WinMessageBox(HWND_DESKTOP,
                           HWND_DESKTOP,
                           pszMessageString,
                           TITLEBAR,
                           ID_MESSAGEBOX,
                           MB_OK | MB_SYSTEMMODAL | MB_MOVEABLE | MB_ERROR);
        break;

   case MSG_WARNING:
        rc =  WinMessageBox(HWND_DESKTOP,
                           HWND_DESKTOP,
                           pszMessageString,
                           TITLEBAR,
                           ID_MESSAGEBOX,
                           MB_MOVEABLE | MB_ICONQUESTION | MB_YESNO | MB_DEFBUTTON1);
        break;

   case MSG_EXCLAMATION:
        rc =  WinMessageBox(HWND_DESKTOP,
                           HWND_DESKTOP,
                           pszMessageString,
                           TITLEBAR,
                           ID_MESSAGEBOX,
                           MB_MOVEABLE | MB_ICONEXCLAMATION | MB_OK | MB_DEFBUTTON1);
        break

   case MSG_INFO:
        rc =  WinMessageBox(HWND_DESKTOP,
                           HWND_DESKTOP,
                           pszMessageString,
                           TITLEBAR,
                           ID_MESSAGEBOX,
                           MB_MOVEABLE | MB_ICONASTERISK | MB_OK | MB_DEFBUTTON1);
        break;
  }
  return rc;
}
```

Figure 2.38   The DisplayMessages function.

REMOVING THE STANDARD FRAME CONTROLS

The SHCOMMON code provided with the sample programs, contains another handy little routine called **HideControls**, that is used to toggle the visibility of the titlebar, action bar, system menu, and minimize/maximize buttons. This function allows the user the ability to display only the BUTTONS control panel without the default frame control windows. The source code for the function is shown in Figure 2.39.

The **HideControls** function takes a single parameter, the handle of the frame window, whose controls are to be removed and works as a toggle. The first time it is called, the controls are hidden. The next time the function is called, the controls are made visible. The function uses a flag called *bHidden* to control the toggle state. The function first obtains the window handles of the controls from their associated frame identifiers. In order to hide the controls, the parent window is changed to HWND_OBJECT via the **WinSetParent** API. The controls are made visible by resetting the parent of the controls to the frame window. Finally, a WM_UPDATEFRAME message is sent to the frame window to inform the frame window that the controls have been updated.

USING THE TITLEBAR CONTROL

The titlebar control window is a very unique control window. Normally, an application should not have a need to alter the titlebar. However, there may be times that an application may require modifying the text displayed in the titlebar. If you are writing an application like a text editor for example, it makes sense to display the edited path and filename within the titlebar. However, if your application is constantly modifying the titlebar text, it can become an eye sore to watch the titlebar constantly changing. Instead of actually modifying the titlebar text, an application can alternatively choose to create a status bar by using the **WinDrawBorder** API.

An application can use the **WinSetWindowText** API to modify the frame window text, causing the titlebar text to change. However, if an application uses the **WinSetWindowText** API, specifying the frame window handle as the first parameter, the titlebar text cannot exceed 60 characters. All characters exceeding 60 will be truncated. This may not be ideal if you are writing an editor program, since HPFS allows for long filenames, and with sub-directories it is easy to exceed the 60 character limit. If you need the titlebar to exceed 60 characters, you need to directly set the window text of the titlebar by calling the **WinSetWindowText** API. Instead of specifying the frame window handle, however, use the titlebar window handle, which can be obtained by calling the **WinWindowFromID** API with the frame window handle and the frame identifier FID_TITLEBAR.

```
VOID HideControls(HWND hwndFrame)
{
    static HWND hwndTitleBar;      // Must be static for initial invocation
    static HWND hwndSysMenu;       // Must be static for initial invocation
    static HWND hwndAppMenu;       // Must be static for initial invocation
    static HWND hwndMinMax;        // Must be static for initial invocation
    static BOOL bHidden = FALSE;   // Must be static for initial invocation

    // If bHidden is not TRUE, this means that we want to hide the controls.  So
    // we will obtains handles to all of the control windows by querying the
    // frame window identifiers.  Then we will remove the controls by setting the
    // parent windows to HWND_OBJECT rather than the frame.  The frame controls
    // are restored by resetting the parent windows back to the frame window.  This
    // allows us to temporily remove the frame control windows without destroying
    // them explicitly.

    if (!bHidden) // Hide Frame Control Windows
      {
      hwndTitleBar = WinWindowFromID(hwndFrame,  FID_TITLEBAR);
      hwndSysMenu  = WinWindowFromID(hwndFrame,  FID_SYSMENU);
      hwndAppMenu  = WinWindowFromID(hwndFrame,  FID_MENU);
      hwndMinMax   = WinWindowFromID(hwndFrame,  FID_MINMAX);

      WinSetParent(hwndTitleBar,  HWND_OBJECT, FALSE);
      WinSetParent(hwndSysMenu,   HWND_OBJECT, FALSE);
      WinSetParent(hwndAppMenu,   HWND_OBJECT, FALSE);
      WinSetParent(hwndMinMax,    HWND_OBJECT, FALSE);

      WinSendMsg(hwndFrame, WM_UPDATEFRAME, (MPARAM)(FCF_TITLEBAR | FCF_MENU | FCF_SYSMENU |
                                            FCF_MINBUTTON), NULL);
      bHidden = TRUE;
      }

    else  // Show Frame Control Windows
      {
      WinSetParent(hwndTitleBar,  hwndFrame, FALSE);
      WinSetParent(hwndSysMenu,   hwndFrame, FALSE);
      WinSetParent(hwndAppMenu,   hwndFrame, FALSE);
      WinSetParent(hwndMinMax,    hwndFrame, FALSE);

      WinSendMsg(hwndFrame, WM_UPDATEFRAME, (MPARAM)(FCF_TITLEBAR | FCF_MENU | FCF_SYSMENU |
                                            FCF_MINBUTTON), NULL );
      bHidden = FALSE;
      }

return;
}
```

Figure 2.39   The HideControls function.

```
// where LONGTITLEBAR represents a string greater than 60 characters
    hwndTitleBar = WinWindowFromID(hwndFrame, FID_TITLEBAR);
    WinSetWindowText(hwndTitleBar, LONGTITLEBAR);
```

Figure 2.40   Setting the titlebar window text.

The 60 character truncation of the titlebar text is a result of the default frame window processing using the MAXNAMEL constant, which is defined as 60. As a result of default frame window processing the frame window receives a WM_SETWINDOWPARAMS message containing the window text that is to be set by the **WinSetWindowText** API. A worker routine truncates the text to the 60 character limit. If the application explicitly modifies the titlebar window text, the default frame window processing is avoided and the limit is the size of the titlebar itself. The code fragment shown in Figure 2.40 allows for the titlebar window text to exceed 60 characters.

SUMMARY

The Presentation Manager environment contains a rich, functional set of controls that allow the developer to provide a consistent user interface to the application end user. The usage of the standard PM controls can make or break an application depending on how the user interacts with the controls. To make the interface as intuitive as possible is the ultimate goal of any PM-based application, and the Presentation Manager itself. The basic PM controls are used throughout the sample programs in this book and should be commonplace to experienced PM developers. The intent of this chapter was to review some of the more important control concepts, and demonstrate how to maximize the effectiveness of the basic PM controls provided by the Presentation Manager components. The concepts discussed throughout the chapter and the source code for the BUTTONS program provide all of the elements required to master the standard PM controls.

CHAPTER 3

Mastering the Keyboard Interface and Scrolling Functionality

E xcept for direct textual input, the pointing device has become the primary mechanism for interacting with PM applications. In fact, applications are often tailored to ensure that significant portions of the application's functionality are accessible with the mouse or other pointing device. Unfortunately, these same applications often neglect to ensure that all functionality is accessible via the keyboard. This omission can be a burden to the user when a machine is not equipped with a pointing device or when the user simply prefers to use the keyboard. In order to help programmers provide keyboard accessibility, this chapter examines how applications receive and process keyboard input.

The chapter also examines scrolling, an important feature for all applications that must present more information than can be conveniently displayed on the screen. The standard keys defined for scrolling with the keyboard and the scroll bar control will both be discussed.

PROCESSING KEYBOARD INPUT

When the system receives input from the keyboard, the input is first stored in the system message queue and then later posted to an application queue in the form of a WM_CHAR message. The queue to which the message is eventually posted is based on the window that has currently been given the input focus when the keystroke is removed from the system message queue.

When the WM_CHAR message is placed in the application's message queue, it contains the raw keyboard scan code and, if one exists, the matching ASCII character or virtual key value. (Virtual keys are common keyboard keys, such as HOME and INSERT, which do not have a defined ASCII representation.) When the application calls **WinGetMessage** or **WinPeekMessage**, the WM_CHAR message is removed from the message queue and a check is made to determine if the character matches an accelerator, or shortcut, key. If so, the message is changed into a WM_SYSCOMMAND, WM_COMMAND, or WM_HELP message. If the WM_SYSCOMMAND or WM_COMMAND message corresponds to a disabled menu item, the message is modified to WM_NULL before being returned to the application.

THE WM_CHAR MESSAGE

Thus, the application need not concern itself with translation and may process any WM_CHAR messages received as actual keystrokes. The **mp1** and **mp2** parameters passed with the WM_CHAR message contain five separate fields of information. Parameter **mp1** contains three fields:

- **fsflags** is the low-order word of **mp1** and holds a number of flags indicating the state of the keyboard when the keystroke was received and the validity of the remaining fields. These flags are enumerated below.
- **ucrepeat** is the low-order byte of the high-order word of **mp1** (accessed using **CHAR3FROMMP**). This field normally contains the value 1; however, when a key is pressed and held for a period of time, the application may not be able to process WM_CHAR messages quickly enough to prevent the system message queue from becoming full. When this happens, the system gathers the duplicated WM_CHAR messages into one message and sets **ucrepeat** to the actual number of keystrokes received.
- **ucscancode** is the high-order byte of the high-order word of **mp1** (accessed using **CHAR4FROMMP**). If the KC_SCANCODE flag is set in **fsflags**, the field contains the actual scan code transmitted by the keyboard.

Parameter **mp2** contains the remaining two fields:

- **usch** is the low-order word of **mp2**. If the appropriate flags are set in **fsflags**, this field contains the ASCII value that maps to the keyboard scan code.
- **usvk** is the high-order word of **mp2**. If the KC_VIRTUALKEY flag is set in **fsflags**, this field contains the virtual key that maps to the keyboard scan code. Virtual keys are defined to match the function, direction, and other nonprintable keys on the keyboard.

The application must examine the **fsflags** field to determine how the keyboard input should be handled. The field contains a set of flag bits defined as:

KC_SCANCODE	0x0004	indicates that the **ucscancode** field contains valid data. This flag is normally set on all input from the keyboard, but would typically be clear when another window posted the WM_CHAR message.
KC_KEYUP	0x0040	indicates that a key has been released. For consistency with the system's translation of accelerators, applications should normally ignore all WM_CHAR messages with this flag set.
KC_PREVDOWN	0x0080	indicates that the previous WM_CHAR message for this key represented a key down event. This flag is set when a key is pressed and held such that multiple keystrokes are received; otherwise, a WM_CHAR message with the KC_KEYUP flag set would have been received.
KC_TOGGLE	0x1000	is set on every other instance of a given key being pressed. While this flag is valid for all keys, it is typically only important for keys such as CAPS LOCK which have a defined on-off state. Note that the toggle state is global—if focus changes between instances of a given key stroke, an application may receive consecutive occurrences of a keystroke without the toggle state changing.
KC_LONEKEY	0x0100	is set in conjunction with KC_KEYUP to indicate that no other key transitions have occurred since the downstroke of the key. For example, pressing the CTRL key followed by an alphabetic key, and then releasing first the alphabetic key followed by the CTRL key, the KC_LONEKEY flag will be set on the WM_CHAR message for the release of the alphabetic key. If the CTRL key is released first, the KC_LONEKEY flag is not set. Note that the system can be forced to perform accelerator translation on the release of a key by setting the LONEKEY flag in the accelerator table entry for the key.
KC_VIRTUALKEY	0x0002	indicates that the **usvk** field contains valid data. If this flag is not set, **usvk** should be ignored. This flag is normally set when a function key or other key that does not have a "normal" ASCII translation is pressed. In a few instances, such as when the TAB or ENTER key is pressed, both KC_VIRTUALKEY and KC_CHAR are set indicating that **usvk** contains the virtual key representation of the key and **usch** contains the ASCII representation for the key. KC_VIRTUALKEY is always set for the numeric keypad keys; if NUMLOCK is in effect, KC_CHAR will also be set.
KC_CHAR	0x0001	indicates that the **usch** field contains valid data and that neither the CTRL or ALT key is pressed.
KC_CTRL	0x0010	indicates that the CTRL key was depressed when the message was generated. If the KC_VIRTUALKEY flag is not also

		set, the **usch** field contains the ASCII character code that would have been generated had the CTRL key not been depressed.
KC_ALT	0x0020	indicates that the ALT key was depressed when the message was generated. If the KC_VIRTUALKEY flag is not also set, the **usch** field contains the ASCII character code that would have been generated had the ALT key not been depressed.
KC_SHIFT	0x0008	indicates that the SHIFT key was depressed when the message was generated.
KC_DEADKEY	0x0200	is set in combination with KC_CHAR to indicate that the key represents a diacritical that must be used in combination with another key. Text processing applications might draw the diacritical mark but not advance the cursor until the following keystroke is entered.
KC_COMPOSITE	0x0400	is set in combination with KC_CHAR to indicate that **usch** contains a character code that represents the combination of the previous KC_DEADKEY character and the current key. The accented vowels of many non-English languages are typically formed as composite keystrokes.
KC_INVALIDCOMP	0x0800	indicates that the current key cannot be combined with the previous key to represent a valid combined character.
KC_INVALIDCHAR	0x2000	indicates that the current keystroke cannot be found in the active translation tables.

Applications that process WM_CHAR messages must check to see that the desired flags are set and that undesired flags are not set. For example, an application that processes a particular control character will only consider WM_CHAR messages with the KC_CTRL flag set. But the application must also ensure that the KC_ALT and KC_VIRTUALKEY flags are not set to avoid processing invalid keystrokes as ordinary control characters. The KC_SHIFT flag is generally not considered in this instance as the control value of ASCII characters is the same for both upper- and lowercase. Figure 3.1 shows an example of the code required to recognize the downstroke of the CTRL+C keystroke.

```
if (!(fsflags & KC_KEYUP)) {
    if( fsflags & KC_CTRL &&
        !(fsflags & (KC_ALT | KC_VIRTUALKEY)) {
        if( usch == `c` || usch == `C` ) {
            /* perform CTRL+C processing */
        }
    }
}
```

Figure 3.1   Detecting CTRL+C.

```
if (!(fsflags & KC_KEYUP)) {  /* normally processed on downstroke */
/* Process Virtual keys */
   if (fsflags & KC_VIRTUALKEY) {
      if (fsflags & KC_CTRL && fsflags & KC_ALT) {
         if (fsflags & KC_SHIFT) { }/* CTRL+ALT+SHIFT+virtual key */
         else { }               /* CTRL+ALT+virtual key */
      } else if (fsflags & KC_CTRL) {
         if (fsflags & KC_SHIFT) { }/* CTRL+SHIFT+virtual key */
         else { }               /* CTRL+virtual key */
      } else if (fsflags & KC_ALT) {
         if (fsflags & KC_SHIFT) { }/* ALT+SHIFT+virtual key */
         else { }               /* ALT+virtual key */
      } else {
         if (fsflags & KC_SHIFT) { }/* SHIFT+virtual key */
         else { }               /* virtual key */
      } /* endif */
   /* Process normal, non-virtual keys */
   } else {
      if (fsflags & KC_CTRL && fsflags & KC_ALT) {
         if (fsflags & KC_SHIFT) { }/* CTRL+ALT+SHIFT+key */
         else { }               /* CTRL+ALT+key */
      } else if (fsflags & KC_CTRL) {
         if (fsflags & KC_SHIFT) { }/* CTRL+SHIFT+key */
         else { }               /* CTRL+key */
      } else if (fsflags & KC_ALT) {
         if (fsflags & KC_SHIFT) { }/* ALT+SHIFT+key */
         else { }               /* ALT+key */
      } else if (fsflags & KC_CHAR) {
         if (fsflags & KC_SHIFT) { }/* SHIFT+key */
         else { }               /* key */
      } /* endif */
   } /* endif */
} else {
   /* handling of KEYUP - normally ignored */
} /* endif */
```

Figure 3.2   General keystroke processing.

An application, such as a word processor, which processes many different keystrokes will normally employ a routine that provides handling for most if not all types of keystrokes. The application could be programmed using a series of IF statements that explicitly check for each combination of set and unset flags. However, a set of nested IF and ELSE clauses similar to that shown in Figure 3.2 will typically use less memory and execute more quickly. The routine first checks to see if the message signifies a downstroke; and if so, it then checks for a virtual key. If the keystroke represents a virtual key, the various combinations of the CTRL and ALT keys are tested, beginning with the most complex combination and working down to the situation where

```
if (!(fsflags & KC_KEYUP)) {
    switch( fsflags &
            (KC_VIRTUALKEY | KC_CHAR | KC_CTRL | KC_ALT | KC_SHIFT)) {
    case KC_VIRTUALKEY | KC_ALT | KC_CTRL | KC_SHIFT: { } break;
    case KC_VIRTUALKEY | KC_ALT | KC_CTRL:            { } break;
    case KC_VIRTUALKEY | KC_ALT | KC_SHIFT:           { } break;
    case KC_VIRTUALKEY | KC_ALT:                      { } break;
    case KC_VIRTUALKEY | KC_CTRL | KC_SHIFT:          { } break;
    case KC_VIRTUALKEY | KC_CTRL:                     { } break;
    case KC_VIRTUALKEY | KC_CHAR | KC_SHIFT:          { } break;
    case KC_VIRTUALKEY | KC_CHAR:                     { } break;
    case KC_VIRTUALKEY | KC_SHIFT:                    { } break;
    case KC_VIRTUALKEY:                               { } break;
    case KC_ALT | KC_CTRL | KC_SHIFT:                 { } break;
    case KC_ALT | KC_CTRL:                            { } break;
    case KC_ALT | KC_SHIFT:                           { } break;
    case KC_ALT:                                      { } break;
    case KC_CTRL | KC_SHIFT:                          { } break;
    case KC_CTRL:                                     { } break;
    case KC_CHAR | KC_SHIFT:                          { } break;
    case KC_CHAR:                                     { } break;
    default:                                          { } break;
    }
} else {
    /* process KEYUP events */
}
```

Figure 3.3 Alternate keystroke processing.

neither key is pressed. This ensures that the proper combination is recognized without having to explicitly check for unset flags. If KC_VIRTUALKEY is not set, then the various combinations of KC_CTRL and KC_ALT are again scanned to process the various possibilities for a normal ASCII character keystroke. Note that the KC_SHIFT flag is checked within the handling for each of the KC_CTRL and KC_ALT combinations. This is particularly important for the ASCII keys, as the shifted state actually modifies the character code in **usch**, eliminating the requirement to check for KC_SHIFT in most instances.

The requirement to process keystrokes based on the most complex flag combination can also be achieved by using a SWITCH statement, as shown in Figure 3.3. In this example, the relevant flags are masked to form the switch value. A case is then provided for each combination of interest. This method uses one logical operation and a series of comparisons and is thus extremely efficient. Since this method explicitly checks for both set and unset flags, the case statement for any combinations that the application does not process can be eliminated, allowing that combination to be processed by the default case and further increasing the efficiency of the operation.

OBTAINING KEYBOARD INPUT

While WM_CHAR messages may be sent from one window to another, the messages are usually received when a window or one of its owned windows is the window that currently has the input focus. PM normally gives the focus to a window when the user clicks the window with the mouse, selects the window from the task list, or uses one of the navigation keys. However, an application can give or take the keyboard focus by calling the **WinSetFocus** API. The prototype for this function is:

```
BOOL APIENTRY WinSetFocus( HWND      hwndDesktop,
                           HWND      hwndFocus );
```

Figure 3.4   The WinSetFocus prototype.

- The **hwndDesktop** parameter is a handle of a desktop window or the HWND_DESKTOP constant.
- The **hwndFocus** parameter is the handle of the window which is to receive the keyboard input focus.

The return value indicates the success of the focus change. The value TRUE indicates that the focus change was successful while a value of FALSE indicates that an error occurred, typically the result of passing an invalid window handle. Use this function with care as an arbitrary change of focus can interrupt work the user is performing in some other application. As a rule, this function should only be called to change focus to another window in the current application and only when requested either directly or indirectly by the user.

A similar API, **WinFocusChange**, can also be used to assign the keyboard input focus to another window. The API takes one additional parameter which allows an application to modify the system's handling of the focus change.

THE KEYBOARD INPUT CURSOR

Just as the mouse pointer shows the user the location affected by mouse input, the keyboard input cursor informs the user of the location that will be affected by keyboard input. However, unlike the mouse pointer, the keyboard input cursor is not automatically handled by the system—application intervention is required. Only one keyboard input cursor is supported, and an existing cursor is deleted when another is created. Thus, for proper integration with other programs, applications that employ a cursor should create the cursor when the window in which the cursor is displayed receives the input focus and should destroy the cursor when the window loses the input focus. The appearance of the cursor is specified by the application when the cursor is created. When operating in insert mode, an application normally creates a narrow, vertical cursor and positions the cursor between the two characters where insertion will occur. When operating in overstrike mode, a cursor that is the width of the character is created and positioned to overlay the character which will be replaced by a character keystroke. The application can specify a blinking or nonblinking cursor which is either solid, half-toned, or transparent.

The **WinCreateCursor** API is used to create and manipulate the cursor. The function is prototyped as shown in Figure 3.5.

- The **hwnd** parameter is the handle of the window where the cursor will be displayed.
- The **lx** parameter is a 32-bit integer specifying the x or horizontal coordinate of the left edge of the cursor specified in window coordinates.
- The **ly** parameter is a 32-bit signed integer specifying the y or vertical coordinate of the bottom edge of the cursor specified in window coordinates.
- The **lcx** parameter is a 32-bit signed integer specifying the width of the cursor in window coordinates. If **lcx** is set to 0, the width is set to the system border width specified by the system value SV_CXBORDER.
- The **lcy** parameter is a 32-bit signed integer specifying the height of the cursor in window coordinates. If **lcy** is set to 0, the height is set to the system border height specified by system value SV_CYBORDER.
- The **ulrgf** parameter is a 32-bit field containing flags that primarily specify the appearance of the cursor. The flags are defined as follows:

CURSOR_SOLID   0x0000   indicates that the cursor is to be displayed as a filled rectangle.

CURSOR_HALFTONE   0x0001   indicates that the cursor is to be displayed as a halftoned filled rectangle.

CURSOR_FRAME   0x0002   indicates that the cursor is to be displayed as a non-filled rectangle.

```
BOOL APIENTRY WinCreateCursor( HWND     hwnd,
                               LONG     lx,
                               LONG     ly,
                               LONG     lcx,
                               LONG     lcy,
                               ULONG    ulrgf,
                               PRECTL   prclClip );
```

Figure 3.5   The WinCreateCursor prototype.

| CURSOR_FLASH | 0x0004 | indicates that the cursor should alternate between visible and hidden, that is blink. |
| CURSOR_SETPOS | 0x8000 | indicates that the cursor should maintain its current characteristics but be moved to the indicated position. **lcx**, **lcy**, and the other bits of **ulrgf** are ignored when this flag is set. |

- The **prclClip** parameter is a pointer to a RECTL structure which specifies the rectangle within which the cursor will be displayed. If the cursor is moved outside this rectangle, it is clipped and not displayed. This parameter may be set to NULL to specify that the clipping rectangle is the area occupied by **hwnd**. The actual clipping region is the intersection of the area specified by **prclClip** and the area occupied by **hwnd**. The coordinates of the clipping rectangle are specified in window coordinates.

WinCreateCursor returns TRUE if the cursor is successfully created. Otherwise, FALSE is returned.

PM maintains a visibility count for the cursor. When this count is zero, the cursor is visible on the display; when the count is nonzero, the cursor is hidden. Following creation, the visibility count is set to 1 and thus the cursor is invisible. The application must call the **WinShowCursor** API in order to reduce the visibility count to zero and make the cursor visible. Each time **WinShowCursor** is called to hide the cursor, the visibility count is incremented; when **WinShowCursor** is called to show the cursor, the visibility count is decremented (unless the current count is already zero). **WinShowCursor** is prototyped as shown in Figure 3.6.

- The **hwnd** parameter is the handle of the window that currently owns the cursor.
- The **fShow** parameter is a Boolean value that indicates the desired visibility of the cursor. If TRUE, the cursor should be shown and the visibility count is decremented; if FALSE, the cursor should be hidden and the visibility count is incremented.

The return value indicates the success of the function. A FALSE return indicates that an error occurred; for example, **hwnd** specified an invalid window handle, or that an attempt was made to show the cursor when it was already

```
BOOL APIENTRY WinShowCursor( HWND    hwnd,
                             BOOL    fShow );
```

Figure 3.6   The WinShowCursor prototype.

```
BOOL APIENTRY WinDestroyCursor( HWND hwnd );
```

Figure 3.7 **The WinDestroyCursor prototype.**

visible. In multithreaded applications, **WinShowCursor** must be called from the same thread that created the cursor.

When an application no longer needs the input cursor or loses the input focus, the cursor should be destroyed with the **WinDestroyCursor** API. The API is prototyped as shown in Figure 3.7.

- The **hwnd** parameter is the handle of the window that currently owns the cursor.

The API return value indicates the success of the function. It will be FALSE if the window specified by **hwnd** is not the current owner of the cursor.

Figure 3.8 shows the WM_SETFOCUS message processing for a window that displays a text insertion cursor. If the window is receiving the focus, the utility function **CalcCurrentPos** is called to obtain the coordinates for displaying the cursor. **WinCreateCursor** is then called to create an input cursor at the calculated location. The **lcx** and **lcy** parameters are set to zero so that the system-defined values are used, and **prclClip** is set to NULL to indicate

```
USHORT    usFocus = SHORT1FROMMP( mp2 );
LONG      lx = 0;
LONG      ly = 0;

case WM_SETFOCUS:
   if (usFocus) {
      /* gaining the focus - create the input cursor */

      /* where should the cursor be positioned */
      CalcCurrentPos( &lx, &ly );

      /* create the cursor */
      WinCreateCursor( hwnd, lx, ly, 0, 0,
                       CURSOR_SOLID | CURSOR_FLASH, NULL );

      /* make the cursor visible */
      WinShowCursor( hwnd, TRUE );
   } else {
      /* losing the focus - destroy the input cursor */
      WinDestroyCursor( hwnd );
   } /* endif */
   return WinDefWindowProc( hwnd, msg, mp1, mp2 );
```

Figure 3.8 **Processing the WM_SETFOCUS message.**

that the window rectangle should serve as the clipping rectangle. Parameter **ulrgf** is set to create a blinking, solid cursor. After the cursor is created, **WinShowCursor** is called with **fShow** set to TRUE to decrement the cursor's visibility count, causing the cursor to become visible. If the window is losing the focus, **WinDestroyCursor** is called to destroy the input cursor.

UPDATING THE DISPLAY

Now that you know the basics of processing keyboard input and managing the input cursor, let's examine how a text-based application can echo keyboard input to the display. One means of achieving this function is to update the text buffers and then repaint the entire window by calling the **WinInvalidateRect** API each time a character is added or deleted. While this method is relatively simple from a programming standpoint, repainting the entire window is a time-consuming process which, repeated frequently, can prevent the user from rapidly entering text.

One alternative is to invalidate only the area of the screen affected by the input. For example, assume that an application inserts received characters into existing text. As each character is received, the application must insert the new character at the proper position in the text and then repaint from the point of insertion to the end of the line containing the new character—no other text in the window is affected and thus does not need to be redrawn. In this case, the application can compute a rectangle which begins at the insertion point and is wide enough to contain the remaining characters on the line. This rectangle is then passed to **WinInvalidateRect** and only that portion of the window is repainted. For maximum efficiency, the application's WM_PAINT processing should locate the text that corresponds to the invalid rectangle and only issue drawing orders for that text.

A second alternative removes the need to call **WinInvalidateRect** and then calculate the proper text for redrawing. With this method, the application obtains a presentation space for the window using the **WinGetPS** API, draws the text, and then releases the presentation space using the **WinReleasePS** API. Figure 3.9 provides an example of the code to implement this method. The function **InsertCharacter** is called from the WM_CHAR processing to place a new character into the text buffer. A pointer to a control structure that maintains the current insert position in the text buffer and a pointer to an array of line data structures that contain the text for each line, are stored in the window instance data. After retrieving the pointer to the structure from the window data, the function sets a pointer to the line data structure for the current line. A new text buffer is then allocated to hold the current text plus the new character and the zero terminator character. The old text before the insertion point is then copied to the new string. The new character is then added and the remainder of the current line is copied to the new buffer. **InsertCharacter** then calls routine **CalcCurrentPos** to determine the coordinate of the lower left corner of the current insertion point. This point is used as the lower left corner of the rectangle to be drawn and, assuming a monospaced font, the upper edge of the rectangle is calculated based on the height of characters; and the right edge is calculated by multiplying the number of characters remaining on the line by the width of a character. The application now has the text to be drawn and the rectangle within which to draw the text.

Next, **WinShowCursor** is called to hide the input cursor to prevent corruption from the display of the cursor. **WinGetPS** is then called to obtain a presentation space for drawing, the text is drawn using the **WinDrawText** API (see Chapter 16 for a detailed treatment of this API), and the presentation space is released with a call to **WinReleasePS**. The operation is completed by freeing the memory for the original text string and changing the text pointer in the current line structure to point to the newly allocated text buffer. The current insertion point is updated to the next column, and the new cursor position is calculated by adding the width of a character to the old position. **WinCreateCursor** is then called with the CURSOR_SETPOS flag to move the cursor to the new location, and **WinShowCursor** is called to make the cursor visible again.

Removing a character is handled in much the same manner. The primary difference is that the rectangle must be extended one character beyond the end of the text to erase the location where the last character of the line was previously displayed.

This discussion has assumed that monospaced fonts are used. These fonts allow the application to assume that the characters are essentially placed on a grid, allowing the display coordinates of a character to be derived with simple mathematical calculations. If the application allows proportional fonts to be used, the position of any given character is best determined by calling the **GpiQueryCharStringPos** API. This function returns an array that contains the coordinates of each character. See Chapter 16 for detailed information on this API.

```
static void InsertCharacter( HWND hwnd, char chInsert )
{
   /* See the sample program accompanying this chapter for a */
   /* full description of the PAPP_DATA and PLINE data types */
   PAPP_DATA   pAppData = (PAPP_DATA)NULL;
   PLINE       pline = (PLINE)NULL;
   HPS         hps;
   PSZ         pszNewText = (PSZ)NULL;
   RECTL       rectlText;
```

Figure 3.9   Drawing inserted characters. **continued**

```
    /* insure that window control data exists and file is open */
pAppData = (PAPP_DATA)WinQueryWindowPtr( hwnd, APP_DATA_POINTER );
if (pAppData != (PAPP_DATA)NULL) {
    /* Get pointer to control structure for current line */
    pline = pAppData->plineCurLine;
    /* allocate a new text buffer */
    pszNewText = (PSZ)malloc( strlen(pline->pszText) + 2 );
    if (pszNewText != (PSZ)NULL) {
        /* copy over old text that is before the current position */
        strncpy( pszNewText, pline->pszText, pAppData->lCurCol );
        /* insert new character */
        pszNewText[ pAppData->lCurCol ] = chInsert;
        pszNewText[ pAppData->lCurCol + 1 ] = '\0';
        /* copy over text following current position */
        strcat( pszNewText, &pline->pszText[ pAppData->lCurCol ] );
        /* get window coordinates of current position */
        CalcCurrentPos( hwnd, pAppData,
                        &rectlText.xLeft, &rectlText.yBottom );
        /* determine width of remaining text and add to current pos */
        rectlText.xRight = strlen(&pszNewText[pAppData->lCurCol]) *
                        pAppData->lWidth + rectlText.xLeft;
        /* add height to current pos */
        rectlText.yTop = rectlText.yBottom + pAppData->lHeight;
        /* hide the cursor during output */
        WinShowCursor( hwnd, FALSE );
        /* obtain presentation space for the window */
        hps = WinGetPS( hwnd );
        /* draw the text */
        WinDrawText( hps, -1, &pszNewText[pAppData->lCurCol], &rectlText,
                    0, 0, DT_TOP | DT_LEFT | DT_TEXTATTRS | DT_ERASERECT );
        /* and release the PS */
        WinReleasePS( hps );
        /* get rid of old buffer and store new one in control struct */
        free( pline->pszText );
        pline->pszText = pszNewText;
        /* advance current location and cursor by one character */
        rectlText.xLeft += pAppData->lWidth;
        pAppData->lCurCol++;
        /* move and redisplay the cursor */
        WinCreateCursor( hwnd, rectlText.xLeft, rectlText.yBottom,
                        0, 0, CURSOR_SETPOS, NULL );
        WinShowCursor( hwnd, TRUE );
    } /* endif */
} /* endif */
return;
}
```

Figure 3.9   Drawing inserted characters.

Function **InsertCharacter** would normally be called whenever a normal ASCII key is received. Receipt of a virtual key would not normally cause this routine to be called, however, some of the virtual keys are typically processed in text editing applications. For example, the keyboard directional keys (arrows, PAGE UP, PAGE DOWN, and so on) are typically assigned to functions that allow the user to move the input cursor within the text and/or to cause different portions of the text to be displayed on the screen. These keys provide keyboard access to the functionality that is available to mouse users via the scroll bar controls. Discussion of the programming techniques for these keys will therefore be deferred to the following section which describes the scroll bar control.

THE SCROLL BAR CONTROL

The scroll bar control graphically represents a finite range of values from which a single value has been selected and allows the user to select a value within the prescribed range. Visually, the control consists of a background area, the bar, representing the entire range of selectable values; a slider representing the currently selected value; and arrow icons at each end of the bar which can be used to incrementally change the selected value. The slider portion of the scroll bar can itself be sized to indicate a range of values within the greater range specified by the bar, for example, the slider can represent the portion of a file which is actually displayed within a window. Scroll bars can be displayed either vertically or horizontally.

In the past, the scroll bar was often used for data input; for example, three scroll bars could be used to represent and select the red, green, and blue components of an RGB color value. New applications should use slider controls (see Chapter 11) for data input and restrict their usage of the scroll bar to its intended purpose, indicating and controlling that portion of a set of data that is displayed within a window.

Scroll bar controls may be explicitly created by an application; however, they are normally included as part of another control type or by specifying the FCF_VERTSCROLL and/or FCF_HORZSCROLL flags when a frame window is created. When created in the latter fashion, horizontal scroll bars extend the width of the client area and vertical scroll bars extend the height of the client area.

Scroll Bar Styles

Five class-specific styles are available to modify the behavior and appearance of the scroll bar. These flags are:

SBS_HORZ   0x0000   causes the control to act as a horizontal scroll bar; issuing
                          WM_HSCROLL notifications, placing the arrows along the

		left and right edges of the bar, and moving the slider between the left and right edges of the control.
SBS_VERT	0x0001	causes the control to act as a vertical scroll bar; issuing WM_VSCROLL notification messages, placing the arrows along the top and bottom edges of the bar, and moving the slider between the top and bottom edges of the bar.
SBS_AUTOTRACK	0x0004	is used by the control when the slider position is directly modified with the mouse. If this style is specified, the entire slider moves with the mouse. If the style is not specified, the slider remains in place and only a shadow of the slider moves with the mouse.
SBS_THUMBSIZE	0x0002	indicates that the slider size should represent the portion of the data displayed in the window. The **cVisible** and **cTotal** elements of the control data for the scroll bar are used for this purpose. The size of the slider in proportion to the length of the bar is matched to the proportion of **cVisible** to **cTotal**.
SBS_AUTOSIZE	0x2000	causes the system to automatically assign a width to vertical scroll bars and a height to horizontal scroll bars.

Scroll Bar Notification Messages

The scroll bar control provides the user with three types of scrolling functions. When the scroll bar is associated with a window displaying text, the user may click on one of the arrow keys to scroll the text by one line or character, click on the bar to scroll the text by a page, or click on and drag the slider to scroll the text to a specific location. If the window is displaying graphical, rather than textual, information, the application must define a suitable equivalent for scrolling by a line or character. Even in textual windows, the application controls the scrolling and can therefore modify the functionality of each scroll type; however, failure to provide the standard functionality may confuse the user. Depending on the scroll bar style, one of two messages is used to transmit the user request to the application. A scroll bar with the SBS_HORZ style sends a WM_HSCROLL message and a scroll bar with the SBS_VERT style sends a WM_VSCROLL message. The message is sent to the window that owns the scroll bar, and frame windows forward the message to the client window. The **mp1** and **mp2** parameters of both messages are identical. Parameter **mp1** contains the window ID of the scroll bar window in the low-order word. Parameter **mp2** is divided into two fields:

- **sslider** is contained in the low-order word. This field identifies the current position of the slider when **uscmd** is set to SB_SLIDERTRACK or SB_SLIDERPOSITION.

- **uscmd** is contained in the high-order word. This field contains a notification code indicating the user action that caused the message to be transmitted.

For a vertical scroll bar, the **uscmd** field may be set to one of the following values:

SB_LINEUP	0x0001	indicating that the up arrow at the top of the scroll bar was clicked.
SB_LINEDOWN	0x0002	indicating that the down arrow at the bottom of the scroll bar was clicked.
SB_PAGEUP	0x0003	indicating that the bar was clicked at a location above the current position of the slider.
SB_PAGEDOWN	0x0004	indicating that the bar was clicked at a location below the current position of the slider.

The **uscmd** field may be set to the following values for messages received from a horizontal scroll bar:

SB_LINELEFT	0x0001	indicating that the left arrow at the left end of the scroll bar was clicked.
SB_LINERIGHT	0x0002	indicating that the right arrow at the right end of the scroll bar was clicked.
SB_PAGELEFT	0x0003	indicating that the bar was clicked at a location to the left of the current slider position.
SB_PAGERIGHT	0x0004	indicating that the bar was clicked at a location to the right of the current slider position.

Both horizontal and vertical scroll bars may also set **uscmd** to the following values:

SB_SLIDERTRACK	0x0005	indicating that the user is dragging the slider. The current position is contained in the **sslider** field. Applications that can update the window quickly process this message to provide direct feedback on the window contents as the slider is moved.
SB_SLIDERPOSITION	0x0006	indicating that the user has completed a drag operation on the slider. The **sslider** field contains the final position of the slider.
SB_ENDSCROLL	0x0007	indicating that the user has clicked and released the mouse on either the bar or an arrow. Since multiple scroll messages will be sent when the user holds the

mouse button down, an application that cannot draw its output quickly may wish to maintain the scrolled position but defer painting until this message is received, indicating that the scrolling operation is complete.

Managing the Scroll Bar

In order to effectively utilize scroll bars, an application must concern itself with three basic functions: maintaining the scroll bar range and, optionally, the size of the slider; processing scroll bar messages and maintaining the slider position; and updating the window contents to track the scroll bar position.

Maintaining the Scroll Bar Range

When a scroll bar is created and no data is displayed in the associated window, the scroll bar range should be set such that both the low and high end of the value range are zero, effectively disabling the scroll bar. As data is added to the window—for instance, by opening a file—the scroll bar range should be modified to reflect the actual amount of data available. The application establishes the scroll bar range by sending an SBM_SETSCROLLBAR message to the scroll bar window. The low-order word of parameter **mp1** is the **sslider** parameter, a signed integer value specifying the position within the range where the slider should be positioned. Parameter **mp2** contains two fields. The low-order word contains parameter **sfirst**, the lowest value in the range, and must be greater than or equal to zero. The high-order word of **mp2** is parameter **slast** and specifies the highest value in the range of values. This value must be greater than or equal to **sfirst**.

Figure 3.10 shows an example of the code that an application could use to initialize the scroll bar after a new file is opened. In this example, a data structure is used that contains elements specifying the number of lines in the file and the number of lines displayed in the window. This latter value is calculated by dividing the size of the window by the height of a character. The code establishes the slider range by sending an SBM_SETSCROLLBAR message to the vertical scroll bar window. The **sslider** parameter is set to

```
/* Update the vertical scroll bar */
WinSendMsg( hwndScroll, SBM_SETSCROLLBAR, 0L,
          MPFROM2SHORT( 0, (SHORT)pAppData->lNumLines - 1));
WinSendMsg( hwndScroll, SBM_SETTHUMBSIZE,
          MPFROM2SHORT( (SHORT)pAppData->lLinesPerPage,
                        (SHORT)pAppData->lNumLines), 0L );
```

Figure 3.10 Setting scroll bar range, position, and thumb size.

zero since the first line of the file will be displayed at the top of the window. Parameter **sfirst** is set to zero, and **slast** is set to the number of lines in the file. This will allow the user to scroll between the first line and the last line.

The optional size of the slider is also set in Figure 3.10 by sending an SBM_SETTHUMBSIZE message to the scroll bar. Parameter **mp1** of this message contains two fields. Field **svisible** is the low-order word of **mp1** and contains a value specifying the number of lines that can be displayed in the window. The units of the value are considered to be the same as the units used to set the scroll bar range. The high-order word of **mp1** is field **stotal** and is set to the number of lines in the file. Parameter **mp2** is reserved and must be set to zero.

Processing Scroll Bar Messages

Let's examine how an application processes messages received from a scroll bar by looking at an example program that displays text files. The vertical scroll bar range represents the number of lines of text in a displayed file and the scroll bar position represents the number of the line displayed at the top of the window. Figure 3.11 shows a switch statement that computes the number of lines of text that correspond to a particular scroll command. Note that an upward scrolling action moves toward the top of the file, reducing the line

```
HWND        hwndScroll;    /* scroll bar window handle */
SHORT       sLinesPerPage; /* lines displayable in window */
SHORT       sDLines = 0;   /* delta display lines */

switch (SHORT2FROMMP(mp2)) {
case SB_LINEUP:
   sDLines = -1;
   break;
case SB_LINEDOWN:
   sDLines = 1;
   break;
case SB_PAGEUP:
   sDLines = (-1) * sLinesPerPage;
   break;
case SB_PAGEDOWN:
   sDLines = sLinesPerPage;
   break;
case SB_SLIDERTRACK:
   sDLines = (SHORT)WinSendMsg( hwndScroll, SBM_QUERYPOS,
                             MPFROMLONG(0L), MPFROMLONG(0L) );
   sDLines = SHORT1FROMMP(mp2) - sDLines;
   break;
} /* endswitch */
```

Figure 3.11 Computing the scroll delta.

number; and scrolling down moves toward the bottom of the file, increasing the line number. Thus an SB_LINEUP command will move the window contents one line closer to the start of the file or a delta of negative one, and an SB_LINEDOWN command will move the window contents one line closer to the end of the file or a delta of positive one. Likewise, an SB_PAGEUP command sets the delta to negative one times the number of lines displayed on a page, and an SB_PAGEDOWN command sets the delta to the number of lines in one page. (The lines per page value is computed by dividing the height of the window by the height of the current font.) The SB_SLIDERTRACK command provides an absolute position, and the value delta is set to the difference between the current position and the SB_SLIDERTRACK position. The current position is retrieved by sending an SBM_QUERYPOS message to the scroll bar window. Parameters **mp1** and **mp2** are both reserved and must be passed as zero. The message returns a 16-bit, signed integer representing the current location of the slider.

Once the delta value has been determined, Figure 3.12 shows code that computes and validates the new top line of the display and then updates the slider position to represent the new value. First the current slider position is queried using the SBM_QUERYPOS message. The delta value is then added

```
SHORT      sCurPos, sSavePos;
LONG       lDy, lFullPage;
RECTL      rectl;

/* Adjust the slider position */
sCurPos = SHORT1FROMMR(WinSendMsg( hwndScroll, SBM_QUERYPOS,
                                   MPFROMLONG(0L), MPFROMLONG(0L) ));
sSavePos = sCurPos;
sCurPos += sDLines;
if( sCurPos < 0 ) sCurPos = 0;
if( (LONG)sCurPos > sNumLines ) sCurPos = sNumLines;
WinSendMsg( hwndScroll, SBM_SETPOS, MPFROMSHORT( sCurPos ), 0l );
sDLines = sCurPos - sSavePos;

/* Update the window contents */
lDy = (LONG)sDLines * lHeight;
lFullPage = (LONG)sLinesPerPage * lHeight;
if (lDy >= lFullPage) {
   WinInvalidateRect( hwnd, NULL, TRUE );
} else {
   WinQueryWindowRect( hwnd, &rectl );
   rectl.yBottom = rectl.yTop - lFullPage;
   WinScrollWindow( hwnd, 0L, lDy, &rectl, &rectl,
                    NULLHANDLE, NULL, SW_INVALIDATERGN );
} /* endif */
```

Figure 3.12   **Updating the display after scrolling.**

to the current position to obtain the new position. If this position is less than zero, the beginning of the file, the position is set back to the beginning of the file. If the position is beyond the last line of the file, the position is set to the last line of the file. An SBM_SETPOS message is then sent to the scroll bar window to establish the new slider position. The low-order word of parameter **mp1** of this message is set to the new slider position. Parameter **mp2** is reserved and must be set to zero.

Updating Window Contents

Also shown in Figure 3.12 is the code to update the data displayed in the window. The code first determines the distance by which the data in the window is to be moved by multiplying the number of lines times the height of a character. If this distance represents a full-page repaint, calling **WinInvalidateRect** with a NULL pointer as the **pRectl** parameter forces the entire window to be redrawn. If the distance is less than a full page, then the **WinScrollWindow** API is used to move the window contents which will still be displayed to their new location, and will redraw only that portion of the window that will show new data, providing a significant performance boost. The prototype for this API is shown in Figure 3.13.

- The **hwnd** parameter is the handle of the window whose contents are to be scrolled.
- The **lDx** parameter is a 32-bit signed integer indicating the horizontal distance by which the window contents are to be scrolled. This distance is expressed in device units. Positive integers cause the window contents to scroll to the right, negative integers cause the window contents to scroll to the left.
- The **lDy** parameter is a 32-bit signed integer which indicates the vertical distance by which the window is to be scrolled. The distance is expressed in device units. A positive integer causes the window contents to scroll upward and a negative integer causes the contents to scroll downward.

```
LONG WinScrollWindow( HWND    hwnd,
                      LONG    lDx,
                      LONG    lDy,
                      PRECTL  prclScroll,
                      PRECTL  prclClip,
                      HRGN    hrgnUpdateRgn,
                      PRECTL  prclUpdate,
                      ULONG   flOptions )
```

Figure 3.13 The WinScrollWindow prototype.

- The **prclScroll** parameter is a pointer to a RECTL structure which identifies the portion of the window's contents to move. If the pointer is NULL, the entire contents of the window are moved.
- The **prclClip** parameter is a pointer to a RECTL structure which, if not NULL, identifies the clip rectangle for the scrolling operation. Only the area of the window within this rectangle is affected by the scroll. For example, if the **prclScroll** rectangle and **prclClip** rectangle identify the same area of the screen, the entire contents of that area will be moved, but the portion that moves beyond the **prclClip** rectangle is discarded.
- The **hrgnUpdateRgn** parameter is a handle to the update region. If this parameter is not NULLHANDLE, the region identified by **hrgnUpdateRgn** will be set to the area uncovered by the scroll operation when the API returns.
- The **prclUpdate** parameter is a pointer to a RECTL structure which the API fills with the coordinates of the bounding rectangle for the area uncovered by the scroll operation. This pointer may be set to NULL if this information is not desired.
- The **flOptions** parameter is a set of flags that identify optional functions to be performed. The valid flags are:

SW_SCROLLCHILDREN   0x0001   causes all child windows of **hwnd** to also be scrolled. If this flag is not set, only the child windows within the rectangle identified by **prclScroll** are scrolled.

SW_INVALIDATEREGION   0x0002   causes the area uncovered by the scrolling operation to be added to the invalid regions for the windows (**hwnd** and children) affected by the scroll. This causes a WM_PAINT message to be generated. If any of the affected windows have class style CS_SYNCPAINT, the WM_PAINT message will be sent before **WinScrollWindow** returns. If this bit is not set, the application should use the **hrgnUpdateRgn** and/or **prclUpdate** parameter return values to paint the uncovered area without the WM_PAINT message.

WinScrollWindow returns a 32-bit integer which indicates the complexity of the area uncovered by the scrolling operation.

RGN_NULL   0x0001   indicates that the operation did not invalidate any portion of the window. This could occur when there is no intersection between **prclScroll** and **prclClip**.

RGN_RECT   0x0002   indicates that a simple rectangle was invalidated. This would normally occur when either **lDx** or **lDy** is zero.

RGN_COMPLEX   0x0003   indicates that a complex region was invalidated. This would normally occur when both **lDx** and **lDy** are nonzero.

RGN_ERROR   0x0000   indicates that an error occurred.

Getting back to the example in Figure 3.12, before **WinScrollWindow** is called, a scroll and clip rectangle is computed which prevents the scrolling operation from moving unwanted data into the area left at the bottom of the window where a full line of text cannot be displayed. This is accomplished first by obtaining the coordinate rectangle for the entire window area. The bottom coordinate of the rectangle is then set to the top coordinate less the distance required to display the number of lines of text that will fit on the screen.

WinScrollWindow is then called with **lDx** set to zero, since this is a vertical scroll; and **lDy** set to the scroll distance computed earlier. The **prclScroll** and **prclClip** pointers are set to reference the computed rectangle which encloses the actual text display rectangle. The SW_INVALIDATEREGION flag of **flOptions** is set so that a WM_PAINT message will be generated to redraw the portion of the window uncovered by the scroll operation. Parameters **hrgnUpdateRgn** and **prclUpdate** are set to NULL since they will not be needed.

The final aspect of the scrolling operation is maintenance of the input cursor position. Applications that display an input cursor typically employ one of two approaches for managing the current input location, and thus the input cursor, during scrolling. The first approach is an independent input cursor which is not affected by scrolling operations. The user is able to freely scroll through the data, perhaps for reference, and quickly return to the current input location whenever a keystroke is entered. This approach does not require any additional processing during scrolling operations, but the application normally must redraw the text when a keystroke is received in order to display the data at the input location.

The second approach moves the input cursor as necessary to ensure that it remains within the displayed portion of the data. For example, in a text application, if the display area is scrolled up such that the input cursor position is below the last displayed line, the cursor is moved to the last line of the displayed area. Figure 3.14 shows code that will handle these calculations.

```
SHORT   sCurLine;

/* adjust the cursor */
if (sCurLine < sCurPos) {
   sCurLine = sCurPos;
} else if (sCurLine >= sCurPos + sLinesPerPage) {
   sCurLine = sCurPos + sLinesPerPage - 1;
} /* endif */
UpdateCursor( hwnd );
```

Figure 3.14   Adjusting the input cursor.

Variables **sCurPos** and **sLinesPerPage** are taken from Figures 3.11 and 3.12. Variable **sCurLine** contains the number of the line that is currently displayed at the top of the window. The first step is to determine if the current input line number is less than the first line displayed in the window. If so, the cursor must be moved to the first displayed line. Next a check is made to see if the current input line number is beyond the last line displayed in the window. If so, the current input line is changed to the last line of the displayed data. At this point, the current input line is known to be within the displayed data, and a utility routine, **UpdateCursor**, is called to display the input cursor at the current input line. This routine computes the x and y coordinates of the cursor based on the current input line and column and then calls **WinCreateCursor** with the CURSOR_SETPOS flag to move the existing cursor to the new position.

PROCESSING THE DIRECTIONAL KEYS

The standard PC keyboard has a number of keys that are typically used in both textual and graphical applications to manipulate the input cursor position. In most instances, if one of these keys moves the input cursor to a position outside the current display area, the display area is adjusted to keep the input cursor in view. While separate routines could be implemented to adjust the display area, the scroll bar message procedures are typically capable of meeting this requirement. Thus the keyboard routines can send an appropriate WM_VSCROLL or WM_HSCROLL message to display the proper data in the window. The following discussion examines the standard functional definitions of the keyboard keys and the coding required to implement this functionality. The discussion is organized into sets of keys based on the modifiers used to obtain the keystroke.

All of the keys normally used for cursor movement are considered virtual keys. The first set of keys are those that are modified by the CTRL key. Thus these are recognized by testing for the presence of the KC_VIRTUALKEY and KC_CTRL flags and the absence of the KC_ALT and KC_SHIFT flags as shown in Figure 3.15. The definitions and processing for these keys are as follows:

CTRL+PAGEUP This keystroke is used to move the cursor one page to the left. The cursor is adjusted by subtracting the number of columns per page from the current cursor position and ensuring that the result is not less than zero. The display area is adjusted by sending a WM_HSCROLL message with **uscmd** set to SB_PAGELEFT.

CTRL+PAGEDOWN This keystroke is used to move the cursor one page to the right. The cursor is adjusted by adding the number of columns per page to the current cursor position and ensuring that the result is not greater than the width of the longest line in the data. The display area is adjusted by sending a WM_HSCROLL message with **uscmd** set to SB_PAGERIGHT.

```
if (fsflags & KC_VIRTUALKEY && fsflags & KC_CTRL &&
    !(fsflags & (KC_ALT | KC_SHIFT))) {
  switch (CHAR3FROMMP(mp2)) {
  case VK_PAGEUP:    /* CTRL+PAGE UP = cursor page left */
     sCurCol -= sColsPerPage;
     if (sCurCol < 0) sCurCol = 0;
     WinSendMsg( hwnd, WM_HSCROLL, (MPARAM)FID_HORZSCROLL,
                 MPFROM2SHORT( 0, SB_PAGELEFT ));
     break;
  case VK_PAGEDOWN: /* CTRL+PAGE DOWN = cursor page right */
     sCurCol += sColsPerPage;
     if (sCurCol > sMaxWidth) {
        sCurCol = sMaxWidth;
     } /* endif */
     WinSendMsg( hwnd, WM_HSCROLL, (MPARAM)FID_HORZSCROLL,
                 MPFROM2SHORT( 0, SB_PAGERIGHT ));
     break;
  case VK_HOME:      /* CTRL+HOME = cursor to start of data */
     sCurLine = 0;
     sCurCol = 0;
     WinSendMsg( hwnd, WM_VSCROLL, (MPARAM)FID_VERTSCROLL,
                 MPFROM2SHORT( 0, SB_SLIDERTRACK ));
     WinSendMsg( hwnd, WM_HSCROLL, (MPARAM)FID_HORZSCROLL,
                 MPFROM2SHORT( 0, SB_SLIDERTRACK ));
     break;
  case VK_END:       /* CTRL+END = cursor to end of data */
     sCurLine = sNumLines - 1;
     sCurCol = strlen(plineLast->pszText );
     sTemp = sCurLine - sLinesPerPage + 1;
     if (sTemp < 0) sTemp = 0;
     WinSendMsg( hwnd, WM_VSCROLL, (MPARAM)FID_VERTSCROLL,
                 MPFROM2SHORT( sTemp, SB_SLIDERTRACK ));
     sTemp = sCurCol - sColsPerPage;
     if (sTemp < 0) sTemp = 0;
     WinSendMsg( hwnd, WM_HSCROLL, (MPARAM)FID_HORZSCROLL,
                 MPFROM2SHORT( sTemp, SB_SLIDERTRACK ));
     break;
  } /* endswitch */
} /* endif */
```

Figure 3.15   Processing CTRL+ directional keys.

CTRL+HOME   This keystroke is used to move the input cursor to the start of the data. The input cursor location is changed to line zero and column zero. The display area is adjusted such that the start of data is displayed in the top left corner of the display by sending both **WM_HSCROLL** and **WM_VSCROLL** messages. For each, **uscmd** is set to SB_SLIDERTRACK and **sslider** is set to zero.

CTRL+END   This keystroke is used to move the input cursor to the end of the data. The current line is set to the last line, the number of lines less one. The current column is set to the length of the last line of text, a value that will place the cursor after the last character on the line. The display area is adjusted to cause the end of data to be displayed at the bottom of the screen. Thus a WM_VSCROLL message is sent with **uscmd** set to SB_SLIDERTRACK and **sslider** set to the number of lines less the number of lines on a page. This value is incremented so that the current line will be the last line in the display area. Similarly, a WM_HSCROLL message is sent with **uscmd** set to SB_SLIDERTRACK and **sslider** set to the length of the text less the number of columns per page.

The next set of keys are lone VIRTUAL keystrokes—the key is pressed without the CTRL, ALT, or SHIFT keys being pressed. As shown in Figure 3.16 the if statement to test for this type of key checks to see that the KC_VIRTUALKEY flag is set and that KC_CTRL, KC_ALT, and KC_SHIFT are not set. On most

```
} else if (fsflags & KC_VIRTUALKEY &&
          !(fsflags & (KC_ALT | KC_CTRL | KC_SHIFT ))) {
   switch (CHAR3FROMMP(mp2)) {
   case VK_UP:
      if (fsflags & KC_CHAR) { /* keypad '8' - insert character */
         InsertCharacter( hwnd, CHAR1FROMMP(mp2) );
      } else {                 /* UP ARROW = cursor up one line */
         if( sCurLine != 0 ) {
            sCurLine--;
            if( sCurLine < sCurTop ) {
               WinSendMsg( hwnd, WM_VSCROLL, (MPARAM)FID_VERTSCROLL,
                           MPFROM2SHORT( 0, SB_LINEUP ));
            } /* endif */
            UpdateCursor( hwnd );
         } /* endif */
      } /* endif */
      break;
   case VK_DOWN:
      if (fsflags & KC_CHAR) { /* keypad '2' - insert character */
         InsertCharacter( hwnd, CHAR1FROMMP(mp2) );
      } else {                 /* DOWN ARROW = cursor down 1 line */
         if( sCurLine != sNumLines - 1 ) {
            sCurLine++;
            if( sCurLine >= sCurTop + sLinesPerPage ) {
               WinSendMsg( hwnd, WM_VSCROLL, (MPARAM)FID_VERTSCROLL,
                           MPFROM2SHORT( 0, SB_LINEDOWN ));
            } /* endif */
            UpdateCursor( hwnd );
         } /* endif */
      } /* endif */
      break;
```

Figure 3.16   Handling the UP and DOWN keys.

keyboards the cursor movement keys in this set are replicated on the numeric keypad. When the keyboard is in numeric mode, these keys will have both the KC_VIRTUALKEY and KC_CHAR flags set. In this instance, the application should treat the keystroke as a normal character as shown in Figures 3.16 through 3.19, which show the code for handling the various keys in this set. The definitions and processing for these keys are as follows:

UP ARROW   This key moves the input cursor up by one line. If the cursor is not already on the first line, line zero, the cursor line is decremented. If the resulting cursor line is above the line currently at the top of the displayed data, a WM_VSCROLL message is sent with the **uscmd** field set to SB_LINEUP.

DOWN ARROW This key moves the input cursor down by one line. If the cursor is not already on the last line of the data, the cursor line is incremented. If the resulting cursor line is below the last line displayed (first line displayed

```
case VK_LEFT:
   if (fsflags & KC_CHAR) { /* keypad '4' - insert character */
      InsertCharacter( hwnd, CHAR1FROMMP(mp2) );
   } else {                 /* LEFT ARROW = cursor left 1 char */
      if( sCurCol != 0 ) {
         sCurCol--;
         if( sCurCol < sCurLeft ) {
            WinSendMsg( hwnd, WM_HSCROLL, (MPARAM)FID_HORZSCROLL,
                     MPFROM2SHORT( 0, SB_LINELEFT ));
         } /* endif */
         UpdateCursor( hwnd );
      } /* endif */
   } /* endif */
   break;
case VK_RIGHT:
   if (fsflags & KC_CHAR) { /* keypad '6' - insert character */
      InsertCharacter( hwnd, CHAR1FROMMP(mp2) );
   } else {                 /* RIGHT ARROW = cursor right 1 char */
      if( sCurCol != sMaxWidth ) {
         sCurCol++;
         if( sCurCol > sCurLeft + sColsPerPage ) {
            WinSendMsg( hwnd, WM_HSCROLL, (MPARAM)FID_HORZSCROLL,
                     MPFROM2SHORT( 0, SB_LINERIGHT ));
         } /* endif */
         UpdateCursor( hwnd );
      } /* endif */
   } /* endif */
   break;
```

Figure 3.17 Handling the LEFT and RIGHT keys.

```
case VK_PAGEUP:
   if (fsflags & KC_CHAR) {    /* keypad '9' - insert character */
      InsertCharacter( hwnd, CHAR1FROMMP(mp2) );
   } else {                    /* PAGEUP = cursor up one page */
      sCurLine -= sLinesPerPage;
      if (sCurLine < 0) sCurLine = 0;
      WinSendMsg( hwnd, WM_VSCROLL, (MPARAM)FID_VERTSCROLL,
                  MPFROM2SHORT( 0, SB_PAGEUP ));
   } /* endif */
   break;
case VK_PAGEDOWN:
   if (fsflags & KC_CHAR) {    /* keypad '3' - insert character */
      InsertCharacter( hwnd, CHAR1FROMMP(mp2) );
   } else {                    /* PAGEDOWN = cursor down one page */
      sCurLine += sLinesPerPage;
      sCurLine = min( sCurLine, sNumLines - 1);
      WinSendMsg( hwnd, WM_VSCROLL, (MPARAM)FID_VERTSCROLL,
                  MPFROM2SHORT( 0, SB_PAGEDOWN ));
   } /* endif */
   break;
```

Figure 3.18   Handling the PAGEUP and PAGEDOWN keys.

plus number of lines displayable), a WM_VSCROLL message is sent with the **uscmd** field set to SB_LINEDOWN.

LEFT ARROW   This key moves the input cursor one character to the left. If the cursor is not already at the leftmost character, the cursor column is decremented. If the resulting column is to the left of the first displayed column, a WM_HSCROLL message is sent with the **uscmd** field set to SB_LINELEFT.

RIGHT ARROW   This key moves the input cursor one character to the right. If the cursor is not already positioned just beyond the rightmost column in the data, the cursor column is incremented. If the resulting cursor column is beyond the rightmost column displayed (leftmost column plus number of columns displayable), a WM_HSCROLL message is sent with the **uscmd** field set to SB_LINERIGHT.

PAGE UP   This key is used to scroll the displayed data area up by one page. In this application, the key also causes the input cursor to move up by one page. The input cursor position is adjusted by subtracting the number of lines per page from the current cursor position. If the result is less than zero, the new cursor position is set to zero. Scrolling is accomplished by sending a WM_VSCROLL message with **uscmd** set to SB_PAGEUP. Note that the cursor position is not updated since the scrolling operation ensures that the cursor will be moved by the scrolling routine.

```
case VK_HOME:
   if (fsflags & KC_CHAR) {    /* keypad '7' - insert character */
      InsertCharacter( hwnd, CHAR1FROMMP(mp2) );
   } else {                     /* HOME = cursor to start of line */
      lCurCol = 0;
      WinSendMsg( hwnd, WM_HSCROLL, (MPARAM)FID_HORZSCROLL,
                 MPFROM2SHORT( 0, SB_SLIDERTRACK ));
      UpdateCursor( hwnd );
   } /* endif */
   break;
case VK_END:
   if (fsflags & KC_CHAR) {    /* keypad '1' - insert character */
      InsertCharacter( hwnd, CHAR1FROMMP(mp2) );
   } else {                     /* END = cursor to end of line */
      lCurCol = strlen(pLines[sCurLine]->pszText);
      WinSendMsg( hwnd, WM_HSCROLL, (MPARAM)FID_HORZSCROLL,
                 MPFROM2SHORT(max(0, lCurCol - lColsPerPage + 1),
                             SB_SLIDERTRACK ));
      UpdateCursor( hwnd );
   } /* endif */
   break;
```

Figure 3.19   Handling the HOME and END keys.

PAGE DOWN   This key is used to scroll the displayed data area down by one page. This application also moves the input cursor down by one page. The new cursor position is calculated by adding the number of lines per page to the current cursor position and taking the minimum of this value and the line number of the last line of data. A WM_VSCROLL message is sent with **uscmd** set to SB_PAGEDOWN to scroll the displayed data area down by one page. No cursor update is necessary since the scrolling operation is guaranteed to move the cursor in this instance.

HOME   This key is used to move the input cursor to the beginning of the current line. The current cursor position is set to column zero and a WM_HSCROLL message with **uscmd** set to SB_SLIDERTRACK and **sslider** set to zero is sent to force display of the leftmost data. The **Update-Cursor** routine is called to ensure that the cursor is properly positioned since the scroll message may not necessarily update the window.

END   This key moves the input cursor to the end of the current line. The column value of the current cursor position is set to the length of the text for the current line. A WM_HSCROLL message is sent with **uscmd** set to SB_SLIDERTRACK. The **sslider** field is set to the maximum of zero and the new cursor position less the number of columns per page plus one to display the maximum amount of data on the line. **UpdateCursor** is called since the scroll message may not necessarily update the window.

For scrolling purposes, all other keystrokes are ignored. The sample program accompanying this chapter contains a routine **wmchar** which combines the processing for all the keystrokes discussed in this chapter. This routine, in combination with Figures 3.15 through 3.19, can be studied to see how a typical keystroke processing routine should test the various elements of fsflags to determine the actual keystroke received.

PAINTING AFTER SCROLLING

Performance gains from using the **WinScrollWindow** API to reduce the area of the window to be repainted were discussed earlier. These gains are realized due to the clipping performed to prevent actual drawing outside the invalidated rectangle. Further gains can be realized if the application's WM_PAINT processing recognizes the invalid rectangle and restricts its calls to the drawing APIs to the minimum necessary. This section examines how the text-based application we have been using can achieve these gains.

Following the normal initialization of the WM_PAINT processing—obtaining the presentation space and filling in the background—the application determines the first line that falls at least partially within the invalid rectangle and then determines the first and last columns that are at least partially within the invalidated area. With these boundaries available, the application draws lines of text until the bottom of the invalid rectangle is reached.

Figure 3.20 shows the code used to compute the first line that requires painting. First, the area of the entire window is obtained. The top of the rectangle less the top of the invalid rectangle provides the area of the window

```
/* calculate first line to draw */
iLineFirst = (LONG)sCurTop;
iLineFirst += (rectlHwnd.yTop - rectl.yTop) / lHeight;

/* set pointer to structure for first line */
if (iLineFirst < (LONG)sNumLines) {
   if (pLines != (PLINE *)NULL) {
      plineDraw = pLines[iLineFirst];
      rectlHwnd.yTop -= (iLineFirst - (LONG)sCurTop ) * lHeight;
   } /* endif */
} /* endif */
```

Figure 3.20 **Calculating the initial y coordinate.**

that does not require painting, and dividing this number by the height of a character, or line, results in the number of whole lines that do not require any repainting. This number is added to the line number of the current top line in the display to determine the line number of the first line to be drawn. If this line number is within the range of the displayed file, pointer **pLineDraw** is set to the structure that describes this line. Then, since the invalidated rectangle may not necessarily fall on the exact coordinates for a line, the top of the drawing rectangle, **rectlHwnd**, is computed by subtracting the space occupied by lines from the top displayed line to the first line to draw from the top of the window rectangle.

Figure 3.21 shows the calculations necessary to obtain the first and last column positions to be drawn. Like the computation of the first line in Figure 3.20, the first column to display is computed by subtracting the left coordinate of the invalid area from the left coordinate of the entire window and dividing by the width of a character. The value is then added to the column number currently displayed at the leftmost position in the window. If the computed first column is beyond the last column position of the longest line in the file, no drawing is necessary and the **pLineDraw** pointer from above is set to NULL. Otherwise, the coordinate of the first column to draw is calculated by adding the space occupied by nondrawn columns to the coordinate of the left edge of the window. Then the number of columns to draw is calculated by subtracting the left edge of the drawing rectangle from the right edge of the invalid rectangle and dividing by the width of a character. The number of columns is incremented to ensure that partial characters at the right edge of the invalid rectangle are drawn.

Figure 3.22 shows the loop that actually draws the text into the window. The control conditional for this loop first checks the pointer to the current line structure for validity. If the pointer is NULL, either this is the entry to the loop and no text is to be drawn (in which case the loop body is never entered) or the last line of the displayed file has been drawn. The conditional

```
/* compute the first column to paint */
lColFirst = (rectl.xLeft - rectlHwnd.xLeft) / lWidth;
lColFirst += lCurLeft;
if (lColFirst > lMaxWidth) {
   plineDraw = (PLINE)NULL;     /* nothing to draw */
} else {
   rectlHwnd.xLeft += (lColFirst - lCurLeft ) * lWidth;
   /* compute the last column to paint */
   lNumCols = (rectl.xRight - rectlHwnd.xLeft) / lWidth;
   lNumCols++;
} /* endif */
```

Figure 3.21 Calculating the initial x coordinate.

```
/* draw while the data fits on the screen */
while (plineDraw != (PLINE)NULL &&
       rectlHwnd.yTop > rectl.yBottom &&
       rectlHwnd.yTop - lHeight >= 0) {
   /* but only if text to be drawn for the current line */
   if (strlen(plineDraw->pszText) > lColFirst) {
      WinDrawText( hps,
                   min(lNumCols,strlen(&plineDraw->pszText[lColFirst])),
                   &plineDraw->pszText[lColFirst],
                   &rectlHwnd, 0, 0, DT_TOP | DT_LEFT | DT_TEXTATTRS );
   } /* endif */
   /* bump down to top position of next line */
   rectlHwnd.yTop -= lHeight;
   /* get next line to draw */
   plineDraw = plineDraw->next;
} /* endwhile */
```

Figure 3.22 Drawing text.

then checks to be sure that the top of the current line does not fall below the invalid rectangle and then ensures that the bottom of the current line falls within the drawing rectangle to prevent a partial line from being drawn at the bottom of the window. The body of the drawing loop checks to see if the text for the current line contains enough characters to require drawing. If so, the **WinDrawText** API (see Chapter 16) is called to draw the text. The second parameter to this API is the number of characters to be drawn, and it is set to the minimum of the computed number of columns to draw or the number of characters remaining in the text for the current line. Once the drawing is complete, the top of the drawing rectangle is lowered by the height of a character to set the starting coordinate for the next line, and the pointer to the line structure is bumped to the next line in the displayed file.

SUMMARY

This chapter has discussed how Presentation Manager applications receive input from the keyboard and process that input to edit text and manipulate the display. In conjunction with the processing of virtual keys, the scroll bar has been discussed, and techniques have been shown for scrolling the information displayed in a window and manipulating the keyboard input cursor. By using and extending these principles and techniques, programmers can create applications that fully exploit the use of the keyboard to access the application's functionality.

CHAPTER 4

Building A Better Mousetrap: Taming the Mouse in PM

There is something about human nature that has made most of us develop an aversion to rodents. It took many years of cartoon culture therapy for the general population to begin to embrace such popular cartoon mice as Mickey and Minnie, Mighty, and of course our pal from the south of the border, Speedy Gonzalez. This fear of mice has even transferred to the computer world, via the graphical programming community. This chapter will attempt to explain how to master programming the mouse under the Presentation Manager environment.

The input pointing device has arguably become the most important tool in the graphical user interface. Some of the early more primitive graphical application interfaces failed because the keyboard interface did not provide quick and easy access to controlling the application, and the keystroke combinations that were required to master the interface were difficult to remember and were not intuitive enough for even advanced users. A hardware device that allowed the user to communicate quickly and effectively was desired. This brought about the invention of the mouse, and completely revolutionized the look and feel of the graphical user interface. Finally users were able to control how applications were started and more easily manipulate text and graphics through the movement of the mouse pointer. Unfortunately, in the early days before graphical programming environments standardized mouse manipulation through the use of the window API, it was difficult for programmers to control the mouse for the user. Luckily, mastering how to program the mouse is relatively simple in the Presentation Manager environment, and once you realize just how simple it is maybe you won't fear our little furry white friends either; well, maybe not, but let's begin mastering the art of programming the computer mouse anyway.

This chapter's sample program combines practical mouse usage with simple drawing functionality that is bound to espouse some nostalgic memories among children from the baby boomer generation. Two favorite toys among children with active imaginations were the Etch-a-Sketch® and the Spirograph®. Both toys were very simple to understand and use, but taught different fundamentals while helping to cultivate cognitive and imaginative learning skills. The sample program CLKDRAW, is designed with similar intentions. Although it is very simple to use, it may not provide as much of an education value as its toy counterpart. It does, however, illustrate some simple pointer programming concepts.

The Etch-a-Sketch® toy was a simple drawing device that allowed children to express their artistic talents, although they really had to be artistically inclined to make anything look good because of the small lines and simple round controls. The toy basically contained two knobs: one that controlled the horizontal movement of the line, and the other that controlled the vertical movement. The sample program demonstrates the technique for capturing the mouse pointer, and through the use of some simple GPI drawing, allows the user to manipulate the mouse buttons to control the drawing.

The Spirograph® made geometry "cool." It allowed you to draw basic geometric shapes simply by using colored pens and various plastic ridged disks with holes. To create an image, the user put a pen through one of the holes on a plastic disk, then rotated the pen within the disk around or within another larger plastic disk, thereby creating a simple yet colorful image. When the user double-clicks on the client area with the right mouse button, an image similar to a Spirograph® is created. The size of the geometric figure created, as well as the circular shape of the image, are based on the current pointer position.

CLKDRAW also demonstrates how to capture the mouse pointer outside of the frame window, giving the user to ability to capture an area of the desktop by highlighting it with a tracking rectangle created by manipulating the mouse pointer. The pointer used to create the tracking rectangle is different from the default mouse pointer, making it easy for the user to distinguish between the captured mouse pointer and the default mouse pointer. The purpose of the program is to demonstrate how to handle mouse messages and use the APIs specific for mouse pointer manipulation to allow the developer to more accurately control the user interface through the input pointing device.

UNDERSTANDING THE USE OF THE MOUSE

Even though the PM graphical user interface allows for keyboard input, using most PM applications without a mouse can become difficult or even awkward.

A well-written application should allow for both keyboard and mouse movement, but most users will definitely agree that using a mouse is much less complex. Have you ever tried using the Workplace Shell without a mouse? It definitely takes time to get used to, whereas the mouse allows the shell to be much more intuitive and friendly.

There are many manufacturers that make the mouse pointing device. Today, some even are designed with ergonomics in mind to allow greater comfort for the user. Variations on the design of the mouse have changed over the years to include trackballs, three-button configurations, and even that funny red eraser thing on the IBM Thinkpad machines. The OS/2 Presentation Manager supports a large variety of pointing devices, thus allowing the PM developer to use the mouse to simplify the application learning curve. Based on the number of buttons on the mouse, developers can take advantage of one, two, or three buttons.

The movement of the mouse is represented in the PM window manager through the use of a bitmapped image on the display called the *mouse pointer*. Obviously, as the mouse moves, the pointer moves. The default PM mouse pointers are shown in Figure 4.1.

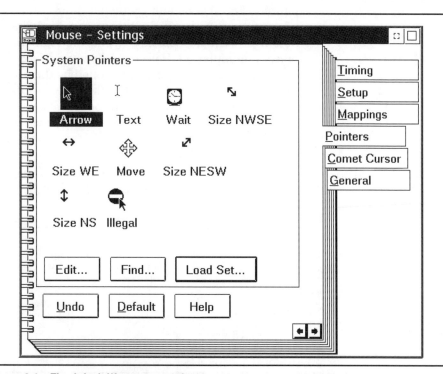

Figure 4.1   The default Warp mouse pointers.

Every mouse pointer has a *hotspot*, which is simply a single pixel within the pointer bitmap that is where the manipulation originates. The very tip of the black arrow is the hotspot on the default mouse pointer. One of the biggest requests of the PM user community has been to allow the user to change the default mouse pointer with ease. The OS/2 Warp system grants this wish by allowing the user to change the default mouse pointer. The mouse pointer file format is essentially a bitmap, and pointers can be drawn using the OS/2 Icon Editor.

QUERYING AND SETTING THE SYSTEM VALUES FOR AN INPUT DEVICE

PM has several default system value flags that can be used to query the resolution of the pointer along with other important characteristics. Figure 4.2 shows some of the system value flags defined in PMWIN.H that affect the mouse pointer. The system values can be queried using the API **WinQuerySysValue** and can be changed using the **WinSetSysValue** API.

SV_SWAPBUTTON   This value is used to change the default function of the mouse buttons. The PM default is for the mouse buttons to be configured for a right-handed user. In the workplace shell, the left button is used for selection while the right button is used for object manipulation. It is generally not advised that this value be changed, since it is usually controlled by the user who can adapt the mouse configuration to fit his or her needs. If this value is set to TRUE, then the mouse buttons have been swapped and the window procedure will get right button messages when the left mouse button is pressed, and left button messages when the right button is pressed.

SV_DBLCLKTIME   This value can be used to change the pointing device's double-click time. PM determines a double-click by two quick single

```
SV_SWAPBUTTON          0
SV_DBLCLKTIME          1
SV_CXDBLCLK           2
SV_CYDBLCLK           3
SV_CXPOINTER         40
SV_CYPOINTER         41
SV_CMOUSEBUTTONS     43
SV_CPOINTERBUTTONS   43
SV_POINTERLEVEL      44
SV_MOUSEPRESENT      48
```

Figure 4.2 Mouse pointer system values.

mouse clicks in succession. The default double-click time is half a second. Using this value, you can modify the default click time. If you decide to change this value, the time is measured in milliseconds. The only time this value should be changed is when you have a controlled user interface—for example, a single application that replaces the workplace shell—and you need to change the double-click time to correspond with the user requirements of the shell.

SV_CXDBLCLK

This is the horizontal length of the double-click sensitive area. In other words, this value is the width of the distance a double click is valid. PM uses the system font character width as the default.

SV_CYDBLCLK

This is the vertical length of the double-click sensitive area. In other words, this value is the height of the distance a double-click is valid. PM uses half the height of the system font character height as the default.

SV_MOUSEPRESENT

If this value returns TRUE, then an input pointing device is present and recognized by the Presentation Manager.

SV_CXPOINTER

This flag can be used to query the horizontal dimensions of the mouse pointer bitmap. The value returned is in pixels wide. This value is based on the resolution of the display driver and cannot be modified.

SV_CYPOINTER

This flag can be used to query the vertical dimensions of the mouse pointer bitmap. The value returned is in pixels high. This value is also based on the resolution of the display driver and cannot be modified.

SV_CMOUSEBUTTONS
or SV_CPOINTERBUTTONS

This value returns the number of buttons on the pointing device. It can be used to query whether the user has a two- or three-button mouse; then, depending on the result, the programmer can assign functionality of the buttons. If a zero is returned, then no mouse device is currently installed. Another method of querying whether a mouse is present is by querying the SV_MOUSEPRESENT flag. This value cannot be modified. The code fragment in Figure 4.3 checks to see if a pointing device is installed and then determines if the pointing device supports a third mouse button.

SV_CXMOTIONSTART

This value flag can be used to set or query the number of pixels that a pointing device can be moved horizontally while the mouse button is depressed before a WM_BUTTONnMOTIONSTART message is sent to the window.

SV_CYMOTIONSTART

This value flag can be used to set or query the number of pixels that a pointing device can be moved vertically while the

```
lButtons = WinQuerySysValue(HWND_DESKTOP, SV_CPOINTERBUTTONS);

if (lButtons == 0)
 {
  return ERROR_MOUSE_NOT_INSTALLED;
 }

else if (lButtons == 3)
 {
  return THREE_BUTTON_MOUSE_INSTALLED;
 }
```

Figure 4.3   Determining the number of buttons.

mouse button is depressed before a WM_BUTTONnMO-TIONSTART message is sent to the window.

*Where n represents the mouse button depressed.

SV_POINTERLEVEL

This flag is used to determine if the mouse pointer is visible or invisible. Often it is not desirable to have a mouse pointer present, so the visibility of the pointer can be changed. For instance, if the user is entering or reading text within a window and has not touched the mouse pointer for a long period of time, it may be desirable to hide the mouse pointer so that it does not appear within the text. Also, screen capture programs may want to hide the mouse pointer until a specific window has been captured. If a zero is returned when specifying this flag, then the pointer is visible. Any other positive value indicates that the pointer is invisible. This value cannot be modified directly using **WinSetSysValue**. The pointer level is actually controlled through the use of the API, **WinShowPointer**. This function is used to either increment or decrement the pointer level usage count.

CHANGING THE VISIBILITY OF THE MOUSE POINTER

The format of the **WinShowPointer** call is as shown in Figure 4.4.

- **hwndDesktop** is the window handle of the desktop window.
- **bVisibility** represents the pointer level visibility indicator. If this value is set to TRUE, then the pointer display level is decremented by one until

```
BOOL WinShowPointer(HWND  hwndDesktop,
                    BOOL  bVisibility);
```

Figure 4.4   The WinShowPointer prototype.

the usage count is zero. When the pointer display level reaches zero, the pointer is made visible. If the value is set to FALSE, then the pointer display level is incremented by one. If the pointer display level is any value greater than one, then the pointer is invisible.

The initial pointer display level is based on the capabilities of the pointing device. If a mouse is detected, the initial pointer display level is set to visible. If no input pointing device is detected, the initial pointer display level is set to invisible.

The code for **WinShowPointer** actually checks the pointer usage count to determine whether the pointer should be made visible. If the pointer should be made visible, it calls a routine in the graphics engine to display the pointer at the next interrupt and then returns FALSE; otherwise, the function call will return TRUE.

CAPTURING THE MOUSE POINTER

The options menu contains a menu item called HideMousePointer that will allow the user to change the visibility of the pointer by modifying the pointer visibility level. Once the user selects the Options/HideMousePointer menu item, the mouse pointer is made invisible by calling **WinShowPointer**. If the Capture Pointer to Window checkbox was not checked prior to hiding the pointer, then the visibility level usage count of the pointer will be decremented every time the mouse is moved outside the bounds of the window. Eventually, the mouse pointer is made visible if you move the mouse around long enough. If the checkbox is checked prior to the Hide pushbutton being selected, the mouse pointer will not be shown until the user selects the Show pushbutton by pressing Enter.

The solution to ensuring that the mouse pointer will not be shown when moved outside the client window boundary is to capture the mouse input. The purpose of capturing the mouse input is to allow mouse messages to be directed to a specific window regardless of the position of the mouse pointer in relation to the desktop. In other words, no matter which window the pointer is positioned over the associated mouse messages are passed on to your window procedure for processing.

Believe it or not, you do not need a mousetrap to capture the mouse pointer. A simple API called **WinSetCapture** does the job without the smelly cheese. This function works by trapping all WM_MOUSEMOVE messages and redirecting them to the capture window. Only one window can become the capture window. The format of the **WinSetCapture** API is shown in Figure 4.5.

- **hwndDesktop** is the handle of the desktop window.
- **hwnd** is the window handle of the capture window.

```
BOOL APIENTRY WinSetCapture(HWND hwndDesktop,
                            HWND hwnd);
```

Figure 4.5   The WinSetCapture prototype.

The **WinSetCapture** function returns TRUE if the mouse pointer is captured. The function will return FALSE if an error occurs. The function will fail if a hard system model window is up and a pointer capture is attempted. The function will also fail if another window is currently set as the capture window.

The **hwnd** parameter is the key value here, since it contains the handle of the window to which the WM_MOUSEMOVE message will be redirected. When capturing the mouse is complete, the capture window can be reset by once again calling **WinSetCapture** and passing a NULL value in the **hwnd** parameter. When the capture window is released, a WM_MOUSEMOVE message is posted to the window regardless of whether the mouse pointer has actually been moved. This is done to ensure that the window currently under the mouse pointer has an opportunity to refresh the pointer.

Applications that need to determine whether the mouse movement message is being captured by a specific window can use the function **WinQueryCapture** to determine the capture window. The function will return the handle of the window that has the mouse input captured.

Figure 4.6 shows the format of the function.

SHOWING THE MOUSE POINTER

The code fragment in Figure 4.7 illustrates the proper use of decrementing the pointer visibility level until the mouse pointer is visible. The code first checks to see if a pointing device is currently installed and then checks the pointer visibility level. If the pointer is currently invisible, the call to **WinQuerySysValue** with the SV_POINTERLEVEL will return a number greater than zero in **lSysVal**. This code fragment will then enter a *for* loop and call **WinShowPointer** with TRUE in the **bVisibility** field, thereby decrementing the pointer level usage count until it finally reaches zero forcing the pointer visible.

```
HWND  APIENTRY WinQueryCapture(HWND hwndDesktop);
```

Figure 4.6   The WinQueryCapture prototype.

```
lSysVal = WinQuerySysValue(HWND_DESKTOP, SV_MOUSEPRESENT);

if (lSysVal != TRUE)
 {
   return ERROR_MOUSE_NOT_INSTALLED;
 } /* endif */

lSysVal = WinQuerySysValue(HWND_DESKTOP, SV_POINTERLEVEL);

for (usCounter = 0; usCounter < lSysVal; usCounter++)
{
 WinShowPointer(HWND_DESKTOP, TRUE);
} /* endfor */
```

Figure 4.7   Making the mouse pointer visible again.

OBTAINING POINTER INFORMATION

There may be times when you need to obtain information about a specific mouse pointer. Obtaining this information is relatively easy since PM maintains a POINTERINFO structure that contains all of the relevant pointer information like the size of the pointer bitmap, the handle of the various bitmap for a specific pointer, and the hotspot coordinates. The format of the POINTERINFO structure is shown in Figure 4.8.

- **fPointer** is used to indicate whether the mouse pointer bitmap is the size of pointer or an icon. If this value contains a 1, then the bitmap is the size of a pointer. If this value contains a 0, then the bitmap is the size of an icon.
- **xHotspot** represents the horizontal coordinate for the primary point of action in relation to the size of the pointer.

```
typedef struct _POINTERINFO     // ptri
 {
  ULONG   fPointer;
  LONG    xHotspot;
  LONG    yHotspot;
  HBITMAP hbmPointer;
  HBITMAP hbmColor;
  HBITMAP hbmMiniPointer;
  HBITMAP hbmMiniColor;
 } POINTERINFO;
typedef POINTERINFO *PPOINTERINFO;
```

Figure 4.8   The POINTERINFO structure.

```
BOOL APIENTRY WinQueryPointerInfo (HPOINTER    hptr,
                                   PPOINTERINFO  pPointerInfo);
```

Figure 4.9   The WinQueryPointerInfo prototype.

- **yHotspot** represents the vertical coordinate for the primary point of action in relation to the size of the pointer.
- **hbmPointer** is the handle of the mouse pointer bitmap.
- **hbmColor** is the handle of the mouse pointer color bitmap.
- **hbmMiniPointer** is the handle of the mouse pointer mini-bitmap.
- **hbmMiniColor** is the handle of the mouse pointer mini-color bitmap.

To obtain the POINTERINFO structure you must first call the **WinQuery-PointerInfo** function specifying the handle of the pointer for which you need the pointer information. This function will return a valid POINTERINFO structure for a valid pointer handle. The format of the **WinQueryPointerInfo** API is given in Figure 4.9.

- **hptr** represents a valid pointer handle.
- **pPointerInfo** represents a pointer to a POINTERINFO structure. This structure is returned if the call is successful.

The function itself will return TRUE if the function is successful and FALSE if an error occurred.

The first parameter to the **WinQueryPointerInfo** API is the pointer handle for which you wish to obtain a POINTERINFO structure. If you need to obtain the current pointer information, you can use the **WinQueryPointer** API to return a pointer handle for the current mouse pointer. The only parameter that this function requires is the desktop window handle. Figure 4.10 has the prototype for **WinQueryPointer**.

- **hwndDesktop** is of course the desktop window handle.

The code fragment in Figure 4.11 obtains the current pointer handle through the use of the **WinQueryPointer** function, then it obtains a POINTER-INFO structure for the pointer by calling the **WinQueryPointerInfo** function.

```
HPOINTER APIENTRY WinQueryPointer(HWND hwndDesktop);
```

Figure 4.10   The WinQueryPointer prototype.

```
hwndStatic = WinWindowFromID(hwnd, ID_STATIC);
hptr = WinQueryPointer(HWND_DESKTOP);
WinQueryPointerInfo(hptr, &ptrinfo);

sprintf(szBuffer, "x = %ld y = %ld", ptrinfo.xHotspot, ptrinfo.yHotspot);
WinSetWindowText(hwndStatic, szBuffer);
```

Figure 4.11   Obtaining current pointer information.

Once a valid POINTERINFO structure is obtained, the hotspot coordinates are displayed in a static text window.

WHERE IS MICKEY?

As the user moves the mouse around the desktop, the Presentation Manager code sends a mouse message to the window that the mouse pointer is currently over. In order to send the right message to the right window, PM must determine where the pointer is in relation to the window hierarchy. Probably, the most important concept to learn about mastering the mouse from a development perspective is how to determine where the mouse pointer is at the right time, and then translate the pointer position into something the user needs to accomplish via the pointer. For example, once you are able to determine the location of the mouse in relation to a user event, it becomes very easy to capture the mouse movement and translate the movement into something that the user can visualize.

The CLKDRAW sample program is the best example of this point. The sample program tracks the movement of the mouse pointer over the client window by processing the WM_MOUSEMOVE message. Once the current pointer position is obtained via a POINTL structure, the movement of the mouse pointer is translated into a line through the use of the **GpiLine** function. There are effectively three methods of obtaining the current mouse pointer position. Each method returns the pointer position in response to a different user event.

There are two PM APIs that are used to determine the current mouse pointer position. The functions **WinQueryPointerPos** and **WinQueryMsgPos** both return the pointer position in screen coordinates, but the two functions return the pointer position based on different events and at different processing times. The **WinQueryPointerPos** function returns the current pointer position immediately, while the **WinQueryMsgPos** function returns the position of the pointer based on when the message that is currently being processed was actually posted to the message queue. The coordinates returned are in the form of a POINTL structure, which contains the valid x and y screen coordinates

```
BOOL APIENTRY WinQueryPointerPos(HWND      hwndDesktop,
                                 PPOINTL   pptl);
```

Figure 4.12   The WinQueryPointerPos prototype.

```
BOOL APIENTRY WinQueryMsgPos(HAB     hab,
                             PPOINTL pptl);
```

Figure 4.13   The WinQueryMsgPos prototype.

of the pointer. The prototype for **WinQueryPointerPos** is shown in Figure 4.12 and the prototype for **WinQueryMsgPos** is in Figure 4.13.

The difference between the layout of the functions is in the first parameter. The first parameter to **WinQueryPointerPos** is the desktop window handle, while the **WinQueryMsgPos** takes an anchor block handle as its first parameter. Both functions return TRUE for success and FALSE for failure.

As previously stated, both of these functions return values in screen coordinates. However, what if you want to determine the position of the pointer in relation to the client window? In order to obtain the coordinates in relation to the window, you must convert the screen coordinates to window coordinates. PM provides two APIs that can be used to do the conversion from one coordinate system to the other. The function **WinMapWindowPoints** can be used to convert or map the screen coordinates which are in relation to the desktop window to a set of coordinates within the client window. Likewise, the function **WinMapDlgPoints** can be used to map window coordinates to dialog coordinates and vice versa. It is extremely useful to understand how these two functions work, since they allow the ability to quickly convert different coordinate schemes. The format of **WinMapWindowPoints** is in Figure 4.14.

- **hwndFrom** represents the handle of the window from which the coordinates are mapped. If you specify the desktop window handle, HWND_DESKTOP, this effectively means that you are converting from screen coordinates to window coordinates.

```
BOOL  APIENTRY WinMapWindowPoints(HWND     hwndFrom,
                                  HWND     hwndTo,
                                  PPOINTL  prgptl,
                                  LONG     cwpt);
```

Figure 4.14   The WinMapWindowPoints prototype.

- **hwndTo** represents the handle of the window to which the coordinates are mapped. If you specify the desktop window handle, HWND_DESKTOP, this effectively means that you are converting from window coordinates to screen coordinates.
- **prgptl** represents the actual coordinates that are being mapped from one coordinate system to the other. The caller specifies the coordinates in the form of a pointer to a POINTL structure. When the function returns, this value contains the converted coordinates.
- **cwpt** represents the count of points to be converted based on the **prgptl** parameter. If the **prgptl** coordinates represent a POINTL structure, then the valid point count is 1. If the **prgptl** coordinates are in the actual form of a RECTL structure, then the point count is 2.

The Configure Spirographs dialog box allows the user to configure the drawing of the spirographs based on window or screen coordinates via a simple radiobutton. As you will notice, unless the window is maximized, the screen coordinates may not be visible in the client window. The program defaults to using window coordinates for drawing the spirographs. The code fragment in Figure 4.15 is used to convert the screen coordinates returned from the function **WinQueryPointerPos** to window coordinates prior to calling the **SpiroGraphBox** function.

Figure 4.15 shows how the pointer coordinates are converted from screen coordinates to window coordinates during the processing of the WM-BUTTON2DBLCLK message. If the bUseWndCoordinates flag is set to TRUE, the coordinates are converted prior to calling the **SpiroGraphBox** routine.

```
case WM_BUTTON2DBLCLK:
    WinQueryPointerPos(HWND_DESKTOP, &ptlCurrent);


    if (bUseWndCoordinates == TRUE)
     {
       WinMapWindowPoints(HWND_DESKTOP, hwndClient, &ptlCurrent, 1);
     }

    hwndStatic = WinWindowFromID(hwndClient, ID_STATIC);

    sprintf(szCoordinates, "x = %ld y = %ld", ptlCurrent.x, ptlCurrent.y);
    WinSetWindowText(hwndStatic, szCoordinates);

    SpiroGraphBox(hwnd, ptlCurrent, usRotAngle, sColor);
    break;
```

Figure 4.15 Mapping screen coordinates to window coordinates.

USING THE WM_MOUSEMOVE MESSAGE

As discussed previously, moving the mouse around the client window generates a mouse movement message called WM_MOUSEMOVE. The WM_MOUSE-MOVE message can also be used to determine the current position of the mouse pointer. The CLKDRAW sample program uses this message to allow the user to draw lines within the client window, thereby creating the etch-a sketch effect. In order to obtain the pointer coordinates during WM_MOUSEMOVE processing, you must extract the coordinates from a mouse message structure that is maintained by PM.

The mouse message structure MSEMSG also provides access to the message parameters for mouse button processing messages, such as button up, button down, and button click messages. PM defines a simple macro in PMWIN.H that can be used to obtain the information contained within the MSEMSG structure. The MOUSEMSG macro is defined as shown in Figure 4.16. The format of the actual MSEMSG structure is in Figure 4.17.

The x and y values correspond to the current pointer position. Within the processing of the WM_MOUSEMOVE message in the sample program, the code will draw a line based on the movement of the mouse. The question is, if the mouse is constantly being moved around the client window, how does PM allow your application to keep up with the processing of the WM_MOUSEMOVE messages?

The code to resolve WM_MOUSEMOVE processing ensures that the current message queue does not get a flurry of wasted mouse movement messages. The messages are posted based on how quickly the message is actually processed by the window procedure. For example, if your application mes-

```
#define MOUSEMSG(pmsg) \
        ((PMSEMSG)((PBYTE)pmsg + sizeof(MPARAM) ))
```

Figure 4.16   The mouse message macro MOUSEMSG.

```
typedef struct _MOUSEMSG        // mousemsg
{
  SHORT   x;                    // mp1
  SHORT   y;
  USHORT  codeHitTest;          // mp2
  USHORT  fsInp;                // input flags
} MSEMSG;
typedef MSEMSG *PMSEMSG;
```

Figure 4.17   The mouse message structure MSEMSG.

```
ptlPointerPos.x = MOUSEMSG(&msg)->x;
ptlPointerPos.y = MOUSEMSG(&msg)->y;
```

Figure 4.18   Obtaining the pointer position within the WM_MOUSEMOVE message.

sage queue is about to process a WM_MOUSEMOVE message, and another WM_MOUSEMOVE message has arrived for processing, PM will automatically replace the message that is already in the message queue so that only the most recent mouse movement message will be processed. The rationale behind this is that the interrupts generated by the mouse movement occur much more frequently than any application could feasibly handle.

The code fragment found in Figure 4.18 uses the MOUSEMSG macro to extract the pointer position.

Determining the Pointer Position in Relation to a Rectangle

Once the pointer position coordinates have been obtained the **WinPtInRect** API can be used to determine whether the coordinates reside within the boundary of a specific rectangle (Figure 4.19).

- The **hab** parameter specifies the anchor block handle.
- The **prcl** parameter specifies a pointer to the rectangle structure that will be used to determine if the point coordinates exist within.
- The **pptl** parameter specifies a pointer to a POINTL structure. This parameter contains the coordinates that will be checked against the rectangle coordinates to determine if the points reside within the rectangle.

Drawing the Spirographs

When the user double-clicks the right mouse button anywhere over the client window, a symmetric image that resembles a spirograph is drawn. The image is drawn based on the current mouse pointer position that is obtained from **WinQueryPointerPosition**. The processing of the right mouse button double-click message is shown in Figure 4.20.

The code fragment shown in Figure 4.20 obtains the current pointer position and stores the coordinates in **ptlCurrent**. The coordinates are then passed to the function **SpiroGraphBox** to draw the image in the client area. The im-

```
BOOL APIENTRY WinPtInRect(HAB    hab,
                          PRECTL  prcl,
                          PPOINTL pptl);
```

Figure 4.19   The WinPtInRect prototype.

```
case WM_BUTTON2DBLCLK:
    WinQueryPointerPos(HWND_DESKTOP, &ptlCurrent);


    hwndStatic = WinWindowFromID(hwndClient, ID_STATIC);
    sprintf(szCoordinates, "x = %ld y = %ld", ptlCurrent.x, ptlCurrent.y);
    WinSetWindowText(hwndStatic, szCoordinates);

    SpiroGraphBox(hwnd, ptlCurrent, usRotAngle, sColor);
    break;
```

Figure 4.20   Processing the WM_BUTTON2DBLCLK message.

age is created simply by drawing a series of boxes on the screen and rotating the boxes in a circle until the image is complete. The current pointer position coordinates are used as the origin for drawing the boxes.

When the user double clicks, the current coordinates that are passed to the function are displayed in a static text window in the lower left corner of the window. Based on these coordinates, this function will draw the image. The higher the y coordinate, the more the corner of the boxes will be visible creating the pointed effect. The lower the y coordinate, the more the image will resemble a circle. The further the image is along the x and y axes, the larger the image will become; and conversely, the closer the image is to the window origin in the lower left corner, the smaller the image will appear. If either the x or y coordinate is less than 30, the image will use a default size for drawing. The function is shown in Figure 4.21.

```
BOOL SpiroGraphBox(HWND hwnd, POINTL ptlCurrent, USHORT usRotAngle, SHORT sDrawColor)
{
    HPS         hps;
    POINTL      ptlDraw;
    MATRIXLF    matrix;
    USHORT      usCounter;
    USHORT      usXValue;
    USHORT      usYValue;
    CHAR        szBuffer[25];
    PSZ         pszCoordinate;

    hps = WinGetPS(hwnd);

    // Set the color of the spirograph
    GpiSetColor(hps, sDrawColor);
```

Figure 4.21   The SpiroGraphBox function.   **continued**

```
// Query the current contents of the model transform
GpiQueryModelTransformMatrix(hps, 9L, &matrix);

usXValue = ptlCurrent.x;
usYValue = ptlCurrent.y;

ptlDraw.x = ptlCurrent.x + (usXValue / 10);
ptlDraw.y = ptlCurrent.y + (usYValue / 10);

// Use default if X or Y is less than 30
if (usXValue < 30 || usYValue < 30)
  {
   ptlDraw.x = ptlCurrent.x + 30;
   ptlDraw.y = ptlCurrent.y + 30;
  }

// The secret of creating the spirographs is simple.  We simply
// start by drawing a series of boxes all the way around a circle
// each time through the loop we will rotate an extra x degrees.
// Where x is the value of the rotational angle that the user
// specifies via usRotAngle.  All the while, we will be replacing
// our transform along the way with the newly calculated transform.
for (usCounter = 0; usCounter < 360; usCounter += usRotAngle)
{
   GpiRotate(hps,                        // Handle to Presentation Space
             &matrix,                    // Transform matrix
             TRANSFORM_REPLACE,          // Transform options
             MAKEFIXED(usCounter, 0),    // Rotation angle
             &ptlCurrent);               // POINTL coordinates for center of rotation

   GpiSetModelTransformMatrix(hps, 9L, &matrix, TRANSFORM_REPLACE);

   GpiSetCurrentPosition(hps, &ptlCurrent);

   // Draw a normal box based on the ptlDraw coordinates that are obtained.
   // The logic that handles the box drawing is totally unaware that the
   // transform will cause the box to be rotated.
   GpiBox(hps,                           // Handle to Presentation Space
          DRO_OUTLINE,                   // Outline and Fill control
          &ptlDraw,                      // POINTL coordinates for box
          0,                             // Horizontal corner rounding
          0);                            // Vertical corner rounding
}

WinReleasePS(hps);
return FALSE;
}
```

Figure 4.21   The SpiroGraphBox function.

Changing the Default Mouse Pointer

Graphics applications will often need to change the default mouse pointer to provide the user an easier interface to accomplish a drawing task. The Options/Capture menu item allows the user the ability to capture a portion of any window on the desktop. The area inside of the captured window is then copied to the client area of the status window, which is simply another window drawn within the client area of the main CLKDRAW window.

The illustratration shown in Figure 4.22 depicts the use of the capture window. When the user selects the Options/Capture menuitem, the pointer is changed to simplify the navigation of the tracking rectangle that is used to capture a portion of the screen. The tracking rectangle is the temporary box that the user will move and size when capturing. When the tracking is complete, the coordinates that composed the tracking rectangle are stored in a RECTL structure. Changing the system mouse pointer is as simple as changing the cheese on a mousetrap, except there's no yucky cheese to dispose of. The mouse pointer is changed by calling the API **WinSetPointer** and specifying the new system pointer to be used.

The prototype for **WinSetPointer** is shown in Figure 4.23.

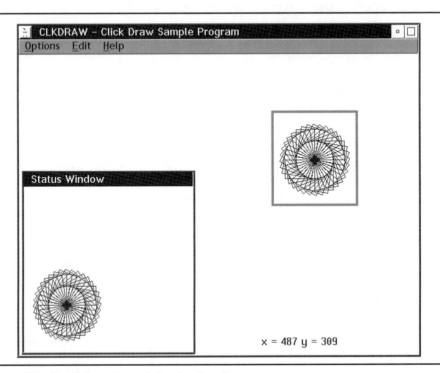

Figure 4.22   Using the capture window functionality.

```
BOOL APIENTRY WinSetPointer(HWND      hwndDesktop,
                            HPOINTER  hptrNew);
```

Figure 4.23   The WinSetPointer prototype.

- The **hwndDesktop** parameter specifies the desktop window handle.
- The **hptrNew** parameter specifies the new pointer that is to be used.

The pointer used by the sample program is a simple cross that is helpful for sizing the tracking rectangle. When the user begins the capture, the pointer is centered within the tracking rectangle to indicate that the tracking can begin. The tracking begins as soon as the user clicks the first mouse button. From there, the north-west quadrant of the cross will correspond to the bottom right end corner of the tracking rectangle. The cross pointer is more intuitive for the user to associate with the tracking rectangle. An application should only modify the system pointer when it provides the user an easier interface to accomplish a specific task.

The cross pointer itself was created by the Icon Editor(ICONEDIT), provided with OS/2. The pointer file is built as a resource into the executable, just like a bitmap or icon.

```
POINTER IDP_TRACKRECT clkdraw.ptr
```

Loading the Pointer

Prior to the pointer being changed, it needs to be loaded from the resource. The API that is used to load the pointer is called, **WinLoadPointer**. Upon success, the **WinLoadPointer** API will return a valid pointer handle that can be used to change the system pointer via a call to **WinSetPointer** (Figure 4.24).

- The **hwndDesktop** parameter specifies the desktop window handle
- The **hmod** parameter specifies the module handle of the module containing the pointer resource. A NULLHANDLE may be used to indicate that the pointer resource is built into the executable.
- The **idres** parameter corresponds to the identifier that represents the pointer to be loaded.

```
HPOINTER APIENTRY WinLoadPointer(HWND     hwndDesktop,
                                 HMODULE  hmod,
                                 ULONG    idres);
```

Figure 4.24   The WinLoadPointer prototype.

```
case IDM_TRACKBOX:
    hptrTrack = WinLoadPointer(HWND_DESKTOP,
                               NULLHANDLE,
                               IDP_TRACKRECT);

    rclTrack = ProcessTrackingRectangle(hptrTrack, HWND_DESKTOP);
```

Figure 4.25 **Loading the cross pointer used for tracking.**

In the code fragment found in Figure 4.25, the pointer is loaded during the processing of the IDM_TRACKBOX command message, and then the **ProcessTrackingRectangle** function is called to set the pointer and handle the tracking rectangle.

Destroying the Pointer

A pointer is a bitmap resource that requires memory from the graphics engine heap. Although the Presentation Manager code should automatically free all of the bitmap resources used by an application when the application terminates, it is a good idea to free the resource as soon as possible. This is especially true, if your application will run for hours without exiting, while the application continuously loads bitmap resources. One common programming error is to repetitively call **WinLoadPointer** without destroying the pointer when it is no longer needed. Eventually, the application will consume the bitmap resources in the graphics engine heap causing all kinds of nasty problems. Therefore, an application should use the **WinDestroyPointer** API to free all loaded pointers that are no longer being used (Figure 4.26).

- The **hptr** parameter specifies the handle of the pointer to be destroyed.

The **WinDestroyPointer** API will return TRUE if the function is successful and FALSE if an error occurred. The calling thread can only destroy the pointer if it was the same thread that created the pointer. Also, a check is done to ensure the current pointer is not destroyed, and that the system pointers are not inadvertantly destroyed. Finally, the worker routine for the API will call a routine in the graphics engine to delete the bitmaps associated to the pointer, *hbmColor*, *hbmMiniPointer* and *hbmMiniColor*.

```
BOOL APIENTRY WinDestroyPointer(HPOINTER hptr);
```

Figure 4.26 **The WinDestroyPointer prototype.**

Creating Pointers Dynamically

Since a pointer is actually composed of multiple bitmaps, an application may choose to manually create a pointer from various bitmaps. Creating the pointer dynamically from the bitmaps is a little bit more complex since it requires working with multiple bitmaps, along with the required presentation space. The pointer is created via a call to the API **WinCreatePointer**, specifying the bitmap required to create the pointer. The API will return a valid pointer handle on success or a NULLHANDLE if an error occurred creating the pointer.

The prototype for the API is shown in Figure 4.27.

- The **hwndDesktop** parameter specifies the desktop window handle.
- The **hbmPointer** parameter specifies the handle of the bitmap that will be used to create the pointer.
- The **fPointer** value is used to indicate whether the specified bitmap represented by **hbmPointer** should be the size of a system pointer or a system icon. If the value is set to TRUE, then the bitmap will be sized to fit the dimensions of a system pointer. If the value is set to FALSE, then the bitmap will be sized to fit the dimensions of a system icon. The icon sized pointer can be used for drag and drop operations.
- The **xHotspot** value is used to indicate the horizontal location of the pointer hotspot. This value is in pels and is based off the lower left corner of the image.
- The **yHotspot** value is used to indicate the vertical location of the pointer hotspot. This value is in pels and is based off the lower left corner of the image.

Processing the Tracking Rectangle

The tracking rectangle provides a visual mechanism for the user to size and move a rectangular box that can be used to track the movement of the pointing device. The tracking rectangle gives the developer a simple method of obtaining the coordinates for a rectangle based on the user's movement of the pointing device.

The manipulation of the tracking rectangle is accomplished through the use of the **WinTrackRect** API. The window manager code makes use of the

```
HPOINTER APIENTRY WinCreatePointer(HWND     hwndDesktop,
                                    HBITMAP  hbmPointer,
                                    BOOL     fPointer,
                                    LONG     xHotspot,
                                    LONG     yHotspot);
```

Figure 4.27   The WinCreatePointer prototype.

```
BOOL APIENTRY WinTrackRect(HWND        hwnd,
                           HPS         hps,
                           PTRACKINFO pti);
```

Figure 4.28   The WinTrackRect prototype.

tracking rectangle for moving and sizing a frame window with a sizeable border.

Figure 4.28 shows the prototype for **WinTrackRect**.

- The **hwnd** parameter specifies the window that the user can use for the tracking. If this parameter is set to HWND_DESKTOP, the user can move the tracking pointer anywhere on the desktop.
- The **hps** parameter specifies the presentation space handle of the area that is to be tracked. If this parameter is a NULLHANDLE then the **hwnd** parameter will be used to determine the presentation space required for tracking.
- The **pti** parameter represents a pointer to the tracking information structure called TRACKINFO, that is used to create the tracking rectangle.

The TRACKINFO structure is shown in Figure 4.29.

- The *cxBorder* element is used to specify the border width of the left and right sides of the tracking rectangle.
- The *cyBorder* element is used to specify the border height of the top and bottom sides of the tracking rectangle.
- The *cxGrid* element is used to specify the horizontal boundary for track movement.

```
typedef struct _TRACKINFO    // trackinfo
  {
    LONG    cxBorder;
    LONG    cyBorder;
    LONG    cxGrid;
    LONG    cyGrid;
    LONG    cxKeyboard;
    LONG    cyKeyboard;
    RECTL   rclTrack;
    RECTL   rclBoundary;
    POINTL  ptlMinTrackSize;
    POINTL  ptlMaxTrackSize;
    ULONG   fs;
  } TRACKINFO;
typedef TRACKINFO *PTRACKINFO;
```

Figure 4.29   The TRACKINFO structure.

- The *cyGrid* element is used to specify the vertical boundary for track movement.
- The *cxKeyboard* element allows the user to use the keyboard arrow keys to move the tracking rectangle. This element specifies the horizontal width that the rectangle will move.
- The *cyKeyboard* element allows the user to use the keyboard arrow keys to move the tracking rectangle. This element specifies the vertical length that the rectangle will move.
- The *rclTrack* element represents a RECTL structure that contains the rectangle coordinates corresponding to the user's movement of the tracking rectangle.
- The *rclBoundary* element specifies the bounding rectangle that the tracking rectangle cannot exceed. This element is used in conjunction with the TF_ALLINBOUNDARY flag.
- The *ptlMinTrackSize* element specifies the minimum tracking size.
- The *ptlMaxTrackSize* element specifies the maximum tracking size.
- The *fs* element contains the tracking flags which are shown in Figure 4.30.

Figure 4.30 shows the tracking rectangle flags.

- The TF_LEFT flag is used to track the left side of the rectangle.
- The TF_TOP flag is used to track the top of the rectangle.
- The TF_RIGHT flag is used to track the right side of the rectangle.
- The TF_BOTTOM flag is used to track the bottom of the rectangle.
- The TF_MOVE flag is used to allow all of the rectangle sides to be tracked.
- The TF_SETPOINTERPOS flag is used in conjunction with the direction tracking flags to determine how the pointer will be positioned.

If no additional direction flag is used, the pointer will be positioned in the center of the tracking rectangle.
If used with the TF_MOVE flag, the pointer will also be positioned in the center of the tracking rectangle.

```
TF_LEFT                0x0001
TF_TOP                 0x0002
TF_RIGHT               0x0004
TF_BOTTOM              0x0008
TF_MOVE                0x000F
TF_SETPOINTERPOS       0x0010
TF_GRID                0x0020
TF_STANDARD            0x0040
TF_ALLINBOUNDARY       0x0080
TF_VALIDATETRACKRECT   0x0100
```

Figure 4.30   The tracking flags.

If used with the TF_LEFT flag, the pointer will be vertically centered at the left of the tracking rectangle.
If used with the TF_RIGHT flag, the pointer will be vertically centered at the right of the tracking rectangle.
If used with the TF_TOP flag, the pointer will be horizontally centered at the top of the tracking rectangle.
If used with the TF_BOTTOM flag, the pointer will be horizontally centered at the bottom of the tracking rectangle.

- The TF_GRID flag is used to restrict the tracking movement to the grid boundaries defined by the cxGrid and cyGrid elements of the TRACKINFO structure.
- The TF_STANDARD flag is used to force cxBorder, cyBorder, cxGrid, cy-Grid, cxKeyboard, and cyKeyboard into multiples of cxBorder and cyBor-der.
- The TF_ALLINBOUNDARY flag is used to ensure that the tracking rectan-gle never extends past the boundary defined by rclBoundary. The default behavior is to ensure that some minimal part of the tracking rectangle is always within the rclBoundary coordinates.
- The TF_VALIDATETRACKRECT flag is used to validate the tracking rect-angle against the size and boundary limits. With the use of this flag no actual tracking occurs. It is only used for validation purposes.

The code fragment in Figure 4.31 handles the tracking rectangle.

The **ProcessTrackingRectangle** routine is used to handle the movement of the tracking rectangle for the user. The first parameter to the function is the handle of the pointer that is to be used for the tracking. The second parameter determines the window area that the user may use for the tracking. For the purposes of the sample program, the tracking is allowed for any window on the desktop by specifying the HWND_DESKTOP constant when calling the function. The first thing the routine does is change the pointer by calling **WinSetPointer** and specifiying the handle of the cross pointer that will be used for tracking. The next thing the function does is call another routine called **GetSysValues**, which uses the **WinQuerySysValue** API to obtain certain system value characteristics that will be used to calculate the tracking rectangle. The **GetSysValues** function is shown in Figure 4.32.

This function populates and returns a structure called SYSVALUES which contains various system defined values that the **ProcessTrackingRectangle** rou-tine will use to determine the coordinates for the tracking rectangle. The border of the tracking rectangle is set to the same size as the border of a standard di-alog box, which is determined by the *lcxDlgFrame* and *lcyDlgFrame* elements. The right and top sides of the tracking rectangle boundary along with the maximum tracking size are set to *lcxScreen* and *lcyScreen* respectively.

```
RECTL ProcessTrackingRectangle (HPOINTER hptrTrack, HWND hwndClientTracking)
{
  RECTL      rclTemp;
  POINTL     ptlTemp;
  TRACKINFO  trackinfo;
  SYSVALUES  sysvals;

  if (hptrTrack)
   {
    WinSetPointer(HWND_DESKTOP, hptrTrack);
   }

  sysvals = GetSysValues();

  // Set up track rectangle for moving
  trackinfo.cxBorder          = sysvals.lcxDlgFrame;      // Tracking rectangle border
  trackinfo.cyBorder          = sysvals.lcyDlgFrame;
  trackinfo.cxGrid            = 0;
  trackinfo.cyGrid            = 0;
  trackinfo.cxKeyboard        = 4;                        // X pels movement by keyboard
  trackinfo.cyKeyboard        = 4;                        // y pels movement by keyboard
  trackinfo.rclBoundary.xLeft   = 0;                      // Tracking rectangle boundary
  trackinfo.rclBoundary.yBottom = 0
  trackinfo.rclBoundary.xRight  = sysvals.lcxScreen;
  trackinfo.rclBoundary.yTop    = sysvals.lcyScreen;
  trackinfo.ptlMinTrackSize.x   = 1;                      // Minimum rectangle width
  trackinfo.ptlMinTrackSize.y   = 1;                      // Minimum rectangle height
  trackinfo.ptlMaxTrackSize.x   = sysvals.lcxScreen;      // Maximum rectangle width
  trackinfo.ptlMaxTrackSize.y   = sysvals.lcyScreen;      // Maximum rectangle height

  WinQueryPointerPos(HWND_DESKTOP, &ptlTemp);

  // Initial position
  trackinfo.rclTrack.xLeft    = ptlTemp.x - sysvals.lcxPointer;
  trackinfo.rclTrack.yBottom  = ptlTemp.y - sysvals.lcyPointer;
  trackinfo.rclTrack.xRight   = ptlTemp.x + sysvals.lcxPointer;
  trackinfo.rclTrack.yTop     = ptlTemp.y + sysvals.lcyPointer;
  trackinfo.fs                = TF_MOVE | TF_STANDARD | TF_SETPOINTERPOS;
  WinTrackRect(hwndClientTracking,   // Track over entire screen
               NULLHANDLE,           // Presentation Space Handle
               &trackinfo);          // Track Information

  // Track rectangle for sizing
  trackinfo.fs = TF_RIGHT | TF_BOTTOM | TF_STANDARD | TF_SETPOINTERPOS;

  WinTrackRect(hwndClientTracking,   // Track over entire screen
               NULLHANDLE,           // Presentation Space Handle
               &trackinfo);          // Track Information

  rclTemp = trackinfo.rclTrack;      // Final rectangle

  // return tracking rectangle coordinates
  return rclTemp;
}
```

Figure 4.31   The Processing of the tracking rectangle.

```
SYSVALUES GetSysValues(VOID)
{
 SYSVALUES sysvalues;

 sysvalues.lcxScreen     = WinQuerySysValue (HWND_DESKTOP, SV_CXSCREEN);
 sysvalues.lcyScreen     = WinQuerySysValue (HWND_DESKTOP, SV_CYSCREEN);
 sysvalues.lcxFullScreen = WinQuerySysValue (HWND_DESKTOP, SV_CXFULLSCREEN);
 sysvalues.lcyFullScreen = WinQuerySysValue (HWND_DESKTOP, SV_CYFULLSCREEN);
 sysvalues.lcxPointer    = WinQuerySysValue (HWND_DESKTOP, SV_CXPOINTER);
 sysvalues.lcyPointer    = WinQuerySysValue (HWND_DESKTOP, SV_CYPOINTER);
 sysvalues.lcxDlgFrame   = WinQuerySysValue (HWND_DESKTOP, SV_CXDLGFRAME);
 sysvalues.lcyDlgFrame   = WinQuerySysValue (HWND_DESKTOP, SV_CYDLGFRAME);
 return sysvalues;
}
```

Figure 4.32   The GetSysValues function.

Using the Clipboard

The CLKDRAW sample program is a very basic drawing utility. Most graphics programs provide a mechanism to exchange the graphical data with other applications, as well as provide the ability to import graphical data from these applications. The PM clipboard is the facility provided by the Presentation Manager to process the exchange of the data. The clipboard is a simple one-time data transfer mechanism, as opposed to the Dynamic Data Exchange (DDE) facility discussed in Chapter 9, which allows for multiple, non-interactive data exchanges.

The clipboard manager uses the cut, copy, and paste metaphors to correspond to the functionality of the clipboard. The cut and copy features allow an application to place data in the clipboard. The difference between cut and copy is simple. Cut deletes the data from an application perspective once the data is copied to the clipboard, while a copy operation leaves the data intact. The paste feature allows an application to retrieve data from the clipboard. All of these clipboard operations must be specifically initiated by the user.

Programming the PM clipboard is a relatively simple task, so we don't spend too much time covering it in this book. However, since the sample program for this chapter is a simple drawing and capture utility, it makes sense to provide the user, the ability to exchange the graphical images created by this program with other programs via the clipboard.

There are essentially three different types of data that the clipboard can support by default: text, bitmaps, and metafiles. An application may choose to copy the same data in multiple data formats so that the application receiving the data can determine which form it requires when it processes the paste operation. Aside from the standard clipboard formats, an application may choose to process data in the clipboard that does not fit into any of the public clipboard data types. In these cases an application may define a private data format to allow other applications the ability to obtain specific data other than the types covered by the public clipboard data types.

In order for an application to use a private clipboard format it must register the format in the system atom table. Once it is registered, the application uses a unique format identification number that identifies the private format. Applications that wish to make use of the private clipboard format must be able to identify the format, either by the format identification number or by querying the system atom table with the private format name.

Figure 4.33 shows the public clipboard data formats.

- The CF_TEXT format is the simplest of all the data formats. It is used to represent an array of characters. A single '\0' character is used to terminate the text and the newline character '\n' can be used to put a line break in the text.
- The CF_BITMAP format is the one used in the sample program. It is used to represent bitmap data.
- The CF_DSPTEXT format is used by the acting clipboard viewer to represent a private data format for text data.
- The CF_DSPBITMAP format is used by the acting clipboard viewer to represent a private data format for bitmap data.
- The CF_METAFILE format is used to represent a metafile.
- The CF_DSPMETAFILE format is used to by the acting clipboard viewer to represent a private data format for metafile data.

Placing Bitmap Data in the Clipboard

The process of putting our bitmap data in the clipboard is a relatively straightforward task since most of the clipboard APIs only take an anchor block handle as a parameter. To gain access to the clipboard, an application needs to first open the clipboard by calling the **WinOpenClipbrd** API. The purpose of this API is to block all other threads in the system from modifying the contents of the data in the clipboard. The function will return TRUE for success and FALSE if an error occurred opening the clipboard as a result of another application having the clipboard open. Also, the API cannot be called twice from the same thread. The function works by simply obtaining access to a special clipboard semaphore.

```
CF_TEXT             1
CF_BITMAP           2
CF_DSPTEXT          3
CF_DSPBITMAP        4
CF_METAFILE         5
CF_DSPMETAFILE      6
```

Figure 4.33   The public clipboard data formats.

```
BOOL APIENTRY WinOpenClipbrd(HAB hab);
```

Figure 4.34 **Opening the clipboard.**

```
BOOL APIENTRY WinEmptyClipbrd(HAB hab);
```

Figure 4.35 **Emptying the contents of the clipboard.**

The prototype for **WinOpenClipbrd** is listed in Figure 4.34.

Once the clipboard is opened by the application, the current contents of the clipboard can be emptied by calling the **WinEmptyClipbrd** API. The prototype for **WinEmptyClipbrd** is shown in Figure 4.35.

The purpose of the **WinEmptyClipbrd** API is to clear the contents of the clipboard and free all of the handles representing data for the clipboard. The function will return TRUE for success and FALSE if an error occurred as a result of the clipboard not being opened or the call being made from a different thread. The function will send a WM_DESTROYCLIPBOARD message to the owner of the clipboard to indicate that it free any CFI_OWNERFREE data. The function works by enumerating through all of the clipboard formats and freeing all of the resources used, like ATOMS, the memory for the clipboard structure, and finally the actual data in the clipboard.

Once the clipboard is emptied, an application can place data in the clipboard by calling the **WinSetClipbrdData** API. The prototype is shown in Figure 4.36.

- The *hab* parameter represents the anchor block handle.
- The *ulData* parameter is used to represent the generic handle of the object that is to be placed in the clipboard.
- The *fmt* parameter represents the clipboard data format.
- The *rgfFmtInfo* parameter is used to identify the type of data that is represented by the *ulData* parameter.

The routine **PutBitmapInClipboard** is used to put the bitmap created by the tracking rectangle into the clipboard. The function will return TRUE for success or FALSE if an error is returned by one of the clipboard API's. The code for this function is shown in Figure 4.37.

```
BOOL APIENTRY WinSetClipbrdData(HAB    hab,
                                ULONG ulData,
                                ULONG fmt,
                                ULONG rgfFmtInfo);
```

Figure 4.36 **The WinSetClipbrdData prototype.**

```
BOOL PutBitmapInClipboard(HBITMAP hbmClipboard)
{
  HAB  habTemp;
  BOOL rc;

  // Obtain anchor block handle
  habTemp = WinQueryAnchorBlock(HWND_DESKTOP);


  // Attempt to open the Clipboard
  rc = WinOpenClipbrd(habTemp);
  if (rc != TRUE)  // If we get an error opening, return FALSE and post message
   {
    DisplayMessages(NULLHANDLE, "Error Opening Clipboard", MSG_ERROR);
    return rc;
   }

  // OK, no error so let's empty the clipboard and
  // place our bitmap in there!
  else
   {
    rc = WinEmptyClipbrd(habTemp);
    if (rc != TRUE)
     {
       DisplayMessages(NULLHANDLE, "Error Emptying Data In Clipboard", MSG_ERROR);
       return rc;
     }

    rc = WinSetClipbrdData(habTemp,          // anchor block handle
                           hbmClipboard,      // bitmap handle
                           CF_BITMAP,         // clipboard data format
                           CFI_HANDLE);       // format information

    if (rc != TRUE)
     {
      DisplayMessages(NULLHANDLE, "Error Placing Data In Clipboard", MSG_ERROR);
      return rc;
     }

    rc = WinCloseClipbrd(habTemp);
    if (rc != TRUE)
     {
      DisplayMessages(NULLHANDLE, "Error Closing Clipboard", MSG_ERROR);
      return rc;
     }
   }
  return TRUE;
}
```

Figure 4.37   Putting a bitmap in the clipboard.

SUMMARY

This chapter demonstrates how to capture and utilize the mouse pointer, mouse pointer position, and pointer resources. The CLKDRAW sample program is a very simplistic drawing tool designed to illustrate various pointer programming techniques. The processing of the mouse button and mouse movement messages along with the pointer manipulation APIs are discussed throughout the chapter. This chapter makes use of the mouse movement and the pointer position concepts by integrating these elements into a fun yet somewhat practical graphics program. The CLKDRAW sample program uses some simple and advanced GPI drawing techniques to illustrate the effective use of the pointer. Learning how to conquer the pointing device issues covered in this chapter is essential to creating well-designed and well-written graphical applications.

SOS for PM Developers: Help Management through the Information Presentation Facility

In the not too distant past, computer users considered extensive, on-line, context-sensitive help a luxury. Now these features have become a necessity. If programmers were forced to build their own help systems from the ground up, the time and expense required to build applications would increase significantly. Fortunately for OS/2 developers, this is not the case—the operating system provides an internal system for managing on-line help data, the Information Presentation Facility, IPF.

Since many of the Presentation Manager applications and utilities for OS/2 utilize IPF to display on-line help, users of the operating system already know how to access help using the IPF facilities. Applications that also use the IPF API to access help provide a consistent user interface which helps give the user a sense of unity and security knowing that help is almost always available and accessible.

For programmers, IPF simplifies the task of providing the proper text based on the context from which the user requests help. For simple applications, the only program code modifications required are three API calls and a set of tables that define the text to be displayed for each element of the application. IPF automatically handles the user's request for help, the display of the help windows, the processing of messages sent to these windows, and the formatting of the text displayed in the windows.

DESIGNING HELP TEXT

The purpose of on-line help is to assist the user in determining how to properly operate an application. Users of an application tend to exhibit a wide range of experience, so the on-line help system must be designed to provide various levels of detail. Experienced users may need only a brief description to jog their memory while a novice may require lengthy explanations and "how to" information.

IPF meets these needs by organizing the help text into *panels* of information. A properly designed system gives the user access to a basic, or general, help panel which describes the application. Hypertext links from this panel lead the novice user to more detailed how-to type information. General help panels can be created for each window of the application to explain the purpose and general functionality of the window. In this instance, hypertext links can lead to additional information about the various elements of the window, such as menus and controls. The text can also be organized such that each element of the window has its own help panel which is immediately accessible when the user is working with that element. Typically, these panels provide concise, expert-level information describing the particular element, and contain a hypertext link to more detailed information when necessary.

Thus the task of the help text designer is twofold: determining the organization of the panels, and determining the text to be displayed in the panel. This second item, the actual text, is largely outside the scope of this book; however, we will describe the *tagging* necessary to define and link panels.

Organization of Panels

The organization of on-line help into panels is largely determined by the structure of the application itself. The main window of the application should have a panel, referred to as the general help panel, which provides an overall description of the application. If desired, this panel can contain hypertext links to additional information; for example, panels that describe the major functional areas of the application and/or how-to panels. The general help panel is displayed when the user requests help via the F1 key and no other application element is currently in use, or when the user selects the General Help item from the Help menu.

Applications that define special uses for the keyboard keys, such as accelerator keys, should provide one or more keys help panels to list these keys and their functions. If appropriate, the keys help panel(s) can contain hypertext links to the panels associated with menu items or other application elements to which the special use keys are mapped. This panel is displayed when the user selects the Keys Help item from the Help menu.

Next, panels should be defined for each element of the main window. These elements include menu items, pushbuttons, and other controls. The panels for primary menu items like File should describe the type of actions performed by the submenu items and contain hypertext links to the panels defined for the submenu items. Panels for the submenu items should describe the action that is taken when that item is selected. If the item causes a secondary window, such as a dialog box to be displayed, a hypertext link to the general help panel for the secondary window should be provided.

After the help panels for the main application window have been defined, help panels for the secondary windows—dialog boxes, message boxes, and so on—should be defined. Panels for these windows are defined similarly to those for the main window: A general help panel is defined to explain the function of the window, and additional panels are defined as required for each control or menu item associated with the window.

While observing the preceding will provide good context-sensitive help for the application, the designer should remember that IPF also generates a table of contents for the panels. Since the table of contents is accessible by the user when a help panel is displayed, some care must be taken to ensure that a logical representation of the panels in the help file is shown. The IPF table of contents is essentially an outline of the help file, organized in the same order as the panels are defined in the help file source and using the title of the panel as the table of contents entry. Panels may be defined with various heading levels, the highest level being level 1. The practice of defining all panels in a help file at level 1, while common, significantly reduces the usefulness of the table of contents. A scheme that defines the general help panels for each window at heading level 1 and the menu and control panels at level 2 or below provides a logical, easy-to-navigate organization. The keys help panel should be defined at level 1. A single how-to panel should be defined at level 1 or, if several are available, define a summary panel at level 1 and the actual help panels below this at level 2.

IPF also allows indexes to be defined which provide access to all panels that reference a particular topic. Indexes should be defined as needed. If no index entries are available, IPF will disable the help index item in the menu of the help window—the application is responsible for removing or disabling this item in its Help menu.

CONSTRUCTING THE IPF SOURCE FILE

Help files are created by constructing a tagged ASCII file containing the help text. Special tags are used to split the text into panels, describe how the text should be formatted, establish links between panels, and so forth. This file is then used as the source for the IPFC compiler, provided in the OS/2 Devel-

```
:userdoc.
:h1.Title
Word
:euserdoc.
```

Figure 5.1 **A minimal help script.**

oper's Toolkit, which produces the help library file used by IPF at runtime. Construction of the help source file can proceed in two phases. In the first phase, the application developer constructs a template file which defines the panels and hypertext links that represent the application architecture. The panel text in this file merely indicates the subject of the help text for the panel. The actual text is added in phase 2 by technical writers or others responsible for this task. As our main concern is the task of the application programmer, let's examine how the template file would be constructed for a sample application, a text editor.

Figure 5.1 shows a basic help source file which consists of three tags and one word of text. This file can be used as the initial template from which to build a full help file for an application. Note that IPF tags begin with a colon and end with a period. The *:userdoc.* tag must be the first tag of the source file and indicates to IPFC that this is the beginning of the document. The *:euserdoc.* tag must be the last tag in the file; text beyond this tag is ignored. The *:h1.* tag defines a level 1 panel which will include all text until another *:hx.* tag or the *:euserdoc.* tag is encountered. "Title" is the text to be displayed in the title bar of the help window when this panel is displayed and is also used to represent this panel in the table of contents. "Word" is the text that will be displayed in body of the help window.

Using this basic file, we begin adding panels as described in the previous section. The first step is defining the general help panel for the main window of the application. Figure 5.2 shows the basic help source file modified to define the general help panel for an application named Editor. In this figure, the basic help file has been modified to include a valid help panel title, and the text of the panel has been changed to a placeholder to be filled in later. Also, the *:h1.* tag now contains a *res=* attribute which provides the panel with a numeric resource ID. This ID is required for IPF to automatically access the appropriate panel when help is requested and must be unique within the help file. When the application coding language permits, the panel IDs can be defined in a

```
:userdoc.
:h1 res=1000.Help for Editor
:p.Insert Editor "General Help" text here.
:euserdoc.
```

Figure 5.2 **Basic help script for Editor.**

separate header file which is used by both the application code and the IPF source file. With this technique, the IPF source file is first passed through the coding language's precompiler and then compiled with IPFC. Be forewarned, however, that IPFC does not perform any arithmetic operations—the definition in the header file must use an explicit numeric value, not a calculation. The sample program accompanying this chapter uses this technique and should be referenced if more detailed information is required.

Now the help panels for the primary menu items and controls associated with the main window need to be defined. Figure 5.3 shows the IPF source file for Editor which defines three primary menu items, File, Edit, and Help, and does not have any embedded controls. Level 2 panels have been added for each of the main menu items using an *:h2.* tag. When the table of contents for this file is displayed, these panels will be displayed under the entry for the main application window general help. In addition, *:link.* and *:elink.* tags have been added to the general help panel. These tags are used to define a hypertext link allowing the user to jump from one panel to another. The text between the two tags is displayed with hypertext highlighting. When the user clicks on this text, the panel defined by the hypertext link is displayed. The *:link.* tag contains two attributes, *reftype=*, which indicates the type of link, and *res=*, which indicates the resource ID of the linked heading. Reftype *hd* indicates that the link is to another help panel. Note that a *:p.*, or paragraph, tag is used to cause the text and each of the links to be displayed on a separate line.

Next, panels for the submenu items of each of the main menu selections are defined. Figure 5.4 illustrates the file following the addition of panels for the File menu. These panels are defined with *:h3.* tags and will thus be displayed under the Help for File Menu entry in the table of contents. The Help for Open Menu panel contains two additional links. The first link references the Level 1 panel for the dialog window used to select a file. By following this link, the user will be able to determine all the information required to actually open the file just by selecting help on the Open menu item. The second link references

```
:userdoc.
:h1 res=1000.Help for Editor
:p.Insert Editor "General Help" text here.
:p.:link reftype=hd res=1100.File:elink.
:p.:link reftype=hd res=1200.Edit:elink.
:p.:link reftype=hd res=1300.Help:elink.
:h2 res=1100.Help for File Menu
:p.Insert FILE menu help here.
:h2 res=1200.Help for Edit Menu
:p.Insert EDIT menu help here.
:h2 res=1300.Help for Help Menu
:p.Insert HELP menu help here.
:euserdoc.
```

Figure 5.3 **Adding Editor's menu items.**

```
:userdoc.
:h1 res=1000.Help for Editor
:p.Insert Editor "Extended Help" text here.
:p.:link reftype=hd res=1100.File:elink.
:p.:link reftype=hd res=1200.Edit:elink.
:p.:link reftype=hd res=1300.Help:elink.
:h2 res=1100.Help for File Menu
:p.Insert FILE menu help here.
:p.:link reftype=hd res=1110.New:elink.
:p.:link reftype=hd res=1120.Open...:elink.
:p.:link reftype=hd res=1130.Save:elink.
:p.:link reftype=hd res=1140.Save as...:elink.
:p.:link reftype=hd res=1150.Exit:elink.
:h3 res=1110.Help for New Menu
:p.Insert FILE NEW menu help here.
:h3 res=1120.Help for Open Menu
:p.Insert FILE OPEN menu help here.
:p.:link reftype=hd res=2000.File Open Dialog Window:elink.
:p.Additional Information
:p.:link reftype=hd res=20010.File Management Concepts:elink.
:h3 res=1130.Help for Save Menu
:p.Insert FILE SAVE menu help here.
:h3 res=1140.Help for Save As Menu
:p.Insert FILE SAVE AS menu help here.
:h3 res=1150.Help for Exit Menu
:p.Insert FILE EXIT menu help here.
:h2 res=1200.Help for Edit Menu
:p.Insert EDIT menu help here.
:h2 res=1300.Help for Help Menu
:p.Insert HELP menu help here.
:h1 res=2000.Help for File Open Dialog Window
:p.Insert extended help for the file open dialog box here.
:h1 res=20000.User's Guide
Insert User's Guide introduction here.
:h2 res=20010.File Management
Insert File Management Concepts section here.
:euserdoc.
```

Figure 5.4   Adding Editor's file menu help.

a Level 2 panel which provides the novice user with additional information on general file management concepts. Links similar to these two should also be provided as appropriate for the other file menu items—the Help for Save as panel should contain a link to the general help panel for the Save as dialog window and all the panels except Help for Exit should provide a link to the file management concepts panel.

When the panels for the Edit and Help submenu items have been added to Figure 5.4, the main application window's help template will be complete. The same process should then be followed to complete the template for other application windows such as the File Open dialog window. Additional general information or how-to panels should be added to the User's Guide section as needed or desired. Finally, a Keys help panel should be provided if the application assigns special functions to the keyboard keys. A link to this panel should be provided from the Keys help submenu item of the Help menu.

The template help source file is now complete. After compilation, the file can be used as is during application development and tested while the actual text is being developed. The file is compiled by invoking the IPFC compiler with the name of the source file as a parameter. Assuming the name of the source file is editor.ipf, the following command line would be used to compile the file:

```
IPFC editor
```

The ipf extension is the default expected by the IPFC compiler; however, other extensions can be used if the file name and extension are both specified on the command line.

The IPFC compiler can also be used to generate on-line documents which are displayed using the OS/2 View utility by adding the /INF parameter to the command line. Generating a viewable document from a help source file is often useful to verify the contents of the file during the development phases.

MAPPING APPLICATION ELEMENTS TO HELP PANELS

In order to provide the correct on-line help panel for each window, control, menu item, dialog box, and so on, IPF requires the application to define a set of tables that map these elements to the proper help panel. Two table types are used: A help table maps help panels to frame windows and help subtables map help panels to control and menu windows within frame windows.

The help table is an array which normally contains one element for each frame window in the application. Each element of the array is a structure of type HELPTABLE which defines the general help panel for the frame window and identifies the help subtable for the nonframe child windows of the frame. The final element of the array must contain a structure whose elements are all set to either zero or NULL. The HELPTABLE structure is defined as shown in Figure 5.5.

```
typedef struct _HELPTABLE {
    USHORT          idAppWindow;
    PHELPSUBTABLE   phstHelpSubTable;
    USHORT          idExtPanel;
} HELPTABLE;
```

Figure 5.5   The HELPTABLE structure.

- The *idAppWindow* element is the window ID of the frame window whose help is mapped with this structure.
- The *phstHelpSubTable* element is a pointer to the first element of the sub-table which maps the frame window's children to their proper help panel.
- The *idExtPanel* element is the resource ID of the help panel to display when general help is requested for the frame window. This value should match one of the *res=* IDs defined in the help source file.

A help subtable is an array of 16-bit values which define the mapping between nonframe child windows and help panels. The first element indicates the number of array elements that are used to represent each entry in the table and is normally set to the value 2. The remainder of the array comprises a number of mapping entries each consisting of the specified number of array elements. Each entry contains at least two 16-bit values: the first is the window ID of a child window, and the second is the resource ID of the help panel to be displayed when help is requested for the child window. Additional 16-bit values may be included in each entry; if so, these values are not used by IPF and are available for application defined use.

Defining Help Tables

The help tables and subtables may be variables within the application's code but normally are defined in the application's resources. The OS/2 Resource Compiler has defined keywords and resource types specifically for generating the help mapping information. The generic syntax for defining a help table is given in Figure 5.6.

The HELPTABLE keyword indicates that the Resource Compiler is to create a HELPTABLE resource. The *helptable_id* is the number that the compiler will assign to the HELPTABLE resource and which applications use to reference the resource. The BEGIN and END keywords are required to signal the start and finish of the individual elements of the help table. Each HELPITEM statement defines one entry. The *window_id* is the ID assigned to a frame window. The *subtable_id* is the resource number assigned to the help subtable which defines the help panel mapping for the nonframe children of the specified frame window. The *extended_help_panel_id* is the help panel resource ID assigned to the panel containing the general help for this window.

```
HELPTABLE helptable_id
BEGIN
HELPITEM   window_id, subtable_id, extended_help_panel_id
END
```

Figure 5.6   Resource file HELPTABLE syntax.

```
HELPTABLE APP_HELPTABLE_ID
BEGIN
    HELPITEM    APP_WINDOW_ID,  APP_SUBHELP_ID,    1000
    HELPITEM    OPEN_DLG,       OPEN_SUBHELP_ID,   2000
    HELPITEM    SAVEAS_DLG,     SAVEAS_SUBHELP_ID, 3000
    HELPITEM    MSGBOX_ID,      0,                 4000
END
```

Figure 5.7   The HELPTABLE for Editor.

Figure 5.7 shows the help table definition statements for the Editor application. The HELPTABLE ID, window IDs, and HELP SUBTABLE IDs are arbitrary and should be defined in a header file for use by the application and the resource compiler. The resource compiler's preprocessor will substitute the actual numeric values at compile time. This technique may also be used for the *extended_help_panel_id* if a preprocessor is available for substituting the appropriate numeric values into the help source prior to compilation by IPFC. In the example, this technique is not used—the panel resource IDs from Figure 5.4 are explicitly specified.

Examining the figure more closely, the HELPTABLE resource is identified as *APP_HELPTABLE_ID*. The table contains one entry for each of the application's frame windows. The first entry is for the main application window which is created with window ID *APP_WINDOW_ID*. A HELPSUBTABLE will be used to provide context-sensitive help for this window's menus; the ID of the subtable will be *APP_SUBHELP_ID*. The help panel with resource ID 1000 will be displayed when the user requests general help for the window. The second entry in the table is for the dialog used to open files. *OPEN_DIALOG* specifies the ID with which the window is created, and *OPEN_SUBHELP_ID* identifies the help subtable that maps the dialog's controls to the correct context-sensitive help panel. Help panel 2000 is displayed when general help is requested for the dialog. The third entry is for the dialog used to save the edited file under a new file name. The fourth entry is for a message box. Note that the help subtable entry for this window is set to zero, indicating that no subtable exists and that specific context-sensitive help is not available. If the user requests help on one of the message box buttons, the general help panel for the message box is displayed.

One further note that can help in organizing help tables: Since the HELPTABLE, window, and HELPSUBTABLES are all different types of entities, they may all be assigned the same ID; for example, *APP_WINDOW_ID* could be used as the *helptable_id* and as the *window_id* and *subtable_id* for the first HELPITEM.

Defining Help Subtables

HELPSUBTABLES must now be defined for each frame window to map the controls, menus, and other nonframe child windows to the appropriate help

```
HELPSUBTABLE helpsubtable_id
SUBITEMSIZE subitem_size
BEGIN
   HELPSUBITEM subwindow_id, help_panel_id
END
```

Figure 5.8   Resource file HELPSUBTABLE syntax.

panels. The resource compiler syntax for defining a help subtable is given in Figure 5.8. The HELPSUBTABLE keyword indicates that the Resource Compiler is to create a HELPSUBTABLE resource. The resource is to be assigned *helpsubtable_id*. The SUBITEMSIZE phrase is optional; if specified, *subitem_size* determines the number of 16-bit values to assign to each HELP-SUBITEM entry in the table—the minimum, and default, value is 2. The BE-GIN and END keywords signal the beginning and end of the list of individual elements in the table. Each HELPSUBITEM statement maps a child element of the frame window to a help panel. The *subwindow_id* field is the ID of the child element to be mapped, and the *help_panel_id* field identifies the resource ID of the help panel to be displayed when help is requested for the child element. If *subitem_size* has been specified, additional values may be added at the end of the line for use as defined by the application.

Figure 5.9 shows the help subtable coding used to provide context-sensitive help for the Editor application's main window. The ID of the subtable is set to *APP_SUBHELP_ID*. Each element of the table is a pair of values specifying a

```
HELPSUBTABLE APP_SUBHELP_ID
BEGIN
    HELPSUBITEM   MENUID_FILE,         1100
    HELPSUBITEM   MENUID_FILENEW,      1110
    HELPSUBITEM   MENUID_FILEOPEN,     1120
    HELPSUBITEM   MENUID_FILESAVE,     1130
    HELPSUBITEM   MENUID_FILESAVEAS,   1140
    HELPSUBITEM   MENUID_FILEEXIT,     1150
    HELPSUBITEM   MENUID_EDIT,         1200
    HELPSUBITEM   MENUID_EDITCOPY,     1210
    HELPSUBITEM   MENUID_EDITCUT,      1220
    HELPSUBITEM   MENUID_EDITPASTE,    1230
    HELPSUBITEM   MENUID_HELP,         1300
    HELPSUBITEM   MENUID_HELPINDEX,    1310
    HELPSUBITEM   MENUID_HELPGENERAL,  1320
    HELPSUBITEM   MENUID_HELPUSING,    1330
    HELPSUBITEM   MENUID_HELPKEYS,     1340
    HELPSUBITEM   MENUID_HELPTUTOR,    1350
    HELPSUBITEM   MENUID_PRODINFO,     1360
END
```

Figure 5.9   The Editor main window help subtable.

menu item ID and the help panel resource ID from the help source file. For example, the first entry specifies the menu ID for the FILE item on the main menu, and help panel resource ID, 1100, for the panel describing the use of the File menu. The second entry specifies the menu ID of the New submenu item under the File menu, and the ID of the help panel describing the function of the new submenu item. Similar subtables would be defined for the dialog boxes used by the editor application.

MENU SUPPORT FOR ON-LINE HELP

Applications that use the IPF feature normally add a Help item to the main menu of the primary application window. The Help menu should normally be added to any frame window or popup menu defined for the application, and it typically contains the following subitems:

Help index   displays a help window that contains the index entries for the help library. Do not include this subitem if the library does not contain any index entries.

General help   displays the general help panel for the application, typically the general help panel for the primary application window.

Using help   displays the OS/2 panel that describes the user interface to IPF.

Keys help   displays a panel that describes special keys defined by the application. This entry should not be included if the panel is not defined or if the application does not use any special keys.

Tutorial   executes the tutorial for the application. Note that this is an executable file provided with the application. If no such executable exists, do not add this menu item.

Product information

displays an application-defined window that identifies the application and provides other pertinent information. Note that this function is not related to IPF; however, CUA guidelines specify that this subitem be placed with the Help menu.

ADDING HELP TO YOUR SOURCE CODE

We have now seen how the help source file is generated and how the help panels are mapped to the application elements via tables defined in the application's resource script. Before IPF will actually provide help, the application must provide IPF with the information required to access the help file and the mapping tables. This information is provided by establishing an instance of IPF for the application and then associating this instance with the application's windows. When the Help menu is provided, code must be added to the application's WM_COMMAND message processing to support the menu items.

```
HWND APIENTRY WinCreateHelpInstance(
                         HAB hab,
                         PHELPINIT phinitHMInitStructure);
```

Figure 5.10   The WinCreateHelpInstance prototype.

Creating an Instance of IPF

An instance of IPF is an object window with which the user and the application communicate to control the display of help information. This object window is called a *help instance* and is created using the **WinCreateHelpInstance** API. This API is prototyped as shown in Figure 5.10.

- The **hab** parameter is the thread's anchor block handle obtained from the **WinInitialize** API.
- The **phinitHMInitStructure** parameter is a pointer to a HELPINIT structure which provides the information that IPF needs to locate and display help for the application. The structure is defined in Figure 5.11.
- The *cb* element specifies the number of bytes contained in the structure. This element should be set to *sizeof(HELPINIT)*.
- The *ulReturnCode* element contains the error code for any error encountered by IPF during creation of the help instance.
- The *pszTutorial* name element is a pointer to a zero-terminated ASCII string containing the name of the executable file that executes the application's tutorial. If this element is non-NULL, IPF will automatically add a Tutorial item to the Help menu of the help windows. If no tutorial is provided, this element should be set to NULL.
- The *phtHelpTable* element can contain either a pointer to a HELPTABLE, which has been constructed in memory, or the ID of the HELPTABLE resource in an executable module. In the latter instance, the high word of *phtHelpTable* is set to 0xFFFF and the low order word is set to the resource

```
typedef struct _HELPINIT {
    ULONG         cb;
    ULONG         ulReturnCode;
    PSZ           pszTutorialName;
    PHELPTABLE    phtHelpTable;
    HMODULE       hmodHelpTableModule;
    HMODULE       hmodAccelActionBarModule;
    ULONG         idAccelTable;
    ULONG         idActionBar;
    PSZ           pszHelpWindowTitle;
    ULONG         fShowPanelId;
    PSZ           pszHelpLibraryName;
} HELPINIT;
```

Figure 5.11   The HELPINIT structure.

ID—set the element to the value (PHELPTABLE)MAKEULONG(resource_id,0xFFFF). Note that element *hmodHelpTable* must also be set when using resources.

- The *hmodHelpTable* module element specifies the module handle of the executable module whose resources contain the help table. Setting this field to NULLHANDLE indicates that the resources are contained in the application's .EXE file. If the resources are contained in a separate DLL, this element should be set to the module handle returned from **DosLoadModule** when the DLL was loaded.

- The *hmodAccelActionBar* module element specifies the module handle of the executable module whose resources contain a customized accelerator table and/or action bar menu. Setting this field to NULLHANDLE indicates that the resources are contained in the application's .EXE file. If the resources are contained in a separate DLL, this element should be set to the module handle returned from **DosLoadModule** when the DLL was loaded. This element should be set to NULLHANDLE if the application does not specify a customized accelerator table or menu.

- The *idAccelTable* element specifies the ID of the accelerator table in the resource file. This element should be set to zero if the application does not specify a custom accelerator table.

- The *idActionBar* element specifies the ID of the customized action bar menu in the resource file. This element should be set to zero if the application does not specify a custom menu.

- The *pszHelpWindowTitle* element is a pointer to a zero-terminated ASCII string which IPF uses as the title for the window in which help information is displayed.

- The *fShowPanelId* element is a flag that is used to cause IPF to display the help panel ID in the title bar of each help panel window. Normally this element is set to CMIC_HIDE_PANEL_ID so that the IDs are not displayed. Setting this element to CMIC_SHOW_PANEL_ID can often be helpful during debugging.

- The *pszHelpLibraryName* element is a pointer to a zero-terminated ASCII string that contains the name(s) of the file(s) where the help panel information is stored. If multiple file names are specified, they should be separated by the space character. Help library files are created from help source files by the IPFC compiler contained in the OS/2 Developer's Toolkit.

The **WinCreateHelpInstance** API returns the handle of the created object window if successful; NULLHANDLE is returned if the API fails. In this instance, the error code for the failure is stored in the *ulReturnCode* element of the HELPINIT structure. The call to **WinCreateHelpInstance** is normally placed in either the main routine of the application or in the routine that processes the WM_CREATE message for the application's main window. Figure

```
HELPINIT   hi;

/* Fill in the help manager initialization structure */
hi.cb = sizeof( HELPINIT );
hi.ulReturnCode = 01;
hi.pszTutorialName = NULL;
hi.phtHelpTable = (PHELPTABLE)MAKEULONG( APP_HELPTAB_ID, 0xffff );
hi.hmodHelpTableModule = NULLHANDLE;
hi.hmodAccelActionBarModule = NULLHANDLE;
hi.idAccelTable = 01;
hi.idActionBar = 01;
hi.pszHelpWindowTitle = "Help for Editor";
hi.fShowPanelId = CMIC_HIDE_PANEL_ID;
hi.pszHelpLibraryName = "EDITOR.HLP";

/* initialize an instance of the help manager for this application */
hwndHelpInstance = WinCreateHelpInstance( WinQueryAnchorBlock(hwnd),
                                          &hi );
if (hwndHelpInstance == NULLHANDLE) {
   ShowError( hi.ulReturnCode );
} /* endif */
```

Figure 5.12 Creating a help instance.

5.12 shows code that the Editor application (discussed earlier) could use to create its help instance.

The application first initializes the HELPINIT structure. Element *cb* is set to the size of the structure, and *ulReturnCode* is initialized to zero. No tutorial application is available, so *pszTutorialName* is set to NULL. Since the help table is contained in the executable's attached resources, the low-order word of *phtHelpTable* is set to *APP_HELPTAB_ID*, the value specified for the help table in the resource script; and the high-order word is set to 0xffff. Element *hmodHelpTableModule* is set to NULLHANDLE, indicating that IPF should search the executable for the HELPTABLE resource. The application does not define a custom accelerator table or help window menu, so elements *idAccelTable* and *idActionBar* are both set to zero, and element *hmodAccelActionBarModule* is set to NULLHANDLE. The help window title bar text is specified by setting element *pszHelpWindowTitle* to a pointer to the string "Help for Editor." Element *fShowPanelId* is set to CMIC_HIDE_PANEL_ID to prevent the resource IDs of the help panels from being displayed. Finally, the *pszHelpLibraryName* is set to point to the string "EDITOR.HLP," the name given to the help library produced from the help source file.

After the structure is initialized, the help instance is created by calling **WinCreateHelpInstance**. The **hab** parameter is obtained by querying the anchor block for the current window; or, if this code is placed in the main routine, to the handle returned for **WinInitialize**. The **phinitHMInitStructure** parameter points to the HELPINIT structure just initialized. If the help instance handle

```
BOOL APIENTRY WinAssociateHelpInstance(HWND hwndHelpInstance,
                                       HWND hwndApp);
```

Figure 5.13 **The WinAssociateHelpInstance prototype.**

returned is NULLHANDLE, an error processing routine is called with the error code passed back to the application in the *ulReturnCode* element of the HELPINIT structure.

Once the help instance has been created, the **WinAssociateHelpInstance** API is called to attach the help instance to the window chain. The prototype for this API is shown in Figure 5.13.

- The **hwndHelpInstance** parameter is the help instance handle returned by **WinCreateHelpInstance**.
- The **hwndApp** parameter is the window handle of the frame window with which the help instance is to be associated. IPF provides help services for this window, all windows descended from this window, and windows owned, either directly or indirectly, by this window. Normally, the help instance is associated with the main frame window of the application, enabling IPF to service all windows of the application that are descended from this window. Passing NULLHANDLE for the parameter removes the association between the window chain and the help instance.

WinAssociateHelpInstance returns TRUE if the association was successful, and FALSE if the association failed. Figure 5.14 provides example code for calling **WinAssociateHelpInstance**. In this example, the **hwndHelpInstance** parameter is set to the handle returned from **WinCreateHelpInstance**. The code is assumed to be within the message processing for the WM_CREATE message, so the **hwndApp** parameter is set to the frame window handle which is the parent of the current window, the application's client window. If an error occurs, a routine is called to obtain and process the current PM error code.

When the help instance has been successfully associated with the window chain, IPF will automatically display help panels as defined in the help tables when the user requests help by pressing the F1 key or by clicking a pushbutton control with the BS_HELP style.

```
/* associate the help instance with the frame window */
if (!WinAssociateHelpInstance( hwndHelpInstance,
                               WinQueryWindow( hwnd, QW_PARENT ))) {
   ShowWinError();
} /* endif */
```

Figure 5.14 **Associating help with a window.**

PROCESSING THE HELP MENU COMMANDS

Most applications that use the IPF facilities add a Help item to the menus of their frame windows. Typical menu items associated with the Help menu were discussed previously; however, IPF does not provide any automated processing for these menu items. The application must handle the menu items when a WM_COMMAND message specifying the menu ID of the menu item is received. This section describes the typical processing used to process the menu items.

The Help Index menu item displays the index window for the application's help library. The WM_COMMAND message processing for this item should send a HM_HELP_INDEX message to the application's help instance. Figure 5.15 shows the WM_COMMAND case statement to accomplish this function.

In the figure, **WinQueryHelpInstance** is called to obtain the handle of the help instance window associated with the window that received the message. **WinSendMsg** is then called to send the HM_HELP_INDEX message to the help instance window. Parameters **mp1** and **mp2** of this message are both reserved and set to zero. IPF displays a window listing the index entries for the current help library when this message is received. If no index entries are contained in the help library, HMERR_INDEX_NOT_FOUND is returned from the **WinSendMsg** call.

The General help menu item is used to display the general help panel for the currently active window, normally the window from which the menu item was chosen. The application should respond to this command by sending an HM_GENERAL_HELP message to the help instance associated with the window. Figure 5.16 shows how this is accomplished.

As before, **WinQueryHelpInstance** is called to obtain the current help instance window handle. **WinSendMsg** is then called to send the HM_GENERAL_HELP message to the help instance. The parameters to this message are both reserved and should be set to zero. When IPF receives this message, it searches the help tables to find the ID of the general help panel for the current window and then displays the panel if found. If the current window does not

```
case MENUID_HELPINDEX:
    {
        HWND      hwndHelp;

        hwndHelp = WinQueryHelpInstance( hwnd );
        if (hwndHelp != NULLHANDLE) {
            WinSendMsg( hwndHelp, HM_HELP_INDEX, 0L, 0L );
        } /* endif */
    }
    break;
```

Figure 5.15 Processing the Help index menu item.

```
case MENUID_GENERALHELP:
  {
    HWND       hwndHelp;

    hwndHelp = WinQueryHelpInstance( hwnd );
    if (hwndHelp != NULLHANDLE) {
       WinSendMsg( hwndHelp, HM_GENERAL_HELP, 0L, 0L );
    } /* endif */
  }
  break;
```

Figure 5.16 **Processing the General help menu item.**

have a general help panel, IPF searches the parent and owner chains until a
frame window with a general help panel is found. If no general help panel
is found, IPF sends an HM_GENERAL_HELP_UNDEFINED message back to
the application which may either ignore the message, in which case no panel
is displayed, or take steps to display an alternate panel or otherwise notify the
user of the failure.

The Using help menu item normally displays an IPF-supplied panel that
describes how on-line help is used. When this command is received, the application should respond by sending an HM_DISPLAY_HELP message to the help
instance. Figure 5.17 provides an example of the required code. After obtaining
the current help instance, the HM_DISPLAY_HELP message is sent by calling
WinSendMsg. In this instance, both parameters to the HM_DISPLAY_HELP
message are set to zero. This particular combination of parameters causes
IPF to display either its own Using help panel or an application-defined panel
that has been specified by sending the HM_REPLACE_USING_HELP message
to the help instance. The low-order word of this message's **mp1** parameter
specifies the help resource ID to be displayed when the Using help panel is
requested via the preceding special instance of the HM_DISPLAY_HELP message or when the user selects the Using help menu item for the help display

```
case MENUID_USINGHELP:
  {
    HWND       hwndHelp;

    hwndHelp = WinQueryHelpInstance( hwnd );
    if (hwndHelp != NULLHANDLE) {
       WinSendMsg( hwndHelp, HM_DISPLAY_HELP,
                   MPFROMLONG(0L), MPFROMLONG(0L));
    } /* endif */
  }
  break;
```

Figure 5.17 **Processing the Using help menu item.**

window. The high-order word of **mp1** and parameter **mp2** are reserved and should be set to zero.

The Keys help menu item should display a help panel that describes any special uses that the application defines for the keyboard. The processing required when this menu item is selected is a bit more complex than that previously discussed. Unlike Using help, IPF does not provide a default panel for Keys help, but does provide a Keys help menu item in the Help window's menu. Therefore, IPF must send a message to the application to determine which panel to display whenever a request for keys help arrives, whether from the application or from the Help window menu. From the application standpoint, when the Keys help menu item is selected, an HM_KEYS_HELP message is sent to the help instance. When IPF receives this message, it sends an HM_QUERY_KEYS_HELP message to the application. The application must then return either the help resource ID for the panel to be displayed or zero to inform IPF that no panel should be displayed. Figure 5.18 shows a section of the window procedure code to perform these functions, ultimately returning the HID_KEYSHELP panel ID for display.

The Tutorial menu item is used to execute an application-defined tutorial. When this command is received, the application does not communicate with IPF but processes the request independently, normally by executing another program using either the **WinStartApp** API or the **DosExecPgm** API—the C Library **system** function is not recommended as it can prevent the application from processing messages until the started program completes execution. If the user selects the Tutorial on the Help window's menu, IPF sends an HM_TUTORIAL message to the application. Parameter **mp1** of this message is a pointer to a string that specifies the name of the tutorial to be executed. The name will be either the name passed in the *pszTutorial* element of the HELPINIT structure or a panel-specific name, added to the panel using the tutorial attribute of the *:hx.* tags.

```
switch (msg) {
case HM_QUERY_KEYS_HELP:
   return (MRESULT)HID_KEYSHELP;
case WM_COMMAND:
   switch (SHORT1FROMMP(mp1)) {
   case MID_KEYSHELP: {
      hwndHelp = WinQueryHelpInstance( hwnd );
      if (hwndHelp != NULLHANDLE) {
        WinSendMsg( hwndHelp, HM_KEYS_HELP,
                  MPFROMLONG(0L), MPFROMLONG(0L));
      } /* endif */
      break;
   } /* endswitch */
} /* endswitch */
```

Figure 5.18 Processing the Keys help menu item.

The Product information menu item is not related to IPF and its processing is entirely up to the application. Typically, an application will respond to this menu item by displaying a dialog box that names the application, provides version information, and displays any additional information that the author of the application deems appropriate.

MULTIPLE FRAME WINDOW CONSIDERATIONS

IPF's mapping of help panels to window elements is based on the activation states of an application's windows. When IPF receives a help request, it first determines the currently active window using the **WinQueryActiveWindow** API. IPF then searches the parent and owner chains for this window to find a frame window that is associated with a help instance. The help table for this instance is then searched for a window ID that matches the active window. If a match is found, IPF then searches the help subtable to find a match for the ID of the element that generated the help request. If a subtable match is found, the panel mapped by that subtable is displayed. If IPF cannot find a matching subtable entry, an HM_HELPSUBITEM_NOT_FOUND message is sent to the application window associated with the help instance. If the application responds to this message by returning FALSE, the general help panel for the matched help table entry is displayed; if the response is TRUE, no help is shown.

Normally, the association of a help instance with the main application frame window is sufficient to allow IPF to map the help panels for all of the application's windows. However, there are two instances that require additional programming for the mapping to function properly. The first instance occurs when the application creates multiple, independent frame windows, windows that are children of the desktop and have no owner relationship. Since these windows do not share a common parent or owner chain with the initial window, IPF will not be able to find a help instance. The application must provide a separate association for each window through one of two methods. A relatively simple method is to merely create an additional help instance to be associated with each window. This, however, may consume significant resources, since IPF must duplicate all of the internal information used to track and display help. The second method involves processing the WM_ACTIVATE message. Whenever one of the windows receives this message indicating that it is becoming the active window, it reassociates a single global help instance with itself by calling **WinAssociateHelpInstance**. Since only one of these independent windows can be active at any given time, this method ensures that help is always available.

The second instance where application assistance is required occurs when an application creates one or more additional frame windows that are children of the window with which the help instance is associated; for example, a word processor that allows the user to open and view multiple documents. With this arrangement, both the parent frame and a child frame may be active at the same time, and IPF's query for the active window will find the parent frame preventing the child frame's help subtable from being searched. IPF provides the HM_SET_ACTIVE_WINDOW message to allow the application to handle this situation by specifying which window to consider the active window and therefore which help subtable to search when help is requested. Parameter **mp1** of this message specifies the handle of the window for IPF to use as the active window. If **mp1** is set to NULLHANDLE, IPF's active window is cleared and IPF again queries PM for the active window. Parameter **mp2** specifies the handle of the window IPF should use for positioning the help window. The application's child windows should process the WM_ACTIVATE message. If the child window is being activated, it should send the HM_SET_ACTIVE_WINDOW message, specifying that its frame window is the active window. When the child window is deactivated, it should send the HM_SET_ACTIVE_WINDOW message to restore the active window to the default. Both the parent and child windows should process the WM_INITMENU message and set the associated frame window as the IPF active window. Figure 5.19 shows the coding for the messages.

MULTIPLE THREAD CONSIDERATIONS

While most applications employ a single thread for all displayable windows, sometimes an application will create additional threads that can also display windows. If the application intends to use the IPF features for displaying help for these windows, a new help instance must be created and associated with the threads' window chain. This should come as no surprise, since the secondary threads must also initialize their own PM environment and create their own message queue. If the secondary threads' windows are identical to the that of the primary thread, the same help tables and other resources may be used when the help instance is created. If the windows are not identical, new help tables and resources may be used for the secondary threads, or the appropriate information may be embedded into the tables and resources used by the primary thread.

SUMMARY

OS/2's Information Presentation Facility is a powerful, yet easy-to-implement means of providing context-sensitive, on-line help for application users. This chapter has examined the basic features of IPF, and it has shown how applications gain access to these features. IPF also provides many additional features that are beyond the scope of this book. These include application control and

```
MRESULT child_wm_activate( HWND hwnd, ULONG msg, MPARAM mp1, MPARAM mp2 )
{
    HWND       hwndHelpInstance;
    HWND       hwndParent;

    hwndHelpInstance = WinQueryHelpInstance( hwnd );
    hwndParent = WinQueryWindow( hwnd, QW_PARENT );
    if (SHORT1FROMMP(mp1)) {
        /* Activating - set the active window to the frame */
        rc = WinSendMsg( hwndHelpInstance, HM_SET_ACTIVE_WINDOW,
                         (MPARAM)hwndParent, (MPARAM)hwndParent );
    } else {
        /* Deactivating - clear the active window */
        rc = WinSendMsg( hwndHelpInstance, HM_SET_ACTIVE_WINDOW,
                         NULLHANDLE, NULLHANDLE );
    } /* endif */
    return WinDefWindowProc( hwnd, msg, mp1, mp2 );
}

MRESULT wm_initmenu( HWND hwnd, ULONG msg, MPARAM mp1, MPARAM mp2 )
{
    HWND       hwndHelpInstance;
    HWND       hwndParent;

    hwndHelpInstance = WinQueryHelpInstance( hwnd );
    hwndParent = WinQueryWindow( hwnd, QW_PARENT );

    WinSendMsg( hwndHelpInstance, HM_SET_ACTIVE_WINDOW,
                         (MPARAM)hwndParent, (MPARAM)hwndParent );

    return WinDefWindowProc( hwnd, msg, mp1, mp2 );
}
```

Figure 5.19   Setting the active help window.

customization of the IPF windows; dynamic data formatting, which allows the application to specify the contents of help panels rather than having the contents read from help libraries; and on-line books, viewable independent of the application. To learn more about these advanced features, see the IPF reference material included in the Developer's Toolkit documentation.

CHAPTER 6

Getting More Power for Your Program: Using OS/2's Multithreading Capabilities

Many Presentation Manager applications suffer from a common malady—failure to *always* process messages in a timely fashion. The failure becomes apparent to the end user when an operation like a database search, which requires a few moments to complete, is requested. The system stops processing input for the duration of the operation such that the workplace shell (and therefore the system) appears to be "hung." In extreme cases, this condition may last for several minutes such that the user hits Ctrl+Esc and terminates the application or, even worse, resets or powers off the computer.

This failure occurs because the application program ignores the manner in which PM handles input from the keyboard and pointing device. Without going into great detail, input events are, in essence, *posted* to the message queue of the window that holds the input focus. But messages are normally retrieved from the message queue one at a time and sent to the window procedure by the **WinDispatchMsg** API. No further messages are retrieved from the queue until the window procedure completes its processing for this message. Thus, input messages that would cause the focus to change are not processed until previous messages have completed their processing. To maintain system responsiveness, all messages should process in a short period of time.

Failing applications typically receive a WM_COMMAND message to trigger some long-running operation and run the operation to its completion before returning from the WM_COMMAND message processing. In this chapter, a program of this type is examined, and then three methods to diminish or avoid the problem are introduced.

A TYPICAL SINGLE THREADED APPLICATION

Applications that exhibit the hung system malady typically provide some type of functionality that requires a significant amount of file access, such as a database or directory search. Other causes include waiting for event or mutex semaphores when the desired event or resource is not immediately available or merely getting stuck in a loop due to bad user parameter specification. The application used as an example provides functionality for initializing the contents of a 1 Megabyte file to zeroes. For demonstration purposes, the initialization function is implemented in less than optimal fashion, performing a separate I/O operation for each byte to be written. Let's examine this application in detail.

The main routine for the application is the typical template: initializing the PM environment, creating a message queue, registering the client window class, creating the application's primary window, and then retrieving and dispatching messages from the application's queue. The client window procedure is shown in Figure 6.1. As usual, this routine is a switch statement that calls worker routines to process the messages. At this stage, only two messages are

```
MRESULT APIENTRY AppWndProc( HWND hwnd, ULONG msg, MPARAM mp1, MPARAM mp2 )
{
    switch (msg) {
    case WM_COMMAND:            return wmCommand( hwnd, msg, mp1, mp2 );
    case WM_PAINT:              return wmPaint( hwnd, msg, mp1, mp2 );
    default:                    return WinDefWindowProc( hwnd, msg, mp1, mp2 );
    } /* endswitch */
}
static MRESULT wmPaint( HWND hwnd, ULONG msg, MPARAM mp1, MPARAM mp2 )
{
    HPS        hps;
    RECTL      rectl;

    hps = WinBeginPaint( hwnd, NULLHANDLE, &rectl );
    if (hps != NULLHANDLE) {
        WinFillRect( hps, &rectl, CLR_BACKGROUND );
        WinEndPaint( hps );
    } /* endif */
    return (MRESULT)0L;
}
```

Figure 6.1   Basic client window procedures.

```
static MRESULT wmCommand( HWND hwnd, ULONG msg, MPARAM mp1, MPARAM mp2 )
{
   char  szFileName[ _MAX_PATH ];

   switch (SHORT1FROMMP(mp1)) {
   case MID_FILEINITIALIZE:
      if (GetFileName( hwnd, szFileName ))
         InitializeFile( hwnd, szFileName );
      break;
   case MID_FILEDELETE:
      if (GetFileName( hwnd, szFileName ))
         DeleteFile( szFileName );
      break;
   case MID_FILEEXIT:
      WinSendMsg( hwnd, WM_CLOSE, MPFROMLONG(0L), MPFROMLONG(0L));
      break;
   } /* endswitch */
   return MRFROMLONG(0L);
}
```

Figure 6.2   The WM_COMMAND worker function.

processed, WM_PAINT and WM_COMMAND; as additional messages are processed throughout the chapter, they will be added in similar fashion. Figure 6.1 also shows the worker routine for the WM_PAINT message, **wmPaint**. This routine fills the client window rectangle with the system background color; no other painting is performed by this application.

The worker routine for the WM_COMMAND message, **wm_command**, is shown in Figure 6.2. This routine is a switch statement based on the menu item selected by the user. When the user selects the File/Initialize menu item, routine **GetFileName** retrieves the name of the file to be initialized. If a file name is entered, routine **InitializeFile** is called to perform the initialization function. Similarly, the File/Delete menu item causes **GetFileName** to be called to select the file to be deleted, and routine **DeleteFile** is called to delete the file. The File/Exit menu item causes a WM_CLOSE message to be posted to the application's message queue to terminate the application.

Routine **GetFileName** is shown in Figure 6.3. This routine uses the **WinFileDlg** API to invoke the standard file dialog and retrieve a file name for the user. After filling the FILEDLG structure with zeroes, the *cbsize* element is set to the size of the structure. The *fl* element is set to FDS_OPEN_DIALOG, allowing the user to select a name from the displayed list of file names, and the dialog title is specified as Select File by setting the *pszTitle* element. The *szFullFile* element is initialized to the * wildcard character, causing all file names in the current directory to be displayed when the dialog box is initialized, and a unique window ID for the dialog is specified in the *usDlgId* element. **WinFileDlg** is then called to display and process the dialog. After the

```
static BOOL GetFileName( HWND hwnd, PSZ pszFileName )
{
   FILEDLG     fd;

   memset( (PVOID)&fd, 0, sizeof(FILEDLG));
   fd.cbSize = sizeof(FILEDLG);
   fd.fl = FDS_OPEN_DIALOG;
   fd.pszTitle = "Select File";
   strcpy(fd.szFullFile, "*" );
   fd.usDlgId = SELECTFILE_ID;

   if ((BOOL)(WinFileDlg( HWND_DESKTOP, hwnd, &fd )) &&
       fd.lReturn == DID_OK ) {
      strcpy( pszFileName, fd.szFullFile );
   } else {
      strcpy( pszFileName, "" );
   } /* endif */
   return (strlen(pszFileName) != 0 );
}
```

Figure 6.3 Using WinFileDlg to select a file.

API call returns, the return value is checked to determine if the user actually selected a file. If the return value is DID-OK, a file name was selected and the file name returned in the *szFullFile* element is copied into the supplied buffer. If the return value is not DID-OK, the user did not select a file and the buffer is set to a NULL string. The function then returns FALSE if the buffer contains a NULL or zero-length string, or TRUE if the buffer contains a valid file name.

Routine **InitializeFile**, shown in Figure 6.4, performs the actual file initialization. The routine first opens the file in write mode causing the file to be created if it does not already exist and setting the file pointer to the beginning of the file. If the file is successfully opened, a dialog containing a progress indicator slider is loaded as a modeless dialog, the title of the dialog is set to the name of the file being initialized, the OK button is temporarily disabled, and the dialog box is made visible. A nested loop is then used to perform the actual initialization. The outer loop executes once for each record in the file, and the inner loop executes once for each byte of an individual record. Each iteration of the inner loop writes one byte of the record to the file. After an entire record is written, the outer loop sends an SLM_SETSLIDERINFO message to the progress indicator slider, updating the shaded portion of the slider bar to reflect the percentage of the initialization operation that has been completed. After all records have been initialized, the file is closed and the OK button in the dialog is enabled providing the user with a positive indication that the operation is complete.

The behavior of the system with this method may be seen by running the sample program, selecting single thread mode, and then initializing a file. While the initialization operation is in progress, no user input is processed and

```
void InitializeFile( HWND hwnd, PSZ pszFileName )
{
    FILE   *file;
    ULONG  record;
    char   buffer = '\0';
    int    i;
    HWND   hwndProgress;

    file = fopen( pszFileName, "w" );
    if (file != (FILE *)NULL) {
        hwndProgress = WinLoadDlg( HWND_DESKTOP, hwnd, ProgDlgProc, NULLHANDLE,
                                   PROGRESS_ID, NULL );
        WinSetWindowText( WinWindowFromID( hwndProgress, DID_FILENAME ),
                          pszFileName );
        WinEnableWindow( WinWindowFromID( hwndProgress, DID_OK ), FALSE );
        WinShowWindow( hwndProgress, TRUE );

        for ( record = 0; record < MAX_RECORD; record++ ) {
            for (i = 0; i < RECORD_SIZE; i++ )
                fwrite( &buffer, 1, 1, file );
            WinSendDlgItemMsg( hwndProgress, DID_PROGRESS, SLM_SETSLIDERINFO,
                               MPFROM2SHORT(SMA_SLIDERARMPOSITION,
                                            SMA_INCREMENTVALUE ),
                               MPFROMLONG( (record * 100) / (MAX_RECORD - 1)));
        } /* endfor */
        fclose( file );
        WinEnableWindow( WinWindowFromID( hwndProgress, DID_OK ), TRUE );
    } /* endif */
}
```

Figure 6.4   The incorrect way to initialize a file.

the only indication that the system is not hung is the update of the progress indicator. Since no user input is processed, no other windows can be selected and the multitasking advantages of OS/2 are essentially nullified for the duration of the operation.

PEEKING AT THE MESSAGE QUEUE

One method of circumventing this problem is to periodically take a peek at the message queue using the **WinPeekMsg** API, which performs the same function as **WinGetMsg**, but does not wait when no message is available. If a message is waiting in the application's message queue, the message is returned and then dispatched to the proper window procedure with the **WinDispatchMsg** API. This allows user input to be processed so that other windows may be selected and prevents the hung system scenario in most cases.

Figure 6.5 shows the previous **InitializeFile** function with a call to the **WinPeekMsg** API (shown in boldface type) added to the outer loop. The API is called once for each record written to the file. If TRUE is returned, the retrieved message is sent to the appropriate window procedure using the **WinDispatchMsg** API.

The results of using this method can be seen by selecting peek loop mode in the sample program before initializing a file. Note that the user is now free to switch away to another task while the initialization function is processing. The user can also select the File/Initialize menu item again; however, the first initialization operation is suspended until the new one finishes. To prevent real or apparent conflicts such as this, many applications that use a peek loop disable the menu items that would result in conflict while an operation is in progress.

```
void InitializeFile( HWND hwnd, PSZ pszFileName )
{
    FILE  *file;
    ULONG record;
    char  buffer = '\0';
    int   i;
    HWND  hwndProgress;
    HAB   hab = WinQueryAnchorBlock( hwnd );
    QMSG  qmsg;

    file = fopen( pszFileName, "w" );
    if (file != (FILE *)NULL) {
        hwndProgress = WinLoadDlg( HWND_DESKTOP, hwnd, ProgDlgProc, NULLHANDLE,
                            PROGRESS_ID, NULL );
        WinSetWindowText( WinWindowFromID( hwndProgress, DID_FILENAME ),
                    pszFileName );
        WinEnableWindow( WinWindowFromID( hwndProgress, DID_OK ), FALSE );
        WinShowWindow( hwndProgress, TRUE );
        for ( record = 0; record < MAX_RECORD; record++ ) {
            for (i = 0; i < RECORD_SIZE; i++ )
                fwrite( &buffer, 1, 1, file );
            WinSendDlgItemMsg( hwndProgress, DID_PROGRESS, SLM_SETSLIDERINFO,
                        MPFROM2SHORT(SMA_SLIDERARMPOSITION,
                                        SMA_INCREMENTVALUE ),
                        MPFROMLONG( (record * 100) / (MAX_RECORD - 1)));
            if (WinPeekMsg(hab, &qmsg, NULLHANDLE, 0L, 0L, PM_REMOVE )) {
                WinDispatchMsg( hab, &qmsg );
            } /* endif */
        } /* endfor */
        fclose( file );
        WinEnableWindow( WinWindowFromID( hwndProgress, DID_OK ), TRUE );
    } /* endif */
}
```

Figure 6.5   Initializing with a peek message.

The peek method works well as long as the operation can be divided into reasonable intervals at which to call **WinPeekMsg**. However, situations can arise where this method is ineffective. In this example, if the file write operation involves a LAN file and problems on the LAN cause delays, the process will be blocked until the write operation is complete. During this time, **WinPeekMsg** will not be called, and the system will again be nonfunctional from the user's viewpoint.

CREATING A NEW THREAD

The only way to ensure that the message processing loop is not interrupted due to an external resource is to place all operations that access these resources in one or more separate threads. This will allow the initial thread to continue operating when external events block the new threads from running. Routine **InitializeFile** is limited to creating the progress indicator dialog and starting the new thread. The actual file operations have been moved to a new thread function, **InitThread**. This thread has been implemented as a non-PM thread since it does not create windows or require a message queue. The only PM API used by the thread is **WinPostMsg** which does not require a PM environment.

Function **InitializeFile** first allocates a block of memory to hold the parameters that will be passed to the new thread and then creates and initializes the progress indicator dialog as before. The format of the thread parameters memory block is defined by the structure shown in Figure 6.6.

- The *hwnd* element is the handle of the main application window. This handle will be used to notify the main window of the completion status of the initialization operation.
- The *hwndSlider* element is the handle of the progress indicator dialog's slider. This window handle is used to update the slider with the current progress of the operation.
- The *szFile* element is the name of the file to be initialized. Note that the actual name and not a pointer to the name is passed in the structure. If a pointer is used and the memory is on the program's stack or is globally accessible, it can be overwritten and affect the operation of the new thread. If a pointer is used to pass information to a new thread, the memory should typically be allocated specifically for this purpose.

```
typedef struct __thread_param__ {
    HWND     hwnd;
    HWND     hwndSlider;
    char     szFile[ _MAX_PATH ];
} TPARM, *PTPARM;
```

Figure 6.6   The TPARM structure.

```
void InitializeFile( HWND hwnd, PSZ pszFileName )
{
   HWND     hwndProgress;
   PTPARM   ptp;

   ptp = (PTPARM)malloc( sizeof(TPARM) );
   if (ptp != (PTPARM)NULL ) {
      hwndProgress = WinLoadDlg( HWND_DESKTOP, hwnd, ProgDlgProc,
                                    NULLHANDLE, PROGRESS_ID, NULL );
      WinSetWindowText( WinWindowFromID( hwndProgress, DID_FILENAME ),
                     pszFileName );
      WinEnableWindow( WinWindowFromID( hwndProgress, DID_OK ), FALSE );
      WinShowWindow( hwndProgress, TRUE );

      ptp->hwndSlider = WinWindowFromID( hwndProgress, DID_PROGRESS );
      ptp->hwnd = hwnd;
      strcpy( ptp->szFile, pszFileName );
      _beginthread( InitThread, 0, 0x2000, (PVOID)ptp );
   } /* endif */
}
```

Figure 6.7   Multiple thread file initialization.

After **InitializeFile**, shown in Figure 6.7, establishes appropriate values for each element of the structure, the C library function **_beginthread** is called to create and start the new thread. It is used in lieu of the **DosCreateThread** API to ensure that the C runtime environment for the new thread is properly established. After this call completes, the main thread returns to processing messages as normal. Note that the allocated memory is not freed as would normally be the case with interprocess communication. Memory is a process-wide resource and can thus be freed by the new thread when no longer needed.

Function **InitThread**, shown in Figure 6.8, first opens the file named by element *szFile* of the TPARM structure. If this operation is successful, the nested loop from the previous examples is used to perform the file initialization. However, instead of using **WinSendMsg** to update the progress indicator slider position, the **WinPostMsg** API is called to place the SLM_SETSLIDERINFO message on the message queue of the main thread. As the main thread processes messages, the SLM_SETSLIDERINFO message will be dispatched to the slider. The return code from **WinPostMsg** is not checked when the API is called within the file initialization loop since missing one of the many positioning messages will not pose a serious problem. After the initialization loop completes, one final SLM_SETSLIDERINFO message is posted. In this case, the return code from **WinPostMsg** is checked to ensure that the final position of the slider reflects 100 percent completion of the operation. After the slider message is successfully posted, a user-defined message, UM_DONE, is posted to the application's main window with the handle of the progress indicator

```
void InitThread( void *param ) {
    PTPARM    ptp = (PTPARM)param;
    HWND      hwndProgress = ptp->hwndSlider;
    FILE      *file;
    ULONG     record;
    char      buffer = '\0';
    int       i;
    ULONG     status = INIT_ERROR;

    file = fopen( ptp->szFile, "w" );
    if (file != (FILE *)NULL) {
        for ( record = 0; record < MAX_RECORD; record++ ) {
            for (i = 0; i < RECORD_SIZE; i++ ) {
                fwrite( &buffer, 1, 1, file );
            } /* endfor */
            WinPostMsg( hwndProgress, SLM_SETSLIDERINFO,
                    MPFROM2SHORT(SMA_SLIDERARMPOSITION, SMA_INCREMENTVALUE ),
                    MPFROMLONG( (record * 100) / (MAX_RECORD - 1)));
        } /* endfor */
        fclose( file );
        while (!(BOOL)WinPostMsg( hwndProgress, SLM_SETSLIDERINFO,
                    MPFROM2SHORT(SMA_SLIDERARMPOSITION, SMA_INCREMENTVALUE ),
                    MPFROMLONG( (record * 100) / (MAX_RECORD - 1))));
        status = INIT_COMPLETE;
    } /* endif */
    while( !(BOOL)WinPostMsg( ptp->hwnd, UM_DONE,
            MPFROMHWND(hwndProgress), MPFROMLONG(status)));
    free(param);
}
```

Figure 6.8   Secondary thread routine to initialize a file.

slider in parameter **mp1** and the completion status of the operation in parameter **mp2**. The thread parameter structure memory is then freed and the thread terminates.

Back in the main application thread, receipt of the UM_DONE message causes a worker routine **umDone** to be called. This function first examines parameter **mp2** of the UM_DONE message to determine if an error occurred. If there was no error, the function implements the final piece of the old **InitializeFile** function by enabling the OK button in the progress indicator dialog. If there was an error, an appropriate message box is displayed with the **WinMsgBox** API and then the progress indicator dialog is destroyed.

The results of this method can be seen when running the sample program by selecting multithread mode and then initializing a file. The user may switch away to another window while the initialization is in progress and additional initialization operations can be performed in parallel. Unlike the peek loop method, messages continue to be processed even if the initialization thread becomes blocked due to a delay or failure in the I/O process.

Be aware that more complicated operations may require access to common resources when multiple threads are executing. The application may need to either synchronize access to these resources or prevent multiple access by disabling some of its functionality for a period of time to prevent concurrent access to resources.

USING AN OBJECT WINDOW

The separate thread method just shown is sufficient for operations like file initialization which do not require any real interaction with PM or the application window. But suppose the operation required that each record be formatted based on information retrieved from a container control. At first glance, one might suppose the application could allocate a large buffer, retrieve the information from the container, and format the records in the buffer before starting the second thread. But this formatting operation itself could take considerable time and qualify as the type of long-running operation which blocks the processing of input messages.

An alternative method is the use of an object window. An object window is a window that is a descendent of the system-defined HWND_OBJECT. Windows of this type are never displayed and cannot receive the input focus, so an object window created in a separate thread with its own message queue is not constrained by the time required to process messages. Note that an object window that shares a thread, and therefore a message queue, with windows descended from HWND_DESKTOP can block the processing of input messages posted to the message queue.

For iterative operations of the type discussed in this chapter, the main application would normally allocate a control structure that tracks the current state of the operation. This structure is passed back and forth as a message parameter between the application window and the object window as the operation proceeds. First the application window posts a message to the object window to initiate the operation and perhaps perform the first iteration. When this is complete, the object window posts a message back to the application. The application window then updates the control structure for the next iteration and posts a message back to the object window. The object window performs the next iteration and again posts a message back to the application. This continues until the entire operation is complete. If necessary, the application can post a final message to the object window to terminate the operation and clean up any resources. If no termination is needed, the application posts no message and goes on about its business. The object window remains idle until another initiation message is posted.

Figure 6.9 shows how the object window and its thread are created during the WM_CREATE processing for the main application window. The **wmCreate** function calls the C library function **_beginthread** to initiate a second thread

```
MRESULT wmCreate( HWND hwnd, ULONG msg, MPARAM mp1, MPARAM mp2 )
{

    _beginthread( InitObjWnd, 0, 0x2000, (PVOID)hwnd );
    return MRFROMLONG(FALSE);
}

void InitObjWnd( void *param ) {
    HAB   hab = (HAB)NULLHANDLE;
    HMQ   hmq = (HMQ)NULLHANDLE;
    QMSG  qmsg;
    HWND  hwndObject = (HWND)NULLHANDLE;
    HWND  hwndMain = (HWND)param;

    do {
        if ((hab = WinInitialize( 0 ) == NULLHANDLE ) break;
        if ((hmq = WinCreateMsgQueue( hab, 0 ) == NULLHANDLE ) break;
        if (!WinRegisterClass( hab, "APPOBJECT", ObjWndProc,0L, 0L )) break;
        hwndObject = WinCreateWindow( HWND_OBJECT, "APPOBJECT", NULL,
                                      0L, 0L, 0L, 0L, 0L, NULLHANDLE,
                                      HWND_TOP, 0L, NULL, NULL );
        if (hwndObject == (HWND)NULLHANDLE) break;
        WinPostMsg( hwndMain, UM_SETOBJ,
                    MPFROMHWND(hwndObject),MPFROMLONG(0L));
        while (WinGetMsg(hab, &qmsg, NULLHANDLE, 0, 0 )) {
            WinDispatchMsg( hab, &qmsg );
        } /* endwhile */
    } while ( false ); /* enddo */
    if (hmq != (HMQ)NULLHANDLE) WinDestroyMsgQueue( hmq );
    if (hab != (HAB)NULLHANDLE) WinTerminate( hab );
}
```

Figure 6.9   Creating the object window.

executing function **InitObjWnd**. Since this thread creates a window and requires a message queue, the thread needs a PM environment and goes through the normal sequence for the **main** routine of a PM application. The only differences, shown in boldface type, are that the object window is created with a call to the **WinCreateWindow** API rather than **WinCreateStdWindow**, and that a message is posted to the main application window to notify it of the object window handle.

Figure 6.10 shows the **InitializeFile** routine for this method. First, the object window handle is retrieved from the window data, where it was placed when the UM_SETOBJ message was posted by the object window. The routine then loads and initializes the progress indicator dialog in the same manner as before and allocates memory for the control parameters structure. The layout of this structure is shown in Figure 6.11 along with the content and initialization of its elements.

```
void InitializeFile( HWND hwnd, PSZ pszFileName )
{
    HWND      hwndProgress;
    POBJPARM  objp;
    FILE      *file;
    HWND      hwndObj = WinQueryWindowULong( hwnd, APP_HWNDOBJ );

    objp = (POBJPARM)malloc( sizeof(OBJPARM));
    if (objp != (POBJPARM)NULL ) {
        hwndProgress = WinLoadDlg( HWND_DESKTOP, hwnd, ProgDlgProc,
                                   NULLHANDLE, PROGRESS_ID, NULL );
        WinSetWindowText( WinWindowFromID(hwndProgress, DID_FILENAME ),
                          pszFileName );
        WinEnableWindow( WinWindowFromID( hwndProgress, DID_OK ), FALSE );
        WinShowWindow( hwndProgress, TRUE );

        objp->hwndProgress = hwndProgress;
        objp->hwnd = hwnd;
        strcpy( objp->szFileName, pszFileName );
        objp->ulRecord = 0;
        objp->cbRecord = RECORD_SIZE;
        memset( objp->record, 0, RECORD_SIZE );
        WinPostMsg( hwndObj, UM_INIT, MPFROMP(objp), MPFROMLONG(0L));
    } /* endif */
}
```

Figure 6.10   Main thread routine to start initialization.

- The *hwnd* element is the window handle of the main application window. The object window will use this handle for communicating with the main thread.
- The *hwndProgress* element is set to the handle of the progress indicator dialog window. This allows the proper indicator to be updated if multiple initialize operations are running concurrently.
- The *szFileName* element is filled with the name of the file to be initialized.
- The **file** parameter is a pointer to a 'C' FILE control structure. This field is filled by the object window when the output file is opened.

```
typedef struct __objwnd_param__ {
    HWND      hwnd;
    HWND      hwndProgress;
    char      szFileName[ _MAX_PATH ];
    FILE      *file;
    ULONG     ulRecord;
    ULONG     cbRecord;
    char      record[ RECORD_SIZE ];
} OBJPARM, *POBJPARM;
```

Figure 6.11   The OBJPARM structure.

- The *ulRecord* element is the record number to be written, and it is initialized to zero.
- The *record* element is the data to be written to the file, and in this case is initialized to zeroes. The record could be filled with data retrieved from a container control or other source at this point.
- The *cbRecord* element specifies the number of bytes contained in the record element.

Once this structure has been initialized, user-defined message UM_INIT is sent to the object window to open the file and begin the operation. Parameter **mp1** of this message contains a pointer to the control parameters structure.

Figure 6.12 shows the window procedure for the object window. When the object window receives the UM_INIT message posted by the **InitializeFile** routine, it attempts to open the specified file. If successful, the handle of the file is stored in the control parameters structure. A UM_WRITE message is then

```
MRESULT APIENTRY ObjWndProc( HWND hwnd, ULONG msg, MPARAM mp1, MPARAM mp2 )
{
   POBJPARM    pObj;
   int         i;

   switch(msg) {
   case UM_INIT:
     pObj = (POBJPARM)mp1;
     pObj->file = fopen( pObj->szFileName, "w" );
     if (pObj->file != (FILE *)NULL) {
        WinPostMsg( hwnd, UM_WRITE, mp1, mp2 );
     } else {
        WinPostMsg( pObj->hwnd, UM_READY, mp1, MPFROMLONG(READY_ERROR) );
     } /* endif */
     return 0L;
   case UM_WRITE:
     pObj = (POBJPARM)mp1;
     for (i = 0; i < pObj->cbRecord; i++ )
        fwrite( &(pObj->record[i]), 1, 1, pObj->file );
     WinPostMsg( pObj->hwnd, UM_READY, mp1, MPFROMLONG(READY_OK));
     return 0L;
   case UM_CLOSE:
     pObj = (POBJPARM)mp1;
     fclose(pObj->file);
     free(pObj);
     return 0L;
   default:
     return WinDefWindowProc( hwnd, msg, mp1, mp2 );
   }
}
```

Figure 6.12 Object window procedure to initialize file.

posted back to the object window to write the first record. Another approach would be to post a message back to the main application window to cause the initial record to be filled. The main application window would then fill the record and post the UM_WRITE message back to the object window.

When the object window receives the UM_WRITE message, it executes the inner loop from our old **InitializeFile** function to write the contents on the record to the file one byte at a time. Once the record has been completely written, a UM_READY message is posted back to the application to indicate that the object window is ready to write the next record.

Figure 6.13 shows the main window processing for the UM_READY message. The routine first verifies the success of the previous write operation, and if there are more records to process, the *ulRecord* element of the control parameters structure is updated to reflect the next record number to write. If the application were actually loading data into the records, the new record data would be inserted into the record element at this point. The position of the progress indicator slider is then updated and a UM_WRITE message is posted back to the object window to cause the new record to be processed. This interchange of the UM_WRITE and UM_READY messages will continue until all records have been processed.

When the main window determines that the final record has been written, the OK button in the progress indicator dialog is enabled and a UM_CLOSE message is sent to the object window. Back in Figure 6.12, the object window processes the UM_CLOSE message by closing the file and deallocating the memory allocated for the control parameters structure.

```
static MRESULT umReady( HWND hwnd, ULONG msg, MPARAM mp1, MPARAM mp2 )
{
    POBJPARM    pObj = (POBJPARM)mp1;
    HWND        hwndObject = WinQueryWindowULong( hwnd, APP_HWNDOBJ );

    if (LONGFROMMP(mp2) == READY_OK && pObj->ulRecord < MAX_RECORD) {
        pObj->ulRecord++;
        WinSendDlgItemMsg( pObj->hwndProgress, DID_PROGRESS, SLM_SETSLIDERINFO,
                           MPFROM2SHORT(SMA_SLIDERARMPOSITION,
                                        SMA_INCREMENTVALUE ),
                           MPFROMLONG( (pObj->ulRecord * 100) /
                                       (MAX_RECORD - 1)));
        WinPostMsg( hwndObject, UM_WRITE, mp1, MPFROMLONG(0L));
    } else {
        WinEnableWindow( WinWindowFromID( pObj->hwndProgress, DID_OK ), TRUE );
        WinPostMsg( hwndObject, UM_CLOSE, MPFROMP(pObj), MPFROMLONG(0L));
    } /* endif */
    return (MRESULT)0L;
}
```

Figure 6.13 Main thread routine to complete initialization.

The results of using this method can be observed in the sample application associated with this chapter by selecting object window mode and then initializing a file. Again, the user may perform other functions while the initialization operation is in progress, including starting another initialization operation. I/O delays or failures only affect the progress of the initialization, not the responsiveness of the system.

This method also tends to be less likely to cause resource conflicts since each step of the operation is an integrated whole and the data required to perform the operation is allocated specifically for each instance of the operation.

SUMMARY

This chapter has shown several methods of performing time-consuming operations. The first two methods leave open the possibility that the application will cease to process input messages for some period of time, preventing the user from doing further work, and perhaps leading to the impression that the application or system is completely hung. The latter two methods employ separate threads to prevent this from occurring. The first of these creates an independent thread capable of performing the complete operation without further intervention and is appropriate when the application does not need to supply data to complete the operation. The last method uses an object window to allow the application window to supply data at various stages of the operation. This method is more appropriate in many cases since it allows for control of the flow of data.

CHAPTER 7

She Sells Sea Shells: Programming the Workplace Shell

O S/2 Version 1 provided the user with a graphical user interface, or GUI, built on the Presentation Manager API. This interface removed the user's dependence on the keyboard by allowing the user to navigate the system's storage devices and start programs using the mouse. The user interface consisted of a desktop, a Program Manager, and Program Groups. The desktop was basically a blank background upon which icons would be painted. They represented running programs that the user had requested to be minimized, or hidden. When the system was started, the Program Manager was automatically started as the base application. This application allowed the user to select a Program Group, an application that displayed a list of programs that the user could execute. Thus the Version 1 GUI was a simple two-level hierarchy allowing the user a relatively limited ability to organize and customize the system. Some additional flexibility was provided by the File Manager application which allowed the user to graphically display the directories on the system's storage devices and to manipulate files and execute programs.

The current user interface, the Workplace Shell, was introduced with OS/2 Version 2. The Workplace Shell is an object-oriented graphical user interface, based on PM and a new technology, SOM, the System Object Model. In this new shell, the distinction between Program Groups, Programs, and Data Files is removed and all types of files are represented as objects. The blank desktop is replaced by the desktop object which is a derivation of a folder object, an object that holds, or contains, an homogenous set of objects such as programs, data, and even other folders. Since folders, and therefore the desktop, can contain other folders, the two-tiered hierarchy of the Version 1 Program Manager/Program Group is replaced by the multitiered hierarchy of folders. This also means that the desktop can contain a mixture of folders, programs, and data files, all of which can be started or opened by clicking the mouse. This organization along with a host of other new features provides the user with an easy-to-operate and highly customizable system.

One of the key concepts of the Workplace Shell is the ability to actually move and otherwise manipulate objects using the mouse. For example, rather than typing a command to copy a file, the user selects the icon representing the file with the mouse and then moves the mouse to the desired folder, dragging the file along. When the user releases the mouse button, the file itself is copied to the new location. Data files can also be dragged in this manner and dropped on an application, causing the application object or program to open and process the dragged file. Workplace Shell *aware* applications should support these direct manipulation features.

Another important feature of the Workplace Shell is its ability to maintain the state of the desktop through an IPL, or reboot, of the system. The Shell assumes responsibility for opening the objects that were open at the time the system was shut down (this feature depends on a user-initiated safe shutdown procedure—if the system is simply powered off, the results are unpredictable and sometimes catastrophic). The objects themselves, for example, folders, application objects, and data files, are responsible for saving and restoring the elements of their internal state, such as window size, presentation parameters, and processing state. Application programmers do not have to design their own individual methods for storing restart data; binary data files, called initialization files, and APIs to manipulate them are provided by the system for this purpose. We will discuss how Workplace Shell aware applications can take advantage of initialization files later in this chapter.

Finally, a brief overview of SOM and the object hierarchy of the Workplace Shell is given to provide a better understanding of how the Workplace Shell works and to assist in the design and implementation of Workplace Shell aware applications.

DIRECT MANIPULATION

Direct manipulation is the Workplace Shell's feature that allows users to manipulate files or other objects using the mouse. The most commonly known direct manipulation operation is called *drag and drop*. The user selects and *drags* an object by placing the mouse pointer over the object, pressing and holding the appropriate mouse button, then moving the mouse. As the mouse moves, an icon representing the object or objects being dragged moves along with the mouse, indicating the current drop location. When the mouse button is released, the object is dropped. The application over which the object is dropped determines what action will be taken—for example, dropping a file on a folder causes the file to be moved or copied to that folder; dropping the same file on a printer object causes the file to be printed.

OS/2 Warp introduced a second direct manipulation operation known as *lazy drag* or *pickup and drop*. The drag-and-drop operation is modal—once the user begins dragging objects, the operation must be completed or cancelled before any other operations can be accomplished. Pickup and drop is a nonmodal operation. After the user has started the operation by picking up an object, other operations may be performed, such as moving a window or opening an application. The picked objects remain available until dropped or the operation is explicitly cancelled. This capability is extremely useful when the source and target of the direct manipulation operation cannot easily be displayed simultaneously.

The low-level activities of direct manipulation are handled by the Presentation Manager. These activities include notifying an application when a direct manipulation operation is requested, moving and painting the icon representing the dragged object and notifying an application when an object has been dropped. Applications are responsible for responding to a direct manipulation request by initiating the operation, notifying PM when they are able to receive a drop, and conversing among themselves using predefined protocols to properly transfer dropped objects.

These application responsibilities can be divided into those performed by source applications and those performed by target applications. A source application is an application that understands PM's notification that a drag operation has been requested and performs the actions necessary to start the operation. An application that performs the actions required to accept a dropped object is a target application. An application that does both can serve as a source application, a target application, or both simultaneously. Before discussing the details of this processing, a grasp of the data structures used to communicate between the source application, PM, and the target application is necessary.

DRAG-AND-DROP DATA STRUCTURES

Four data structures are used during the processing of direct manipulation operations. The DRAGINFO structure is the base structure that contains the controlling information for the operation. Linked to the DRAGINFO structure are DRAGITEM structures that provide detailed information about each object being dragged. The DRAGIMAGE structure is used by the source application to inform PM which image or images are to be used to represent the dragged objects during a drag and drop operation. The DRAGTRANSFER structure is used for communication between the source and target applications after a drop has occurred and objects are being rendered. Except for DRAGIMAGE, these structures must be accessible by multiple applications running as different processes and thus must be allocated in shared memory. Rather than have the applications manage the memory themselves, PM provides APIs for allocating, accessing, and freeing the memory associated with these structures. In the following sections, we will examine the elements of the structures and the APIs provided for manipulation.

The DRAGINFO Structure

The DRAGINFO structure is the basic, controlling entity for the drag operation and contains generic information about the operation as a whole. The format of the structure is shown in Figure 7.1.

- The *cbDraginfo* element specifies the length of the DRAGINFO structure in bytes. The element is initialized by PM and must not be modified by the application.
- The *cbDragitem* element specifies the length of the DRAGITEM structures associated with this DRAGINFO structure. This element is initialized by PM and must not be modified by the application.
- The *usOperation* element specifies the default function to be performed when the dragged objects are dropped. PM initializes this field to DO_ DEFAULT. The application may modify this element to specify DO_COPY, DO_LINK, DO_MOVE or another application-defined operation. This is the only element of the DRAGINFO structure that the application should modify.
- The *hwndSource* element specifies the handle of the window that is the source window for the drag-and-drop operation. PM initializes this element to the window over which the mouse pointer was positioned when the drag-and-drop operation was initiated.
- The *xDrop* element contains an unspecified value at initialization. This element contains the x coordinate of the mouse pointer position after a drop occurs. This element should not be modified by the application.

```
typedef struct _DRAGINFO {
    ULONG    cbDraginfo;
    USHORT   cbDragitem;
    USHORT   usOperation;
    HWND     hwndSource;
    SHORT    xDrop;
    SHORT    yDrop;
    USHORT   cditem;
    USHORT   usReserved;
} DRAGINFO;
```

Figure 7.1   The DRAGINFO structure.

```
PDRAGINFO APIENTRY DrgAllocDraginfo(ULONG cditem);
```

Figure 7.2   The DrgAllocDraginfo prototype.

- The *yDrop* element contains an unspecified value at initialization. This element contains the y coordinate of the mouse pointer position after a drop occurs. This element should not be modified by the application.
- The *cditem* element specifies the number of DRAGITEM structures that are associated with this DRAGINFO structure. The number of DRAGITEM structures indicates the number of objects being dragged. This field is initialized to the value specified in the **cDitem** parameter of the **DrgAlloc-Draginfo** API. This element should not be modified by the application.
- The *usReserved* element is reserved and should not be modified by the application.

Five APIs are provided for managing the DRAGINFO structure. These APIs allow an application to allocate the structure, resize the structure, free the structure, give another application access to the structure, and obtain access to the structure.

The source application uses the **DrgAllocDraginfo** API to allocate and initialize the structure. PM responds to this API by allocating the DRAGINFO structure and the specified number of DRAGITEM structures within shared memory. The prototype for this API is shown in Figure 7.2.

- The **cditem** parameter is the number of objects to be dragged and is used to allocate space for the DRAGITEM structures associated with the allocated DRAGINFO structure.

The API returns a pointer to the allocated DRAGINFO structure if successful; otherwise, NULL is returned.

When a pickup-and-drag operation is in progress, additional objects can be added to the set of objects being dragged after the initial call to **DrgAlloc-Draginfo**. In this instance, additional space for DRAGITEM structures will be required so the DRAGINFO structure must be reallocated. The **DrgRealloc-Draginfo** API accomplishes this function. The prototype of the API is in Figure 7.3.

- The **pdinfoOld** parameter is the address of the current DRAGINFO structure obtained from a prior call to **DrgAllocDraginfo** or **DrgReallocDrag-Info**.

```
PDRAGINFO APIENTRY DrgReallocDrgInfo( PDRAGINFO pdinfoOld,
                                      ULONG cdItem );
```

Figure 7.3   The DrgReallocDrgInfo prototype.

```
BOOL APIENTRY DrgAccessDraginfo(PDRAGINFO pdinfo);
```

Figure 7.4 **The DrgAccessDraginfo prototype.**

- The **cdItem** parameter is the total number of DRAGITEM structures to be associated with the new DRAGINFO structure.

   DrgReallocDragInfo returns a pointer to the newly allocated DRAGINFO structure. The memory for the previous DRAGINFO structure is freed and should not be accessed further. The application is responsible for maintaining the DRAGITEMs. **DrgReallocDragInfo** makes no attempt to save the existing structures.
   When PM sends a notification message to a potential target application, a pointer to the DRAGINFO structure is sent as one of the parameters. However, the application is not automatically given access to the memory containing the structure. The **DrgAccessDraginfo** API must be called to gain access to the DRAGINFO structure. The prototype of this API is in Figure 7.4.

- The **pdinfo** parameter is a pointer to the DRAGINFO structure to be accessed.

The API returns TRUE if access is granted or FALSE if an error occurs.
   The **DrgFreeDraginfo** API must be called to release an application's access to the DRAGINFO memory when the application has finished using the DRAGINFO structure. When the structure has been freed by all applications, it is deallocated. The **DrgFreeDraginfo** API is prototyped as shown in Figure 7.5.

- The **pdinfo** parameter is a pointer to the DRAGINFO structure to be freed.

The API returns TRUE if the structure was successfully freed and FALSE if an error occurs. If the source and target applications are the same application and the **DrgDrag** API is still active, the DRAGINFO structure will not be freed and **DrgFreeDraginfo** will return FALSE. In this instance, the PM error code will be set to PMERR_SOURCE_SAME_AS_TARGET. This prevents accidental deallocation of the structure while it is still in use.
   The **DrgPushDraginfo** API is used to directly give access to the DRAGINFO structure to another process. This API should be used with caution. If the process receiving access is unaware that access has been given and does not

```
BOOL APIENTRY DrgFreeDraginfo(PDRAGINFO pdinfo);
```

Figure 7.5 **The DrgFreeDraginfo prototype.**

```
BOOL APIENTRY DrgPushDraginfo(PDRAGINFO pdinfo,
                             HWND hwndDest);
```

Figure 7.6   The DrgPushDraginfo prototype.

release its access with the **DrgFreeDraginfo** API, the memory will never be released until the process terminates. This type of behavior results in a loss of system memory and can eventually cause the system to cease operating due to a lack of resources. The prototype of the **DrgPushDraginfo** API is in Figure 7.6.

- The **pdinfo** parameter is a pointer to the DRAGINFO structure to be given.
- The **hwndDest** parameter is the handle of a window whose process is to receive access to the DRAGINFO structure.

DrgPushDraginfo returns TRUE if access is successfully granted and FALSE if an error occurs.

The DRAGITEM Structure

The DRAGITEM structure is used to convey information about the individual objects involved in a direct manipulation operation. The source and target applications use this information to negotiate the transfer of the object. The format of the structure is given in Figure 7.7.

- The *hwndItem* element is the handle of the source window for this item. This element is typically initialized to a value equal to the *hwndSource* element of the DRAGINFO structure. Source applications that require a DM_RENDERPREPARE message from the target may use a different

```
typedef struct _DRAGITEM {
    HWND    hwndItem;
    ULONG   ulItemID;
    HSTR    hstrType;
    HSTR    hstrRMF;
    HSTR    hstrContainerName;
    HSTR    hstrSourceName;
    HSTR    hstrTargetName;
    SHORT   cxOffset;
    SHORT   cyOffset;
    USHORT  fsControl;
    USHORT  fsSupportedOps;
} DRAGITEM;
```

Figure 7.7   The DRAGITEM structure.

window to perform the rendering operation and will modify this element so that the target can establish a conversation with the new window.

- The *ulItemID* element is a 32-bit value used by the source application to identify the object to which this DRAGITEM structure pertains.
- The *hstrType* element is a handle to a string that specifies the type, or format, of the object; for example, plain text, executable, or metafile. A set of predefined types are included in the Developer's Toolkit header and include files as DRT_ constants; additional types may be defined by applications. Some objects may correctly be defined as having multiple types; for instance, a C program source file could be defined as C Code and Plain Text. All possible types should be listed, separated by commas. The first type in the list should be the type that best describes the object. This type is known as the *true* type of the object. In the example, C Code would be the true type.
- The *hstrRMF* element is a handle to a string that specifies the mechanism(s) and format(s) that may be used to transfer the object between the source and target applications. The mechanism is the manner in which the object is transferred; for example, DRM_OS2FILE indicates that the object is stored as a file and thus may be transferred with the file system API functions used to manipulate files while DRM_DDE indicates that the Dynamic Data Exchange (DDE) protocol may be used to transfer the data. Format refers to the structure of the data, for example, a bitmap structure or plain text. These items are formatted in the string as pairs, either explicitly as a mechanism/format pair enclosed in angle brackets (< >) or as a cross product of one or more mechanisms and one or more formats separated by an (x) and enclosed in parentheses ( ). Multiple pairs or multiple items in a cross product are separated by commas. In order for a transfer to take place, both the source and target applications must agree on both the transfer mechanism and format. As an example, suppose a source application supports transfer of a graphical object in both bitmap format and metafile format; however, it can only render the bitmap format via a DDE interchange and the metafile format through an external data file. If the target can only accept a bitmap format but does not support DDE, then no transfer can occur. An example of an RMF string is:

```
(DRM_OS2FILE x DRF_METAFILE, DRF_BITMAP),<DRM_DDE,DRF_BITMAP>
```

The first pair, either explicit or formed by a cross product, must be the native, or natural, mechanism and format for the object. In the example, the native mechanism is DRM_OS2FILE and the native format is DRF_METAFILE. In general, the native format provides the truest representation of the object. Thus a graphical drawing program would be likely to specify DRF_METAFILE as the native format over DRF_BITMAP since the metafile format retains the lines and other graphical elements, whereas the bitmap format only provides the visual image of the graphic. The native mechanism generally provides the most natural means of transferring the data.

Since most programmers are familiar with file manipulation, DRM_ OS2FILE is likely to be a common native mechanism and should generally be supported by all applications that provide direct manipulation capability. Additional formats and/or mechanisms may also be provided and may be desirable when direct manipulation is provided between a set of interrelated applications.

- The *hstrContainerName* element is a handle to a string that provides the location of the object. For objects transferred as files this might be a directory; for objects that are parts of a file, say a range of cells in a spreadsheet, a full path (directory and file name) to the spreadsheet file might be specified; for an object transferred through interprocess communications, this might be the name of a shared memory area. Note that this latter method is not one of the predefined mechanisms but could perhaps be an application-defined extension.

- The *hstrSourceName* element is a handle to a string that identifies the object to be transferred; for example, the file name for objects transferred as a file, or the cell range for a portion of a spreadsheet. *hstrSourceName* may be passed as NULLHANDLE by the source when the source wishes to be notified of the transfer before rendering occurs, or wishes to handle the rendering itself.

- The *hstrTargetName* element is a handle to a string provided by the source application to suggest the identity of the object after the transfer. This might be the name of the file after the transfer or the range into which spreadsheet cells are to be transferred. This element is optional; the target can always decide the name for itself.

- The *cxOffset* element is the offset in the direction of the x axis from the pointer's hotspot to the origin of the image used to represent this object. This element is used when the spatial representation of the dragged objects is to be maintained at the target and is copied from the DRAGIMAGE structure which provides the representation of the object.

- The *cyOffset* element is the offset in the direction of the y axis from the pointer's hotspot to the origin of the image used to represent this object. This element is used when the spatial representation of the dragged objects is to be maintained at the target and is copied from the DRAGIMAGE structure which provides the representation of the object.

- The *fsControl* element is a set of flags that specify various attributes of the object being dragged. These flags are defined as:

DC_OPEN	0x0001	the object is currently open.
DC_REF	0x0002	the dragged object is a reference to another object.
DC_GROUP	0x0004	the dragged object is a group of objects.

DC_CONTAINER   0x0008   the dragged object is a container of other objects, for example, a directory.

DC_PREPARE   0x0010   a DM_RENDERPREPARE message must be sent to the source application before the transfer begins in order to ready the object for transfer; for example, a text editor might set this flag so that it could copy a selected block of text to a file.

DC_REMOVABLEMEDIA   0x0020   the dragged object is either on removable media or cannot be recovered at the source following a move operation.

- The *fsSupportedOps* element is a set of flags that indicate the operations allowed by the source. These flags are:

DO_COPYABLE   0x0001   indicates that the object may be copied. A new object is created at the target. The source object is not affected.

DO_MOVEABLE   0x0002   indicates that the object may be moved. The object is transferred to the target and is no longer available at the source.

DO_LINKABLE   0x0004   indicates that the object may be linked. A new object is created at the target and a connection to the original object at the source is established, typically so that both copies of the object may be kept synchronized.

Three APIs are provided for managing and accessing DRAGITEM structures. These APIs allow an application to copy a local DRAGITEM structure to the shared memory associated with the DRAGINFO structure, to fill a local DRAGITEM structure from the shared memory, and to obtain a pointer to a DRAGITEM structure in the shared memory.

The **DrgSetDragitem** API is used to copy the contents of a DRAGITEM structure provided by the application into one of the DRAGITEM structures associated with the DRAGINFO structure. The prototype of this API is shown in Figure 7.8.

- The **pdinfo** parameter is a pointer to the DRAGINFO structure associated with the shared memory to which the DRAGITEM structure will be copied.

```
BOOL APIENTRY DrgSetDragitem(PDRAGINFO pdinfo,
                             PDRAGITEM pditem,
                             ULONG cbBuffer,
                             ULONG iItem);
```

Figure 7.8   The DrgSetDragitem prototype.

```
BOOL APIENTRY DrgQueryDragitem(PDRAGINFO pdinfo,
                               ULONG cbBuffer,
                               PDRAGITEM pditem,
                               ULONG iItem);
```

Figure 7.9 The DrgQueryDragitem prototype.

- The **pditem** parameter is a local pointer to the DRAGITEM structure to be copied.
- The **cbBuffer** parameter is the length in bytes of the DRAGITEM structure pointed to by **pditem**.
- The **iItem** parameter is the zero-based index within the array of DRAGITEM structures allocated with **pdinfo** to which **pditem** should be copied.

DrgSetDragitem returns TRUE if successful and FALSE if an error occurred.

The **DrgQueryDragitem** API is used to copy all or part of a DRAGITEM structure from the shared memory associated with a DRAGINFO structure. The prototype for this call is in Figure 7.9.

- The **pdinfo** parameter is a pointer to the DRAGINFO structure which identifies the shared memory area containing the desired DRAGITEM structure.
- The **cbBuffer** parameter is the length in bytes of the structure pointed to by **pditem**. This may be less than the length of the DRAGITEM structure if the entire structure is not desired.
- The **pditem** parameter is a pointer to the location in local memory to which the desired DRAGITEM structure is copied.
- The **iItem** parameter identifies the zero-based index of the desired DRAGITEM structure within the array of DRAGITEM structures allocated to **pdinfo**.

DrgQueryDragitem returns TRUE if successful or FALSE if an error occurred.

DrgQueryDragitemPtr is used to obtain a pointer to a drag item within the shared memory area. Unlike **DrgQueryDragitem**, which makes a local copy of the structure, this API allows the application to modify the actual structure in DRAGINFO. The syntax of the API call is in Figure 7.10.

```
PDRAGITEM APIENTRY DrgQueryDragitemPtr(PDRAGINFO pdinfo,
                                       ULONG ulIndex);
```

Figure 7.10 The DrgQueryDragitemPtr prototype.

- The **pdinfo** parameter is a pointer to the DRAGINFO structure which identifies the shared memory area containing the desired DRAGITEM structure.
- The **ulIndex** parameter is the zero-based index of the desired DRAGITEM structure within the array of DRAGITEM structures allocated with **pdinfo**.

This function returns a pointer to the DRAGITEM structure indicated by parameter **ulIndex**.

The **DrgQueryDragitemCount** API returns the number of DRAGITEM structures allocated for a given DRAGINFO structure. The API is defined as shown in Figure 7.11.

- The **pdinfo** parameter is a pointer to the DRAGINFO structure for which the number of DRAGITEM structures is desired.

The function returns the number of DRAGITEM structures allocated for the DRAGINFO structure identified by **pdinfo**.

The DRAGIMAGE Structure

The DRAGIMAGE structure is used to describe the graphic image used to represent one or more of the objects being dragged during a drag-and-drop operation. For compatibility, DRAGIMAGE structures may be specified for pickup-and-drop operations, but are ignored. An application may associate one or more DRAGIMAGE structures with a DRAGINFO structure. If the total number of DRAGIMAGEs is less than the number of dragged objects or DRAGITEM structures, then the first *n* DRAGIMAGE structures are used to represent the first *n* DRAGITEM structures; DRAGIMAGE structure *n* is then used to represent the remaining DRAGITEM structures. The DRAGIMAGE structure may also be used to convey spatial information to the target application so that objects may retain their original orientation to one another when dropped. The DRAGIMAGE structure is defined as shown in Figure 7.12.

- The *cb* element is the length of the DRAGIMAGE structure in bytes.
- The *cptl* element is the number of points in the array pointed to by *hImage* when the image is a polygon (see *fl*); otherwise, this element is ignored.
- The *hImage* element identifies the image to be drawn. The *fl* element determines how this element is interpreted.

```
ULONG APIENTRY DrgQueryDragitemCount(PDRAGINFO pdinfo);
```

Figure 7.11 The DrgQueryDragitemCount prototype.

```
typedef struct _DRAGIMAGE
{
    USHORT  cb;
    USHORT  cptl;
    LHANDLE hImage;
    SIZEL   sizlStretch;
    ULONG   fl;
    SHORT   cxOffset;
    SHORT   cyOffset;
} DRAGIMAGE;
```

Figure 7.12   The DRAGIMAGE structure.

- The *sizlStretch* element is a SIZEL structure that defines the size of the image. If the appropriate flag is set in *fl*, the image will be stretched or compressed to match this size; if the *fl* flag is not set, this field is not used.
- The *fl* element is a set of flags that define the type of image and how the image will be displayed. The valid flags are:

DRG_ICON   0x0001   specifies that a graphic pointer is used to represent the associated object. *hImage* is interpreted as an HPOINTER.

DRG_BITMAP   0x0002   specifies that a bitmap is used to represent the associated object. *hImage* is interpreted as an HBITMAP.

DRG_POLYGON   0x0004   specifies that a polygon (or series of connected points) is used to represent the associated object. *hImage* is interpreted as a pointer to an array containing at least *cptl* POINTL structures.

DRG_STRETCH   0x0008   when ORed with either DRG_ICON or DRG_BITMAP, causes the image to be stretched or compressed as necessary to match the size specified in *sizlStretch*.

DRG_TRANSPARENT   0x0010   when ORed with DRG_ICON, causes an outline of the pointer to be created and displayed instead of the actual pointer.

DRG_CLOSED   0x0020   when ORed with DRG_POLYGON causes the first and last points of the *hImage* array to be connected so that the image is a closed polygon.

- The *cxOffset* element specifies the position of the image's origin in relation to the pointer hotspot measured as the distance between the two points along the x axis. This element is copied to the *cxOffset* element of the associated DRAGITEM before the target application is notified of a drop.
- The *cyOffset* element specifies the position of the image's origin in relation to the pointer hotspot measured as the distance between the two points

along the y axis. This element is copied to the *cyOffset* element of the associated DRAGITEM structure before the target application is notified of a drop.

An array of one or more DRAGIMAGE structures is passed as a parameter to the **DrgDrag** API to define the default images that represent the dragged objects. As the objects are dragged over a potential target, the target may use the **DrgSetDragImage** API to cause a different image or set of images to be displayed while the pointer is located over its window. The prototype for this API is given in Figure 7.13.

- The **pdinfo** parameter is a pointer to the DRAGINFO structure for the current drag and drop operation. This value is normally passed to the target application as one of the MPARAM parameters of a message.
- The **pdimg** parameter is a pointer to an array of DRAGIMAGE structures which define the graphical images to display while the pointer is over this target window.
- The **cdimg** parameter specifies the number of structures in the array pointed to by *pdimg*.
- The **pRsvd** parameter is a reserved parameter and must be set to NULL.

The API returns TRUE if successful and FALSE if an error occurred.

The DRAGTRANSFER Structure

The DRAGTRANSFER structure is used to pass information during the ensuing conversation between the source and target applications after a drop occurs. The definition of the structure is given in Figure 7.14.

- The *cb* element is the length of the structure in bytes.
- The *hwndClient* element is the handle of the target application window with which the source application communicates.
- The *pditem* element is a pointer to the DRAGITEM structure that describes the object being rendered. The DRAGITEM structure pointed to by this element must exist within the shared memory identified by the DRAG-INFO structure for the direct manipulation operation. This pointer should normally be obtained by calling the **DrgQueryDragitemPtr** API.

```
BOOL APIENTRY DrgSetDragImage(PDRAGINFO pdinfo,
                              PDRAGIMAGE pdimg,
                              ULONG cdimg,
                              PVOID pRsvd);
```

Figure 7.13   The DrgSetDragImage prototype.

```
typedef struct _DRAGTRANSFER
{
    ULONG       cb;
    HWND        hwndClient;
    PDRAGITEM   pditem;
    HSTR        hstrSelectedRMF;
    HSTR        hstrRenderToName;
    ULONG       ulTargetInfo;
    USHORT      usOperation;
    USHORT      fsReply;
} DRAGTRANSFER;
```

Figure 7.14   The DRAGTRANSFER structure.

- The *hstrSelectedRMF* element is a handle to a string that specifies the rendering mechanism and format that the target has selected for the operation. Note that this string must be formatted as a single mechanism/format pair enclosed in angle brackets (< >).
- The *hstrRenderToName* element is a handle to a string that identifies the location where the source should store the rendered object. If this item is a file name, the full path should be specified.
- The *ulTargetInfo* element is a 32-bit value reserved for use by the target application.
- The *usOperation* element defines the rendering operation to be performed. The standard, predefined values for this field are:

DO_COPY   0x0010   creates a new instance of the object and passes to the target.

DO_MOVE   0x0020   passes the object to the target; the object is no longer available to the source.

DO_LINK   0x0018   provides the target with a means of accessing the existing copy of the object.

Additional operations may be defined by applications; however, the operation will not be performed unless both the source and target understand the operation.

- The *fsReply* element is a set of flags that the source application uses to communicate its success or failure in performing the rendering operation. The valid flags are:

DMFL_NATIVERENDER   0x0004   indicates that the source will not render this object and that the target should use the native mechanism and format to render the data.

DMFL_RENDERRETRY   0x0008   indicates that the source is able to render the object but does not support the selected mechanism and format. The target may retry with a different mechanism and format if desired.

```
PDRAGTRANSFER APIENTRY DrgAllocDragtransfer(ULONG cdxfer);
```

Figure 7.15   The DrgAllocDragtransfer prototype.

Two APIs are provided for managing DRAGTRANSFER structures; one API is used to allocate one or more structures in an array, the other is used to free an allocated array of structures. While the structures may be allocated as an array, they are passed to the source application individually. Therefore, **DrgFreeDragtransfer** allows the structures to be freed on an individual basis and does not free the shared memory until all structures have been freed.

The **DrgAllocDragtransfer** API must be called by the target application to allocate DRAGTRANSFER structures in shared memory so that they can be properly accessed by both the source and target applications. The API is prototyped as in Figure 7.15.

- The **cdxfer** parameter specifies the number of DRAGTRANSFER structures to be allocated.

The API returns a pointer to an array containing **cdxfer** DRAGTRANSFER structures. Again, while multiple DRAGTRANSFER structures may be allocated, the drag-and-drop protocols process the array one element at a time.

The **DrgFreeDragtransfer** API frees the memory allocated by the **DrgAllocDragtransfer** API. This API must be called by both the source and target applications since the memory allocated for the DRAGTRANSFER structure is given to the source application. The prototype for the API is in Figure 7.16.

- The **pdxfer** parameter is a pointer to the DRAGTRANSFER structure to free. When all structures allocated by a call to **DrgAllocDragtransfer** have been freed, the memory is freed.

The API returns TRUE if successful and FALSE if an error occurred.

STRING HANDLES

Like most of the memory used during a direct manipulation operation, the text needed to complete the operation must be accessible to multiple processes and cannot therefore be allocated in the local memory of any one application. Rather than require the applications to allocate and manage memory for the

```
BOOL APIENTRY DrgFreeDragtransfer(PDRAGTRANSFER pdxfer);
```

Figure 7.16   The DrgFreeDragtransfer prototype.

```
HSTR APIENTRY DrgAddStrHandle(PSZ psz);
```

Figure 7.17   The DrgAddStrHandle prototype.

strings, an API is provided, which copies the text into memory managed by PM and returns a unique handle with which applications can identify the string. Another API is provided, which copies the string associated with a given handle from PM's memory back into the local memory of an application. Of course, an API is provided to remove the string from PM's memory and free the handle. These string handles are stored in the direct manipulation data structures instead of the strings themselves.

The API used to copy the text into PM's memory and assign the string handle is **DrgAddStrHandle**. The prototype for this function is in Figure 7.17.

- The **psz** parameter is a pointer to the NULL-terminated string for which a handle is desired.

DrgAddStrHandle returns NULLHANDLE if an error occurs or the handle assigned to the text string if successful.

The **DrgQueryStrName** API copies the text associated with a string handle into a buffer in the application's local memory. The prototype for the API is in Figure 7.18.

- The **hstr** parameter specifies the string handle representing the desired string.
- The **cbBuffer** parameter is the length of the local buffer in bytes. The number of bytes required to accommodate the entire string may be obtained with the **DrgQueryStrNameLen** API (upcoming).
- The **pBuffer** parameter is a pointer to the local memory to which the string should be copied.

DrgQueryStrName returns the number of bytes copied to **pBuffer**. If **hstr** is invalid, zero is returned.

The length of the string associated with a given string handle may be obtained by calling the **DrgQueryStrNameLen** API, which is prototyped as in Figure 7.19.

```
ULONG APIENTRY DrgQueryStrName(HSTR hstr,
                               ULONG cbBuffer,
                               PSZ pBuffer);
```

Figure 7.18   The DrgQueryStrName prototype.

```
ULONG APIENTRY DrgQueryStrNameLen(HSTR hstr);
```

Figure 7.19   The DrgQueryStrNameLen prototype.

- The **hstr** parameter is the handle to the string whose length is desired.

The API returns the number of bytes in the string associated with **hstr**, but does not include the NULL character terminating the string.

The **DrgDeleteStrHandle** API frees the resources associated with a string handle obtained via the **DrgAddStrHandle** API and invalidates the handle. The prototype for this API is shown in Figure 7.20.

- The **hstr** parameter is the handle that identifies the string to delete.

The API returns TRUE if successful and FALSE if an error occurred.

String handles may also be removed with the **DrgDeleteDraginfoStrHandles** API. This API provides a shortcut for the programmer by deleting all the string handles referenced in the DRAGITEM structures associated with a DRAGINFO structure. The prototype for this API is in Figure 7.21.

- The **pdinfo** parameter is a pointer to the DRAGINFO structure associated with the DRAGITEM structures whose string handles are to be freed.

The API returns TRUE is successful or FALSE if an error occurred.

DIRECT MANIPULATION CODING

Now that you have at least a basic understanding of the data structures used for direct manipulation, we can turn our attention to the coding required for an application to support direct manipulation. In order to clearly see the complete flow of the operation, we will begin with the coding required for a window to act as the source of a drag-and-drop operation and then proceed to the coding that allows a window to be a target. After examining the drag-and-drop programming, we will examine the additional code required to also act as the source or target of a pickup-and-drop operation.

The application used for the examples provides direct manipulation capability for a listbox control that displays a list of the file names in a directory. The application creates the listbox control as the client window of a standard

```
BOOL APIENTRY DrgDeleteStrHandle(HSTR hstr);
```

Figure 7.20   The DrgDeleteStrHandle prototype.

```
BOOL APIENTRY DrgDeleteDraginfoStrHandles(PDRAGINFO pdinfo);
```

Figure 7.21   The DrgDeleteDraginfoStrHandles prototype.

frame and then subclasses the control to provide menu support and direct manipulation functionality. See Chapter 10 for additional information on subclassing.

Starting the Drag and Drop Operation

The source application in a drag-and-drop operation is the application that controls the window from which objects are dragged. This application is responsible for initiating the drag operation, informing the system which objects are being dragged, specifying the graphical image(s) used to represent the object(s) during the operation, specifying the rendering mechanism(s) and format(s) that it supports, and rendering the object(s) using the mechanism and in the format selected by the target application.

A drag-and-drop operation is initiated when the user presses and holds the drag-and-drop button on the pointing device and then moves the pointing device. PM responds to the user action by sending a WM_BEGINDRAG message to the window over which the mouse pointer is positioned. An application capable of acting as a source application responds to this message by allocating and initializing the data structures for the operation and then calling the **DrgDrag** API function.

Figure 7.22 provides an example of the code for processing the WM_BEGIN DRAG message. First the number of items being dragged must be determined so that the correct number of DRAGITEM structures can be allocated along with the DRAGINFO structure. The application determines this number by calling a utility function, **QuerySelectionCount**, to scan the items in the listbox and determine how many are selected. Once the number of selected items is known, **DrgAllocDraginfo** is called to allocate the DRAGINFO structure and the proper number of DRAGITEM structures. If this function is successful, another utility function, **SetDragItems**, is called to initialize a DRAGITEM structure for each selected element of the listbox.

Next, one or more DRAGIMAGE structures must be initialized to inform PM how to graphically represent the dragged objects during the drag operation. This application displays a single image no matter how many objects are dragged, but the image varies depending on whether there is one object or multiple objects. First the DRAGIMAGE structure is cleared, then the size of the structure is stored in the cb element. Next, the fl flag for the type of graphical representation is set; in this instance, a pointer is used so the DRG_ICON flag is set. The $hImage$ element is set to a system-defined pointer handle obtained via a call to the **WinQuerySysPointer** API. The handle to the SPTR_FILE pointer

```
static MRESULT wm_begindrag( HWND hwnd, ULONG msg, MPARAM mp1, MPARAM mp2 )
{
    ULONG       cFiles;
    DRAGIMAGE   dImage;
    PDRAGINFO   pDinfo = NULL;
    SHORT       sItem = LIT_FIRST;
    HWND        hwndTarget;

    do {
        if ((cFiles = QuerySelectionCount( hwnd )) == 0) break;
        if ((pDinfo = DrgAllocDraginfo( cFiles )) == (PDRAGINFO)(NULL))
            break;
        SetDragItems( pDinfo, hwnd, cFiles );
        memset( &dImage, 0, sizeof(DRAGIMAGE));
        dImage.cb = sizeof(DRAGIMAGE);
        dImage.fl = DRG_ICON;
        dImage.hImage = (LHANDLE)WinQuerySysPointer( HWND_DESKTOP,
                            cFiles == 1 ? SPTR_FILE : SPTR_MULTFILE,
                            FALSE );
        gpSrcDinfo = pDinfo
        gulSrcCount = cFiles;
        hwndTarget = DrgDrag( hwnd, pDinfo, &dImage, 1, VK_ENDDRAG, NULL );
        if (hwndTarget == NULLHANDLE) {
            DrgDeleteDraginfoStrHandles( pDinfo );
            DrgFreeDraginfo( pDinfo );
        } /* endif */
    } while ( false ); /* enddo */
    return (MRESULT)TRUE;
}
```

Figure 7.22   Handling the WM_BEGINDRAG message.

is used if a single listbox item is selected; the handle to the SPTR_MULTFILE pointer is used if multiple listbox items are selected. The remaining elements of the structure remain at their default values since the program does not wish to modify the size of the pointer, and no spatial orientation is possible with only one image.

After initializing the DRAGIMAGE structure, the application saves the DRAGINFO pointer and the number of dragged items in global variables. These values are used after a drop occurs to determine when the target application has completed its processing of all items so that the source application may release its access to the DRAGINFO structure.

The **DrgDrag** API is then called to initiate PM's processing of the drag operation. The prototype for the **DrgDrag** API is shown in Figure 7.23.

- The **hwndSource** parameter is the window handle of the source window for the operation, normally the window that received the WM_BEGINDRAG message.

```
HWND APIENTRY DrgDrag(HWND hwndSource,
                      PDRAGINFO pdinfo,
                      PDRAGIMAGE pdimg,
                      ULONG cdimg,
                      LONG vkTerminate,
                      PVOID pRsvd);
```

Figure 7.23   The DrgDrag prototype.

- The **pdinfo** parameter is the pointer to the DRAGINFO structure and associated DRAGIMAGE structures that convey the information necessary to complete the drag-and-drop operation.
- The **pdimg** parameter is a pointer to the DRAGIMAGE structure or array of DRAGIMAGE structures that inform PM how to graphically represent the dragged objects during the drag portion of the operation.
- The **cdimg** parameter indicates the number of DRAGIMAGE structures in the array pointed to by **pdimg**.
- The **vkTerminate** parameter indicates the pointing device button whose release will terminate the drag-and-drop operation. Possible values for this parameter are:

VK_ENDDRAG 0x0038   indicates that the system-defined button must be released. **vkTerminate** should normally be set to this value.

VK_BUTTON1 0x0001   indicates that releasing button 1 of the pointing device terminates the operation.

VK_BUTTON2 0x0002   indicates that releasing button 2 of the pointing device terminates the operation.

VK_BUTTON3 0x0003   indicates that releasing button 3 of the pointing device terminates the operation.

- The **pRsvd** parameter is reserved and must be set to NULL.

The **DrgDrag** API returns the handle to the window on which the objects were dropped, or NULLHANDLE if the operation was cancelled or an error occurred. Note that this API starts a modal operation and does not return until the objects are dropped or the operation is cancelled. PM handles processing of the message queue in the same manner as when the **WinDlgBox** API is called. When the drag operation ends by dropping the objects, a DM_DROP message is sent to the target window before the **DrgDrag** API returns. If **DrgDrag** returns NULLHANDLE, the DRAGINFO structure is freed immediately by calling the **DrgDeleteDraginfoStrHandles** and **DrgFreeDraginfo** APIs. The **wm_begindrag** function then returns TRUE to indicate that the WM_BEGINDRAG message was processed.

Figure 7.24 shows the code for routine **SetDragItems** which was mentioned earlier. This routine is responsible for initializing the DRAGITEM structures with the required information to identify the objects being dragged. A prototype DRAGITEM structure is allocated in the routine's local memory as a stack variable. After the prototype structure is cleared, the elements of the structure that remain constant for every object are set to appropriate values. Then a loop is executed which scans the selected items in the listbox, storing appropriate values in the varying elements of the DRAGITEM structure and copying the completed DRAGITEM structure to the shared memory allocated for the operation's DRAGINFO structure.

The constant elements of the DRAGITEM structure in this example are the string handle for the rendering mechanism and format, the supported operations flags, and the source window handle. This application only supports transferring objects as files, thus the rendering mechanism is set to DRM_OS2FILE. Since this application does not concern itself with the format in which files are stored and does no translation of the file format, the rendering format is set to DRF_UNKNOWN. These two selections are merged into the RMF string "<DRM_OS2FILE,DRF_UNKNOWN>" for which a string handle is allocated and stored in the *hstrRMF* element of the DRAGITEM structure. The application will allow files to be moved or copied, but does not support linking; therefore, the DO_COPYABLE and DO_MOVEABLE flags are set in the *fsSupportedOps* element.

The loop in **SetDragItems** scans the listbox for selected items. When an item is found, the text of the item is retrieved from the listbox. A string handle is allocated for this text and stored in the *hstrSourceName* element of the DRAGITEM structure. Since the application expects the name to remain the same when transferred to the target, the *hstrTargetName* element is also set to this handle (the target name is a suggestion, the target application may change the name). Next, routine **QueryType** is called to obtain the type of the file from the extended attributes associated with the file. The routine sets this value as the native type of the file and appends the DRT_UNKNOWN type for applications that are not concerned about the actual file type. A string handle is allocated for the resulting string and stored in element *hstrType*. Finally, the name of the current directory is obtained and a string handle allocated for the text. This handle is then stored in the *hstrContainerName* element. At this point, the prototype structure has been filled and **DragSetDragitem** is called to copy the prototype to the operation's shared memory area.

We will return to the source application later to examine how the rendering operation is handled, but first, let's examine how target applications handle the messages received during the drag portion of the operation.

Responding to the Drag Operation

After **DrgDrag** is called, PM assumes control of the drag operation and modifies the mouse pointer to include the graphic image or images that represent the

```
static void SetDragItems( PDRAGINFO pDinfo, HWND hwnd, ULONG cFiles )
{
    SHORT       sItem;
    SHORT       cbItem;
    PSZ         pszFileName;
    PSZ         pszType;
    PSZ         pszContainer;
    DRAGITEM    dItem;

    memset( &dItem, 0, sizeof(DRAGITEM));
    dItem.hstrRMF = DrgAddStrHandle( "<DRM_OS2FILE,DRF_UNKNOWN>" );
    dItem.fsSupportedOps = DO_COPYABLE | DO_MOVEABLE;
    dItem.hwndItem = hwnd;

    sItem = LIT_FIRST;
    while ((sItem = SHORT1FROMMR( WinSendMsg( hwnd, LM_QUERYSELECTION,
                          MPFROMSHORT( sItem ), 0L ))) != LIT_NONE ) {

        cbItem = SHORT1FROMMR( WinSendMsg( hwnd, LM_QUERYITEMTEXTLENGTH,
                          MPFROMSHORT( sItem ), 0L )) + 1;
        if ((pszFileName = (PSZ)malloc( cbItem )) != (PSZ)NULL) {
            WinSendMsg( hwnd, LM_QUERYITEMTEXT,
                      MPFROM2SHORT( sItem, cbItem ), pszFileName );
            dItem.hstrSourceName = dItem.hstrTargetName =
                                          DrgAddStrHandle( pszFileName );
            if ((pszType = QueryType( pszFileName )) != NULL) {
                dItem.hstrType = DrgAddStrHandle( pszType );
                free( pszType );
            } else {
                dItem.hstrType = NULLHANDLE;
            } /* endif */
            if ((pszContainer = QueryCurrentDirectory()) != NULL) {
                dItem.hstrContainerName = DrgAddStrHandle( pszContainer );
                free( pszContainer );
            } else {
                dItem.hstrContainerName = NULLHANDLE;
            } /* endif */

            DrgSetDragitem( pDinfo, &dItem, sizeof( DRAGITEM ), --cFiles );

            free( pszFileName );
        } /* endif */
    } /* endwhile */
    return;
}
```

Figure 7.24 Initializing the DRAGITEM structures.

dragged objects. As the pointer moves over a window, PM sends messages to the window to notify it of the drag operation. Windows that are capable of being targets of the drag operation must respond to these messages.

One of these messages is the DM_DRAGOVER message. This message informs a window that it is the current target of a direct manipulation operation and is sent as the pointer moves into and within the window, allowing a window with multiple target areas, such as a container, to respond based on the capabilities of the area under the pointer. Parameter **mp1** of the message is a pointer to the DRAGINFO structure for the operation. Parameter **mp2** contains the current location of the pointer in desktop coordinates; the x coordinate is in the low-order 16 bits of the parameter and the y coordinate is in the high-order 16 bits. The application's response to the message depends on the ability of the application to act as a target for the current drag operation and set of dragged objects.

When an application receives the DM_DRAGOVER message, it should provide some type of emphasis indicating that the current window is the current target. While this emphasis can take many forms, a thin border is normally drawn around the inner edge of the window; or, if the window supports multiple target areas, the portion of the window that is the current target. After emphasis is provided, the application obtains access to the DRAGINFO structure and determines if the current operation is supported for all elements of the set of dragged objects. In making this determination, the application should examine the type of operation in the **usOperation** field of the DRAGINFO structure and the object type, rendering mechanism, and format in each of the DRAGITEM structures associated with the DRAGINFO structure. In order to accept a drop of the current set of objects, the application should be able to support all of these items. Once this determination is made, the application should release its access to the DRAGINFO structure and prepare a response to the message.

The return code for the DM_DRAGOVER message consists of two fields. The lower-order 16 bits, **usDrop**, indicate the application's ability to accept the dragged objects; and the high-order 16 bits, **usDefaultOp**, indicate the default operation that the application will perform. **usDefaultOp** is only necessary when the drop can be accepted and the **usOperation** field of the DRAGINFO structure is set to DO_DEFAULT or DO_UNKNOWN. Field **usDrop** may be set to the following values:

DOR_DROP   0x0001   indicates that the application is capable of supporting a drop of the current set of objects.

DOR_NODROP   0x0000   indicates that the application is capable of supporting a drop of the current set of objects, but is not able to do so at this time; possibly because the application is busy with some other operation.

DOR_NODROPOP   0x0002   indicates that the application is capable of supporting a drop of the objects, but does not support the requested operation.

DOR_NEVERDROP   0x0003   indicates that the application cannot accept a drop of the objects.

The **usDefaultOp** field may be assigned the following values:

DO_COPY   0x0010   indicates that a copy operation will be performed.

DO_MOVE   0x0020   indicates that a move operation will be performed.

DO_LINK   0x0018   indicates that a link operation will be performed.

other   indicates that an application-defined operation will be performed. Application-defined operations should be assigned a value greater than DO_UNKNOWN (0xBFFF).

Figure 7.25 shows the code our example application uses to process the DM_DRAGOVER message. The application can serve as the target for dropping OS/2 files of any type in any format. If not already applied by a prior DM_DRAGOVER message, the routine first establishes target emphasis for the window and then determines if the current drag operation and objects are supported.

If checking the window data determines that target emphasis is needed, the emphasis is supplied by drawing a border around the interior of the window. To accomplish this, a presentation space is obtained by calling the **DrgGetPS** API. This API takes one parameter, the handle of the window in which drawing will occur, and returns a handle to the presentation space. **WinQueryWindowRect** is then called to obtain the area occupied by the window and the coordinates are adjusted to account for scroll bar controls and the size of the border to be drawn. Next, **WinDrawBorder** is called to draw the actual border, and the window data is updated to indicate that emphasis has been applied. The presentation space is then released by calling **DrgReleasePS** and by passing the handle to the presentation space obtained earlier. The prototype for the **WinDrawBorder** API is shown in Figure 7.26.

- The **hps** parameter is the handle of the presentation space where drawing is to occur.
- The **prcl** parameter is a pointer to a rectangle describing the area around which the border is to be drawn.
- The **cx** parameter specifies the width of the border.
- The **cy** parameter specifies the height of the border.
- The **clrFore** parameter specifies the foreground color for the border.
- The **clrBack** parameter specifies the background color for the border.

```
static MRESULT dm_dragover( HWND hwnd, ULONG msg, MPARAM mp1, MPARAM mp2 )
{
    PDRAGINFO       pdInfo = (PDRAGINFO)NULL;
    USHORT          usDrop = DOR_NEVERDROP;
    USHORT          usDefaultOp;
    PDRAGITEM       pdItem = NULL;
    ULONG           lItem = 0;
    HPS             hps;
    RECTL           rclRect;

    do {
        if (!WinQueryWindowULong(WinQueryWindow(hwnd,QW_OWNER),WL_EMPHASIZED)){
            hps = DrgGetPS( hwnd );
            if (hps == NULLHANDLE) break;
            WinQueryWindowRect( hwnd, &rclRect );
            rclRect.xLeft += WinQuerySysValue(HWND_DESKTOP, SV_CXBORDER);
            rclRect.yTop -= WinQuerySysValue(HWND_DESKTOP, SV_CYBORDER);
            rclRect.xRight -= WinQuerySysValue(HWND_DESKTOP, SV_CXVSCROLL);
            rclRect.yBottom += WinQuerySysValue(HWND_DESKTOP, SV_CYBORDER) + 1;
            WinDrawBorder(hps,&rclRect,1,1,01,01,DB_DESTINVERT|DB_STANDARD);
            WinSetWindowULong( WinQueryWindow( hwnd, QW_OWNER ),
                               WL_EMPHASIZED, (LONG)TRUE );
            DrgReleasePS( hps );
        } /* endif */
        pdInfo = (PDRAGINFO)mp1;
        if (!DrgAccessDraginfo( pdInfo )) pdInfo = (PDRAGINFO)NULL; break;
        usDrop = DOR_DROP;
        switch(pdInfo->usOperation){
        case DO_COPY: usDefaultOp = DO_COPY; break;
        case DO_MOVE: usDefaultOp = DO_MOVE: break;
        case DO_DEFAULT: usDefaultOp = DO_MOVE; break;
        case DO_UNKNOWN: usDefaultOp = DO_MOVE; break;
        default: usDrop = DOR_NODROPOP;
        }
        for( lItem = 0; lItem < pdInfo->cditem; lItem++ ) {
            if( (pdItem = DrgQueryDragitemPtr(pdInfo, lItem)) != NULL ) {
                if( !DrgVerifyRMF( pdItem, "DRM_OS2FILE", NULL )) {
                    usDrop = DOR_NEVERDROP; /* can't handle this object */
                    break;
                }
                /* do type here if necessary - bad type = DOR_NEVERDROP */
                if( usDefaultOp == DO_COPY &&
                    !(pdItem->fsSupportedOps & DO_COPYABLE )) {
                    usDrop = DOR_NODROPOP;
                } else if( usDefaultOp == DO_MOVE &&
                           !(pdItem->fsSupportedOps & DO_MOVEABLE )) {
                    usDrop = DOR_NODROPOP;
                }
            }
        }
    } while ( false ); /* enddo */
    if (pdInfo != (PDRAGINFO)NULL) DrgFreeDraginfo( pdInfo );
    return MRFROM2SHORT( usDrop, usDefaultOp );
}
```

Figure 7.25 Handling the DM_DRAGOVER message.

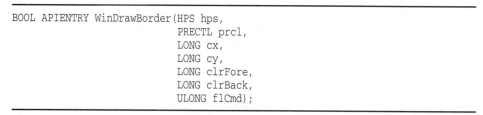

```
BOOL APIENTRY WinDrawBorder(HPS hps,
                            PRECTL prcl,
                            LONG cx,
                            LONG cy,
                            LONG clrFore,
                            LONG clrBack,
                            ULONG flCmd);
```

Figure 7.26   The WinDrawBorder prototype.

- The **flCmd** parameter is a set of flags that modify the operation of the function. These are defined as:

DB_PATCOPY	0x0000	uses the current pattern to draw the border.
DB_PATINVERT	0x0001	exclusive ORs the current pattern with the existing presentation space data.
DB_DESTINVERT	0x0002	inverts the destination.
DB_AREAMIXMODE	0x0003	uses the current mix mode for drawing the border area.

Note that the above four flags are collectively known as DB_ROP and are mutually exclusive. The remaining flags may be ORed with one of these.

DB_INTERIOR	0x0008	causes the area within the *prcl* rectangle that is not part of the border specified by **cx** and **cy** to be drawn.
DB_AREAATTRS	0x0010	causes the current area attributes to be used rather than the specified foreground and background colors.
DB_STANDARD	0X0100	specifies that the **cx** and **cy** parameters are to be multiplied by SV_CXBORDER and SV_CYBORDER to obtain the width and height of the border.
DB_DLGBORDER	0x0200	specifies that a dialog border is to be drawn. The border is drawn in the active title bar color if DB_PATCOPY is specified and in the inactive title bar color if DB_PATINVERT is specified. If DB_INTERIOR is specified, the interior is drawn using the **clrFore** and **clrBack** parameters; the **DB_ROP** and **DB_AREAATTRS** parameters are ignored for interior drawing.

WinDrawBorder returns TRUE if successful and FALSE if an error occurs. In the example code, the API is used to show emphasis by inverting a narrow border around the inside edge of the window.

After the emphasis has been applied, the application obtains access to the shared memory containing the DRAGINFO and DRAGITEM structures by calling the **DrgAccessDraginfo** API with the pointer passed as **mp1** of the

DM_DRAGOVER message. The application then verifies that the operation specified in the *usOperation* element of the DRAGINFO structure is supported. A switch statement is used to handle this verification and to set the *usDefaultOp* variable if the operation is supported. Copy and move operations are supported and merely assign DO_COPY or DO_MOVE to *usDefaultOp*. The default and unknown operations are also supported and set *usDefaultOp* to the default for this application, DO_MOVE. All other operations are not supported by this application, so the default case sets the *usDrop* variable to DOR_NODROPOP. Assuming that the objects themselves are supported, this value indicates that the application does not support the current operation.

After the operation type is verified, the application scans the DRAGITEMs connected to the DRAGINFO structure to verify that the individual objects can be rendered. In order to make this determination, the application calls the **DrgVerifyRMF** API to ensure that the objects can be rendered using the DRM_OS2FILE mechanism—this application is not concerned with the file format, so the format string parameter is set to NULL. If an object does not support the OS/2 file mechanism, the *usDrop* variable is set to DOR_NEVERDROP to indicate that the application cannot support a drop of the current set of objects, and the loop to check the dragged objects is terminated. The prototype for the **DrgVerifyRMF** API is given in Figure 7.27.

- The **pditem** parameter is a pointer to the DRAGITEM to be tested.
- The **pszMech** parameter is a pointer to a zero-terminated string of characters representing the mechanism for which to search. Specifying a NULL pointer will match any mechanism.
- The **pszFmt** parameter is a pointer to a zero-terminated string of character representing the format for which to search. Specifying a NULL pointer will match any format.

The **DrgVerifyRMF** API returns TRUE if the desired mechanism and format are supported for the object and FALSE if the mechanism and format pair are not supported. The API obtains the string represented by element *hstrRMF* of the DRAGITEM structure and expands any cross products into their individual pairs. The resulting set of paired mechanisms and formats are tested for the desired pair.

Normally, an application that processes the object's contents would verify the type passed in *hstrType* at this stage; but, since this application does

```
BOOL APIENTRY DrgVerifyRMF(PDRAGITEM pditem,
                           PSZ pszMech,
                           PSZ pszFmt);
```

Figure 7.27   The DrgVerifyRMF prototype.

not interpret the contents of the file, the file type is unimportant and is not verified. The final step for verifying the objects is to ensure that the current operation is supported for the object. This is accomplished by testing the *fs-SupportOps* element of the DRAGITEM structure for the bit that corresponds to the current operation. If the corresponding bit is not set, *usDrop* is set to DOR_NODROPOP, once again indicating that transfer of the objects may be supported, but not using the current operation. When all objects have been checked, the application releases its access to the DRAGINFO structure and returns *usDrop* and *usDefaultOp* to PM.

Once a DM_DRAGOVER message has been received, the application will receive either a DM_DRAGLEAVE message or a DM_DROP message. The DM_DRAGLEAVE message indicates that either the pointer has left the window or the direct manipulation operation has been cancelled. When this message is received, the target emphasis applied to the window should be removed. Parameter **mp1** of the DM_DRAGLEAVE message is a pointer to the DRAG-INFO structure, allowing the application to query information about the operation or the dragged objects if necessary. The target application will receive a DM_DROPHELP message in addition to the DM_DRAGLEAVE message if a drag-and-drop operation is cancelled as the result of the user pressing the Help key, F1. This message allows the application to display help explaining how it handles a drop operation and/or why it cannot accept a drop for the currently dragged objects.

The DM_DROP message indicates that the user has requested that the dragged objects be dropped on the window that receives the message. When the application receives this message, it should remove the target emphasis from the window, obtain access to the DRAGINFO structure pointed to by parameter **mp1** of the message, and take steps to initiate the rendering of the objects; for example, by posting a message to itself to perform the rendering. The application should not wait until the objects have actually been rendered before responding to the DM_DROP message. After the target application returns from DM_DROP, the **DrgDrag** API will return to the source application.

Figure 7.28 provides an example of the target application processing of the DM_DROP message. In this example, the target first obtains access to the DRAGINFO structure using the **DrgAccessDraginfo** API. An application-defined message is then posted to an object window associated with the target application to handle the task of communicating with the source window to render the objects. This method allows the rendering to occur on a separate thread so that the application's user interface remains active. After posting the message, the emphasis set in the processing for the DM_DRAGOVER message is removed by using the same code to again invert the border around the edge of the window. The emphasis flag in the window instance data is then cleared so that future DM_DRAGOVER messages from another drag operation will be able to establish the emphasis. The function then returns and PM allows the source application to return from the **DrgDrag** API call.

```
static MRESULT dm_drop( HWND hwnd, ULONG msg, MPARAM mp1, MPARAM mp2 )
{
    HPS         hps;
    PDRAGINFO   pdInfo = (PDRAGINFO)mp1;
    RECTL       rclRect;
    HWND        hwndMain = (HWND)WinQueryWindow( hwnd, QW_OWNER );
    HWND        hwndObj = (HWND)NULLHANDLE;

    if (DrgAccessDraginfo( pdInfo )) {
        hwndObj = (HWND)WinQueryWindowULong( hwndMain, WL_HWNDOBJECT );
        WinPostMsg( hwndObj,UM_RECEIVEDROP,MPFROMHWND(hwnd),MPFROMP(pdInfo));
    } /* endif */

    if (WinQueryWindowULong( hwndMain, WL_EMPHASIZED)) {
        hps = DrgGetPS( hwnd );
        if (hps != NULLHANDLE) {
            WinQueryWindowRect( hwnd, &rclRect );
            rclRect.xLeft += WinQuerySysValue(HWND_DESKTOP, SV_CXBORDER);
            rclRect.yTop -= WinQuerySysValue(HWND_DESKTOP, SV_CYBORDER);
            rclRect.xRight -= WinQuerySysValue(HWND_DESKTOP, SV_CXVSCROLL);
            rclRect.yBottom += WinQuerySysValue(HWND_DESKTOP, SV_CYBORDER) + 1;
            WinDrawBorder(hps,&rclRect,1,1,0l,0l,DB_DESTINVERT|DB_STANDARD);
            WinSetWindowULong( WinQueryWindow( hwnd, QW_OWNER ),
                               WL_EMPHASIZED, (LONG)FALSE );
            DrgReleasePS( hps );
        } /* endif */
    } /* endif */

    return MRFROMLONG( 0L );
}
```

Figure 7.28   Handling the DM_DROP message.

RENDERING OBJECTS

When the application-defined message posted during DM_DROP processing is received by the target's object window, the rendering stage of the drag-and-drop operation begins. During this stage, the target application processes each of the dragged objects, determines which of the available rendering formats to use, and performs the rendering operation according to the protocol for the selected mechanism. The DRM_OS2FILE mechanism protocol uses established direct manipulation messages to converse with the source and perform rendering. This mechanism is discussed in detail next. The DRM_DDE mechanism uses the standard DDE messages and protocol to perform the rendering. See Chapter 9 for a complete description of the DDE protocol. When the DRM_PRINT mechanism is selected, the target sends a DM_PRINTOBJECT message to the source after filling a PRINTDEST structure. The source is then expected to complete the rendering operation by printing the object or by directing the target to print the object. A target that supports the DRM_DELETE mechanism sends a DM_DELETEOBJECT message to the source. The source may either delete the object or request that the target perform the deletion. These are the predefined mechanisms—applications may define additional protocols; however, these will not be selected unless both the source and target applications are capable of supporting the mechanism.

Our examples have specified the DRM_OS2FILE mechanism. This mechanism allows objects to be rendered as common OS/2 file system files, a concept understood by most programmers. When this mechanism is used, the conversation between the source and target applications is conducted using messages native to the direct manipulation support. While the actual conversation varies depending on the exact actions required, the general flow of the conversation is:

1. If requested by the source application, the target sends a DM_RENDER PREPARE message to the source window. This allows the source to perform actions to prepare for the rendering operation. For example, the source may wish to create an object window to perform the operation; or, in the case of an editor, it may need to save a portion of the text to a file.
2. The target sends a DM_RENDER message to request that the source perform the rendering operation.
3. The source sends a DM_RENDERCOMPLETE message to the target to indicate that the rendering operation has been completed.
4. The target sends a DM_ENDCONVERSATION message to the source to indicate that no further action is necessary for the current object and that the source may release any resources it has allocated to perform the rendering of the object.

When the target application chooses DRM_OS2FILE as the rendering mechanism for a particular dropped object and DRM_OS2FILE is the native mechanism, it may choose to render the object itself without involvement from the source. This is possible if the source has provided all information necessary to complete the rendering operation. The primary requirement is that the source has provided both the *hstrContainerName* and *hstrSourceName* elements of the DRAGITEM structure for the object. Additionally, the target must be able to understand the native format and true type of the object. When these conditions are met, the target may perform the rendering operation and then send the DM_ENDCONVERSATION message without sending the DM_RENDER message.

If the conditions for target rendering are not met, or if the target chooses, a DM_RENDER message is sent to the source application to request that the source render the object. The source responds to this message indicating that:

it will perform the rendering; rendering cannot be performed; or the target should either perform the rendering or retry the operation. Since the source can elect the third option, the easiest course for a target application is to first request that the source render objects, and then if the source cannot perform the rendering, attempt to render the objects itself.

Figure 7.29 shows an example of the processing that a target application performs in response to the message to begin rendering of objects. The example application supports the DRM_OS2FILE mechanism. The routine first stores the DRAGINFO pointer in a global variable for later use. Normally, the **DrgQueryDraginfoPtrFromHwnd** or **DrgQueryDraginfoPtr-FromDragitem** API could be used to obtain the DRAGINFO pointer, but unfortunately, the original release of WARP has a nasty bug in the latter API, so a global variable is used instead. The routine allocates a counter and initializes it to the number of objects dropped. This counter will be decremented each time an object is rendered. When the count reaches zero, all of the objects have been rendered and the application can release its access to the DRAGINFO structure. A for loop is used to process each of the objects dragged. As each object is processed, the **DrgQueryDragitemPtr** API is used to obtain a pointer to the DRAGITEM structure for the object. A utility routine, **MakeXfer**, is then called to allocate and fill the DRAGTRANSFER structure for rendering the object.

After the DRAGTRANSFER structure is allocated and initialized, an attempt is made to allow the source to render the object. If the source has indicated that it needs to prepare for the rendering, a DM_RENDERPREPARE message is sent to the source and the conversation window handle is set to the value returned from the source as the *hwndItem* element of the DRAGITEM structure. A DM_RENDER message is then sent to the source using the **DrgSendTransferMsg** API. In addition to sending the message, this API gives the source access to the DRAGTRANSFER structure. If the response to DM_RENDER indicates that the source will perform the rendering operation, the target suspends processing of the current object until notified that the source has finished its processing.

The prototype of the DrgSendTransferMsg API is shown in Figure 7.30.

- The **hwnd** parameter specifies the handle of the window that is to receive the message.
- The **msg** parameter is the message to be sent.
- The **mp1** parameter is a value defined by the message being sent.
- The **mp2** parameter is a value defined by the message being sent.

DragSendTransferMsg returns FALSE if the message could not be sent to **hwnd**; otherwise, the MRESULT response from **hwnd** is returned. This API specifically addresses the requirements for sending messages involving DRAG-

```
HWND            hwndTarget = HWNDFROMMP(mp1);
HWND            hwndRender;
PDRAGINFO       pDraginfo = (PDRAGINFO)mp2;
PDRAGITEM       pDragitem = (PDRAGITEM)NULL;
USHORT          usDragitem = 0;
PUSHORT         pusToDo;
PDRAGTRANSFER   pDragXfer = (PDRAGTRANSFER)NULL;

gpDraginfo = pDraginfo;
pusToDo = (PUSHORT)malloc( sizeof(USHORT) );
*pusToDo = pDraginfo->cditem;
for( usDragitem = 0; usDragitem < pDraginfo-> cditem; usDragitem++ ) {
    pDragitem = DrgQueryDragitemPtr( pDraginfo, (ULONG)usDragitem );
    pDragXfer = MakeXfer(hwnd, pDragitem, pDraginfo->usOperation, pusToDo);
    hwndRender = pDraginfo->hwndSource;
    if( pDragitem->fsControl & DC_PREPARE ) {
        if(!DrgSendTransferMsg( pDraginfo->hwndSource, DM_RENDERPREPARE,
                                MPFROMP( pDragXfer ), MPFROMLONG( 0l ))) {
            KillXfer( pDragXfer );
            --(*pusToDo);
            continue;
        } /* endif */
        hwndRender = pDragitem->hwndItem;
    } /* endif */
    if( DrgSendTransferMsg ( hwndRender, DM_RENDER,
                             MPFROMP( pDragXfer), MPFROMLONG( 0l ))) {
        continue;
    } /* endif */
    if( pDragXfer->fsReply & DMFL_RENDERRETRY ) {
        /* no different ops supported - try target render */
    } /* endif */
    if (RenderFile( pDragXfer )) {
        DrgSendTransferMsg( hwndRender, DM_ENDCONVERSATION,
                MPFROMSHORT(usDragitem), MPFROMSHORT(DMFL_TARGETSUCCESSFUL));
    } else {
        DrgSendTransferMsg( hwndRender, DM_ENDCONVERSATION,
                MPFROMSHORT(usDragitem), MPFROMSHORT(DMFL_TARGETFAIL));
    } /* endif */
    KillXfer( pDragXfer );
    --(*pusToDo );
} /* endfor */
if( *pusToDo == 0 ) {
    free( pusToDo );
    DrgDeleteDraginfoStrHandles( pDraginfo );
    DrgFreeDraginfo( pDraginfo );
} /* endif */
}
```

Figure 7.29 **Target process to render objects.**

```
MRESULT APIENTRY DrgSendTransferMsg(HWND hwnd,
                                    ULONG msg,
                                    MPARAM mp1,
                                    MPARAM mp2);
```

Figure 7.30   The DrgSendTransferMsg prototype.

TRANSFER structures between applications by setting the *fsReply* element of the DRAGTRANSFER structure to zero and by giving access to the DRAG-TRANSFER structure to the source application when a DM_RENDER message is sent.

Continuing with Figure 7.29, if the source did not perform the rendering, the target application attempts to either retry the operation or render the object itself. If, following the DM_RENDER message, the DMFL_RENDERRETRY flag of the *fsReply* element of the DRAGTRANSFER structure is set, the target can change the rendering mechanism/format pair and then resend the DM_RENDER message. The application in the example opts to ignore the DMFL_RETRY flag and perform the rendering itself. Normally, this processing would only occur if the source had set the DMFL_NATIVERENDER flag in *fsReply*; however, some applications, most notably, the Workplace Shell, do not set this flag even when target rendering is possible. Thus the application ignores the *fsReply* field and calls a utility routine **Render-File** to perform the operation. If the rendering operation was successful, a DM_ENDCONVERSATION message is sent to the source, indicating that the rendering for this object is complete and allowing the source to release any resources dedicated to rendering the specified object. The DRAGTRANSFER structure is then released by routine **KillXfer** and the next object is processed. When all objects have been processed through the loop, if the current count of objects being rendered is zero, the counter itself is freed along with the DRAGINFO structures. If the count is not zero, the source is still in the process of rendering objects, so none of the items associated with the DRAGINFO structure is freed.

Routine MakeXfer is shown in Figure 7.31. This routine is responsible for allocating and initializing a DRAGTRANSFER structure for use in rendering an object. The routine uses the **DrgAllocDragtransfer** API to obtain the DRAGTRANSFER structure, which is then initialized to all zero values using the **memset** library function. Element *cb* is set to the size of the structure. Element *hwnd* is set to the handle of the object window which serves as the target window for the rendering conversation. A pointer to the DRAGITEM structure is stored in element *pditem*. The *hstrSelectedRMF* element is initialized to a string handle representing the DRM_OS2FILE mechanism and DRF_UNKNOWN file format, indicating that this application will accept any OS/2 file. The routine then obtains the name of the source file by querying the

```
static PDRAGTRANSFER MakeXfer( HWND hwnd, PDRAGITEM pdi,
                               USHORT usOp, PUSHORT pusToDo )
{
   PDRAGTRANSFER  pXfer;
   ULONG          len;
   PSZ            pszSource;
   PSZ            pszTarget;

   pXfer = DrgAllocDragtransfer( 1 );
   if( pXfer != (PDRAGTRANSFER)NULL ) {
      memset( pXfer, 0, sizeof( DRAGTRANSFER ));
      pXfer->cb = sizeof( DRAGTRANSFER );
      pXfer->hwndClient = hwnd;
      pXfer->pditem = pdi;
      pXfer->hstrSelectedRMF = DrgAddStrHandle("<DRM_OS2FILE,DRF_UNKNOWN>");
      len = DrgQueryStrNameLen( pdi->hstrSourceName ) + 1;
      pszSource = (PSZ)malloc(len);
      DrgQueryStrName( pdi->hstrSourceName, len, pszSource );
      pszTarget = _fullpath( NULL, pszSource, _MAX_PATH );
      pXfer->hstrRenderToName = DrgAddStrHandle( pszTarget );
      free( pszSource );
      free( pszTarget );
      pXfer->ulTargetInfo = (ULONG)pusToDo;
      pXfer->usOperation = usOp;
      } /* endif */
   return pXfer;
}
```

Figure 7.31   Initializing the DRAGTRANSFER structure.

string associated with *hstrSourcename* in the DRAGITEM structure and calling the **_fullpath** function to append the name to the current directory, forming the full path name of the target file. This string is then converted to a string handle and stored in the *hstrRenderToName* element of the DRAGTRANSFER structure. The memory allocated to hold the source and target names is then freed. The *ulTargetInfo* element is set to a pointer to the count of items to render, allowing the DM_RENDERCOMPLETE message processing to access this element and free the resources used for the drag operation when the render count goes to zero. The initialization is completed by setting the *usOperation* element to the current drag operation. The function returns a pointer to the DRAGTRANSFER structure.

When the application is finished with the DRAGTRANSFER structure, routine **KillXfer**, shown in Figure 7.32, is called to release the resources associated with the transfer operation. The routine first uses the **DrgDeleteStrHandle** function to free the string handles stored in the *hstrSelectedRMF* and *hstrRenderToName* elements. The DRAGTRANSFER structure is then freed by calling the **DrgFreeDragtransfer** API.

```
static void KillXfer( PDRAGTRANSFER pDragXfer )
{
   if (pDragXfer->hstrSelectedRMF != (HSTR)NULL)
      DrgDeleteStrHandle( pDragXfer->hstrSelectedRMF );
   if (pDragXfer->hstrRenderToName != (HSTR)NULL)
      DrgDeleteStrHandle( pDragXfer->hstrRenderToName );
   DrgFreeDragtransfer( pDragXfer );
}
```

Figure 7.32   **Releasing the DRAGTRANSFER structure.**

When the rendering is performed by the source, the target must wait to complete the rendering operation and free the resources until a DM_RENDER COMPLETE message is received from the source. If this message indicates that the source failed to render the object, the target may attempt to retry the operation, provided the source indicates retries are allowed. Otherwise, if the target chooses not to retry a failed operation or if the operation was successful, the target should perform any additional processing required to complete the rendering, send a DM_ENDCONVERSATION message to the source, and then free any resources it has allocated to handle the rendering of the object. This processing is shown in Figure 7.33. Since this application is not concerned about retries, the function first posts the DM_ENDCONVERSATION message to the source. A pointer to the count of items to render is then obtained

```
MRESULT dm_rendercomplete( HWND hwnd, ULONG msg, MPARAM mp1, MPARAM mp2 )
{
   PDRAGTRANSFER      pDragXfer = (PDRAGTRANSFER)PVOIDFROMMP( mp1 );
   USHORT             usFlags = SHORT1FROMMP( mp2 );
   PUSHORT            pusToDo;
   PDRAGINFO          pDraginfo;

   WinPostMsg( pDragXfer->pditem->hwndItem, DM_ENDCONVERSATION,
            MPFROMLONG(pDragXfer->pditem->ulItemID),
            MPFROMSHORT(DMFL_TARGETSUCCESSFUL));
   pusToDo = (PUSHORT)pDragXfer->ulTargetInfo;
   KillXfer( pDragXfer );
   if( --(*pusToDo) == 0 ) {
      free( pusToDo );
      pDraginfo = DrgQueryDraginfoPtrFromDragitem( pDragXfer->pditem );
      DrgDeleteDraginfoStrHandles( pDraginfo );
      DrgFreeDraginfo( pDraginfo );
   } /* endif */
   return (MRESULT)0L;
}
```

Figure 7.33   **Handling the DM_RENDERCOMPLETE message.**

from the *ulTargetInfo* element of the DRAGTRANSFER structure before that structure is freed by calling **KillXfer**. The number of items is decremented, and if this item was the last item, a pointer to the DRAGINFO structure for the entire drag operation is obtained. The **DrgDeleteDraginfoStrHandles** API is called to release all string handles associated with the operation, and then **DrgFreeDraginfo** is called to release the DRAGINFO structure, completing the target's processing of the direct manipulation operation.

The source application processing to handle the rendering operation is shown in Figure 7.34. As shown by this routine, the source application's processing should determine if the requested rendering can be performed. If not, the *fsReply* element of the DRAGTRANSFER structure is set to an appropriate value and FALSE is returned. If the source can handle the rendering, it returns TRUE after initiating the operation—the rendering operation is not performed while processing the DM_RENDER message from the target application.

The routine in Figure 7.34 first presets the *fsReply* element to zero to indicate that if the rendering operation cannot be performed, the target is not allowed to retry the operation. The routine then verifies that a target file name

```
static MRESULT dm_render( HWND hwnd, ULONG msg, MPARAM mp1, MPARAM mp2 )
{
    HWND            hwndMain = WinQueryWindow( hwnd, QW_OWNER );
    HWND            hwndObj = WinQueryWindowULong( hwndMain, WL_HWNDOBJECT );
    PDRAGTRANSFER   pDT;
    MRESULT         mrRetVal = (MRESULT)FALSE;
    ULONG           cRMF;
    PSZ             pszRMF;

    do {
        pDT->fsReply = 0;
        if (pDT->hstrRenderToName == (HSTR)NULLHANDLE) break;
        if (pDT->hstrSelectedRMF == (HSTR)NULLHANDLE) break;
        if (pDT->usOperation != DO_COPY && pDT->usOperation != DO_MOVE ) break;
        pDT->fsReply = DMFL_RENDERRETRY;
        if ((cRMF = DrgQueryStrNameLen( pDT->hstrSelectedRMF )) == 0) break;
        if ((pszRMF = (PSZ)malloc(++cRMF)) == (PSZ)NULL) break;
        if (DrgQueryStrName(pDT->hstrSelectedRMF, cRMF, pszRMF) == 0) break;
        if (!strstr( pszRMF, "DRM_OS2FILE" || !strstr( pszRMF, "DRF_UNKNOWN"))
            break;
        WinPostMsg( hwndObj, UM_RENDER, mp1, mp2 );
        pDT->fsReply = 0;
        mrRetVal = (MRESULT)TRUE;
    } while ( FALSE ); /* enddo */
    if( !mrRetVal ) DrgFreeDragtransfer( pDT );
    return mrRetVal;
}
```

Figure 7.34 Handling the DM_RENDER message.

and RMF value are specified and that the rendering operation is supported. If not, the function immediately returns—the operation cannot be performed. Otherwise, *fsReply* is preset to indicate that the target can either perform native rendering itself or retry the operation—indicating that the source does not support the requested rendering mechanism or format. The string associated with the *hstrSelectedRMF* element of the DRAGTRANSFER structure is then obtained and checked for the DRM_OS2FILE rendering mechanism since this application only deals with files. The RMF string is then checked to ensure that the rendering format is DRF_UNKNOWN—this application does not know and cannot change the internal format of the file; thus, DRF_UNKNOWN is the only supported format. If the RMF is supported, the routine posts a message to an object window to actually perform the rendering. The **fsReply** field is set to zero—since no target rendering is necessary—and the result code is set to TRUE. As the routine exits, if the result code is FALSE, the DRAGTRANSFER structure is freed as it will no longer be used. If the result code is TRUE, access to the DRAGTRANSFER structure is maintained for use by the object window procedure.

Figure 7.35 shows the processing that the object window uses to perform the actual rendering operation. As an alternative to the normal method of allocating string handle string buffers, this function preallocates fixed-length character buffers then verifies that the string handle strings will fit in the buffers. The function first obtains the string associated with the *hstrRender-ToName* element of the DRAGTRANSFER structure as the target name of the file and then obtains the source file directory and name from the *hstrCon-tainerName* and *hstrSourceName* elements of the DRAGITEM structure. These two are concatenated to form the full path name of the source file. The function then uses the **DosCopy** API to copy the source file to the target file. If the rendering operation was a move, **DosDelete** is called to delete the source file. Note that the **DosMove** API is not used, because it does not allow movement between different drives. If no errors have occurred, the return value is changed from its preset value of DMFL_RENDERFAIL to DMFL_RENDEROK, and the DMFL_RENDERRETRY flag is set so that the target can try again if it cannot complete the rendering. A DM_RENDERCOMPLETE message is then posted to the target with the return value and the DRAGTRANSFER structure is released.

When the target application receives the DM_RENDERCOMPLETE message, it should respond with a DM_ENDCONVERSATION message. This message informs the source that the rendering operation for a given target is complete and any resources allocated to support the rendering can be released. For example, a word processor might store a portion of a document in a temporary file during the rendering. When the DM_ENDCONVERSATION message is received, the temporary file can be deleted. Figure 7.36 shows the code used by the example application we have been studying. This function

```
static MRESULT dm_render( HWND hwnd, ULONG msg, MPARAM mp1, MPARAM mp2 )
{
    PDRAGTRANSFER       pDT = (PDRAGTRANSFER)PVOIDFROMMP(mp1);
    char                pszSource[ CCHMAXPATH ];
    char                pszTarget[ CCHMAXPATH ];
    char                pszSourceDir[ CCHMAXPATHCOMP ];
    char                pszSourceFile[ CCHMAXPATHCOMP ];
    ULONG               cString;
    USHORT              usRetVal = DMFL_RENDERFAIL;

    do {
        if ((cString = DrgQueryStrNameLen( pDT->hstrRenderToName )) >=
                CCHMAXPATH) break;
        DrgQueryStrName( pDT->hstrRenderToName, ++cString, pszTarget);
        if ((cString = DrgQueryStrNameLen( pDT->pditem->hstrContainerName)) >=
                CCHMAXPATHCOMP ) break;
        DrgQueryStrName( pDT->pditem->hstrContainerName, ++cString,
                            pszSourceDir);
        if ((cString = DrgQueryStrNameLen( pDT->pditem->hstrSourceName)) >=
                CCHMAXPATHCOMP ) break;
        DrgQueryStrName( pDT->pditem->hstrSourceName, ++cString,
                pszSourceFile);
        if (strlen(pszSourceFile) + strlen(pszSourceFile) + 1 > CCHMAXPATH)
            break;

        strcpy( pszSource, pszSourceDir );
        strcat( pszSource, pszSourceFile );
        if (DosCopy( pszSource, pszTarget, DCPY_EXISTING) != NO_ERROR) break;
        if (pDT->usOperation == DO_MOVE)
            if (DosDelete(pszSource) != NO_ERROR) break;

        usRetVal = DMFL_RENDEROK | DMFL_RENDERRETRY;
    } while ( FALSE ); /* enddo */
    DrgPostTransferMsg( pDT->hwndClient, DM_RENDERCOMPLETE, pDT,
                    (ULONG)usRetVal, 0L, TRUE );
    DrgFreeDragtransfer( pDT );
    return (MRESULT)0L;
}
```

Figure 7.35   Source application object rendering.

```
static MRESULT dm_endconversation( HWND hwnd, ULONG msg,
                                    MPARAM mp1, MPARAM mp2 )
{
    if( --gulDragCount == 0 ) {
        DrgFreeDraginfo( gpSrcDinfo );
    }
    return MRFROMLONG(0L);
}
```

Figure 7.36   Handling the DM_ENDCONVERSATION message.

decrements the global count established when the drag operation was initiated. When the count reaches zero, indicating that all items have been rendered, **DrgFreeDraginfo** is called to release the source application's access to the structure pointed to by the global pointer stored when the direct manipulation operation was started. Deletion of the associated string handles is left to the target application.

This completes the coding for the drag-and-drop direct manipulation function. In the next section we will see how to modify this code to include support for the pickup-and-drop, or lazy drag operation.

SUPPORTING PICKUP AND DROP

While the new OS/2 WARP pickup-and-drop direct manipulation uses the same basic structure as drag and drop, some modifications are required due to the new APIs that are provided to implement this feature. This section details the additions and changes necessary to add pickup-and-drop support to the examples used in our discussion of drag and drop.

Pickup-and-drop operations can be initiated by pointing device button clicks or by menu selection, which will be discussed later. When the proper pointing device click is received, PM sends a WM_PICKUP message to the application window. Parameter **mp1** provides the pointing device coordinates at the time of the click. Parameter **mp2** is not used. This message corresponds to the WM_BEGINDRAG message of the drag-and-drop operation. Rather than coding a whole new routine to initiate an operation when WM_PICKUP is received, the initiation code can be moved to a separate function which is called by both the WM_BEGINDRAG and WM_PICKUP message processing. The new message processing routines are shown in Figure 7.37. Each routine calls the initiation routine passing the window handle, and a flag that is set to TRUE if a pickup-and-drop operation has been requested.

```
MRESULT wm_begindrag( HWND hwnd, ULONG msg, MPARAM mp1, MPARAM mp2 )
{
    StartDragOp( hwnd, FALSE );
    return (MRESULT)TRUE;
}

MRESULT wm_pickup( HWND hwnd, ULONG msg, MPARAM mp1, MPARAM mp2)
{
    StartDragOp( hwnd, TRUE );
    return (MRESULT)TRUE;
}
```

Figure 7.37   Handling the WM_PICKUP message.

The **StartDragOp** function is the original WM_BEGINDRAG processing function modified to support pickup-and-drop, or lazy drag, operations. Only two major changes are required. First, if a lazy drag has been requested, the **DrgLazyDrag** API must be called to initiate the operation. Second, additional objects can be added to a lazy drag object set after the operation is initiated. When this occurs, the DRAGINFO structure must first be reallocated and then **DrgLazyDrag** must again be called to restart the operation with the new set of objects.

Figure 7.38 shows the **StartDragOp** function with the major changes highlighted in boldface type. The first change is the inclusion of a new Boolean variable that indicates when the DRAGINFO structure must be updated to add new objects during a pickup-and-drop operation. The second change occurs at the point where the DRAGINFO structure is normally allocated. Now, if the request is for a pickup-and-drop operation and an operation is already in progress, the existing DRAGINFO structure is queried. If the structure belongs to a different window, the operation is cancelled since pickup from multiple windows is not currently allowed. Otherwise, the reallocation flag is set to indicate that an item is being added to the current set. If no operation is currently in progress, the code follows the previous path and allocates a new DRAGINFO structure. The next change involves modifications to the **SetDragItems** function call. The first parameter has been changed to a pointer to the location where the DRAGINFO structure pointer is stored, allowing the routine to reallocate the structure as necessary and pass back the new value; an additional parameter has been added to indicate to the function when reallocation is required. The final change in **StartDragOp** occurs at the point where the operation is initiated. If a lazy drag has been requested, **DrgLazyDrag** is called instead of **DrgDrag**.

The prototype for the DrgLazyDrag API is shown in Figure 7.39.

- The **hwndSource** parameter is the window handle of the source window for the operation, normally the window that received the WM_PICKUP message.
- The **pdinfo** parameter is a pointer to the DRAGINFO structure and associated DRAGITEM structures which convey the information necessary to complete the drag-and-drop operation.
- The **pdimg** parameter is a pointer to a DRAGIMAGE structure or array of DRAGIMAGE structures. This parameter is provided to maintain compatibility with the **DrgDrag** API but is not used for image display during lazy drag operations.
- The **cdimg** parameter indicates the number of DRAGIMAGE structures in the array pointed to by **pdimg**.
- The **pRsvd** parameter is reserved and must be set to NULL.

```
void StartDragOp( HWND hwnd, BOOL fLazy )
{
    ULONG       cFiles;
    DRAGIMAGE   dImage;
    PDRAGINFO   pDinfo = NULL;
    HWND        hwndDest;
    SHORT       sItem = LIT_FIRST;
    BOOL        fLazyRealloc = FALSE;

    do {
        if ((cFiles = QuerySelectionCount( hwnd )) == 0) break;
        if (fLazy && DrgQueryDragStatus() == DGS_LAZYDRAGINPROGRESS) {
            pDinfo = DrgQueryDraginfoPtrFromHwnd(hwnd);
            if (pDinfo == NULL) break;
            fLazyRealloc = TRUE;
        } else {          /* do drag and drop */
            if ((pDinfo = DrgAllocDraginfo( cFiles )) == (PDRAGINFO)(NULL))
                break;
        } /* endif */
        SetDragItems( &pDinfo, hwnd, cFiles, fLazyRealloc );
        memset( &dImage, 0, sizeof(DRAGIMAGE));
        dImage.cb = sizeof(DRAGIMAGE);
        dImage.fl = DRG_ICON;
        dImage.hImage = (LHANDLE)WinQuerySysPointer( HWND_DESKTOP,
                                cFiles == 1 ? SPTR_FILE : SPTR_MULTFILE,
                                FALSE );
        gulDragCount = pDinfo->cditem;
        gpSrcDinfo = pDinfo;
        if (fLazy) {
            DrgLazyDrag( hwnd, pDinfo, &dImage, 1, 0L );
        } else {
            hwndDest = DrgDrag( hwnd, pDinfo, &dImage, 1, VK_ENDDRAG, NULL );
            if (hwndDest == NULLHANDLE ) {
                DrgDeleteDraginfoStrHandles( pDinfo );
                DrgFreeDraginfo( pDinfo );
            } /* endif */
        } /* endif */
    } while ( false ); /* enddo */
}
```

Figure 7.38 The StartDragOp function.

```
BOOL APIENTRY DrgLazyDrag( HWND hwndSource,
                           PDRAGINFO pdinfo,
                           PDRAGIMAGE pdimg,
                           ULONG cdimg,
                           PVOID pRsvd );
```

Figure 7.39 The DrgLazyDrag prototype.

The **DrgLazyDrag** API returns TRUE if the drag operation is successfully initiated and FALSE if an error occurs. Unlike the **DrgDrag** API, which initiates a modal operation and does not return until the dragged objects are dropped, **DrgLazyDrag** returns immediately after starting the drag as a modeless operation.

The new **SetDragItems** routine is shown in Figure 7.40. As noted, the parameters to the routine have changed to pass a pointer to the location of the pointer to the DRAGINFO structure and a flag, which indicates that a lazy drag is in progress and reallocation of the DRAGINFO structure may be necessary. Three internal changes are necessary. First, when a lazy drag is in progress, routine **GetItemForFile** is called to determine if the new object is already in the drag set; and, if so, the object is skipped—no need to drag the same object twice. Later, before the object is added to the drag set, if a lazy drag is already in progress, routine **ReallocDragInfo** is called to reallocate the DRAGINFO structure and maintain the set of DRAGITEM structures. The final change is the addition of the *litem* variable. This value is used to track the actual item number to be inserted into the DRAGINFO structure since the object count in *cFiles* is no longer directly related to the number of DRAGITEMs associated with the DRAGINFO structure.

The code for routine **GetItemForFile** is shown in Figure 7.41. This function scans the DRAGITEMs associated with a DRAGINFO structure to determine if a particular object is a member of the set of dragged objects. Within the loop that enumerates each item, a pointer to the current item is obtained by calling **DrgQueryDragitemPtr**. **DrgQueryStrNameLen** and **DrgQueryStrName** are then called to retrieve the name of the object associated with the DRAGITEM. The C library function **strcmp** is used to determine if the object name matches the requested name; if so, the loop exits. When the loop terminates, a check is made to determine if a valid item was found; if so, the item number is returned; if not, the value −1 is returned.

The code for routine **ReallocDraginfo** is shown in Figure 7.42. This routine is used to perform reallocation of the DRAGINFO structure when items are added to the dragged set during a pickup-and-drop operation. Unfortunately, PM does not automatically copy the DRAGITEM set when reallocating the structure, so the application must either maintain a separate list of the objects comprising the drag set or, as shown here, retrieve the DRAGITEM structures before reallocating the DRAGINFO structure. **ReallocDraginfo** first allocates sufficient memory to hold the DRAGITEMs currently associated with the DRAGINFO structure, and then copies them from the DRAGINFO using the **DrgQueryDragitem** API. When all the items have been retrieved, **DrgReallocDraginfo** is called to associate an additional DRAGITEM with the DRAGINFO structure. The saved DRAGITEMs are then reassociated with the DRAGINFO structure by calling **DrgSetDragitem**. After freeing the memory, the function returns.

```
void SetDragItems( PDRAGINFO *ppDinfo, HWND hwnd, ULONG cFiles, BOOL fLazy )
{
    SHORT       sItem;
    SHORT       cbItem;
    PSZ         pszFileName;
    PSZ         pszType;
    PSZ         pszContainer;
    DRAGITEM    dItem;
    ULONG       litem;
    PDRAGINFO   pDinfo = *ppDinfo;

    memset( &dItem, 0, sizeof(DRAGITEM));
    dItem.hstrRMF = DrgAddStrHandle( SUPPORTED_RMF );
    dItem.hwndItem = hwnd;
    dItem.fsSupportedOps = DO_COPYABLE | DO_MOVEABLE;
    litem = 0;
    sItem = LIT_FIRST;
    while ((sItem = SHORT1FROMMR( WinSendMsg( hwnd, LM_QUERYSELECTION,
                        MPFROMSHORT( sItem ), 0L ))) != LIT_NONE ) {
        cbItem = SHORT1FROMMR( WinSendMsg( hwnd, LM_QUERYITEMTEXTLENGTH,
                        MPFROMSHORT( sItem ), 0L ));
        cbItem++;
        if ((pszFileName = (PSZ)malloc( cbItem )) != (PSZ)NULL) {
            WinSendMsg( hwnd, LM_QUERYITEMTEXT,
                    MPFROM2SHORT( sItem, cbItem ), pszFileName );
            if (!fLazy || GetItemForFile( pDinfo, pszFileName) == -1) {
                dItem.hstrSourceName = dItem.hstrTargetName =
                                        DrgAddStrHandle( pszFileName );
                if ((pszType = QueryType( pszFileName )) != NULL) {
                    dItem.hstrType = DrgAddStrHandle( pszType );
                    free( pszType );
                } else {
                    dItem.hstrType = NULLHANDLE;
                } /* endif */
                if ((pszContainer = QueryCurrentDirectory()) != NULL) {
                    dItem.hstrContainerName = DrgAddStrHandle( pszContainer );
                    free( pszContainer );
                } else {
                    dItem.hstrContainerName = NULLHANDLE;
                } /* endif */
                if (fLazy) {
                    *ppDinfo = pDinfo = ReallocDraginfo( pDinfo );
                    litem = pDinfo->cditem - 1;
                } /* endif */
                DrgSetDragitem( pDinfo, &dItem, sizeof( DRAGITEM ), litem++ );
            } /* endif */
            free( pszFileName );
        } /* endif */
        --cFiles;
    } /* endwhile */
    return;
}
```

Figure 7.40 Modified SetDragItems routine.

```
SHORT GetItemForFile( PDRAGINFO pDinfo, PSZ pszFileName )
{
    SHORT       item;
    PSZ         pszSource;
    ULONG       cbSource;
    PDRAGITEM   pDitem;

    for (item = 0; item < pDinfo->cditem; item++) {
        pDitem = DrgQueryDragitemPtr( pDinfo, item );
        cbSource = DrgQueryStrNameLen( pDitem->hstrSourceName );
        pszSource = (PSZ)malloc( ++cbSource );
        DrgQueryStrName( pDitem->hstrSourceName, cbSource, pszSource );
        if( !strcmp( pszFileName, pszSource )) break;
    } /* endfor */
    if( item == pDinfo->cditem ) item = -1;
    return item;
}
```

Figure 7.41   Determining presence of a file in a drag set.

Post-Drop Notification

When a pickup-and-drop operation is in progress and the objects are dropped
or the operation is cancelled, the source application receives a DM_DROPNOTI-
FY message. Parameter **mp1** of this message is the DRAGINFO pointer for the
drag operation, and parameter **mp2** is the handle of the target window. The
OS/2 documentation indicates that the application should free the DRAGINFO
structure when this message is received. The apparent intent is that the **Drg-
QueryDraginfoPtrFromHwnd** and **DrgQueryDraginfoPtrFromDragitem** APIs

```
PDRAGINFO ReallocDraginfo( PDRAGINFO pDinfo )
{
    PDRAGITEM   pdItem;
    ULONG       cdItem = pDinfo->cditem;
    ULONG       iItem;

    pdItem = (PDRAGITEM)malloc(cdItem * sizeof(DRAGITEM));
    for (iItem = 0; iItem < cdItem; iItem++)
        DrgQueryDragitem( pDinfo, sizeof(DRAGITEM), &pdItem[iItem], iItem );
    pDinfo = DrgReallocDraginfo( pDinfo, cdItem + 1 );
    for (iItem = 0; iItem < cdItem; iItem++)
        DrgSetDragitem( pDinfo, &pdItem[iItem], sizeof(DRAGITEM), iItem );
    free(pdItem);
    return pDinfo;
}
```

Figure 7.42   Reallocating the DRAGINFO structure.

should be used to obtain the address of the DRAGINFO structure during the rendering operations. Unfortunately, the bug in the latter of these APIs makes this impossible. The method shown earlier of storing the object count and releasing the DRAGINFO structure when DM_ENDCONVERSATION messages have been received for all objects should be used until this bug is resolved. However, if the DM_DROPNOTIFY message is received with parameter **mp2** set to NULLHANDLE, the DRAGINFO structure should be released by calling **DrgFreeDraginfo** since no post-drop conversation will occur. Note that neither the target application drop procedures nor the rendering operations require any changes for pickup-and-drop support.

Menu Support for Pickup and Drop

As mentioned at the beginning of this section, a pickup-and-drop operation can also be initiated from a menu choice. Applications that provide this choice normally include additional items to support dropping objects and cancelling the operation. Figure 7.43 shows the WM_COMMAND message routine which

```
MRESULT wm_command( HWND hwnd, ULONG msg, MPARAM mp1, MPARAM mp2 )
{
    POINTL      ptl = {0,0};
    PDRAGINFO   pdi;

    switch (SHORT1FROMMP(mp1)) {
    case MID_PICKUP:
        WinSendMsg( hwnd, WM_PICKUP, MPFROMP(&ptl), MPFROMLONG(0L));
        break;
    case MID_DROPCOPY:
        if ((pdi = DrgQueryDraginfoPtr(NULL)) != NULL ) {
            DrgAccessDraginfo( pdi );
            DrgLazyDrop( hwnd, DO_COPY, &ptl );
        } /* endif */
        break;
    case MID_DROPMOVE:
        if ((pdi = DrgQueryDraginfoPtr(NULL)) != NULL ) {
            DrgAccessDraginfo( pdi );
            DrgLazyDrop( hwnd, DO_MOVE, &ptl );
        } /* endif */
        break;
    case MID_CANCEL:
        DrgCancelLazyDrag( );
        break;
    } /* endswitch */
    return MRFROMLONG(0L);
}
```

Figure 7.43   Handling pickup-and-drop menu items.

supports these menu items for the listbox application we have been using for a sample.

The MID_PICKUP menu emulates the pointing device click to initiate the lazy drag operation by sending a WM_PICKUP message. Since the position is not important, parameter **mp1** points to a POINTL structure containing coordinates (0, 0).

The MID_DROPCOPY and MID_DROPMOVE items indicate that the user is requesting that the current set of objects be dropped. MID_DROPCOPY indicates that a copy operation is desired, and MID_DROPMOVE indicates that a move operation is desired. The processing for these items first queries the current DRAGINFO structure. If one exists, indicating that a drag operation is in progress, access to the DRAGINFO structure is obtained and API **DrgLazy-Drop** is called to perform the drop operation. The prototype for this API is given in Figure 7.44.

- The **hwndTarget** parameter is the handle of the window that is to serve as the target of the drag operation, normally the client window of the application.
- The **ulOperation** parameter indicates the operation to be performed. Valid values for this parameter are the same as those for the *usOperation* element of the DRAGINFO structure.
- The **pptlDrop** parameter is a pointer to a POINTL structure indicating the desired drop coordinates.

DrgLazyDrop returns TRUE if the drop is successful or FALSE if an error occurs. Be sure to access the DRAGINFO structure before calling this API; otherwise a trap will occur if the source and target windows are not part of the same application.

The MID_CANCEL item indicates that the user wishes to cancel the current pickup-and-drop operation. This request is fulfilled by calling the **DrgCancel-LazyDrag** API. This API requires no parameters, returns TRUE if the operation is successfully cancelled, and returns FALSE if an error occurs.

Direct Manipulation Summary

This completes the discussion of the direct manipulation features. These features provide the user with a powerful, yet easy-to-use means of manipulating

```
BOOL APIENTRY DrgLazyDrop( HWND hwndTarget,
                           ULONG ulOperation,
                           PPOINTL pptlDrop );
```

Figure 7.44   The DrgLazyDrop prototype.

objects, and they are applicable to most applications. The programming requirements may initially seem quite complex; but the effort to understand and implement these features will be handsomely rewarded with applications that are easy to use and that integrate well with the standard operations of the OS/2 Workplace Shell.

INITIALIZATION FILES

Another of the important features of the Workplace Shell, which applications should provide, is its ability to maintain the state of applications and the entire system between invocations, including a complete shutdown of the system. Contrary to what many think, very little of the work required to implement this feature is actually performed by the Workplace Shell, which primarily maintains a list of the objects that were open at the time of shutdown, and restarts or reopens these objects when the system is rebooted. The data required for an object or application to restore its size and position on the screen and, in some instances, other aspects of its termination state, must be maintained by the object or application.

There are a number of avenues open to applications for storing the necessary information. Applications that process private data file formats may store the required information within the data file. Word processors and spreadsheets often use this technique to return the user to the same location in the file and reestablish options when a file is opened. Applications that process common format files, such as ASCII text, can accomplish this same type of functionality by storing the required information in the data file's extended attributes. Private configuration files can also be used by applications for storing global options and other restart information. This method would not normally be used for storing information about individual data files since the application would need to provide functionality for removing information for data files that are no longer available.

OS/2, PM, and the Workplace Shell, along with the Workplace Shell objects and many OS/2 applications, use configuration files of a specific type called initialization, or INI, files to store their internal state information. These files have a defined structure for storing and organizing variable length data, and a set of APIs is provided that allow applications to store and retrieve specific data records. Internally, OS/2 uses two INI files, known as the USER and SYSTEM INI files. The names of the files are established in the system CONFIG.SYS file by setting the environment variables USER_INI for the USER file and SYSTEM_INI for the SYSTEM file. Applications may use either of these files or create private INI files of their own, though, as a rule, applications should use the USER INI file, not the SYSTEM INI file, for private variables.

Data in the initialization files is organized into named sections. The section name is referred to as the application name since an application will normally, but not necessarily, store all of its data within one section. The records within each section are stored as tuples in the form name = value. The name portion of the tuple, known as the key name, is an ASCII string that the application must specify when accessing the record. Key names are unique; when the application stores data and specifies a key name that already exists, the value portion of the tuple is overwritten with the new data. The value portion of the tuple may be in the form of either an ASCII string or binary data.

In this section we will examine the code required to use initialization files to save and restore an application's primary window size and position. We will also see how the application can store and retrieve additional data to restore its internal state.

Restoring the Window State

PM provides two specific API's for saving and restoring the size and position of a window. These APIs also store and retrieve the presentation parameters associated with the window, allowing an application to easily maintain its fonts and colors. These APIs access the USER initialization file.

The **WinStoreWindowPos** API is used to store the window state. In many cases this API is called during an application's WM_CLOSE processing to save the final state of the window for restoration when the application is next invoked. Another popular method is to provide a menu item that allows the user to specify when the window state should be saved. The prototype for the API is given in Figure 7.45.

- The **pszAppName** parameter is the name of the application key under which the window state information is to be stored.
- The **pszKeyName** parameter is the name of the key under which the window state information is to be stored.
- The **hwnd** parameter is the handle of the window whose state is to be saved.

WinStoreWindowPos returns TRUE if successful or FALSE if an error occurred.

Figure 7.46 shows the WM_CLOSE message processing for the example program from the direct manipulation discussion. This application uses **Win-CreateStdWindow** to create a frame window and a listbox window in the client

```
BOOL APIENTRY WinStoreWindowPos( PSZ  pszAppName,
                                 PSZ  pszKeyName,
                                 HWND hwnd );
```

Figure 7.45 The WinStoreWindowPos prototype.

```
#define INIAPPNAME    "SAMPLE"
#define INIFRMPOSKEY "FRAMEPOS"
#define INILBXPOSKEY "LISBOXPOS"

MRESULT wm_close( HWND hwnd, ULONG msg, MPARAM mp1, MPARAM mp2 )
{
   HWND   hwndParent = WinQueryWindow( hwnd, QW_PARENT);

   WinStoreWindowPos( INIAPPNAME, INIFRMPOSKEY, hwndParent );
   WinStoreWindowPos( INIAPPNAME, INILBXPOSKEY, hwnd );
   return pLBDefProc( hwnd, msg, mp1, mp2 );
}
```

Figure 7.46   Saving the window size and position.

area of the frame. The sample code saves the positioning and presentation parameters of each of these windows. The initialization file application and key names are predefined so that they may be easily reused when the window positions are restored. The **wm_close** function is called when the WM_CLOSE message is received by the client area listbox. The function first obtains the window handle of the frame window by querying the listbox window's parent. The position and presentation parameters of the frame window and its controls are then stored with the key name defined by INIFRMPOSKEY. The data for the listbox and its controls are stored under the key name defined by INILBXPOSKEY. The normal listbox window procedure is then called to complete the WM_CLOSE processing.

After the window data has been saved, the application can call the **WinRestoreWindowPos** API to return the window to the saved state. This function is normally called at application startup to restore the state of the window when the application was last terminated. Some applications also provide menu items or other input mechanisms that allow the user to specifically request that the window be returned to its saved state. The prototype of the **WinRestoreWindowPos** API is defined as shown in Figure 7.47.

- The **pszAppName** parameter is a pointer to a zero-terminated array of characters containing the application name under which the window state was saved.
- The **pszKeyName** parameter is a pointer to a zero-terminated array of characters containing the key under which the window state was saved.

```
BOOL APIENTRY WinRestoreWindowPos(  PSZ pszAppName,
                                    PSZ pszKeyName,
                                    HWND hwnd );
```

Figure 7.47   The WinRestoreWindowPos prototype.

- The **hwnd** parameter is a handle to the window whose state is to be restored.

WinRestoreWindowPos returns TRUE if the state is successfully restored or FALSE if an error occurs.

Coding that can be used to restore the window position when the application is started is shown in Figure 7.48. This code is a segment of the application and window initialization code normally found in the application's main routine. The **WinCreateStdWindow** call is the usual, except that the WS_VISIBLE style is not set to prevent the window from being displayed prior to the state restoration. After the frame and client windows have been created, **WinRestoreWindowPos** is called to restore the state of the frame window and then the listbox control window that acts as this application's client area. The windows' states are then changed to visible using the **WinShowWindow** API. Last, the system's active window is set to the frame window by calling **WinSetActiveWindow**. If this last step is not executed, focus will not be given to the application when it is started from a Workplace Shell icon.

Accessing Initialization Files

APIs are also available that allow applications to store additional information in the USER, the SYSTEM, or private initialization files. In order to access an initialization file, an application must have a handle for the file. The standard INI files have predefined constant handles; HINI_USERPROFILE is the handle to the USER initialization file, HINI_SYSTEMPROFILE is the handle to the SYSTEM initialization file, and HINI_PROFILE is a pseudo handle that accesses both the USER and SYSTEM files when reading, and accesses the USER file when writing. Applications obtain a handle to a private initialization file by calling the **PrfOpen** API. This API is prototyped as shown in Figure 7.49.

```
hwndFrame = WinCreateStdWindow( HWND_DESKTOP,
                                OL,
                                &flStyle,
                                WC_LISTBOX,
                                "Sample Application",
                                LS_MULTIPLESEL | LS_EXTENDEDSEL,
                                NULLHANDLE,
                                RID_APPLICATION,
                                &hwndClient );
if (hwndFrame == NULLHANDLE) break;
WinRestoreWindowPos( INIAPPNAME, INIFRMPOSKEY, hwndFrame );
WinRestoreWindowPos( INIAPPNAME, INILBXPOSKEY, hwndClient );
WinShowWindow( hwndFrame, TRUE );
WinSetActiveWindow( HWND_DESKTOP, hwndFrame );
```

Figure 7.48 Restoring the window size and position.

```
HINI APIENTRY PrfOpenProfile(HAB hab,
                             PSZ pszFileName);
```

Figure 7.49 The PrfOpenProfile prototype.

- The **hab** parameter is the anchor block handle for the application. This handle is provided by the **WinInitialize** API or may be queried with the **WinQueryAnchorBlock** API.
- The **pszFileName** parameter is the name of the initialization file to open. If this file does not already exist, it is created.

PrfOpenProfile returns the handle to the initialization file if successful and returns NULLHANDLE if a failure occurs.

Two APIs are provided to allow an application to write data to initialization files. Both of these APIs require that the application supply an application name and a key name with which to associate the data. Depending on which API is chosen, the data may be presented in the form of an ASCII string or as binary data. The **PrfWriteProfileString** API is used to store data in the form of an ASCII string. The prototype for this API is given in Figure 7.50.

- The **hini** parameter is the handle of the initialization file to receive the data.
- The **pszApp** parameter is a pointer to a zero-terminated array of characters that specify the application name under which the data is to be stored. The content of the string is defined by the application; however, names beginning with PM_ are reserved for system use.
- The **pszKey** parameter is a pointer to a zero-terminated array of characters that specify the key name with which the data is to be associated.
- The **pszData** parameter is a pointer to a zero-terminated array of characters to be associated with application name **pszApp** and key name **pszKey**.

PrfWriteProfileString returns TRUE if successful or FALSE if an error occurred.

Blocks of binary data may be written to initialization file records using the **PrfWriteProfileData** API. The prototype for this API is in Figure 7.51.

- The **hini** parameter is the handle of the initialization file to receive the data.

```
BOOL APIENTRY PrfWriteProfileString( HINI hini,
                            PSZ  pszApp,
                            PSZ  pszKey,
                            PSZ  pszData );
```

Figure 7.50 The PrfWriteProfileString prototype.

```
BOOL APIENTRY PrfWriteProfileData(HINI  hini,
                                  PSZ   pszApp,
                                  PSZ   pszKey,
                                  PVOID pData,
                                  ULONG cchDataLen);
```

Figure 7.51   The PrfWriteProfileData prototype.

- The **pszApp** parameter is a pointer to a zero-terminated array of characters that specify the application name under which the data is to be stored. The content of the string is defined by the application; however, names beginning with PM_ are reserved for system use.
- The **pszKey** parameter is a pointer to a zero-terminated array of characters that specify the key name with which the data is to be associated.
- The **pData** parameter is a pointer to the binary data to be associated with application name **pszApp** and key name **pszKey**.
- The **cchDataLen** parameter is the number of bytes of data to write from the location pointed to by **pData**.

PrfWriteProfileData returns TRUE if successful or FALSE if an error occurred.

Both of these APIs first perform a case-sensitive search of the initialization file to determine if a record with the specified application name/key name pair already exists. If an existing record is found, the value portion of the record tuple is updated with the new data specified in the API call. If an existing record is not found, a new record is added with the specified application name/key name pair and the data specified by the function call.

These APIs may also be used to remove records from an initialization file. If the **pszData** parameter or **pData** parameter is specified as a NULL pointer and a record matching the values in **pszApp** and **pszKey** is found, the record is deleted. All records associated with a given application name may be deleted by passing the **pszKey** parameter as a NULL pointer.

Four APIs are available for application use when reading initialization file records. The first of these, **PrfQueryProfileSize**, is a utility function that returns the length of the value portion of an INI file record or the length of an enumeration list. The remaining three APIs allow the application to retrieve the value from an initialization file record as an integer value, **PrfQueryProfileInt**; an ASCII string, **PrfQueryProfileString**; or a block of binary data, **PrfQueryProfileData**. The latter two APIs also allow the application to receive an enumerated list of the application names in an initialization file or the key names associated with an application name.

The **PrfQueryProfileSize** API provides an application with the size of the value portion of an initialization file record or the total length of an enumeration buffer. If both an application name and a key name are provided, and a record matching these parameters is found, the function returns the length of the value portion of the record in bytes. If the key name or application name is NULL, the length of an enumerated list of key names or application names is returned. Note that the value returned for an enumeration list is the total length of the buffer, including the final NULL character terminator, which is not included in the length returned by the APIs that perform the enumeration. Typical uses for this API include determining the number of bytes of memory to allocate for buffers, verifying that an initialization value will fit in a local buffer, and avoiding corrupted data by verifying that a value is of the expected size. The prototype for the API is shown in Figure 7.52.

- The **hini** parameter is the handle of the INI file where the data is stored.
- The **szApp** parameter is a pointer to a zero-terminated array of characters specifying the application name for which to search. Set this parameter to NULL to determine the length of an enumeration of all application names.
- The **szKey** parameter is a pointer to a zero-terminated array of characters specifying the key name for which to search. Set this parameter to NULL to determine the length of an enumeration of all key names for the given application name.
- The **pulReqLen** parameter is a pointer to a ULONG where the length of the profile data is stored. This value includes the zero-termination character for data stored as an ASCII string.

PrfQueryProfileSize returns TRUE if successful or FALSE if an error occurs, including not finding a match for the supplied **pszApp** and **pszKey**. The length of the data is returned in the location pointed to by **pulReqLen**.

When retrieving data from an initialization file, it is important to remember that the internal representation of the data in the initialization file is always binary. Thus, a record written with **PrfWriteProfileString** may be retrieved as binary data, and data written with **PrfWriteProfileData** may be retrieved with **PrfReadProfileString**. In fact, **PrfQueryProfileData** and **PrfQueryProfileString** always return identical data for any given initialization file record, but **PrfQueryProfileString** allows the application to supply a default value if the requested initialization file record does not exist.

The **PrfQueryProfileData** API is normally used to retrieve the value portion of an initialization file record as a block of binary data. The API may also be used to enumerate the key names associated with an application by passing

```
BOOL APIENTRY PrfQueryProfileSize( HINI   hini,
                                   PSZ    szApp,
                                   PSZ    szKey,
                                   PULONG pulReqLen );
```

Figure 7.52   The PrfQueryProfileSize prototype.

the key name field as a NULL pointer or to enumerate the application names in an initialization file by passing the application name as a NULL pointer. Enumerations are returned as a set of variable length, zero-terminated ASCII strings followed by a final zero character (the end of the buffer is signaled by a double NULL character). The returned length of the enumeration does not include the final NULL terminator. If the return buffer size is not sufficient to contain the entire enumeration, the list is truncated at the buffer size. No effort is made to ensure that a NULL termination character is provided, so the application must rely on the returned buffer length.

The prototype for the **PrfQueryProfileData** API is given in Figure 7.53.

- The **hini** parameter is the handle of the INI file where the data is stored.
- The **pszApp** parameter is a pointer to a zero-terminated array of characters specifying the application name for which to search. Set this parameter to NULL to retrieve a list of all application names contained in the initialization file.
- The **pszKey** parameter is a pointer to a zero-terminated array of characters specifying the key name for which to search. Set this parameter to NULL to retrieve a list of all key names for the application name specified by **pszApp**.
- The **pBuffer** parameter is a pointer to the location where the retrieved data is to be stored. This buffer should contain at least the number of bytes indicated by **pulBuffLen**.
- The **pulBuffLen** parameter is a pointer to a location that on input contains a value specifying the maximum number of bytes to retrieve. The number of bytes actually copied to **pBuffer** is stored in this location when the function returns.

PrfQueryProfileData returns TRUE if the function is successful and returns FALSE if an error occurs.

The **PrfQueryProfileString** API performs essentially the same function as **PrfQueryProfileData** but allows the specification of a default value to return if the specified application name or key name is not found in the initialization file. Since the function is designed to primarily return a zero-terminated ASCII string, the value specified for the default value must be zero-terminated. Attempting to specify binary data for this parameter that is not zero-terminated

```
BOOL APIENTRY PrfQueryProfileData(HINI    hini,
                                  PSZ     pszApp,
                                  PSZ     pszKey,
                                  PVOID   pBuffer,
                                  PULONG  pulBuffLen);
```

Figure 7.53 The PrfQueryProfileData prototype.

```
ULONG APIENTRY PrfQueryProfileString(HINI  hini,
                                     PSZ   pszApp,
                                     PSZ   pszKey,
                                     PSZ   pszDefault,
                                     PVOID pBuffer,
                                     ULONG cchBufferMax);
```

Figure 7.54   The PrfQueryProfileString prototype.

can lead to catastrophic results. Like **PrfQueryProfileData**, this function will return an enumerated list if the application name parameter or the key name parameter is specified as a NULL pointer.

The prototype for PrfQueryProfileString() is shown in Figure 7.54.

- The **hini** parameter is the handle of the INI file where the data is stored.
- The **pszApp** parameter is a pointer to a zero-terminated array of characters specifying the application name for which to search. Set this parameter to NULL to retrieve a list of all application names contained in the initialization file.
- The **pszKey** parameter is a pointer to a zero-terminated array of characters specifying the key name for which to search. Set this parameter to NULL to retrieve a list of all key names for the application name specified by **pszApp**.
- The **pszDefault** parameter is a pointer to a zero-terminated ASCII string to return in **pBuffer** if the name specified in **pszApp** or **pszKey** cannot be found.
- The **pBuffer** parameter is a pointer to the location where the retrieved data is to be stored. This buffer should contain at least the number of bytes indicated by **cchBufferMax**.
- The **cchBufferMax** parameter specifies the maximum number of bytes to store into **pBuffer**.

PrfQueryProfileString returns the number of bytes copied into **pBuffer**, or zero if an error occurs.

The final API for retrieving initialization file record data is **PrfQueryProfileInt**. This API interprets the value portion of the record as a numeric ASCII string and converts the string to an integer. The first non-numeric character in the data terminates the conversion. Like the **PrfQueryProfileString** API, a default value is returned if the specified application name and key name combination is not found in the initialization file.

PrfQueryProfileInt is prototyped as shown in Figure 7.55.

- The **hini** parameter is the handle of the INI file where the data is stored.
- The **pszApp** parameter is a pointer to a zero-terminated array of characters specifying the application name for which to search.

```
LONG APIENTRY PrfQueryProfileInt(HINI hini,
                                 PSZ   pszApp,
                                 PSZ   pszKey,
                                 LONG  sDefault);
```

Figure 7.55   The PrfQueryProfileInt prototype.

- The **pszKey** parameter is a pointer to a zero-terminated array of characters specifying the key name for which to search.
- The **sDefault** parameter specifies the default value to return if the application name or key name is not contained in the initialization file.

PrfQueryProfileInt returns the converted value of the initialization file data corresponding to **pszApp** and **pszKey** or the value passed in **sDefault** if **pszApp** or **pszKey** cannot be found.

When an application no longer requires access to a private initialization file, the **PrfCloseProfile** API should be called to release the file. This API is prototyped as in Figure 7.56.

- The **hini** parameter is the handle of the private initialization file to close.

PrfCloseProfile returns TRUE if the function was successful and FALSE if an error occurred. Note that this API cannot be used to close the system-defined initialization files, thus the constants HINI_USERPROFILE, HINI_SYSTEM PROFILE, and HINI_PROFILE are not valid when this API is called.

Figure 7.57 shows two routines used by our example program to maintain the displayed directory between applications. Routine **IniToDir** resets the current disk drive and directory to the directory that was displayed when the application was last closed. The routine first queries the current drive and directory for use as the defaults should the initialization file records not be present, as would occur on the first invocation of the program. **PrfQueryProfileInt** is then called to obtain the saved disk number, and **PrfQueryProfileString** is called to retrieve the directory. Note that the **pBuffer** parameter is set to point to the second character of the output string. This allows the backslash character to be placed in front of the directory so that **DosSetCurrentDir** will set the new current directory relative to the root directory of the drive rather than to the current directory. Once the initialization file data, or appropriate defaults, are obtained, the DOS API functions to set the default drive and current directory are called.

```
BOOL APIENTRY PrfCloseProfile( HINI hini );
```

Figure 7.56   The PrfCloseProfile prototype.

```
#define INIAPPNAME    "CHAPT6"
#define INICURDSKKEY "CURRENT DISK"
#define INICURDIRKEY "CURRENT DIR"

MRESULT IniToDir( HWND hwnd, ULONG msg, MPARAM mp1, MPARAM mp2 )
{
    ULONG     ulDiskNum;
    ULONG     ulDiskMap;
    char      szCurDir[ _MAX_PATH];
    char      szIniDir[ _MAX_PATH];
    ULONG     cbCurDir = _MAX_PATH;

    DosQueryCurrentDisk( &ulDiskNum, &ulDiskMap );
    DosQueryCurrentDir( ulDiskNum, szCurDir, &cbCurDir );
    ulDiskNum = PrfQueryProfileInt( HINI_USERPROFILE, INIAPPNAME, INICURDSKKEY,
                                    ulDiskNum );
    PrfQueryProfileString( HINI_USERPROFILE, INIAPPNAME, INICURDIRKEY,
                           szCurDir, &szIniDir[1], _MAX_PATH );
    szIniDir[ 0 ] = '\\';
    DosSetDefaultDisk( ulDiskNum );
    DosSetCurrentDir( szIniDir );
}

MRESULT DirToIni( HWND hwnd, ULONG msg, MPARAM mp1, MPARAM mp2 )
{
    ULONG     ulDiskNum;
    ULONG     ulDiskMap;
    char      szCurDir[ _MAX_PATH];
    char      szIniDir[ _MAX_PATH];
    char      szDisk[ 3 ];
    ULONG     cbCurDir = _MAX_PATH;

    DosQueryCurrentDisk( &ulDiskNum, &ulDiskMap );
    szDisk[ 0 ] = (CHAR)(ulDiskNum/10) + 0x30;
    szDisk[ 1 ] = (CHAR)(ulDiskNum % 10) + 0x30;
    szDisk[ 2 ] = '\0';
    PrfWriteProfileString( HINI_USERPROFILE, INIAPPNAME, INICURDSKKEY,
                           szDisk );
    DosQueryCurrentDir( ulDiskNum, szCurDir, &cbCurDir );
    PrfWriteProfileString( HINI_USERPROFILE, INIAPPNAME, INICURDIRKEY,
                           szCurDir );
    return MRFROMLONG(0L);
}
```

Figure 7.57 **Saving and restoring application data.**

Routine **DirToIni** saves the default drive and current directory to the initialization file. **DosQueryCurrentDisk** returns the default drive as an integer number. This value is then converted to a zero-terminated ASCII string and saved into the initialization file with the **PrfWriteProfileString** API. **DosQueryCurrentDir** is then called to obtain the current directory and the resulting string is written to the initialization file by again calling **PrfWriteProfileString**.

Routine **IniToDir** is called during the startup of the program prior to the initial filling of the listbox. In many applications, these types of values would be retrieved from within the WM_CREATE message processing or from inside the **main** routine. Routine **DirToIni** is called from within the WM_CLOSE message processing, which is the normal routine for saving this type of information. In some instances, it may be more convenient to store the information to the initialization file when the values are changed rather than waiting for the application to terminate.

SOM

SOM, an acronym for System Object Model, is an architecture and methodology for implementing language-independent, extendable systems of classes and objects. Unlike systems built by most object-oriented programming languages, object classes that conform to this model may be implemented as separate units of executable code, possibly developed using different high-level languages. SOM defines the manner in which interactions between classes are resolved, such as when a method in a parent class is called via an object of a derived class. When using C++ and other object-oriented programming languages, this type of interaction is often resolved statically when the executable module is linked. The SOM model allows this interaction to be resolved dynamically at runtime. This requires some additional overhead, but provides significant flexibility in the construction of object classes.

OS/2 provides functionality for run-time resolution of the interfaces between SOM-compatible objects and also provides a base set of SOM classes from which programmers can derive their own SOM-compatible classes. The OS/2 Developer's Toolkit provides the SOM Compiler, which converts source files containing class definitions written in IDL, Interface Definition Language, into language-specific headers and source files. The source files contain stubs for each object method, which the programmer can then expand to implement the object functionality. The Toolkit also provides the language headers and IDL specifications for the SOM base classes so that additional classes may be derived by the programmer.

The base classes provided with OS/2 are SOMObject, a class that defines the basic functionality of a SOM-compatible object; SOMClass, a class derived from SOMObject that provides the basic functionality of a SOM metaclass;

and SOMClassMgr, a class that provides registration functions for classes and objects within a process.

SOMObject

Class SOMObject is the base class from which all SOM-compliant classes must be descended. This class defines and implements the basic functionality required for SOM compliance. Methods are provided to manage instance data, to retrieve information about an object's class, to determine the type and derivation of an object's class, to dump debug information, and most important, to dynamically access methods of the class.

Three methods are provided for managing object data; somInit, somUninit, and somFree. Since SOMObject does not define any data, these methods do nothing for the base object. The somInit method should normally be overridden by classes that define instance data in order to ensure that the data is in a known state after the object is created. The somUninit method should be overridden by classes that define instance data requiring cleanup when the object is destroyed; for instance, a pointer to allocated memory. Method somFree releases the memory used by the object and should not normally require an overriding method.

Four additional methods are provided for dynamically accessing methods of the class; somDispatchA, somDispatchD, somDispatchL, and somDispatchV. The method called depends on the return value of the accessed method: somDispatchA is used to access methods that return a pointer; somDispatchD is used to access methods that return a floating point number; somDispatchL is used to access methods that return an integer; and somDispatchV is used to access methods that return void, or no value. These routines locate and call a stub routine for the target method, which parses a variable length argument list and then calls the actual target method with these parameters. These methods define OS/2's standard methodology for dynamically accessing the methods of a given object and are not normally overridden; however, the methods may be overridden if a different access method is desired.

SOMClass

Within the SOM model, a method must operate on an established instance of a class, that is, an existing object. Thus, object constructor methods cannot be defined in the class whose objects are being instantiated. Rather, the constructor method must be defined in some class for which an object already exists. In SOM terminology, the class defining the constructor method is known as the *metaclass* of a class, and an instantiation of this class is known as a *class object*. A class's metaclass may either be explicitly defined or inherited from its parent class. The root metaclass is SOMClass, which by definition is its own metaclass and is also the metaclass for SOMObject, from which it is derived.

Since SOMClass is derived from SOMObject, it inherits all the methods of SOMObject. It also defines a number of new methods used in the construction of objects. Four methods are defined for creating objects: somNew constructs and initializes a new object by invoking somInit; somNewNoInit constructs an object but does not perform initialization; somRenew constructs and initializes an object in memory provided by its caller; and somRenewNoInit constructs an object in caller-provided memory without invoking the initialization method somInit. These methods may be overridden to perform special initialization or construction as required for a particular class.

Metaclasses derived from SOMClass may also define additional data and/or methods for use by all objects of a given class.

SOMClassMgr

Class SOMClassMgr is derived from SOMObject to provide methods for registering new classes and, in OS/2, for loading and unloading the Dynamic Link Libraries (DLLs) that contain the classes. Only one instance of SOMClassMgr or a class derived from SOMClassMgr is allowed per process. If a derived class is used, it should invoke the somMergeInto method to replace the SOMClassMgr object created during SOM initialization.

DISTRIBUTED SOM

The version of SOM provided with OS/2 version 2.0 was limited to a single process. Thus, an application was not allowed to directly access the data or methods of a Workplace Shell object. OS/2 Warp contains a workstation implementation of the Distributed System Object Model. This model allows an application to create and access objects that are defined and supported by another process. In general, this allows applications to create and manipulate Workplace Shell objects without themselves being part of the shell.

Workplace Classes

The Workplace Shell is an object-oriented environment implemented as a hierarchy of SOM-compliant classes. The Workplace class hierarchy begins with class WPObject, which is derived from SOMObject, to define the basic behavior of all Workplace objects. Next in the hierarchy are the three Workplace storage classes: WPTransient, WPAbstract, and WPFileSystem. In general, all Workplace objects must be derived from one of these three storage classes.

Hierarchy

Class WPObject, itself derived from SOMObject, is the root class from which all Workplace Shell classes are derived. This class defines the "normal" behavior for a Workplace object. As might be expected, WPObject defines a large number of methods. These methods implement functionality that includes managing the settings notebook, saving and restoring an object's state, or data, displaying and handling popup menus, modifying and querying object data, handling errors, managing memory, and direct manipulation of objects. Because this functionality is provided by WPObject, new Workplace classes may be developed without a great deal of concern for the Workplace environment. Typically, new classes will override the methods that provide appearance or configuration information, such as title text, icons, or help information, but the functional behavior methods are typically inherited.

Immediately below WPObject in the Workplace class hierarchy are the storage classes. These are so named because they provide different methods of saving an object's state or data. New Workplace classes must be derived from a storage class, and while additional storage classes can be developed, the three provided with OS/2—WPTransient, WPAbstract, and WPFilesystem—are normally used for deriving new classes.

The first of the storage classes, WPTransient, is used to derive classes that represent objects that are temporary in nature and do not require their state to be saved. Objects instantiated from these classes are not automatically re-created when the system is booted, but in some instances will be reinstantiated from data available on the system. A good example of a class derived from WPTransient is the class that is used to represent a print job, WPJob. As output is sent to a printer, a pair of files are created on the system storage device to retain the data until it can actually be output. The printer object representing this printer creates objects of class WPJob to represent the files that are waiting to be sent to the printer. When a file has been completely processed, it is deleted along with its object. If the system is restarted while spool files are still present on the storage device, the WPJob objects must be re-created by the printer object—they are not automatically generated by the Workplace startup procedure. Another good use for a class derived from WPTransient would be a class used to represent records in a database. In most instances, objects representing these records can be easily re-created from the data in the record and therefore should not require additional storage in the initialization files, as provided by WPAbstract. Also, since the records are not individual files on the disk, objects derived from WPFileSystem are not appropriate.

The second storage class provided with OS/2 is WPAbstract. Classes are derived from WPAbstract in order to create objects that must be re-created after the system is booted but which are not properly represented by a single file (or directory) on the system storage device(s). WPAbstract provides methods that save the state of the object in the USER initialization file, normally, OS2.INI. WPProgram, which is used to represent a reference to a program (not the program executable file), is an example of such a class. Objects created from WPProgram represent a particular state of the referenced program. For instance, one WPProgram object might be used to perform a backup function using XCOPY.EXE, while another WPProgram object, which also references XCOPY.EXE, performs a restore function. Thus the WPProgram object represents more than just the executable file; it represents the program performing a function. All the information necessary to cause the executable to perform the desired function is stored in the initialization file.

The final storage class provided with OS/2 is WPFileSystem. Classes derived from this class are used to represent files (including directories) stored on the system storage device(s). The state of objects created from these classes is stored with the files, typically in the directory entry and extended attributes for the file. An example of a class derived from WPFileSystem is WPProgramFile, which represents an executable file on the disk. Unlike the WPProgram class just discussed, whose title is not necessarily related to the executable program, the title for WPProgramFile objects is the name of the executable—changing the object's title changes the executable file name. Also, when a WPProgram object is moved or copied, the executable file is not touched; when a WPProgramFile object is moved or copied, the file itself is moved or copied. Thus objects created from classes derived from WPFileSystem directly represent files on the storage device, and manipulating these objects manipulates the file.

Programmers may use these classes, or the specific classes derived from them, to produce new Workplace Shell classes that perform application functions. In time, many popular types of applications may be implemented as one or more Workplace Shell objects, rather than as separate executable programs. The details of how to implement these classes is beyond the scope of this book, but the information presented here should serve as a starting point to understand how the Workplace Shell is implemented.

SUMMARY

This chapter has described OS/2's object-oriented, graphical user interface, the Workplace Shell. Drag-and-drop manipulation and initialization files, essential functionality required for Workplace-aware PM applications, have been described in detail. A brief introduction to SOM and the object hierarchy of the Workplace Shell has been provided.

CHAPTER 8

Mastering Dialogs, Menus, and Other PM Resources

The intent of the graphical user interface is to provide the user with a clear, concise, and consistent way of navigating through the application to accomplish a desired function. Unfortunately, because of the overwhelming power and complexity of the Presentation Manager, it is all too easy to design applications that confuse the user due to poor resource management. For instance, application menus that do not flow logically or dialogs cluttered with controls can frustrate the user who only wants to create a simple text file. Applications that make poor use of the simplicity of the graphical user interface will probably not succeed in the marketplace. Today's computer user demands complex functionality with a simple look and feel. The software development community is keenly aware of this desire, and thus it has become increasingly important to master the art of using PM resources. This chapter will focus on making the best use of menus, dialogs, and other simple PM resources.

THE PURPOSE OF THE SAMPLE PROGRAM

The sample program for this chapter may seem similar to the OS/2 System Editor, E.EXE. The sample program PMEDIT.EXE, like the E Editor, also draws an MLE control within the client area that acts as the editor window. The MLE control was introduced in Chapter 2.

The sample is intended to demonstrate the proper use of menus, dialogs, and various other PM resources, such as string tables and accelerators. The program uses a combination of menus and dialog boxes along with various other PM resources.

APPLICATION MENUS

Virtually any application that requires some sort of user input will require an application menu; therefore, designing the menu is an extremely important element of a successful PM program. Menus that make sense can have a great impact on the learning curve that the user will have to endure when initially using the application. Menus should be grouped in a scheme that makes sense functionally. A menu that contains file operations—for example, open, save, and search functions—should not contain clipboard operations as well. Users should be able to visualize the groupings in their head. This becomes increasingly important the more menuitems there are on a menu. The associations between a submenu, menuitem, and menu function should be distinguishable. For example, a submenu labeled File would be the logical place to find an Open File menuitem, which would signify to users that this is where they need to click to be able to open a text file.

Developers should be cognizant of the user learning curve, and envision themselves using the application for the first time. Menuitems that contain similar or identical functionality are useless because they impede the user's ability to associate a function with a menuitem selection. Thus, the next time the user is confronted with finding the option he or she needs, it will again be necessary to evaluate which menuitem will perform the necessary function.

The purpose of the Presentation Manager is to provide a common interface to the user. So, to some extent, every single application designed and developed for PM should share a common look and feel. In the programmer's best of all possible worlds, every PM application would look so similar to the next that the user would automatically know exactly what to do next. In reality, complex menu interfaces can destroy the usability of any application.

A *menu* is a control window that provides the user with the ability to make a selection that will perform some type of function or operation. There are three types of application menus that appear on virtually every main window of an application. The most primitive form of a menu is the minimize and maximize buttons, located in the upper right-hand corner of the main frame window. These two bitmapped windows are menus by definition because they allow the user to modify the appearance of the entire frame window by minimizing, maximizing, or restoring the window coordinates for the window. The programming functionality of these control windows is limited: the programmer can choose via frame control flags whether to display one or both of these windows or remove them entirely from the frame window. The implementation of these control windows corresponds directly to their equivalent menuitems on the system menu. The other two types of application menus are the system menu and the action bar menu. Before we discuss these two types, however, it is important to understand the composition of the menu window.

Menu Messages

There are several menu control messages designed to allow the developer to alter the appearance of a particular menu window. Once an application starts, it is usually initialized with an action bar menu and a system menu through the frame control flags FCF_MENU and FCF_SYSMENU, respectively. However, there may be times that the application will have to change the contents of a particular menu based on input from the user. For example, if you examine the sample program PMEDIT, you will notice that the clipboard options in the Edit submenu will either be enabled or disabled based on the data contained in the clipboard. It makes sense that if a menuitem is not functional, that the menuitem is disabled, preventing the user from selecting it. Also, menuitems that will never be used should be deleted entirely, and menuitems that illustrate some kind of a default selection should have a check mark associated with them. All of these menu characteristics are known as *menu item attributes*. The menu control messages provide the vehicle to change the attributes associated with a particular menuitem.

Figure 8.1 lists the menu control messages. It is extremely important to understand the message parameters associated with each of the menu control messages. The message parameters **mp1** and **mp2** are actually a 4-byte area of storage that can be used to hold various pieces of information based on

MM_INSERTITEM	0x0180
MM_DELETEITEM	0x0181
MM_QUERYITEM	0x0182
MM_SETITEM	0x0183
MM_QUERYITEMCOUNT	0x0184
MM_STARTMENUMODE	0x0185
MM_ENDMENUMODE	0x0186
MM_REMOVEITEM	0x0188
MM_SELECTITEM	0x0189
MM_QUERYSELITEMID	0x018a
MM_QUERYITEMTEXT	0x018b
MM_QUERYITEMTEXTLENGTH	0x018c
MM_SETITEMHANDLE	0x018d
MM_SETITEMTEXT	0x018e
MM_ITEMPOSITIONFROMID	0x018f
MM_ITEMIDFROMPOSITION	0x0190
MM_QUERYITEMATTR	0x0191
MM_SETITEMATTR	0x0192
MM_ISITEMVALID	0x0193
MM_QUERYITEMRECT	0x0194
MM_QUERYDEFAULTITEMID	0x0431
MM_SETDEFAULTITEMID	0x0432

Figure 8.1   Menu control messages.

the message type. Most of the menu control messages do not use the entire 4-byte storage area and actually may use both the low word and high word for storage. The storage is divided based on the data type that is stored in the message parameters. For example:

- If the data type is NULL, then all four bytes are equal to zero.
- If the data type is a SHORT variable, then the value of the message parameter is stored in the low word, and the sign is placed in the high word.
- If the data type is a BOOL or USHORT variable, then the value of the message parameter is stored in the low word, and the high word equals zero.

We already know that a menu is a control window in its purest form, therefore, menus contain characteristics of other windows, including window styles and attributes. Figure 8.2 is a chart indicating the different menu control styles that can be used to define a menu window. A definition of their usage is provided, along with their hexadecimal values defined in PMWIN.H. The menu control styles can be used to create different types of menu controls, each with their own distinct behavior.

MS_ACTIONBAR	0x00000001L	Used to implement the Action Bar Submenu concept, this style displays menuitems side by side. Although menus with this style may be used to perform some function, they are usually used to display the actual pull-down menu that is associated with the submenu.
MS_TITLEBUTTON	0x00000002L	Used to implement menus that may be drawn within the title bar. This menu style needs to be used in conjunction with MS_ACTIONBAR.
MS_VERTICALFLIP	0x00000004L	Used when a submenu's pull-down window cannot be entirely displayed within the desktop's presentation space.
MS_CONDITIONALCASCADE	0x00000040L	This style was introduced with OS/2 2.0. It is used to implement a conditional cascade menu. A conditional cascade menu is a menu that is only revealed when the user selects the cascade via a bitmap arrow on the menuitem with the conditional cascade.

Figure 8.2   Menu control styles.

The conditional cascade menu, like a regular cascade menu, is designed to show the user a selection of similar menuitems that correspond to a single menuitem choice. The difference is that the user must press the arrow button, located to the right of the menuitem to display the pull-down menuitems. One of the menuitems in the pull-down may be selected as a default choice. The default menuitem option is marked by a check mark. An example of this menu style is illustrated in Figure 8.3. The PMEDIT sample program uses a conditional cascade menu to allow the user to select color choices for the edit window.

The best example of the difference between a cascade menu and a conditional cascade menu is found in OS/2's desktop popup menu. This menu contains a typical example of the cascade and conditional cascade menu usage. In Figure 8.3, the Open menuitem uses the conditional cascade control style. As you can see, the menuitem contains an arrow within a button that, when selected, will reveal the different views of the container for the desktop folder. When the user selects this item, an additional popup menu is revealed. This popup menu contains a default selection identified by a check mark. A standard cascade menu is used for the Select menuitem. When this menuitem is selected, it reveals two choices, Select all or Deselect all, in its popup menu. If there is no default choice in a menu, you should use the Cascade menu. If a default choice is required, use the conditional cascade. Creating the conditional cascade is simple. The first step is to create a simple cascade menu. The

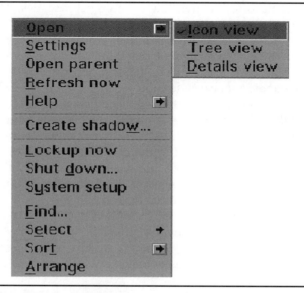

Figure 8.3 **The conditional cascade menu.**

```
SUBMENU "~Options",                            ID_OPTIONSMENU
 {
  MENUITEM "Change Font Selection",               IDM_EDITFONT
  SUBMENU  "Change Foreground Color",          ID_COLORMENU
  {
   MENUITEM "Red",                                 IDM_RED
   MENUITEM "Blue",                                IDM_BLUE
   MENUITEM "Green",                               IDM_GREEN
   MENUITEM "Yellow",                              IDM_YELLOW
 }
}
```

Figure 8.4   Defining a cascade menu.

code fragment in Figure 8.4 is from the resource script file and it represents the Options submenu. Within this submenu, a cascade menu is created that is used to change the foreground color of the editor.

The cascade is essentially a submenu embedded within another submenu, in this case, the Change Foreground Color submenu within the Options submenu. The master submenu is the Options submenu. It contains one menuitem, IDM_EDITFONT, and the embedded submenu represented by ID_COLORMENU. The ID_COLORMENU submenu contains several menuitems that represent the individual foreground color selections.

Be very careful not to embed too many cascade menus, as it becomes very difficult to follow the flow of multiple cascades. The goal of any application menu is to get the application to perform the task that the user wants to initiate as quickly and easily as possible. When you start to embed too many cascade windows, it works against that goal.

The code fragment in Figure 8.5 converts the cascade menu by using the conditional cascade control style. The function *CreateConditionalCascade-Menu* takes three parameters. The first parameter **hwndMenu** is the window handle of the menu that contains the cascade menu. The second parameter is a SHORT variable, **sSubMenu**, that represents the identifier of the submenu that is to be converted to the conditional cascade. The final parameter is another SHORT, **sDefault**, that is used to identify the default selection within the conditional cascade menu. The default selection is represented by a check mark next to the menuitem.

The function first sends a MM_QUERYITEM message to the menu window represented by **hwndMenu**. The first message parameter, **mp1**, contains the identifier of the submenu, which in the preceeding sample would be ID_COLORMENU. The second message parameter returns a valid MENU-ITEM structure.

The MENUITEM structure is shown in Figure 8.6.

```
BOOL CreateConditionalCascadeMenu(HWND hwndMenu, SHORT sSubMenu, SHORT sDefault)
  {
    HWND      hwndSubMenu;
    ULONG     ulSubMenuStyle;
    MENUITEM  menuitem;

    WinSendMsg(hwndMenu,
               MM_QUERYITEM,
               MPFROM2SHORT(sSubMenu, TRUE),
               MPFROMP(&menuitem));

    hwndSubMenu = menuitem.hwndSubMenu;
    ulSubMenuStyle = WinQueryWindowULong(hwndSubMenu, QWL_STYLE);

    WinSetWindowULong(hwndSubMenu,
                      QWL_STYLE,
                      ulSubMenuStyle | MS_CONDITIONALCASCADE);

    WinSendMsg(hwndSubMenu,
               MM_SETDEFAULTITEMID,
               MPFROMSHORT(sDefault),
               NULL);
    return FALSE;
  }
```

Figure 8.5   The CreateConditionalCascadeMenu function.

- The *iPosition* element is used to indicate the position of the menuitem.
- *afStyle* represents the menu style flags. The menu style flags are listed in Figure 8.7, and are prefixed by MIS_.
- *afAttribute* represents the menu attribute flags. The menu attribute flags are listed in Figure 8.8, and are prefixed by MIA_.
- *id* is the window identifier.
- *hwndSubMenu* is the window handle of the submenu.
- *hItem* is the item handle.

```
typedef struct _MENUITEM     // mi
{
 SHORT   iPosition;
 USHORT  afStyle;
 USHORT  afAttribute;
 USHORT  id;
 HWND    hwndSubMenu;
 ULONG   hItem;
} MENUITEM;
typedef MENUITEM *PMENUITEM;
```

Figure 8.6   The MENUITEM structure.

MIS_TEXT	0x000	The simplest of menuitem styles, this is used for all menuitems that display a simple ASCII text string.
MIS_BITMAP	0x0002	This menuitem should only be used when a graphical image is needed to simplify the explanation of the menuitem. It is used to display a bitmapped image within a menuitem.
MIS_SEPARATOR	0x0004	This menuitem can only be used within a SUBMENU pull-down. Its purpose is to graphically represent a change in the contextual flow of the menu. This menuitem serves no functional purpose other than to display the horizontal separator line. The keyword SEPARATOR, when used in a resource script file, signifies this menuitem style.
MIS_OWNERDRAW	0x0008	This menuitem style is left to the developer to customize. Notification messages are sent to the owner for manipulating the item's appearance.
MIS_SUBMENU	0x0010	This menuitem is used to draw SUBMENUs. A SUBMENU is a menuitem that usually does not perform a function on its own other than reveal a pull-down menu with additional menuitem options. The keyword SUBMENU, when used in a resource script file, signifies this menuitem style.
MIS_SYSCOMMAND	0x0040	This menuitem style is used when the menu window needs to send a WM_SYSCOMMAND to its owner. It is used primarily in the system menu context.
MIS_HELP	0x0080	When this menuitem style is used, a WM_HELP message is posted to the owner when the item is selected.
MIS_STATIC	0x0100	This menuitem is used to indicate that a given menuitem cannot be selected.
MIS_BUTTONSEPARATOR	0x0200	This item is used to simulate a button. When used, the user cannot move to the item via the keyboard, but can use an accelerator key or pointing device to make the selection. The item can be used to display the HELP SUBMENU, and is drawn with a vertical separator bar.
MIS_BREAK	0x0400	This menuitem style is used to denote the start of a new column or row.
MIS_BREAKSEPARATOR	0x0800	This item is the functional equivalent of the MIS_BREAK menuitem style, except it also physically draws a separator bar. It is used in the context of the action bar submenu.

Figure 8.7 The menuitem styles.

230

MIA_NODISMISS	0x0020	If this menuitem attribute is used, the specified item's sub-menu pull-down is not dismissed until the user explicitly dismisses the menu via a selection using the keyboard or mouse, or by pressing the Esc key.
MIA_FRAMED	0x1000	When this attribute is used, a visible frame is drawn around the item.
MIA_CHECKED	0x0004	When this attribute is set, a check mark appears to the left of the menuitem. This menuitem attribute is used to indicate the current selection in a cascade or multiple-choice menu.
MIA_DISABLED	0x4000	When this attribute is used, the menuitem is disabled and therefore cannot be selected by the user.
MIA_HILITED	0x8000	This attribute is used to highlight the menuitem when it is selected.

Figure 8.8   The menuitem attributes.

The function then stores the *hwndSubMenu* element of the structure in the variable *hwndSubMenu* through the following assignment:

```
hwndSubMenu = menuitem.hwndSubMenu;
```

The next step is to obtain the style flags that are stored in the window words of the submenu window. The style flags are obtained by calling the **WinQueryWindowULong** function with the QWL_STYLE index value. The resulting style flags for the window are returned in the ULONG variable *ulSubMenuStyle*. Conversely, the style flags are set by calling the function **WinSetWindowULong** with the QWL_STYLE index value. The following code fragment sets the style flags by ORing the current style flags with the MS_CONDITIONALCASCADE menu style flag. This is the code that actually creates the conditional cascade menu:

```
WinSetWindowULong(hwndSubMenu,
            QWL_STYLE,
            ulSubMenuStyle | MS_CONDITIONALCASCADE);
```

The final step in the function is to set the default selection in the conditional cascade menu. This is done by sending an MM_SETDEFAULTITEMID message and passing the sDefault value that was passed to the function. The **CreateConditionalCascadeMenu** function will return FALSE if it can successfully create the conditional cascade menu. If the function encounters an error along the way, like an invalid **hwnd** passed in **hwndMenu**, the function will return TRUE representing an error that occurred.

Altering the System Menu

The System menu, which is located in the upper left-hand corner of the frame window by default, contains a drop-down that performs system operations that manipulate the frame window's appearance or identity. The System menu contains menuitems that can maximize, minimize, restore, hide, move, size, or close the frame window. The System menu menuitems can be manipulated based on the functionality of the frame window. For example, frame windows that should not be closed can have the close menuitem removed from the System menu.

The menuitem text for the Close option can be altered or removed entirely along with any other menuitem in the list. Also, if the frame window requires some additional function, menuitems can be added to the System menu. A routine in the PMEDIT sample program called **SetTheSysMenu** is used to remove the menuitems that are redundant for the given window. This routine also shows how to change a system menuitem by modifying the Close option. But take care when changing system menuitems, because foreign language versions of OS/2 use the SC_CLOSE menuitem to correspond to the language equivalent of the word close.

The Composition of the System Menu

The actual System menu as we know it, is composed of two distinct windows. The first is the small window located in the upper left-hand corner of a frame window. This window contains a small bitmapped image that denotes that it can reveal a pull-down menu. This window receives a WM_BUTTON1DOWN message to indicate that it should display another window with the pull-down menuitems. The second window is the pull-down window itself, revealing the System menu items. The combination of both of these windows form the basis for the System menu functionality.

The frame identifier for the system menu is defined in PMWIN.H as FID_SYSMENU:

```
#define FID_SYSMENU             0x8002
```

The goal of the **SetTheSysMenu** function is to remove all unnecessary menuitems in the System menu. Since the Search dialog box does not have sizing capabilities, the restore, minimize, and maximize options are useless in the System menu. The function first obtains the handle of the System menu window from the frame window identifier representing the system menu by calling the **WinWindowFromID** API and specifying the FID_SYSMENU frame identifier. The handle to the System menu is then stored in the *hwndSysMenu* variable and subsequently will be used to send messages to the System menu window.

The first message sent is the MM_QUERYITEM message, whose purpose is to obtain a valid MENUITEM structure for the System menu pull-down window. The first message parameter, **mp1**, contains the System menu constant SC_SYSMENU and a TRUE indicating that it is not necessary to search all submenus. The MENUITEM structure is returned in the second message parameter, **mp2**. Once we have obtained the valid MENUITEM structure representing the system menu, we can query information regarding the current menuitems, or change the menuitems by sending additional menu messages.

The next message sent to the System menu submenu window is MM_ QUERYITEMCOUNT. This message is used to determine the number of menuitems contained within the submenu for the System menu. The number of items is returned and stored in the *sNumItems* variable. Then, for every item within the submenu, the code enters a **while** loop to determine the menuitem identifiers for each item by sending the MM_ITEMIDFROMPOSITION message. This message returns the menuitem identifiers based on the position of the item within the System menu.

The code that removes unnecessary system menu items is shown in Figure 8.9.

Figure 8.10 lists the overall layout of the System menu including the positions, which should give you a better understanding of how the System menu works.

```
VOID SetTheSysMenu(HWND hwnd, PCH szCloseItem)
{
    HWND        hwndSysMenu;
    MENUITEM    menuitem;
    ULONG       ulMenuID;
    SHORT       sNumItems;
    SHORT       sIndex = 0;
    BOOL        bDontChangeClose = FALSE;

    if (!szCloseItem)
      {
      bDontChangeClose = TRUE;
      }
    // Obtain the system menu window handle from the identifier
    // and find out how many items exist in the menu.

    hwndSysMenu = WinWindowFromID(hwnd, FID_SYSMENU);

    WinSendMsg(hwndSysMenu,
            MM_QUERYITEM,
            MPFROM2SHORT(SC_SYSMENU, FALSE),
            MPFROMP((PCH) &menuitem));

    sNumItems = SHORT1FROMMR(WinSendMsg(menuitem.hwndSubMenu,
                                MM_QUERYITEMCOUNT,
```

Figure 8.9   The SetTheSysMenu function.   **continued**

```
                                        (MPARAM)NULL,
                                        (MPARAM)NULL));

      while (sNumItems--)
      {
       ulMenuID = (ULONG) WinSendMsg(menuitem.hwndSubMenu,
                              MM_ITEMIDFROMPOSITION,
                              MPFROM2SHORT(sIndex, TRUE),
                              (MPARAM)NULL);

       switch (SHORT1FROMMP(ulMenuID))
        {
         case SC_MOVE:      // DO NOT REMOVE THE MOVE  MENUITEM
         case SC_CLOSE:     // DO NOT REMOVE THE CLOSE MENUITEM
              sIndex++;
              break;

         default:           // DELETE ALL OTHER MENUITEMS
              WinSendMsg(menuitem.hwndSubMenu,
                       MM_DELETEITEM,
                       MPFROM2SHORT(ulMenuID, TRUE),
                       (MPARAM)NULL);
        }
      }

      if (bDontChangeClose != TRUE)
       {
        WinSendMsg(hwndSysMenu,
                  MM_SETITEMTEXT,
                  (MPARAM)SC_CLOSE,
                  MPFROMP(szCloseItem));
       }
}
```

Figure 8.9   The SetTheSysMenu function.

Window Name	WM_SYSCOMMAND	Identifier	Menuitem Styles	
SysMenu Bitmap Window	SC_SYSMENU	0x8007	MIS_SUBMENU	MIS_BITMAP
SysMenu Pulldown Restore	SC_RESTORE	0x8008	MIS_TEXT	MIS_SYSCOMMAND
SysMenu Pulldown Move	SC_MOVE	0x8001	MIS_TEXT	MIS_SYSCOMMAND
SysMenu Pulldown Size	SC_SIZE	0x8000	MIS_TEXT	MIS_SYSCOMMAND
SysMenu Pulldown Minimize	SC_MINIMIZE	0x8002	MIS_TEXT	MIS_SYSCOMMAND
SysMenu Pulldown Maximize	SC_MAXIMIZE	0x8003	MIS_TEXT	MIS_SYSCOMMAND
SysMenu Pulldown Hide	SC_HIDE	0x802a	MIS_TEXT	MIS_SYSCOMMAND
SysMenu Pulldown Separator		-2	MIS_SEPARATOR	
SysMenu Pulldown Close	SC_CLOSE	0x8004	MIS_TEXT	MIS_SYSCOMMAND
SysMenu Pulldown Separator		-3	MIS_SEPARATOR	
SysMenu Pulldown WindowList	SC_TASKMANAGER	0x8011	MIS_TEXT	MIS_SYSCOMMAND

Figure 8.10   The composition of the system menu.

After we have all of the System menu identifiers, we enter a switch statement to filter out those menuitems that we want to remove and identify those we want to keep. Since we want to keep the Move and Close menuitems, we increment the sIndex counter and break out of the switch statement. All other menuitem identifiers are handled by the default case statement, which sends an MM_DELETEITEM message indicating that those menuitem options are to be removed from the System menu.

The final step in this routine involves changing the Close menuitem text. The caller of this function can pass a string containing the text to replace the standard Close menuitem. The code works by sending a MM_SETITEMTEXT message for the SC_CLOSE identifier, to change the menuitem text of the System menu Close option. If a valid value is passed in to the routine in the *szCloseItem* variable, we will set the Close item text to reflect the user-passed string. If the value passed into the routine is NULL, then we will not modify the Close menuitem option.

Removing the System Menu Separators

The system menu contains two menuitem separators, one before the Close menuitem and one after. The identifiers for these separators are shown in Figure 8.10. The code fragment shown in Figure 8.11 removes the separators from the system menu. The code works by sending a MM_QUERYITEM message to the System menu window to obtain the MENUITEM structure for the system menu. The MENUITEM structure is needed to obtain the window handle of the submenu. The last step involves sending two MM_DELETEITEM messages to the submenu specifying the separator identifiers, −2 and −3.

Replacing the System Menu Entirely

The PMEDIT sample program also contains a routine called ***ReplaceTheSystemMenu*** that is used to replace the default System menu bitmap with the old-fashioned System menu bitmap, which was a straight horizontal bar. Those

```
hwndSysMenu = WinWindowFromID(hwnd, FID_SYSMENU);
WinSendMsg(hwndSysMenu,                               // Window Handle
           MM_QUERYITEM,                              // Message
           MPFROM2SHORT(SC_SYSMENU, FALSE),           // Message Parameter 1
           MPFROMP(&menuitem));                        // Message Parameter 2

WinSendMsg(menuitem.hwndSubMenu, MM_DELETEITEM, MPFROM2SHORT(-2, TRUE), (MPARAM)NULL);
WinSendMsg(menuitem.hwndSubMenu, MM_DELETEITEM, MPFROM2SHORT(-3, TRUE), (MPARAM)NULL);
```

Figure 8.11 **Removing the system menu separators.**

of you familiar with the OS/2 1.x PM or Windows 3.x graphical user interface will remember this System menu. The OS/2 2.x Presentation Manager keeps this bitmap around for compatability with previous versions.

This routine not only changes the actual System menu bitmap, but also does pretty much the same thing as the **SetTheSysMenu** routine by removing all unnecessary System menu items. It accomplishes the same goal through a totally different route; it starts with no System menu, then adds values for the Move and Close menuitems, SC_MOVE and SC_CLOSE respectively.

The routine starts by obtaining an object window through a call to **WinQueryObjectWindow**. We need to have an object window to set the actual System menu pull-down's parent, since the System menu pull-down is not a child of the frame, but is owned by the System menu. It is important to understand the window relationship in the entire System menu. The System menu bitmap window is owned by and is a child of the frame window. The system menu pull-down window is owned by the System menu bitmap window and is a child of our object window that we obtain from the desktop. The System menu bitmap window has a sibling window, the title bar window. The handle of the title bar window is obtained by calling **WinWindowFromID** with the frame identifier FID_TITLEBAR; the handle is stored in the HWND variable *hwndSibling*.

For backward compatibility, the current versions of PM still maintain all of the older system bitmaps. They can be found in the PMWIN.H header file, prefixed SBMP, along with all of the current System bitmaps. To implement our 1.x system menu bitmap, we obtain the handle to the bitmap by calling **WinGetSysBitmap** with the SBMP_OLD_SYSMENU value.

The next steps involve actually populating the MENUITEM data structures and adding them to our newly created menu windows via calls to MM_INSERTITEM. The code for this is given in Figure 8.12.

```
VOID ReplaceTheSystemMenu(HWND hwndFrame)
 {
   HWND      hwndSysMenu;
   HWND      hwndPullDown;
   HWND      hwndObject;
   HWND      hwndSibling;
   HBITMAP   hbm;
   MENUITEM  menuitem;
   CHAR      szMoveText[] = "~Move\tAlt+F7";
   CHAR      szCloseText[] = "~Close Product Information\tAlt+F4";

   hwndObject  = WinQueryObjectWindow(HWND_DESKTOP);
   hwndSibling = WinWindowFromID(hwndFrame, FID_TITLEBAR);
   hbm         = WinGetSysBitmap(HWND_DESKTOP, SBMP_OLD_SYSMENU);
```

Figure 8.12   The ReplaceTheSystemMenu function.   **continued**

```
      hwndSysMenu = WinCreateWindow(hwndFrame,
                                    WC_MENU,
                                    NULL,
                                    MS_ACTIONBAR | MS_TITLEBUTTON,
                                    0, 0, 0, 0,
                                    hwndFrame,
                                    hwndSibling,
                                    FID_SYSMENU,
                                    NULL,
                                    NULL ) ;

    hwndPullDown = WinCreateWindow(hwndObject,
                                   WC_MENU,
                                   NULL,
                                   NULLHANDLE,
                                   0, 0, 0, 0,
                                   hwndSysMenu,
                                   HWND_BOTTOM,
                                   FID_SYSMENUPOP,
                                   NULL,
                                   NULL ) ;

// Populate MENUITEM structure
  menuitem.iPosition   = MIT_END;
  menuitem.afStyle     = MIS_BITMAP  | MIS_SUBMENU;
  menuitem.afAttribute = NULLHANDLE;
  menuitem.id          = SC_SYSMENU;
  menuitem.hwndSubMenu = hwndPullDown;
  menuitem.hItem       = hbm;

  WinSendMsg(hwndSysMenu,       // Window Handle to send message to
             MM_INSERTITEM,     // Menu Message
             &menuitem,         // mp1 = MENUITEM structure
             NULL);             // mp2 = Text for Menuitem
  menuitem.iPosition   = MIT_END;
  menuitem.afStyle     = MIS_TEXT  | MIS_SYSCOMMAND;
  menuitem.afAttribute = NULLHANDLE;
  menuitem.id          = SC_MOVE;
  menuitem.hwndSubMenu = NULLHANDLE;
  menuitem.hItem       = NULLHANDLE;

  WinSendMsg(hwndPullDown,      // Window Handle to send message to
             MM_INSERTITEM,     // Menu Message
             &menuitem,         // mp1 = MENUITEM structure
             szMoveText);       // mp2 = Text for Menuitem

  menuitem.id          = SC_CLOSE;
  WinSendMsg(hwndPullDown,      // Window Handle to send message to
             MM_INSERTITEM,     // Menu Message
             &menuitem,         // mp1 = MENUITEM structure
             szCloseText);      // mp2 = Text for Menuitem
}
```

Figure 8.12 The ReplaceTheSystemMenu function.

The Action Bar Menu

The most important type of menu in an application is the action bar menu. It provides the user with choices that will execute the functionality of the program. Each option on the menu corresponds to a WM_COMMAND message that contains the instructions that the menu item will perform when selected. Figure 8.13 is the action bar menu for the PMEDIT sample program, where you can see that the File submenu has been selected, thus revealing the pull-down list of menuitems.

The sample application shown in this figure contains several submenus, including File and Edit. The submenu is generally not used to perform an application function, but rather to display additional menu item choices that will associate with a given function. The File submenu in this figure contains six menuitems that perform functions that are related to file operations such as opening a file and saving a file.

An action bar menu is usually defined as a resource in the resource script file and then built into the executable. A menu is identified in the resource file by the MENU keyword. Figure 8.14 is a sample of the action bar menu used in the PMEDIT sample. The action bar menu is included as part of the frame window by including the FCF_MENU frame creation flag when creating the frame window. The identifier specified in the MENU template in the resource file should correspond to the frame window identifier.

An application can choose to selectively create and load a menu by dynamically creating a menu by populating a MENUTEMPLATE(MT) structure in memory, and then create a window of the WC_MENU class.

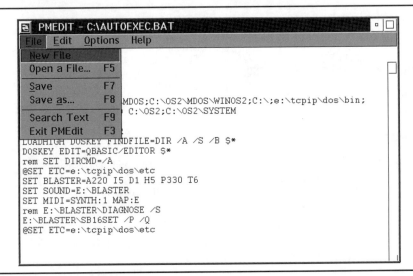

Figure 8.13   A sample action bar menu.

```
MENU ID_MAINWINDOW PRELOAD
{
 SUBMENU "~File",                            ID_FILEMENU, MIS_TEXT
  {
   MENUITEM "Create a ~New File",                IDM_FILENEW
   MENUITEM "Open a File...\tF5",                IDM_FILEOPEN
   MENUITEM SEPARATOR
   MENUITEM "~Save\tF7",                         IDM_FILESAVE
   MENUITEM "Save ~as...\tF8",                   IDM_FILESAVEAS
   MENUITEM SEPARATOR
   MENUITEM "Search...\tF9",                     IDM_FILESEARCH
   MENUITEM "Exit PMEdit\tF3",                   IDM_EXIT
  }

 SUBMENU "~Edit",                            ID_EDITMENU, MIS_TEXT
  {
   MENUITEM "~Undo\tAlt+Backspace",              IDM_EDITUNDO
   MENUITEM SEPARATOR
   MENUITEM "Cu~t\tShift+Delete",                IDM_EDITCUT
   MENUITEM "~Copy\tCtrl+Insert",                IDM_EDITCOPY
   MENUITEM "~Paste\tShift+Insert",              IDM_EDITPASTE
   MENUITEM SEPARATOR
   MENUITEM "Cl~ear\tDelete",                    IDM_EDITCLEAR
  }
}
```

Figure 8.14 **Sample of PMEDIT's action bar menu definition.**

```
typedef struct _mt        // mt
 {
  ULONG  ulLength;        // Length of template in bytes
  USHORT usCodepage;      // Codepage
  USHORT reserved;        // Reserved
  USHORT cMti;            // Count of template items
  MTI    rgMti[1];        // Array of template items
 } MT;
typedef MT *LPMT;
```

Figure 8.15 **The menu template structure MT.**

The MENUTEMPLATE structure that is defined in PMWIN.H is shown in Figure 8.15.

- *ulLength* is the length of the menu template in bytes.
- *usCodepage* represents the code page used for the menu.
- *reserved* is reserved.
- *cMti* is the total number of items in the template.

- *rgMti[1]* is an array of template items based on a menu template item structure MTI.

When a menu window is created by calling **WinCreateWindow** with the WC_MENU window class, the control data structure, specified by the **pCtlData** parameter of **WinCreateWindow**, should contain the menu template. Although using this method for creating a menu is not as simple as using the menu resource, it does provide more control for maintaining multiple menus.

The menu can be loaded dynamically by calling the **WinLoadMenu** API and sending menu messages to the window to change the menuitems. Menuitem messages are signified in PM by the prefix MM_. The *ToggleMenuItem* routine uses several of these messages to dynamically update the menuitems for the PMEDIT action bar menu. The format of the **WinLoadMenu** API is given in Figure 8.16.

The actual menu window code processes most messages needed for the menu so that maintaining a menu is relatively simple; the developer does not have to send paint messages to the frame for handling menu code. There are instances when creating or loading a menu window may require updating the frame window. This can be done by sending a WM_UPDATEFRAME message to force the frame to update the menu, after the menu has been modified.

Adding an Action Bar Menu to a Dialog Box

The purist PM programmer views the dialog box as a functional frame window that automates several of the complexities involved in frame window processing. Most dialogs are used as a simple user input mechanism, or as a vehicle to display information to the user. If complex drawing is required within the window, a dialog does not offer the flexibility of a frame window.

Therefore, most applications will create their own frame window by calling the function *WinCreateStdWindow*, and since most applications do not require additional action bar menus, there is usually no need to add one to a dialog window. Many purists believe that to add a menu to a dialog window contradicts the purpose and functionality of the dialog box because it is not intended to provide that type of interface. However, if you are writing a simple utility program that really doesn't do much, it may be easier to use a dialog window instead of a frame because of the various advantages offered by the dialog manager code within PMWIN (the code for which resides in PMMERGE.DLL in OS/2 WARP). Fortunately, adding an action bar menu to

```
HWND APIENTRY WinLoadMenu(HWND      hwndFrame,
                          HMODULE   hmod,
                          ULONG     idMenu);
```

Figure 8.16 The WinLoadMenu API.

```
MENU ID_DIALOGMENU
  {
   SUBMENU "~File",                    ID_FILEMENU
    {
     MENUITEM "Run Chkdsk",            IDM_CHKDSK
     MENUITEM "Exit This Dialog",      IDM_EXITDLG
    }
  }
```

Figure 8.17   The menu template for a dialog box.

a dialog is a relatively painless task. Besides, the differences between a dialog and a standard frame window are transparent to the application user.

To add an action bar menu to a dialog, define a MENU template in the resource script file as you would for any action bar menu. For this menu, do not use the same resource identifier as the frame window. The code is given in Figure 8.17.

The dialog procedure for the dialog box has to explicitly load the menu by calling the **WinLoadMenu** function, specifying the identifier for the dialog menu, which in this case is ID_DIALOGMENU. The procedure loads the menu as part of the initialization of the dialog, during the processing of the WM_INITDLG message. Once the menu is loaded, you must send a WM_UPDATEFRAME message to notify the frame window that the menu is added. The code fragment in Figure 8.18 is a dialog procedure that loads the action bar menu.

```
MRESULT EXPENTRY DialogMenuDlgProc (HWND hwnd, ULONG msg, MPARAM mp1, MPARAM mp2)
 {
  switch (msg)
   {
    case WM_INITDLG:
         WinLoadMenu (hwnd, NULLHANDLE, ID_DIALOGMENU);
         WinSendMsg  (hwnd, WM_UPDATEFRAME, 0,0);
         break;

    case WM_COMMAND:
         switch (COMMANDMSG(&msg)->cmd)
           {
            case DID_OK:
                 WinDismissDlg (hwnd, TRUE) ;
                 break;
           }
          break ;
    }
 return WinDefDlgProc (hwnd, msg, mp1, mp2) ;
 }
```

Figure 8.18   Adding an action bar menu to a dialog window.

```
MENU ID_MAINWINDOW PRELOAD
{
 PRESPARAMS PP_MENUFOREGROUNDCOLORINDEX, CLR_RED

 SUBMENU "~Classes",                            ID_OPTIONS, MIS_TEXT

   MENUITEM "~Math...\tF5",                     IDM_MATH
   MENUITEM "~Science...\tF6",                  IDM_SCIENCE
   MENUITEM "~Reading...\tF7",                  IDM_READING
   }
```

Figure 8.19   Changing the colors of a menu.

Using Presentation Parameters in Menu Templates

It is possible to change the presentation parameters for a menu window like if an application ever has a need to change the colors of an action bar menu. However, changing the presentation parameters for a menu window is not advisable, and contradicts CUA interface guidelines. The action bar menu, should be consistent among all PM applications, and the user should be responsible for configuring the appearance of the action bar menu. However, if the environment that you are developing the application for is specific to a defined set of users, it may be acceptable to change the menu colors to provide a simple customized interface. For example, if you are writing an application that will be the only application a user will ever run on their machine, like a machine used to control a plant-floor environment, the user will likely never use the workplace shell or any other application. So if you absolutely must, here is how it is done. The code fragment shown in Figure 8.19 changes the foreground color of the action bar menu and all of the menuitems.

POPUP MENUS

There are times that your application may need additional menu functionality outside the context of the action bar menu. For example, applications that create workplace objects that will interface with other objects will require a menu specific to that object. In this case, a popup menu provides the functionality for a particular object, since the menu is specific to that object. The popup menu is an integral part of the Workplace Shell paradigm, as it allows every object to have a unique menu. The format of the **WinPopupMenu** function is given in Figure 8.20.

```
BOOL APIENTRY WinPopupMenu(HWND    hwndParent,
                           HWND    hwndOwner,
                           HWND    hwndMenu,
                           LONG    lx,
                           LONG    ly,
                           LONG    idItem,
                           ULONG   usOptions);
```

Figure 8.20   The WinPopupMenu prototype.

- The **hwndParent** parameter is the window handle representing the parent window.
- The **hwndOwner** parameter is the window handle representing the owner window.
- The **hwndMenu** is the window handle representing the popup menu. The popup menu is typically created through the use of the **WinLoadMenu** API. The window handle returned by **WinLoadMenu** corresponds to this window handle.
- The **lx** parameter is the x coordinate representing the position of the popup menu in the window based on the origin of its parent window.
- The **ly** parameter is the y coordinate representing the position of the popup menu in the window based on the origin of its parent window.
- The **idItem** parameter represents a menuitem identifier within the popup menu that can be selected based on whether the PU_POSITIONITEM flag or the PU_SELECTITEM flag is set in the **usOptions** parameter.
- The **usOptions** parameter contains a series of flags that are combined to determine or set the position of the popup, the initial popup menu state, the selection state, as well as the horizontal or vertical constraints of the popup. There are also flags that determine the user input method that can be used to control the popup menu.

The **WinPopupMenu** function returns TRUE if the function is successful and FALSE if an error occurred. Figure 8.21 lists the valid option flags for **usOptions**.

Creating the Popup Menu

Adding a popup menu to your application is extremely simple. For the most part, the menu is constructed the same way as a standard action bar menu in the resource script file. The code fragment in Figure 8.22 from the resource script file is used to create the popup menu and the code fragment in Figure 8.23 loads the popup menu.

```
// Popup Menu position flag
            PU_POSITIONONITEM          0x0001

// Popup Menu constraint flags
            PU_HCONSTRAIN              0x0002
            PU_VCONSTRAIN              0x0004

// Popup Menu initial state flags
            PU_NONE                    0x0000
            PU_MOUSEBUTTON1DOWN        0x0008
            PU_MOUSEBUTTON2DOWN        0x0010
            PU_MOUSEBUTTON3DOWN        0x0018

// Popup Menu selection flags
            PU_SELECTITEM              0x0020

// Popup Menu user input method flags
            PU_MOUSEBUTTON1            0x0040
            PU_MOUSEBUTTON2            0x0080
            PU_MOUSEBUTTON3            0x0100
            PU_KEYBOARD                0x0200
```

Figure 8.21   The WinPopupMenu option flags.

```
MENU ID_POPUPMENU
{
 SUBMENU  "Change ~Attributes",      ID_ATTRIBS,,MIA_NODISMISS
  {
   MENUITEM "~Normal",               IDM_NORMAL,,MIA_CHECKED
   MENUITEM "~Bold",                 IDM_BOLD
   MENUITEM "~Italic",               IDM_ITALIC
   MENUITEM "~Underline",            IDM_UNDERLINE
  }

 SUBMENU  "Change Text ~Colors",     ID_COLORS,
  {
   MENUITEM "Default",               IDM_DEFAULT
   MENUITEM "Red",                   IDM_RED
   MENUITEM "Blue",                  IDM_BLUE
   MENUITEM "Green",                 IDM_GREEN
   MENUITEM "Yellow",                IDM_YELLOW
  }

 MENUITEM SEPARATOR
 MENUITEM "~Settings...",            IDM_SETTINGS
 MENUITEM "~Exit PMEDIT",            IDM_EXIT
}
```

Figure 8.22   Defining the popup menu.

```
MRESULT EXPENTRY MLESubclassProc(HWND hwnd, ULONG msg, MPARAM mp1, MPARM mp2)
{
 MRESULT rc;
 ULONG   ulOptions;
 POINTL  ptlCurrent;
 CHAR    szFont[30];

 static HWND    hwndPopup;

 // if the user presses the first mouse button anywhere in the MLE obtain
 // the position of the cursor and update the line numbers.
 if (msg == WM_BUTTON1DOWN)
  {
   rc = ((*OldMLEProc) (hwnd, msg, mp1, mp2));
   UpdateLineNumbers();
   return rc;
  }

 else if (msg == WM_BUTTON2DOWN)
  {
   WinQueryPointerPos(HWND_DESKTOP, &ptlCurrent);
   WinMapWindowPoints(HWND_DESKTOP, hwnd, &pt1Current, 1);

   if (hwndPopup)
    {
     WinDestroyWindow(hwndPopup);
    }

   hwndPopup = WinLoadMenu (hwnd, NULLHANDLE, ID_POPUPMENU);

   ulOptions = PU_NONE | PU_MOUSEBUTTON1 | PU_KEYBOARD | PU_HCONSTRAIN | PU_VCONSTRAIN;

   // set the font of the popup menu
   strcpy(szFont, "8.Courier");
   WinSetPresParam(hwndPopup, PP_FONTNAMESIZE, sizeof(szFont + 1, szFont);

   WinPopupMenu (hwnd,          // Parent Window is MLE
                 hwndClient,    // Owner is Client Window
                 hwndPopup,     // Window handle of Popup Menu
                 ptlCurrent.x,  // x coordinate
                 ptlCurrent.y,  // y coordinate
                 0,             // Item identity
                 ulOptions);    // Option Flags

   return ((*OldMLEProc) (hwnd, msg, mp1, mp2));
  }
 else
  {
   return ((*OldMLEProc) (hwnd, msg, mp1, mp2));
  }
}
```

Figure 8.23   Using the WinPopupMenu API.

```
ACCELTABLE ID_MAINWINDOW PRELOAD
{
VK_F2, IDM_ABOUT,        VIRTUALKEY
VK_F3, IDM_EXIT,         VIRTUALKEY
VK_F5, IDM_FILEOPEN,     VIRTUALKEY
VK_F7, IDM_FILESAVE,     VIRTUALKEY
VK_F8, IDM_FILESAVEAS,   VIRTUALKEY
VK_F9, IDM_FILESEARCH,   VIRTUALKEY
```

Figure 8.24   The Accelerator Table.

KEYBOARD ACCELERATORS

Making an application menu cooperate with the keyboard is an important part of designing a successful user interface. End users often associate particular functions with keys more easily than they can navigate through menuitems. Therefore, it is critical to provide a corresponding keyboard interface to your application menu. This functionality is known as the keyboard accelerator table. Essentially a keyboard accelerator is a shortcut key that allows the user quick access to the function of a particular menuitem. Since the accelerator represents a particular menuitem, it is important that the accelerator key make sense to the user selection.

It has become programming commonplace to reserve the F1 and F3 function keys for the specific functions Help and Exiting the application. (Consult the Common User Access (CUA) guidelines for complete keystroke recommendations.)

The easiest way to use keyboard accelerators is to specify the keyboard accelerator table as a resource in the resource script file, then include the resource when creating the frame window by using the frame control flag FCF_ACCELTABLE. Figure 8.24 is a sample ACCELERATOR table from the PMEDIT resource script file.

MENU MNEMONICS

OK, this is definitely a tongue twister. Try saying menu mnemonics five times really fast. Trust me, Menu Mnemonics are far easier to implement than having to say menu mnemonics. Although they are often taken for granted, and some users don't know what they provide, menu mnemonics offer a simple method for obtaining access to menuitem functions. The mnemonic keys are identified by an underscore character in one letter of the menu. The user can use make a selection with the keyboard quicker by pressing the mnemonic key as a shortcut. A mnemonic key on an action bar menu is accessed by pressing the

```
MENUITEM "~Save\tF7",        IDM_FILESAVE
MENUITEM "Save ~as...\tF8",  IDM_FILESAVEAS
```

Figure 8.25 MenuMnemonics.

key in conjunction with the Alt key. From a pulldown menu the user only needs to press the mnemonic key to make the selection from the keyboard. Like the accelerator keys, mnemonics need to make sense to the user. The mnemonic keys are defined by using a tilde character before the key to be used as a mnemonic in the menu. For example, the fragment shown in Figure 8.25 defines the mnemonic key "s" for the File/Save and "a" for File/Save as menuitems.

STANDARD DIALOGS

Virtually every PM application will somehow manipulate a file to perform some function within the application. The need to open and save files to a fixed disk prompted the development of a common user interface so that users could immediately become familiar with the opening and saving of files without being dependent on the application to provide the interface. Similarly, most applications that make heavy use of text or graphics need to provide an interface to the user to change fonts. Because of these demands, OS/2 2.0 introduced two new standard dialog windows, the standard file dialog, and the standard font dialog. We will focus primarily on the standard file dialog here. The standard font dialog is covered in detail in Chapter 16.

The Standard File Dialog

In previous versions of the Presentation Manager, it was up to the programmer to provide the interface for manipulating files to the user. In order to do this, the developer had to manually create dialog boxes with listbox and pushbutton controls, and then call file system functions such as ***DosQueryCurrentDisk***, ***DosQueryCurrentDir***, and ***DosFindFirst*** to fill the listboxes with the proper drive, directory, and file information. Therefore, almost every PM application available to the user had a different look and feel for opening and saving files. Although many file dialogs were elaborate, it took a great deal of programming time and effort on the part of the developer to provide a simple interface to the user.

The standard file dialog requires little coding on the part of the developer, and it is also simple to use. To create the standard file dialog, the developer simply calls one API, ***WinFileDlg***, and passes a pointer to a structure called FILEDLG, which contains all of the options available for the standard file dialog. The programmer also specifies the parent and owner windows, when calling **WinFileDlg**. The standard file dialog (SFD) can be used for either opening or saving a nonnamed file. These functions usually correspond to an Open or Save As option within a File submenu. The PMEDIT program uses the standard file dialog for both the Open and Save As functions.

The SFD is an extremely powerful dialog window, since it can be customized to accommodate the needs of the user. It may contain a help pushbutton, include extended attribute information, and it can even allow for multiple file selections. An example of the standard file dialog is shown in Figure 8.26.

The routine *StandardFileDialog* is called from within both the **FileOpen** and **FileSaveAs** routines, based on the specific type of dialog required for either opening or saving a nonnamed file. This routine takes parameters that coordinate the appearance of the standard file dialog by filling in the important elements of the FILEDLG structure.

The routine initially sets all of the elements of the structure to zero by calling the **memset** function, then calls **WinFileDlg** to draw the file dialog. The important elements of the FILEDLG structure that are specific to the appearance of our file dialog are filled in based on the parameters passed to **StandardFileDialog**. Specifically, we are interested in the title bar text of the dialog, the OK pushbutton text, and the flags that indicate whether an Open or Save As dialog is required. The final parameter is the filter parameter that tells the file dialog with which filetype extensions to filter the file listbox. This is useful when programs that only work with a specific filetype only want the user to see files of this type. For example, a graphics program may only want to fill the file listbox with .BMP files, rather than every single file in a

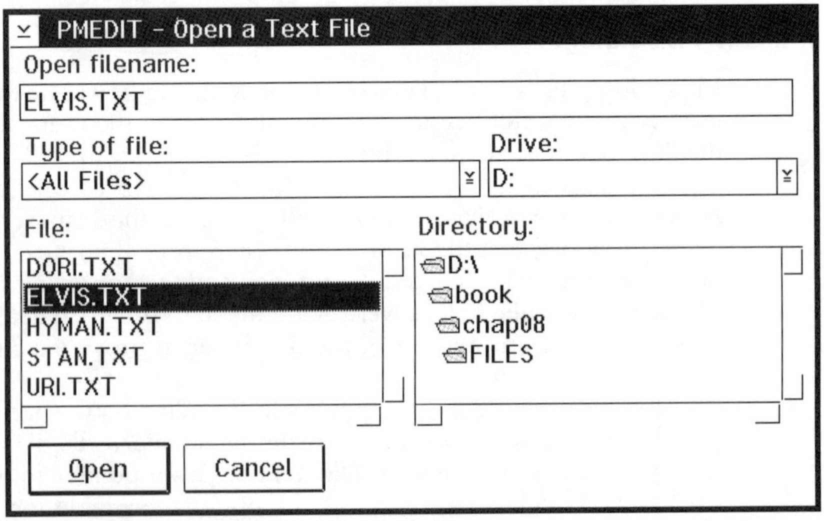

Figure 8.26 The Open File standard file dialog.

```
HWND APIENTRY WinFileDlg(HWND      hwndParent,
                         HWND      hwndOwner,
                         PFILEDLG  pfiledlg);
```

Figure 8.27 The WinFileDlg prototype.

given directory; this makes sense since only .BMP files will be read by the
program. Figure 8.27 has the function prototype for **WinFileDlg** as defined in
the PMSTDDLG.H header file.

- *hwndParent* is the window handle of the parent window.
- *hwndOwner* is the window handle of the owner window.
- *pfiledlg* is a pointer to a file dialog structure FILEDLG.

The **WinFileDlg** API will return a valid window handle representing the
standard file dialog if the FDS_MODELESS flag was specified, indicating that
the dialog is to be modeless. If the FDS_MODELESS flag is not specified,
then the function will return TRUE if the call completes successfully. Regardless of whether the FDS_MODELESS flag is set, the function will return a
NULLHANDLE if the dialog cannot be created successfully.

The file dialog structure FILEDLG is defined in PMSTDDLG.H as shown
in Figure 8.28.

```
typedef struct _FILEDLG      //filedlg
{
    ULONG     cbSize;
    ULONG     fl;
    ULONG     ulUser;
    LONG      lReturn;
    LONG      lSRC;
    PSZ       pszTitle;
    PSZ       pszOKButton;
    PFNWP     pfnDlgProc;
    PSZ       pszIType;
    PAPSZ     papszITypeList;
    PSZ       pszIDrive;
    PAPSZ     papszIDriveList;
    HMODULE   hMod;
    CHAR      szFullFile[CCHMAXPATH];
    PAPSZ     papszFQFilename;
    ULONG     ulFQFCount;
    USHORT    usDlgId;
    SHORT     x;
    SHORT     y;
    SHORT     sEAType;
} FILEDLG;
typedef FILEDLG FAR *PFILEDLG;
```

Figure 8.28 The FILEDLG structure.

- *cbSize* is the size of the FILEDLG structure.
- The *fl* element represents the file dialog flags. The flags are used to control the appearance and behavior of the standard file dialog. There are two basic types of standard file dialogs, the Open SFD and the Save As SFD. Therefore, this parameter must contain either the FDS_OPEN_DIALOG or FDS_SAVEAS_DIALOG flag. You must specify at least one of these flags, but you cannot specify both.

    All of the file dialog flags are listed here:

FDS_CENTER	0x00000001L	The use of this flag indicates that the dialog will be positioned in the center of its parent window. The use of this flag will supercede any specified x and y coordinates.
FDS_CUSTOM	0x00000002L	This flag is used to override the default appearance of the SFD by allowing the application to define a custom dialog template that will be used to replace the SFD. If this flag is used, the **hMod** and **usDlgID** fields of the structure must be valid.
FDS_FILTERUNION	0x00000004L	This flag is used to control the filtering of the FILES listbox. If this flag is set, the SFD uses a "union" of the EA type filter specified by **pszlType** and the string filter, which can be specified in the **szFullFile** character array.
FDS_HELPBUTTON	0x00000008L	This flag is used to add a Help pushbutton to the SFD. The pushbutton is created using the BS_HELP | BS_NOPOINTER FOCUS button styles by default, and a WM_HELP message is sent to the owner window specified by **hwndOwner**, in the call to **WinFileDlg**. The Help pushbutton's identifier is defined as DID_HELP_PB.
FDS_APPLYBUTTON	0x00000010L	This flag is used to add an Apply button to the dialog. The purpose of the Apply button is to allow the user to view the changes made through the use of the standard dialog, without actually dismissing the standard file dialog. Essentially, it performs the same functionality that the OK pushbutton performs, without dismissing the dialog. This button is typically designed for the modeless SFD, since the application

		input is not tied to the standard file dialog when using a modeless window; therefore, the user can move back and forth between the SFD and the window.
FDS_PRELOAD_VOLINFO	0x00000020L	The use of this flag allows the SFD to preload the volume information for the drives, and also to set the current default directory for every drive.
FDS_MODELESS	0x00000040L	This flag is used to make the standard file dialog a modeless dialog window.
FDS_INCLUDE_EAS	0x00000080L	This flag is used to force the dialog to search for extended attribute information every time it populates the FILES listbox.
FDS_OPEN_DIALOG	0x00000100L	This flag is used to indicate that the SFD is an Open dialog.
FDS_SAVEAS_DIALOG	0x00000200L	This flag is used to indicate that the SFD is a Save As dialog.
FDS_MULTIPLESEL	0x00000400L	This flag is used to give the user the ability to select multiple files from the FILES listbox.
FDS_ENABLEFILELB	0x00000800L	This flag is used to allow the FILES listbox on a Save As SFD to be enabled.

- The *ulUser* element is reserved for use by the application. This field is useful for applications that will end up subclassing the file dialog.
- The *lReturn* element is the actual value returned when the dialog is dismissed. If an error occurs during the processing of the dialog, this field is set to zero. Otherwise, the pushbutton identifier used to dismiss the dialog is returned.
- The *lSRC* element is the system return code. This element is used to provide more detailed information with regard to why the SFD failed. Figure 8.29 lists the return codes defined in PMSTDDLG.H.
- The *pszTitle* element is used to set the title of the standard file dialog window.
- The *pszOKButton* element is used to set the pushbutton text for the DID_OK pushbutton.
- The *pfnDlgProc* value represents a dialog window procedure that is to be used if the application is subclassing the standard file dialog. If this element contains a value, then the value should point to the dialog procedure that will handle the standard file dialog; otherwise, this value is set to NULL to indicate that the defualt standard file dialog procedure will do all of the dialog processing.

FDS_SUCCESSFUL	0
FDS_ERR_DEALLOCATE_MEMORY	1
FDS_ERR_FILTER_TRUNC	2
FDS_ERR_INVALID_DIALOG	3
FDS_ERR_INVALID_DRIVE	4
FDS_ERR_INVALID_FILTER	5
FDS_ERR_INVALID_PATHFILE	6
FDS_ERR_OUT_OF_MEMORY	7
FDS_ERR_PATH_TOO_LONG	8
FDS_ERR_TOO_MANY_FILE_TYPES	9
FDS_ERR_INVALID_VERSION	10
FDS_ERR_INVALID_CUSTOM_HANDLE	11
FDS_ERR_DIALOG_LOAD_ERROR	12
FDS_ERR_DRIVE_ERROR	13

Figure 8.29   The standard file dialog system return codes.

- The *pszIType* element contains a pointer to the EA type filter.
- The *papszlTypeList* value is a somewhat complex element. It is actually a pointer to a table of pointers that represent the extended attribute types. Every pointer in the table represents a different EA type and is actually a NULL-terminated string. The table is concluded with a NULL pointer. The EA types are sorted in ascending order in the Type of file combobox.
- The *pszlDrive* value contains a pointer to a string that represents the initial drive.
- The *papszlDriveList* element contains a pointer to a table of pointers representing the drives. Every pointer in the table is a NULL-terminated string that represents a valid drive. The drive table specified will be sorted in ascending order in the "Drive" combobox.
- The **hMod** parameter represents the DLL module containing the dialog resource. This value is only valid if the FDS_CUSTOM flag has been specified. A NULLHANDLE value indicates that the dialog resource is to be extracted from the executable.
- The *szFullFile* element specifies an array of CCMMAXPATH size. Prior to calling **WinFileDlg** this value contains a string containing the file filter extension. For example, a graphics program will only need to search for files with a .BMP extension. After the function completes, this value contains the fully qualified path and file name of the user selection.
- *papszFQFilename* is the pointer to a table of pointers leading to fully-qualified file names. This value is returned to SFD's that provide for multiple selections. This table of pointers is storage space allocated by the file dialog. When the application finishes opening or saving all of the files, the calling application must use the **WinFreeFileDlgList** API to free the memory allocated by the file dialog.
- *ulFQFCount* is the number of files that the user selected. Obviously, a single selection standard file dialog will return a value of 1.

- *usDlgID* is used only if a custom dialog template is requried for the standard file dialog. If the FDS_CUSTOM file dialog style is set, this value contains the window identifier of the representing the customized dialog template.
- *x;* is the horizontal position coordinate. The FDS_CENTER flag overrides this position and will automatically center the dialog in its parent.
- *y;* is the vertical position corrdinate. The FDS_CENTER flag overrides this position and will automatically center the dialog in its parent.
- *sEAType* is the extended-attribute type and is only used for the Save As standard file dialog. This element will contain a −1 value for an Open standard file dialog.

DIALOG BOXES

As a PM developer, you should already be familiar with many of the intricacies involved in creating and processing a dialog box. Therefore, since you already know how to display dialog boxes and process messages in a dialog window procedure, we will only review some of the more interesting dialog box issues. A dialog box is a special type of defined frame window, designed to provide the user with most of the functionality of a frame window, while being far easier to create. The dialog box itself is used to display information to the user or obtain information from the user. On occasion, it may be more practical to use a dialog window rather than create a frame window via **WinCreateStdWindow** as the main window of your program. This depends entirely on what the main window must do. After all, dialogs provide a tremendous benefit to application programming, since they automate much of the window processing code.

The dialog box will generally contain other control windows drawn within its client area. This is where much of the benefit of the dialog box can be obtained, as the complex control window processing is virtually eliminated. The control windows used within the dialog box are created through the use of the dialog template, and most of the processing for the controls is done automatically. The dialog manager code within the window manager (PMWIN) is responsible for creating, sizing, and setting the position of the control windows. The dialog box template is created in the resource script file via the DLGTEMPLATE keyword.

Processing the WM_INITDLG Message

The WM_INITDLG message is the dialog window equivalent of WM_CREATE. The first message parameter, **mp1** contains the window handle of the control window that will initially receive the input focus within the dialog. Typically, this window handle corresponds to the first control window that specifies the WS_TABSTOP window style. If an application needs to modify the focus window to change it to another control window within the dialog, it can change the focus within the context of the WM_INITDLG message. However, if the focus is changed within the processing of the WM_INITDLG, the message must return TRUE. A return value of TRUE is used to indicate that the default focus has been changed while a return value of FALSE indicates that the focus was not changed. The focus change will not occur unless the processing of the WM_INITDLG message returns TRUE. The second message parameter, **mp2** contains a pointer to application specific data that can be passed in the **pCreateParams** parameter of the dialog box functions: **WinLoadDlg**, **WinCreateDlg**, and **WinDlgBox**. Figure 8.30 illustrates a sample dialog template.

Another of the benefits derived from using a dialog box instead of creating a frame window is that the dialog manager provides a comprehensive keyboard interface. This interface provides the user the ability to navigate through the various controls on the dialog with relative ease by using the Tab key and the cursor movement (arrow) keys. The developer does not have to implement code to handle the shifting of the keyboard input focus when the user presses a key on the keyboard.

Understanding TabStops and Groups

One of the biggest benefits derived from using a dialog box instead of creating a frame window is that the dialog manager code in PMWIN provides a comprehensive keyboard interface. This interface provides the user the ability to navigate through the various controls on the dialog with relative ease by using the Tab key and the cursor movement (arrow) keys. The developer does

```
DLGTEMPLATE ID_SEARCH LOADONCALL MOVEABLE DISCARDABLE
{

DIALOG  "PMEDIT - Text Search Facility", ID_SEARCH, 75, 75, 250, 100, FS_NOBYTEALIGN | WS_VISIBLE,
                                                                 FCF_SYSMENU | FCF_TITLEBAR

  {
  LTEXT          "Search For:"                     -1,   25, 70, 55,  8
  ENTRYFIELD     "",                   IDE_SEARCHTEXT,   95, 70, 60,  8, ES_MARGIN

  LTEXT          "Replace With:"                   -1,   25, 50, 55,  8
  ENTRYFIELD     "",                   IDE_REPLACETEXT,  95, 50, 60,  8, ES_MARGIN

  AUTOCHECKBOX   "Case Sensitive",     IDC_CASECHECK,    90, 30, 90, 10, WS_GROUP
  DEFPUSHBUTTON  "~Find"               IDD_FIND,         40,  8, 45, 15, WS_GROUP
  PUSHBUTTON     "~Replace"            IDD_REPLACE,      90,  8, 45, 15,
  PUSHBUTTON     "~Cancel"             DID_OK,          140,  8, 45, 15,
  }
}
```

Figure 8.30   Sample dialog box template.

not have to implement code to handle the shifting of the keyboard input focus when the user presses a key on the keyboard.

A *tabstop* is specified with the WS_TABSTOP window style. It is used to determine the order in which the input focus will be changed when the user presses the Tab key. As a result of the user pressing the Tab key on a dialog window, the input focus is switched to the next control window that has specified the WS_TABSTOP style. Once the last tabstop is reached, the tabstop processing wraps around to the first tabstop window again. The button control windows defined by the DEFPUSHBUTTON, PUSHBUTTON, AUTOCHECK-BOX, and CHECKBOX specifiers are declared with the WM_TABSTOP style by default. Other control window specifiers like LISTBOX and ENTRYFIELD use the tabstop style as well.

The tabstop window style can be removed from within the context of a program by using the **WinSetWindowBits** API, specifying the QWL_STYLE index to modify the value stored in the window words. The code fragment shown in Figure 8.31 removes the tabstop style from three checkbox buttons. The code uses a *for* loop to scan through each of the checkboxes. The checkbox identifiers are defined in numeric order beginning with IDC_SUPLOGO. The *ulcounter* variable is used to index each of the individual button identifiers. For each button identifier, the **WinWindowFromID** API is used to set each member of the *hwndCheckbox* array to the corresponding window handle for the checkboxes.

A group is similar to a tabstop, except it defines how the input focus will be changed when the user manipulates the cursor movement keys on the keyboard. The group itself is identified by the first control window that specifies the WS_GROUP window style, until the next control that specifies the WS_GROUP style. All control windows between are part of the group, meaning that the user can move the arrow keys to cycle through all of the controls declared within the group.

Sizing a Dialog Window

A dialog procedure handles the sizing of a window a little bit differently from a client window procedure. A dialog window procedure will not get a WM_SIZE message, so if your dialog procedure contains a WM_SIZE message it will never be received and thus never processed. The WM_SIZE message

```
for (ulCounter = 0; ulCounter < 3; ulCounter++)
  {
  hwndCheckBox[ulCounter] = WinWindowFromID(hwnd, IDC_SUPLOGO + ulCounter);
  WinSetWindowBits(hwndCheckBox[ulCounter], QWL_STYLE, 0, WS_TABSTOP);
  }
```

Figure 8.31   Using the WinSetWindowBits API.

that is sent to a client window procedure originates from the default window procedure as a result of a WM_WINDOWPOSCHANGED message being received. A dialog window procedure will not get this message because the frame window processing for the dialog does not pass the message along to the window procedure. Therefore, a dialog procedure should process the WM_WINDOWPOSCHANGED message directly if it requires the window to be sized. It is important to note; however, that a typical dialog window should not be sizeable because the FCF_DLGBORDER frame control flag, which is typically used by dialog boxes, does not allow for sizing.

Avoiding a Common Error

The MLE control provides the foundation for the editor. Essentially, the sample program draws an MLE within the contents of the client area. Therefore, since the MLE is the primary source of input, it is expected and desired that the MLE contain the edit control cursor—the vertical I beam cursor—when the program is started, so that the user can immediately start entering text via the keyboard, rather than having to explicitly give the MLE control input focus.

The quick and dirty solution would be to simply add a call to the**WinSet-Focus** API to modify the focus chain by setting the MLE control window to the primary focus window when the application is started. For example, in the routine *CreateEditWindow* you could add the code in Figure 8.32 after the **WinCreateWindow** function has successfully returned the hwndMLE handle.

At first glance, this resolution seems to work without a flaw. However, you must proceed with caution anytime you explicitly modify the focus window, since it can alter the focus chain for other situations. This solution is flawed, as it forces the input focus to the MLE window every time the application is started and the MLE control window is created. What if the user did not want the application to start in the foreground? For example, the user could use the START command to invoke the editor in the background as shown here:

```
[C:\PMEDIT]  START PMEDIT.EXE /B
```

Although the session manager will attempt to start the session in the background, the call to **WinSetFocus** will force the focus to the MLE window every time the application is started. This effectively changes the behavior that the user was attempting to accomplish.

A better solution is to not directly modify the current focus window, but instead modify the focus chain so that the child windows of the frame window are

---

```
WinSetFocus(HWND_DESKTOP, hwndMLE);
```

Figure 8.32 Setting the focus to the MLE window.

```
WinSetWindowULong(hwndFrame, QWL_HWNDFOCUSSAVE, hwndMLE);
```

Figure 8.33   **Altering the child window focus for a frame window.**

changed to indicate that the MLE window is the next window that should get the input focus. In order to accomplish this, use the QWL_HWNDFOCUSSAVE flag to alter the window words as shown in Figure 8.33.

By changing this value in the window words, you are telling the frame that the MLE control window was the last child window of **hwndFrame** to have the input focus prior to the frame window being deactivated. In effect this will allow the MLE control to have the input cursor without forcing it to have focus every time it is created, since the MLE window is the first child window in the focus chain for that frame. Now, if you use the START command again to start the editor in the background, you will notice that with this code the editor can successfully be started in the background because the MLE window does not automatically steal the input focus.

SUMMARY

The application interface is the most important part of any program. Even the most technically advanced software package will not succeed if it offers a poor user interface. Making the best use of PM resources like those described in this chapter is critical to developing an easy-to-use piece of software. The Presentation Manager provides powerful resource functionality, but it is up to the application development community to ensure that the application user interface is easy to use.

CHAPTER 9

Communication Between Applications Using PM's Dynamic Data Exchange Protocol

In the age of the information superhighway and other powerful networking systems, the need for applications to communicate effectively and efficiently with one another is paramount to the success of any operating system. The ability for independent processes to share resources has become known as Interprocess Communication or IPC. The purpose of Interprocess Communication is to allow multiple independent programs to share information with one another. OS/2 provides several methods of Interprocess Communication within the operating system. Of the various methods of Interprocess Communication supported by OS/2, only one provides a robust set of features for the Presentation Manager environment; it is known as the Dynamic Data Exchange, or DDE for short. Dynamic Data Exchange is actually a message-based protocol that operates on a window granular basis, meaning that information is exchanged between one window called the DDE server and another window called the DDE client.

Through the use of DDE, unrelated programs that run within the Presentation Manager screen group can effectively share information with one another. Because this communication is dynamic, unlike that of the PM Clipboard, the information sharing is totally transparent to the user since the user is not responsible for processing the communication transaction. This means that as long as two or more applications provide for the communication within the program code by using the DDE protocol, they can obtain information from one another without any user interaction.

DDE has long been a powerful, yet often misunderstood programming concept. Unfortunately, few software development companies have realized the true potential of DDE and how it can assist in making multiple applications cooperate with one another. One huge benefit of the power of DDE is demonstrated in this chapter's sample program. The sample program shows how DDE can be used to bridge the application porting gap, by allowing one large software vendor with a new 32-bit PM application to communicate with an existing Windows-based application running in the WIN-OS/2 environment. DDE can provide the powerful link between PM and Windows applications, because the DDE message protocol is essentially the same in both programming environments.

The DDE protocol was designed to provide the PM development community with an architected data exchange process. In and of itself, DDE is not a complete interprocess communications layer. The DDE protocol still requires the use of shared memory and pipes internally to accomplish the goal of exchanging information between the communicating processes. The actual information exchange occurs through the use of shared memory. One of the communicating processes will be responsible for giving the other process access to the memory via a pointer to the memory. This ensures that the communicating processes can freely exchange information through this common piece of memory.

The actual DDE protocol is nothing more than a series of window functions and messages designed to help the communicating processes talk to one another. Through the use of the pre-defined DDE messages, the communicating processes can decide how, when, and where the information will be exchanged. A single window within each of the processes is responsible for handling the communication. The window that initiates the exchange by requesting data is known as the DDE client. The window that provides the information to the client is known as the DDE server.

IMPLEMENTING THE DDE COMMUNICATION ARCHITECTURE

If the seamless Windows concept was to be a success for IBM, the seamless development and design phases would have to ensure that any Windows application be able to communicate effectively with any other application running within the Presentation Manager screen group. Since the Dynamic Data Exchange protocol is extremely similar between the Windows and PM environments, DDE would provide a powerful communications link to application developers to allow applications within different user-interface platforms to share information. To fulfill the common Dynamic Data Exchange philosophy, an intermediary component would have to bridge the gap between the PM and Windows DDE implementations; therefore, the Windows DDE Agent was created.

There were two limitations that the Windows DDE agent was created to address. The first was the obvious desire for Windows applications to communicate with PM applications through the use of the Dynamic Data Exchange. The second was to allow Windows applications that run in independent Virtual DOS Machine (VDM) sessions to communicate with each other; since applications running within different VDMs do not share resources, the standard Windows DDE protocol would not allow these Windows applications to share information. The Windows DDE agent, named WINSDDE.DLL, acts as the interface to resolve both limitations. On the PM side, a module called PMDDE.DLL contains the code for the super agent code. Among other things, the super agent code contains a routine that is responsible for spawning a communication thread that will communicate with each VDM. The actual code for the DDE API functions is contained within the window manager, PMWIN.DLL.

THE PURPOSE OF THE SAMPLE PROGRAM

Just when you thought you would never have to look at Windows code again, along comes this chapter and the programming example. For those of you who are entering the PM development environment without the benefit of previous programming experience in Windows, this chapter will provide you the ability to briefly evaluate some of the similarities and differences between the two graphical programming interfaces.

This chapter actually contains two sample programs. The first is a simple PM-based application which functionally resembles a spreadsheet. The application is called PMSTATS and is used to track customer satisfaction survey information. As with any spreadsheet, PMSTATS is used to collect numerical data from the user. The numerical data is entered via the spreadsheet dialog window, which is invoked by selecting an option from the application menu.

The spreadsheet dialog window contains various entryfield control windows representing monthly customer satisfaction percentages. The user can enter the monthly statistical information for a product by filling in the entryfields with the information for the corresponding month. The data can be entered only as numeric characters 1 through 100, since it is percentage based. The information entered is based on a complete calendar year. Once the information is completed, it can be saved to a file or sent to a charting program to create a visual representation of the numeric data. For the purposes of our sample, we will create a simple Windows-based program that will chart customer satisfaction.

The entryfields used to enter the monthly sales information are subclassed so that only numeric information will be accepted, thereby preventing the user from entering any character other than a whole number. The process of filtering out all non-numeric characters other than a space is done through the **FilterEntryFieldProc** window procedure. The code is in Figure 9.1.

The purpose of this routine is to evaluate all WM_CHAR messages that are sent to the entryfield windows. The C library macro **isdigit** can be used to determine whether the character just entered by the user is a number. If the character entered is a valid number, then the function will return a pointer to the original subclassed entryfield procedure, so that the processing of this character can continue through the entryfield default window procedure as normal. If the character is not a number, then the user will get the beloved raspberry tone generated by calling the **WinAlarm** function with the WA_ERROR beep tone. Subclassing is explained in further detail in Chapter 10.

The second sample program is a 16-bit Windows-based application called WINCHART. The source code was built using the WATCOM compiler for Windows. If you do not have a DOS-based compiler and the Windows Software Development Kit (SDK), don't worry, you will at least be able to see the DDE interaction by using the WINCHART executable; that is, you will be able to see how the communication works between the PM and WIN-OS/2 application, assuming that you have WIN-OS/2 support installed and that your video adapter can support seamless windows.

The purpose of these sample programs is to show how effectively DDE can be used to communicate between PM and Windows. The WINCHART executable, based on the information provided by PMSTATS (see Figure 9.2), will draw a chart illustrating the customer information.

```
MRESULT EXPENTRY FilterEntryFieldProc(HWND hwnd, ULONG msg, MPARAM mp1, MPARAM mp2)
{
 if (msg == WM_CHAR)
  {
   if (!(CHARMSG(&msg)->fs & KC_VIRTUALKEY))
    if (CHARMSG(&msg)->fs & KC_CHAR)
     if (isdigit(CHARMSG(&msg)->chr))
      {
       return ((*OldEntryFieldProc)(hwnd, msg, mp1, mp2));
      }

    else
      {
       WinAlarm(HWND_DESKTOP, WA_ERROR);
       return FALSE;
      }
   }
  } /* endif WM_CHAR */
 return (*OldEntryFieldProc)(hwnd, msg, mp1, mp2);
}
```

Figure 9.1   Subclassing the entryfields.

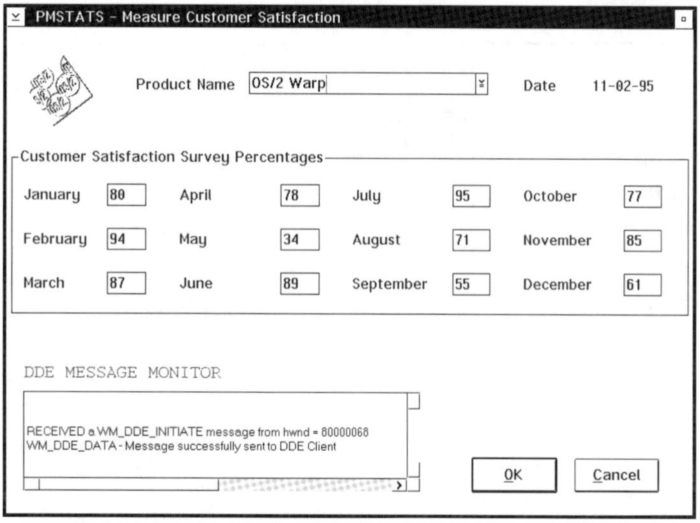

Figure 9.2   The PMSTATS data entry facility.

Understanding the Client and Server Interaction

Any DDE server can send data to multiple DDE clients simultaneously, and likewise, any DDE client can actually get data from multiple DDE servers. In the case of these sample programs, the Windows application WINCHART is the client application, since it is requesting the monthly numbers that it needs to draw a chart to visualize the statistical information. The PM-based application PMSTATS is the server since it will be providing the numerical information to the Windows program. The actual user will only be entering data in the PMSTATS application. The WINCHART program will obtain the numeric information from PMSTATS via the data exchange; therefore, the user does not actually have to enter any numbers in WINCHART. It is important to note that the communication does not have to terminate with just the single interaction with the server and client. Once it receives its data, The DDE client can now in turn act as a server by passing its information on to another window, which would be the new client. For example, the sample program WINCHART can take the entire chart that it composed and save the information as a bitmap image. The bitmap could then be transferred to a word processor which, when combined with other text, can create a document. In this case, the WINCHART program would then be providing the information to the word processor. The word processor would be the one that initiated the DDE communication to WINCHART, making the WINCHART program the server and the word processor the client. Figure 9.3 illustrates this communication.

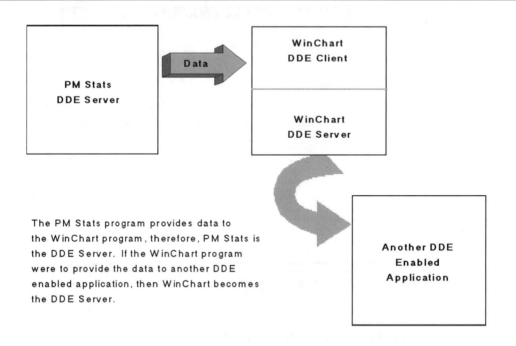

The PM Stats program provides data to the WinChart program, therefore, PM Stats is the DDE Server. If the WinChart program were to provide the data to another DDE enabled application, then WinChart becomes the DDE Server.

Figure 9.3 Understanding the DDE client/server communication process.

Understanding the Data Transfer Hierarchy

As discussed, DDE is a method enabling two independent applications to share information with one another. The DDE client is the application that is requesting data from another application, while the DDE server is the application that is providing the information. The DDE client usually knows the type of information that is needed to complete the transaction, along with which applications the data can be requested from. Therefore, the DDE communication starts with an *application link*, which is the process of using a string name to represent an application that is used by the DDE client to identify from which DDE server information is needed.

The application name string is a NULL-terminated ASCII string used to identify the DDE server; therefore, the application name string can usually be the same as the application itself. Each DDE client application that wants to communicate with any DDE server must typically know the name of the application string, although, as you will soon find out, it is possible for the DDE client to communicate with any DDE-empowered application by not specifying an application name string.

DDE MESSAGES

There are currently 12 DDE messages defined in PMWIN.H. Of the 12 only 10 are commonly used. The other two DDE messages, WM_Dde_FIRST and WM_DDE_LAST, are used internally by the **WinDdePostMsg** function to validate that you are actually passing 1 of 10 messages numerically between WM_DDE_FIRST and WM_DDE_LAST. If you have the debug version of PMWIN and attempt to pass any other message, you will get an invalid parameter message returned from **WinDDEPostMsg**. The DDE messages are defined in PMWIN.H as shown in Figure 9.4.

Initiating a DDE Conversation Using WM_DDE_INITIATE

WM_DDE_INITIATE is used to establish the communication link between the client and server windows. It is sent by the DDE client window to the server. In WINCHART.C, it is used to establish the connection to the data contained in the spreadsheet window for PMSTATS. It can be done from almost anywhere within the window's client window procedure. For example, for dynamic connection, it can be done whenever a window is created by sending the message in the WM_CREATE or WM_INITDLG messages. The problem with doing the communication this way is that if the server window is not started, then the initiation will fail. You can circumvent this by setting a timer and continuously sending the WM_DDE_INITIATE message until the proper connection with the server is established. If the server is still not started, then at some time interval you can alert the user that the DDE connection cannot be established, prompting the user to start the DDE server application or the client application can start the server by calling **DosStartSession**. The easiest way to establish the DDE communication link is by sending the WM_DDE_INITIATE message as a result of receiving a WM_COMMAND message.

```
WM_DDE_FIRST            0x00A0
WM_DDE_INITIATE         0x00A0
WM_DDE_REQUEST          0x00A1
WM_DDE_ACK              0x00A2
WM_DDE_DATA             0x00A3
WM_DDE_ADVISE           0x00A4
WM_DDE_UNADVISE         0x00A5
WM_DDE_POKE             0x00A6
WM_DDE_EXECUTE          0x00A7
WM_DDE_TERMINATE        0x00A8
WM_DDE_INITIATEACK      0x00A9
WM_DDE_LAST             0x00AF
```

Figure 9.4   The DDE messages.

```
if (szApplication && szTopic)
 {
  SendMessage (HWND_BROADCAST,              // Broadcast to all
               WM_DDE_INITIATE,             // Message
               (WORD)hwnd,                  // DDE client window
               MAKELONG(szApplication,      // Appname and Topic
                        szTopic));
 }
```

Figure 9.5   Sending a WM_DDE_INITIATE message to the DDE server.

In the window procedure **DrawChartDlgProc** (see WINCHART.C), DDE communication is requested through the following processing of the DID_OK identifier. This WM_COMMAND message is processed when the user clicks on the Connect pushbutton. The code is shown in Figure 9.5.

In this code sample, we are actually using the **SendMessage** API, which is the Windows equivalent of **WinSendMsg**, to send a WM_DDE_INITIATE message to the DDE server PMSTATS to request a DDE conversation. This is not the way to initiate a DDE conversation in the PM environment, but it does the trick for the purposes of our demonstration program. In PM, an application initiates a DDE data conversation by using the **WinDdeInitiate** API.

Although the **SendMessage** function differs slightly from its PM counterpart, the parameters used to send the message are similar. The first parameter is the window to which the message is being sent. In our case, the constant HWND_BROADCAST with a value of −1 decimal or 0xFFFF hexadecimal is the window handle we are sending the message to, which means that the message is going to be broadcast to all top-level frame windows. A top-level frame window is simply any frame window whose parent is the desktop window. All top-level windows are registered with the class style of CS_FRAME.

PM will enumerate all children of the desktop looking for windows that are registered with the frame class style. The first message parameter sent in the message is the window handle of the DDE client window. The second message parameter contains two strings which were created as ATOMS. The strings **szApplication** and **szTopic** contain the application name and topic name of the DDE server with which our DDE client window is attempting to communicate. In our case, the application name is PM_Stats and the topic that we are interested in is called ChartTopic.

Using WinDdeInitiate to Initiate the DDE Conversation

For the purposes of illustrating how effective DDE can be to communicate between the PM and Windows environments, the DDE client in our sample program is a Windows application. Therefore, we are forced to manually send an initiation message. Other DDE client applications written for PM can call the **WinDdeInitiate** API instead of sending the WM_DDE_INITIATE message. Functionally, using the **WinDdeInitiate** function is the same as sending the message from the DDE client since this function will also initiate a DDE conversation by sending the WM_DDE_INITIATE message. Using this function, any DDE client application can initiate a DDE conversation with a specified national conversation context, thereby supporting multiple language data exchanges.

The format of the **WinDdeInitiate** function is given in Figure 9.6.

- The **hwndDDEClient** parameter is the window handle of the DDE client window.
- The **pszAppname** parameter is the application name string which is used to identify the DDE server that the DDE client is attempting to communicate with. Under the current PM implementation, this string cannot contain slashes or backslashes. A zero-length string signifies that any DDE server application can respond to the initiation.
- The **pszTopicName** parameter specifies the name of the topic that DDE client is seeking support for. A zero-length string signifies that each responding DDE server application will respond once for every topic name that it knows how to support.
- The **pConvContext** parameter is a pointer to a DDE Conversation Context structure.

Using Unnamed Application and Topic Name Strings

The actual DDE data exchange revolves around the communicating applications knowing the application name string and the topic name string for the DDE data conversation. As the parameters from the **WinDdeInitiate** function illustrate, the **pszAppName** and **pszTopicName** strings can be zero-length strings. A zero length string simply implies that the DDE client is willing to communicate with any DDE server and using multiple topics of conversation. This allows the DDE client to communicate with DDE servers that it does not know the application name string for, since it can identify all active DDE servers, and can also identify all the topics supported by a particular DDE server.

```
BOOL APIENTRY WinDdeInitiate(HWND          hwndDDEClient,
                             PSZ           pszAppName,
                             PSZ           pszTopicName,
                             PCONVCONTEXT  pConvContext);
```

Figure 9.6   The WinDdeInitiate API.

Using the System Topics

Since the DDE protocol is public domain, it makes sense that there is a global system topic and associated topic name strings. It makes good programming practice to use these predefined items, since it allows the DDE client to initiate the DDE conversation based on an existing topic name string, thereby potentially saving the time needed for DDE initiation. The reason for this is that the DDE server will not have to acknowledge the initiation with a WM_DDE_INITIATEACK message for each and every topic it supports, as it must do with a DDE client that specifies an unnamed topic name string in **pszTopicName**. The pre-defined system topic and item name strings are listed in Figure 9.7.

A Dynamic Data Exchange conversation can be initiated through the use of the **WinDdeInitiate** function or, as was done in WINCHART, through the sending of the WM_DDE_INITIATE message. Regardless of the method of DDE initiation, a DDE initiation structure (DDEINIT) is populated for the application initiating the communication. All the caller needs to specify is the DDE client that will be requesting the initiation along with the application and topic name strings for which the DDE client application will be seeking support.

When the DDE server application responds positively to an initiation request, the worker routine for **WinDdeRespond** calls another routine that initializes the initiation data appropriate for the response and then sends an acknowledgement message in the form of WM_DDE_INITIATEACK back to the DDE client. When the message is received by the DDE client, the message contains the handle of the DDE server window along with a pointer to the actual populated DDEINIT structure. The DDE client application can determine whether to begin a data conversation based on the **pszTopic** name string in the DDEINIT structure.

Most applications do not need to explicitly fill in the DDEINIT structure since it is done automatically by the initiation process, although applications

```
#define SZDDESYS_TOPIC                "System"
#define SZDDESYS_ITEM_TOPICS          "Topics"
#define SZDDESYS_ITEM_SYSITEMS        "SysItems"
#define SZDDESYS_ITEM_RTNMSG          "ReturnMessage"
#define SZDDESYS_ITEM_STATUS          "Status"
#define SZDDESYS_ITEM_FORMATS         "Formats"
#define SZDDESYS_ITEM_SECURITY        "Security"
#define SZDDESYS_ITEM_ITEMFORMATS     "ItemFormats"
#define SZDDESYS_ITEM_HELP            "Help"
#define SZDDESYS_ITEM_PROTOCOLS       "Protocols"
#define SZDDESYS_ITEM_RESTART         "Restart"
```

Figure 9.7   The standard system topic and item name strings.

should be aware of the structure since they can obtain the application and topic name strings from the structure when receiving either a WM_DDE_INITIATE or WM_DDE_INITIATEACK message in their client window procedure.

The Reason for a Common DDE Protocol

Before an established DDE protocol was complete and understood by programmers, DDE messages could actually be used outside of the context of a DDE conversation. In other words, applications could initiate the DDE process without using the DDE protocol. As a result, any two applications that had a private protocol and had access to the other applications window handle could exchange DDE messages with one another, since the only place that the DDE messages are validated is in the **WinDdePostMsg** API. Using this method to initiate data exchanges and send DDE messages is bad news, because the DDE structures are subject to change, and although elements of the structures may change, the structures' support will always be backward-compatible through the use of the DDE APIs and messages. But applications that explicitly rely on values in the structure may not work in future releases of the Presentation Manager.

DDEINIT Structure

The DDEINIT structure is defined within PMWIN.H as shown in Figure 9.8.

- The *cb* element is the size of the entire DDEINIT structure.
- The *pszAppname* element is the application name string, which is used to identify the DDE server that the DDE client is attempting to communicate with. Under the current 2.x PM implementation, this string cannot contain slashes or backslashes.
- The *pszTopic* element is a pointer to a NULL-terminated string that is used to signify the topic of communication.
- The *offConvContext* element is a ULONG value, which represents the offset into a CONVCONTEXT structure.

```
typedef struct _DDEINIT    /* ddei */
 {
  ULONG    cb;             /* sizeof(DDEINIT) */
  PSZ      pszAppName;
  PSZ      pszTopic;
  ULONG    offConvContext;
} DDEINIT;
typedef DDEINIT *PDDEINIT;
```

Figure 9.8   The DDE initiation structure.

```
typedef struct _CONVCONTEXT     /* cctxt */
{
   ULONG cb;               /* sizeof(CONVCONTEXT) */
   ULONG fsContext;
   ULONG idCountry;
   ULONG usCodepage;
   ULONG usLangID;
   ULONG usSubLangID;
} CONVCONTEXT;
typedef CONVCONTEXT *PCONVCONTEXT;
```

Figure 9.9   The DDE conversation context structure.

A CONVCONTEXT structure contains language-specific information so that developers can build applications based on National Language Support (NLS). The information within this structure identifies country and code page information. The format of the structure is given in Figure 9.9.

- The *cb* element is the size of the structure.
- The *fsContext* element is a ULONG containing the conversation context flags. This flag field can contain the following constant defined in PMWIN.H:

DDECTXT_CASESENSITIVE   0x0001   This is used to indicate that the strings in this conversation are case-sensitive.

- The *idCountry* element is a ULONG containing the country code.
- The *usCodepage* element is actually defined as a ULONG, but it only contains the code page information for the country.
- The *usLangID* element is the language identifier. If this element is zero, then no language information is present.
- The *usSubLangID* element is the sublanguage identifier. If this element is zero, then no sublanguage information is present.

The **WinDdeInitiate** function will also automatically broadcast a WM_DDE_INITIATE message to all top-level windows, looking for a DDE server that can support the requested application name and topic name strings. In WINCHART, we used the Windows API **SendMessage** to send the WM_DDE_INITIATE message. The worker routine for **WinDdeInitiate** also sends the message to the DDE server. Therefore, since the message is sent and not posted to the DDE server, all DDE server window procedures that choose to process the WM_DDE_INITIATE message must respond to the message before returning control to the requesting DDE client.

Since the WM_DDE_INITIATE message is broadcast to all top-level frame windows (all windows that are registered with the class style CS_FRAME), this means that the receipient DDE server should be the main PMSTATS window. Therefore, the WM_DDE_INITIATE message should be processed within the context of the client window procedure **ClientWndProc** in PMSTATS.C, rather than in a dialog procedure. This is why the code to handle the DDE messages is within the client window procedure not the spreadsheet dialog procedure.

In the PMSTATS sample program, the WM_DDE_INITIATE message is received and processed by the client window procedure. When the message is received, **mp1** contains the window handle of the DDE client window that is making the request to initiate the DDE conversation. The **mp2** parameter contains a pointer to a DDEINIT structure which contains the application and topic name strings.

PMSTATS will process the WM_DDE_INITIATE message by checking the application name. If the application name is correct, then it will send a positive response back to the DDE client. The relevent code is given in Figure 9.10.

Using WinDdeRespond

Once the DDE server processes the conversation inititation, it can send an acknowledgment to the DDE client by using the **WinDdeRespond** API. This function is used to respond to the DDE client by informing the DDE client window that the server can support the specified topic names. Using this call is the same as responding with a WM_DDE_INITIATEACK message to the DDE client that originally requested the initiation through aWM_DDE_INITIATE message.

The format of **WinDdeRespond** is as shown in Figure 9.11.

- The **hwndDDEClient** parameter is the window handle of the DDE client window, which is the window that is receiving the response.

```
case WM_DDE_INITIATE:
    if (!(strcmp(((PDDEINIT)mp2)->pszAppName, APPNAME)))
    {
    hwndDDEClient = (HWND)mp1;
    sprintf(szBuffer,"RECEIVED a WM_DDE_INITIATE message from hwnd = %8.8X",
            hwndDDEClient);
    SendTextToMLE(szBuffer);

    WinDdeRespond(hwndDDEClient,    // DDE Client Window Handle
                  hwnd,             // DDE Server Window Handle(our client window)
                  APPLICATION,      // Application name
                  TOPIC,            // Topic name
                  (PCONVCONTEXT)0); // Conversation Context
    }
    break;
```

Figure 9.10 Processing the WM_DDE_INITIATE message.

```
MRESULT APIENTRY WinDdeRespond(HWND        hwndDDEClient,
                               HWND        hwndDDEServer,
                               PSZ         pszAppName,
                               PSZ         pszTopicName,
                               PCONVCONTEXT pcctxt);
```

Figure 9.11   The WinDdeRespond API.

- The **hwndDDEServer** parameter is the window handle of the DDE server window, which is the window that is sending the response. If the DDE server is responding to more than one topic, a unique window must be used for each topic that will be responded to.
- The **pszAppName** parameter is the application name string, which is used to identify the DDE server that the DDE client is attempting to communicate with. Under the current 2.x PM implementation, this string cannot contain slashes or backslashes. This parameter cannot contain a zero-length string.
- The **pszTopicName** parameter specifies the name of the topic that the DDE server can support. Like the **pszAppname** parameter, it cannot contain a zero-length string.
- The **pcctxt** parameter is a pointer to a DDE conversation context structure.

In PMSTATS, this function is called inside the WM_DDE_INITIATE message processing to tell the WINCHART application that the PMSTATS DDE server can handle the communication of information based on the ChartTopic topic name.

If the DDEINIT structure used in the DDE initiate contains a zero-length application name string in the **pszAppName** field, then any DDE server can respond to the request. If the **pszTopic** field contains a zero-length string, then each supporting DDE server would respond one time for every supported topic. In the two sample programs, we use a single application name PM_Stats, so that only the DDE client knows how to connect to the PMSTATS server. Also, since we are only interested in obtaining one specific type of information from the DDE server, then we are only interested in processing one topic name. If the PMSTATS application actually wanted to process different types of topics for the DDE client, then the application would respond for each of the topics that PMSTATS would support.

WM_DDE_INITIATEACK

In our sample, we use only a single topic for communication between the DDE server and the DDE client, but what if we wanted to share information based on multiple topics? The answer is that the DDE server can send a WM_DDE_INITIATEACK message for each topic that the DDE server can support. So, if the WINCHART program requested different information based on the type of chart it would draw, we could use a different topic name to get the different information. For example, let's assume that the spreadsheet window in PMSTATS contained more entryfields with different types of information, like models sold and color. The criteria for drawing the charts is different. For example, you may only need a subset of the numbers to draw a pie chart, whereas a bar would require that different numerical data be plotted. The applications could use different topic names to get different pieces of information from the DDE server.

Unlike the WM_INITIATE message, you cannot pass zero-length strings for the **pszAppName** and **pszTopic** fields respectively, since these fields are needed to validate the data. This message is sent by the server so the **mp1** parameter will contain the window handle of the DDE server window. The **mp2** parameter contains a pointer to a DDEINIT structure, which has the valid **pszAppName** and **pszTopic** information. The DDEINIT structure must be in a shareable memory segment, and this memory must be freed after the DDE client processes this information.

Using Window Words to Store Transaction-specific Data

It is important that the DDE server application provide a unique window handle for every response to an initiation message. An application can use the window words of the window to store a pointer to the DDEINIT structure, assuming that the DDE server does not free the memory object that contains the DDEINIT structure after it finishes processing the WM_DDE_INITIATE message. This allows the communicating application to obtain the topic of conversation from the DDEINIT structure via the window words.

The DDE Communication Process

The DDE communication process consists of three steps: the initiation, the data conversation, and finally the termination of the communication. The DDE initiation process is the term used to describe how the DDE client establishes the communications link with the DDE server. The initiation consists of two parts: the initiate itself followed by the response or initiate acknowledgment. After the initiation is complete and the specified DDE server has agreed to communicate with the DDE client, the DDE client and DDE server applications each know the topic of communication and the window handle of the corresponding communicating window.

Once the DDE conversation is initiated by the DDE client and acknowledged by the DDE server, the data conversation can begin. The data conversation denotes how the information from the DDE server will be communicated to the DDE client. It is the responsibility of the DDE client to terminate all data conversations that it does not want to take part in, since terminating the DDE server will prevent all other DDE clients from communicating to that server until the data connection is reestablished through the DDE initiation process. For example, think of a DDE conversation as several people talking over a telephone—a miniature conference call. Imagine one person, your boss, providing information regarding the state of your department and what everyone will be doing for the next week. The provider of the information, your boss, is the DDE server, and the rest of the department are DDE clients. Once enough information is obtained about what you will be doing or if you just get really bored, you can hang up the telephone, thereby terminating the conversation. If your boss decided to hang up the phone without telling everyone about what they would be doing, then the connection would be lost and nobody would know what was going on. The connection to all other DDE clients would be terminated and they would have to initiate a new conversation by calling your boss again. Although as far as PM is concerned, the data conversation does not end automatically when the server goes away.

Terminating the DDE Conversation

The DDE data conversation may be terminated at any time either by the DDE client or DDE server by simply posting a WM_DDE_TERMINATE message. Either communicating window can receive the termination message at any time during message processing. Under normal circumstances, the termination should not occur until the data recipient has received all of the information required by this data exchange. For example, in the case of the sample programs, we would not want to terminate the data conversation until the WINCHART program had all of the numbers needed from PMSTATS to build the graph within its window. Using this message terminates all transactions for the current data exchange and signals to the other communicating window that since no more data will be passed, it can do its cleanup and terminate its window when ready. The other communicating window that receives the message can only respond to this message with a WM_DDE_TERMINATE message of its own.

When both the DDE server and DDE client process the termination messages, the DDE communication is complete. If the window that posted the original termination message receives any other DDE message from the other communicating window before the other communicating window responds with a WM_DDE_TERMINATE message of its own, care must be taken to ensure that the window handle of the window is still valid before responding to the message, since the sender of the message may have already destroyed the window as a result of the termination.

The responsibility of terminating a DDE conversation is left with the communicating applications. The Dynamic Data Exchange code does not maintain a list of all of the communicating processes; therefore, the Presentation Manager is unaware that any two applications are exchanging information via the

DDE protocol. The DDE code is not magic; it is only designed to establish a communication protocol that allows the communicating applications to exchange information like the handle of the windows that will be exchanging information.

Well-designed applications that make use of DDE must ensure that the communication link is terminated properly if an application abends or exits prematurely. For example, if one of the communicating application traps, the communication link is not terminated; hence, as far as PM is aware, the two applications are still communicating. The WM_DDE_TERMINATE message is not posted automatically when the process terminates. Since exit list processing is called as a result of normal or abnormal process termination, applications can use an exit list routine to determine whether the termination occurred normally or abnormally and terminate the data conversation if required.

Building a DDE Message Spy Window

The spreadsheet dialog window used by PMSTATS contains a simple Multi-Line Entry field control window that is used to display the important DDE message processing between the DDE server and DDE client. Although this MLE window would not be practical in a real-time application design, it is helpful in understanding the flow of messages between the communicating windows. Every time a message is processed, an update is made to the MLE showing what just occurred and where it came from. The MLE code is similar to that used in the Chapter 8 PMEDIT sample program, except that the MLE is created via a dialog template in the resource script file. To send a text message to the MLE, we created the routine **SendTextToMLE()**. This routine is used simply by passing the text string to be displayed. In WM_DDE_INITIATE, we will print the DDE client window handle in the MLE using this routine.

PROVIDING FOR THE CLIENT/SERVER DATA EXCHANGE

The actual data exchange between the client and server is accomplished through the use of a giveable shared memory object. The DDE server application is responsible for allocating the memory that will be needed for the data transfer, and is also responsible for ensuring that the memory is available to all potential DDE clients. Each of the DDE client applications must be able to access this memory to receive the data from the DDE server.

A DDE structure containing all of the information that is to be provided to the DDE client is copied into the shared memory object, allowing the client to access the information in the structure. The format of the DDE structure is shown in Figure 9.12.

The **cbData** parameter is the actual size of the data that is to be exchanged. If no data is to be exchanged, this parameter should be set to zero.

```
typedef struct _DDESTRUCT      /* dde */
  {
    ULONG    cbData;
    USHORT   fsStatus;
    USHORT   usFormat;
    USHORT   offszItemName;
    USHORT   offabData;
  } DDESTRUCT;
  typedef DDESTRUCT *PDDESTRUCT;
```

Figure 9.12   The Dynamic Data Exchange structure.

The **fsStatus** parameter contains flags that are used to indicate the status of the data exchange. The purpose of these flags is to allow applications to query the state of the flag, and then, depending on the current state, take some action. The predefined status flags along with their defined hexadecimal value are listed in Figure 9.13. Note: The upper 8 bits of the **fsStatus** parameter are not used and may actually be used by applications to store information that is specific to the application.

The **usFormat** parameter is the format of the data being exchanged; in other words, it is the type of information that we will be sending from the DDE server to the DDE client. For the most part, exchanging text will be sufficient; however, there will be times that other exchange formats may be needed to transfer binary data between applications. PMWIN allows applications to

DDE_FACK	0x0001	This flag is used to indicate a positive acknowledgment.
DDE_FBUSY	0x0002	This flag is set to indicate that the communicating application is currently busy.
DDE_FNODATA	0x0004	This flag is used to indicate that no actual data has been exchanged.
DDE_FACKREQ	0x0008	This flag is used to indicate to the communicating applications that an acknowledgment is being requested.
DDE_FRESPONSE	0x0010	This flag is used to respond to a WM_DDE_REQUEST message.
DDE_NOTPROCESSED	0x0020	This flag is used to indicate that the DDE message was not handled.
DDE_FRESERVED	0x00C0	This flag is reserved for application-defined use.
DDE_FAPPSTATUS	0xFF00	This is a single byte bit field that can be used by applications for specific return information.

Figure 9.13   The DDE status flags.

register their own unique data formats. To register a unique data format for an application, the system atom table can be used, since it will return a unique identification number for the atom name string that represents the unique data format name. This ensures that all applications that use the same data can use the same atom to represent the unique format. The defined data exchange formats are shown below.

Valid predefined data exchange formats include:

DDEFMT_TEXT	Simple text exchange format. This value is defined as 0x0001.
SZFMT_TEXT	This exchange format is used to pass an array of characters, which can include the newline ('\n') character. The NULL character ('\0') signifies the end of the text.
SZFMT_BITMAP	The OS/2 bitmap file exchange format.
SZFMT_DSPTEXT	This exchange format is a private format that is used for text.
SZFMT_DSPBITMAP	This exchange format is a private format that is used for bitmaps.
SZFMT_METAFILE	The OS/2 metafile exchange format.
SZFMT_DSPMETAFILE	This data exchange format is a private format that is used for metafile information.
SZFMT_PALETTE	This exchange format is used for palette information.
SZFMT_SYLK	This exchange format signifies that the data is in the synchronous link file format.
SZFMT_DIF	This exchange format signifies that the data is in the data image file format.
SZFMT_TIFF	This exchange format signifies that the data is in the tag image file format.
SZFMT_OEMTEXT	This exchange format signifies that the data is in the OEM text format.
SZFMT_DIB	This exchange format is for a device independent bitmap.
SZFMT_CPTEXT	This data exchange format is the code page text format and is only used by applications that need to handle multiple language text strings without changing the conversation context.

The *offszItemName* element is a USHORT value that is simply the offset to the item name from the start of the DDESTRUCT structure. The item name must always be a NULL-terminated string, meaning that if no item name is used, the string must at least contain a single NULL character.

The *offabData* element is a USHORT value that represents the offset to the actual data block. This offset will need to be calculated whether or not actual data exists. The developer can add a check for valid data, since if we have valid data, the **cbData** field will be non-zero.

The DDE Shared Memory Object

Since the DDE memory object must reside within the shared arena, it must be allocated with a call to the **DosAllocSharedMem** API. The size of the object must be large enough to hold the entire DDESTRUCT structure, along with the item name string and the actual data that will be transferred to the DDE recipient.

The usage of the shared memory object is the most important part of the data transfer since it is the method whereby the information will be exchanged. Unfortunately, it is often the most difficult to understand since the DDE participants are responsible for its maintenance, and the offsets to the information are left to the user to calculate. In the windows implementation of DDE, memory management is quite different.

Once the DDE conversation is initiated, the DDE client and servers communicate with one another via DDE transactions. The DDE client can start the transaction process by allocating a shared memory object to hold information regarding the type of information that will be needed from the DDE server. Once the given information is copied into the shared memory, the DDE client can call **WinDdePostMsg** to post a transaction message to the respective DDE server, thereby signaling the DDE server to perform some kind of an action based on the information from the DDE client. Along with the message, the DDE server receives the handle of the window for the DDE client along with a pointer to the shared memory containing the information. The DDE server can use this pointer to obtain the information.

Once the DDE server deciphers what the DDE client requires, it can respond to the transaction process by also allocating a shared memory object of its own, copying its response data to the memory and posting a DDE response message back to the DDE client with which it is communicating.

Since the applications are responsible for allocating the shared memory and populating the DDE structure that will reside in the memory, a worker function should be created to handle the task of creating a DDE shared memory object. The routine **BuildDDEDataStructure** within PMSTATS does exactly that by allocating a shared giveable memory object, populating a DDESTRUCT structure and returning a pointer to the DDE structure. The pointer to the structure is then given to the WINCHART program through subsequent calls to **WinDdePostMsg**.

The prototype for the **BuildDDEDataStructure** routine has the format shown in Figure 9.14.

- The **usDataFormat** parameter is the DDE data format that is to be used. In the case of being called from within PMSTATS, this format will be set to the standard text format DDEFMT_TEXT.
- The **pszTopicName** parameter is the actual topic name string based upon which the DDE server and DDE client will be communicating information.

```
PDDESTRUCT EXPENTRY BuildDDEDataStructure (USHORT usDataFormat,
                                           PSZ    pszTopicName,
                                           PVOID  pvData,
                                           USHORT usData,
                                           USHORT usStatusFlags);
```

Figure 9.14 **Building the DDE data object.**

- The **pvData** parameter is declared as a pointer to VOID. This pointer will actually point to the start of the data that will be sent to the DDE client application.
- The **usData** parameter is actually the length of the data that will be communicated to the DDE client.
- The **usStatusFlags** parameter is used to fill the **fsStatus** field of the DDE-STRUCT structure. This field is used to indicate the type of acknowledgment.

The routine will return a pointer to the DDESTRUCT structure that it will populate based on the information that was passed to it. If an error occurs during the processing of this routine, then the function will return FALSE to the caller.

The first thing that this routine must do is allocate the giveable shared memory object that will be used for the DDE data transfer. The code for allocating the DDE shared memory object is given in Figure 9.15. The first step was to allocate the unnamed memory object. The size of the object is equal to the length of the topic name string plus one. The memory must be committed before we can write to it, so we use the PAG_COMMIT flag on the allocation. You could alternatively choose not to commit the memory at allocation time, in which case you could use the **DosSetMem** function to commit the memory. In any case, the memory must be committed before we write to the memory

```
ulObjectSize = (USHORT)(strlen(pszDDETopicName) + 1);
rc = DosAllocSharedMem(((PPVOID)&pulSharedObj),         // Pointer to Base Address
                       (PSZ)0,                          // Un-Named Shared Memory
                       ulObjectSize,                    // Size of the Object
                       PAG_COMMIT | PAG_READ |          // Memory Flags
                       PAG_WRITE  | OBJ_GIVEABLE);

if (rc != NULLHANDLE)
 {
  DisplayMessages(NULLHANDLE, "Error Allocating the DDE Memory", MSG_ERROR);
  return (PDDESTRUCT)FALSE;
 }
```

Figure 9.15 **Allocating the DDE memory object.**

to avoid a page fault. The OBJ_GIVEABLE flag tells the memory manager that the memory can be given to other processes in the system.

The contents of the shared memory object should include the populated DDESTRUCT structure, the topic name string, and the actual data that is going to be passed to the communicator process. It is extremely important to ensure that the offset fields in the DDESTRUCT structure correctly point to the valid application name string and the beginning of the data block.

Using the Same Memory Object for a Response

An application can choose to create a new shared memory object for a transaction and the resulting response, or attempt to reuse the same memory object to hold the DDESTRUCT structure. For example, if one application processes the transaction, it gets a DDESTRUCT structure that was passed to it via **Win-DdePostMsg**. The receiving application will in turn have to return a positive acknowledgment by specifying the DDE_FACK flag in the **fsStatus** field of the DDESTRUCT structure, which implies that a new memory object is required to post the WM_DDE_ACK message. At this point, the application can create a new shared memory object to hold the structure or reuse the existing object by updating only the DDE_FACK flag of the structure.

Using the same memory object makes sense in most cases, especially on a WM_DDE_EXECUTE, since the positive acknowledgment must contain the command strings for this message. It is far easier to just reuse the data structure then repopulate it for the same information. Ultimately, regardless of whether the object is re-created or reused, the application that receives the memory object containing the structure is responsible for freeing the memory when it is done with it. As you will see, the **WinDdePostMsg** function contains a flag that can be used to indicate if the structure should be automatically freed. This is extremely important since the function can free the memory that was used for the DDESTRUCT on the responding WM_DDE_ACK. It is critical that applications understand the responsibility associated with freeing the memory object. It is a common mistake for applications to not free this memory properly, resulting in shared memory growth eventually causing abnormal swapper growth.

THE DDE COMMUNICATION MESSAGES

Once the DDE initiation process is complete, the actual data conversation can begin. The data conversation is composed of a series of transaction messages initiated by the DDE client, followed by subsequent response messages from the DDE server. These messages form the basis for the data communication; therefore, the combination of both transaction and response messages is known as the communication messages. The format of both of these message types is essentially the same. The first message parameter, **mp1**, contains the handle of the window that generated the message. The second message parameter contains a pointer to the DDE shared memory object.

One of the major differences between the Windows DDE convention and the PM implementation is in regard to the contents of the second message parameter. In Windows, the second message parameter is dependant on the message being posted, while in PM the second message parameter is always a pointer to the DDE shared memory object containing a DDE structure. The first message parameter in both environments is the window handle of the communicating application.

There are several specific types of transactions that the DDE client will use to obtain information from the DDE server. All of the transaction messages are posted from the DDE client to the DDE server's message queue. The various types of transaction messages are described in the next sections.

WM_DDE_REQUEST

This message is used by the DDE client to request that data be provided by the DDE server. The DDE server will then respond to this message by posting a WM_DDE_DATA message if there is data to communicate. If the DDE server cannot provide data to the client, it should respond with a negative acknowledgment using the WM_DDE_ACK message. Assuming the DDE server has data to transfer, the data is communicated one time for every data request. The process of this single, one-time exchange is known as the *cold link* exchange.

- **mp1** is the DDE server's window handle.
- **mp2** contains the pointer to the DDESTRUCT structure. The *offszItem-Name* element of the structure is used to identify the type of data that is being requested. The *usFormat* element is important since it represents the type of format for the data.

It is important to note that in the context of the WM_DDE_REQUEST message, the data contained in the DDESTRUCT structure, represented by *offab-Data*, is undefined. Therefore, both the *cbData* and *offabData* elements should contain zero. Also, if your application will be communicating with a Windows-based DDE-enabled application, OS/2 will not fill in the data elements of the structure since there is no data area associated with the WM_DDE_REQUEST message.

It is possible to calculate where the data will start even if there is no valid data to begin with. Therefore, even if this element contains a value, there may still be no data. The *cbData* element is used to verify that data exists since it contains the actual size of the data. The purpose of doing this calculation, regardless of whether valid data exists, is to safeguard an ill-behaved application from corrupting a portion of the DDESTRUCT structure in memory. This ugly scenario is possible if the application does not properly validate the data, since it operates under the assumption that the actual offset to the data starts at zero.

WM_DDE_DATA

This message is used by the communicating applications to handle unsolicited data. When the client window receives the WM_DDE_DATA message to fulfill the request, it can then process the data.

- **mp1** is the window handle of the communicating application.
- **mp2** contains the pointer to the DDESTRUCT structure.

The important element of the structure is the **usStatus** field since it contains the status word that determines whether an acknowledgment message is needed. If the DDE_FACKREQ bit is set to TRUE, the DDE client is expected to respond with a positive WM_DDE_ACK. If the bit is FALSE, then no acknowledgment is required. The DDE_FRESPONSE bit is used to determine exactly for which message the data is being processed. If this bit is TRUE, then the data originates from a WM_DDE_REQUEST message. If this bit is FALSE, then the data originates from a WM_DDE_ADVISE message. Remember, the *offszItemName* element of the structure is used to identify the type of data that is registered in the format represented by the *usFormat* element.

WM_DDE_POKE

This message is used by the communicating applications to handle unsolicited data or data that the DDE application may not have requested. As with the other messages listed, this message is always posted using **WinDdePostMsg**. The parameters of the message are:

- **mp1** is the window handle of the window that posted the message.
- **mp2** contains the pointer to the DDESTRUCT structure.

The *offszItemName* element of the struture is the topic of the DDE conversation while the actual data starts at the *offabData* element of the structure. The format type that identifies the data is represented by the **usFormat** field of the structure. The window procedure that processes this message can choose to accept the data for further processing. If the window procedure accepts the data, it should post a positive acknowledgment back to the other communicating window via the WM_DDE_ACK message. It can send a negative acknowledgment if it does not want the data.

WM_DDE_ADVISE

This message is used to tell the DDE server to dynamically notify the DDE client whenever the corresponding data has changed. This allows for dynamic updates to the information and gives the DDE client application the ability to detect the changes automatically, rather than having to determine if the communicated data has changed, and then once again request the data. The parameters of the message are:

- **mp1** is the window handle of the window that posted the message.
- **mp2** contains the pointer to the DDESTRUCT structure.

The easiest way to visualize the use of this transaction is to imagine a spreadsheet as the DDE server and a chart drawing program as the DDE client, much like the sample programs, PMSTATS and WINCHART. If the user changes some of the numbers in the entry fields in PMSTATS, through the use of the WM_DDE_ADVISE message, the chart drawn in WINCHART could automatically be updated instantly without the user having to initiate any further communication.

Hot Data Link vs. Warm Data Link

The process of this automatic transfer of data is also known as a *hot link*. The hot link is viewed as a permanent method of communicating between the DDE server and DDE client, since the link is valid until the link is explicitly broken. The hot link is designed to allow small pieces of data to be transferred quickly and automatically. During the processing of the hot link, actual data is transferred from the DDE server to the DDE client. The WM_DDE_ADVISE message can also be used to alert the DDE client application that the data has changed, without actually transferring the data from the DDE server to the DDE client. This notification process is known as a *warm link*. The warm link is designed for larger pieces of data which would be too tedious to continually transfer. Functionally, the only real difference between a warm link and a hot link is that no actual data is transferred with the warm link.

The DDE server replies to the WM_DDE_ADVISE message with a positive acknowledgment if it can supply the data, or a negative acknowledgement if it cannot, using the WM_DDE_ACK message. If the server responds postively, it will "advise" the DDE client that the data is changing by continually posting the WM_DDE_DATA message with the data object. The DDE client will continue to receive the data until the hot link is broken or the data conversation is terminated. Therefore, the WM_DDE_DATA message that the DDE client receives will contain the data object as part of the DDESTRUCT structure in **mp2**. If the structure received contains no actual data, then the WM_DDE_DATA message is being used for a warm link rather than a hot link. The *cbData* element of the DDESTRUCT structure can be used to determine the size of the data.

The DDE client application requests that a warm data link be provided by setting the DDE_FNODATA status flag, set within the *fsStatus* element within the DDESTRUCT structure that will be passed on the WM_DDE_ADVISE message. When the DDE server application processes this request, it does not send any data, but does post a WM_DDE_DATA message back to the DDE client with zero bytes of data and the DDE_FNODATA status flag also set. Once the DDE client gets the warm link notification, it can choose to not obtain the information since it may not be necessary at this time, or it can request the information from the server by posting a WM_DDE_REQUEST message. Figure 9.16 is an illustration of the hot data link process, and Figure 9.17 shows the warm data link process.

Controlling the Flow of Data Messages

If an application is making use of the hot data link to transfer data repetitiously, it is possible to fill the application message queue, since the DDE client may not have had an opportunity to process all of the WM_DDE_DATA messages. In order to safeguard the overflow of WM_DDE_DATA messages to the DDE client, the DDE protocol provides the DDE_FACKREQ status flag. The DDE_FACKREQ flag is set in the *fsStatus* element of the DDESTRUCT for the WM_DDE_ADVISE message. If the DDE_FACKREQ flag is set, the application receiving the WM_DDE_ADVISE message should in turn set the flag on the corresponding WM_DDE_DATA message. Basically, the purpose of this flag is to allow an application to wait until it receives a WM_DDE_ACK message as an acknowledgment before posting another WM_DDE_DATA message containing the data, thus controlling the flow of the data.

WM_DDE_UNADVISE

This message is used by the DDE client to notify the DDE server that the information that was being dynamically updated by the advise message should no longer be updated. This message as its name implies, effectively reverses the WM_DDE_ADVISE message. The DDE server replies to this message with either a positive or negative acknowledgment using the WM_DDE_ACK message.

Posting DDE Messages

All transaction and response messages are posted to the receiver's message queue. Since the purpose of these messages is to facilitate the data transfer, a special PM API is used to post the message to the communicating applica-

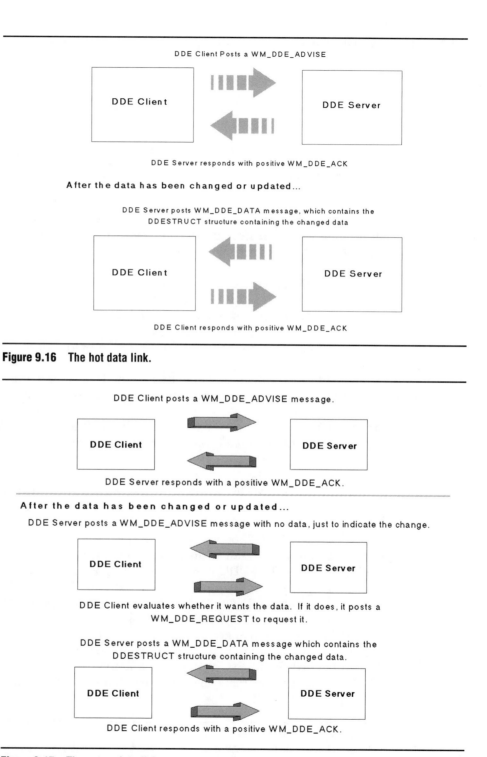

DDE Client Posts a WM_DDE_ADVISE

DDE Client

DDE Server

DDE Server responds with positive WM_DDE_ACK

After the data has been changed or updated...

DDE Server posts WM_DDE_DATA message, which contains the DDESTRUCT structure containing the changed data

DDE Client

DDE Server

DDE Client responds with positive WM_DDE_ACK

Figure 9.16   The hot data link.

DDE Client posts a WM_DDE_ADVISE message.

DDE Client

DDE Server

DDE Server responds with a positive WM_DDE_ACK.

After the data has been changed or updated...

DDE Server posts a WM_DDE_ADVISE message with no data, just to indicate the change.

DDE Client

DDE Server

DDE Client evaluates whether it wants the data. If it does, it posts a WM_DDE_REQUEST to request it.

DDE Server posts a WM_DDE_DATA message which contains the DDESTRUCT structure containing the changed data.

DDE Client

DDE Server

DDE Client responds with a positive WM_DDE_ACK.

Figure 9.17   The warm data link.

```
BOOL APIENTRY WinDdePostMsg(HWND       hwndTo,
                            HWND       hwndFrom,
                            ULONG      wm,
                            PDDESTRUCT pddest,
                            ULONG      ulOptions);
```

Figure 9.18   The WinDdePostMsg API.

tion, along with a pointer to the shared memory object that will contain the information to be transferred. **WinDdePostMsg** is the API used to post these messages. Its format is shown in Figure 9.18.

- The **hwndTo** parameter is the window handle of the window whose message queue the message will be posted to.
- The **hwndFrom** parameter is the window handle of the window that is attempting to post the DDE message.
- The **wm** parameter is the actual transaction or response message that is being posted.
- The **pddest** parameter is the pointer to the DDESTRUCT structure that is being passed to the receiving application. This parameter is always passed as a 16-bit address.
- The **ulOptions** parameter is used to tell the Presentation Manager code what to do if the posted message cannot be received by the Windows message queue. Like the regular API used for posting a message, **WinPostMsg**, the **WinDdePostMsg** function will fail if the message queue associated with the window is full. The developer can specify the behavior that PM should take if the function fails by passing one of two parameters.

The DDEPM_RETRY option is used to specify whether the message should be continually posted until it finally reaches the destination message queue (see Figure 9.19). The DDE message will be posted in one-second intervals until it finally is successfully posted. The DDE code safeguards the message processing by establishing a message loop of its own to prevent deadlocks.

The worker routine for **WinDdePostMsg** first checks to see if the retry flag is set. If the retry flag was not specified, then it immediately exists. Otherwise, the code checks to ensure that the only error it will continue processing for is PMERR_QUEUE_FULL, which indicates that the receipient's message queue is full. For all other errors that can cause the function to fail, the **WinDdePostMsg**

```
DDEPM_RETRY       0x00000001L
DDEPM_NOFREE      0x00000002L
```

Figure 9.19   The WinDdePostMsg retry options.

function will return FALSE. Once the check for the retry flag is complete, the sender is thrown into a modal message loop to avoid a deadlock situation. The receiver of the DDE message may actually be waiting on the sender to receive a DDE message. Also, a deadlock may arise if two applications have full message queues and post a DDE message to each other while using the retry option. The code then calls the **WinCallMsgFilter** API, and specifies the MSGF_DDEPOSTMSG option, which allows those applications that filter messages prior to the **WinPeekMsg** function to use the **WinSetHook** function to detect whether the code has entered this message loop processing.

The modal loop is a simple **WinPeekMsg/WinDispatchMsg** loop. The loop is designed to allow messages from other applications to be received. In other words, the application can receive Dynamic Data Exchange messages, or any other messages for that matter, while the application continues to post the DDE message through **WinDdePostMsg**. The **WinPeekMsg** function actually specifies the **PM_REMOVE** parameter to ensure that the message is removed from the queue. If a WM_QUIT message is received while inside this loop, the message is posted back to the application's message queue for processing by the main message loop, and this loop is exited.

The DDEPM_NOFREE option is used to allow the caller to free the shared memory object rather than the worker code for **WinDdePostMsg**. If this parameter is not used, the default behavior ensures that the memory is automatically freed. The purpose of using this parameter is performance; for example, if several calls to **WinDdePostMsg** will occur, the same shared memory object can be used for each of the calls to the function. Once the processing is complete, the application code will have to free the memory object.

The code fragment in Figure 9.20 first obtains a pointer to the DDESTRUCT structure containing the data that will be trasferred to the WINCHART application. The structure is then passed to the application through the use of the **WinDdePostMsg** API. The DDEPM_RETRY option is specified to continually post the message if the WINCHART application's message queue is full.

WM_DDE_ACK

The final message in the DDE protocol is the acknowledgment message, WM_DDE_ACK. This message is used to synchronize the communication messages and provide information for the communicating applications with regard to when a particular message was received and whether it was actually processed. This message is extremely important because it provides the signal to the DDE client or DDE server to either continue processing the data exchange or take some other action like waiting for another event. Like the communication messages, this message is posted using **WinDdePostMsg**. In the processing of this message, the first message parameter, **mp1**, contains the handle of the window that initiated the message, while the second message parameter, **mp2**, contains a pointer to the DDESTRUCT structure.

```
pddes = BuildDDEDataStructure(DDEFMT_TEXT,        // Format
                              TOPIC,              // Topic Name String
                              (PVOID)pszSendString,  // Data to be exchanged
                              sizeof(pszSendString),  // Size of Data
                              0);

if (pddes = 0)
 {
  SendTextToMLE("DDEERROR: DDE Structure is empty");
 }


bSuccess = WinDdePostMsg(hwndDDEClient,  // DDE Client Window Handle
                         hwndClient,     // DDE Server Window Handle
                         WM_DDE_DATA,    // DDE message
                         pddes,          // Pointer to DDE structure
                         DDEPM_RETRY);   // Retry Post

SendTextToMLE("Posting WM_DDE_DATA message to DDE Client");

if (bSuccess == TRUE)   // No Error
 {
  SendTextToMLE("WM_DDE_DATA - Message successfully sent to WINOS2 session...");
 }

else
 {
  WinAlarm(HWND_DESKTOP, WA_ERROR);
  SendTextToMLE("DDEERROR: Error Sending WM_DDE_DATA");
 }
```

Figure 9.20 Using WinDdePostMsg.

The acknowledgment comes in the form of the **fsStatus** field of the DDE-STRUCT structure. The communicating application that wants to acknowledge a particular message uses this field as the source of the notification by modifying the field to reflect the state of the acknowledgment when the particular message is received. The receiving window procedure can check the value of this field to determine whether the other communicating application has actually posted valid data. In the Windows DDE implementation of the DDE protocol, the status flags are stored in the low order byte of the DDEACK structure. Also, unlike its PM counterpart, the Windows implementation uses this message to respond to a WM_DDE_INITIATE request since the WM_DDE_INITIATEACK message is undefined for Windows.

Back on the PM side, the DDE_FACK flag is used to indicate whether the acknowledgement is positive, while the DDE_FBUSY flag indicates that the communicating application is currently busy processing something else indicating that the request should be retried.

```
// DDE helper macros

#define DDES_PSZITEMNAME(pddes) \
(((PSZ)pddes) + ((PDDESTRUCT)pddes)->offszItemName)

#define DDES_PABDATA(pddes)        \
(((PBYTE)pddes) + ((PDDESTRUCT)pddes)->offabData)

#define DDEI_PCONVCONTEXT(pddei)        \
((PCONVCONTEXT)((PBYTE)pddei + pddei->offConvContext))
```

Figure 9.21   The DDE helper macros.

The WM_DDE_ACK message is ineffective by itself, its only purpose is to respond to other DDE messages in either a positive or negative manner and to alert the other application to take some appropriate action. The acknowledgment is based on the *offszItemName* element of the DDESTRUCT structure, so acknowledgments are based on what is being communicated.

THE DDE HELPER MACROS

PMWIN.H defines three macros that are used to help calculate offsets into the various DDE structures. The first two macros are used to calculate offsets into the DDESTRUCT structure. The third macro is used to calculate an offset into a DDEINIT structure. Using these macros you can easily obtain the offset by knowing the pointer to the structure. The macros are given in Figure 9.21.

The **DDES_PSZITEMNAME** macro is used to calculate the offset for the item name from the start of the DDESTRUCT structure pointed to by **pddes**. Through the use of this macro you can easily copy the topic name string into the **offszItemName** element of the DDESTRUCT structure. The macro works by first obtaining the address of the beginning of the DDESTRUCT structure and then adding the offset to the item name string. Finally, the resulting address is returned. PMSTATS uses this macro in the **BuildDDEDataStructure** routine to place the topic name string within the DDESTRUCT structure.

The topic name string is passed into the function and then copied within the structure through the use of the **strcpy** function, as you can see in Figure 9.22.

```
pdde->offszItemName = (USHORT)sizeof(DDESTRUCT);
strcpy(DDES_PSZITEMNAME(pdde), pszItemName);
```

Figure 9.22   Using the DDES_PSZITEMNAME macro.

The value returned is a pointer to a string. The pointer is only valid if the *offszItemName* element of the DDESTRUCT structure contains a valid non-zero value. It is important to note that a non-zero string is very much different from a zero-length string, which is actually valid, although not commonly expected.

The **DDES_PABDATA** macro is used to calculate the offset for the actual data block from the start of the DDESTRUCT structure pointed to by **pddes**. This macro provides easy access to the offset for the data that will be exchanged. The macro works by first obtaining the address to the start of the DDESTRUCT structure and adding the offset to the data. The pointer returned by this macro is only valid if within the DDESTRUCT structure the *cbData* element contains a non-zero value. If the value is zero, then no actual data exists and the pointer returned is invalid.

The **DDEI_PCONVCONTEXT** macro is used to calculate the offset for the national language conversation context. This macro, unlike the other two DDE helper macros, calculates the offset into the CONVCONTEXT structure and takes a pointer to a DDEINIT structure as input to the macro.

The source code fragment shown in Figure 9.23 is used to post the WM_DDE_DATA message containing the data to the WINCHART DDE client sample.

```
case WM_COMMAND:
    switch (SHORT1FROMMP(mp1))
    {
    case DID_OK:
        cbText = 0;
        for (usCounter = IDE_MONTH01; usCounter < IDE_MONTH13; usCounter++)
        {
            cbText += WinQueryDlgItemTextLength( hwnd, (ULONG)usCounter );
            cbText++;      // room for separator - terminator
        }

        // allocate string
        pszSendString = malloc(cbText + 1);
        pszSendString[0] = '\0';

        for (usCounter = IDE_MONTH01; usCounter < IDE_MONTH13; usCounter++)
        {
            WinQueryDlgItemText(hwnd, usCounter, sizeof(szTextFromEF), szTextFromEF);

            // OK, since our sample program deals with satisfaction percentages,
            // we can only have the user enter a number up to 100 percent.  So
            // we will validate the number the user entered in the entryfield.
            // If the number is above 100, sound the error tone, put an error message
            // in the status window, and finally reset the focus to the entryfield
            // that is in error.
```

Figure 9.23   Transferring the data from the DDE server.   continued

```
    usNumber = atoi(szTextFromEF);
    if (usNumber > 100)
      {
      WinAlarm(HWND_DESKTOP, WA_ERROR);
      SendTextToMLE("ERROR: Number in Entryfield must be percentage up to 100%");
      hwndEntryfield = WinWindowFromID(hwnd, usCounter);
      WinSetFocus(HWND_DESKTOP, hwndEntryfield);
      return FALSE;
      }


    strcat(pszSendString, szTextFromEF );

    // pass one big comma delimited string over to the
    // DDE client containing all of the data
    if(usCounter != IDE_MONTH12)
      {
      strcat(pszSendString, ",");
      }
  }

if (pszSendString[0])
  {
  pDDEStruct = BuildDDEDataStructure(DDEFMT_TEXT,
                                     TOPIC,
                                     (PVOID)pszSendString,
                                     sizeof(pszSendString),
                                     DDE_FACK);

  bSuccess = WinDdePostMsg(hwndDDEClient,  // DDE Client Window Handle
                           hwndClient,     // DDE Server Window Handle
                           WM_DDE_DATA,    // DDE message to be posted
                           pDDEStruct,     // Pointer to DDE structure
                           DDEPM_RETRY);   // Options


  if (bSuccess == TRUE)    // No Error
    {
    SendTextToMLE("WM_DDE_DATA - Message successfully posted...");
    }

  else
    {
    WinAlarm(HWND_DESKTOP, WA_ERROR);
    SendTextToMLE("DDEERROR: Error posting WM_DDE_DATA message");
    }
  }
free(pszSendString);
return FALSE;
```

Figure 9.23   Transferring the data from the DDE server.

EXCHANGING THE SAMPLE PROGRAM DATA

The code shown in Figure 9.23 is the actual code used to transfer the monthly percentage data from the PMSTATS program to the WINCHART program. The data is transferred when the user clicks the OK pushbutton; therefore, the processing of the data exchange occurs within the context of the DID_OK pushbutton. The PMSTATS application will transfer the numeric data as one large comma delimited string, with the comma separating each of the monthly numbers. Applications should use caution when transferring text data using the DDEFMT_TEXT data exchange format between a PM application and a Windows application. For some strange reason, a worker routine in PMDDE that is used to translate the codepage information between PM and Windows, truncates a text buffer at the first NULL character. So if your PM application passes strings that are NULL delimited only the first string would be passed on to the Windows side.

The first *for* loop in the code is used to obtain the length of the string that will be transferred. The code then uses the C runtime call **malloc** to allocate storage for the string. The code then loops through each of the entryfields in the spreadsheet dialog by using the **WinQueryDlgItemText** API with the identifier of the entryfield. If any of the entryfields contains a number that is greater than 100, an error tone will sound and the cursor will be placed on the entryfield containing the invalid number. Remember, the entryfields are subclassed to only take numbers in the **FilterEntryFieldProc** subclass procedure. The C runtime function **strcat** is used to insert the commas into the string. The next step is to create the shared memory object and obtain a pointer to the DDESTRUCT structure containing the data to be exchanged within the memory. The final step in this code is to actually transfer the data by posting a WM_DDE_DATA message to the DDE client, passing the pointer to the DDESTRUCT structure. The code fragment uses the DDEPM_RETRY option to continue posting if the first time was not successful. If an error occurs, the user will hear a beep and see the error in the MLE window. The processing of the DID_OK pushbutton concludes by freeing the memory for the string using the **free** function.

The code fragment shown in Figure 9.24 contains the previously discussed routine used to create the shared memory object and return a pointer to the populated DDESTRUCT structure containing the data.

```
PDDESTRUCT EXPENTRY BuildDDEDataStructure(USHORT usFormat, PSZ pszItemName, PVOID  pvData,
     USHORT cbData, USHORT fsStatus)
{
APIRET    rc;
ULONG     ulObjSize = 0;
PVOID     pvBuffer;
```

Figure 9.24   The BuildDDEDataStructure routine.   **continued**

```
PCHAR       szBuffer   = NULL;
PDDESTRUCT  pDDEStruct = NULL;

// Allocate shared memory and ensure its giveable
ulObjSize = strlen(pszItemName) + 1;

rc = DosAllocSharedMem(&pvBuffer,
                       NULL,
                       ulObjSize,
                       PAG_COMMIT | PAG_READ | PAG_WRITE | OBJ_GIVEABLE);

if (rc != NULLHANDLE)
 {
  DisplayMessages(NULLHANDLE, "Error Allocating Shared Memory for DDE Data", MSG_ERROR);
  return (PDDESTRUCT)NULL;
 }

// Populate the DDESTRUCT
pDDEStruct                = (PDDESTRUCT)pvBuffer;
pDDEStruct->usFormat      = usFormat;
pDDEStruct->offszItemName = (USHORT)sizeof(DDESTRUCT);

// Copy the item name into the structure
strcpy(DDES_PSZITEMNAME(pDDEStruct), pszItemName);

pDDEStruct->cbData        = cbData;
pDDEStruct->offabData     = pDDEStruct->offszItemName + strlen(pszItemName) + 1;
pDDEStruct->fsStatus      = fsStatus;

if (usFormat == DDEFMT_TEXT)
 {
  if (pvData == NULL || cbData == 0)
   {
    // This will only happen if the caller of the routine
    // for whatever reason passed us no data
    DisplayMessages(NULLHANDLE, "No data to exchange", MSG_ERROR);
    return (PDDESTRUCT)NULL;
   }

  else
   {
    szBuffer = pvData;
    strcpy(DDES_PABDATA(pDDEStruct), szBuffer);
   }
 }

else
 {
  DisplayMessages(NULLHANDLE, "This routine currently only supports the DDEFMT_TEXT format",
    MSG_ERROR);
 }

return pDDEStruct;
}
```

Figure 9.24 The BuildDDEDataStructure routine.

The code fragment listed in Figure 9.25 shows the processing of the
WM_DDE_DATA message by the WINCHART application.

```
case WM_DDE_DATA:
    hMsgMem = (HANDLE)LOWORD(lParam);
    pdde = (DDEDATA FAR *)GlobalLock(hMsgMem);
    GlobalUnlock(hMsgMem);

    // Received data from our DDE Server, show the data
    // string in the static text window
    SetDlgItemText(hwnd, ID_DATA, pdde->Value);

    // Parse out the fields in the data string
    for (nMonth = 0; nMonth < 12; nMonth++)
     {
       if (nMonth)
        {
         pszToken = strtok(NULL, ",");
        }

       else
        {
         pszToken = strtok(pdde->Value, ",");
        }

       if (pszToken == NULL)
        {
         break;
        }

       nChartData[ nMonth ] = atoi( pszToken );
     }

    // Now send an acknowledgement back to the PM side
    pdde = (DDEDATA FAR *)GlobalLock(hMem);
    pdde->cfFormat = CF_TEXT;

    strcpy(pdde->Value, "\tWINCHART received data");
    GlobalUnlock(hMem);

    // Post a WM_DDE_DATA message back to DDE Server
    PostMessage(hwndDDEServer,
                WM_DDE_DATA,
                hwnd,
                MAKELONG(hMem, aItem));

    break;
```

Figure 9.25   The DDE client receiving the data.

CHARTING THE DATA

The code shown in Figure 9.26 illustrates how the DDE client application makes use of the WM_DDE_DATA message. The data string received from the DDE server is displayed in a static text window via the **SetDlgItemText** routine. Once the string is displayed in the window, the code then strips the commas out of the passed string and converts each string separated by a comma into an integer. The numeric information is then stored in an array that will be used to draw the chart. The painting of the chart is done within the context of the WM_PAINT message.

The logic used to draw the chart is relatively simple. The code used to paint the window simply draws colorful rectangles to create the chart. The rectangles are drawn by using the Windows **Rectangle** API. The text information used to

```
case WM_PAINT:
    hdc = BeginPaint(hwnd, &ps);
    hpen = SelectObject (hdc, CreatePen(PS_SOLID, 1, 0L)) ;

    xOrigin = (LONG)cxClient / 10L;
    xDelta  = ((LONG)cxClient - (xOrigin * 2L))/12L;
    yOrigin = (LONG)cyClient - ((LONG)cyClient / 10L);
    yDelta  = ((LONG)cyClient / 10) * 8L;

    for (nMonth = 0; nMonth < 12; nMonth++)
     {
      hbrush = CreateSolidBrush(clrTable[nMonth%6]);
      SelectObject(hdc, hbrush);
      xLeft = xOrigin;
      xRight = xOrigin + xDelta;
      yBottom = yOrigin;
      yTop = yOrigin - ((yDelta * nChartData[nMonth]))/100L;
      Rectangle (hdc, (int)xLeft, (int)yTop, (int)xRight, (int)yBottom );
      itoa( nChartData[nMonth], szpct, 10 );
      rect.left = (int)xLeft;
      rect.right = (int)xRight;
      rect.bottom = (int)(yOrigin - yDelta);
      rect.top = rect.bottom - 20;
      DrawText( hdc, szpct, strlen(szpct), &rect, DT_CENTER);
      rect.top = (int)yOrigin + 5;
      rect.bottom = rect.top + 20;
      DrawText( hdc, szMonth[nMonth], 3, &rect, DT_CENTER);
      xOrigin += xDelta;
     }
    EndPaint (hwnd, &ps) ;
    return FALSE;
```

Figure 9.26   Drawing the chart.

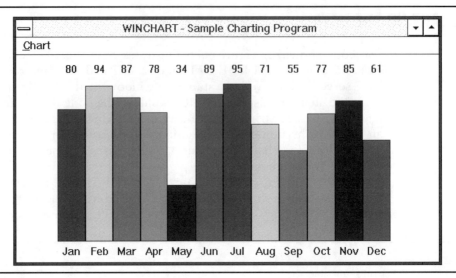

Figure 9.27   The chart showing the data.

show the percentages and the months is drawn by calling the Windows API
DrawText. The illustration in Figure 9.27 shows the final product, the bar chart
showing the data.

SUMMARY

Dynamic Data Exchange is not an automated data transfer facility. It is, however, a powerful message-based protocol that allows developers to share information with other DDE-enabled applications. The DDE protocol enables unrelated applications to communicate effectively providing more power to the user since any enabled application that runs in the context of the Presentation Manager can transfer data to another DDE-enabled application. With all of the PM- and Windows-based applications that exist in today's software community, many applications provide a method for data to be exchanged via DDE. Applications that effectively use the Dynamic Data Exchange protocol enable their application to communicate with several popular vendor applications, thereby creating a wealth of information to be shared by the user. Creating a DDE-enabled application provides the user with a powerful communication interface that is totally transparent to them. Few users truly appreciate the benefits of DDE, while few developers can deny the benefits that DDE brings to the user.

Getting to the Head of the Class: Understanding Subclassing

P M programmers seem to have an unreasonable fear of using subclassing in their programs. Even highly talented and experienced individuals have expressed their ignorance of the methods of subclassing. This fear probably stems from the belief that a methodology as powerful as subclassing must inherently be extremely complicated. In many instances, however, subclassing is an extremely simple task. This chapter will explain the subclassing concept and, hopefully, ease many of the associated fears so that you can take full advantage of this concept in your programs.

Subclassing is a mechanism that allows an application to intercept messages intended for a particular window or a class of windows for the purpose of modifying or extending the behavior of the window or class. This mechanism is similar to the inheritance property of object-oriented systems. In fact, PM may be considered as a rudimentary object-oriented programming environment. Applications register object classes and then create instances of the classes known as windows. The instance data associated with each window is the object data. Object methods are invoked by sending messages to the object. In this light, the window procedure is merely the mechanism used to invoke methods. PM defines an implied base class whose data is the system-defined window data accessible through **WinQueryWindowShort**, **WinQueryWindowLong**, and **WinQueryWindowPtr**. The methods of the base class are invoked by calling the **WinDefWindowProc** API. Thus, every application that invokes **WinDefWindowProc** to provide default message processing is actually subclassing the PM base window class, and most PM programmers employ subclassing without being aware of the action.

This chapter examines two forms of subclassing commonly used in PM programs. The simpler form merely replaces the window procedure of an existing window and allows the application to override the methods, or message processing functions, of the original class. This method was used in Chapter 7 to allow a listbox control to function as an application client window and to provide direct manipulation support for the listbox. The second form of subclassing is very similar to the derivation of classes in object-oriented programming languages and allows an application to extend both the data and methods of an existing class to form a new class. As simple as this sounds, there are complications due to the fact that class derivation was not a major concern in the implementation and documentation of the PM-defined classes.

REPLACING A WINDOW'S WINDOW PROCEDURE

The simplest and most commonly used form of subclassing replaces the window procedure of an existing window in order to modify the behavior of the window. This section describes two examples where this method is used. In the first, the existing window class is specifically designed to allow a subclassing procedure to modify its behavior. In the second, a message normally processed by the existing class is intercepted in order to modify the functionality of the existing class.

The **WinSubClassWindow** API replaces the current function that PM calls for processing a window's messages and returns the address of the current function. The prototype for this API is given in Figure 10.1.

- The **hwnd** parameter specifies the window whose window procedure is to be replaced.
- The **pfnwp** parameter specifies the address of the new window procedure to be called when **hwnd** receives a message.

The new window procedure should normally call the old procedure to perform the window class's normal processing for any unprocessed messages or for messages that only modify but do not replace the original functionality. This is identical to the subclassing of the base window class wherein application window procedures call the **WinDefWindowProc** API.

```
PFNWP APIENTRY WinSubclassWindow(HWND hwnd,
                                 PFNWP pfnwp);
```

Figure 10.1   The WinSubclassWindow API.

The first example subclasses the container control in order to modify the background of the control. The container explicitly supports this subclassing function by sending itself a CM_PAINTBACKGROUND message whenever the background requires updating and the CA_OWNERPAINTBACKGROUND attribute is set (see Chapter 12 for a detailed discussion of the container window). If the container has not been subclassed, it returns FALSE when this message is received, causing the background to be drawn in the normal manner. If the container has been subclassed and the new window procedure processes the message, TRUE is returned to indicate that the new window procedure has drawn the background. This return value prevents the container control from redrawing the background and erasing the work of the application.

Parameter **mp1** of the CM_PAINTBACKGROUND message contains a pointer to an OWNERBACKGROUND structure which contains the information required to draw the background. Parameter **mp2** is reserved and should not be used by the application. The definition of the OWNERBACKGROUND structure is given in Figure 10.2.

- The *hwnd* element is the handle of the container window.
- The *hps* element is a handle to a presentation space established by the container for drawing the background.
- The *rclBackground* element is a RECTL structure that specifies the area to be drawn.
- The *idWindow* element is the window identifier for the container window and allows the application to identify the window being painted.

Figure 10.3 shows coding that can be used to draw a bitmap onto the background of the container control. After the container is created, **WinSubclassWindow** is called to replace the container's normal window procedure with routine **cnrSubclassProc**. The address of the original routine is stored in a global variable, *pfnCnrProc*.

After the **WinSubclassWindow** call, all messages for the container are first processed by **cnrSubclassProc**. The routine casts the value in parameter **mp1** to a pointer to an OWNERBACKGROUND structure for use if the incoming message is CM_PAINTBACKGROUND. If this is indeed the message, the func-

```
typedef struct _OWNERBACKGROUND       /* ownbckg */
{
   HWND    hwnd;
   HPS     hps;
   RECTL   rclBackground;
   LONG    idWindow;
} OWNERBACKGROUND;
```

Figure 10.2   The OWNERBACKGROUND structure.

```
/************** From window creation processing ************/
     hwndCnr = WinCreateWindow( hwnd, WC_CONTAINER, "Just a test",
                                CCS_AUTOPOSITION | WS_VISIBLE,
                                0, 0, 0, 0, hwnd, HWND_TOP,
                                CID_REGISTER, NULL, NULL );
     pfnCnrProc = WinSubclassWindow( hwndCnr, cnrSubclassProc );
/************** End from window creation processing ************/

MRESULT APIENTRY cnrSubclassProc(HWND hwnd,ULONG msg,MPARAM mp1,MPARAM mp2)
{
    POWNERBACKGROUND    pob = (POWNERBACKGROUND)mp1;
    static HBITMAP      hbm = NULLHANDLE;
    RECTL               rectl;
    POINTL              ptl;
    MRESULT             rc;

    if (msg == CM_PAINTBACKGROUND) {
        if( pob->idWindow != CID_REGISTER &&
            pob->idWindow != CID_LEFTDVWND &&
            pob->idWindow != CID_RIGHTDVWND )
          return MRFROMLONG(FALSE);
        if( hbm == NULLHANDLE ) {
          WinQueryWindowRect( hwnd, &rectl );
          hbm = LoadBitmap(pob->hps, &rectl);
        }
        ptl.x = pob->rclBackground.xLeft;
        ptl.y = pob->rclBackground.yBottom;
        WinDrawBitmap( pob->hps, hbm, &(pob->rclBackground), &ptl,
                       01, 01, DBM_NORMAL );
        return MRFROMLONG(TRUE);
    }
    if (msg == WM_VSCROLL || msg == WM_HSCROLL) {
        WinLockWindowUpdate( HWND_DESKTOP, hwnd );
        rc = (*pfnCnrProc)(hwnd, msg, mp1, mp2 );
        WinLockWindowUpdate( HWND_DESKTOP, NULLHANDLE );
        return rc;
    }
    if (msg == WM_SIZE ) {
        GpiDeleteBitmap( hbm );
        hbm = NULLHANDLE;
    }
    return (*pfnCnrProc)(hwnd, msg, mp1, mp2);
}
```

Figure 10.3   Subclassing the Container.

tion examines the *idWindow* element of the OWNERBACKGROUND structure to determine if the background being drawn is either the background of the container window itself or one of the data windows of the details view (the container child window IDs are defined in pmstddlg.h). If the background is not for one of these windows, FALSE is returned to allow the container to paint the background. Otherwise, if the bitmap has not already been loaded, **LoadBitmap** is called to establish a bitmap sized to fill the window. (See Chapter 15 for additional bitmap programming information.) When the bitmap is available, a point structure is initialized to indicate the starting point of the drawing operation, and **WinDrawBitmap** is called to repaint the requested portion of the window background. After the drawing is complete, the function returns TRUE to prevent the container from redrawing the background.

Three additional messages are processed by the container subclass procedure. The WM_VSCROLL message and WM_HSCROLL message must be processed to prevent the background from becoming corrupted due to the use of the **WinScrollWindow** API by the container. The processing for these messages uses the **WinLockWindowUpdate** API to prevent output to the window while the container is performing the scrolling operation. The standard container window procedure is then called to perform the scrolling operation. When the scrolling is complete, **WinLockWindowUpdate** is again called to allow output to the window. The WM_SIZE message is processed so that the bitmap can be resized to fit the window. When the message is received, the function deletes the bitmap so that it will be reloaded and resized when another background drawing request is received. WM_SIZE and all other unprocessed messages are passed to the standard container window procedure for normal processing.

The ability to subclass the container control and paint its background is this easy because the control provides the CM_PAINTBACKGROUND message. If this message were not available, this functionality would be impossible since there would be no way to prevent the container from drawing the background during its WM_PAINT processing short of completely rewriting the paint function. Even with the message, the functionality is not as straightforward as it might first appear, as evidenced by the need to process the scrolling and sizing messages. Since this type of message is not universally available, subclassing is more commonly used to either prevent certain messages from being processed by the standard window procedure for a class or to process additional messages that are not normally processed by a class's standard window procedure.

The second example shows how an entry field can be subclassed to prevent the standard window procedure from receiving WM_CHAR messages representing non-numeric characters, resulting in a numeric-only entry field. Figure 10.4 shows code that can be used to accomplish this function for an entry field in a dialog box. Routine **SubentryDlgProc** is the dialog procedure for the dia-

```
MRESULT APIENTRY SubentryDlgProc(HWND hwnd,ULONG msg,MPARAM mp1,MPARAM mp2)
{
    HWND      hwndEntry;

    switch (msg) {
    case WM_INITDLG:
        hwndEntry = WinWindowFromID( hwnd, ID_ENTRYFIELD );
        pfnEntry = WinSubclassWindow( hwndEntry, entrySubProc );
        return MRFROMLONG(FALSE);
        break;
    default:
        return WinDefDlgProc( hwnd, msg, mp1, mp2 );
        break;
    } /* endswitch */
}

MRESULT APIENTRY entrySubProc( HWND hwnd, ULONG msg, MPARAM mp1, MPARAM mp2 )
{
    if (msg == WM_CHAR) {
        if ((SHORT1FROMMP(mp1) & (KC_CHAR|KC_VIRTUALKEY)) == KC_CHAR) {
            if (CHAR1FROMMP(mp2) < '0' || CHAR1FROMMP(mp2) > '9') {
                return MRFROMLONG(FALSE);
            } /* endif */
        } /* endif */
    } /* endif */
    return (*pfnEntry)(hwnd, msg, mp1, mp2 );
}
```

Figure 10.4   Subclassing the entry field.

log box. The WM_INITDLG processing for this dialog first obtains the window handle of the entry field, then calls **WinSubclassWindow** to replace the standard entry field window procedure with routine **entrySubProc**. The standard window procedure is stored in a global variable for use by the subclassing procedure.

Routine **entrySubProc** forwards all messages except WM_CHAR to the standard entry field window procedure. If the WM_CHAR message is for a keystroke that produces a nonvirtual keystroke, a comparison is made to determine if the character falls into the numeric range. If not, the routine returns without forwarding the message to the standard entry field procedure. WM_CHAR messages that represent virtual keys or numeric characters are forwarded to the standard entry field procedure for normal processing.

CREATING A NEW CLASS

So far we have discussed examples where only one window is subclassed. When many windows require the same subclass functionality, subclassing through

```
BOOL APIENTRY WinQueryClassInfo(HAB hab,
                                PSZ pszClassName,
                                PCLASSINFO pClassInfo);
```

Figure 10.5 The WinQueryClassInfo API.

the creation of a whole new class may prove beneficial. In addition, a new class is necessary if the subclass functionality requires additions to the window instance data defined for the existing class. The new class retains the overall behavior of the existing class, but adds its own enhanced functionality or data. When this method is used, windows are created as instances of the new class and the **WinSubclassWindow** API is not required.

This approach to subclassing is very similar to what occurs in object-oriented environments when a new object class is derived from an existing class. The methods and data of the original class are maintained but the new class typically adds or replaces some methods and extends the object data. When a window class subclasses, or is derived from, an existing class, the new class must maintain a link to the methods of the existing class and must maintain the window instance data required by the existing class. The new class obtains this information by calling the **WinQueryClassInfo** API. The prototype of this function is shown in Figure 10.5.

- The **hab** parameter is the handle to the process's or thread's anchor block.
- The **pszClassName** parameter specifies the class for which information is desired. The parameter is specified in the same manner as the class name of the **WinCreateWindow** API, which is a class name constant to obtain information for the OS/2 system-defined classes or a pointer to a zero-terminated string for application-defined classes.
- The **pClassInfo** parameter is a pointer to a CLASSINFO structure in which the class definition information is returned.

WinQueryClassInfo returns TRUE if successful or FALSE if the class does not exist.

The CLASSINFO structure returned by **WinQueryClassInfo** is defined as in Figure 10.6.

```
typedef struct _CLASSINFO
{
    ULONG    flClassStyle;
    PFNWP    pfnWindowProc;
    ULONG    cbWindowData;
} CLASSINFO;
```

Figure 10.6 The CLASSINFO structure.

- Element *flClassStyle* is the defined class style used for creating windows of the class.
- The *pfnWindowProc* element is the window procedure that implements the methods for the class. The window procedures of derived classes normally call this procedure rather than **WinDefWindowProc** for messages that are not completely processed by the derived class.
- Element *cbWindowData* specifies the number of bytes of window instance data reserved for the class. Derived classes must specify the reservation of at least this many bytes of window instance data.

To see how this form of subclassing is performed, let's examine the coding required to implement a static text field, which may be edited under special conditions (similar to the icon text of Workplace Shell objects). This type of control might be used in a WYSIWYG forms editor in which the field labels are normally displayed as static text. When the user wishes to modify the label text, the label is changed to an entry field. When the modifications are complete, the entry field returns to a static text control. All of this could be accomplished within the application code, but isolating the control functionality in a derived class reduces application complexity and allows the control functionality to be easily included in other applications.

Before the new class can be used to create a window, it must be registered. To avoid complications in the main application, a function is provided to accomplish this task. This function is shown in Figure 10.7. The new control class is actually implemented using two derived classes: the class derived from the entry field, which is known to the application; and a class derived from the static text control, which is used internally by the derived entry field class. Function **RegisterMyClass** first calls **WinQueryClassInfo** to obtain the class specifications for both the entry field and the static text control. **WinRegisterClass** is then called to register the new entry field class. A new

```
void RegisterMyClass( HAB hab )
{
   WinQueryClassInfo( hab, WC_STATIC, &ciStatic );
   WinQueryClassInfo( hab, WC_ENTRYFIELD, &ciEntry );
   WinRegisterClass( hab, "MYCLASS",
           MyClassWndProc, (ULONG)(ciEntry.flClassStyle) & ~CS_PUBLIC,
           ciEntry.cbWindowData + SIZE_WINDOW_DATA);
   WinRegisterClass( hab, "MYCLASSSTATIC",
           MyClassStaticWndProc,
           (ULONG)(ciStatic.flClassStyle)&~CS_PUBLIC,
           ciStatic.cbWindowData );
}
```

Figure 10.7   Registering a new class.

window procedure, **MyClassWndProc**, is specified as the window procedure for the class; the class style is set to the style of the entry field, less the CS_PUBLIC style. The number of bytes of window instance data is set to the amount required by the base entry field class plus room for two additional ULONG values required by the new class. The new static text field class is then registered. The window procedure is set to **MyClassStaticWndProc**; the style is set to the base static text control style, less the CS_PUBLIC style. The number of bytes of reserved instance data is set equal to the number of bytes required by the base class; no additional window instance data is required. The CS_PUBLIC style is removed since the derived classes are not global classes.

After the new class has been registered and the application creates windows of this class, **MyClassWndProc** begins to receive messages sent to the new control windows. The first message that the new class processes is the WM_CREATE message. The code that processes this message is shown in Figure 10.8. The primary function of this routine is the creation of the static text control associated with the new window. The function first converts parameter **mp2** to a CREATESTRUCT pointer. The style of the new window is then extracted and used to compile the style flags for the static text control. The style of the entry field control is then modified. The ES_MARGIN style is set to draw a border around the entry field, and the ES_READONLY style is reset—the static text field now provides this functionality. The static text window is then

```
case WM_CREATE:
    pCS = (PCREATESTRUCT)PVOIDFROMMP(mp2);
    if (!(pCS->flStyle & (MC_CENTER | MC_RIGHT))) flStaticStyle |= DT_LEFT;
    if (pCS->flStyle & MC_CENTER) flStaticStyle |= DT_CENTER;
    if (pCS->flStyle & MC_RIGHT) flStaticStyle |= DT_RIGHT;
    if (pCS->flStyle & MC_AUTOSIZE) flStaticStyle |= SS_AUTOSIZE;

    flEntryStyle = WinQueryWindowULong( hwnd, QWL_STYLE );
    flEntryStyle |= ES_MARGIN;
    flEntryStyle &= ~ES_READONLY;
    WinSetWindowULong( hwnd, QWL_STYLE, flEntryStyle );

    hwndStatic = WinCreateWindow( pCS->hwndParent, "MYCLASSSTATIC",
                                  pCS->pszText, flStaticStyle,
                                  pCS->x, pCS->y + 2, pCS->cx, pCS->cy,
                                  hwnd, pCS->hwndInsertBehind,
                                  pCS->id | 0x8000L, NULL,
                                  pCS->pPresParams );
    WinSetWindowULong( hwnd, WD_HWNDSTATIC, hwndStatic );
    WinSetWindowULong( hwnd, WD_HWNDPARENT, pCS->hwndParent );
    WinPostMsg( hwnd, MC_ALLOWEDIT, MPFROMLONG(FALSE), 0);
    return (*(ciEntry.pfnWindowProc))(hwnd, msg, mp1, mp2 );
```

Figure 10.8   **Processing the WM_CREATE message for the new class.**

created. The parent window is set to the parent of the new entry field control and the owner window is set to the new control. The ID is set equal to the ID used to create the entry field control with the top bit set (hopefully moving the ID out of the range normally used by applications). After the static text window is created, the handles of the static text window and the parent window are stored in the new fields of the entry field's window instance data. Finally, an MC_ALLOWEDIT message is posted back to the new entry field to cause the initial state to be read-only, thereby causing the static field text to be displayed in the application window. Note that this message is actually a redefinition of the base entry field EM_SETREADONLY message. Again, there is no need to make the entry field itself read-only since the static text field is used to display the text in this mode.

The entry field's processing of the MC_ALLOWEDIT message, shown in Figure 10.9, handles the switch from the static text control to the entry field control and back. Parameter **mp1** of the message is a Boolean value that indicates if editing is allowed. The code first obtains the handle of the associated static text control and then checks the value of **mp1**. If **mp1** indicates that editing is allowed, the static text control is hidden, the entry field control is enabled and displayed, and focus is set to the entry field control. If **mp1** is FALSE, the current text of the entry field is retrieved and used to change the text in the static text control. The entry field is then disabled and hidden and the static text field is made visible.

While the application can send the MC_ALLOWEDIT message, the control itself defines functionality which switches between the static text control and the entry field. The window procedure for the static text control sends an MC_ALLOWEDIT message with **mp1** set to TRUE when it receives a WM_BUTTON2DOWN message. Thus the user can enter edit mode by press-

```
case MC_ALLOWEDIT:
    hwndStatic  = WinQueryWindowULong( hwnd, WD_HWNDSTATIC );
    if ((BOOL)mp1) {
        WinShowWindow( hwndStatic, FALSE );
        WinEnableWindow( hwnd, TRUE );
        WinShowWindow( hwnd, TRUE );
        WinSetFocus( HWND_DESKTOP, hwnd );
    } else {
        WinQueryWindowText( hwnd, 256, szText );
        WinSetWindowText( hwndStatic, szText );
        WinShowWindow( hwnd, FALSE );
        WinEnableWindow( hwnd, FALSE );
        WinShowWindow( hwndStatic, TRUE );
    } /* endif */
    return (MRESULT)TRUE;
```

Figure 10.9   Processing the MC_ALLOWEDIT message.

```
MRESULT APIENTRY MyClassStaticWndProc( HWND hwnd, ULONG msg,
                                       MPARAM mp1, MPARAM mp2 );
{
   HWND          hwndEntry = WinQueryWindow( hwnd, QW_OWNER );

   switch (msg) {
   case WM_BUTTON2DOWN:
      WinSendMsg( hwndEntry, MC_ALLOWEDIT, (MPARAM)TRUE, 01 );
      return (MRESULT)TRUE;
   default:
      return (*(ciStatic.pfnWindowProc))(hwnd, msg, mp1, mp2 );
   } /* endswitch */
}
```

Figure 10.10   The MyClassStaticWndProc window procedure.

ing mouse button 2 over the static text field. **MyClassStaticWndProc** is shown
in Figure 10.10. If the received message is not WM_BUTTON2DOWN, the
message is forwarded to the window procedure of the base static text control.

   When the entry field control has been enabled to allow editing of the text
and then loses the input focus, read-only mode is resumed. As shown in Figure
10.11, **MyClassWndProc** processes the WM_SETFOCUS message to perform
this function. If parameter **mp2** is set to FALSE, the control is losing the focus
and an MC_ALLOWEDIT message is sent with **mp1** set to FALSE to disable the
entry field and display the associated static text control. The WM_SETFOCUS
message is then forwarded to the base entry field window procedure in order
to allow proper functioning of the input cursor.

SUMMARY

Subclassing of windows and classes allows new features to be added to existing
controls without requiring a complete rewrite of the basic control functionality.
Though often misunderstood, this mechanism is relatively easy to use. In many
cases, the new features can be implemented by merely intercepting messages
sent to the base control. In more complicated cases, a new control class is

```
case WM_SETFOCUS:
   if (!(BOOL)mp2) {
      WinSendMsg( hwnd, MC_ALLOWEDIT, (MPARAM)FALSE, 0 );
   } /* endif */
   return( *(ciEntry.pfnWindowProc))(hwnd, msg, mp1, mp2 );
```

Figure 10.11   Processing the WM_SETFOCUS message.

derived from an existing class. The primary difficulties encountered when subclassing are the determination of which features may be subclassed and overcoming any side effects that may be caused by subclassing, as we saw in the container control example. In most cases, a little forethought and some intelligent experimentation allow these difficulties to be successfully managed.

CHAPTER 11

Improving Your Control: Using the Advanced OS/2 Controls

O S/2 2.0 and later versions have introduced a number of new controls into the PM library. Among these are the notebook, the value set, and the linear and circular sliders. The notebook control provides a convenient mechanism for presenting multiple pages of information to the user. The value set provides the ability to display a set of mutually exclusive choices to the user in graphic form. The sliders enable the user to select a value based on its relative location within a range of acceptable values. This chapter discusses each of these controls in detail.

NOTEBOOKS

From an application standpoint, the notebook control provides a means of presenting the user with multiple pages of information and/or dialog without the hassle of controlling the user's manipulation of the pages to find the desired information. From the user's standpoint, the notebook control is a computerized version of a physical notebook, providing an easy means of accessing any portion of a large set of data. The value of the control from both the user and application standpoints can be easily seen by comparing the notebook representation of a set of dialogs with the old method of presenting the dialogs one at a time and closing each dialog before another is opened. With the notebook, the application opens all the dialogs at once and the user simply pages through the various bits of information without requiring further support from the application code until a change in the data occurs. Of course, the application must take action at this time to validate the change and update its internal copy of the information.

The notebook control is different from most other controls in one important respect. Other controls, like the static text control and the entry field, are used to display data or to obtain input from the user. The notebook does not directly provide this type of functionality. Its intended and normal purpose is to provide a means of organizing other windows for the display of data or dialog. The notebook is similar to the dialog box in this respect, but, by providing multiple, easily accessible pages, it overcomes the limitations inherent in the normal usage of the dialog box.

Several examples of using notebook controls are readily available in OS/2's Workplace Shell. The most common example is the settings notebook associated with Workplace objects. The pages of these notebooks are dialogs that allow the user to configure the object. Tabs allow quick access to the section of the notebook that addresses the desired options. Another example is the Master Help Index. This notebook provides a listbox that displays the various topics comprising the help index. Separate pages are used to provide tabs, which allow the user to quickly move to the first index entry for each letter of the alphabet. Unlike most notebooks, the Master Help Index displays the same data on every page—the pages and tabs merely allow the user to move to different locations in the displayed data.

The graphical representation of the notebook is a picture of a real-world notebook, without covers; it has a binding along one edge; optional section, or major, tabs opposite the binding; and optional subsection, or minor, tabs on one of the other unbound edges. Two arrow buttons are displayed in one corner of the notebook. When enabled, these buttons allow the user to move back and forth through the pages. Optional status text may be displayed in the area horizontally adjacent to the arrow buttons. The three-dimensional appearance of the notebook is achieved by recessing two of the edges of the upper pages to reveal the back pages. These two page edges are always adjacent, and their intersection, known as the back page intersection, defines the overall appearance of the control.

Just as the appearance and functionality of the notebook mimic its real-world counterpart, so too do the operations that an application performs to present the notebook to the user. First, an empty notebook must be obtained by creating the notebook window. Then, blank pages are added to the notebook by sending messages to insert new pages. Finally, the empty pages are scribed with information by indicating which window to display on the page. The following discussion describes each of these operations in detail.

Selecting a Notebook Style

The available styles for the notebook control allow the programmer to control six aspects of the control's appearance: the back page intersection location, the tab and binding positions, the binding type, the tab appearance, the justification of text within the tabs, and the justification of the status text. The complete appearance of the notebook may be specified by the logical OR of one flag chosen from the set available for each aspect.

Four style flags are provided for specifying the location of the back page intersection:

BKS_BACKPAGESBR   0x0001   indicates that the back page edges are to intersect at the bottom right corner.

BKS_BACKPAGESBL   0x0002   indicates that the back page edges are to intersect at the bottom left corner.

BKS_BACKPAGESTR   0x0004   indicates that the back page edges are to intersect at the top right corner.

BKS_BACKPAGESTL   0x0008   indicates that the back page edges are to intersect at the top left corner.

Four style flags are available for specifying the location of the major tabs; however, since the major tabs must always be placed on a edge adjacent to the back page intersection, only two flags are valid for any given back page intersection style flag specified. If an invalid combination is specified, the major tab style is ignored and the major tabs are placed on the nearest edge clockwise from the intersection point. Minor tabs are displayed along the remaining edge adjacent to the back page intersection, and the binding is always displayed on the edge opposite the major tabs. The major tab location flags are:

BKS_MAJORTABRIGHT   0x0010   places the major tabs on the right edge of the notebook.

BKS_MAJORTABLEFT   0x0020   places the major tabs on the left edge of the notebook.

BKS_MAJORTABTOP   0x0040   places the major tabs on the top edge of the notebook.

BKS_MAJORTABBOTTOM   0x0080   places the major tabs on the bottom edge of the notebook.

The notebook binding may be displayed as a solid binding or a spiral binding. The chosen style is specified by one of the following style flags:

BKS_SOLIDBIND   0x0000   causes the binding to display as a solid cover binding.

BKS_SPIRALBIND   0x0400   causes the binding to display as a spiral binding.

The tab appearance is specified by one of the following three style flags.

BKS_SQUARETABS   0x0000   causes the ends of the tabs to be square.

BKS_ROUNDEDTABS   0x0100   causes the ends of the tabs to taper off and appear rounded.

BKS_POLYGONTABS   0x0200   is similar to the rounded style, causing the ends of the tabs to taper off, but flattens the end of the tab.

The tab text may be left- or right-justified or centered in the tab. The following three flags are used to specify the tab text justification:

BKS_TABTEXTCENTER	0x8000	centers the text within the tab.
BKS_TABTEXTLEFT	0x0000	left-justifies the text within the tab.
BKS_TABTEXTRIGHT	0x4000	right-justifies the text within the tab.

The status line text is left-justified, right-justified, or centered based on the specification of one of the following three style flags:

BKS_STATUSTEXTLEFT	0x0000	left-justifies the text on the status line.
BKS_STATUSTEXTRIGHT	0x1000	right-justifies the text on the status line.
BKS_STATUSTEXTCENTER	0x2000	centers the text on the status line.

While an application is free to explicitly specify each aspect of the control's appearance, only those styles that vary from the default need be specified. The defaults supplied by the control are defined by the following programming construct:

```
BKS_BACKPAGESBR | BKS_MAJORTABRIGHT | BKS_SOLIDBIND |
BKS_SQUARETABS | BKS_TABTEXTLEFT | BKS_STATUSTEXTLEFT
```

This produces a notebook with a solid binding on the left-hand side, major tabs on the right-hand side, and minor tabs on the bottom. Tabs are displayed with square ends and centered text, and the status line text is left-justified.

Creating the Notebook

The notebook control may be created as an element of a dialog box or as an independent control, depending on the needs of the application and the preferences of the programmer. Since the control is used to organize other controls, dialogs, and windows, it will often occupy the entire client area of a surrounding frame or dialog window. If the control is part of a dialog box, it might share the client area with pushbuttons that allow the user to explicitly inform the application when to read the information back from the windows controlled by the notebook.

The resource script statement for including a notebook control in a dialog template is shown in Figure 11.1.

```
NOTEBOOK  id, x, y, cx, cy, style
```

Figure 11.1 Notebook control resource script statement.

- *id* is the numeric identifier assigned to the dialog element.
- *x* specifies the x coordinate of the origin of the notebook relative to the origin of the dialog window. The value is expressed in dialog units.
- *y* specifies the y coordinate of the origin of the notebook relative to the origin of the dialog window. The value is expressed in dialog units.
- *cx* specifies the width of the control in dialog units.
- *cy* specifies the height of the control in dialog units.
- *style* specifies the style of the control composed of the style flags discussed previously and the standard WS_ window styles.

The coding required to create a notebook as an independent control is shown in Figure 11.2. This example shows one method of filling the client area of an application frame window with a control. Function **wmCreate** is called when the client window procedure receives the WM_CREATE message. The function creates the notebook control window by calling the **WinCreateWindow** API. No notebook styles are specified in the **flstyle** parameter so the default notebook styles are used. The WS_VISIBLE flag is set so that the window will be displayed when the client becomes visible. The size of the client is unknown during WM_CREATE processing, therefore the size and position parameters are set to zero. The remainder of the function contains code to customize the notebook appearance and initialize the notebook pages; the details of these functions are discussed next.

When the application window size is established later in the creation process, a WM_SIZE message is sent to the client window. When this message is received, function **wmSize** is called to resize the notebook control to be the same size as the client window. The function retrieves the handle of the notebook window based on its ID and then calls the **WinSetWindowPos** API to set the position of the notebook to the origin of the client window, (0, 0), and the width and height of the notebook to the new size of the client window. Parameter **mp2** of the WM_SIZE message contains the width of the window in its low-order word, and the height of the window in its high-order word.

Customizing the Notebook

When the notebook is initially created, the tab sizes are set to a height and width that is approximately the size required to display one character in the currently selected font for the notebook's presentation space. Applications that display multiple characters in the tabs must modify the tab dimensions if all characters are to be visible. This is accomplished by sending a BKM_SETDIMENSIONS message to the notebook control window. This message allows the application to modify the dimensions of the major tabs, minor tabs, or page arrow buttons. Parameter **mp1** specifies the new dimensions: the low-order word specifies the width and the high-order word specifies the height. These dimensions are specified in world coordinates. If both the width and height are set to zero, the specified notebook element will be hidden. Parameter **mp2** of the message

```
#define NOTEBOOK_ID    100

MRESULT APIENTRY wmCreate( HWND hwnd, ULONG msg, MPARAM mp1, MPARAM mp2 )
{
    HWND            hwndNote;

    hwndNote = WinCreateWindow( hwnd,
                                WC_NOTEBOOK,
                                "",
                                WS_VISIBLE,
                                0, 0, 0, 0,
                                hwnd, HWND_TOP,
                                NOTEBOOK_ID, NULL, NULL );
    SetTabLen( hwndNote );
    AdjustNotebookColors( hwndNote );
    DoSamplePages( hwndNote );
    AddNotebookPages( hwndNote );
    CreateVSIntro( hwndNote, pgData[PGI_MLE1].ulPageID );
    CreateCalen( hwndNote, pgData[PGI_VS1].ulPageID );
    CreateClrEdit( hwndNote, pgData[PGI_VS2].ulPageID );
    CreateSampDlg( hwndNote, pgData[PGI_SAMPDLG].ulPageID );
    hwndPage = CreateAppWnd( hwndNote );
    if (hwndPage != NULLHANDLE) {
        WinSendMsg( hwndNote, BKM_SETPAGEWINDOWHWND,
                    MPFROMLONG( pgData[PGI_APPWND1].ulPageID ),
                    MPFROMLONG( hwndPage ));
        WinSendMsg( hwndNote, BKM_SETPAGEWINDOWHWND,
                    MPFROMLONG( pgData[PGI_APPWND2].ulPageID ),
                    MPFROMLONG( hwndPage ));
    }
    return (MRESULT)FALSE;
}

MRESULT wmSize( HWND hwnd, ULONG msg, MPARAM mp1, MPARAM mp2 )
{
    HWND     hwndNote = WinWindowFromID( hwnd, NOTEBOOK_ID );

    WinSetWindowPos( hwndNote, NULLHANDLE, 0, 0,
                     SHORT1FROMMP( mp2 ), SHORT2FROMMP( mp2 ),
                     SWP_SIZE | SWP_MOVE );
    return WinDefWindowProc( hwnd, msg, mp1, mp2 );
}
```

Figure 11.2   Creating a notebook control.

specifies the notebook element to change and may contain one of the following values:

BKA_MAJORTAB	0x0001	changes the dimensions of the major tabs.
BKA_MINORTAB	0x0002	changes the dimensions of the minor tabs.
BKA_PAGEBUTTON	0x0100	changes the dimensions of the page arrow buttons.

Figure 11.3 provides example coding for adjusting the size of a tab to fit the text to be displayed. The **WinDrawText** API is used to determine the required dimensions—see Chapter 16 for a detailed description of this API. Function **SetTabSize** takes three parameters: the handle to the notebook window, a pointer to an array of strings, and the type of tab, either BKA_MAJORTAB or BKA_MINORTAB. The function first obtains the handle to the presentation space for the notebook and then establishes a rectangle the size of the screen for use with **WinDrawText**. A loop is then entered to scan each of the strings passed in the array. Within the loop, a copy of the screen rectangle is passed to **WinDrawText**. On return from the API, this rectangle is modified to reflect the area required to just surround the text. If either the height or width of the current string is greater than the previous maximum, the maximum is changed to the value for the current string. The loop terminates when a NULL pointer is encountered, signaling the end of the array of strings. Both the height and width are then adjusted to leave space for the tab border and the selection cursor. The minimum factor of 7 indicated in the operating system documentation is sometimes insufficient. A factor of 8 should be added to the height

```
void SetTabSize( HWND hwndNote, PSZ *pszText, ULONG ulType)
{
    HPS         hps;
    SHORT       cx = 0, cy = 0;
    RECTL       rcl, rcl1;

    hps = WinGetPS( hwndNote );
    if (hps != NULLHANDLE) {
        memset( (PVOID)&rcl1, 0, sizeof(RECTL));
        rcl1.xRight = WinQuerySysValue( HWND_DESKTOP, SV_CXSCREEN );
        rcl1.yTop = WinQuerySysValue( HWND_DESKTOP, SV_CYSCREEN );
        while( *pszText != NULL ) {
            rcl = rcl1;
            WinDrawText( hps, strlen(pgData[i].pszTabText),
                         pgData[i].pszTabText, &rcl, 0, 0,
                         DT_LEFT | DT_BOTTOM | DT_QUERYEXTENT );
            if( (SHORT)(rcl.xRight) > cx ) cx = (SHORT)(rcl.xRight);
            if( (SHORT)(rcl.yTop) > cy ) cy = (SHORT)(rcl.yTop);
            pszText++;
        }
        cx += 24;
        cy += 8;
        WinSendMsg( hwndNote, BKM_SETDIMENSIONS,
                    MPFROM2SHORT( cx, cy ), (MPARAM)ulType );
        WinReleasePS( hps );
    } /* endif */
    return;
}
```

Figure 11.3　Modifying the notebook tab size.

NOTEBOOK ELEMENT	DEFAULT COLOR	PRESENTATION PARAMETERS
Border	SYSCLR_WINDOWFRAME	PP_BORDERCOLOR PP_BORDERCOLORINDEX
Window background	SYSCLR_FIELDBACKGROUND	PP_BACKGROUNDCOLOR PP_BACKGROUNDCOLORINDEX
Selection cursor	SYSCLR_HILITEBACKGROUND	PP_HILITEBACKGROUNDCOLOR PP_HILITEBACKGROUNDCOLORINDEX
Status text	SYSCLR_WINDOWTEXT	PP_FOREGROUNDCOLOR PP_FOREGROUNDCOLORINDEX

Figure 11.4 **Notebook colors changed with WinSetPresParam.**

of top and bottom tabs to prevent clipping when the BKS_ROUNDEDTABS style is specified. The factor to be added to the width of left and right tabs is dependent on the tab style. Use a factor of 8 for the BKS_SQUARETABS style, a factor of 14 for the BKS_ROUNDEDTABS style, and a factor of 21 for the BKS_POLYGONTABS style. After these adjustments have been made, **WinSendMsg** is called to send the BKM_SETDIMENSIONS message to the notebook. Parameter **mp1** is set to the combined width and height values, and parameter **mp2** is set to the tab type parameter passed to **SetTabSize**. The presentation space is then released and the function returns.

The color used to paint various elements of the notebook control can also be controlled by the application. These elements may be organized into two groups based on the method the application uses to modify the color. The first group is modified by calling the **WinSetPresParam** API. The notebook elements comprising this group are listed in Figure 11.4 along with the default color of the element and the presentation parameters that are used to modify the color of the element. The BKM_SETNOTEBOOKCOLORS message is used to modify the color of the elements in the second group. Figure 11.5 lists these elements, their default colors, and the color identifiers that will change the

NOTEBOOK ELEMENT	DEFAULT COLOR	BKM_SETNOTEBOOKCOLORS mp2
Major tab background	SYSCLR_PAGEBACKGROUND	BKA_BACKGROUNDMAJORCOLOR BKA_BACKGROUNDMAJORCOLORINDEX
Major tab text	SYSCLR_WINDOWTEXT	BKA_FOREGROUNDMAJORCOLOR BKA_FOREGROUNDMAJORCOLORINDEX
Minor tab background	SYSCLR_PAGEBACKGROUND	BKA_BACKGROUNDMINORCOLOR BKA_BACKGROUNDMINORCOLORINDEX
Minor tab text	SYSCLR_WINDOWTEXT	BKA_FOREGROUNDMINORCOLOR BKA_FOREGROUNDMINORCOLORINDEX
Page background	SYSCLR_PAGEBACKGROUND	BKA_BACKGROUNDPAGECOLOR BKA_BACKGROUNDPAGECOLORINDEX

Figure 11.5 **Notebook colors changed with BKM_SETNOTEBOOKCOLORS.**

element color. Parameter **mp1** of the BKM_SETNOTEBOOKCOLORS message specifies either an RGB color or a color index value depending on the value of **mp2**, the color identifier.

Figure 11.6 provides sample code for changing the color of notebook areas. This example first calls **WinSetPresParam** to set the border color to the RGB value 0x00FF0000. This value sets the red component of the color to its maximum value and the green and blue components to their minimum value; thus the notebook border will be red. Next, **WinSetPresParam** is called to set the notebook background to a color index. The index value is CLR_GREEN which is green in the default palette; however, this could be any color if the palette has been changed. The first call to **WinSendMsg** sends the BKM_SETNOTEBOOKCOLORS message to set the background of the major tabs to the RGB color 0x000000FF producing a blue background color since the blue component is set to its maximum value and the red and green components are set to their minimum value. The second call to **WinSendMsg** sets the minor tab background color to the value specified by the color index CLR_YELLOW. If the palette has not been modified, the color is yellow.

Adding Pages to the Notebook

Like a newly acquired three-ring binder, the notebook is empty when first created. Before the notebook can be used to display information to the user, pages must be inserted. The application sends one or more BKM_INSERTPAGE messages to the notebook control window to accomplish this function. Parameter **mp1** of this message is the identifier assigned for an existing page and is used when the new page is to be inserted before or after the given page. Parameter **mp2** is composed of two fields: the low-order word specifies the style of the

```
ulParam = 0x00ff0000;
WinSetPresParam( hwndNote, PP_BORDERCOLOR, sizeof( ULONG ),
            (PVOID *)&ulParam );

ulParam = CLR_GREEN;
WinSetPresParam( hwndNote, PP_BACKGROUNDCOLORINDEX, sizeof( ULONG ),
            (PVOID *)&ulParam );

ulParam = 0x000000ff;      /* blue */
WinSendMsg( hwndNote, BKM_SETNOTEBOOKCOLORS, (MPARAM)ulParam,
          (MPARAM)BKA_BACKGROUNDMAJORCOLOR );

ulParam = CLR_YELLOW;
WinSendMsg( hwndNote, BKM_SETNOTEBOOKCOLORS, (MPARAM)ulParam,
          (MPARAM)BKA_BACKGROUNDMINORCOLORINDEX );
```

Figure 11.6 Changing notebook colors.

page, and the high-order word specifies the location in which the new page is inserted. The style in the low-order word may specify the following flags:

BKA_MAJOR   0x0040   indicates that the new page should be given a major tab. Note that only one type of tab may be specified per page—do not set both the BKA_MAJOR and BKA_MINOR flags. The BKM_SETTABTEXT message is used to set the text displayed on the tab.

BKA_MINOR   0x0080   indicates that the new page should be given a minor tab. Do not set both BKA_MAJOR and BKA_MINOR for a single page. The BKM_SETTABTEXT message is used to set the text displayed on the tab.

BKA_STATUSTEXTON   0x0001   indicates that the status line field should be turned on for the page. The field remains blank until filled by the BKM_SETSTATUSLINETEXT message.

BKA_AUTOPAGESIZE   0x0100   indicates that the notebook control automatically maintains the size and position of the window that is eventually assigned to the page.

The location of the new page is specified by setting one of the following four flags in the high-order word of **mp2**:

BKA_FIRST   0x0004   indicates that the new page should be inserted as the first page in the notebook. Parameter **mp1** is ignored.

BKA_PREV   0x0010   indicates that the new page should be inserted in front of the page specified by parameter **mp1**.

BKA_NEXT   0x0008   indicates that the new page should be inserted behind the page specified by parameter **mp1**.

BKA_LAST   0x0002   indicates that the new page should be inserted as the last page in the notebook. Parameter **mp1** is ignored.

The return value from the BKM_INSERTPAGE message is the unique page ID assigned to the new page, or zero if an error occurred and the page could not be inserted. This value should be stored for later use when accessing the page.

The BKM_SETTABTEXT message is sent to the notebook control to assign text to the tab associated with a page that was inserted with either the BKA_MAJOR or BKA_MINOR style. Parameter **mp1** identifies the page whose tab text is to be set; the page identifier is the value returned by BKM_INSERTPAGE when the page was inserted. Parameter **mp2** is a pointer to a zero-terminated array of characters to be displayed on the tab.

Instead of displaying text, an application can display a bitmap on the tab by sending the BKM_SETTABBITMAP message to the notebook control.

Parameter **mp1** again specifies the page ID of the page whose tab bitmap is to be set. Parameter **mp2** is a handle to the bitmap to be displayed.

Message BKM_SETSTATUSLINETEXT may be sent to a page inserted with the BKA_STATUSTEXTON style to specify the text to display on the status line. Parameter **mp1** is the page ID of the page whose status line text is to be set. Parameter **mp2** is a pointer to the text to be displayed.

Figure 11.7 shows one approach for inserting pages and setting the appropriate tab and status text. In this example, an array of structures defines how each page is created and reserves room to store the page ID for newly inserted pages. Each element of the array is processed by a loop. The first action in the loop sends a BKM_INSERTPAGE message to the notebook to insert a new last page into the notebook. Parameter **mp2** specifies the page style from the current array structure and the BKA_LAST flag. Parameter **mp1** is not used when the BKA_LAST flag is set and is assigned the value zero. The return value from the message is saved back into the array structure for later use. If the page was successfully inserted, a check is made to see if tab text has been defined for the page; if so, a BKM_SETTABTEXT message is sent to indicate the text to be displayed. Parameter **mp1** specifies the stored page ID from the structure, and parameter **mp2** is set to the *pszTabText* element of the current structure. If status line text has been defined for this page, a BKM_SETSTATUSLINETEXT message is sent to the notebook. Parameter **mp1** is again set to the stored page ID. Parameter **mp2** is set to the *pszStatusText* element of the current array structure.

Presenting Information on the Pages

When pages have been added to the notebook, the basic structure of the notebook is complete. The application must now present information to the user on these pages. This is accomplished by sending a message to the notebook control to associate a window with each page. Windows associated with notebook pages become children of the notebook page window; a child of the notebook control window that defines the area in which the page information is displayed. The owner of the associated window is not affected, allowing the application to establish whatever notification hierarchy is required. When the page is displayed at the top of the notebook, the associated window is displayed and receives activation and the input focus. The examples following illustrate the manner in which various types of windows may be associated with the notebook control and processed.

The most common window type associated with notebook pages may well be the dialog box. Figure 11.8 illustrates the coding requirements for creating a dialog and associating it with a notebook page. Routine **CreateClrEdit** is passed the handle of the notebook window and the identifier of the page where the dialog is to be shown. The routine first creates a modeless dialog box using the **WinLoadDlg** API. The routine then sends a BKM_SETPAGEWINDOWHWND

```
typedef struct __NPAGE_DATA__ {
    ULONG    ulPageID;
    ULONG    ulPageStyle;
    PFNWP    pfnWP;
    char     *pszTabText;
    char     *pszStatusText;
} NPAGE, *PNPAGE;

NPAGE pgData[] = {
    0, BKA_MAJOR | BKA_STATUSTEXTON, NULL, "Section 1", "Page 1 of 3",
    0, BKA_MINOR | BKA_STATUSTEXTON, NULL, "Subsection A", "Page 2 of 3",
    0, BKA_MINOR | BKA_STATUSTEXTON, NULL, "Subsection B", "Page 3 of 3",
    0, BKA_MAJOR,                    NULL, "Section 2", "",
    0, BKA_MAJOR | BKA_STATUSTEXTON, NULL, "Section 3", "Page 1 of 5",
    0, BKA_STATUSTEXTON,             NULL, "", "Page 2 of 5",
    0, BKA_MINOR | BKA_STATUSTEXTON, NULL, "Subsection a", "Page 3 of 5",
    0, BKA_STATUSTEXTON,             NULL, "", "Page 4 of 5",
    0, BKA_MINOR | BKA_STATUSTEXTON, NULL, "Subsection b", "The last page"
};

#define NUM_PAGES  (sizeof(pgData)/sizeof(NPAGE))

void AddPages( HWND hwndNote )
{
    int    i;

    for (i=0; i<NUM_PAGES; i++) {
        pgData[i].ulPageID = (ULONG)WinSendMsg( hwndNote, BKM_INSERTPAGE, 0L,
                    MPFROM2SHORT( pgData[i].ulPageStyle, BKA_LAST ));
        if (pgData[i].ulPageID) {
            if (strlen(pgData[i].pszTabText))
                WinSendMsg( hwndNote, BKM_SETTABTEXT,
                            (MPARAM)pgData[i].ulPageID,
                            (MPARAM)pgData[i].pszTabText );
            if (strlen(pgData[i].pszStatusText))
                WinSendMsg( hwndNote, BKM_SETSTATUSLINETEXT,
                            (MPARAM)pgData[i].ulPageID,
                            (MPARAM)pgData[i].pszStatusText );
        } /* endif */
    } /* endfor */
}
```

Figure 11.7   Adding pages to a notebook.

```
void CreateClrEdit( HWND hwndNotebook, ULONG ulPageID )
{
   HWND       hwndPage;

   /* Create the dialog for editing colors */
   hwndPage = WinLoadDlg( hwndNotebook, hwndNotebook, ClrEditDlgProc,
                    NULLHANDLE, ID_CLREDIT, NULL );

   /* Associate the dialog window with a notebook page */
   if( hwndPage != NULLHANDLE) {
      WinSendMsg( hwndNotebook, BKM_SETPAGEWINDOWHWND,
               MPFROMLONG( ulPageID ),
               MPFROMLONG( hwndPage ));
   } /* endif */
}
```

Figure 11.8   **Associating a dialog window with a notebook page.**

message to associate the dialog box with the specified notebook page. Parameter **mp1** of this message specifies the page ID for the association, and parameter **mp2** specifies the window handle to be associated. The resource file dialog template is modified to remove the FS_DLGBORDER style. This prevents the normal dialog frame border from being displayed on the notebook page. This is not absolutely necessary but it is common practice.

Dialog boxes associated with notebook pages in this manner must be modeless and require slightly different processing from the modal dialog boxes normally used by applications. Applications normally create modal dialog boxes with the **WinDlgBox** API. These dialogs block execution of the main application until the dialog box is closed. The main application is notified by the return from **WinDlgBox** that the user has finished the dialog and that the user's input can be processed.

Modeless dialogs must be used with the notebook. These dialogs allow the main application to continue processing, so the dialog must alert the main application when significant events occur. In some instances, the dialog merely updates a data structure provided by the main application, and the changes in data values are reflected when the main application next uses the data. Alternately, the dialog may send a user-defined message to the application when changes occur or when the user takes a specific action, such as pressing a Save pushbutton.

Single controls can also be associated with notebook pages. Figure 11.9 shows how this is accomplished by associating a multiline edit, or MLE, control with a notebook page. Routine **CreateIntro** is passed the notebook control window handle and the notebook page ID as parameters. The routine first obtains the client window handle by querying the parent of the notebook control. The MLE is then created using the **WinCreateWindow** API. The parent window is the notebook control, and the owner window

```
void CreateIntro( HWND hwndNote, ULONG ulPageID )
{
   HWND      hwndPage;
   HWND      hwndOwner = WinQueryWindow( hwndNote, QW_PARENT );

   hwndPage = WinCreateWindow( hwndNote, WC_MLE,
     "This is a sample MLE on a notebook control page.\nThis section contains"
     " examples of value sets and sliders.", MLS_WORDWRAP | MLS_READONLY,
     0, 0, 0, 0, hwndOwner, HWND_TOP, ID_MLE1, NULL, NULL );
   if (hwndPage != NULLHANDLE) {
     WinSendMsg( hwndNote, BKM_SETPAGEWINDOWHWND,
                 MPFROMLONG( ulPageID ),
                 MPFROMLONG( hwndPage ));
   } /* endif */
}
```

Figure 11.9   Associating a control window with a notebook page.

is the application client window. Since the page to which this item is assigned was inserted with the BKA_AUTOPAGESIZE style, the size and position parameters of the **WinCreateWindow** call are set to zero. The notebook
will adjust the size and position of the control to match the notebook page.
Once the control is created, it is associated with the specified notebook page
via the BKM_SETPAGEWINDOWHWND message. Since the client window
is the owner, it will receive any notifications from the control and should
normally process these messages in the same manner as it would a control
associated directly with the client window without the intervening notebook.

The next example shows how a window of an application-defined class is
associated with a notebook page. This example also demonstrates how a window may be associated with multiple notebook pages and how the processing
can be varied depending on which of the associated pages is the top page of
the notebook. Routine **CreateAppWnd** is shown in Figure 11.10. The function
takes three parameters: the notebook window handle and two notebook page
identifiers. After retrieving the anchor block handle for the current thread and
the notebook's parent window, the application client window, the class for the
new application window is registered. Next, assuming the page was inserted
without the BKA_AUTOPAGESIZE style, the required size of the new window
is determined by first obtaining the window rectangle for the notebook window
and then sending a BKM_CALCPAGERECT message to convert the notebook
rectangle to the notebook page rectangle. The resulting rectangle is used to
compute the width and height of the new window.

The BKM_CALCPAGERECT message may be used as shown to determine
the page rectangle from the notebook rectangle and may also be used to
obtain the size of the notebook window when the page rectangle is known.
Parameter **mp1** is a pointer to the rectangle to be converted. Parameter **mp2**

```
HWND CreateAppWnd( HWND hwndNote, ULONG ulPage1, ULONG ulPage2 )
{
   HAB   hab;
   HWND  hwndPage;
   RECTL rectl;

   do {
      if( (hab = WinQueryAnchorBlock( hwndNote )) == NULLHANDLE) break;
      if (!WinRegisterClass( hab, "APPLICATION1", App1WndProc,
                  CS_SYNCPAINT | CS_CLIPSIBLINGS | CS_CLIPCHILDREN,
                  APP1_WINDOW_DATA_SIZE)) break;
      WinQueryWindowRect( hwndNote, &rectl );
      WinSendMsg( hwndNote, BKM_CALCPAGERECT, (MPARAM)&rectl, (MPARAM)TRUE );
      hwndPage = WinCreateWindow( hwndNote,
                              "APPLICATION1",
                              "SAMPLE TEXT",
                              WS_VISIBLE,
                              0, 0,
                              rectl.xRight - rectl.xLeft,
                              rectl.yTop - rectl.yBottom,
                              WinQueryWindow(hwndNote,QW_PARENT),
                              HWND_TOP,
                              APPWND_ID, NULL, NULL );
      WinSendMsg( hwndNote, BKM_SETPAGEWINDOWHWND,
                  MPFROMLONG( ulPage1 ),
                  MPFROMLONG( hwndPage ));
      WinSendMsg( hwndNote, BKM_SETPAGEWINDOWHWND,
                  MPFROMLONG( ulPage2 ),
                  MPFROMLONG( hwndPage ));
   } while (false);   /* endwhile */

   return hwndPage;
}
```

Figure 11.10 **Associating an application-defined window with a notebook page.**

indicates which conversion to perform; if set to TRUE, the notebook rectangle is converted to the page rectangle; if set to FALSE, the page rectangle is converted to the notebook rectangle.

After the required size of the new window is obtained, **WinCreateWindow** is called to create the window. The parent is set to the notebook and the owner to the application client window. The window is positioned at location (0, 0) of its eventual parent window, the page rectangle. The width is set to the difference in the x coordinates of the page rectangle, and the height is set to the difference in the y coordinates. After successful creation, BKM_SETPAGEWINDOWHWND messages are sent to associate the window with the specified notebook pages.

In instances like this where BKA_AUTOPAGESIZE is not specified, if the application wishes to adjust the size of the window when the notebook size changes, the BKN_NEWPAGESIZE notification must be processed. Figure 11.11 shows the WM_CONTROL processing of the application client window that accomplishes this function. The function first verifies that the proper notification code was received and that the sender was the notebook control. The window handle of the notebook is then queried by its ID, and the application window to be sized is obtained from the notebook by sending a BKM_QUERYPAGEWINDOWHWND message. Parameter **mp1** of this message is the page identifier of the page whose window handle is to be returned; parameter **mp2** is reserved and set to zero. The new notebook size is then queried and converted to the page rectangle. The resulting rectangle is used to compute the new width and height of the application window associated with the notebook page, and the **WinSetWindowPos** API is used to resize the application window. Since the application window was associated with multiple pages, any of these pages could have been used when obtaining the window handle.

Association of a window with multiple pages normally indicates that the information in the window will vary in some manner depending on which of the associated pages is the top page of the notebook. There are several ways to determine which page is currently displayed and thereby what information to display in the application window associated with the page. First, when a new page is selected, the notebook sends a BKN_PAGESELECTEDPENDING

```
MRESULT APIENTRY wmControl( HWND hwnd, ULONG msg, MPARAM mp1, MPARAM mp2 )
{
    RECTL     rectl;
    HWND      hwndNote;
    HWND      hwndPage;

    if (SHORT2FROMMP(mp1) == BKN_NEWPAGESIZE &&
        SHORT1FROMMP(mp1) == NOTEBOOK_ID) {
      hwndNote = WinWindowFromID( hwnd, NOTEBOOK_ID );
      hwndPage = (HWND)WinSendMsg( hwndNote, BKM_QUERYPAGEWINDOWHWND,
                             (MPARAM)(ulAppWndPage1),
                             (MPARAM)0l );
      WinQueryWindowRect( hwndNote, &rectl );
      WinSendMsg( hwndNote, BKM_CALCPAGERECT, (MPARAM)&rectl, (MPARAM)TRUE );
      WinSetWindowPos( hwndPage, NULLHANDLE, 0, 0,
                       rectl.xRight - rectl.xLeft,
                       rectl.yTop - rectl.yBottom,
                       SWP_SIZE | SWP_MOVE );
    } /* endif */
    return (MRESULT)0;
}
```

Figure 11.11 **Processing notebook size changes.**

```
typedef struct _PAGESELECTNOTIFY {
   HWND    hwndBook;
   ULONG   ulPageIdCur
   ULONG   ulPageIdNew
} PAGESELECTNOTIFY;
```

Figure 11.12   The PAGESELECTNOTIFY structure.

notification. Parameter **mp2** of this message is a pointer to a PAGESELECT-NOTIFY structure. This structure is defined as shown in Figure 11.12.

- The *hwndBook* element is the handle of the notebook window.
- The *ulPageIdCur* element is the page identifier of the current top page of the notebook.
- The *ulPageIdNew* element is the page identifier of the page that is becoming the top page of the notebook.

If the application sets the *ulPageIdNew* element of this structure to zero before responding to the message, the new page will not be selected.

After the new page has been brought to the top of the notebook, a BKN_PAGESELECTED notification is sent. This message also passes a pointer to a PAGESELECTNOTIFY structure as parameter **mp2**. The application can use the *ulPageIdNew* element from either of these messages to establish a determinate state for drawing information when the notebook causes the window to be updated. Alternately, the window procedure of the associated window can determine the current top page and draw the proper information when an update request is received in the form of a WM_PAINT message. The page identifier of the current top page is obtained by sending a BKM_QUERYPAGEID message to the notebook with the low-order word of parameter **mp2** set to BKA_TOP.

Figure 11.13 shows application coding that implements the latter method within the procedure for handling the WM_PAINT message. This routine first obtains the notebook window handle that is the parent of the page window, which is the parent of this window—the window associated with the page. **WinBeginPaint** is then called to obtain the presentation space for drawing, and **WinQueryWindowRect** is called to obtain the window rectangle. The BKM_QUERYPAGEID message is sent to the notebook window to obtain the page identifier of the current top page. This value is passed to a local routine that scans the page information structures used earlier to determine which ordinal page number in the section this page identifier represents. The resulting value is formatted into a string that is then drawn in the center of the window with the **WinDrawText** API. The presentation space is released with the **WinEndPaint** API, and the function exits.

```
static MRESULT wm_paint( HWND hwnd, ULONG msg, MPARAM mp1, MPARAM mp2 )
{
   HPS      hps;
   HWND     hwndNote;
   RECTL    rectl;
   ULONG    ulPageID;
   ULONG    ulPageNum;
   char     szText[ 50 ];

   hwndNote = WinQueryWindow( hwnd, QW_PARENT );
   hwndNote = WinQueryWindow( hwndNote, QW_PARENT );
   hps = WinBeginPaint( hwnd, NULLHANDLE, &rectl );
   if (hps != NULLHANDLE ) {
      WinQueryWindowRect( hwnd, &rectl );
      ulPageID = (ULONG)WinSendMsg( hwndNote,
                                    BKM_QUERYPAGEID,
                                    (MPARAM)0L,
                                    MPFROM2SHORT(BKA_TOP,0));
      ulPageNum = QueryPgNumFromID( ulPageID );
      sprintf( szText, "Sample - Page %ld", ulPageNum );
      WinDrawText( hps, -1L, szText, &rectl, 0, 0,
                   DT_ERASERECT | DT_CENTER | DT_VCENTER | DT_TEXTATTRS );
      WinEndPaint( hps );
   } /* endif */
   return (MRESULT)01;
}
```

Figure 11.13   Drawing to the same window on multiple notebook pages.

The Modular Approach

The approach taken above for initializing the notebook pages, while perfectly acceptable and particularly useful for illustrating the required steps, can be difficult to maintain since the portions of the code that deal with a particular page are scattered. A modular approach, which gathers the initialization steps for each section and page into functional units, allows the programmer to easily perform modifications for a given page and/or add pages or sections as required. In this section, we will examine the resulting code to reimplement the preceding examples. The new code also uses a new message introduced with OS/2 WARP, which performs most of the page initialization in one easy step.

Let's first examine how the WM_CREATE message processing code has changed. The original code was shown in Figure 11.2 and the new routine is shown in Figure 11.14. The new code creates the notebook window, customizes the notebook colors, and then calls three functions that handle the initialization of the three sections of the notebook. The functionality to establish the dimensions of the tabs is now called from within the page initialization routines.

```
MRESULT APIENTRY wmCreate( HWND hwnd, ULONG msg, MPARAM mp1, MPARAM mp2 )
{
   HWND            hwndNote;

   hwndNote = WinCreateWindow( hwnd,
                               WC_NOTEBOOK,
                               "SAMPLE TEXT",
                               WS_VISIBLE,
                               0, 0, 0, 0,
                               hwnd, HWND_TOP,
                               NOTEBOOK_ID, NULL, NULL );
   AdjustNotebookColors( hwndNote );
   AddValueSetSection( hwndNote );
   AddSampleSection( hwndNote );
   AddAppWndSection( hwndNote );
   return (MRESULT)FALSE;
}
```

Figure 11.14   Creating a notebook using the modular approach.

The routines that handle initialization of the notebook sections are shown
in Figure 11.15. These routines are shown together for convenience; in the
actual code, the routines would normally be placed into individual source files
that contain code related to the specific section. Routine **AddValueSetSection**

```
void AddValueSetSection( HWND hwndNote )
{
   CreateIntro( hwndNote );
   CreateCalen( hwndNote );
   CreateClrEdit( hwndNote );
}

void AddSampleSection( HWND hwndNote )
{
   CreateSampDlg( hwndNote );
}

void AddAppWndSection( HWND hwndNote )
{
   hwndAppWnd = CreateAppWnd( hwndNote );

   AddAppWndPage( hwndNote, hwndAppWnd, "App. Window", 1, 5 );
   AddAppWndPage( hwndNote, hwndAppWnd, NULL, 2, 5 );
   AddAppWndPage( hwndNote, hwndAppWnd, "Subsection A", 3, 5 );
   AddAppWndPage( hwndNote, hwndAppWnd, NULL, 4, 5 );
   AddAppWndPage( hwndNote, hwndAppWnd, "Subsection B", 5, 5 );
}
```

Figure 11.15   Creating sections of the notebook.

calls three more routines, one for each of the pages in the section. **AddSample-Section** only calls one other routine because the section consists of only one page. This is a bit of overkill, but allows additional pages to be added later without modifying the structure of the program. Routine **AddAppWndSection** is slightly different since a single window is associated with all the pages in this section. The routine first creates the application window and then for each page of the section calls a routine to add the page and associate the created window with the page.

The new **CreateClrEdit** routine, which replaces the one shown in Figure 11.8, is shown in Figure 11.16. This routine first adds a page to the notebook with styles for displaying a minor tab, displaying status text, and automatic resizing of the window. The function then initializes a structure for the BKM_SETNOTEBOOKINFO message. This message, new to OS/2 WARP, allows an application to set the page data, the associated window, the status text, and the tab text, all with one **WinSendMsg** API call. Parameter **mp1** of the message is the identifier of the page whose information is modified. Parameter **mp2** is a pointer to a BOOKPAGEINFO structure which indicates the

```
void CreateClrEdit( HWND hwndNotebook )
{
    ULONG           ulPageID;
    USHORT          usStyle=BKA_MINOR | BKA_STATUSTEXTON | BKA_AUTOPAGESIZE;
    HWND            hwndPage;
    BOOKPAGEINFO    bpi;
    char            szStatusText[] = "Page 3 of 3";
    char            szTabText[] = "Edit Colors";

    ulPageID = LONGFROMMR(WinSendMsg( hwndNotebook, BKM_INSERTPAGE,
                                      MPFROMLONG(0L),
                                      MPFROM2SHORT( usStyle, BKA_LAST )));
    memset( (PVOID)&bpi, 0, sizeof( BOOKPAGEINFO ));
    bpi.cb = sizeof( BOOKPAGEINFO );
    bpi.fl = BFA_PAGEFROMDLGRES | BFA_STATUSLINE | BFA_MINORTABTEXT;
    bpi.bLoadDlg = FALSE;
    bpi.pfnPageDlgProc = (PFN)ClrEditDlgProc;
    bpi.idPageDlg = ID_CLREDIT;
    bpi.hmodPageDlg = NULLHANDLE;
    bpi.cbStatusLine = strlen( szStatusText );
    bpi.pszStatusLine = szStatusText;
    bpi.cbMinorTab = strlen( szTabText );
    bpi.pszMinorTab = szTabText;
    WinSendMsg( hwndNotebook, BKM_SETPAGEINFO,
                MPFROMLONG( ulPageID ),
                MPFROMP( &bpi ));
    SetTabLen( hwndNotebook, szTabText, FALSE );
}
```

Figure 11.16   Adding a page for a dialog window.

information to be changed and the new values to be assigned. Note that the original OS/2 WARP documentation incorrectly indicates that this is a PAGE-INFO structure that is used by the Workplace Shell to specify information for object settings pages. The BOOKPAGEINFO structure can be found in the header files and its layout is described next. After **CreateClrEdit** establishes the page parameters with the BKM_SETPAGEINFO message, routine **SetTabLen** is called to ensure that the tab text for this page will fit in the displayed tabs.

This routine also illustrates another new feature of the OS/2 WARP notebook, which is available when the BKM_SETPAGEINFO message is used to associate windows with notebook pages. This feature allows the application to associate dialog boxes with pages by specifying the resource ID of a dialog template or a pointer to a dialog template in memory. PM then handles the creation of the dialog box and can actually delay the dialog creation until the page associated with the dialog is brought to the top of the notebook. This can significantly decrease the load time of a notebook which displays several dialogs, giving the impression of significantly improved performance.

The BOOKPAGEINFO structure is defined as shown in Figure 11.17.

- The *cb* element is the size of the structure in bytes and should be set to sizeof(BOOKPAGEINFO).
- The *fl* element is a set of flags that indicate which of the structure elements should actually be used to update the information for the notebook page. The valid flags are:

```
typedef struct _BOOKPAGEINFO
{
    ULONG       cb;
    ULONG       fl;
    BOOL        bLoadDlg;
    ULONG       ulPageData;
    HWND        hwndPage;
    PFN         pfnPageDlgProc;
    ULONG       idPageDlg;
    HMODULE     hmodPageDlg;
    PVOID       pPageDlgCreateParams;
    PDLGTEMPLATE pdlgtPage;
    ULONG       cbStatusLine;
    PSZ         pszStatusLine;
    HBITMAP     hbmMajorTab;
    HBITMAP     hbmMinorTab;
    ULONG       cbMajorTab;
    PSZ         pszMajorTab;
    ULONG       cbMinorTab;
    PSZ         pszMinorTab;
    PVOID       pBidiInfo;
} BOOKPAGEINFO;
```

Figure 11.17   The BOOKPAGEINFO structure.

BFA_PAGEDATA	0x0001	indicates that the *ulPageData* element should be used to update the page's user data information. This replaces the functionality of the BKM_SETPAGEDATA message.
BFA_PAGEFROMHWND	0x0002	indicates that the window handle to associate with the page is contained in the *hwndPage* element. This replaces the functionality of the BKM_SETPAGEWINDOWHWND message.
BFA_PAGEFROMDLGTEMPLATE	0x0004	indicates that the window to associate with the page is a dialog window whose template is stored in memory. Element *pdlgtPage* contains a pointer to the dialog template. This replaces the BKM_SET PAGEWINDOWHWND message functionality.
BFA_PAGEFROMDLGRES	0x0008	indicates that the window to associate with the page is a dialog window whose template is stored in an executable module's resources. Element *idPageDlg* contains the resource ID, and *hmodPageDlg* contains the module handle where the resource is located. This replaces the BKM_SETPAGEWINDOWHWND message functionality.
BFA_STATUSLINE	0x0010	replaces the BKM_SETSTATUSLINETEXT message functionality. Element *cbStatusLine* is expected to contain the number of characters in the text, and element *pszStatusLine* is expected to contain a pointer to an array of characters to display on the page's status line.
BFA_MAJORTABBITMAP	0x0020	replaces the BKM_SETTABBITMAP functionality. Element *hbmMajorTab* should contain the handle of the bitmap to display on the page's major tab.
BFA_MINORTABBITMAP	0x0040	replaces the BKM_SETTABBITMAP functionality. Element *hbmMinorTab* should contain the handle of the bitmap to display on the page's minor tab.
BFA_MAJORTABTEXT	0x0080	replaces the BKM_SETTABTEXT functionality for pages with BKA_MAJOR

style. Element *cbMajorTab* specifies the number of characters in the tab text, and element *pszMajorTab* contains a pointer to the array of characters to display on the page's major tab.

BFA_MINORTABTEXT   0x0100   replaces the BKM_SETTABTEXT functionality for pages with BKA_MINOR style. Element *cbMinorTab* specifies the number of characters in the tab text, and element *pszMinorTab* contains a pointer to the array of characters to display on the page's minor tab.

BFA_BIDIINFO   0x0200   specifies that bidirectional language support information is set in element *pBidiInfo*. Programmers interested in BIDI should consult the *OS/2 Bidirectional Language Support Development Guide*.

- Element *bLoadDlg* is a flag that controls the loading of dialog boxes when BFA_PAGEFROMDLGRES or BFA_PAGEFROMDLGTEMPLATE is specified. If the flag is set to FALSE, the dialog window will not be created until the page is brought to the top of the notebook. If the flag is TRUE, the dialog window is created when the BKM_SETPAGEINFO message is received.
- Element *ulPageData* specifies the value to store in the page's data area reserved for application use. This element is ignored if the BKA_PAGEDATA flag is not set in element *fl*. The application data area may also be modified using the BKM_SETPAGEDATA message.
- The *hwndPage* element specifies the handle of the window to be associated with the page, but is ignored if the BKA_PAGEFROMHWND flag is not set. Message BKM_SETPAGEWINDOWHWND may also be called to associate a window with a page.
- Element *pfnPageDlgProc* is used to specify the window procedure for the created dialog box when the BKA_PAGEFROMDLGTEMPLATE or BKA_PAGEFROMDLGRES flag is set.
- The *idPageDlg* element specifies the resource identifier for the template used to create the dialog box when the BFA_PAGEFROMDLGRES flag is set.
- The *hmodPageDlg* element specifies the module handle of the executable containing the dialog template resource when the BFA_PAGEFROMDLGRES flag is set.
- Element *pPageDlgCreateParams* specifies a pointer to the dialog creation parameters when the BFA_PAGEFROMDLGTEMPLATE or BFA_PAGE

FROMDLGRES flag is set. This value is used as the **pCreateParams** parameter for the **WinLoadDlg** function.

- Element *pdlgtPage* is a pointer to the memory resident dialog template used to create the dialog window when the BFA_PAGEFROMDLGTEMPLATE flag is set.
- The *cbStatusLine* element specifies the number of characters pointed to by the *pszStatusLine* element and is used when the BFA_STATUSLINE flag is set.
- The *pszStatusLine* element is a pointer to the characters to display on the status line. The element is ignored unless the BFA_STATUSLINE flag is set.
- Element *hbmMajorTab* specifies the bitmap handle to display on the major tab for the page. This element is ignored if the BFA_MAJORTABBITMAP flag is not set.
- The *hbmMinorTab* element specifies the bitmap handle to display on the minor tab for the page. This element is ignored if the BFA_MINORTABBITMAP flag is not set.
- Element *cbMajorTab* specifies the number of characters pointed to by *pszMajorTab* when the BFA_MAJORTABTEXT flag is specified.
- Element *pszMajorTab* is a pointer to the characters to display on the page's major tab when the BFA_MAJORTABTEXT flag is set.
- The *cbMinorTab* element specifies the number of characters pointed to by *pszMinorTab* when the BFA_MINORTABTEXT flag is specified.
- The *pszMinorTab* element is a pointer to the characters to display on the page's minor tab when the BFA_MINORTABTEXT flag is set.
- Element *pBidiInfo* is reserved for use by bidirectional language support. Interested programmers should reference the *OS/2 Bidirectional Language Support Development Guide* for more information.

CreateClrEdit provides a good example of how this structure is initialized and used by an application. The page that this function creates is used to display a dialog box and has the style flags set to show status text and a minor tab. The routine first clears the BOOKPAGEINFO structure using the C library **memset** function. The *cb* element is then set to the size of the structure. The *fl* element is set to indicate that the structure contains status line text, minor tab text, and information to associate a dialog template from a resource file with the page. The **bLoadDlg** function is set to FALSE to delay creation of the dialog until the page is displayed. Element *pfnPageDlgProc* is set to point to the dialog window procedure; element *idPageDlg* is set to the dialog template's resource ID; and element *hmodPageDlg* is set to NULLHANDLE to indicate that the resource is located in the application's executable. The *cbStatusLine* element is set to the length of the status line text as determined by the C library **strlen** function (note that the terminating zero is not included in the count).

Element *pszStatusLine* is set to point to the status line text. In similar fashion, elements *cbMinorTab* and *pszMinorTab* are specified for the minor tab text.

The new routine for creating an MLE control and associating it with a notebook page is shown in Figure 11.18. This routine replaces the original **CreateIntro** shown in Figure 11.9. This function follows the same basic flow as **CreateClrEdit**. First, a page is inserted into the notebook. Then the handle of the notebook's parent, the application client area, is obtained. This window will be set as the owner of the control so that notification messages can be received and processed. Next, the control window itself is created since only dialogs may be created automatically. The BOOKPAGEINFO structure is then cleared and initialized. The *cb* element is again set to the size of the structure, and the *fl* element flags are set to specify association of an existing window with the page, setting of the status line text, and setting of the major tab text.

```
void CreateIntro( HWND hwndNote )
{
    ULONG           ulPageID;
    HWND            hwndPage;
    HWND            hwndOwner;
    USHORT          usStyle = BKA_MAJOR | BKA_STATUSTEXTON | BKA_AUTOPAGESIZE;
    BOOKPAGEINFO    bpi;
    char            szStatusText[] = "Page 1 of 3";
    char            szTabText[] = "Value Set";

    ulPageID = LONGFROMMR( WinSendMsg( hwndNote, BKM_INSERTPAGE,
                                       MPFROMLONG(0L),
                                       MPFROM2SHORT( usStyle, BKA_LAST )));
    hwndOwner = WinQueryWindow( hwndNote, QW_PARENT );
    hwndPage = WinCreateWindow(hwndNote, WC_MLE, "This is a sample MLE on a "
                            "notebook control page.\nThis section contains"
                            " examples of value sets and sliders.",
                            MLS_WORDWRAP | MLS_READONLY,
                            0, 0, 0, 0, hwndOwner, HWND_TOP,
                            ID_MLE1, NULL, NULL );
    memset( (PVOID)&bpi, 0, sizeof(BOOKPAGEINFO) );
    bpi.cb = sizeof(BOOKPAGEINFO);
    bpi.fl = BFA_PAGEFROMHWND | BFA_STATUSLINE | BFA_MAJORTABTEXT;
    bpi.hwndPage = hwndPage;
    bpi.cbStatusLine = strlen(szStatusText);
    bpi.pszStatusLine = szStatusText;
    bpi.cbMajorTab = strlen(szTabText);
    bpi.pszMajorTab = szTabText;
    WinSendMsg( hwndNote, BKM_SETPAGEINFO, MPFROMLONG(ulPageID),
            MPFROMP(&bpi));
    SetTabLen( hwndNote, szTabText, TRUE );
}
```

Figure 11.18 Adding a page for a control window.

The *hwndPage* element is set to the handle of the control just created, and the elements associated with the status line and major tab text are set in same manner as seen in **CreateClrEdit**. The BKM_SETPAGEINFO message is then sent to transfer the information to the notebook, and **SetTabLen** is called to ensure the proper sizing for the tabs.

The routine for adding windows of an application-defined class is shown in Figure 11.19. Remember from Figure 11.15 that the window is created in a separate routine. This routine, **CreateAppWnd**, is the same as the original shown in Figure 11.10 except that the BKM_SETPAGEWINDOWHWND messages have been removed. Routine **AddAppWndPage** is a bit different from the

```
void AddAppWndPage( HWND hwndNote, HWND hwndApp, PSZ pszTab,
                    ULONG ulPage, ULONG ulOfPage )
{
    ULONG          ulPageID;
    USHORT         usStyle = BKA_STATUSTEXTON;
    BOOKPAGEINFO   bpi;
    char           szStatusText[ 128 ];

    sprintf( szStatusText, "Page %ld of %ld", ulPage, ulOfPage );
    if( pszTab != NULL )
        usStyle |= (ulPage == 1 ? BKA_MAJOR : BKA_MINOR );
    ulPageID = LONGFROMMR( WinSendMsg( hwndNote, BKM_INSERTPAGE,
                                       MPFROMLONG(0L),
                                       MPFROM2SHORT( usStyle, BKA_LAST )));
    memset( (PVOID)&bpi, 0, sizeof(BOOKPAGEINFO) );
    bpi.cb = sizeof(BOOKPAGEINFO);
    bpi.fl = BFA_PAGEFROMHWND | BFA_STATUSLINE | BFA_PAGEDATA;
    bpi.bLoadDlg = TRUE;
    bpi.ulPageData = ulPage;
    bpi.hwndPage = hwndApp;
    bpi.cbStatusLine = strlen(szStatusText);
    bpi.pszStatusLine = szStatusText;
    if( usStyle & BKA_MAJOR ) {
        bpi.fl |= BFA_MAJORTABTEXT;
        bpi.cbMajorTab = strlen(pszTab);
        bpi.pszMajorTab = pszTab;
        SetTabLen( hwndNote, pszTab, TRUE );
    } else if( usStyle & BKA_MINOR ) {
        bpi.fl |= BFA_MINORTABTEXT;
        bpi.cbMinorTab = strlen(pszTab);
        bpi.pszMinorTab = pszTab;
        SetTabLen( hwndNote, pszTab, FALSE );
    } /* endif */
    WinSendMsg( hwndNote, BKM_SETPAGEINFO, MPFROMLONG(ulPageID),
                MPFROMP(&bpi));
}
```

Figure 11.19 **Adding a page for an application-defined window.**

previous two functions discussed in that the same window is being associated with several pages. If only one page were associated with the window, the flow of the function would be identical to that shown for the MLE control. In this instance, however, some additional parameters are passed to the routine. These parameters specify the window handle of the application window, the tab text—if any—to associate with the page, the current page number within the section, and the total number of pages within the section. The latter two parameters are used to build the status line text and to determine the type of tab to associate with the page; a major tab is associated with the first page of the section and minor tabs are associated with any subsequent pages for which tab text is specified. A new page is then added to the notebook with the appropriate tab style. Next the BOOKPAGEINFO structure is initialized. Again, this operation is basically the same as that used for the MLE control, though some additional complexity has been added to build the tab text and *fl* elements of the structure depending on the tab type. After the structure is initialized, the BKM_SETPAGEINFO message is sent and the function returns.

The function **SetTabLen** is shown in Figure 11.20 and replaces the **SetTab-Size** function shown in Figure 11.3. The new version of the function has been rewritten to maintain the current size of the tabs in global variables and to determine if a new tab size is needed as each page is added to the notebook. The function takes three parameters: the notebook window handle, the tab text to be tested, and a flag that indicates when the text is associated with a major tab. After obtaining a presentation space for the window, the function initializes a rectangle, which covers the entire area of the screen and then calls the **WinDrawText** API to determine the actual size of the rectangle required to surround the text. The resulting rectangle is then adjusted by the appropriate factors for the tab style. This rectangle is compared to the appropriate global variables for the tab type and if the current rectangle is larger, the new width and height are formatted into an MPARAM value, mpDims. This value is then passed to the notebook with a BKM_SETDIMENSIONS message. The presentation space is released before the function returns.

VALUE SETS

The value set control, like the radio button, provides the user with the ability to select one choice from a set of available options. Unlike the radio button, which only displays textual choices, the value set presents the available options to the user in a graphical format. This makes the value set particularly useful for displaying graphics-related choices, such as colors, patterns, or line styles. The value set also allows display of textual information, but this use should be limited to short strings such as those that might be used to select a CD track or a day of the month. Longer textual choices should normally be displayed with the radio button.

```
void SetTabLen( HWND hwndNote, PSZ pszText, BOOL fMajor )
{
    HPS         hps;
    MPARAM      mpDims = MPFROMLONG(0L);
    RECTL       rcl, rcl1;
    INT         i;

    hps = WinGetPS( hwndNote );
    if (hps != NULLHANDLE) {
        memset( (PVOID)&rcl1, 0, sizeof(RECTL));
        rcl1.xRight = WinQuerySysValue( HWND_DESKTOP, SV_CXSCREEN );
        rcl1.yTop = WinQuerySysValue( HWND_DESKTOP, SV_CYSCREEN );
        rcl = rcl1;
        WinDrawText( hps, strlen(pszText), pszText, &rcl, 0, 0,
                     DT_LEFT | DT_BOTTOM | DT_QUERYEXTENT );
        rcl.xRight += 21;
        rcl.yTop += 8;

        if (fMajor) {
            if ((USHORT)rcl.xRight > usMajorWidth ) usMajorWidth = rcl.xRight;
            if ((USHORT)rcl.yTop > usMajorHeight ) usMajorHeight = rcl.yTop;
            mpDims = MPFROM2SHORT( usMajorWidth, usMajorHeight );
        } else {
            if ((USHORT)rcl.xRight > usMinorWidth ) usMinorWidth = rcl.xRight;
            if ((USHORT)rcl.yTop > usMinorHeight ) usMinorHeight = rcl.yTop;
            mpDims = MPFROM2SHORT( usMinorWidth, usMinorHeight );
        } /* endif */
        WinSendMsg( hwndNote, BKM_SETDIMENSIONS, mpDims,
                    MPFROMLONG(fMajor ? BKA_MAJORTAB : BKA_MINORTAB));
        WinReleasePS( hps );
    } /* endif */
}
```

Figure 11.20   Alternate method for setting notebook tab sizes.

The choices depicted by a value set are arranged into rows and columns and may display bitmaps, icons, text, RGB colors, or index-based colors from a color palette. If desired, each choice may display a different type of object; thus, bitmaps, icons, text, and colors may all be displayed in the same value set. The value set also supports disabling of individual items and automatic resizing of the items to fit within the size of the value set. However, some items will be clipped if the size of the value set window is reduced such that all items do not fit.

Creating and Initializing the Value Set

Value set controls may be included as items in a dialog template or explicitly created using the **WinCreateWindow** API. In the latter case, the **pCtlData** parameter must point to a VSCDATA structure initialized to indicate the number of rows and columns to be displayed in the window. This structure is defined as shown in Figure 11.21.

- The *cbSize* element is the number of bytes in the structure and should be set to sizeof(VCSDATA).
- Element *usRowCount* is a 16-bit, unsigned integer indicating the number of rows of items to display.
- The *usColumnCount* is a 16-bit, unsigned integer indicating the number of items to display in each row.

The **flStyle** parameter to **WinCreateWindow** may specify a combination of the WS_ style flags and/or the value set style flags. The value set style flags are:

VS_BORDER	0x0020	causes a thin border to be drawn around the control and is most often used to delineate the area occupied by the control.
VS_ITEMBORDER	0x0040	causes a thin border to be drawn around each individual item in the control. This style is often used to enhance items that are otherwise difficult to distinguish.
VS_RIGHTTOLEFT	0x0100	causes the treatment of column numbers to be reversed. Normally, column one is the leftmost column, and the numbers increase moving to the right. When this style is set, the rightmost column is column one, and the numbers increase moving to the left. The columns selected by the home and end keys are also affected by this flag.
VS_SCALEBITMAPS	0x0080	causes the bitmap displayed for items with the VIA_BITMAP or VIA_ICON attributes to be scaled rather than centered (for bitmaps smaller than the item) or clipped (for bitmaps larger than the item).
VS_OWNERDRAW	0x0200	causes a WM_DRAWITEM message to be sent to the owner window whenever the background of the control requires painting.

One of the following flags may be set to indicate the type of data that the application intends to provide for each item in the control. Note that this flag

```
typedef struct _VSCDATA
{
    ULONG   cbSize;
    USHORT  usRowCount;
    USHORT  usColumnCount;
} VSCDATA;
```

Figure 11.21   The VSCDATA structure.

sets the default data type for all items; individual items may be set to a different type with the WM_SETITEMATTR message.

VS_BITMAP   0x0001   sets the VIA_BITMAP attribute for each item in the control. The control expects each item to be set to a bitmap handle.

VS_ICON   0x0002   sets the VIA_ICON attribute for each item in the control. The control expects each item to be set to a pointer handle.

VS_TEXT   0x0004   sets the VIA_TEXT attribute for each item in the control. The control expects each item to be set to a pointer to a zero-terminated array of characters.

VS_RGB   0x0008   sets the VIA_RGB attribute for each item in the control. The control expects each item to be set to an RGB color value. The default value, zero, causes a black box to be displayed.

VS_COLORINDEX 0x0010   sets the VIA_COLORINDEX attribute for each item in the control. The control expects each item to be set to an index value for the current color palette. The default value, zero, causes a white box to be displayed when the default palette is used.

Figure 11.22 shows an example of the code used to create a value set control with the **WinCreateWindow** API. In this example, the value set is used to represent a month on a calendar. First, the VSCDATA structure is initialized with the size of the structure—six rows for the possible weeks in a month and seven columns to represent the days in each week. Next, the desired style of the value set is initialized. VS_TEXT is set to indicate that the data for each

```
VSCDATA    vscd;
ULONG      ulStyle;

vscd.cbSize = sizeof( VSCDATA );
vscd.usRowCount = 6;              /* possible weeks in month */
vscd.usColumnCount = 7;          /* days per week */
ulStyle = VS_TEXT | VS_BORDER | VS_OWNERDRAW;
hwndVS = WinCreateWindow( hwndNote,
                          WC_VALUESET,
                          (PSZ)NULL,
                          ulStyle,
                          0, 0, 100, 100,
                          WinQueryWindow( hwndNote, QW_PARENT ),
                          HWND_TOP,
                          201,
                          &vscd,
                          (PVOID)NULL );
```

Figure 11.22   **Creating a value set control.**

item should be interpreted as a pointer to a text string. VS_BORDER is set to draw a border around the entire control, and VS_OWNERDRAW is set to allow the application to paint the control background. **WinCreateWindow** is then called to create the control.

Following creation, the value set displays as an empty box with the item in the upper left position selected. Before the control is useful, the application must assign a graphical object to each item. This is accomplished by sending a VM_SETITEM message to the control. Parameter **mp1** passed with this message contains the row number of the item in the low-order 16 bits, and the column number of the item in the high-order 16 bits. Parameter **mp2** specifies the graphical object to associate with the item. The content of **mp2** varies depending on the style selected; for example, a pointer to a character string is expected when the VS_TEXT style is specified, and a bitmap handle is expected when the VS_BITMAP style is specified.

Figure 11.23 shows example code for filling in the calendar value set created earlier. The sample code uses C library functions to determine the current date. Utility function **mkwkday** determines the weekday of the first day of the month, and **getnumdays** returns the number of days in the month. The weekday number is used to determine the column number of the item in the value set that represents the first day of the month. The row number is normally set to two to center the month in the calendar; however, months

```
time( &curTime );
curTM = *localtime( &curTime );
wkday = mkwkday( curTM.tm_mon, curTM.tm_year + 1900 );
scolumn = wkday + 1;
srow = 2;
if (getnumdays(curTM.tm_mon) == 31 && wkday >= 5) srow = 1;
if (getnumdays(curTM.tm_mon) == 30 && wkday == 6) srow = 1;
row = srow, column = scolumn;

for (day = 0; day < getnumdays(curTM.tm_mon); day++) {
   WinSendMsg( hwndVS, VM_SETITEM,
             MPFROM2SHORT(row, column),
             MPFROMP(daytext[day]));
   if (column++ == 7) {
      column = 1;
      row++;
   } /* endif */
} /* endfor */

WinSendMsg( hwndVS, VM_SELECTITEM,
          MPFROM2SHORT(srow, scolumn),
          (MPARAM)0 );
```

Figure 11.23   **Initializing the value set control.**

that start on Friday or Saturday may span all six rows. Where this occurs, the initial row value is set to one. Once the starting position has been determined, a loop is entered to send a VM_SETITEM message for each day of the month. The message parameters specify the current row and column and a pointer to a text string containing the numeric digits for the current day. Following the message, the column and row values are updated as necessary. At the end of the loop, a VM_SELECTITEM message is sent to the value set to select the item at the row and column representing the first day of the month. Parameter **mp1** of this message specifies the row and column number of the item to select; the row number is contained in the low-order 16 bits, and the column number is contained in the high-order 16 bits. Parameter **mp2** is reserved and should be set to zero.

Now our calendar actually contains the days of the month. The items that are blank can still be selected by the user. The VM_SETITEMATTR message may be used to prevent selection of these items and to change the graphic display of the item so that the user is aware that the items are unselectable. The VM_SETITEMATTR message allows the application to customize individual value set items by changing the global attributes assigned when the value set was created. Thus individual items may be enabled or disabled or display different data types. Parameter **mp1** contains the item row number in the low-order 16 bits, and the column number in the high-order 16 bits. Parameter **mp2** contains the attribute(s) to be changed in the low-order 16 bits and a flag indicating whether to set or clear the attribute in the high-order 16 bits. One of the following attributes may be used to specify the data type:

VIA_BITMAP	0x0001	data associated with the item is interpreted as a bitmap handle.
VIA_COLORINDEX	0x0010	data associated with the item is interpreted as a color index value.
VIA_ICON	0x0002	data associated with the item is interpreted as a pointer handle.
VIA_RGB	0x0008	data associated with the item is interpreted as an RGB color value.
VIA_TEXT	0x0004	data associated with the item is interpreted as a pointer to a zero-terminated text string.

Specifying one of these attributes to be set causes the other attributes in the group to be cleared. Clearing all attributes causes the default attribute, VIA_BITMAP, to be set. Additionally, one or more of the following attributes may be set or cleared:

VIA_DISABLED	0x0040	prevents the item from being set to the selected state. The selection cursor may still be moved to the object, but no

VN_SELECT notification is sent to the owner. If the F1 key is pressed, however, a VN_HELP notification is sent.

VIA_DRAGGABLE 0x0080 indicates that the application supports dragging of the item.

VIA_DROPONABLE 0x0100 indicates that the application accepts data being dropped on the item.

VIA_OWNERDRAW 0x0020 indicates that the application should be notified when the item needs to be painted.

In Figure 11.24, code has been added to the calendar example to modify the attributes of the blank items to prevent selection and to display an icon indicating that the items are unavailable. The new code is placed around the original loop that scanned the days of the month. Preceding the original loop

```
row = column = 1;
while( row < srow || column < scolumn ) {
    WinSendMsg( hwndVS, VM_SETITEMATTR,
                MPFROM2SHORT( row, column ),
                MPFROM2SHORT( VIA_ICON | VIA_DISABLED, TRUE ));
    WinSendMsg( hwndVS, VM_SETITEM,
                MPFROM2SHORT( row, column ),
                (MPARAM)hptr );
    if (column++ == 7) {
        column = 1, row++;
    } /* endif */
} /* endwhile */

for (day = 0; day < getnumdays(curTM.tm_mon); day++) {
    WinSendMsg( hwndVS, VM_SETITEM,
                MPFROM2SHORT(row, column),
                MPFROMP(daytext[day]));
    if (column++ == 7) {
        column = 1, row++;
    } /* endif */
} /* endfor */

while( row < 7 ) {
    WinSendMsg( hwndVS, VM_SETITEMATTR,
                MPFROM2SHORT( row, column ),
                MPFROM2SHORT( VIA_ICON | VIA_DISABLED, TRUE ));
    WinSendMsg( hwndVS, VM_SETITEM,
                MPFROM2SHORT( row, column ),
                (MPARAM)hptr );
    if (column++ == 7) {
        column = 1, row++;
    } /* endif */
} /* while */
```

Figure 11.24 Modifying value set items.

is another loop that scans the value set items that precede the first day of the month. For each item, the VM_SETITEMATTR message is sent to change the state of the item to disable and the type of element displayed by the item to an icon graphic. This message is followed by a VM_SETITEM message, which assigns a pointer handle to the item. After the day number items are set by the original loop, another loop scans the remaining items in the value set. Like the first loop, this one disables each item and assigns a pointer to be displayed.

Processing Value Set Input

The previous section dealt with initializing a value set control to display a set of choices to the user. In most applications, this is just the beginning of the problem. Once the choices are displayed, the application must accept and process the user's selections. The value set's functionality provides a variety of methods for the application to recognize user input. In some methods, selections by the user are processed immediately, either as the selected item changes or when the user indicates that the currently selected choice should be used by either double-clicking the choice or pressing the Enter key. In other cases, the application does not process the selection immediately, but waits for some other event, such as a focus change or pressing the OK button in a dialog. This section will examine the mechanisms that are available for recognizing the user's selection and the code required to access these mechanisms.

Let's look first at an example dialog that acts as a miniature color palette and processes user input to the value set immediately as it occurs. The dialog is placed on a notebook page and contains a 16-item value set and three slider controls. The value set items display colors. When an item is selected, the RGB components of the item's color are reflected in the sliders, which may then be used to modify the color of the item. If the user double-clicks an item or presses the Enter key while the value set has focus, the color from the selected value set item is used to change the color of the notebook control's background.

The coding required to implement this functionality is shown in Figure 11.25. The dialog box procedure receives notification of the value set events by way of the WM_CONTROL message. When the notification code in the message is VN_SELECT, a different value set item has been selected and the sliders must be updated to reflect the RGB color represented by the new item. The row and column of the selected item are passed to the dialog procedure in parameter **mp2** of the WM_CONTROL message. The row is contained in the low-order 16 bits, and the column is contained in the high-order 16 bits. In this instance, however, there is no need to split these values out of **mp2** since the same construct is used when sending messages to the value set to obtain data. A VM_QUERYITEMATTR message is first sent to the value set to determine the type of data stored in the selected item. Parameter **mp1** of this message is the row and column of the desired item, and parameter **mp2** is reserved and set to

```
MRESULT APIENTRY ClrEditDlgProc(HWND hwnd, ULONG msg, MPARAM mp1, MPARAM mp2)
{
    ULONG    rgb;
    ULONG    ulAttrs;
    HWND     hwndNote;

    switch (msg) {
    case WM_CONTROL:
        if (SHORT2FROMMP(mp1) == VN_SELECT ) {
            usAttrs = SHORT1FROMMR(WinSendDlgItemMsg( hwnd, ID_VSCOLORS,
                              VM_QUERYITEMATTR, mp2, MPFROMLONG(0L)));
            if( usAttrs & VIA_RGB ) {
                rgb = LONGFROMMR(WinSendDlgItemMsg( hwnd, ID_VSCOLORS,
                            VM_QUERYITEM, mp2, MPFROMLONG(0L)));
                UpdateSliders( hwnd, rgb );
            } /* endif */
        } else if ( SHORT2FROMMP(mp1) == VN_ENTER ) {
            hwndNote = WinQueryWindow( hwnd, QW_PARENT );
            hwndNote = WinQueryWindow( hwndNote, QW_PARENT );
            usAttrs = SHORT1FROMMR(WinSendDlgItemMsg( hwnd, ID_VSCOLORS,
                              VM_QUERYITEMATTR, mp2, MPFROMLONG(0L)));
            if( usAttrs & VIA_RGB ) {
                rgb = LONGFROMMR(WinSendDlgItemMsg( hwnd, ID_VSCOLORS,
                            VM_QUERYITEM, mp2, MPFROMLONG(0L)));
                WinSetPresParam( hwndNote, PP_BACKGROUNDCOLOR, sizeof( ULONG ),
                            (PVOID *)&rgb );
            } /* endif */
        } /* endif */
        return MRFROMLONG(0L);
    } /* endswitch */
    return WinDefDlgProc( hwnd, msg, mp1, mp2 );
}
```

Figure 11.25   Processing value set notifications.

zero. The low-order word of the value returned by the message is a set of flags indicating the attributes of the value set item. These flags are interpreted in the same manner as described for the VM_SETITEMATTR message. (Note that in this example, all items have the same, known attributes so that this message is not really required—the code is shown here for illustrative purposes.) If the value in the item is an RGB color, a VM_QUERYITEM message is sent to the value set to retrieve the color value. Parameter **mp1** of this message is again the row and column of the desired item. If the item attribute is VIA_TEXT, parameter **mp2** is a pointer to a VSTEXT structure; otherwise this value is not used and should be set to zero. The VSTEXT structure is defined in Figure 11.26.

- The *pszItemText* element is a pointer to the location to store the text of the item's value.

```
typedef struct _VSTEXT
{
    PSZ        pszItemText;
    ULONG      ulBufLen;
} VSTEXT;
```

Figure 11.26 The VSTEXT structure.

- The *ulBufLen* element is the length of the buffer pointed to by *pszItem-Text*. If this value is set to zero, the required buffer length is returned by the VM_QUERYITEM message. The returned length excludes the null termination character.

The value returned from VM_QUERYITEM depends on the type of data stored in the item. If the item contains text, the number of bytes copied to the *pszItemText* element of the VSTEXT structure is returned. If the item contains a bitmap, the bitmap handle is returned. In the example, the item contains an RGB color value and this value is returned. The RGB color is then sent to routine **UpdateSliders** to split out the red, green, and blue components and to set the values of the sliders representing these colors.

When the user presses the Enter key while the value set has focus, or double-clicks one of the value set items with the mouse, a WM_CONTROL message is sent to the dialog procedure with the VN_ENTER notification. Receipt of this message indicates that the background of the notebook should be changed to the color of the item whose row and column are passed in parameter **mp2** of the message. The dialog procedure first obtains the window handle of the notebook window by querying the parent of the dialog to obtain the notebook page window and then querying the parent of the page window. The value of the value set item is then queried in the same manner as with the VN_SELECT notification code. This value is then used to change the value of the PP_BACKGROUNDCOLOR presentation parameter for the notebook window.

If the application knows the row and column of a value set item, the code from the previous example can be used to retrieve the data from the selection. Thus, an application that does not process selections immediately but waits for some external event also uses this code. The primary difference between immediate and delayed handling is in the event that triggers the request for the data and the method of obtaining the item number to retrieve. For example, an application may not immediately process each selection but wait until the user leaves the value set before determining what the final selection was. In this instance, the application would process WM_CONTROL messages with the VN_KILLFOCUS notification code. Parameter **mp2** of this message is the handle of the value set window. As shown in Figure 11.27, the application processes the message by first querying the currently selected item using the VM_QUERYSELECTEDITEM message. The **mp1** and **mp2** parameters of this

```
MRESULT APIENTRY ClrEditDlgProc(HWND hwnd, ULONG msg, MPARAM mp1, MPARAM mp2)
{
    ULONG    rgb;
    ULONG    ulAttrs;
    HWND     hwndNote;

    switch (msg) {
    case WM_CONTROL:
        if ( SHORT2FROMMP(mp1) == VN_KILLFOCUS ) {
            hwndNote = WinQueryWindow( hwnd, QW_PARENT );
            hwndNote = WinQueryWindow( hwndNote, QW_PARENT );
            vsitem = LONGFROMMR(WinSendMsg(HWNDFROMMP(mp2),VM_QUERYSELECTEDITEM,
                           MPFROMLONG(0L), MPFROMLONG(0L)));
            usAttrs = SHORT1FROMMR(WinSendDlgItemMsg( hwnd, ID_VSCOLORS,
                              VM_QUERYITEMATTR, vsitem, MPFROMLONG(0L)));
            if( usAttrs & VIA_RGB ) {
                rgb = (ULONG)WinSendDlgItemMsg( hwnd, ID_VSCOLORS,
                          VM_QUERYITEM, (MPARAM)vsitem, (MPARAM)0L );
                WinSetPresParam( hwndNote, PP_BACKGROUNDCOLOR, sizeof( ULONG ),
                          (PVOID *)&rgb );
        } /* endif */
        return MRFROMLONG(0L);
    } /* endswitch */
    return WinDefDlgProc( hwnd, msg, mp1, mp2 );
}
```

Figure 11.27   Processing a value set selection when focus changes.

message are both reserved values and must be set to zero. The return value from this message is the item ID of the currently selected item in the usual row/column format. This item ID is then used to query the item data in the same manner as shown earlier.

Applications may also obtain the value set data based on some event external to the value set, such as clicking the OK button in a dialog. In this case, if the value of the currently selected item is required, the code would be same as shown for the VN_KILLFOCUS notification message. An application might also need to process the data in all the items when the external event occurs. For example, in the previous color editor example, the current values of all the colors might be retrieved and stored in an initialization file as a small color palette for the application. In this case, the code could contain two loops similar to those used to create and initialize the value set in the calendar example. The current row and column of the loop is used to form the item ID, and the value is queried in the same manner as always.

Direct Manipulation of Value Set Items

The value set control class supports drag-and-drop direct manipulation operations by notifying its owner whenever it receives a direct manipulation message. The pickup-and-drop operation is not supported in this manner in the original OS/2 WARP release.

Initiation of a drag operation by receipt of the WM_BEGINDRAG message is reported to the owner window via the WM_CONTROL message with a VN_INITDRAG notification code when the pointing device is located over an item that has the VIA_DRAGGABLE attribute. Parameter **mp1** of the message contains the control ID and notification code as usual. Parameter **mp2** contains a pointer to a VSDRAGINIT structure, which is defined as shown in Figure 11.28.

- The *hwnd* element is the handle of the value set window.
- The *x* element is the x coordinate of the mouse pointer on the desktop.
- The *y* element is the y coordinate of the mouse pointer on the desktop.
- The *cx* element is the horizontal distance from the mouse pointer hotspot to the origin of the item that is the object of the direct manipulation operation.
- The *cy* element is the vertical distance from the mouse pointer hotspot to the origin of the item that is the object of the direct manipulation operation.
- Element *usRow* is the row number containing the object of the direct manipulation operation.
- Element *usColumn* is the column number containing the object of the direct manipulation operation.

The value set control also notifies its owner when objects are dragged over the value set window. The VN_DRAGOVER notification is sent when the value set receives a DM_DRAGOVER message; the VN_DRAGLEAVE notification is sent when the value set receives the DM_DRAGLEAVE message; and the VN_DRAGHELP notification is sent when the value set receives the DM_DRAGHELP message. If the value set receives a DM_DROP message and the pointing device is over an item that has the VIA_DROPONABLE attribute set, a VN_DROP notification is sent to the owner window. All of these notifications are sent via the WM_CONTROL message. Parameter **mp2** of the message contains a pointer to a VSDRAGINFO structure, defined as shown in Figure 11.29.

```
typedef struct _VSDRAGINIT
{
    HWND     hwnd;
    LONG     x;
    LONG     y;
    LONG     cx;
    LONG     cy;
    USHORT   usRow;
    USHORT   usColumn;
} VSDRAGINIT;
```

Figure 11.28   The VSDRAGINIT structure.

```
typedef struct _VSDRAGINFO
{
    PDRAGINFO pDragInfo;
    USHORT    usRow;
    USHORT    usColumn;
} VSDRAGINFO;
```

Figure 11.29   The VSDRAGINFO structure.

- Element *pDragInfo* is a pointer to the DRAGINFO structure for the current drag operation.
- The *usRow* element identifies the row containing the item under the mouse pointer.
- The *usColumn* element identifies the column containing the item under the mouse pointer.

For additional information on direct manipulation programming, see Chapter 7.

Owner Draw and the Value Set

The value set control provides for application drawing of the value set background and various components of the items that comprise the selection set. Drawing of the control background is enabled by setting the VS_OWNERDRAW style flag, and drawing of individual items is enabled by setting the VIA_OWNERDRAW attribute of the item. When an enabled component requires painting, a WM_DRAWITEM message is forwarded to the value set control window's owner. Parameter **mp1** of this message is the window ID of the value set window, and parameter **mp2** is a pointer to an OWNERDRAW structure. The *idItem* element of this structure indicates which component is to be painted. The valid values are:

VDA_BACKGROUND	0x0004	indicates that the background of the value set needs to be painted.
VDA_SURROUNDING	0x0003	indicates that the area surrounding an item needs to be redrawn.
VDA_ITEMBACKGROUND	0x0002	indicates that the background of an item needs to be painted.
VDA_ITEM	0x0001	indicates that the value set item must be repainted.

The *hItem* element contains the item identifier with the row number in the low-order 16 bits and the column number in the high-order 16 bits.

SLIDERS

The slider control class provides a graphical mechanism for representing and choosing a specific value within a range of values. By definition, the slider is kin to the scroll bar, but to avoid confusion, the latter should only be used for its intended purpose, manipulating the data displayed in a window. The slider control, with features such as tick marks, detents, and annotation, provides a much better facility for obtaining user input, and in its read-only form, is an excellent mechanism for reporting progress toward a goal, such as the completion percentage of a print operation or installation procedure.

There are two types of slider controls, the linear slider and the circular slider. The linear slider resembles the scroll bar control, having a slider that moves along a bar or shaft. The circular slider resembles the control knobs on stereo equipment and is useful when screen space is limited. In this section, we will examine both types of slider control, beginning with the linear slider.

The Linear Slider

The basic linear slider consists of a bar or shaft, a slide arm that moves along the bar, and two directional buttons. Annotated tick marks may be displayed at fixed intervals along the bar as helpful references for determining the current value of the slider. Detent marks can also be displayed and allow the user to quickly select a specific value for the slider by clicking on the detent mark. The ribbon strip, the area of the slider shaft between the origin and the current value, may be drawn with a different color than the normal background. A read-only slider removes the slide arm and directional buttons and is often used for display of values that tend to vary within a given range.

Creating Linear Sliders

Linear sliders may be created as stand-alone controls or as elements of a dialog in a dialog template. When creating stand-alone sliders, the application must specify the style of the control and must provide a SLDCDATA structure as the **pCtlData** parameter of the **WinCreateWindow** API. The **pszClass** parameter of the API call must be set to WC_SLIDER.

The SLDCDATA structure determines the range of values that the slider represents and the overall size of the slider. The structure is defined as shown in Figure 11.30.

- Element *cbSize* is the length of the structure in bytes and should be set to sizeof(SLDCDATA).
- The *usScale1Increments* element specifies the number of incremental values along the default scale. Since the home, or lowest, value reported back

```
typedef struct _SLDCDATA
{
    ULONG   cbSize;
    USHORT  usScale1Increments;
    USHORT  usScale1Spacing;
    USHORT  usScale2Increments;
    USHORT  usScale2Spacing;
} SLDCDATA;
```

Figure 11.30   The SLDCDATA structure.

to the application is zero, the maximum incremental value that the slider reports is one less than this value.

- The *usScale1Spacing* element specifies the number of pixels between each increment. If a value of zero is specified, the slider control automatically calculates the spacing based on the number of increments and the size of the control window.
- Element *usScale2Increments* specifies the number of incremental values along the alternate scale.
- Element *usScale2Spacing* specifies the number of pixels between each incremental value along the alternate scale.

A number of predefined constants are available for specifying the bits comprising the control-specific style flags for the slider. Those constants that have a defined value of zero are the default styles for the control. The primary style flag constants are:

SLS_HORIZONTAL	0x0000	specifies that the slider shaft is parallel to the x axis.
SLS_VERTICAL	0x0001	specifies that the slider shaft is parallel to the y axis.
SLS_PRIMARYSCALE1	0x0000	indicates that the *usScale1Increments* and *usScale1Spacing* elements of the SLDCDATA structure are to be used, and that tick marks, annotation, and detent marks are to be displayed above horizontal sliders or to the right of vertical sliders.
SLS_PRIMARYSCALE2	0x0400	indicates that the *usScale2Increments* and *usScale2Spacing* elements of the SLDCDATA structure are to be used, and that tick marks, annotation, and detent marks are to be displayed below horizontal sliders or to the left of vertical sliders.
SLS_SNAPTOINCREMENT	0x0008	causes the slider arm to be moved to the nearest incremental value if it is placed at a pixel position that is between increments.
SLS_READONLY	0x0080	causes a read-only slider to be created. This type of slider may be used to indicate progress toward

		some goal and does not allow user input. When this style is specified, the slider arm is not displayed.
SLS_RIBBONSTRIP	0x0100	specifies that a ribbon strip is to be drawn along the shaft between the home position and the current value of the slider. The ribbon strip is merely a shaft of a different color than the normal shaft. This style is especially useful for indicating the current value of read-only sliders, since no slider arm is drawn.
SLS_OWNERDRAW	0x0040	specifies that the slider's owner window is to be notified via a **WM_DRAWITEM** message whenever the shaft, ribbon strip, slider arm, or slider background is to be drawn.

The remaining style flags each have a dual constant definition. The defined constant normally used is dependent on the orientation of the slider, horizontal or vertical. The style constant definitions for horizontal sliders are:

SLS_CENTER	0x0000	indicates that the slider shaft is drawn in the center of the area defined for the control window.
SLS_BOTTOM	0x0002	indicates that the slider shaft is drawn at the bottom of the area defined for the control window.
SLS_TOP	0x0004	indicates that the slider shaft is drawn at the top of the area defined for the control window.
SLS_HOMELEFT	0x0000	specifies that the left end of the shaft is the home, or zero value, position.
SLS_HOMERIGHT	0x0200	specifies that the right end of the shaft is the home, or zero value, position.
SLS_BUTTONSLEFT	0x0010	indicates that the directional movement buttons are to be drawn and placed to the left of the slider shaft.
SLS_BUTTONSRIGHT	0x0020	indicates that the directional movement buttons are to be drawn and placed to the right of the slider shaft.

The style constant definitions for vertical sliders are:

SLS_CENTER	0x0000	indicates that the slider shaft is drawn in the center of the area defined for the control window.
SLS_LEFT	0x0002	indicates that the slider shaft is drawn at the left side of the area defined for the control window.
SLS_RIGHT	0x0004	indicates that the slider shaft is drawn at the right side of the area defined for the control window.
SLS_HOMEBOTTOM	0x0000	specifies that the bottom end of the shaft is the home, or zero value, position.

SLS_HOMETOP   0x0200   specifies that the top end of the shaft is the home, or zero value, position.

SLS_BUTTONSBOTTOM 0x0010   indicates that the directional movement buttons are to be drawn and placed at the bottom of the slider shaft.

SLS_BUTTONSTOP   0x0020   indicates that the directional movement buttons are to be drawn and placed at the top of the slider shaft.

As an example of creating the linear slider, let's look at a slider that represents degrees Centigrade between the freezing point (0 degrees) and boiling point (100 degrees) of water. Since both endpoints are included in the range, the total number of degrees, and therefore increments, displayed on the slider is 101. Initially, each increment will be one pixel, so the spacing will be set to 1. Figure 11.31 shows the code for creating this slider. The SLDCDATA structure is initialized to set scale 1 to the number of increments and spacing described. The structure is then passed to the **WinCreateWindow** API. The **flStyle** parameter sets the slider styles SLS_VERTICAL to display a vertical slider, SLS_BUTTONSBOTTOM to place the directional buttons at the bottom of the slider, and SLS_LEFT to place the bar at the left of the control window leaving room for tick marks and annotation to the right along scale 1. The width of the window is set to 50 pixels, or screen coordinates, allowing for the width of the slider and for the tick marks and annotation, which will be added later. The height of the window is set to 130 pixels, 100 pixels for the slide bar and 30 pixels for the buttons.

```
HWND  hwndSlider;
SLDCDATA cData;

cData.cbSize = sizeof(SLDCDATA);
cData.usScale1Increments = 101;
cData.usScale1Spacing = 1;
cData.usScale2Increments = 0;
cData.usScale2Spacing = 0;

hwndSlider = WinCreateWindow( hwndParent,
                             WC_SLIDER,
                             NULL,
                             SLS_BUTTONSBOTTOM | SLS_VERTICAL | SLS_LEFT,
                             0, 0, 100, 40,
                             hwndOwner,
                             HWND_TOP,
                             500,
                             &cData,
                             NULL );
```

Figure 11.31   Creating a linear slider.

Customizing the Linear Slider

Notice that the WS_VISIBLE style was not set when the slider was created in Figure 11.31. Before showing the slider to the user, tick marks and annotation will be added so that the range and current value of the slider can be easily determined. Figure 11.32 shows the basic code used for the thermometer slider created in Figure 11.31. Tick marks are added every two degrees, and a longer tick mark and degree value text are placed every 10 degrees. Since the spacing between slider increments is one, which places an increment at every pixel, if a tick were placed at every degree, or pixel, the tick marks would be indistinguishable and a solid black rectangle would be drawn. The for loop in Figure 11.32 scans every other increment of the slider, starting with value zero. If the increment value is not a multiple of 10, the SLM_SETTICKSIZE message is sent to change the tick size from the default of zero to five pixels. Parameter **mp1** of this message contains two fields; the low-order 16 bits specify the slider increment whose tick size is to be modified; the high-order 16 bits specify the length of tick in pixels. Parameter **mp2** is reserved and must be set to zero. For increment values that are a multiple of 10, the tick size is set to 10 pixels and an SLM_SETSCALETEXT message is sent to annotate the tick mark. The low-order 16 bits of parameter **mp1** specify the slider increment to annotate. Parameter **mp2** is a pointer to a zero-terminated array of characters to display as the annotation for the increment.

The code in Figure 11.32 causes annotation to be drawn every 10 pixels. While there is no overlap in this particular case, the resulting text appears rather crowded. The overall appearance of the slider can be improved by drawing the ticks on both sides of the slider and alternating the text from side to side. This is accomplished by drawing the ticks and text for one of the slider scales, then modifying the style of the slider and drawing the ticks and text for the other side of the slider. Note that this requires that the increment and spacing for both scales be initialized in the SLDCDATA structure when the

```
for( i = 0; i <= cData.usScale1Increments; i += 2 ) {
   if( i % 10 ) {
      WinSendMsg( hwndSlider, SLM_SETTICKSIZE,
                  MPFROM2SHORT( i, 5 ), MPFROMLONG(0));
   } else {
      WinSendMsg( hwndSlider, SLM_SETTICKSIZE,
                  MPFROM2SHORT( i, 10), MPFROMLONG(0L));
      _itoa( i, szScaleText, 10 );
      WinSendMsg( hwndSlider, SLM_SETSCALETEXT,
                  MPFROMSHORT( i ), MPFROMP(szScaleText));
   }
} /* endfor */
```

Figure 11.32   Annotating the linear slider.

window is created. Figure 11.33 shows the code to create and annotate the temperature slider in this manner.

The first portion of Figure 11.33 is a slightly modified version of the code from Figure 11.31. Note that the values for both slider scales are now specified. In this case, both scales are the same since the only reason for two scales is to improve the appearance of the annotation. The width of the slider is increased, and the SLS_LEFT style is removed in the **WinCreateWindow** call to center the slider and make room for the additional tick marks and annotation. The code from Figure 11.32 follows the **WinCreateWindow** call. The only modification to this initial loop is an if statement to determine if an even or odd multiple of 10 increments has been encountered. Only the odd multiples are drawn on scale one. Following this loop, the style of the slider is modified such that scale two becomes the primary scale. This is accomplished by querying the current style from the window data for the slider, ORing in the SLS_PRIMARYSCALE2 style, and then storing the new value back into the window words. A for loop similar to that for annotating scale one is then executed to annotate scale two. This loop only specifies annotation for increment values that are even multiples of 10. When this loop completes, the slider is ready for display, and **WinShowWindow** is called to make the slider visible.

Additional customization of the slider may also be performed. Common or frequently selected increment values may be represented with detents, allowing these values to be selected with a single pointing device click. Detent marks are added to the slider by sending an SLM_ADDDETENT message to the control. The low-order 16 bits of parameter **mp1** specify the number of pixels from the home position to place the detent. Parameter **mp2** is reserved and should be set to zero. The return value of the message is a unique detent identifier, which must be passed as parameter **mp1** of the SLM_REMOVEDETENT message to remove the detent from the slider. This identifier is also passed as parameter **mp1** of the SLM_QUERYDETENTPOS message used by the application to determine the location of the detent. The return value from this message contains the position of the detent as the number of pixels from the slider home position in the low-order 16 bits and the scale on which the detent is positioned in the upper 16 bits. The scale value is SMA_SCALE1 or SMA_SCALE2. These last two messages are not required in typical applications since movement of the slider arm to a detent position is reported back to the application in the same manner as any other value.

The size and position of the slide bar and the slide arm may be modified with the SLM_SETSLIDERINFO message. This functionality is discussed later in the section on using the slider as a progress indicator.

Obtaining Information with the Slider

The application may obtain the current value of the slider by processing notifications from the slider or by directly querying the value via a message to

```
HWND CreateSliderWnd( HWND hwnd )
{
    HWND     hwndSlider = NULLHANDLE;
    SLDCDATA cData;
    char     szScaleText[33];
    int      i;

    do {
        cData.cbSize = sizeof(SLDCDATA);
        cData.usScale1Increments = cData.usScale2Increments = 101;
        cData.usScale1Spacing = cData.usScale2Spacing = 1;
        hwndSlider = WinCreateWindow( hwnd,
                                      WC_SLIDER,
                                      NULL,
                                      SLS_BUTTONSBOTTOM | SLS_VERTICAL,
                                      0, 0, 90, 130,
                                      hwnd,
                                      HWND_TOP,
                                      500,
                                      &cData,
                                      NULL );
        for( i = 0; i <= cData.usScale1Increments; i += 2 ) {
            if( i % 10 ) {
                WinSendMsg( hwndSlider, SLM_SETTICKSIZE,
                            MPFROM2SHORT( i, 5 ), MPFROMLONG(0));
            } else {
                WinSendMsg( hwndSlider, SLM_SETTICKSIZE,
                            MPFROM2SHORT( i, 10), MPFROMLONG(0L));
                if( (i/10)%2 ) {
                    _itoa( i, szScaleText, 10 );
                    WinSendMsg( hwndSlider, SLM_SETSCALETEXT,
                                MPFROMSHORT( i ), MPFROMP(szScaleText));
        } } } /* endfor */
        ulStyle = WinQueryWindowULong( hwndSlider, QWL_STYLE );
        ulStyle |= SLS_PRIMARYSCALE2;
        WinSetWindowULong( hwndSlider, QWL_STYLE, ulStyle );
        for( i = 0; i <= cData.usScale2Increments; i += 2 ) {
            if( i % 10 ) {
                WinSendMsg( hwndSlider, SLM_SETTICKSIZE,
                            MPFROM2SHORT( i, 5 ), MPFROMLONG(0));
            } else {
                WinSendMsg( hwndSlider, SLM_SETTICKSIZE,
                            MPFROM2SHORT( i, 10), MPFROMLONG(0L));
                if (!((i/10)%2)) {
                    _itoa( i, szScaleText, 10 );
                    WinSendMsg( hwndSlider, SLM_SETSCALETEXT,
                                MPFROMSHORT( i ), MPFROMP(szScaleText));
        } } } /* endfor */
        WinShowWindow( hwndSlider, TRUE );
    } while (false);   /* endwhile */
    return hwndSlider;
}
```

Figure 11.33 Annotating both slider scales.

the slider. As with all controls, notifications are sent via the WM_CONTROL message with the notification code in the high-order 16 bits of **mp1**. Two notification codes are of particular interest when retrieving values from the slider:

- The SLN_CHANGE notification is sent to the application whenever the value of the slider changes (but not while the slider is being dragged). The current value of the slider, expressed as the number of pixels from the home location to the current position of the slider, is contained in parameter **mp2**. This notification would normally be processed by an application that provides immediate feedback of the effects of slider value changes.
- The SLN_SLIDERTRACK notification allows the application to provide feedback while the slide arm is being dragged along the bar. The value of the current position of the slider is given in parameter **mp2**.

Applications that do not provide any form of immediate feedback but are only interested in the current value of the slider when some event occurs—for example, when the user clicks the OK button in a dialog—can retrieve the current value by sending an SLM_QUERYSLIDERINFO message to the control window. For this operation, the low-order 16 bits of parameter **mp1** should be set to SMA_SLIDERARMPOSITION, and the high-order 16 bits should be set to either SMA_RANGEVALUE to query the number of pixels from the home position or to SMA_INCREMENT to determine the tick mark where the arm is positioned. In the first instance, SMA_RANGEVALUE, the return value contains the current position of the slider arm in the low-order 16 bits, and the total pixels for the bar in the high-order 16 bits. If SMA_INCREMENT is specified, the low-order 16 bits of the return value contain the tick mark, or increment value, where the arm is positioned, and the high-order 16 bits are not used. If the slide arm is located between increment values, the value returned is rounded to the nearest increment value.

As an example, consider how an application might process changes to the temperature slider. In this instance, changing the slider value might cause an I/O operation to occur that changes the setting of a thermostat. Since temperature changes do not normally occur instantaneously, there is no need to process the SLN_SLIDERTRACK notification. Instead, the SLN_CHANGE notification is processed to change the thermostat each time a change is made in the slider value. Figure 11.34 shows the coding used to implement this functionality.

The **wmControl** function is called by the window procedure of the slider's owner window when the WM_CONTROL message is received. If the message is a notification from the slider, the slider's WM_CONTROL processing function, **wmControlSlider**, is called. The routine first checks to see if the message is an SLN_CHANGE notification. If so, two methods of obtaining the current value of the slider are shown. The first method merely obtains the pixel value of

```
MRESULT APIENTRY wmControl( HWND hwnd, ULONG msg, MPARAM mp1, MPARAM mp2 )
{
   if (SHORT1FROMMP(mp1) == 500 )
      wmControlSlider( hwnd, msg, mp1, mp2 );
   return (MRESULT)0;
}

void wmControlSlider( HWND hwnd, ULONG msg, MPARAM mp1, MPARAM mp2 )
{
    SHORT    pixTemp;
    SHORT    incrTemp;
    MRESULT  ulValue;

    if( SHORT2FROMMP( mp1 ) == SLN_CHANGE ) {
       pixTemp = SHORT1FROMMP( mp2 );
       ulValue = WinSendMsg( hwndSlider, SLM_QUERYSLIDERINFO,
          MPFROM2SHORT(SMA_SLIDERARMPOSITION, SMA_INCREMENTVALUE),
          MPFROMLONG(01));
       incrTemp =  SHORT1FROMMR(ulValue);
       SetTemp( incrTemp );
    } /* endif */
}

void SetTemp( USHORT usNewTemp )
{
   printf( "Changing temperature to %d degrees \n", usNewTemp );
}
```

Figure 11.34   **Processing slider value changes.**

the slider by examining the low-order 16 bits of parameter **mp2**. In cases like this one, where the increment spacing is one pixel, this value is equal to the increment value. In other cases, the pixel value may need to be converted to an increment. This could be accomplished by using a mathematical calculation, or as shown in the example, by querying the increment value from the slider. The value is retrieved by sending an SLM_QUERYSLIDERINFO message to the slider. Parameter **mp1** is set to query the slider arm position, the current value of the slider, as an increment value. The low-order 16 bits of the return value from the message is the current increment value of the slider. This value is then passed to routine **SetTemp** to change the thermostat. For the purposes of this example, **SetTemp** merely prints the value to the standard output device. This output can be seen by redirecting standard output to a file when the program is invoked.

Using Read-Only Linear Sliders

Linear sliders are also commonly used to display the current value of a datum that tends to vary within some fixed range. Examples of this usage include a temperature or pressure gauge, or an audio device volume meter. Another common usage is a progress meter, in which the slider displays the percent achievement of some goal, such as formatting a diskette or installing a program. To demonstrate this use of the slider, we will examine code that implements a read-only slider to display the seconds component of the current time. As an added benefit, the OWNERDRAW features of the slider will be used to display a bitmap in the ribbon strip of the slider.

Figure 11.35 shows the code used to create the slider window. The SLDCDATA structure is initialized to create a slider with 60 increments having two pixels per increment. Several style flags are passed to **WinCreateWindow** to create a slider with the desired appearance and behavior. The SLS_READONLY style prevents user input and hides the slide arm, replacing it with a narrow line across the breadth of the slider to indicate the current value. Style SLS_RIBBONSTRIP causes the slider to display the area between the home position of the slider and the current value in a different color. The SLS_OWNERDRAW style causes the slider to send a WM_DRAWITEM message to its owner when the slider's background, slide bar, slide arm, or ribbon strip require painting. This example uses the WM_DRAWITEM message to paint a bitmap in the ribbon strip rather than just changing the color. WM_DRAWITEM messages for the other portions of the slider are not processed, allowing the slider to draw these elements as normal.

After the slider window is created, a for loop is used to set the tick mark sizes and to annotate the slider at every 10th tick mark. An SLM_SETSLIDER INFO message is then sent to modify the breadth of the slider to match the size of the bitmap that is drawn into the ribbon strip. Parameter **mp1** of this message specifies the slider component to be modified. The following values are valid:

SMA_SHAFTDIMENSIONS	0x0000	sets the breadth of the slider. This is the width of vertical sliders or the height of horizontal sliders. The low-order 16 bits of parameter **mp2** specify the breadth in pixels.
SMA_SHAFTPOSITION	0x0001	sets the x and y coordinates of the lower left corner of the slide bar. This allows the application to move the slide bar to a nonstandard location within the slider window. The low-order 16 bits of parameter **mp2** specify the x coordinate, and the high-order 16 bits specify the y coordinate. The coordinates must be specified as window coordinates.
SMA_SLIDERARMDIMENSIONS	0x0002	modifies the size of the slide arm. The low-order 16 bits of parameter **mp2** specify the length of the arm; the arm width for horizontal sliders and the arm height for vertical

```
HWND CreateClockWindow( HWND hwndNote )
{
    HWND      hwndSlider = NULLHANDLE;
    SLDCDATA  cData;
    char      szScaleText[33];
    int       i;

    cData.cbSize = sizeof(SLDCDATA);
    cData.usScale1Increments = 60;
    cData.usScale1Spacing = 2;
    cData.usScale2Increments = 0;
    cData.usScale2Spacing = 0;
    hwndSlider = WinCreateWindow( hwndNote,
                                  WC_SLIDER,
                                  NULL,
                                  SLS_READONLY | SLS_RIBBONSTRIP |
                                  SLS_BOTTOM | SLS_OWNERDRAW,
                                  0, 0, 130, 70,
                                  WinQueryWindow(hwndNote,QW_PARENT),
                                  HWND_TOP,
                                  600,
                                  &cData,
                                  NULL );
    for( i = 0; i <= 60; i += 2 ) {
        if( i % 10 ) {
            WinSendMsg( hwndSlider, SLM_SETTICKSIZE,
                        MPFROM2SHORT( i, 5 ), MPFROMLONG(0));
        } else {
            WinSendMsg( hwndSlider, SLM_SETTICKSIZE,
                        MPFROM2SHORT( i, 10), MPFROMLONG(0L));
            _itoa( i, szScaleText, 10 );
            WinSendMsg( hwndSlider, SLM_SETSCALETEXT,
                        MPFROMSHORT( i ), MPFROMP(szScaleText));
        }
    } /* endfor */
    WinSendMsg( hwndSlider, SLM_SETSLIDERINFO,
                MPFROMSHORT( SMA_SHAFTDIMENSIONS ), MPFROMSHORT( 32 ));
    WinStartTimer( WinQueryAnchorBlock(hwndSlider),
                   WinQueryWindow(hwndNote,QW_PARENT),
                   TID_USERMAX - 1, 1000 );
    return hwndSlider;
}
```

Figure 11.35   Creating a read-only slider.

sliders. The high-order 16 bits specify the breadth of the arm; the arm height for horizontal sliders and the arm width for vertical sliders. All measurements are expressed as pixels.

SMA_SLIDERARMPOSITION   0x0003   modifies the position of the slider arm, which equates to the value of the slider. The low-order 16 bits of parameter **mp2** specify the new value of the slider. The value is expressed as either the number of pixels from the home position or as an increment value, depending on the value in the high-order 16 bits of parameter **mp1**, which may be set to:

SMA_RANGEVALUE   0x0000   indicates that the new value is expressed as the number of pixels from the home position.

SMA_INCREMENTVALUE   0x0001   indicates that the new value is expressed as an increment value.

Once the slider size has been adjusted, API **WinStartTimer** is called to create a timer that will be used for updating the slider value. This timer sends a WM_TIMER message to the slider's owner once per second. The owner window then calls routine **AppWndTimer**, shown in Figure 11.36, to set the slider value to the seconds component of the current time.

Routine **AppWndTimer** first verifies that the WM_TIMER message is from the timer created by routine **CreateClockWindow**. If so, the routine calls the **WinGetCurrentTime** API to retrieve the millisecond counter from the system clock. This value is then converted to a seconds value between 1 and 60 which is used to update the slider position with the SLM_SETSLIDERINFO message. Parameter **mp1** of the message indicates that the slider component to update

```
MRESULT AppWndTimer( HWND hwnd, ULONG msg, MPARAM mp1, MPARAM mp2 )
{
   ULONG     ulMs;
   USHORT    usS;

   if( SHORT1FROMMP(mp1) == TID_USERMAX - 1 ) {
      ulMs = WinGetCurrentTime( WinQueryAnchorBlock( hwnd ));
      usS = (USHORT)((ulMs / 1000) % 60);
      WinSendMsg( hwndClock, SLM_SETSLIDERINFO,
                  MPFROM2SHORT( SMA_SLIDERARMPOSITION, SMA_INCREMENTVALUE ),
                  MPFROMSHORT( usS ));
   } /* endif */
   return MRFROMLONG(0L);
}
```

Figure 11.36   Modifying the slider value.

is the arm position and that the new position is specified as an increment value.

Under most circumstances, this would be the end of the code for this slider; however, changing the slider position causes the ribbon strip to be redrawn. Since the SLS_OWNERDRAW style was specified, the slider's owner window receives a WM_DRAWITEM message when the slide arm position changes. The owner window calls routine **AppWndDrawClock**, shown in Figure 11.37, to handle this message. Parameter **mp2** of the WM_DRAWITEM message, which is forwarded to this routine, is an OWNERITEM structure that provides the application with information about the item to be drawn. The definition of this structure as it relates to drawing slider components is shown in Figure 11.38.

- Element *hwnd* is the window handle of the slider window.
- Element *hps* is the handle of a presentation space that allows drawing in the area that requires painting. Any drawing outside this area is clipped. The coordinates used for drawing are based on the origin of the presentation space.
- The *fsState* element contains the slider style flags.

```
MRESULT AppWndDrawClock( HWND hwnd, ULONG msg, MPARAM mp1, MPARAM mp2 )
{
    POWNERITEM  pOD = (POWNERITEM)PVOIDFROMMP(mp2);
    HBITMAP     hbm = NULLHANDLE;
    MRESULT     ulInfo;
    POINTL      ptl;
    USHORT      usSlWidth;

    if( pOD->idItem == SDA_RIBBONSTRIP ) {
        hbm = GpiLoadBitmap(pOD->hps,
                            NULLHANDLE,
                            IDB_CLOCK,
                            32, 32);
        ulInfo = WinSendMsg( pOD->hwnd, SLM_QUERYSLIDERINFO,
                            MPFROM2SHORT(SMA_SLIDERARMPOSITION, SMA_RANGEVALUE),
                            MPFROMLONG(0L));
        usSlWidth = SHORT1FROMMR(ulInfo);
        ptl.x = pOD->rclItem.xLeft; ptl.y = pOD->rclItem.yBottom;
        do {
            WinDrawBitmap( pOD->hps, hbm, NULL, &ptl, 0, 0, DBM_NORMAL );
            ptl.x += 32;
            usSlWidth -= (usSlWidth > 32 ) ? 32 : usSlWidth;
        } while( usSlWidth != 0 );
        GpiDeleteBitmap( hbm );
        return MRFROMLONG(1L);
    }
    return MRFROMLONG(0L);
}
```

Figure 11.37   Drawing the slider background.

```
typedef struct _OWNERITEM
{
    HWND    hwnd;
    HPS     hps;
    ULONG   fsState;
    ULONG   fsAttribute;
    ULONG   fsStateOld;
    ULONG   fsAttributeOld;
    RECTL   rclItem;
    LONG    idItem;
    ULONG   hItem;
} OWNERITEM;
```

Figure 11.38   The OWNERITEM structure.

- The *fsAttribute* element is reserved and not used for the slider.
- Element *fsStateOld* is reserved and not used for the slider.
- Element *fsAttributeOld* is reserved and not used for the slider.
- The *rclItem* element is a rectangle that defines the area of the item requiring update. The coordinates are specified in window coordinates. Note that this rectangle identifies the entire area of the item, not just the region being updated, in coordinates relative to the origin of the presentation space.
- The *idItem* element identifies which portion of the slider is being updated. Valid values for this element are:

SDA_SLIDERSHAFT   0x0002   the slider shaft is being updated.

SDA_RIBBONSTRIP   0x0001   the ribbon strip is being updated.

SDA_SLIDERARM   0x0004   the slider arm is being updated.

SDA_BACKGROUND   0x0003   the background of the slider window is being updated.

- The *hItem* element is reserved and not used for the slider.

Routine **AppWndDrawClock** is only capable of painting the ribbon strip, so it first checks the *idItem* element of the OWNERDRAW structure to ensure that this component of the slider is being updated. If not, the routine returns zero to allow the slider to update whichever other portion of the window is being drawn. When the ribbon strip is being updated, the function first loads the bitmap used to fill the ribbon strip from the application's resources. An SLM_QUERYSLIDERINFO message is then sent to the slider to obtain the current slider arm position. This represents the maximum x coordinate to be drawn. A POINTL structure is then filled with the x and y coordinates of the lower left corner of the ribbon strip as indicated by the *rclItem* element of the OWNERITEM structure. A loop is then entered to draw multiple copies of the bitmap using the **WinDrawBitmap** API. As each copy is drawn, the

POINTL structure, which acts as the origin for drawing the bitmap, is updated to place the next copy adjacent to the previous copy. When the entire ribbon strip area has been filled, the loop terminates, the bitmap is deleted, and a nonzero value is returned to indicate that the ribbon strip has been updated.

Note that this routine could be optimized by calculating the portions of one or more copies of the bitmap that actually fall into the area requiring update and then only drawing these portions. However, in this and many instances, the performance gain is relatively small and typically not worth the additional code complexity that extends the initial development time and hampers maintenance efforts.

Circular Sliders

The circular slider provides the same basic functionality as its partner, the linear slider. The circular slider's graphic representation resembles a rotating control knob like that found on most modern stereo equipment. Like the physical knob, the circular slider typically requires less room than its linear counterpart. This makes the control well suited to situations where several sliders are required. Unlike the linear slider, the presentation options for the circular slider are somewhat limited, making it less well suited for use in display-only situations or where annotation is required.

The graphic representation of the slider consists of the round slider, optional value text within the slider, optional tick marks around the slider, optional directional buttons on each side of the slider, optional text to label the slider, and an indicator that marks the current value of the slider.

The circular slider was originally part of the Multimedia Developer's Toolkit, but in OS/2 WARP it has been moved into the mainstream of the Presentation Manager and enhanced to provide more flexibility. The reference documentation for the slider can now be found in the *Presentation Manager Guide and Reference*, and the definitions and declarations used to program the slider have been moved to pmstddlg.h. If you are maintaining code written for earlier versions of the operating system and using circular sliders, the programs must be modified to point to the new header before recompiling.

Creating Circular Sliders

The circular slider can be included as an item in a dialog template or created using the **WinCreateWindow** or **WinCreateStdWindow** APIs. Several control-specific styles are available for modifying the appearance and behavior of the slider. These styles are defined as:

CSS_NOTEXT   0x0002   removes the text that is otherwise displayed below
                                        the slider to label the slider.

CSS_NONUMBER	0x0004	removes the text that is otherwise displayed in the center of the slider to indicate the current value of the slider.
CSS_NOBUTTON	0x0001	removes the directional buttons that are otherwise displayed on each side of the slider.
CSS_360	0x0010	allows the slider to rotate through a full 360 degrees rather than the default 180 degrees.
CSS_MIDPOINT	0x0020	causes the tick marks at the endpoints and the midpoint of the slider's range to be elongated.
CSS_POINTSELECT	0x0008	modifies the scrolling movement of the slider when values are selected with the mouse. If this style is not specified, the slider is moved to the location clicked with the mouse in a smooth motion. When this style is set, using the mouse to select a value causes the value to be immediately selected.
CSS_CIRCULARVALUE	0x0100	changes the value indicator for the slider from its normal radius line to a small circular indention near the edge of the slider dial.
CSS_PROPORTIONALTICKS	0x0040	causes the length of the tick marks to be a percentage of the size of the slider radius rather than a constant value. This can be particularly useful for small sliders by allowing the size of the slider itself to occupy additional space within the area allocated for the slider control window.
CSS_NOTICKS	0x0080	prevents the tick marks from being displayed.

Unless the CSS_NOTEXT flag is set, the window text (the **pszTitle** or **pszName** parameters of the APIs) is displayed as a label below the dial portion of the slider window. When creating the slider with the **WinCreateWindow** API, the control data for the slider, CSBITMAPDATA, should not be passed as the **pCtlData** parameter since it does not conform to the documented requirement that the first two bytes of the structure specify the length of the data. If non-default button bitmaps are required, use the CSM_SETBITMAPDATA message to specify the new bitmaps after the window is created.

Customizing the Circular Slider

Figure 11.39 shows an example of the code needed to create and customize a circular slider for use as a volume control dial. The slider value will vary between 0 and 100, representing the percent of maximum volume, and custom bitmaps are used for the slider buttons to demonstrate the use of the CSBITMAP structure.

```
HWND CreateDialWindow( HWND hwndNote )
{
    CSBITMAPDATA cData;
    HPS      hps;

    hwndDial = WinCreateWindow( hwndNote,
                                WC_CIRCULARSLIDER,
                                "Volume",
                                WS_VISIBLE | CSS_CIRCULARVALUE,
                                0, 0, 130, 130,
                                WinQueryWindow(hwndNote,QW_PARENT),
                                HWND_TOP, 600, NULL, NULL );
    hps = WinGetPS( hwndDial );
    cData.hbmRightUp = GpiLoadBitmap(hps, NULLHANDLE, IDB_UP, 10, 10);
    cData.hbmRightDown = GpiLoadBitmap(hps, NULLHANDLE, IDB_UP1, 10, 10 );
    cData.hbmLeftUp = GpiLoadBitmap(hps, NULLHANDLE, IDB_DOWN, 10, 10);
    cData.hbmLeftDown = GpiLoadBitmap(hps, NULLHANDLE, IDB_DOWN1 10, 10);
    WinReleasePS( hps );
    WinSendMsg( hwndDial, CSM_SETBITMAPDATA, MPFROMP(&cData), MPFROMLONG(01));
    WinSendMsg( hwndDial, CSM_SETRANGE, MPFROMSHORT(0), MPFROMSHORT(100));
    WinSendMsg( hwndDial, CSM_SETVALUE, MPFROMSHORT(50), MPFROMLONG(01));
    WinSendMsg( hwndDial, CSM_SETINCREMENT, MPFROMSHORT(1), MPFROMSHORT(10));
    return hwndDial;
}
```

Figure 11.39   Creating a circular slider.

The routine creates the slider by calling the **WinCreateWindow** API. The **pszClass** parameter is set to WC_CIRCULARSLIDER, the constant identifying the circular slider class; **pszName** is set to a pointer to "Volume," which will be displayed as a label below the slider dial. The **flStyle** parameter specifies that the control will be visible and that the value indicator will appear as a circular indention rather than a radius. The created slider will thus display the label text, tick marks which are uniform in length, the value text, and the directional buttons. When the user directly selects a new value on the slider, the slider scrolls rather than jumping immediately. This prevents equipment, and possibly eardrum, damage which might occur if the volume were to suddenly snap from minimum to maximum. Other applications might require a rapid change, which can be easily accomplished by setting the CSS_POINTSELECT style when the window is created.

After the window is created, the application modifies the bitmaps that are displayed to allow the user to increment and decrement the value of the slider. A presentation space handle is obtained by calling the **WinGetPS** API. Four bitmaps are then loaded from the application's resource file, and the handles for the bitmaps are stored in the appropriate elements of the CSBITMAP structure. The screen area occupied by the bitmaps is 10 pixels by 10 pixels; bitmaps of other sizes are stretched or compressed to fill this area. After the

```
typedef struct _CSBITMAPDATA
{
    HBITMAP hbmLeftUp;
    HBITMAP hbmLeftDown;
    HBITMAP hbmRightUp;
    HBITMAP hbmRightDown;
} CSBITMAPDATA;
```

Figure 11.40   The CSBITMAPDATA structure.

bitmaps are loaded, the presentation space is released. The definition of the CSBITMAP structure is given in Figure 11.40.

- The *hbmLeftUp* element specifies the bitmap to use when the button to the left of the slider is in the up position.
- The *hbmLeftDown* element specifies the bitmap to use when the button to the left of the slider is in the down position.
- The *hbmRightUp* element specifies the handle of the bitmap to use when the button to the right of the slider is in the up position.
- The *hbmRightDown* element specifies the handle of the bitmap to use when the button to the right of the slider is in the down position.

After the bitmap structure is initialized, a CSM_SETBITMAPDATA message is sent to the slider to change the displayed bitmaps. Parameter **mp1** of this message specifies a pointer to the initialized CSBITMAPDATA structure. Parameter **mp2** is reserved and set to the value zero. Note that though the default bitmaps appear to be buttons, they are merely bitmaps. Application-defined bitmaps should normally maintain this appearance. Also, if either the up or down bitmap is specified as NULLHANDLE, only one bitmap is displayed; the default is no longer used after the CSM_SETBITMAPDATA message is received by the slider.

After the bitmaps have been specified, the range of values represented by the slider is changed to begin at 0 and end at 100. This allows the application to use the value of the slider as a percent of the maximum volume. The slider range is set by sending a CSM_SETRANGE message. The low-order 16 bits of parameter **mp1** specify the minimum value that the slider can assume, and the low-order 16 bits of parameter **mp2** specify the maximum value of the slider. If this message is not sent, the default range of the slider is from 0 to 30.

The initial value of the slider is established by sending a CSM_SETVALUE message. The new value is passed as the low-order 16 bits of parameter **mp1**. If this message is not sent, the default initial value is 15. In many applications, the initial value will be set to either a stored value or the current value of the entity controlled by the slider. In this example, we have arbitrarily chosen the midpoint of the slider range as the initial value. The CSM_SETVALUE message may be sent at any time the application wishes to change the slider value, not just at initialization time.

A CSM_SETINCREMENT message is then sent to the slider. The low-order 16 bits of parameter **mp1** specify the movement delta for the slider. When the CSS_POINTSELECT style is not specified, this value is used to determine how many increments are added or subtracted each time the value is changed while scrolling to the final destination when the mouse is used to directly select a value or when a directional button is pressed and held. The amount of movement caused when a directional button is clicked is not affected by the movement delta and always remains one. The low-order 16 bits of parameter **mp2** specify the number of increments between tick marks.

Retrieving Data from the Slider

As with most controls, the circular slider defines messages that may be sent to determine its current value. The slider also sends messages to its owner window whenever the value changes. This allows the application to process the changes dynamically as they occur or to wait until some later time, such as when a dialog is dismissed or the slider loses focus, to read the value of the slider.

Applications that provide dynamic feedback as the circular slider changes value normally process the CSN_TRACKING and CSN_CHANGED notifications. These notifications are sent to the slider window's owner when the slider value changes. The CSN_TRACKING notification is sent when the slider is scrolling from one value to the next. The CSN_CHANGED notification is sent when the slider has reached a final destination. In both cases, the current value of the slider is contained in the low-order 16 bits of parameter **mp2**. Figure 11.41 shows WM_CONTROL processing, which could be used to handle these messages. The code merely verifies the notification code and the ID of

```
MRESULT wmControlCSlider( HWND hwnd, ULONG msg, MPARAM mp1, MPARAM mp2 )
{
    USHORT       usValue;

    if( SHORT1FROMMP(mp1) == 600 ) {
        if( SHORT2FROMMP(mp1) == CSN_TRACKING ||
            SHORT2FROMMP(mp1) == CSN_CHANGED ) {
            SetVolume( SHORT1FROMMP(mp2));
        }
    }
    return MRFROMLONG(0L);
}
```

Figure 11.41   Processing circular slider value changes.

the control where the message originated and then calls a routine to change the volume to the current slider value.

Other applications may not need to provide this type of dynamic feedback. These applications can send the CSM_QUERYVALUE message to the slider to obtain the current value when desired. Parameter **mp1** of the message is a pointer to the location to store the new value. Parameter **mp2** is reserved and should be set to zero.

CHANGING THE CIRCULAR SLIDER BACKGROUND COLOR

Whenever the slider needs to be painted, a WM_CONTROL message is sent to the slider's owner window with the CSN_QUERYBACKGROUNDCOLOR notification code. The application can then return a color index value, CLR_ or SYSCLR_, to modify the background color of the slider. This feature can be used to provide additional feedback to the user; for instance, the background color could normally be drawn as green, change to yellow when the value approaches a critical point, and then change to red when the value has exceeded safe limits. However, the only means of forcing the slider to paint the background is to force a WM_PAINT message to be sent to the slider by calling **WinInvalidateRect**. This will normally cause the window to blink as it is being repainted, an effect that is normally not desirable.

SUMMARY

This chapter has examined several of the new control classes that were introduced beginning with OS/2 version 2.0. These controls allow application programmers to efficiently organize and present information to the user in graphical forms that emulate familiar real-world objects. The notebook control organizes large amounts of information into convenient pages. The value set provides a graphical representation of a set of mutually exclusive choices. The linear slider provides a precise means of entering numeric values and avoids the confusion that existed when the scroll bar was used for this function in addition to its designed window scrolling function. The linear slider also provides a convenient means for displaying progress and similar information. The circular slider provides the same input functionality as the linear slider in a compact form. Use of these controls helps to produce efficient, user-friendly applications.

CHAPTER 12

Containing Your Excitement: Making Use of the Container Control

The container is one of the newest and most visually complex controls provided by PM. Though the control is typically touted as a means of displaying and manipulating sets of objects, the internal design of the control is similar to a small database manager. Records in the database are composed of predefined elements, which describe the graphical representation(s) of the record, and application-defined elements, which may be displayed in the DETAIL view of the database. Because of this design, the container is an effective tool for displaying and manipulating almost every type of data.

The container control provides functionality for displaying the set of data records in various formats or views. The DETAIL view allows the application to format and display the contents of the data records. The remaining three views provide a single graphical and/or textual representation of each data record and allow an hierarchical display of the relationship between the records. The container also allows user editing of the textual fields of the data records and supports direct manipulation of the records.

Common examples of container usage are the folder objects of the Workplace Shell. The implementation of folders uses the container to display and manipulate a variety of object types including directories, data files, abstract objects, and transient objects. Any application that processes data records is a candidate for using the container and, as familiarity with the control grows, its usage will also expand.

This chapter discusses the various container views, the primary data structures used with the container and the application coding required to use the container.

CONTAINER VIEWS

The container provides four different views, or representations, of the data records associated with the control. The ICON and NAME views provide an annotated graphical representation of each data record, while the TEXT view uses a single text string to represent each record. In DETAIL view, the elements of each data record are represented as a row in a multiple-column display.

Depending on the view chosen, three additional modes may be available. In MINI mode, the ICON and NAME views display an alternate, typically smaller, version of the icon or bitmap, allowing more objects to be displayed in a given space. FLOW mode is used with either the NAME or TEXT views to display objects in multiple columns. TREE mode is used with the NAME, ICON, or TEXT modes to display a hierarchical view of the objects.

The ICON view represents objects, or data records, by displaying an icon or bitmap above a text string. Positioning of the objects is normally determined by the application and is not restricted. The CCS_AUTOPOSITION style causes the container to determine the position of the objects as they are added to the container. Sending a CM_ARRANGE message to the container causes the objects to be positioned in multiple rows such that no two objects overlay each other. The MINI mode is supported for this view in order to display a smaller icon or bitmap. In TREE mode, the ICON view represents objects by displaying them vertically on the page with an expanded/collapsed icon displayed to the left of the object's icon or bitmap, and the object's text displayed to the right of the object's icon.

The NAME view representation of objects is similar to that of the ICON view except that the text is displayed to the right of the object's icon or bitmap. NAME view automatically positions the representations in a single vertical column in the window, adding a vertical scroll bar when required. The MINI mode is supported for this view in order to display a smaller icon or bitmap.

This view may also be displayed in FLOW mode. In this mode, the object representations are arranged in multiple vertical columns, and a horizontal scroll bar is added if needed. In TREE mode, the normal expanded/collapsed graphic is not used; instead, parent objects may be displayed with a different graphic which can vary depending on whether the object is expanded or collapsed; objects with no children are displayed using the normal graphic.

In TEXT view, objects are represented with text only, there is no graphic associated. Like the NAME view, the objects are automatically positioned in a single vertical column, and a vertical scroll bar is displayed when needed. When FLOW mode is selected, the text representing objects is arranged in multiple vertical columns, and a horizontal scroll bar is added as required. In TREE mode, the expanded/collapsed icon is displayed to the left of the text string for the object.

The DETAIL view displays each object as a row of horizontal data arranged in columns defined by the application. Each column may be defined to display data contained in the core record structure provided by the container or data contained in an application-defined extension to this basic structure. This view is typically used to display data from a homogenous set of objects, such as the records in a database or the entries in a file directory; however, the view can also be used to display common data from a heterogeneous set of objects.

CONTAINER DATA STRUCTURES

The container control utilizes four primary data structures to control the appearance and function of the container and to store the data records that the container manipulates. The CNRINFO structure contains elements that apply to the container as a whole. These items include information such as the title of the container, the view to be displayed, and the type of graphical object used to represent data records. The RECORDCORE structure and its smaller counterpart, the MINIRECORDCORE structure, are used to store the data records for the container; the FIELDINFO structure is used to describe and format the columns of information when the container displays the DETAIL view.

CNRINFO

The control data for the container is defined by the CNRINFO structure. The contents of this structure control many aspects of the container's appearance and operation, and most applications will need to specify the value of at least some elements. Because of the size and complexity of the structure, it is not normally passed with the **WinCreateWindow** API, but is allowed to assume default values when the control is created and then modified with the CM_SETCNRINFO message. Parameter **mp2** of this message contains a set of flags indicating which elements are being modified. The description of the structure in Figure 12.1 indicates the flag which modifies each element.

- The *cb* element specifies the size of the structure in bytes. This element is read-only and cannot be modified with the CM_SETCNRINFO message.
- The *pSortRecord* element is a pointer to the comparison function used when records in the container are sorted. This value is modified by setting the CMA_PSORTRECORD (0x0020) flag in **mp2** of the CM_SETCNRINFO message. The function identified by this element should be of the form:

```
typedef struct _CNRINFO
{
    ULONG       cb;
    PVOID       pSortRecord;
    PFIELDINFO  pFieldInfoLast;
    PFIELDINFO  pFieldInfoObject;
    PSZ         pszCnrTitle;
    ULONG       flWindowAttr;
    POINTL      ptlOrigin;
    ULONG       cDelta;
    ULONG       cRecords;
    SIZEL       slBitmapOrIcon;
    SIZEL       slTreeBitmapOrIcon;
    HBITMAP     hbmExpanded;
    HBITMAP     hbmCollapsed;
    HPOINTER    hptrExpanded;
    HPOINTER    hptrCollapsed;
    LONG        cyLineSpacing;
    LONG        cxTreeIndent;
    LONG        cxTreeLine;
    ULONG       cFields;
    LONG        xVertSplitbar;
} CNRINFO;
```

Figure 12.1   The CNRINFO structure.

```
SHORT EXPENTRY function( PRECORDCORE p1,
    PRECORDCORE p2, PVOID pStorage );
```

and returns a negative number if p1 is less than p2, zero if p1 equals p2, a positive number if p1 is greater than p2.

- Element *pFieldInfoLast* is a pointer to the FIELDINFO structure which describes the last column to be displayed in the left side of a split DETAIL view. By default, the value is NULL and the view is not split. This value is modified by setting the CMA_PFIELDINFOLAST (0x0010) flag in **mp2** of the CM_SETCNRINFO message.
- Element *pFieldInfoObject* is a pointer to the FIELDINFO structure which describes the column of the DETAIL view, which will show "in use" emphasis. The specified column must contain icon or bitmap data. By default, the leftmost column is used. Set the CMA_PFIELDINFOOBJECT (0x200) flag in **mp2** of the CM_SETCNRINFO message to modify this value.
- The *pszCnrTitle* element is a pointer to a zero-terminated array of characters to display as the container's title. If the value is NULL, no title is displayed. Set the CMA_CNRTITLE (0x0001) flag in **mp2** of the CM_SETCNRINFO message to modify this value.
- The *flWindowAttr* element is a set of flag bits that determine various attributes of the container including the view displayed, the type of graphic

displayed, and the appearance of the title. This value is modified by setting the CMA_FLWINDOWATTR (0x0004) flag in **mp2** of the CM_SETCNRINFO message. The valid attribute flags are listed here:

- CV_ICON (0x00000004) displays the container's ICON view. Records are depicted in rows of icons or bitmaps paired with text that is displayed below the graphical element.
- CV_NAME (0x00000002) displays the container's NAME view. Records are depicted as a column of icons or bitmaps paired with text that is displayed beside the graphic element. If the CV_FLOW flag is also set, the record representations are displayed in multiple columns.
- CV_TEXT (0x00000001) displays the container's TEXT view. Records are depicted as a column of text. If the CV_FLOW flag is also set, the record representations are displayed in multiple columns.
- CV_DETAIL (0x00000008) displays the container's DETAIL view. Each record is displayed as a single row of multicolumnar data. The content and format of the data displayed in the columns is defined by the FIELDINFO structures passed to the container.
- CV_MINI (0x00000020) is used with the ICON and NAME views to cause the graphical elements to be displayed in a normally smaller size, based on the SV_CYMENU system value. This flag is ignored if the CV_TREE attribute flag or the CCS_MINIRECORDCORE style bit is set.
- CV_FLOW (0x00000010) causes the NAME and TEXT views to be displayed as multiple columns. Normally, these views are displayed in a single column.
- CV_TREE (0x00000040) causes the ICON, NAME, and TEXT views to be displayed in a TREE format. In this format, the hierarchy of the records is displayed, with each level of the hierarchy indented by the value contained in the *cxTreeIndent* element of CNRINFO. Records at lower levels are only displayed when their parent record is expanded. Note that CV_TREE can be specified without the other view attributes. In this event, the ICON view is used. This flag cannot be used with the CV_MINI and CV_FLOW attributes.
- CA_DRAWICON (0x00040000) causes the container to use the *hptr* elements of the record for the graphic representation, and the *hptr* elements of CNRINFO for the TREE mode expand and collapse graphics.
- CA_DRAWBITMAP (0x00020000) causes the container to use the *hbm* elements of the record for the graphic representation, and the *hbm* elements of CNRINFO for the TREE mode expand and collapse graphics.
- CA_ORDEREDTARGETEMPH (0x00100000) causes the container to indicate that a drop is permitted by underlining a record's representation when in NAME, TEXT, or DETAIL view, indicating that a new drop may occur between records but not on a record. This attribute

might be used when a drop would insert a new record in a database, but could not be used to change the values in an existing record. If neither CA_ORDERTARGETEMPH nor CA_MIXEDTARGETEMPH is specified, then drops occur on records and would normally be expected to modify the contents of the records.

- CA_MIXEDTARGETEMPH (0x00200000) allows a drop to occur either on a record or between two records. The container draws a line between two objects when the drop would occur between the objects and draws a line around the object representation when the drop would occur on a data record. If neither CA_ORDERTARGET-EMPH nor CA_MIXEDTARGETEMPH is specified, then drops occur on records and would normally be expected to modify the contents of the records.
- CA_TREELINE (0x00400000) causes lines to be drawn showing the relationship between records in TREE view.
- CA_OWNERDRAW (0x00004000) indicates that the application will draw the container records. When a record requires painting, the container sends a WM_DRAWITEM message to the container window's owner.
- CA_OWNERPAINTBACKGROUND (0x00100000) indicates that the application is subclassing the container in order to paint the background. When set, the container sends a CM_PAINTBACKGROUND message to itself and thereby the subclass procedure.
- CA_CONTAINERTITLE (0x00000200) when set, indicates that the application is providing a title for the container.
- CA_TITLEREADONLY (0x00080000) causes the title of the container to be read-only. By default, the user can edit the container title.
- CA_TITLESEPARATOR (0x00000400) causes a line to be drawn separating the title and the representations of the container's records.
- CA_TITLECENTER (0x00002000) when set, causes the title to be horizontally centered in the container window.
- CA_TITLELEFT (0x00000800) when set, causes the title to be drawn at the left of the container.
- CA_TITLERIGHT (0x00001000) when set, causes the title to be drawn at the right of the container.
- CA_DETAILSVIEWTITLES (0x00008000) causes column headings to be displayed in DETAIL view.

- Element *ptlOrigin* is a POINTL structure that describes the origin location of the viewable area within the total area of the container when in ICON view. This value is modified when the CMA_PTLORIGIN (0x0040) flag is set in **mp2** of the CM_SETCNRINFO message.
- The *cDelta* element specifies a number of records from either end of the container's linked list of records. When either of the records at this delta position is scrolled into view in all but the ICON view, the container

sends a CN_QUERYDELTA notification, allowing the application to remove records at the opposite end of the list and then append additional records at the end near the delta record. This field is typically used when the total number of records to be displayed cannot reasonably be held in memory simultaneously. Pass the CMA_DELTA (0x0002) flag with the CM_SETCNR-INFO message to modify this value.

- Element *cRecords* is the number of records currently held in the container. This element is read-only and cannot be modified with the CM_SETCNRINFO message.

- Element *slBitmapOrIcon* is a SIZEL structure that specifies the size of the graphical elements used to represent the container's records. The structure contains the *cx* and *cy* delta values in pels. Set the CMA_SLBITMAPORICON (0x0080) flag in **mp2** of the CM_SETCNRINFO message to modify this value.

- The *slTreeBitmapOrIcon* element is a SIZEL structure that specifies the display size in pels of the expanded/collapsed graphical element in TREE mode. This value is modified by setting the CMA_SLTREEBITMAPORICON (0x4000) flag in **mp2** of the CM_SETCNRINFO message.

- Element *hbmExpanded* specifies the handle for a bitmap to be used to represent expanded items in TREE mode. The default if neither this element nor *hptrExpanded* is set is a bitmap minus sign. This value is modified by setting the CMA_TREEBITMAP (0x0800) flag in **mp2** of the CM_SETCNRINFO message.

- The *hbmCollapsed* element specifies the handle for a bitmap to be used to represent collapsed items in TREE mode. The default if neither this element nor *hptrCollapsed* is set is a bitmap plus sign. Set the CMA_TREEBITMAP (0x0800) flag in **mp2** of the CM_SETCNRINFO message to modify this value.

- Element *hptrExpanded* specifies the handle for the icon to be used to represent expanded items in TREE mode. The default if neither this element nor *hbmExpanded* is set is a bitmap minus sign. Set the CMA_TREEICON (0x0400) flag in **mp2** of the CM_SETCNRINFO message to modify this value.

- The *hptrCollapsed* element specifies the handle for the icon to be used to represent collapsed items in TREE mode. If neither this element nor *hbmCollapsed* is set, the default is a bitmap plus sign. Set the CMA_TREEICON (0x0400) flag in **mp2** of the CM_SETCNRINFO message to modify this value.

- The *cyLineSpacing* element specifies the number of pels used to vertically separate records. This value is modified by setting the CMA_LINESPACING (0x0008) flag in **mp2** of the CM_SETCNRINFO message.

- Element *cxTreeIndent* specifies the number of pels to indent each level of the TREE mode. This value is modified by setting the CMA_CXTREEINDENT (0x1000) flag in **mp2** of the CM_SETCNRINFO message.

- Element *cxTreeLine* specifies the width of the lines drawn to show the relationship between elements in TREE mode. Set the CMA_CXTREE-LINE (0x2000) flag in **mp2** of the CM_SETCNRINFO message to modify this value.
- The *cFields* element specifies the number of columns (FIELDINFO structures) displayed in DETAIL view. This element is read-only and cannot be modified with the CM_SETCNRINFO message.
- Element *xVertSplitBar* specifies the position of the vertical bar that separates the left and right windows in DETAIL view. Set the CMA_XVERT-SPLITBAR (0x0100) flag in **mp2** of the CM_SETCNRINFO message to modify this value.

Messages may be sent to the container to obtain the current CNRINFO structure contents and to modify the contents. The CM_QUERYCNRINFO message is used to obtain the current value of the structure elements. Parameter **mp1** of this message is a pointer to the location where the structure contents are to be stored. Parameter **mp2** indicates how many bytes of storage are reserved at this location. Normally, **mp2** is set to the size of the structure but may be less if the entire structure is not to be retrieved. The message returns the number of bytes copied to the buffer.

The CM_SETCNRINFO message is used to modify the contents of the container's internal copy of the structure. Parameter **mp1** of this message is a pointer to a CNRINFO structure containing the desired values. Parameter **mp2** is a set of flags that indicate which elements of the structure are to be modified.

Figure 12.2 provides sample code that causes the container to display the NAME view. The current structure is retrieved using the CM_QUERYCNR-INFO message. The *flWindowAttr* element is then modified by first clearing all the view flags and then setting the CV_NAME flag. The structure is copied back to the container with the CM_SETCNRINFO message. Parameter **mp2** is set to CMA_FLWINDOWATTR so that only the window attribute flags are modified.

RECORDCORE and MINIRECORDCORE

Data records added to the container must be composed of a core structure followed by optional application-defined data. The core structures define the

```
WinSendMsg( hwndCnr, CM_QUERYCNRINFO,
          MPFROMP(&cnrInfo), MPFROMLONG(sizeof(CNRINFO)));
cnrInfo.flWindowAttr &= ~(CV_ICON | CV_NAME | CV_TEXT | CV_DETAIL);
cnrInfo.flWindowAttr |= CV_NAME;
WinSendMsg( hwndCnr, CM_SETCNRINFO,
          MPFROMP(&cnrInfo), MPFROMLONG(CMA_FLWINDOWATTR));
```

Figure 12.2   Modifying CNRINFO.

information required to represent the records in all but the DETAIL view. Depending on the application requirements, the structure used for the core portion of the data record may be either a RECORDCORE structure or a MINIRECORDCORE structure.

The RECORDCORE structure allows the application to vary the representation of the data record in the various views. The structure allows both normal and MINI mode icons and bitmaps to be defined and provides for different text in each of the ICON, NAME, and TEXT views. The MINIRECORDCORE structure is a subset of the RECORDCORE structure. When this structure is used, the graphic representation of the data record is limited to a normal size icon and the same text is used in ICON, NAME, and TEXT views. Both structures define a set of record attribute flags and the position of the record's representation in ICON view. The container determines which structure is in use based on the setting of the CCS_MINIRECORDCORE style flag. The MINIRECORD-CORE structure is normally used when the flexibility of the RECORDCORE structure is not required and/or memory usage is a significant consideration. The RECORDCORE structure is defined as shown in Figure 12.3.

- The *cb* element is the size of the structure in bytes, including any data appended by the application. This value is supplied by the container control when the record is allocated and should not be modified by the application.
- The *flRecordAttr* element is a set of flag bits which specify various attributes for the individual record such as whether the record is selected. The valid flags are listed here:

CRA_SELECTED   (0x00000001)   indicates that selected state emphasis is applied to the record.

CRA_TARGET   (0x00000002)   indicates that target emphasis is applied to the record.

```
typedef struct _RECORDCORE
{
    ULONG               cb;
    ULONG               flRecordAttr;
    POINTL              ptlIcon;
    struct _RECORDCORE  *preccNextRecord;
    PSZ                 pszIcon;
    HPOINTER            hptrIcon;
    HPOINTER            hptrMiniIcon;
    HBITMAP             hbmBitmap;
    HBITMAP             hbmMiniBitmap;
    PTREEITEMDESC       pTreeItemDesc;
    PSZ                 pszText;
    PSZ                 pszName;
    PSZ                 pszTree;
} RECORDCORE;
```

Figure 12.3   **The RECORDCORE structure.**

CRA_CURSORED	(0x00000004)	indicates that the keyboard cursor emphasis is applied to the record.
CRA_INUSE	(0x00000008)	indicates that in-use emphasis is applied to the record.
CRA_FILTERED	(0x00000010)	indicates that the record is filtered and therefore not displayed.
CRA_DROPONABLE	(0x00000020)	indicates that the record may be the target of a direct manipulation operation.
CRA_RECORDREADONLY	(0x00000040)	indicates that the record text may not be edited.
CRA_EXPANDED	(0x00000080)	indicates, in tree mode, that the children of the record are displayed.
CRA_COLLAPSED	(0x00000100)	indicates, in tree mode, that the children of the record are hidden.
CRA_PICKED	(0x00000200)	indicates that picked emphasis is applied to the record.
CRA_SOURCE	(0x00004000)	indicates that source menu emphasis is applied to the record.
CRA_DISABLED	(0x00001000)	indicates that disabled emphasis is applied to the record.

- The *ptlIcon* element is a POINTL structure that contains the coordinates at which the representation of the record is displayed in ICON view. The location can be specified by the application or supplied by the container when an arrange operation occurs.
- The *preccNextRecord* element is a pointer to the next record in a linked list of records and is normally used by the application to access the next record when multiple records are allocated with one CM_ALLOCRECORD message.
- Element *pszIcon* is a pointer to a null-terminated array of characters, which are displayed beneath the icon that represents the record when the container is in ICON view.
- Element *hptrIcon* is a pointer handle that specifies the icon to be displayed for this record in the ICON and NAME views when the CA_DRAWICON flag is set in element *flWindowAttr* of the CNRINFO structure.
- The *hptrMiniIcon* element is a pointer handle that specifies the icon to be displayed for this record in the ICON and NAME views when the CA_DRAWICON and CV_MINI flags are set in the *flWindowAttr* element of the CNRINFO structure.
- Element *hbmBitmap* is a bitmap handle that specifies the bitmap to be displayed for this record in the ICON and NAME views when the CA_DRAWBITMAP flag is set in the *flWindowAttr* element of the CNRINFO structure.

- The *hbmMiniBitmap* element is a bitmap handle that specifies the bitmap to be displayed for this record in the ICON and NAME views when the CA_DRAWBITMAP and CV_MINI flags are set in element *flWindowAttr* of the CNRINFO structure.
- The *pTreeItemDesc* element is a pointer to a TREEITEMDESC structure that is used when the container displays the NAME view in TREE mode. The elements of this structure specify the icons and bitmaps displayed to indicate when a record is in expanded or collapsed mode. The icons specifications are used when the container is in ICON mode, and the bitmaps are used when the container is in BITMAP mode. If this element is NULL, the bitmap or icon normally used for records is used for parent as well as child records.
- Element *pszText* is a pointer to a null-terminated array of characters that are used to represent the record in TEXT view.
- The *pszName* element is a pointer to a null-terminated array of characters that are displayed beside the graphical representation of the record in NAME view.
- The *pszTree* element is a pointer to a null-terminated array of characters that are displayed beside the graphical representation of the record in TREE mode.

The TREEITEMDESC structure pointed to by element *pTreeItemDesc* is defined in Figure 12.4.

- Element *hbmExpanded* is the handle for the bitmap used to represent a parent record when its children are displayed and the container's CV_DRAWBITMAP window attribute flag is set.
- Element *hbmCollapsed* is the handle for the bitmap used to represent a parent record when its children are not displayed and the container's CV_DRAWBITMAP window attribute flag is set.
- Element *hptrExpanded* is the handle for the icon used to represent a parent record when its children are displayed and the container's CV_DRAWICON window attribute flag is set.
- Element *hptrCollapsed* is the handle for the icon used to represent a parent record when its children are not displayed and the container's CV_DRAWICON window attribute flag is set.

```
typedef struct _TREEITEMDESC
{
   HBITMAP      hbmExpanded;
   HBITMAP      hbmCollapsed;
   HPOINTER     hptrExpanded;
   HPOINTER     hptrCollapsed;
} TREEITEMDESC;
```

Figure 12.4 The TREEITEMDESC structure.

```
typedef struct _MINIRECORDCORE
{
    ULONG                    cb;
    ULONG                    flRecordAttr;
    POINTL                   ptlIcon;
    struct _MINIRECORDCORE *preccNextRecord;
    PSZ                      pszIcon;
    HPOINTER                 hptrIcon;
} MINIRECORDCORE;
```

Figure 12.5   The MINIRECORDCODE structure.

The definition of the alternate core record, the MINIRECORDCORE structure, is shown in Figure 12.5.

- The *cb* element indicates the length of the structure in bytes. This value is set by the container and should not be modified by the application.
- The *flRecordAttr* element is a set of flag bits specifying various attributes of the record. See the description of this element under the RECORDCORE structure for details.
- Element *ptlIcon* is a POINTL structure that contains the coordinates at which the representation of the record is displayed in ICON view.
- The *preccNextRecord* element is a pointer to the next record in a linked list of records.
- Element *pszIcon* is a pointer to a null-terminated array of characters used as the text for the record representation in the ICON, NAME, and TEXT views.
- Element *hptrIcon* is a pointer handle for the icon used to represent the record in the ICON and NAME views.

The core records must be allocated by the container on behalf of the application. This is accomplished by sending a CM_ALLOCRECORD message to the container. Parameter **mp1** of this message indicates the number of bytes of application data to allocate for each record. Parameter **mp2** indicates the number of records to allocate. The return value from the message is a pointer to the allocated record or to the first record in a linked list of records if multiple records were requested. This pointer is NULL if an error occurred.

After the records are allocated, the application must fill in the data and then add the record to the container by sending either CM_INSERTRECORD or CM_INSERTRECORDARRAY messages to the container. The CM_INSERTRECORD message inserts a linked list of records while the CM_INSERTRECORDARRAY message uses an array of pointers to records. Parameter **mp1** of the CM_INSERTRECORD message is a pointer to the first or only record in the linked list. Additional records are accessed via the *preccNextRecord* element of the core structure. Parameter **mp1** of the CM_INSERTRECORD-ARRAY message is a pointer to an array in which each element is a pointer to a record structure to be inserted. The **mp2** parameter of both messages is a pointer to a RECORDINSERT structure, which describes the relationship of the new records to records that may already exist in the container. The definition of this structure is given in Figure 12.6.

- Element *cb* is the length of the structure in bytes and should be set to sizeof(RECORDINSERT).
- The *pRecordOrder* element specifies the placement of the records within the container's linked list of records. If this element is set to a pointer to a record currently in the container's list, the new records are inserted following this record. Setting this element to CMA_FIRST causes the record(s) to be inserted at the beginning of the list of children of the record specified by *pRecordParent*, or at the beginning of the container's list if *pRecordParent* is set to NULL. Likewise, when this element is given the value CMA_END, the record or list of records is inserted at the end of the children of *pRecordParent* or at the end of the container's list. **CAUTION:** Do not confuse CMA_END and CMA_LAST—if this element is set to CMA_LAST, your application will not receive an error message; a trap will occur.
- Element *pRecordParent* specifies the parent record of the records to be inserted. This field is only valid when *pRecordOrder* is set to CMA_FIRST or CMA_END. This field is used to establish the record hierarchy for TREE mode. Records inserted as children will not be visible if TREE mode is not selected.
- Element *fInvalidateRecord* is used to indicate whether the container is updated after the record or list of records is inserted. When set to TRUE, the container display is automatically updated when the records are inserted. When set to FALSE, the application must explicitly inform the container to perform the update with the CM_INVALIDATE message.
- The *zOrder* element specifies the record's z-order position with respect to records already inserted into the container. The value CMA_TOP places the

```
typedef struct _RECORDINSERT
{
    ULONG       cb;
    PRECORDCORE pRecordOrder;
    PRECORDCORE pRecordParent;
    ULONG       fInvalidateRecord;
    ULONG       zOrder;
    ULONG       cRecordsInsert;
} RECORDINSERT;
```

Figure 12.6   The RECORDINSERT structure.

record(s) at the top of the z-order, and the value CMA_BOTTOM places the record(s) at the bottom of the z-order.

- Element *cRecordsInsert* specifies the number of records pointed to by the **mp1** parameter.

Figure 12.7 shows a sample for inserting a container record. In this sample, the icons used to represent records are declared as global variables. The TREEITEMDESC structure is also a preinitialized global variable. The parent record and the text to be associated with the new record are supplied by the application.

The function first initializes the *cb* element of the RECORDINSERT structure and determines the length of the text supplied by the application. The CM_ALLOCRECORD message is then sent to obtain the record buffer from the container. Parameter **mp1** is passed as the length of the text in order to obtain enough extra storage to maintain the text in the record. This memory could be allocated independently; however, using this method allows the container to completely manage the storage and does not require additional memory

```
TREEITEMDESC    tid;

PRECORDCORE AddCnrRecord( HWND hwndCnr, PSZ pszText, PRECORDCORE pPRec )
{
    PRECORDCORE     pRec;
    RECORDINSERT    ri;
    ULONG           cbText;

    ri.cb = sizeof( RECORDINSERT );
    cbText = strlen(pszText) + 1;
    pRec = WinSendMsg( hwndCnr, CM_ALLOCRECORD,
                    MPFROMLONG(cbText), MPFROMLONG(1L));
    pRec->pszIcon = (PSZ)(pRec + 1);
    strcpy(pRec->pszIcon, pszText );
    pRec->hptrIcon = hptrIcon;
    pRec->hptrMiniIcon = hptrMiniIcon;
    pRec->pTreeItemDesc = &tid;
    pRec->pszText = pRec->pszName = pRec->pszTree = pRec->pszIcon;
    ri.pRecordOrder = (PRECORDCORE)CMA_END;
    ri.pRecordParent = pPRec;
    ri.fInvalidateRecord = TRUE;
    ri.zOrder = CMA_TOP;
    ri.cRecordsInsert = 1;

    WinSendMsg( hwndCnr, CM_INSERTRECORD, MPFROMP(pRec), MPFROMP(&ri));
    return pRec;
}
```

Figure 12.7   Adding records to a container.

management code in the application. Note that items to which the container record points should be either global or allocated, not a stack variable. The container does not maintain an internal copy of the data but uses the pointer to reference the data.

After allocation, the record structure is initialized. The *pszIcon* element is set to point to the text string that is copied into the record buffer. The *hptrIcon* and *hptrMiniIcon* elements are copied from the appropriate global variables, and the *pTreeItemDesc* element is set to point to the global tree item description structure. The remaining text elements are then set to point to the text string stored in the record buffer.

The RECORDINSERT structure is then initialized. The *pRecordOrder* element is set to CMA_END, forcing the record to the end of its parent's children or to the end of the container. The *pRecordParent* element is set to the parent record pointer provided by the application. Element *fInvalidateRecord* is set to TRUE to cause a repaint after the record is inserted, allowing the user to see the progress of the container being filled. The setting of this element during initial loading will depend on the application. In some instances, repainting will cause significant performance degradation and should be postponed until after the container is completely filled. The *zOrder* element is set to place the new record at the top of the z-order, and *cRecordsInsert* is set to the number of records being inserted—one. A CM_INSERTRECORD message is then sent to the container to add the record into the container's contents. The pointer to the record is then returned to the application.

The CM_REMOVERECORD message is used to delete a record from the container's list. Parameter **mp1** is a pointer to an array of pointers to one or more record structures to remove from the container's list of records. If a parent record is specified in the array, its children are also removed. Parameter **mp2** is composed of two 16-bit values. The low-order 16 bits specify the number of elements in the array pointed to by **mp1**; in other words, the number of records to be removed. If this value is set to zero, parameter **mp1** is ignored and all records are removed. The high-order 16 bits contain the following two flags:

CMA_FREE	0x0001	causes the records to be free after removal.
CMA_INVALIDATE	0x0002	causes the container to be redrawn after the operation.

If the CMA_FREE flag is not set when records are removed from the container, the message CM_FREERECORD must be sent to the container to deallocate the memory associated with the records. Parameter **mp1** is a pointer to an array of pointers to the records that are to be freed. The low-order 16 bits of **mp2** contain the number of records to be deallocated. NOTE: The application is responsible for deallocating memory that is referenced by pointers in the record structure.

FIELDINFO

The FIELDINFO structure is only required when the application displays the container's DETAIL view. The structure describes the content and format of the data displayed in each column. The definition of this structure is shown in Figure 12.8.

- Element *cb* specifies the length of the structure in bytes. This element is filled by the container and should not be modified by the application.
- The *flData* element is a set of flags that specify attributes to be applied to the column data. The valid flags are listed here:
  - CFA_BITMAPORICON specifies that the data in the column is a bitmap or an icon.
  - CFA_STRING specifies that the column data is a pointer to a zero-terminated array of characters.
  - CFA_ULONG specifies that the column data is an unsigned long integer.
  - CFA_DATE specifies that the column data is a date in the form of a CDATE structure.
  - CFA_TIME specifies that the column data is a time in the form of a CTIME structure.
  - CFA_HORZSEPARATOR, if set, indicates that a line is drawn between the column heading and the column data.
  - CFA_SEPARATOR, if set, indicates that this column and the next should be separated by a vertical line.
  - CFA_OWNER, if set, specifies that the data is OWNERDRAWN. A WM_DRAWITEM message is sent to the owner whenever the column data requires repainting.
  - CFA_INVISIBLE, if set, specifies that the column is hidden.
  - CFA_READONLY indicates that the column data cannot be edited. This flag is only used if the CFA_STRING flag is set. Other data types are read-only by definition.

```
typedef struct _FIELDINFO
{
    ULONG              cb;
    ULONG              flData;
    ULONG              flTitle;
    PVOID              pTitleData;
    ULONG              offStruct;
    PVOID              pUserData;
    struct _FIELDINFO  *pNextFieldInfo;
    ULONG              cxWidth;
} FIELDINFO;
```

Figure 12.8   The FIELDINFO structure.

- CFA_TOP indicates that the column data is drawn at the top of the vertical area reserved for displaying the data record.
- CFA_BOTTOM indicates that the column data is drawn at the bottom of the vertical area reserved for displaying the data record.
- CFA_VCENTER indicates that the column data is drawn in the center of the vertical area reserved for displaying the data record.
- CFA_CENTER indicates that the column data is drawn in the center of the horizontal area reserved for the column data.
- CFA_LEFT indicates that the column data is drawn at the left of the area reserved for displaying the column data.
- CFA_RIGHT indicates that the column data is drawn at the right of the area reserved for displaying the column data.
- The *flTitle* element is a set of flags that specify attributes to be applied to the title for the column. The valid flags are listed here:
  - CFA_BITMAPORICON specifies that the title is a bitmap or an icon.
  - CFA_TITLEREADONLY indicates that the title data cannot be edited.
  - CFA_TOP indicates that the title is drawn at the top of the vertical area reserved for displaying the column titles.
  - CFA_BOTTOM indicates that the title is drawn at the bottom of the vertical area reserved for displaying the column titles.
  - CFA_VCENTER indicates that the title is drawn in the center of the vertical area reserved for displaying the column titles.
  - CFA_CENTER indicates that the title is drawn in the center of the horizontal area reserved for the column.
  - CFA_LEFT indicates that the title is drawn at the left of the area reserved for displaying the column.
  - CFA_RIGHT indicates that the title data is drawn at the right of the area reserved for displaying the column.
- The *pTitleData* element contains the data to be displayed in the title area of the column. If the CFA_BITMAPORICON flag is set in *flTitle*, then this element should contain a handle to a bitmap if the CA_DRAWBITMAP flag is set in the *flWindowAttr* element of the CNRINFO structure, or a handle to an icon if the CA_DRAWICON flag is set in the *flWindowAttr* element of the CNRINFO structure. If CFA_BITMAPORICON is not set, this element should contain a pointer to a null-terminated string to be displayed as the column heading.
- Element *offStruct* specifies the offset into the data record at which the data may be found. The offset may be within the RECORDCORE or MINIRECORDCORE structure of the data record or within the application-defined area appended to the core structures.
- Element *pUserData* is a 4-byte data area reserved for use by the application.
- The *pNextFieldInfo* element is a pointer to the next FIELDINFO structure in a linked list of structures.

- The *cxWidth* element specifies the width of the column. If this field is set to zero, the column dynamically changes size to match the width of the widest data.

As with the RECORDCORE structures, several messages are provided for the application to allocate and manage FIELDINFO structures. The CM_ALLOCDETAILFIELDINFO message is used to allocate FIELDINFO structures. CM_INSERTDETAILFIELDINFO is used to place FIELDINFO structures into the container's active list. Message CM_REMOVEDETAIL-FIELDINFO is used to remove structures from the container's active list, and CM_FREEDETAILFIELDINFO is used to deallocate FIELDINFO structures. CM_INVALIDATEFIELDINFO is used to repaint the container view when a FIELDINFO structure has been inserted, modified, or removed; and CM_QUERYDETAILFIELDINFO is used to scan the container's list of active FIELDINFO structures.

Message CM_ALLOCDETAILFIELDINFO is sent to the container to allocate a list of one or more FIELDINFO structures. The low-order 16 bits of parameter **mp1** should contain an unsigned integer indicating the number of FIELDINFO structures to be allocated. Parameter **mp2** is reserved and should be set to zero. The container's response to the message is either zero, indicating that an error occurred, or a pointer to the first FIELDINFO structure in the list of allocated structures. The additional structures are linked via the *pNextFieldInfo* element of the structure.

Once the application has allocated and filled the FIELDINFO structure(s), message CM_INSERTDETAILFIELDINFO is sent to the container to add the structure(s) to the container's active list. Parameter **mp1** is a pointer to the FIELDINFO structure to be inserted or to the first in a list of FIELDINFO structures when more than one is being inserted. Parameter **mp2** is a pointer to a FIELDINFOINSERT structure that describes where the insertion is to occur. The elements of this structure are given in Figure 12.9.

- The *cb* element specifies the length of the structure in bytes.
- Element *pFieldInfoOrder* specifies where the insertion occurs. Setting this field to CMA_FIRST causes the structure(s) to be inserted at the beginning

```
typedef struct _FIELDINFOINSERT
{
    ULONG       cb;
    PFIELDINFO  pFieldInfoOrder;
    ULONG       fInvalidateFieldInfo;
    ULONG       cFieldInfoInsert;
} FIELDINFOINSERT;
```

Figure 12.9 The FIELDINFOINSERT structure.

of the container's list of FIELDINFO structures so that the columns are displayed at the left of the container. If this element is set to CMA_END, the structure(s) is/are inserted at the end of the container's list and the columns are displayed at the right of the container. When this element is filled with a pointer to a FIELDINFO structure that is currently in the container's list, the new structure(s) is/are inserted into the list following this structure.

- The *fInvalidateFieldInfo* is a flag that, when set to TRUE, causes the container to be refreshed following the insertion. If this flag is set to FALSE, then the CM_INVALIDATEDETAILFIELDINFO message must be sent to the container to force the refresh and display the new columns.
- Element *cFieldInfoInsert* is a 32-bit unsigned integer that specifies the number of structures in the list to which parameter **mp1** points.

Figure 12.10 is an example of the code required to allocate and insert a FIELDINFO structure into the container's active list. As the example shows, filling the FIELDINFO structures can be—and usually is—a tedious process since most of the effort involves assigning constant values to the various elements of the structure. The programming burden can be eased somewhat by predefining FIELDINFO structures in the application's data area and then copying the predefined structures into those allocated by the container. Be careful when using this method to preserve the *cb* and *pNextFieldInfo* elements of the structures provided by the container.

Message CM_REMOVEDETAILFIELDINFO is sent to the container to remove FIELDINFO structures from the container's active list. The **mp1** parameter for this message is a pointer to an array of one or more pointers to FIELDINFO structures to be removed. Parameter **mp2** is composed of two 16-bit fields. The low-order 16 bits are an unsigned integer identifying the number of pointers in the array pointed to by **mp1**. If set to zero, all FIELD-INFO structures are removed from the container's list and parameter **mp1** is ignored. The high-order 16 bits contain two flags that affect the removal process; flag CMA_FREE causes the FIELDINFO structures to be freed after they are removed; flag CMA_INVALIDATE causes the container to refreshed following the remove operation. The container's response to this message is the number of structures actually removed from the list. If the response is zero, then an error occurred and no structures were removed.

The CM_FREEDETAILFIELDINFO tells the container to deallocate one or more FIELDINFO structures. Parameter **mp1** is a pointer to an array of pointers to the FIELDINFO structures to be deallocated. Parameter **mp2** is the number of structures that are to be deallocated. Note that if a structure still resides in the container's active list, an error response is returned and the structure is not deallocated. The container's response to this message is the number of structures that were deallocated, or zero if an error occurred.

```
typedef struct {
    RECORDCORE    core;
    struct {
        char    *psz;
    } data;
} APP_REC;
void AddColumn( ) {
    PFIELDINFO         pFieldInfo = NULL;
    PFIELDINFO         pField = NULL;
    PFIELDINFO         pFieldNext;
    FIELDINFOINSERT    fii;

    pFieldInfo = WinSendMsg( hwndCnr, CM_ALLOCDETAILFIELDINFO,
                        MPFROMSHORT( N_FIELDS ),
                        MPFROMLONG( 01 ));
    if (pFieldInfo != (PFIELDINFO)NULL) {
        pField = pFieldInfo;
        pField->flData = CFA_STRING | CFA_HORZSEPARATOR | CFA_SEPARATOR;
        pField->flTitle = CFA_FITITLEREADONLY;
        pField->pTitleData = "Column 1";
        pField->offStruct = (ULONG)FIELDOFFSET( APP_REC, data.psz );
        pField->cxWidth = 0;

        pField = pField->pNextFieldInfo;
        fii.cb = sizeof( FIELDINFOINSERT );
        fii.pFieldInfoOrder = (PFIELDINFO)CMA_FIRST;
        fii.fInvalidateFieldInfo = TRUE;
        fii.cFieldInfoInsert = N_FIELDS;

        WinSendMsg( hwndCnr, CM_INSERTDETAILFIELDINFO, pFieldInfo, &fii );
    } /* endif */
}
```

Figure 12.10 Defining detail view columns.

Message CM_INVALIDATEDETAILFIELDINFO causes the container to be refreshed. Both **mp1** and **mp2** should be set to zero when this message is sent. While CM_INVALIDATEDETAILFIELDINFO is normally sent when a FIELDINFO structure is inserted, removed, or modified, it may be sent at any time to force a refresh of the container's display.

The application uses the CM_QUERYDETAILFIELDINFO to traverse the container's linked list. Parameter **mp1** is a pointer to a FIELDINFO structure. Parameter **mp2** is a value that specifies the traversal action to perform. Valid values for **mp2** are:

CMA_FIRST   0x0010   returns a pointer to the first FIELDINFO structure in the container's list. **mp1** is ignored.

CMA_LAST   0x0020   returns a pointer to the last FIELDINFO structure in the container's list. **mp1** is ignored.

CMA_NEXT   0x0100   returns a pointer to the FIELDINFO structure following the FIELD-INFO structure pointed to by **mp1**.

CMA_PREV   0x0080   returns a pointer to the FIELDINFO structure preceding the FIELDINFO structure pointed to by **mp1**.

The container's response to this message is a pointer to a FIELDINFO structure if no errors occurred, a NULL pointer if no structure was available (for example, when specifying a pointer to the last structure in the list and CMA_NEXT), or a negative one (0xffffffff) if an error occurred.

CREATING CONTAINERS

As usual, the container control may be included as an item in a dialog template. The control may also be created using the **WinCreateWindow** API. In either case, the only control-specific information required is the setting of the window style. The container control defines the following styles:

CCS_AUTOPOSITION   0x0008   specifies that objects displayed in the ICON view will be automatically positioned by the container when required; for example, when objects are inserted or deleted or when the size of the window changes. If this attribute is not set, the application must provide the positioning either by setting the *ptlIcon* element of the record structure or by issuing the CM_ARRANGE message.

CCS_MINIRECORDCORE   0x0040   specifies that objects added to the container are represented with the MINIRECORDCORE structure rather than the RECORDCORE structure.

CCS_READONLY   0x0020   specifies that none of the text fields in the container may be edited. Additional field-specific flags are available to specify read-only status for the individual parts of the container. These are contained in the various field-specific structures.

CCS_VERIFYPOINTERS   0x0010   specifies that the container should check all pointers provided by the application to ensure that they have been added to the container's internal linked list. This attribute should normally be used only during development and then removed from the final product.

CCS_SINGLESEL	0x0004	forces one and only one container object to be selected. This is the default value if none of the selection attributes is explicitly set.
CCS_EXTENDEDSEL	0x0001	forces at least one container object to be selected, but allows multiple objects to be selected.
CCS_MULTIPLESEL	0x0002	allows no objects or multiple objects to be selected.

While an initialized CNRINFO structure may be passed as a parameter when creating a container control, the normal practice is to pass a NULL pointer, allowing the container to establish default values, and then modify specific elements using the procedures outlined earlier in the section dealing with the CNRINFO data structure.

Figure 12.11 shows how an application might create the container control and then modify the CNRINFO structure to display bitmaps, the NAME view, and a title. **WinCreateWindow** is called to create a window of class WC_CONTAINER. Since this window does not support window text, the **pszName** parameter is set to NULL. The **flStyle** parameter indicates that the control will be visible and will automatically handle positioning of the data record representation in ICON view. After the window has been created, CM_QUERYCNRINFO is sent to obtain the default CNRINFO structure. The *flWindowAttr* element is masked to remove the undesired view attributes and the CA_DRAWICON attribute. Attributes for displaying NAME view, bitmaps, and a title are then set. The *pszCnrTitle* element is set to point to the text to display as the container title. Note that like pointers in the data records, the text

```
hwndCnr = WinCreateWindow( hwnd,
                           WC_CONTAINER,
                           NULL,
                           CCS_AUTOPOSITION | WS_VISIBLE
                           x, y, cx, cy,
                           hwnd,
                           HWND_TOP,
                           CID_REGISTER,
                           NULL,
                           NULL );
WinSendMsg( hwndCnr, CM_QUERYCNRINFO,
            MPFROMP(&cnrInfo), MPFROMLONG(sizeof(CNRINFO)));
cnrInfo.flWindowAttr &= ~(CV_ICON | CV_TEXT | CV_DETAIL);
cnrInfo.flWindowAttr &= ~CA_DRAWICON;
cnrInfo.flWindowAttr |= CV_NAME | CA_DRAWBITMAP | CA_CONTAINERTITLE;
cnrInfo.pszCnrTitle = "Title Text";
WinSendMsg( hwndCnr, CM_SETCNRINFO,
            MPFROMP(&cnrInfo), MPFROMLONG(CMA_FLWINDOWATTR));
```

Figure 12.11 Creating a container control.

pointed to by *pszCnrTitle*, should be in a constant area like allocated memory, a global variable, or a constant. The CNRINFO structure is then passed back to the container with the CM_SETCNRINFO message with parameter **mp2** set to update the internal copy of the *flWindowAttr* element and the pointer for the title text.

LOADING CONTAINER DATA

After creating the container, the application will normally fill the container with data records. Figure 12.7 showed a basic function for allocating and inserting data records that is completely adequate for many applications. When designing the portion of the application that utilizes this code, the programmer should be aware of the time required to load the container. In most instances, the data for the records must be read from a file or other device and then inserted into the container. In cases of even a few records, this type of operation will normally require more time than allowed for processing a single message. The programmer should consider the methods described in Chapter 6 and/or posting a message to the application window for loading each container record. This will allow the system to remain responsive even when loading large numbers of records. If the application uses the DETAIL view, the FIELDINFO structures must also be inserted into the container. The code required for this function was shown in Figure 12.10.

PROCESSING USER INPUT

Once the container has been created and loaded with data, the application must respond to the user's interactions with the control. These interactions include selecting records, editing text, requesting menus, expanding and collapsing parent items in TREE mode, scrolling, and direct manipulation. This section will examine how the application is notified of these interactions and some typical responses.

Record Emphasis

Emphasis is the graphical effect that the container uses to indicate the state of a particular record to the user. The container provides emphasis for many states of the record; for example, the change of graphic that occurs when a record is expanded or collapsed in TREE mode is a form of emphasis, as are the borders and underlines that accompany an object being dragged over container items. Emphasis is also available to show when an object has been added to a direct manipulation pickup set, when an object is in use, or when an object is affected by a popup menu. The container also automatically provides emphasis to indicate which record or records have been selected and which record is the current target of keyboard interaction.

Except for changes in the direct manipulation and expanded/collapsed emphasis, the container sends a WM_CONTROL message with the CN_EMPHASIS notification whenever a record's emphasis changes. Applications normally use this message to handle any processing required when a record is selected or when the keyboard cursor moves to a different record, though processing can also be included for other types of emphasis. Parameter **mp2** of the message is a pointer to a NOTIFYRECORDEMPHASIS structure that indicates the record and type or types of emphasis that changed. This structure is defined in Figure 12.12.

- Element *hwndCnr* is the handle of the container window sending the message.
- The *pRecord* element is a pointer to the record whose emphasis has changed.
- The *fEmphasisMask* element contains flags that indicate which emphasis attributes have changed. The defined flags are:

CRA_CURSORED   (0x0004)   changes when a record gains or loses the keyboard focus.

CRA_SELECTED   (0x0001)   changes when a record is selected or deselected.

CRA_INUSE   (0x0008)   changes when the application modifies the in-use emphasis, typically when processing of a record begins or ends.

CRA_SOURCE   (0x4000)   changes when the application modifies the source emphasis, typically when a popup menu is displayed or hidden.

CRA_PICKED   (0x0200)   changes when the application modifies the picked-up emphasis, typically in response to a WM_PICKUP message or when a pickup-and-drop operation is completed or cancelled.

Note that the *fEmphasisMask* settings indicate which emphasis attributes have changed, not the current state of the attribute. The attribute state must be examined via the *flRecordAttr* element of the record. To ensure that the current attributes are reflected in this element when records have been inserted into

```
typedef struct _NOTIFYRECORDEMPHASIS
{
    HWND        hwndCnr;
    PRECORDCORE pRecord;
    ULONG       fEmphasisMask;
} NOTIFYRECORDEMPHASIS;
```

Figure 12.12   **NOTIFYRECORDEMPHASIS structure.**

```
case CN_EMPHASIS:
  {
    PNOTIFYRECORDEMPHASIS   pEmphasis = (PNOTIFYRECORDEMPHASIS)mp2;

    WinSendMsg( pEmphasis->hwndCnr, CM_QUERYRECORDINFO,
            MPFROMP(&(pEmphasis->pRecord)), MPFROMSHORT(1));
    /* If this record is selected - save it */
    if (pEmphasis->fEmphasisMask & CRA_SELECTED  &&
        pEmphasis->pRecord->flRecordAttr & CRA_SELECTED) {
      WinSetWindowPtr( hwnd,WP_SELRECORD,(PVOID)(pEmphasis->pRecord) );
    } /* endif */
  }
  break;
```

Figure 12.13   CN_EMPHASIS processing.

multiple containers, the application must send a CN_QUERYRECORDINFO message to the container window to allow it to update the state of the record accessible by the application. Parameter **mp1** of this message is a pointer to an array of pointers to records, and the low-order 16 bits of parameter **mp2** indicate the number of records in the array. Figure 12.13 shows how an application might process the CN_EMPHASIS notification to handle changes in the selection state.

This figure shows the case statement for the CN_EMPHASIS notification code of the WM_CONTROL message. A pointer to the NOTIFYRECORDEMPHASIS structure is obtained from the message's **mp2** parameter. Then the record attributes are updated with the CM_QUERYRECORDINFO message. Parameter **mp1** of this message is set to a pointer to the pointer to the record in the NOTIFYRECORDEMPHASIS structure to simulate a pointer to an array of pointers. After the record has been updated, *fEmphasisMask* is checked to see if the selection state has changed, and *flRecordAttr* is checked to see if the state has been set. If so, a pointer to the record is stored in the instance data for the container's owner window. Note from this example that the application always has access to the record data once it has been allocated. Inserting the record into a container does not remove the application's access to the data. Changes in the other emphasis states may be processed in the same manner.

The application may also defer its processing of the emphasis states until some other event such as an OK button click occurs. The application can then determine which record or records is set to a particular state by sending a CM_QUERYRECORDEMPHASIS message to the container. This message causes the container to scan its records until a record with the desired emphasis has been found. Parameter **mp1** of the message is a pointer to the record after which the search is to begin. This parameter may be set to CMA_FIRST to begin the search with the first record in the container. Parameter **mp2** is a set of flags that indicate the emphasis state or states that constitute a match.

The return value from the message is NULL if no records satisfy the search criteria, or a pointer to the next record in the container that does match the criteria, or (0xffffffff) if an error occurred.

While the container is generally allowed to automatically handle the selection and keyboard cursor attributes, the in-use, source, and picked attributes must be established by the application. These emphasis attributes are changed by sending a CM_SETRECORDEMPHASIS message to the container. Parameter **mp1** of this message is a pointer to the record whose emphasis attributes are to be changed. The low-order 16 bits of parameter **mp2** are set to TRUE if the attributes are to be set or to FALSE if the attributes are to be cleared. The high-order 16 bits of **mp2** indicate which attribute to modify. An example that manages the CMA_SOURCE attribute is shown in the upcoming section on processing context menus.

Field Editing

Another important feature of the container control is the user's ability to edit text fields displayed within the container. However, this capability relies on the application to process the edited data; if the application does not update the data pointed to by the record, then no modification occurs. In order to accomplish useful editing, the application must respond to three notification messages from the container.

Message CN_BEGINEDIT informs the application that the user has started to edit a field. When this message is received, the application should no longer send any message to the container window until a CN_ENDEDIT message has been received. Receipt of any other messages may cause unpredictable results. Parameter **mp2** of the CN_BEGINEDIT message is a pointer to a CNREDITDATA structure.

The CN_REALLOCPSZ notification message is sent to the application when the edit operation has been completed, but before the text has been copied back to the memory area pointed to by the RECORDCORE structure. This message allows the application to allocate sufficient space to hold the edited version of the text and modify the pointer in the record if necessary. Again, a pointer to a CNREDITDATA structure is passed to the application as parameter **mp2** of the message.

The CN_ENDEDIT notification indicates that direct editing of the container text has ended and that the application can once again send messages to the container. Parameter **mp2** is once again a pointer to a CNREDITDATA structure.

Container text editing is normally triggered by a user mouse click, but the application can also programmatically control the editing feature. The application starts an edit operation by sending a CM_OPENEDIT message to the container and terminates the edit operation by sending a CM_CLOSEEDIT message. Parameter **mp1** of the CM_OPENEDIT message is pointer to a

CNREDITDATA structure; parameter **mp2** is reserved and must be set to zero. Both parameters of the CM_CLOSEEDIT message are reserved and should be set to zero.

The CNREDITDATA structure used by all of these messages is defined in Figure 12.14.

- The *cb* element is the length of the structure in bytes and should be set to sizeof(CNREDITDATA).
- Element *hwndCnr* is the window handle of the container window that contains the text field.
- Element *pRecord* is a pointer to the record containing the edited field.
- The *pFieldInfo* element is a pointer to the FIELDINFO structure for the edited column. This field is only used when the container is in DETAIL view and the container title is not being edited. Otherwise the element should be set to NULL.
- Element *ppszText* is a pointer to a pointer to the text string being edited. This element is not used for the CM_OPENEDIT message and should be set to NULL.
- The *cbText* element is the number of bytes in the new text string for the CN_REALLOCPSZ and CN_ENDEDIT messages. Otherwise, this element should be set to zero.
- The *id* element is the window ID of the container subwindow that contains the text. This element may be one of the following values:

CID_CNRTITLEWND	(0x7ff5)	for the container title window.
CID_LEFTDVWND	(0x7ff7)	for the left DETAIL view data window.
CID_RIGHTDVWND	(0x7ff8)	for the right DETAIL view data window.
CID_LEFTCOLTITLEWND	(0x7ff0)	for the left DETAIL view column title window.
CID_RIGHTCOLTITLEWND	(0x7ff1)	for the right DETAIL view column title window.

Other values indicate that the window is the container window itself.

```
typedef struct _CNREDITDATA
{
    ULONG        cb;
    HWND         hwndCnr;
    PRECORDCORE  pRecord;
    PFIELDINFO   pFieldInfo;
    PSZ          *ppszText;
    ULONG        cbText;
    ULONG        id;
} CNREDITDATA;
```

Figure 12.14 **The CNREDITDATA structure.**

```
case CN_BEGINEDIT:
   fInEdit = TRUE;
   break;
case CN_REALLOCPSZ:
   {
       PCNREDITDATA   pced = (PCNREDITDATA)PVOIDFROMMP(mp2);
       PSZ            newpsz = NULL;

       free( *(pced->ppszText) );
       newpsz = (PSZ)malloc( pced->cbText );
       *(pced->ppszText) = newpsz;
       return MRFROMLONG(TRUE);
   }
case CN_ENDEDIT:
   fInEdit = FALSE;
   break;
```

Figure 12.15   Editing container text.

Figure 12.15 shows how an application might process an edit operation involving the container text. The CN_BEGINEDIT message processing merely sets a flag that informs the application that an edit operation is in progress. The application should not receive additional messages from the container until the edit operation is complete, but this flag should be checked prior to sending messages to the container during the processing of keyboard, mouse, or other events that might otherwise require sending messages to the container. The processing for the CN_REALLOCPSZ notification first frees the existing text buffer and then allocates a new buffer. The address of the new buffer is then stored back into the CNREDITDATA structure, and TRUE is returned to indicate that the container should copy the edited text back to the new buffer. Finally, the CN_ENDEDIT processing clears the flag that indicates that an edit is in progress.

Context Menus

The container provides support for handling the WM_CONTEXTMENU message in order to allow the application to pop up a context-sensitive menu. When the context menu mouse click or keyboard key is received, PM sends a WM_CONTEXTMENU message to the window over which the mouse click occurred or to the window that has the keyboard focus. If this window is a container control, a WM_CONTROL message containing the CN_CONTEXTMENU notification code is sent to the container's owner. Parameter **mp2** of the WM_CONTROL message is a pointer to the record that either has cursored emphasis when the WM_CONTEXTMENU is sent as the result of a keyboard event, or that the mouse pointer is over when the WM_CONTEXTMENU is sent as the result of a mouse event. If the mouse pointer is not over an object, the pointer value is NULL.

Figure 12.16 provides an example of how an application can process the CN_CONTEXTMENU notification to raise a popup menu. Note that an application can display a menu related to the container as a whole if the menu is requested by clicking the mouse over the container's white space. In this example, however, a menu is only displayed if the request is related to a data record. Thus the application first checks **mp2** to ensure that a data record pointer was received. If so, the application saves the pointer to the record in its window instance data for later use. A message is then sent to set the source emphasis on the record. Then, if not already available, the menu is loaded from the application's resources. Next, the current position of the mouse pointer is obtained and converted to the coordinates of the current window. The menu is then raised at the location of the pointer.

Once the menu is raised, the application will later receive a WM_MENUEND message. If the menu window handle passed with this message matches the menu window handle for the popup menu, the source emphasis for the record should be removed. If the user actually selected one of the menu items, a WM_COMMAND message will then be received with the menu identifier of the selected menu item. In the example, the WM_COMMAND

```
case CN_CONTEXTMENU:
   {
       PRECORDCORE     prec = (PRECORDCORE)mp2;
       HWND            hwndMenu;
       POINTL          pt;

       if (prec != (PRECORDCORE)NULL) {
          WinSetWindowPtr( hwnd, WP_MENURECORD, (PVOID)prec );
          WinSendMsg( WinWindowFromID(hwnd,SHORT1FROMMP(mp1)),
                      CM_SETRECORDEMPHASIS, MPFROMP(mp2),
                      MPFROM2SHORT( TRUE, CRA_SOURCE));
          hwndMenu = (HWND)WinQueryWindowULong( hwnd, WL_MENUHWND );
          if (hwndMenu == NULLHANDLE) {
             hwndMenu = WinLoadMenu( hwnd, NULLHANDLE, MID_POPUP );
             WinSetWindowULong( hwnd, WL_MENUHWND, hwndMenu );
          } /* endif */
          WinQueryPointerPos( HWND_DESKTOP, &pt );
          WinMapWindowPoints( HWND_DESKTOP, hwnd, &pt, 1 );
          WinPopupMenu( hwnd, hwnd, hwndMenu, pt.x, pt.y, 0,
                  PU_KEYBOARD | PU_MOUSEBUTTON1 );
       } /* endif */
   }
   break;
```

Figure 12.16   Raising a context menu.

processing would take action on the data record stored in the window instance data. Other applications might use the CM_QUERYRECORDEMPHASIS message to perform some action on all selected records.

TREE Mode

When the container is displaying the TREE mode, notifications are sent to the application whenever the user expands or collapses items in the tree, allowing the application to take any necessary action. These notifications are sent to the application via the WM_CONTROL message. The notification code is set to CN_COLLAPSETREE when a record is collapsed or to CN_EXPANDTREE when a record is expanded. The **mp2** parameter is a pointer to the affected data record.

The application may also programmatically expand and collapse records by sending messages to the container. The CM_COLLAPSETREE message is used to hide the children of a record, and the CM_EXPANDTREE message is used to display a record's children. Parameter **mp2** of these messages is a pointer to the parent record that is to be expanded or collapsed. If set to NULL, all parent records are set to the desired state.

Scrolling

The container control automatically handles the window operations needed to scroll through the set of data records inserted into the container. However, in cases where there are more records than can be reasonably added to the container record simultaneously, the container sends a WM_CONTROL message with notification code CN_QUERYDELTA to allow the application to add records to the end of the container near the currently displayed data and remove records from the opposite end of the container's list. Parameter **mp2** of this message is a pointer to a NOTIFYDELTA structure. This structure is defined in Figure 12.17.

- The *hwndCnr* element is the handle of the affected container window.
- The *fDelta* element indicates the type of scrolling operation and where new records should be inserted. The valid flags are:

```
typedef struct _NOTIFYDELTA
{
    HWND        hwndCnr;
    ULONG       fDelta;
} NOTIFYDELTA;
```

Figure 12.17   The NOTIFYSCROLL structure.

CMA_DELTATOP   (0x0001)   indicates that records should be added at the beginning of the current container list.

CMA_DELTABOT   (0x0002)   indicates that records should be added at the end of the current container list.

CMA_DELTAHOME   (0x0004)   indicates that the container has been scrolled to the home position and that records should be added such that the first record is visible.

CMA_DELTAEND   (0x0008)   indicates that the container has been scrolled to the end position of the container and that records should be added such that the last record is visible.

Drag and Drop

The container provides full support for direct manipulation operations by intercepting the messages associated with the initiation of the operation and the manipulation of objects and sending these messages to the application in the form of WM_CONTROL notifications.

The WM_PICKUP and WM_INITDRAG messages are reflected in the CN_PICKUP and CN_INITDRAG notifications. Parameter **mp2** of the WM_CONTROL message containing these notification codes contains a pointer to a CNRINITDRAG data structure. This structure is defined in Figure 12.18.

- The *hwndCnr* element is the handle of the container window that received the direct manipulation initiation message.
- Element *pRecord* is a pointer to the record associated with the direct manipulation operation. If NULL, the operation was initiated with the mouse over a white space area of the container.
- The *x* and *y* elements provide the coordinates of the mouse pointer at the time the operation was initiated.
- Element *cx* and *cy* provide the offset from the mouse pointer to the origin of the representation of the record.

```
typedef struct _CNRDRAGINIT
{
    HWND        hwndCnr;
    PRECORDCORE pRecord;
    LONG        x;
    LONG        y;
    LONG        cx;
    LONG        cy;
} CNRDRAGINIT;
```

Figure 12.18   **The CNRINITDRAG structure.**

```
typedef struct _CNRDRAGINFO
{
   PDRAGINFO   pDragInfo;
   PRECORDCORE pRecord;
} CNRDRAGINFO;
```

Figure 12.19   The CNRDRAGINFO structure.

The DM_DRAGLEAVE and DM_DRAGHELP messages are sent as notification codes CN_DRAGLEAVE and CN_DRAGHELP. The DM_DRAGOVER message may be reflected as either a CN_DRAGAFTER or CN_DRAGOVER notification. The CN_DRAGAFTER notification is sent when the drop point is placed between two records. The CN_DRAGOVER message is sent when the drop point is placed on a record. The placement of the drop point depends on the target emphasis attribute in the *flWindowAttr* element of the CNRINFO structure. The container sends the CN_DROP notification when the DM_DROP message is received. The **mp2** parameter of these WM_CONTROL messages is a pointer to a CNRDRAGINFO structure which is defined in Figure 12.19.

- The *pDragInfo* element is a pointer to the DRAGINFO structure for the operation.
- The *pRecord* element is a pointer to the affected record. This element is set to NULL for the CN_DRAGLEAVE notification and to the record preceding the insertion point for the CN_DRAGAFTER notification.

For complete information on direct manipulation programming, see Chapter 7.

SUMMARY

The container control is a powerful tool for displaying and manipulating sets of objects that may be defined as data records. Since much of the data processed by computer programs falls into this category, the container control is finding wide acceptance as new applications are developed. In fact, the rich set of display modes and the functionality provided by the control make it destined to be one of the most prevalent classes used in PM programming. Become familiar with this control and, in many cases, the PM portion of application development will be greatly simplified.

CHAPTER 13

What's New with OS/2: Getting a Look at the Multimedia Controls

T he Multimedia Presentation Manager, or MMPM, code and tools were originally a separate add-on product for OS/2, but with the release of Version 2.1, though still separate, the MMPM code was shipped with the OS/2 product and the development tools were added to the OS/2 Developer's Toolkit. With OS/2 WARP, the MMPM code has been completely integrated into the operating system code and the development tools are an integral part of the toolkit.

The MMPM components can now be used with confidence by developers; they provide features that can often be quite beneficial. The graphic button control provides the functionality of a pushbutton with significantly enhanced visual features, including animation. Secondary windows provide the convenience of dialog boxes in addition to the freedom of normal frame windows, and secondary message boxes (as provided by MMPM or the **WinMessageBox2** API) provide a more flexible presentation of information to the user than the original message box.

GRAPHIC BUTTONS

The graphic button control was originally designed for use in windows that serve as control panels for multimedia devices and is thus particularly well suited to this type of functionality. Since the controls for most audio and video devices in the real world use symbols to indicate the functionality of their controls, application designers needed to emulate these symbols on the computerized controls for these devices. The graphic pushbutton allows both text and graphical symbols to be displayed; thus an application can display a fast forward button with the commonly recognized double arrow symbol and, if desired, also display text, such as FF or Fast Forward, both of which indicate the functionality of the button.

The buttons used by most real-world devices also provide several types of functionality that the graphic button has been designed to emulate. A Play button, for example, usually starts the device when pushed and then does nothing until the device is stopped. A Pause button, on the other hand, toggles between pausing the action of the device and starting the action of the device each time it is depressed. A third type of button, such as a Cue button, causes the device to play only while the button is depressed and stops the device when the button is released. The graphic button control allows an application to easily emulate all three types of button functionality.

Of course, the computerized versions of the device control buttons do not merely emulate the real-world buttons but improve upon them. The graphic button control allows different graphic information to be displayed depending on the state of the button. Thus a Pause button could display one bitmap graphic when the device is playing normally and a different bitmap when the device is in the paused state. Furthermore, the control provides the capability to sequence through a set of bitmaps to produce an animation effect allowing the double arrows of a Fast Forward button to appear to move across the face of the button when the device is fast forwarding.

Normal PM applications that have nothing to do with multimedia devices can also take advantage of these features to improve their own appearance and functionality. For example, graphic buttons can be used to implement the increasingly popular button bars, which supplement the functionality of menus. Graphic buttons can also replace checkboxes, radio buttons, and pushbuttons to give a better visual representation of the selection's functionality.

REGISTERING THE GRAPHIC BUTTON CLASS

The graphic button class, WC_GRAPHICBUTTON, is not a part of the standard PM control class library and must be registered before any graphic button windows can be created. Registration of the class is accomplished by calling the **WinRegisterGraphicButton** API. This function, which takes no parameters, handles all the work necessary to register the WC_GRAPHICBUTTON class for the application. Normally a call to this API is issued from within the application's main routine when the other classes required by the application are being registered.

CREATING GRAPHIC BUTTONS

Like other controls, graphic buttons may be created explicitly by an application or may be defined in a resource file, typically as an element of a dialog template. In either case, the programmer must make some preliminary decisions as to how the button will appear and behave before creating the window. The style of the button must be determined based on the desired appearance and behavior of the control. Depending on the style(s) chosen, the button control data must be defined to support this style.

The first two style flags affect the states that the button may assume. By default, graphic buttons have one steady state, known as the UP state. A temporary state, known as HILITE state, is assumed when the pointing device cursor is placed over the control and the selection button is pressed. When the selection button is released or the mouse cursor is moved off the button, the button returns to the steady state. The HILITE state is also assumed when a graphic button has the input focus and the Spacebar is pressed on the keyboard. The button will remain in the HILITE state until the Spacebar is released. The graphic button may assume another steady state, known as the DOWN state, if either of the following two style flags are set:

GBS_TWOSTATE   0x1000   allows the application to set the button to the DOWN state. If the state is being set in response to user input, the application should process the WM_COMMAND message for the button and toggle the state as necessary. In normal practice, the UP state is associated with inactive or idle functionality, while the DOWN state indicates active functionality.

GBS_AUTOTWOSTATE   0x2000   enables the DOWN state for the button but causes the state of the button to toggle when pressed. Thus, when the button is pressed, the state changes from UP to DOWN when the button is in the UP state and from DOWN to UP when the button is in the DOWN state. With this style, the application can process the WM_CONTROL message to determine when the state of the button changes and act appropriately.

Normally, a single bitmap is shown for each state of the graphic button—different bitmaps may be selected for each state by sending the GBM_SETBIT MAPINDEX message, but only one static bitmap is displayed per state. The next two style flags allow a series a bitmaps to be shown, producing the effect of animated motion.

GBS_ANIMATION   0x4000   enables the animation feature of the button. The application must explicitly start and stop the animation by sending the GBM_ANIMATION message to the button control.

GBS_AUTOANIMATION   0x8000   enables the animation feature but causes the animation to be automatically toggled whenever the state changes from UP to DOWN or DOWN to UP. By default, the button is created in the UP state and animation is started when the button transitions to the DOWN state. However, if the application explicitly enables animation while the button is in the UP state, the animation will be stopped when the button transitions to the DOWN state and restarted when the button returns to the UP state.

The next two style flags allow additional static bitmaps to be displayed when the button is in the HILITE state or when the button control window is disabled:

GBS_HILITEBITMAP   0x0020   enables the button to display a specific bitmap when the button is in HILITE state. The bitmap to display is selected by sending a GM_SETBITMAPINDEX message to the button control.

GBS_DISABLEBITMAP   0x0010   causes the graphic button to display a different bitmap when the graphic button control window is disabled. The bitmap to display is selected by sending a GBM_SET BITMAPINDEX message to the button control window.

The final group of style flags control how the optional text is displayed on the button. If none of the style bits are set, the text is displayed such that it appears flat on the face of the button. One of the following two style flags may be set to modify this appearance:

GBS_3D_TEXTRAISED   0x0080   causes the text to appear raised above the surface of the button.

GBS_3D_TEXTRECESSED   0x0040   causes the text to appear below the surface of the button as if engraved.

The final style flag affects the size of the graphic button:

GBS_MINIBUTTON   0x0001   reduces the space occupied by the button borders, resulting in a smaller button while maintaining the displayed size of the graphic and text associated with the button.

```
typedef struct _GBTNCDATA
{
    USHORT   usReserved;
    PSZ      pszText;
    HMODULE  hmod;
    USHORT   cBitmaps;
    USHORT   aidBitmap[1];
} GBTNCDATA;
```

Figure 13.1   Application program control data.

Once the style has been selected, the control data for the graphic button can be defined. The basic contents of the control data are the text, if any, to be displayed on the button and the resource ID(s) of the bitmap(s) to be displayed. The actual layout of the control data varies depending on whether the data is defined in the resource file or as a structure in the application program. If the control data is defined as a structure within the application program, the format in Figure 13.1 is used.

- The *usReserved* element identifies the type of structure and must be set to GB_STRUCTURE.
- Element *pszText* may be set to NULL if no text is displayed. Otherwise, this element points to a zero-terminated array of characters to be displayed as the button text.
- Element *hmod* identifies the module handle of the executable that contains the bitmap resources to be displayed on the button. Setting this field to NULLHANDLE indicates that the bitmap resources are located in the application executable.
- The *cBitmaps* element indicates the number of elements in the aidBitmaps array.
- Element *aidBitmap* is a variable-length array whose elements are the resource IDs of the bitmaps that the button can display.

When the button is defined as a resource using a CONTROL statement in the resource definition file, the resource compiler structures the control data as shown in Figure 13.2.

```
struct {
    USHORT       usReserved;
    char         szText[];
    USHORT       cBitmaps;
    USHORT       aidBitmaps[];
};
```

Figure 13.2   Resource control data.

- The *usReserved* element identifies the type of structure and is set to GB_RESOURCE.
- Element *szText* is a zero-terminated, variable-length array of characters to be displayed as the button text.
- Element *cBitmaps* indicates the number of elements in the aidBitmaps array.
- The *aidBitmaps* element is a variable-length array whose elements are the resource IDs of the bitmaps that the button can display.

Note that in either case, the array of bitmap IDs can contain duplicates—the *cBitmaps* element represents the number of elements in the array, not the number of unique bitmaps.

After the style has been determined and the control data initialized, the graphic button can be created. In many cases, the graphic button is created implicitly when a dialog template is loaded. Figures 13.3 and 13.4 show the coding necessary to create a graphic button as an element of a dialog window. Figure 13.3 shows the source code for the application, which consists of a main routine and a dialog procedure. The main routine is typical, initializing

```
MRESULT EXPENTRY DlgProc( HWND hwnd, ULONG msg, MPARAM mp1, MPARAM mp2 )
{
    if (msg == WM_COMMAND ) {
       return 01;
    } else {
       return WinDefDlgProc( hwnd, msg, mp1, mp2 );
    } /* endif */
}

main(int argc, char *argv[], char *envp[])
{
    HAB      hab;
    HMQ      hmq;

    do {
       hab = WinInitialize(0);
       if (hab == NULLHANDLE) break;
       hmq = WinCreateMsgQueue( hab, 0 );
       if (hmq == NULLHANDLE) break;
       WinRegisterGraphicButton();
       WinDlgBox( HWND_DESKTOP, HWND_DESKTOP, DlgProc, NULLHANDLE,
             DLGID, NULL );
    } while ( 0 ); /* enddo */
    if (hmq != (HMQ)NULLHANDLE) WinDestroyMsgQueue( hmq );
    if (hab != (HAB)NULLHANDLE) WinTerminate( hab );
}
```

Figure 13.3 **Graphic button dialog sample.**

```
#include "dialog.h"

DLGTEMPLATE DLGID LOADONCALL MOVEABLE DISCARDABLE
BEGIN
    DIALOG  "Sample", DLGID, 12, 37, 239, 108, WS_VISIBLE,
            FCF_SYSMENU | FCF_TITLEBAR
    BEGIN
        CONTROL             "", 100, 5, 8, 0, 0, WC_GRAPHICBUTTON,
                            WS_VISIBLE | GBS_AUTOTWOSTATE | GBS_AUTOANIMATION
                            CTLDATA GB_RESOURCE, "Sample", 6,
                                1, 100, 101, 102, 103, 104, 0
    END
END

bitmap    1   1.bmp
bitmap  100   ap1.bmp
bitmap  101   ap2.bmp
bitmap  102   ap3.bmp
bitmap  103   ap4.bmp
bitmap  104   ap5.bmp
```

Figure 13.4 Graphic button dialog template.

the PM environment and creating a message queue. Next, the **WinRegister-GraphicButton** API is called to register the graphic button class and enable button controls to be created. **WinDlgBox** is then called to create and process the dialog box. When the API returns, the application is terminated. The dialog procedure for this application is quite simple, calling **WinDefDlgProc** for most of the messages received. The WM_COMMAND message is not forwarded to **WinDefDlgProc** to prevent the dialog from closing when the graphic button is clicked.

Figure 13.4 shows the resource script used to build the dialog template. The file contains the dialog template and the statements to create the bitmap resources that will be displayed by the graphic button. The button is defined within the dialog template using the CONTROL statement. Note that the text portion of the control statement is specified as a NULL string and the text for the graphic button is specified in the CTLDATA portion of the statement. The style of the button is set to enable GBS_AUTOTWOSTATE and GBS_AUTOANIMATION allowing the button to sequence through the defined bitmaps when clicked. The CTLDATA portion of the statement specifies GB_RESOURCE, indicating that the control data is defined in a resource file, sets the text to be displayed as "Sample", indicates that six bitmaps are to be used, and identifies the six bitmap resources. The bitmap ID array is terminated with a zero to indicate to the resource compiler that the list is complete. If the number of bitmaps contained in the list does not match the number in the array, the smaller number will actually be used by the button control when displaying bitmaps. The dimensions specified for the size and width of the control, both being zero, are also noteworthy. The minimum width of the control is determined by the space required to hold the bitmap, and the minimum height is determined by the space required to display both the bitmap and text, if defined. Be sure when creating buttons to allow sufficient space to display the button with these minimum sizes.

Figure 13.5 shows how this button could be created by specifying the control data as an application structure and using the **WinCreateWindow** API. The main routine of the application is unchanged and the resource file is the same except that the CONTROL statement has been removed from the dialog template. Instead, the graphic button control is created during the processing of the WM_INITDLG message. The control data for the control is defined as global data by specifying a structure that contains the basic control data structure, GBTNCDATA, followed by an array large enough to hold all but the first of the bitmap IDs—space for the first ID is reserved in the GBTNCDATA structure. This structure is then initialized with the data that was previously specified in the resource file. Note that the value of the *usReserved* element is set to GB_STRUCTURE and that the text is now initialized as a pointer to a string. Since the bitmap resources are located in the application's executable, the *hmod* element is set to NULLHANDLE. When the WM_INITDLG message is received, **WinCreateWindow** is called to create the graphic button control. The **pszName** parameter is set to NULL since the text for the button must be specified in the control data. The style for the button is passed in the **flStyle** parameter.

CONTROLLING THE GRAPHIC BUTTON

Once the button is created, the application can use the button to perform many different functions. For example, the graphic button can be used like a normal pushbutton to cause an action to occur when the button is pressed. The button can also be used to cause some action to occur while the button is depressed and then stop the action when the button is released. A third use of the graphic button is as a toggle switch. An action begins when the button is first clicked and terminates when the button is clicked again. Different graphics are usually displayed for each state in this instance. A fourth use of the button replaces the standard checkbox or radio button, allowing the user to provide a graphic representation of the choices available rather than relying solely on text. This section will examine the programming required to implement these functions.

To begin, let's enhance the earlier sample to include two buttons, one labeled Start and one labeled Stop, with appropriate bitmaps. The buttons will be used to start and stop some abstract operation. The operation could be playing an audio CD, running a model train, performing a computerized simulation, or even running an assembly line in an automobile factory. The

```
HWND       gbtnhwnd;

#pragma pack(1)
struct {
   GBTNCDATA   btndata;
   USHORT      bitmaps[5];
} gbtndata = { GB_STRUCTURE, "Sample", NULLHANDLE, 6,
               1, 100, 101, 102, 103, 104 };
#pragma pack()

MRESULT EXPENTRY DlgProc( HWND hwnd, ULONG msg, MPARAM mp1, MPARAM mp2 )
{
   if (msg == WM_COMMAND ) {
      return 01;
   } else if (msg == WM_INITDLG) {
      gbtnhwnd = WinCreateWindow( hwnd,
                 WC_GRAPHICBUTTON, NULL,
                 WS_VISIBLE | GBS_AUTOTWOSTATE | GBS_AUTOANIMATION,
                 5, 8, 0, 0, hwnd, HWND_TOP, 100,
                 &gbtndata, NULL );
      WinSetFocus( HWND_DESKTOP, gbtnhwnd );
      return (MRESULT)FALSE;
   } else {
      return WinDefDlgProc( hwnd, msg, mp1, mp2 );
   } /* endif */
}

main(int argc, char *argv[], char *envp[])
{
   HAB       hab;
   HMQ       hmq;
   QMSG      qmsg;

   do {
      hab = WinInitialize(0);
      if (hab == NULLHANDLE) break;
      hmq = WinCreateMsgQueue( hab, 0 );
      if (hmq == NULLHANDLE) break;
      WinRegisterGraphicButton();
      WinDlgBox( HWND_DESKTOP, HWND_DESKTOP, DlgProc, NULLHANDLE,
                 DLGID, NULL );
   } while ( 0 ); /* enddo */
   if (hmq != (HMQ)NULLHANDLE) WinDestroyMsgQueue( hmq );
   if (hab != (HAB)NULLHANDLE) WinTerminate( hab );
}
```

Figure 13.5 Graphic button window creation.

only requirement is that the operation can be started and stopped. To avoid confusion, only one button will ever be enabled. If the operation is currently stopped, the Start button will be enabled; if the operation is running, the Stop button will be enabled.

The resource file for this example is similar to that shown in Figure 13.4. A second graphic button control is added, the GBS_AUTOTWOSTATE and GBS_AUTOANIMATION flags are removed, and a GBS_DISABLEBITMAP flag is added to enable display of a different bitmap when the button is disabled. Also, the number of bitmaps per button is decreased to two, one for display when the button is enabled and one for display when the button is disabled. In this case, the disabled bitmap is the same as the enabled bitmap with less intense colors.

Figure 13.6 shows the dialog window procedure to implement the desired functionality. When the WM_INITDLG message is received, a GBM_SETBIT MAPINDEX message is sent to each of the buttons to modify the bitmap that will be displayed when the button is disabled. The low-order 16 bits of parameter **mp1** of this message are a set of flags that indicate the state for which the index is to be set. Here are the valid flags:

```
MRESULT EXPENTRY DlgProc( HWND hwnd, ULONG msg, MPARAM mp1, MPARAM mp2 )
{
   if (msg == WM_INITDLG) {
      WinSendDlgItemMsg( hwnd, DID_START, GBM_SETBITMAPINDEX,
                         MPFROMSHORT(GB_DISABLE), MPFROMSHORT(1));
      WinSendDlgItemMsg( hwnd, DID_STOP, GBM_SETBITMAPINDEX,
                         MPFROMSHORT(GB_DISABLE), MPFROMSHORT(1));
      WinEnableControl( hwnd, DID_STOP, FALSE );
      return (MRESULT)0L;
   } else if (msg == WM_COMMAND ) {
      if (SHORT1FROMMP(mp1) == DID_START ) {
         WinEnableControl( hwnd, DID_START, FALSE );
         WinEnableControl( hwnd, DID_STOP, TRUE );
         Start_Operation();
      } else if (SHORT1FROMMP(mp1) == DID_STOP ) {
         WinEnableControl( hwnd, DID_START, TRUE );
         WinEnableControl( hwnd, DID_STOP, FALSE );
         Stop_Operation();
      }
      return 01;
   } else {
      return WinDefDlgProc( hwnd, msg, mp1, mp2 );
   } /* endif */
}
```

Figure 13.6 Two-button dialog example.

GB_UP	0x0001	sets the index of the bitmap to display when the button is in the UP state.
GB_DOWN	0x0002	sets the index of the bitmap to display when the button is in the DOWN state.
GB_HILITE	0x0004	sets the index of the bitmap to display when the button is in the HILITE state.
GB_DISABLE	0x0003	sets the index of the bitmap to display when the button is in the disabled state.
GB_ANIMATIONBEGIN	0x000c	sets the index of the first bitmap to display when the button is changed to the animation state.
GB_ANIMATIONEND	0x000d	sets the index of the last bitmap to display when the button is in the animation state. This value should be equal to or greater than the animation begin index. The animation will cycle through the bitmaps between the begin animation and end animation indices.
GB_CURRENTSTATE	0x000b	sets the index of the bitmap to display when the button is in the state that matches the current state.

The low-order 16 bits of parameter **mp2** of the GBM_SETBITMAPINDEX message specify the index to be assigned to the button state. The valid values are:

GB_INDEX_FORWARD	−1	sets the index to the next index beyond the current value. The value wraps back to index 0 if the current index is the last bitmap in the bitmap array.
GB_INDEX_BACKWARD	−2	sets the index to the index prior to the current index value. The value wraps to the last item in the array if the current index is zero.
GB_INDEX_FIRST	−3	sets the index to the first element of the array of bitmaps.
GB_INDEX_LAST	−4	sets the index to the last element of the array of bitmaps.
other		sets the index to the indicated index.

In the example, parameter **mp1** is set to GB_DISABLE to indicate that the bitmap for the disabled state is being set. Parameter **mp2** is set to 1 to indicate that the second bitmap in the array is to be displayed when the button is in this state. Since the operation is assumed to be stopped when the application first executes, the Stop button is disabled using the **WinEnableControl** API.

When a graphic button is clicked, a WM_COMMAND message is sent to the button window's owner. When the WM_COMMAND message is received, the application determines which button was clicked. If the Start button was clicked, **WinEnableControl** is called once to disable the Start button and then a second time to enable the Stop button. Function **Start_Operation** is then called to perform whatever is necessary to begin the operation. Likewise, if the Stop button was clicked, **WinEnableControl** is called to enable the Start button and disable the Stop button. Function **Stop_Operation** is called to halt the operation.

With the exception of setting the disabled bitmap index, this coding is identical to that which would be used with a normal pushbutton. The primary advantage of the graphic button is its ability to automatically display different bitmaps for different states. As we will see shortly, the Start button could display an animated bitmap to show that the operation runs when the button is pressed, and the Stop button could be left with a static bitmap to show that clicking the button stops the operation.

In the second example, a single button is used. Rather than clicking the button, the user depresses the button by holding down the mouse selection button or the Spacebar, causing the operation to run. When the mouse button or Spacebar is released, the operation stops. Operations supported by this type of button could include cue/review functions for audio or video equipment, an automotive braking system, or the flippers and shooter in a computerized pinball game.

In order to implement this functionality, the button's HILITE state will be used. When the button is depressed, the button is in HILITE state; when the button is released, it returns to UP state. Depending on the application, the button style could be set to GBS_HILITEBITMAP to display a different bitmap when the button is depressed or to GBS_ANIMATION to allow animation when the button is depressed. In the example, an animated button will be used to perform the cue/review function. When the button is in the UP state, a single bitmap depicting an arrow will be displayed. When the button is depressed, the arrow will move across the face of button to show that the device is in motion. The resource script, shown in Figure 13.7, has been modified to provide five bitmaps for the animation. Note that the width of the button has been specified to accommodate the minimum width needed to display the button text.

Figure 13.8 shows the dialog window procedure used to implement this button. In this case, the processing for the WM_INITDLG message sends two GBM_SETBITMAPINDEX messages to the button control. The first message sets the bitmap index at which animation will start and the second message sets the bitmap index at which animation will end. A GBM_SETANIMATIONRATE message is sent to cause the button to change the bitmap every 200 milliseconds when animation is enabled. Parameter **mp1** of this message specifies the number of milliseconds for the button to delay between bitmap changes. Parameter **mp2** is reserved and must be set to zero.

In this example, the WM_CONTROL message is used to track the changing state of the graphic button. When the message indicates that the button is in the HILITE state, a GBM_ANIMATION message is sent to start ani-

```
#include "dialog.h"

DLGTEMPLATE DLGID LOADONCALL MOVEABLE DISCARDABLE
BEGIN
    DIALOG  "Sample", DLGID, 12, 37, 239, 108, WS_VISIBLE,
            FCF_SYSMENU | FCF_TITLEBAR
    BEGIN
        CONTROL         "", DID_REVIEW, 5, 8, 46, 0, WC_GRAPHICBUTTON,
                        WS_VISIBLE | WS_TABSTOP | GBS_ANIMATION
                        CTLDATA GB_RESOURCE, "Review", 6,
                        1, 2, 3, 4, 5, 6, 0
    END
END


bitmap 1 start.bmp
bitmap 2 play1.bmp
bitmap 3 play2.bmp
bitmap 4 play3.bmp
bitmap 5 play4.bmp
bitmap 6 play5.bmp
```

Figure 13.7   Press and hold sample resource.

mation on the button. Parameter **mp1** of this message starts the animation when set to TRUE and stops animation when set to FALSE. Parameter **mp2** is set to TRUE to start animation at the index following the currently displayed index or to FALSE to start with the defined animation start index. In the example, parameter **mp1** is set to TRUE to indicate that animation should be started, and parameter **mp2** is set to FALSE to indicate that the animation should start at the GB_ANIMATIONBEGIN bitmap index. When the end of the animation sequence is reached, the next bitmap shown would be that designated as the GB_ANIMATIONBEGIN bitmap index. After the animation is started, **Start_Operation** is called to begin the operation. When the WM_CONTROL message indicates that the button has returned to the UP state, a GBM_ANIMATION message is sent to the button with parameter **mp1** set to FALSE to stop the animation, and **Stop_Operation** is called to halt the animation. Since this is the only button in this dialog box, the WM_COMMAND message is processed by returning a zero result. If this message were forwarded to the **WinDefDialogProc** API, the dialog would be dismissed.

The next example uses a two-state button, acting as a toggle switch. When the button is in the DOWN state, the operation is in progress; when the button is in the UP state, the operation has been halted. This functionality is very similar to the previous example except that now the user can click the button, walk

```
MRESULT EXPENTRY DlgProc( HWND hwnd, ULONG msg, MPARAM mp1, MPARAM mp2 )
{
    if (msg == WM_INITDLG) {
        WinSendDlgItemMsg( hwnd, DID_REVIEW, GBM_SETBITMAPINDEX,
                           MPFROMSHORT(GB_ANIMATIONBEGIN), MPFROMSHORT(1));
        WinSendDlgItemMsg( hwnd, DID_REVIEW, GBM_SETBITMAPINDEX,
                           MPFROMSHORT(GB_ANIMATIONEND), MPFROMSHORT(5));
        WinSendDlgItemMsg( hwnd, DID_REVIEW, GBM_SETANIMATIONRATE,
                           MPFROMLONG(200L), MPFROMLONG(0L));
        return (MRESULT)0L;
    } else if (msg == WM_CONTROL ) {
        if (SHORT2FROMMP(mp1) == GBN_BUTTONHILITE ) {
            WinSendDlgItemMsg( hwnd, DID_REVIEW, GBM_ANIMATE,
                               MPFROMSHORT(TRUE), MPFROMSHORT(FALSE));
            Start_Operation();
        } else if (SHORT2FROMMP(mp1) == GBN_BUTTONUP ) {
            WinSendDlgItemMsg( hwnd, DID_REVIEW, GBM_ANIMATE,
                               MPFROMSHORT(FALSE), MPFROMSHORT(FALSE));
            Stop_Operation();
        }
        return 01;
    } else if (msg == WM_COMMAND) {
        return 01;
    } else {
        return WinDefDlgProc( hwnd, msg, mp1, mp2 );
    } /* endif */
}
```

Figure 13.8   Press and hold button example.

away, or do some other task while the operation is running, and come back to stop the operation when desired. Operations of this type include the pause button used with audio or video equipment; the selection of a font attribute, such as bold or italic, as seen in word processors; or single button control of processes, such as a factory floor (as opposed to the two-button approach discussed in the first example). Rather than starting fresh, let's use the code from the previous example to create a fast forward button that forwards an audio device when clicked and stops the device when clicked again. The same bitmaps and animation will be used, but the resource script has been modified to add the GBS_TWOSTATE style to the button.

Figure 13.9 shows the dialog window procedure for controlling the button. The processing for the WM_INITDLG message is same as in Figure 13.8, setting the bitmap indexes for animation and the animation rate. The processing for the WM_COMMAND message handles the button state transitions. When the message is received, a GBM_QUERYSTATE message is sent to the button to determine the current state. Both **mp1** and **mp2** are reserved and set to zero.

```
MRESULT EXPENTRY DlgProc( HWND hwnd, ULONG msg, MPARAM mp1, MPARAM mp2 )
{
   ULONG ulState;

   if (msg == WM_INITDLG) {
      WinSendDlgItemMsg( hwnd, DID_FF, GBM_SETBITMAPINDEX,
                         MPFROMSHORT(GB_ANIMATIONBEGIN), MPFROMSHORT(1));
      WinSendDlgItemMsg( hwnd, DID_FF, GBM_SETBITMAPINDEX,
                         MPFROMSHORT(GB_ANIMATIONEND), MPFROMSHORT(5));
      WinSendDlgItemMsg( hwnd, DID_FF, GBM_SETANIMATIONRATE,
                         MPFROMLONG(200L), MPFROMLONG(0L));
      return (MRESULT)0L;
   } else if (msg == WM_COMMAND) {
      ulState = LONGFROMMR(WinSendDlgItemMsg( hwnd, DID_FF, GBM_QUERYSTATE,
                                  MPFROMLONG(0L), MPFROMLONG(0L)));
      if (ulState == GB_UP) {
         WinSendDlgItemMsg( hwnd, DID_FF, GBM_SETSTATE,
                            MPFROMSHORT(GB_DOWN), MPFROMSHORT(FALSE));
         WinSendDlgItemMsg( hwnd, DID_FF, GBM_ANIMATE,
                            MPFROMSHORT(TRUE), MPFROMSHORT(FALSE));
         Start_Operation();
      } else if (ulState == GB_DOWN) {
         WinSendDlgItemMsg( hwnd, DID_FF, GBM_ANIMATE,
                            MPFROMSHORT(FALSE), MPFROMSHORT(FALSE));
         WinSendDlgItemMsg( hwnd, DID_FF, GBM_SETSTATE,
                            MPFROMSHORT(GB_UP), MPFROMSHORT(TRUE));
         Stop_Operation();
      }
      return 0l;
   } else {
      return WinDefDlgProc( hwnd, msg, mp1, mp2 );
   } /* endif */
}
```

Figure 13.9   Toggle button example.

If the button is in the UP state, a GBM_SETSTATE message is sent to change the button to the DOWN state. Parameter **mp1** contains the value for the new state, in this case, GB_DOWN. Parameter **mp2** may be set to TRUE to cause an immediate repaint of the button or, as in the example, may be set to FALSE to prevent repainting until a paint message is received. Since the subsequent animation will repaint the button, **mp2** is set to FALSE. Next, a GBM_ANIMATE message is sent to start the animation, and **Start_Operation** is called to start the fast forward operation. If the button is in the DOWN state when the WM_COMMAND message arrives, a GBM_ANIMATE message is sent to the button to stop the animation. Then a GBM_SETSTATE message is sent that changes the button to the UP state by using GB_UP for **mp1**, and repaints the button by setting **mp2** to TRUE. **Stop_Operation** is called to halt the fast forward operation.

Figure 13.10 shows an alternate window procedure for accomplishing this functionality when the button style contains the GBS_AUTOTWOSTATE and GBS_AUTOANIMATE styles. Since the button now handles the state transition and animation, the dialog procedure only needs to recognize changes in the state when the WM_CONTROL notification message is received. If the notification indicates a change to the DOWN state, **Start_Operation** is called. If the notification indicates a change to the UP state, **Stop_Operation** is called. The WM_COMMAND message is still processed to prevent the dialog from being dismissed.

In the final example, the graphic button is used to replace the functionality of a set of checkbox controls. This implementation conserves space in the dialog box and provides a graphic, rather than textual representation of the choices available. An example of this type of functionality would be the attribute section of a font selection dialog. Normally, there would be at least three checkboxes, one each for bold, italic, and underline. Rather than use checkboxes, graphic buttons could be used that actually depict how a character looks when the attribute is applied.

```
MRESULT EXPENTRY DlgProc( HWND hwnd, ULONG msg, MPARAM mp1, MPARAM mp2 )
{
   if (msg == WM_INITDLG) {
      WinSendDlgItemMsg( hwnd, DID_FF, GBM_SETBITMAPINDEX,
                         MPFROMSHORT(GB_ANIMATIONBEGIN), MPFROMSHORT(1));
      WinSendDlgItemMsg( hwnd, DID_FF, GBM_SETBITMAPINDEX,
                         MPFROMSHORT(GB_ANIMATIONEND), MPFROMSHORT(5));
      WinSendDlgItemMsg( hwnd, DID_FF, GBM_SETANIMATIONRATE,
                         MPFROMLONG(200L), MPFROMLONG(0L));
      return (MRESULT)0L;
   } else if (msg == WM_CONTROL) {
      if (SHORT2FROMMP(mp1) == GB_DOWN) {
         Start_Operation();
      } else if (SHORT2FROMMP(mp1) == GB_UP) {
         Stop_Operation();
      }
      return 0l;
   } else if (msg == WM_COMMAND) {
      return 0l;
   } else {
      return WinDefDlgProc( hwnd, msg, mp1, mp2 );
   } /* endif */
}
```

Figure 13.10   **Toggle button with automatic animation.**

```
#include "dialog.h"

DLGTEMPLATE DLGID LOADONCALL MOVEABLE DISCARDABLE
BEGIN
    DIALOG  "Sample", DLGID, 12, 37, 239, 108, WS_VISIBLE,
            FCF_SYSMENU | FCF_TITLEBAR
    BEGIN
        CONTROL           "", DID_BOLD, 5, 8, 0, 0, WC_GRAPHICBUTTON,
                          WS_VISIBLE | WS_TABSTOP | GBS_AUTOTWOSTATE
                          CTLDATA GB_RESOURCE, "", 2, 1, 5, 0
        CONTROL           "", DID_ITALIC, 28, 8, 0, 0, WC_GRAPHICBUTTON,
                          WS_VISIBLE | WS_TABSTOP | GBS_AUTOTWOSTATE
                          CTLDATA GB_RESOURCE, "", 2, 2, 6, 0
        CONTROL           "", DID_UNDER, 51, 8, 0, 0, WC_GRAPHICBUTTON,
                          WS_VISIBLE | WS_TABSTOP | GBS_AUTOTWOSTATE
                          CTLDATA GB_RESOURCE, "", 2, 3, 7, 0
        CONTROL           "", DID_STRIKE, 74, 8, 0, 0, WC_GRAPHICBUTTON,
                          WS_VISIBLE | WS_TABSTOP | GBS_AUTOTWOSTATE
                          CTLDATA GB_RESOURCE, "", 2, 4, 8, 0
        CONTROL           "OK", DID_OK, 120, 8, 20, 12, WC_BUTTON,
                          WS_VISIBLE | WS_TABSTOP | BS_PUSHBUTTON
    END
END


bitmap 1 bold.bmp
bitmap 2 italic.bmp
bitmap 3 under.bmp
bitmap 4 strike.bmp
bitmap 5 boldd.bmp
bitmap 6 italicd.bmp
bitmap 7 underd.bmp
bitmap 8 striked.bmp
```

Figure 13.11   Checkbox replacement resource definition.

Figure 13.11 shows the resource script for this example. The script defines the OK pushbutton and four graphic buttons, each of which has the GBS_AUTOTWOSTATE style flag set and two bitmaps defined. The first bitmap is used for the UP state. The second bitmap is used for the DOWN state and reverses the contrast between the foreground and background of the bitmap image to further inform the user that the button is selected.

The dialog procedure shown in Figure 13.12 shows how a set of graphic buttons for selecting bold, italic, underline, and strike-through attributes would be processed. An OK pushbutton has been added to finish the selection. When the WM_INITDLG message is received, a GBM_SETBITMAPINDEX message is sent to each of the graphic buttons to establish the bitmap to be displayed

```
MRESULT EXPENTRY DlgProc( HWND hwnd, ULONG msg, MPARAM mp1, MPARAM mp2 )
{
   if (msg == WM_INITDLG) {
      WinSendDlgItemMsg( hwnd, DID_BOLD, GBM_SETBITMAPINDEX,
                         MPFROMSHORT(GB_DOWN), MPFROMSHORT(1));
      WinSendDlgItemMsg( hwnd, DID_ITALIC, GBM_SETBITMAPINDEX,
                         MPFROMSHORT(GB_DOWN), MPFROMSHORT(1));
      WinSendDlgItemMsg( hwnd, DID_UNDER, GBM_SETBITMAPINDEX,
                         MPFROMSHORT(GB_DOWN), MPFROMSHORT(1));
      WinSendDlgItemMsg( hwnd, DID_STRIKE, GBM_SETBITMAPINDEX,
                         MPFROMSHORT(GB_DOWN), MPFROMSHORT(1));
      return (MRESULT)0L;
   } else if (msg == WM_COMMAND) {
      if (SHORT1FROMMP(mp1) == DID_OK) {
         flAttrs = 0;
         if (WinSendDlgItemMsg( hwnd, DID_BOLD, GBM_QUERYSTATE,
                            MPFROMLONG(0L), MPFROMLONG(0L)))
            flAttrs |= FL_BOLD;
         if (WinSendDlgItemMsg( hwnd, DID_ITALIC, GBM_QUERYSTATE,
                            MPFROMLONG(0L), MPFROMLONG(0L)))
            flAttrs |= FL_ITALIC;
         if (WinSendDlgItemMsg( hwnd, DID_UNDER, GBM_QUERYSTATE,
                            MPFROMLONG(0L), MPFROMLONG(0L)))
            flAttrs |= FL_UNDER;
         if (WinSendDlgItemMsg( hwnd, DID_STRIKE, GBM_QUERYSTATE,
                            MPFROMLONG(0L), MPFROMLONG(0L)))
            flAttrs |= FL_STRIKE;
         WinDismissDlg (hwnd, TRUE);
      }
      return (MRESULT)01;
   } else {
      return WinDefDlgProc( hwnd, msg, mp1, mp2 );
   } /* endif */
}
```

Figure 13.12   Checkbox replacement example code.

when the button is in the DOWN state. No further processing of the buttons is necessary as the GBS_AUTOTWOSTATE style was selected. When the WM_COMMAND message is sent by the OK pushbutton, the global variable *flAttrs* is initialized to zero. The state of each of the graphic buttons is then queried by sending a GBM_QUERYSTATE message. If the button is in the DOWN state, the bit corresponding to that button's attribute is set in *flAttrs*. After all the buttons have been queried, the dialog box is dismissed.

These four examples have shown how different styles and processing can be combined to produce several types of functionality with the graphic button.

These are by no means the only combinations allowed, but they do serve to show the power of the graphic button and should provide a good basis for development of further variations.

ADDITIONAL GRAPHIC BUTTON MESSAGES

The previous sections examined the graphic button styles and most of the messages used to modify or set the various features of the graphic button. The button also supports messages that query the various settings, and this section provides an overview of the remaining messages.

The GBM_QUERYANIMATEACTIVE message allows an application to determine if the button is currently animating a series of bitmaps. Both **mp1** and **mp2** for this message are reserved values and should be set to zero. The return value is set to TRUE if the button is currently animating a series of bitmaps and FALSE if no animation is in progress.

The GBM_QUERYANIMATIONRATE message returns the number of milliseconds a bitmap is displayed before the next bitmap in an animation sequence is displayed. Parameters **mp1** and **mp2** are both reserved and should be set to zero.

Message GBM_QUERYBITMAPINDEX returns the zero-based index value of the bitmap that will be displayed for a given state. Parameter **mp1** contains the state value to be queried in the low-order 16 bits. Valid values are the same as those specified for the **mp1** parameter of the GBM_SETBITMAPINDEX message. Parameter **mp2** is reserved and should be set to zero.

Should an application need to change the bitmaps associated with a graphic button after the button is created, a new control data structure can be passed to the button by sending the GBM_SETGRAPHICDATA message. Parameter **mp1** for this message is a pointer to a GBTNCDATA structure containing the new control data. Note that when this message is sent, the button is reinitialized, losing all information regarding the current state of the button, so if only the text of the button is to be changed, the **WinSetWindowText** API should be called.

Normally, the text of the graphic button is displayed below the bitmap. Message GBM_SETTEXTPOSITION can be used to move the text to a position above the bitmap. The low-order 16 bits of parameter **mp1** are used to designate the desired position. If set to GB_TEXTBELOW (1), the text is positioned below the bitmap. If set to GB_TEXTABOVE (2), the text is displayed above the bitmap. Parameter **mp2** is reserved and should be set to zero. The current position of the text can be determined by sending the GBM_QUERYTEXTPOSITION message. Both parameter **mp1** and parameter **mp2** of this message are reserved and should be set to zero. The return value for the message is GB_TEXTABOVE if the text is displayed above the bitmap or GB_TEXTBELOW if the text is displayed below the bitmap.

SECONDARY WINDOWS

Many programmers have found occasion to forgo the standard window for an application and merely load a dialog box from the main routine. This is a particularly viable solution when the client window of the application presents a number of controls; for example, an application that is the control panel for playing audio CD-ROMs. By using the dialog box, the creation and handling of the controls is the responsibility of the dialog box manager rather than the application program. Unfortunately, the standard dialog box does not provide some features users normally expect of an application window; primarily, the ability to change the window to a convenient size and then scroll through the contents as necessary. This type of functionality must be handled by the application and can be quite complicated.

The Secondary Window Manager provided by the multimedia tools overcomes this and other limitations of the standard dialog box manager. Secondary windows automatically handle displaying scroll bars when the size of the window is reduced below the area specified by the dialog template; and, when the scroll bars are displayed, the Secondary Window Manager also handles all processing necessary to scroll the contents of the window. As an additional feature, the application can request that a menu item be added to the system menu, which allows the user to easily return the window to its default size such that all information is visible. After the menu item is added, the Secondary Window Manager handles the sizing when the menu item is selected. Finally, the secondary window allows both an icon and a menu to be associated with the window, thereby providing all the functionality of a normal application window with the programming ease of a dialog box.

The secondary window accomplishes this dual functionality by creating a standard frame window with its associated controls. However, rather than using an application-defined window class as the client area, the secondary window uses a dialog window with an invisible frame. This implementation gives the secondary window the characteristics of both the standard frame window and the dialog frame window. Instead of the normal client window procedure of most applications, the secondary window procedure is implemented as a dialog procedure since the client window is actually a dialog window.

Using Secondary Windows

Building the dialog template is the first step in creating a secondary window. This may be accomplished in the same manner as a normal dialog: by creating the template as part of the application program, by manually building the template as part of the application's, or a DLL's, resource script, or by using the dialog editor to build the template for inclusion in the resource script. In order to take advantage of the features of the secondary window, style flags and frame creation flags must be specified in addition to those normally associated with a dialog box. The sizing and scrolling functions of the secondary window are enabled by specifying the FS_SIZEBORDER style and the FCF_VERTSCROLL and FCF_HORZSCROLL frame creation flags. Specifying the FCF_ICON and FCF_MENU flags cause the application icon and a menu bar to be displayed. Note that these latter two flags cannot be set with the dialog editor but must be added manually. Figure 13.13 is an example of the resource script for a secondary window for which sizing and scrolling is enabled and which displays both an icon and a menu bar. Note that an ICON and MENU whose IDs match the dialog template ID are also included.

Once the dialog template has been completed, the application can raise a secondary window using the dialog template. APIs are provided that mirror the functionality for creation and manipulation of dialog boxes. For example, an application that displays itself as a dialog box would be modified to replace the **WinDlgBox** API call with a call to the **WinSecondaryWindow** API. The parameters and functionality are identical except for the type of window created. This particular API causes the secondary window to be displayed and processed immediately. The API does not return until the secondary window is dismissed.

```
DLGTEMPLATE DLGID LOADONCALL MOVEABLE DISCARDABLE
BEGIN
    DIALOG  "Secondary Sample", DLGID, 29, 65, 153, 87, NOT FS_DLGBORDER |
        FS_SIZEBORDER | WS_VISIBLE, FCF_SYSMENU | FCF_TITLEBAR |
        FCF_MINBUTTON | FCF_MAXBUTTON | FCF_VERTSCROLL | FCF_HORZSCROLL |
        FCF_ICON | FCF_TASKLIST | FCF_MENU
    BEGIN
        CTEXT           "Secondary Window Example", 101, 8, 72, 137, 8, NOT
                        WS_GROUP
        LISTBOX         DID_LB, 7, 26, 137, 40
        PUSHBUTTON      "OK", DID_OK, 6, 4, 40, 14
        PUSHBUTTON      "Cancel", DID_CANCEL, 56, 4, 40, 14
        PUSHBUTTON      "Help", DID_HELP, 106, 4, 40, 14
    END
END

ICON DLGID  SWT.ICO

MENU DLGID
BEGIN
    MENUITEM "Save", MID_SAVE
END
```

Figure 13.13   Secondary window dialog template.

```
BOOL EXPENTRY WinInsertDefaultSize(HWND hwnd,
                                   PSZ pszDefaultSize)
```

Figure 13.14   WinInsertDefaultSize.

A secondary window may also be processed by calling the **WinLoadSecondaryWindow** API to create the window, **WinProcessSecondaryWindow** to handle the user interaction, and then **WinDestroySecondaryWindow** to destroy the window after processing is complete. This sequence is analogous to calling **WinLoadDlg**, **WinProcessDlg**, and then **WinDestroyWindow** for a dialog box. The secondary window may also be processed as a modeless window, in parallel with another application window, by calling **WinLoadSecondaryWindow** and making the window visible. In this case, there is no need to call **WinProcessSecondaryWindow**. If the dialog template is built in memory instead of residing in a resource, **WinCreateSecondaryWindow** is called instead of **WinLoadSecondaryWindow**. This function is the secondary window replacement for the **WinCreateDlg** API. The equivalent of the **WinDismissDlg** API for the secondary window is the **WinDismissSecondaryWindow** API.

The window procedure specified when the secondary window is created is programmed in the same manner as a dialog window procedure. In fact, a dialog window procedure can be converted to a secondary window procedure merely by replacing all calls to **WinDefDlgProc** with calls to **WinDefSecondaryWindowProc**, the default window procedure that defines the behavior of the secondary window. All the normal dialog helper APIs and macros, such as **WinSendDlgItemMsg** and **WinQueryDlgItemText**, which access controls as dialog items may be used in the secondary window procedure.

If an application is intended to enable the default sizing feature of the secondary window, a call to the **WinInsertDefaultSize** API should be issued, normally from within the WM_INITDLG processing. The prototype for this API is shown in Figure 13.14.

- The **hwnd** parameter is the secondary window's frame window handle.
- The **pszDefaultSize** parameter is a pointer to the text to be displayed on the menu item.

If this function is called from within the window procedure of the secondary window, the handle of the frame window can be obtained from the window procedure's **hwnd** parameter by calling the **WinQuerySecondaryHWND** API, which is prototyped as shown in Figure 13.15.

```
HWND EXPENTRY WinQuerySecondaryHWND(HWND hwnd,
                                    ULONG ulFlag);
```

Figure 13.15   WinQuerySecondaryHWND.

- The **hwnd** parameter is the handle of the source window for the API.
- The **ulFlag** parameter indicates the type of translation. If this parameter is set to QS_FRAME, **hwnd** should be set to the dialog window handle, and the handle of the secondary window's frame window is returned. If this parameter is set to QS_DIALOG, **hwnd** should be set to the frame window, and the handle of the dialog is returned.

The application may also programmatically set the window to its default size by calling the **WinDefaultSize** API. The prototype for this function is shown in Figure 13.16.

- The **hwnd** parameter is the window handle of the secondary window's frame window.

Figure 13.17 shows the program code that handles the dialog template from Figure 13.13 as the main window for the application. The only changes between this secondary window implementation and a normal dialog box implementation are shown in boldface type.

Secondary Message Boxes

The secondary window tools also provide an enhanced form of the standard message box called a secondary message box. This message box allows the programmer to create message boxes with application-defined buttons and a custom icon. The message box is created by calling the **WinSecondaryMessageBox** API. This function is prototyped as shown in Figure 13.18.

- Parameter **hwndParent** is the window handle of the window that will be the parent of the message box.
- Parameter **hwndOwner** is the window handle of the window that will be the owner of the message box.
- The **pszText** parameter is a pointer to a zero-terminated array of characters that will be displayed as the text of the message box.
- The **pszCaption** parameter is a pointer to a zero-terminated array of characters that will be displayed in the title bar of the message box.
- The **idWindow** parameter is the window ID of the message box.
- Parameter **psmbInfo** is a pointer to a SMBINFO structure that describes the custom features of the message box.

```
BOOL EXPENTRY WinDefaultSize(HWND hwnd);
```

Figure 13.16   WinSetDefaultSize.

```
MRESULT EXPENTRY DlgProc( HWND hwnd, ULONG msg, MPARAM mp1, MPARAM mp2 )
{
   if (msg == WM_INITDLG) {
      WinSendDlgItemMsg( hwnd, DID_LB, LM_INSERTITEM,
                         MPFROMLONG(LIT_END), MPFROMP( "Line 1" ));
      WinSendDlgItemMsg( hwnd, DID_LB, LM_INSERTITEM,
                         MPFROMLONG(LIT_END), MPFROMP( "Line 2" ));
      WinSendDlgItemMsg( hwnd, DID_LB, LM_INSERTITEM,
                         MPFROMLONG(LIT_END), MPFROMP( "Line 3" ));
      /* Enable the default size processing */
      WinInsertDefaultSize( WinQuerySecondaryHWND( hwnd, QS_FRAME ),
                            "Default Size" );
      return (MRESULT)0L;
   } else if (msg == WM_COMMAND) {
      if (SHORT1FROMMP(mp1) == DID_OK)
         WinDismissSecondaryWindow( hwnd, TRUE );
      if (SHORT1FROMMP(mp1) == DID_CANCEL)
         WinDismissSecondaryWindow( hwnd, FALSE );
      if (SHORT1FROMMP(mp1) == 10000 ) {
         /* Handle menu command */
      }
      return (MRESULT)0l;
   } else {
      return WinDefSecondaryWindowProc( hwnd, msg, mp1, mp2 );
   } /* endif */
}

main(int argc, char *argv[], char *envp[])
{
   HAB      hab;
   HMQ      hmq;
   QMSG     qmsg;

   do {
      if ((hab = WinInitialize(0)) == NULLHANDLE) break;
      if ((hmq = WinCreateMsgQueue( hab, 0 )) == NULLHANDLE) break;
      WinSecondaryWindow( HWND_DESKTOP, HWND_DESKTOP, DlgProc, NULLHANDLE,
               DLGID, NULL );
   } while ( 0 ); /* enddo */
   if (hmq != (HMQ)NULLHANDLE) WinDestroyMsgQueue( hmq );
   if (hab != (HAB)NULLHANDLE) WinTerminate( hab );
}
```

Figure 13.17   Programming with the secondary window.

```
ULONG EXPENTRY WinSecondaryMessageBox(HWND      hwndParent,
                                      HWND      hwndOwner,
                                      PSZ       pszText,
                                      PSZ       pszCaption,
                                      ULONG     idWindow,
                                      PSMBINFO psmbinfo);
```

Figure 13.18   WinSecondaryMessageBox.

WinSecondaryMessageBox returns a ULONG that identifies the pushbutton that was pressed to dismiss the message box.

The SMBINFO structure is used to describe the customization features of the message box and contains the items shown in Figure 13.19.

- Element *hIcon* is an HPOINTER that identifies the custom icon to display in the message box. This element is only used when the *flStyle* element contains the MB_ICONCUSTOM flag.
- Element *cButtons* is the number of buttons that have been defined for the message box. This represents the number of elements in the array pointed to by element *psmbd*.
- The *flStyle* element is a set of flags that indicate the type of icon to display in the message box. This can be one of the standard PM message box icons or the value MB_ICONCUSTOM to display the icon identified by the *hIcon* element.
- The *hwndNotify* element is reserved and should be set to NULLHANDLE.
- Element *psmbd* is a pointer to an array of SMBD structures that describe the buttons to be displayed in the message box.

The SMBD structure contains the three elements shown in Figure 13.20.

- The *achText* element is an array of characters that will be displayed as the button text. The size of the array and therefore the maximum length of the text is defined by the constant MAX_SMBTEXT. The portion of the array to be displayed should be followed by a null character terminator.

```
typedef struct _SMBINFO
{
   HPOINTER hIcon;
   ULONG    cButtons;
   ULONG    flStyle;
   HWND     hwndNotify;
   PSMBD    psmbd;
} SMBINFO;
```

Figure 13.19   The SMBINFO structure.

```
typedef struct _SMBD
{
   CHAR    achText[MAX_SMBDTEXT + 1];
   ULONG   idButton;
   LONG    flStyle;
} SMBD;
```

Figure 13.20 The SMBD structure.

- The *idButton* element is the window ID to assign to the button. If this button is clicked, this window ID will be returned to the application.
- Element *flStyle* is a set of flags that define the style of the button. The valid styles are the normal pushbutton style flags.

Figure 13.21 provides an example of the code required to initialize the structures, create the message box, and process the return value. An array of SMBD structures are defined as a global variable and initialized with text, return value IDs, and styles for the message box. The SMBINFO structure is also defined as a global variable and is initialized to indicate that the message box will contain three buttons and a custom icon. The *hIcon* element of the SMBINFO structure is initialized in the WM_INITDLG processing for the secondary window, which raises this message box. Within the WM_COMMAND processing, the ID_SHOWMESSAGE command causes the **WinSecondaryMessageBox** API to be called. Upon return from the message box processing, a switch statement is used to provide handling based on the button used to dismiss the message box. If the default size button was pressed, **WinDefaultSize** is called to return the secondary window to its default size. If the exit application button was pressed, **WinDismissSecondaryWindow** is called to close the secondary window and the application.

OS/2 Warp added the **WinMessageBox2** API. This API provides the same functionality as the original multimedia secondary message box, which is being retained for compatibility with existing applications. New programs should use **WinMessageBox2**. The SMBINFO structure has been renamed to MB2INFO and the SMBD structure has been renamed to MB2D; otherwise, the two APIs are identical.

SUMMARY

The graphic button control, secondary window class, and secondary message box provide application programmers with new, more flexible ways to perform old functions. The graphic button may be used to enhance functionality and appearance in instances where a pushbutton or checkbox would normally

```
SMBD   smbData[3] = { "Set Default Size", ID_DEFAULTSIZE, BS_DEFAULT,
                      "Exit Application", ID_EXITAPP, 0,
                      "Return", ID_RETURN, 0 };

SMBINFO smbInfo = { NULLHANDLE, 3, MB_ICONCUSTOM, NULLHANDLE, smbData };

MRESULT EXPENTRY SecWndProc( HWND hwnd, ULONG msg, MPARAM mp1, MPARAM mp2 )
{

   /* Process initialization message */
   if (msg == WM_INITDLG) {
     /* Load custom ICON for secondary message box */
     smbInfo.hIcon = WinLoadPointer( HWND_DESKTOP, NULLHANDLE, DLGID );
     return (MRESULT)0L;
   } else if (msg == WM_COMMAND) {
     /* if command is request to load secondary message box */
     if( SHORT1FROMMP(mp1) == ID_SHOWMESSAGE )
       /* Load and process the secondary message box */
       choice = (ULONG)WinSecondaryMessageBox( HWND_DESKTOP,
                     HWND_DESKTOP,
                     "What do you want to do?",
                     "Secondary Message Box Sample",
                     ID_MSGBOX, &smbInfo );
       switch( choice ) {
       case ID_DEFAULTSIZE:
          /* Set secondary window to default size */
          WinDefaultSize( WinQuerySecondaryHWND( hwnd, QS_FRAME ));
          break;
       case ID_EXITAPP:
          /* Exit the secondary window processing */
          WinDismissSecondaryWindow( hwnd, TRUE );
          break;
       }
       return (MRESULT)0L;
   }
   } else {
     return WinDefSecondaryWindowProc( hwnd, msg, mp1, mp2 );
   }
}
```

Figure 13.21   Secondary message box example.

be used. Additional features and operational modes of the button provide functionality such as press and hold which are not readily available in other PM controls. The secondary window is particularly useful for providing the user interface of a standard frame window for applications or major functions whose client areas are composed of a set of controls. With the secondary window, these applications can be structured as dialog boxes and reduce the application complexity required to manage the controls while retaining the full functionality of the standard frame window. The secondary message box provides the ease of use of a regular message box, but provides functionality that allows the application to customize the buttons and icon displayed in the box. Without the secondary message box, an application requiring this functionality would have to implement a dialog box or other window, a much more complicated task. Explore the window classes discussed in this chapter. They can easily add a bit of pizzazz to your applications.

CHAPTER 14

PM, Your Kingdom Awaits: Creating Your Own Controls

N ow that we've examined all the controls provided by PM, you're probably saying to yourself that PM provides everything an application programmer could ever desire. Right? No!? You would like to have just one more control that performs the function you always needed. In that case, you'll just have to develop the control yourself. And this chapter explains how.

PM control windows are no different than other windows created by an application, though they are normally more limited in functionality than the windows that application programmers are accustomed to creating. This chapter will describe the implementation of control classes using an example control. The TUTORIAL control is intended to provide an application the ability to easily generate and manipulate simple panels for providing explanatory information to the user. Since a picture is said to be worth a thousand words, the tutorial control allows the application to display bitmap graphics, text, or a combination of the two. The control does not accept any real input, but does notify the application of keyboard and mouse activity that the application can use to sequence through a set of panels.

DESIGNING THE CONTROL WINDOW APPLICATION INTERFACE

When designing a control class, bear in mind that the windows of the class will normally interface with other windows such as a dialog box or application client window. This interface consists of the control-specific styles, the control's externally visible data, control-specific messages that may be sent to the control, and control notification messages that are sent from the control to its owner. Certain types of messages and notifications are almost universally present in the PM controls and should normally be implemented in custom controls. For example, most controls provide notifications when gaining or losing the focus.

Any optional behavior or appearance of the control is normally managed by the class-specific flags of the window style. These flags are located in the low-order 16 bits of the window style and should be defined for the application. The TUTORIAL control provides the capability to display either one or two panels with each panel capable of displaying either text or a bitmap. If multiple panels are displayed, the control window may be split either vertically or horizontally. The control also provides functionality to automatically notify the application to change the panel contents after a specified amount of time. This capability must be enabled with a style flag before the automatic operation is started. The style flags defined by the control to support these capabilities are:

TS_SPLITHORZ	(0x0001)	causes the control to split the window horizontally and display panel 1 at the top of the window and panel 2 at the bottom of the window.
TS_SPLITVERT	(0x0002)	causes the control to split the window vertically and display panel 1 in the left side of the window and panel 2 in the right side of the window. This style is ignored if TS_SPLITHORZ is set.
TS_PANL1BITMAP	(0x0004)	causes the control to display a bitmap in panel 1. If this style is not set, text is displayed. Panel 1 is defined to be the entire window if the control is not split.
TS_PANL2BITMAP	(0x0008)	causes the control to display a bitmap in panel 2. If this style is not set, text is displayed. This style is ignored if the window is not split.
TS_AUTO	(0x0010)	enables the automatic notifications to be sent to the control's owner. A TM_AUTOMATE message must be sent to the control to begin the notification process.

The control data for the control typically contains all the information that the control class needs to handle processing for a window of the class. Remember that an application may create several instances of a control, which means that several instances of the control data will exist simultaneously. Thus, the data cannot be simply stored in a global variable, because the different control instances would receive the same data area and conflict with each other. The control data is typically stored in the window instance data for the control window or alternately in allocated memory. In the second case, a pointer to the memory is stored in the window instance data.

If the control allows applications to process the control data as an aggregate—for instance, by passing initial values in the **pCtlData** parameter of the **WinCreateWindow** API—a control data structure should be defined for public consumption. The first element of the structure must be a 16-bit value that defines the length of the structure in order to meet the requirements of the **pCtlData** parameter. The remaining elements are dependent on the control. The structure defined for the TUTORIAL class is shown in Figure 14.1.

- Element *cb* specifies the length of the structure in bytes.
- Element *hPnl1Data* specifies the data to be displayed in panel 1 of the control. This value is interpreted as a bitmap handle if the style flag TS_PNL1BITMAP is set, or as a pointer to text if the style flag is not set. If the TS_SPLITHORZ style is active, the data is displayed in the top half of the control. If the TS_SPLITVERT style is active, the data is displayed in the left half of the control.
- Element *hPnl2Data* specifies the data to be displayed in panel 2 of a split control. This value is interpreted as a bitmap handle if the style flag TS_PNL2BITMAP is set, or as a pointer to text if the style flag is not set. The data is displayed in the bottom half of the control if the TS_SPLITHORZ style is active, or in the right half of the control if the TS_SPLITVERT style is active.
- Element *ulTimerMS* specifies the number of milliseconds that the control will delay between TN_ENTER notifications when the TS_AUTO style is active.

Next, the control-specific messages that the control processes must be defined. These messages are defined with numeric values equal to or greater than WM_USER. Note that messages in this range may suffer from two potential problems that are not typically encountered by the PM controls whose messages reside below WM_USER: First, ill-behaved applications may inadvertently send these messages to unknown windows by calling the **WinBroadcastMsg** API; second, multiple custom controls may define the same message. Applications that use these controls must be especially careful that the proper messages are sent to the proper windows. The controls themselves should also do everything possible to ensure that parameters passed with the messages carry valid data.

```
typedef struct __TUTORCDATA__ {
    USHORT      cb;
    PVOID       hPnl1Data;
    PVOID       hPnl2Data;
    ULONG       ulTimerMS;
} TUTORCDATA, *PTUTORCDATA;
```

Figure 14.1   TUTORIAL control data.

When defining the messages for a particular control, avoid duplication of the functionality provided by the standard Presentation Manager messages and APIs. Duplication is confusing to programmers using the control and can increase the complexity of the control's coding when attempting to implement the same or similar functionality for different messages. The control messages defined for the TUTORIAL control are:

- TM_SETDATA—This message sets the bitmap handle or text pointer for either of the control's panels. The low-order 16-bits of parameter **mp1** indicate the panel whose data is to be set; a value of 1 indicates panel 1, and a value of 2 indicates panel 2. The high-order 16-bits of **mp1** are treated as a Boolean value, which indicates that the control is to be redrawn after the data is changed. If the value is zero or FALSE, no redrawing occurs. This allows the application to update both panels before invalidating the window for repainting. Parameter **mp2** is either a bitmap handle or a pointer to text, depending on the style flags. The return value is TRUE if the operation is successful or FALSE if an error occurred.
- TM_AUTOMATE—This message is used to start and stop the automation feature of the control. Parameter **mp1** is a Boolean value that, when TRUE, starts automation and, when FALSE, stops automation. Parameter **mp2** is a ULONG value that specifies the number of milliseconds between occurrences of the notification message from the control. If zero, the existing value in the control data is retained. Parameter **mp2** is ignored when **mp1** is FALSE. The return value is TRUE if the operation is successful or FALSE if an error occurred.
- TM_QUERYDATA—This message is used to retrieve the current bitmap handle or text pointer for a specified panel. The low-order 16 bits of parameter **mp1** indicate which panel's data is to be retrieved, and is set to 1 for panel 1 and 2 for panel 2. Parameter **mp2** is a pointer to the location to store the retrieved information. The return value from the message is TF_TEXT if the data is a text pointer, TF_BITMAP if the data is a bitmap handle, or TF_ERROR if an error occurred.
- TM_QUERYSTATE—This message is used to retrieve the automation state of the control. Parameters **mp1** and **mp2** are reserved and must be set to zero. The return value is zero if automation is not currently in progress; otherwise, the time interval between notifications is returned.
- TM_QUERYERROR—This message is used to retrieve the last error condition reported by the control and should be used in conjunction with an error return from a control message. This message duplicates the PM **WinGetLastError** API functionality because custom controls do not have access to the PM error reporting mechanism.

Last, but by no means least, the notifications that the control sends to its owner window must be specified. As you may have noticed, almost every control sends notifications when it receives or loses the focus. As a rule, custom controls should also provide these notifications. Custom notifications should also be provided for any other significant events in the control's processing, such as receipt of special keys. No special considerations are necessary when defining the actual numeric value of the notifications. Since the ID of the window is provided along with the notification code, the application is responsible for determining the actual notification code based on the control type if conflicts occur. The notifications provided by the tutorial control are:

- TN_SETFOCUS indicates that the control has received the focus.
- TN_KILLFOCUS indicates that the control has lost the focus.
- TN_CLICKED indicates a single click of mouse button 1 over the window or the Spacebar being pressed while the control has focus.
- TN_ENTER indicates a double-click of mouse button 1 over the window or the Enter key being pressed while the control has focus. This notification is also sent by the control's automation process when the specified time has elapsed.

These notification codes are sent to the control's owner window as the high-order 16 bits of parameter **mp1** of the WM_CONTROL message. The control must pass its ID as the low-order 16 bits of parameter **mp1**. Additional notification code-specific information may be passed in parameter **mp2**. Parameter **mp2** for the TUTORIAL notifications is set to the window handle of the control to facilitate messages sent from the application during processing of the notifications.

Custom controls should also send several predefined notification messages to the owner window. The WM_CONTROLPOINTER message is sent to the owner when the control receives a WM_MOUSEMOVE message to allow the owner to specify a change in the mouse pointer if necessary. This can allow the control to appear as part of the larger window rather than have the pointer change as it moves over the control. This also permits the application to modify the pointer to provide special emphasis alerting the user when the pointer is over a particular control. Controls should also forward WM_COMMAND, WM_HELP, and WM_SYSCOMMAND messages directly to the owner window.

CODING THE CUSTOM CONTROL

This section examines the code behind the TUTORIAL control. Of course, the code for any given control will vary depending of the functionality of the class, but many of the general principles remain the same. The TUTORIAL control provides a function, **RegisterTutorialControl**, that applications can call to register the TUTORIAL class. As shown in Figure 14.2, the TUTORIAL's function merely calls the **WinRegisterClass** API. This is the only public function

```
BOOL EXPENTRY RegisterTutorialControl(HAB hab)
{
    return WinRegisterClass( hab, "TUTORIAL", TutorWinProc, 0, C_WINWORDS );
}
```

Figure 14.2 Registering the TUTORIAL control class.

that the class makes available to applications. All other interaction between applications and the class occur through normal PM APIs or messages.

After the class has been registered, applications can create instances of the class by calling **WinCreateWindow**. This causes PM to create the window and send a WM_CREATE message. The control should handle this message by retrieving any control data passed to the API and using this data to initialize its own internal copy of the data. If no control data is passed, the control should initialize its internal copy of the data to default values. The TUTORIAL control's processing of this message is shown in Figure 14.3.

The *wmCreate* function extracts a pointer to the control data from parameter **mp1** of the WM_CREATE message and then the window style from the window instance data. If control data was passed, the function saves the data for panel 1 in the window instance data. If the window style indicates that the window is to be split into two panels, the data for panel 2 is also stored in

```
MRESULT wmCreate( HWND hwnd, MPARAM mp1, MPARAM mp2 )
{
    PTUTORCDATA pTCD = (PTUTORCDATA)mp1;
    ULONG       flStyle = WinQueryWindowULong( hwnd, QWL_STYLE );
    MRESULT     mr = MRFROMLONG(FALSE);

    if (pTCD != NULL) {
        if (pTCD->cb == sizeof( TUTORCDATA)) {
            WinSetWindowPtr( hwnd, WINWORD_WIN1DATA, pTCD->hWin1Data );
            if (flStyle & (TS_SPLITHORZ | TS_SPLITVERT)) {
                WinSetWindowPtr( hwnd, WINWORD_WIN2DATA, pTCD->hWin2Data );
            } /* endif */
            if (flStyle & TS_AUTO) {
                WinSetWindowULong( hwnd, WINWORD_TIMERMS, pTCD->ulTimerMS );
            } /* endif */
        } else {
            mr = MRFROMLONG(TRUE);
        } /* endif */
    } /* endif */
    return mr;
}
```

Figure 14.3 Processing WM_CREATE in a custom control.

the window data. Next, if the automation mode has been enabled, the interval time is stored in the window instance data (note that the animation is not started). The application must send the TM_AUTOMATE message to start the notification timer.

Let's next examine how the control paints itself. One of the main differences between control windows and normal application windows is the need for the control window to handle the definition and painting of its borders, focus emphasis, and so on, in addition to its contents. The **wmPaint** routine in Figure 14.4 shows an abbreviated version of how the TUTORIAL control handles painting for a control window that displays text and is not split.

The **wmPaint** routine first loads the style flags from the window instance data. Painting then begins when the **WinBeginPaint** routine is called to obtain a presentation space for drawing. The invalidated rectangle is then filled with the background color. The control now retrieves the coordinates of the rectangle, which define the entire window area so that the following calculations affect the entire window, not just the invalid area.

With the rectangle available, the control draws its borders. In this case, the border consists of several bands that vary in intensity and provide a thick, three-dimensional appearance. Each band is drawn by calling the **WinDrawBorder** API. **WinInflateRect** is then called to shrink the drawing rectangle in preparation for drawing the next band. When the border is complete, **WinInflateRect** is called one final time to compute the drawing rectangle for the control contents. This final calculation leaves a bit of space between the border and the text or bitmap to be displayed in the body of the window.

The routine now checks the style flags for the first panel to determine the type of data to be drawn. If the bitmap flag is not set, then text is drawn into the window. The pointer to the text is obtained from the window instance data and validated. If valid, **GpiQueryFontMetrics**, assuming for the moment that an image font is in use, is called to make available the vertical space required for each line of text. The function then begins scanning the text in a nested loop. The outer loop runs as long as the zero-termination character has not been found and executes once for each line of text. As the text is drawn, the top of the drawing rectangle is decremented by the height of the text from the FONTMETRICS structure. The inner loop scans the text for the newline character. Each time a new line is found, the characters for the current line are drawn into the presentation space with the **WinDrawText** API. After all the text has been drawn, **WinEndPaint** is called to release the presentation space and terminate the paint operation.

Finally, let's take a look at how the control handles the WM_SETFOCUS message by sending notification messages to the owner window and displaying the keyboard cursor. The code for the control's **wmSetFocus** routine is shown in Figure 14.5. The routine first obtains the owner window handle and the window ID assigned to the control from the window instance data. If the

```
MRESULT wmPaint( HWND hwnd, MPARAM mp1, MPARAM mp2 )
{
   HPS      hps;
   RECTL    rectl;
   PSZ      pszText;
   PSZ      pszText1;
   ULONG    cchText;
   FONTMETRICS fm;
   ULONG    flStyle = WinQueryWindowULong( hwnd, QWL_STYLE );

   if ((hps=WinBeginPaint(hwnd, NULLHANDLE, &rectl)) != NULLHANDLE ) {
      WinFillRect( hps, &rectl, SYSCLR_DIALOGBACKGROUND );
      WinQueryWindowRect( hwnd, &rectl );
      WinDrawBorder( hps, &rectl, 1, 1, CLR_DARKGRAY, CLR_WHITE, 0 );
      WinInflateRect( WinQueryAnchorBlock(hwnd),&rectl, -1, -1 );
      WinDrawBorder( hps, &rectl, 1, 1, CLR_PALEGRAY, CLR_WHITE, 0 );
      WinInflateRect( WinQueryAnchorBlock(hwnd),&rectl, -1, -1 );
      WinDrawBorder( hps, &rectl, 1, 1, CLR_WHITE, CLR_WHITE, 0 );
      WinInflateRect( WinQueryAnchorBlock(hwnd),&rectl, -1, -1 );
      WinDrawBorder( hps, &rectl, 1, 1, CLR_PALEGRAY, CLR_WHITE, 0 );
      WinInflateRect( WinQueryAnchorBlock(hwnd),&rectl, -1, -1 );
      WinDrawBorder( hps, &rectl, 1, 1, CLR_DARKGRAY, CLR_WHITE, 0 );

      WinInflateRect( WinQueryAnchorBlock(hwnd),&rectl, -5, -5 );
      if( !(flStyle & TS_PANL1BITMAP)) {
         pszText = (PSZ)WinQueryWindowPtr( hwnd, WINWORD_WIN1DATA );
         if( pszText != NULL ) {
            GpiQueryFontMetrics( hps, sizeof(FONTMETRICS), &fm );
            pszText1 = pszText;
            while (*pszText1 && rectl.yTop > 0 ) {
               cchText = 0;
               while (*pszText1 && *pszText1++ != '\n' ) cchText++;
               if( cchText ) {
                  WinDrawText( hps, cchText, pszText, &rectl, CLR_BLACK,
                              CLR_WHITE, DT_TEXTATTRS | DT_WORDBREAK );
               } /* endif */
               rectl.yTop -= fm.lMaxBaselineExt;
               pszText = pszText1;
            } /* endwhile */
         } /* endif */
      } /* endif */
      WinEndPaint( hps );
   } /* endif */
   return MRFROMLONG(0L);
}
```

Figure 14.4   Painting the TUTORIAL control.

```
MRESULT wmSetFocus( HWND hwnd, MPARAM mp1, MPARAM mp2 )
{
    HWND      hwndOwner = WinQueryWindow( hwnd, QW_OWNER );
    USHORT    usId = WinQueryWindowUShort( hwnd, QWS_ID );
    RECTL     rectl;

    if (SHORT1FROMMP(mp2)) {
        if (hwndOwner != NULLHANDLE) {
            WinSendMsg( hwndOwner, WM_CONTROL,
                        MPFROM2SHORT( usId, TN_SETFOCUS ),
                        MPFROMHWND( hwnd ));
        } /* endif */
        WinQueryWindowRect( hwnd, &rectl );
        WinInflateRect( WinQueryAnchorBlock(hwnd), &rectl, -5, -5 );
        WinCreateCursor( hwnd, rectl.xLeft, rectl.yBottom,
                         rectl.xRight - rectl.xLeft,
                         rectl.yTop - rectl.yBottom,
                         CURSOR_FRAME, NULL );
        WinShowCursor( hwnd, TRUE );
    } else {
        if (hwndOwner != NULLHANDLE) {
            WinSendMsg( hwndOwner, WM_CONTROL,
                        MPFROM2SHORT( usId, TN_KILLFOCUS ),
                        MPFROMHWND( hwnd ));
        } /* endif */
        WinDestroyCursor( hwnd );
    } /* endif */
    return MRFROMLONG(0L);
}
```

Figure 14.5   The WM_SETFOCUS message.

control is receiving the focus, the low-order 16 bits of **mp2** are TRUE, and the control attempts to notify the owner and establish cursor emphasis. Before sending the WM_CONTROL message, the control first ensures that an owner window was provided. If so, the WM_CONTROL message is sent to the owner window. The low-order 16 bits of parameter **mp1** are set to the control's window ID, and the high-order 16 bits are set to the TN_SETFOCUS notification code. Parameter **mp2** is set to the window handle of the control. When the owner window completes its processing of the WM_CONTROL message, the control creates a keyboard cursor that frames the window contents. The window rectangle is first queried and then deflated to the area inside the border with **WinInflateRect**. **WinCreateCursor** is called to establish a frame cursor around the edge of the resulting rectangle, and **WinShowCursor** is called to make the cursor visible.

If parameter **mp2** of the WM_SETFOCUS message is FALSE, the control window is losing focus. After checking the owner window handle, the

WM_CONTROL message is again formatted, but in this instance uses the TN_KILLFOCUS notification code. After the owner window finishes with the WM_CONTROL message, the keyboard cursor is destroyed by calling WinDestroyCursor.

A Few Words of Caution

The previous discussion, while far from giving a complete implementation of the TUTORIAL control, covers the basics of control design and implementation. The remaining details can be gleaned from the sample program for this chapter. We will next see how the control is packaged for efficient reuse in many applications. But first, let's review a few key points.

Remember that an application will often create multiple instances of a control. Be careful to avoid global data and other situations that can produce unwanted interaction between controls. Also, since the control is normally perceived to be an integral part of a larger window, avoid operations that could affect the overall function of the larger window. For instance, a control should not normally take or give the keyboard focus but should allow the owner or parent window to determine which control, if any, has focus.

Also be careful to release any system resources that the control allocates and to test the control's operation thoroughly. Since a control, once implemented, is likely to find use in many applications, any deficiencies in its operation can make a whole family of applications appear bad.

Packaging the Control

Once your control is implemented, you will need to package it for use by applications. If the control is very specific to a particular application, the source for the control can be included as part of the application source code and compiled along with the rest of the application. If, on the other hand, the control is used in several applications, you will want to handle the control much as you might any other subset of function code modules. This can be accomplished by providing header files and object modules or libraries, but this method embeds the control's executable code into each application. To avoid this duplication, package the control's executable code as a Dynamic Link Library, providing a header and library to the application developer's and a DLL module to ship with the application executable.

The header file should provide all the information for using the control, including the control's class name; constant definitions for the control's styles, messages, and notifications; the control data structure definition; and any application entry points into the control's executable code. The header file for the TUTORIAL class is shown in Figure 14.6 as an example.

```
/* Define a class name constant */
#define  WC_TUTORIAL    ("TUTORIAL")

/* Define the messages which can be sent to the control */
#define  TM_SETDATA     WM_USER
#define  TM_AUTOMATE    (TM_SETDATA + 1)
#define  TM_QUERYDATA   (TM_AUTOMATE + 1)
#define  TM_QUERYSTATE  (TM_QUERYDATA + 1)
#define  TM_QUERYERROR  (TM_QUERYSTATE + 1 )

/* Define the control styles */
#define  TS_SPLITHORZ   0x00000001
#define  TS_SPLITVERT   0x00000002
#define  TS_PANL1BITMAP 0x00000004
#define  TS_PANL2BITMAP 0x00000008
#define  TS_AUTO        0x00000010

/* Define the WM_CONTROL notification codes */
#define  TN_SETFOCUS    1
#define  TN_KILLFOCUS   2
#define  TN_CLICKED     3
#define  TN_ENTER       4

/* Define the control data structure */
typedef struct __TUTORCDATA__ {
    USHORT      cb;
    PVOID       hWin1Data;
    PVOID       hWin2Data;
    ULONG       ulTimerMS;
} TUTORCDATA, *PTUTORCDATA;

/* Prototype callable functions */
BOOL EXPENTRY RegisterTutorialControl(HAB hab);
```

Figure 14.6   The public header for control.

SUMMARY

The mechanics of creating a control class are actually quite simple, requiring little more effort than the implementation of any PM window. Of course, controls may be implemented that provide functionality that makes implementation difficult—consider the code that must be behind the container control—but this is a result of the functionality, not the mechanics of control implementation. This chapter has provided you with the basic information needed to journey into the wonderful world of control programming, so take the information and go implement that one control you always wished PM had provided.

CHAPTER 15

Win, Lose, or Draw:
The Art of Drawing Bitmaps

A large part of the success of any graphical programming environment is the ability for the developer to master the visual effect. It is imperative that a strong programming interface exist, so that the developer can communicate successfully with the operating system and provide a powerful and simple interface to the user. Several of the early GUIs failed because, although they contained advanced graphical programming capabilities, there was no architected method to fully exploit the power of the graphics subsystem.

THE PM GRAPHICS SUBSYSTEM

Three OS/2 components form the nucleus of the PM graphics subsystem. PMGPI.DLL, is the developer interface or Graphical Programming Interface. It contains all of the code to handle the graphical API layer. All of the code for the API calls prefixed with Gpi are contained within this library. Through the use of these APIs, the application developer can draw and manipulate graphical images.

The second component is the window manager or PMWIN.DLL. This library also contains simplified versions of various APIs that are available to the application developer to manipulate both text and graphic images. Also, this library contains the code to resolve PM's usage of bitmaps. For example, the various control windows used throughout PM contain graphical images stored in bitmap files; PMWIN uses these bitmaps to respond to different user events and adjust the behavior accordingly. The movement of a scroll bar, the positioning of a frame window, or the click on the minimize button are all examples of how PM uses bitmaps to illustrate the effect of a given function.

Finally, probably the most important graphical component is the graphics engine, PMGRE.DLL. This library contains no API support, so application developers have no direct interaction with the functions contained in the engine, although most of the graphics-related functions resolve to worker functions contained in the graphics engine. The graphics engine contains the actual worker routines for bitmap manipulation, including calls to create, load, and bit block transfer a bitmap, as well as the code required for the presentation spaces and device contexts.

Since no GRE API exists, all calls into the engine come through a single 16- and 32-bit entry point. The 16-bit entry point is a routine called **Dispatch16**, and the 32-bit entry point is a routine called **Dispatch32**. If you ever are debugging a graphical application and want to trace the calls in and out of the engine, you can use this breakpoint to track entry and exit through the engine routines.

The 2.1 and 2.11 releases of the operating system contain 32-bit versions of PMGRE and PMGPI while the PMWIN code is still 16-bit (although the API layer is 32-bit, the actual worker routines are still 16-bit). OS/2 WARP is the first release of the operating system to contain a complete 32-bit window manager. Because of the changes made to PMWIN, many of the limitations that plagued the 16-bit PMWIN have been fixed. As discussed in Chapter 2, PMGRE and PMWIN are now contained in PMMERGE.DLL.

The term *graphics engine* does not even begin to express the complete functionality of the PM graphics engine component. The engine is probably one of the most important components to the entire operating system, and it interacts with virtually all of the graphical subsystem components. The engine contains a powerful memory subsystem that allocates shared memory on behalf of virtually every PM process.

THE PURPOSE OF THE SAMPLE PROGRAM

The workplace shell provides the ability to view a bitmap file as the background of any folder (container), including the desktop. Also, the workplace shell allows the user the ability to view a bitmap file while the workplace lockup feature is enabled. Although the usability that the workplace shell provides is great, using a workplace folder as purely a bitmap viewer is tedious at best. The sample program SHOWOFF is a simple bitmap viewer that allows the user to preview bitmap files quickly and easily. It also allows the user the ability to change the desktop bitmap.

The code for the program also illustrates how to create the memory device context and required presentation space, along with the necessary code for painting the client area with the bitmapped image. The program provides the keys for mastering the display and manipulation of bitmaps along with other basic graphic file formats and the painting of graphic images.

THE COMPOSITION OF A BITMAP FILE

One of the most powerful graphics file formats is inherent to the Presentation Manager; this file format is known as the bitmap file. The bitmap is, quite literally, a union of binary data (bits), that form the basis of a graphical image on a raster device. In more simplistic terms, a bitmap is a series of bits that, when put together, form an image on your screen or printer. Bitmaps are actually device-dependent, meaning that the visual representation of the image is based on the type of device upon which the image will be displayed. Therefore, bitmaps use device coordinates rather than world coordinates when the image is displayed.

EXAMINING THE CONTENTS OF BITMAP DATA

To understand what a bitmap looks like, let's create a simple monochrome bitmap from scratch. Each bit in the bitmap corresponds to a pixel or pel (pixel and pel both mean the same thing, it just depends on which side of the IBM terminology track you are on). The bits are stored as a BYTE array. The bottom row of bits in the array is stored first in the bitmap; the top row of bits is stored last. The bytes are stored from left to right so that the first byte is the first eight pixels from left to right. For example, consider the primitive arrow bitmap drawn in the grid in Figure 15.1.

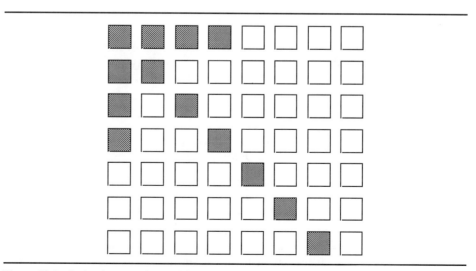

Figure 15.1 A simple monochrome bitmap.

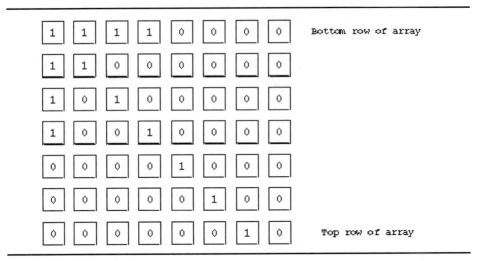

Figure 15.2   The bitmap bits.

Figure 15.1 represents a basic 8 x 8 bitmap; nothing magical here. Now, if you replace all of the black squares in the grid with a 1, to represent black, and all the white squares in the grid with a 0, to represent white, you have a series of bits that represents the bitmap (See Figure 15.2).

Now, to create our bitmap array for our bitmap, we convert all of the bits in the bitmap to hexadecimal and store it as a **BYTE** array. The bottom row of the bitmap actually corresponds to the top row of the array (See Figure 15.3).

The Bitmap File Format Structures

The Presentation Manager user interface makes frequent use of the bitmaps to simulate moving controls across the screen. For the most part, the bitmap file format is relatively similar between PM versions 1.x, 2.x, OS/2 WARP, and

```
BYTE abArrow[] = {
            0x02 0x00 0x00 0x00
            0x04 0x00 0x00 0x00
            0x08 0x00 0x00 0x00
            0x90 0x00 0x00 0x00
            0xa0 0x00 0x00 0x00
            0xc0 0x00 0x00 0x00
            0xf0 0x00 0x00 0x00
          }
```

Figure 15.3   Turning the bitmap into an array.

even the Microsoft Windows bitmap file format; pointers and icons are also composed of bitmaps. There are three important structures that all bitmaps use. The definitions of the bitmap data structures are resolved in PMBITMAP.H.

NOTE: The bitmap structures have changed from previous versions of PM, but PM still contains support for the old structure formats for compatibility with 1.x PM applications. The new 2.x bitmap structure formats contain a "2" at the end of the structure name. Unless you are writing an application that needs the compatibility, it is beneficial to use the new structure format.

The BitmapInfoHeader Structure

The **BitmapInfoHeader** structure contains the information regarding the physical composition of the bitmap image. The format of the complete data structure is given in Figure 15.4. Since the first five parameters of the structure are the really important elements with regard to the characteristics of the bitmap, the structure may be truncated after the *cBitCount* element.

- The **cbFix** parameter is the size of the stucture.
- The *cx* element of the structure is the horizontal width of the bitmap in pels.
- The *cy* element of the structure is the vertical height of the bitmap in pels.

```
typedef struct _BITMAPINFOHEADER2      // bmp2
  {
    ULONG   cbFix;
    ULONG   cx;
    ULONG   cy;
    USHORT  cPlanes;
    USHORT  cBitCount;
    ULONG   ulCompression;
    ULONG   cbImage;
    ULONG   cxResolution;
    ULONG   cyResolution;
    ULONG   cclrUsed;
    ULONG   cclrImportant;
    USHORT  usUnits;
    USHORT  usReserved;
    USHORT  usRecording;
    USHORT  usRendering;
    ULONG   cSize1;
    ULONG   cSize2;
    ULONG   ulColorEncoding;
    ULONG   ulIdentifier;
  } BITMAPINFOHEADER2;
typedef BITMAPINFOHEADER2 FAR *PBITMAPINFOHEADER2;
```

Figure 15.4   The BitmapInfoHeader2 data structure.

- The *cPlanes* element of the structure contains the number of bit planes within the bitmap.
- The *cBitCount* element contains the number of bitmap bits per pel within the bit plane.
- The *ulCompression* element contains the type of compresssion algorithm that can be used to compress the size of the bitmap. The compression constants are defined in PMBITMAP.H as:

BCA_UNCOMP	0L	uncompressed.
BCA_HUFFMAN1D	3L	a modified form of Huffman compression that is used for a 1-bit per pel bitmap.
BCA_RLE4	2L	represents a 4-bit per pel run-length encoded bitmap.
BCA_RLE8	1L	represents an 8-bit per pel run-length encoded bitmap.
BCA_RLE24	4L	represents a 24-bit per pel run-length encoded bitmap.

- The *cbImage* element is the length in bytes of the bitmap storage area. If no form of bitmap compression is used, this parameter should be zero.
- The *cxResolution* element corresponds to the horizontal resolution of the output device that the bitmap will be displayed on. The resolution is in the form of the units specified in the **usUnits** field of the structure.
- The *cyResolution* element corresponds to the vertical resolution of the output device that the bitmap will be displayed on.
- The *cclrUsed* element represents the number of color indexes that will be used in the bitmap.
- The *cclrImportant* element is the smallest number of color indexes that are required to display the bitmap on the output device. Although more colors can be in the bitmap, it is overkill to assign them to the palette of the device.
- The *usUnits* element represents the unit of measure for the resolution of the output device that the bitmap will be displayed on. The default value is the only measurement unit defined in PMBITMAP.H, BRU_METRIC, which implies the metric unit of measurement.
- The *usReserved* element is reserved and must be zero if this element of the structure is used.
- The *usRecording* element specifies the algorithm that is used to record the bitmap data. The default is BRA_BOTTOMUP, which indicates that the scan lines are actually recorded from the bottom up.
- The *usRendering* element specifies the algorithm that is used to record bitmap data that has been altered through digital halftoning. The following constants are defined for halftoning.

BRH_NOTHALFTONED	0L	the default value indicating no halftoning.
BRH_ERRORDIFFUSION	1L	indicates that the error diffusion algorithm has been used for halftoning.

BRH_PANDA   2L   represents the Processing Algorithm for Non-Coded Document Acquisition.

BRH_SUPERCIRCLE   3L   indicates that the super circle algorithm has been used for halftoning.

- The *cSize1* value is used in conjunction with the halftoning element. If the *usRendering* value is either BRH_PANDA or BRH_SUPERCIRCLE, then this value represents the horizontal size of the pattern in pels. If the *usRendering* value is BRH_ERRORDIFFUSION, then this value is used to represent the error damping percentage.
- The *cSize2* value is the vertical size of the pattern in pels if either the BRH_PANDA or BRH_SUPERCIRCLE halftoning algorithms is applied. If the BRH_ERRORDIFFUSION halftoning algorithm is used, then this value is not relevent.
- The *ulColorEncoding* element specifies the color encoding that is to be used. The valid values are:

BCE_RGB   0L   the default value indicating that each element in the color array is based off an RGB2 structure.

BCE_PALETTE   1L   indicates that each element in the color array is derived from the palette.

- The *ulIdentifier* element is not used and is reserved for application use.

There is also a **BitmapInfo2** structure defined in PMBITMAP.H which is virtually the same as the **BitmapInfoHeader2** structure except that it contains an additional element, an RGB2 data structure.

The 32-bit BitmapFileHeader Structure

The second important bitmap structure is the **BitmapFileHeader2** structure which contains information regarding the format of the actual bitmap file. The last element of this structure is the **BitmapInfoHeader2** structure. The format of this structure is shown in Figure 15.5.

```
typedef struct _BITMAPFILEHEADER2     // bfh2
  {
    USHORT    usType;
    ULONG     cbSize;
    SHORT     xHotspot;
    SHORT     yHotspot;
    ULONG     offBits;
    BITMAPINFOHEADER2 bmp2;
  } BITMAPFILEHEADER2;
typedef BITMAPFILEHEADER2 FAR *PBITMAPFILEHEADER2;
```

Figure 15.5   **The BitmapFileHeader2 structure.**

- The *usType* element is used to represent the type of bitmap file format. The valid file type formats include:

BFT_ICON	0x4349	// 'IC' Icon File Type
BFT_BMAP	0x4d42	// 'BM' Bitmap File Type
BFT_POINTER	0x5450	// 'PT' Pointer File Type
BFT_COLORICON	0x4943	// 'CI' Color Icon File Type
BFT_COLORPOINTER	0x5043	// 'CP' Color Pointer File Type
BFT_BITMAPARRAY	0x4142	// 'BA' Bitmap Array File Type

- The *cbSize* element is the size of the structure in bytes. Applications can query this value to determine if the bitmap file is using the 32-bit format or the older 16-bit format.
- The *xHotSpot* is the horizontal coordinate representing the point of action for an icon or pointer. This field is ignored for bitmaps.
- The *yHotspot* is the vertical coordinate representing the point of action for an icon or pointer. This field is ignored for bitmaps.
- The *offBits* element is the offset in bytes from the beginning of the file to the beginning of the actual bitmap data.

Although there are several different types of bitmap files that were described, only two of the six bitmap file types actually end in the .BMP file extension, indicating that the file is a standard bitmap image file. The BFT_BMAP format is composed of a single bitmap file, thus it contains a **BitmapFile-Header2** data structure, the RGB color table structure, and the actual bitmap data. The BFT_BITMAPARRAY file type is used to store several individual bitmaps in a single bitmap file. Since bitmaps are device-dependent graphical images, the bitmap array file type is designed to allow the developer to store multiple versions of the same image that are modified to provide the best resolution on multiple video displays or other raster devices. This allows a different bitmap of the same image to be displayed so that a 640 x 480 version of the image is displayed on VGA video devices, while a 1024 x 768 version of the image is displayed on a SVGA or XGA display that supports that resolution. Physically, the only difference between the two file formats is that the bitmap array file format contains one additional structure—the bitmap array file header structure. The format of the structure is shown in Figure 15.6.

- The *usType* element represents the type of bitmap file format.
- The *cbSize* element is the actual size of the structure in bytes.
- The *offNext* element is the offset to the next bitmap array file header structure from the start of the file.
- The *cxDisplay* element represents the horizontal resolution of the the device that the bitmap is to be displayed on.

```
typedef struct _BITMAPARRAYFILEHEADER2    // bafh2
 {
  USHORT          usType;
  ULONG           cbSize;
  ULONG           offNext;
  USHORT          cxDisplay;
  USHORT          cyDisplay;
  BITMAPFILEHEADER2 bfh2;
 } BITMAPARRAYFILEHEADER2;
typedef BITMAPARRAYFILEHEADER2 FAR *PBITMAPARRAYFILEHEADER2;
```

Figure 15.6   The BitmapArrayFileHeader2 structure.

- The *cyDisplay* element represents the vertical resolution of the device that the bitmap is to be displayed on.
- The *bfh2* element is a **BitmapFileHeader2** structure.

THE COLOR TABLE STRUCTURE

Virtually every color on the face of the earth is derived from some combination of the colors red, blue, and green. Thus, it is easy to combine different variances of these colors to form other colors (See Figure 15.7). The first 8 bits correspond to red, while the second 8 bits correspond to green, and the last 8 bits are blue.

DRAWING WITHIN A PM WINDOW

The *presentation space* (PS) is the paradigm provided by the Presentation Manager to allow the application the ability to draw within a window. All drawing within a PM application is done through the presentation space. Any PM application can create and maintain multiple presentation spaces; each PS defines a different environment for drawing. In order to draw within a presentation space, an application obtains a presentation space handle, or HPS.

The presentation space is the canvas that is used for drawing within the PM environment. Any given window that is used to illustrate the drawing may only be showing a subset of the image that is contained within the presentation space. A presentation space is associated to a particular *device context* (DC) to represent where the drawing will be displayed. The device context is the paradigm used to represent the actual physical output device on which the drawing will occur. The device context can represent either printers or video devices.

Color	RGB Value		
Red	0xFF0000	• All Red, no Green or Blue.	255, 0, 0
Green	0x00FF00	• All Green, no Red or Blue.	0, 255, 0
Blue	0x0000FF	• All Blue, no Red or Green.	0, 0, 255
Black	0x000000	• Black is the absence of color.	
White	0xFFFFFF	• White is the complete presence of red, green and blue. 255, 255, 255.	
Yellow	0xFFFF00	• Yellow is the presence of red and green, but the absence of blue. 255, 255, 0.	
Cyan	0x00FFFF	• Cyan is the presence of green and blue, but the absence of red. 0, 255, 255.	
Magenta	0xFF00FF	• Magenta is the presence of red and blue, but the absence of green. 255, 0, 255.	

• **You can create different colors by varying the RGB values**

Orange	0xFF7F00	• A form of Orange can be derived from the presence of red, some green and the absence of blue. 255, 127, 0.
Gray	0x7F7F7F	• The color Gray can be derived from half of red, green and blue. 127, 127, 127.

• **The RGB structure looks like this:**

```
typedef struct _RGB2        // rgb2
  {
   BYTE bBlue;              // Blue component of the color definition
   BYTE bGreen;            // Green component of the color definition
   BYTE bRed;              // Red component of the color definition
   BYTE fcOptions;         // Reserved, must be zero
  } RGB2;
typedef RGB2 *PRGB2;
```

Standard Bitmap Formats:

Format	Bits per pel
2 color bitmap (monochrome)	1
16 color bitmap	4
256 color bitmap	8
16.7 million color bitmap	24

Figure 15.7   Creating colors.

The purpose of the device context is to interpret and then translate all graphics commands used by the presentation space into the visible image that will appear on the output device. An application must obtain a device context handle to represent the device context. The device context handle is also known as the HDC. The PS and DC combination allow the developer the luxury of not worrying about displaying graphics on individual physical devices, since the same graphics functions provided by the PM graphical programming interface (Gpi) can be used for different display types.

The different display drivers contain the necessary code to handle the translation of the graphical image to the raster device. In reality, a printer device driver is nothing more than a display driver. Under the 1.x version of OS/2, the DISPLAY.DLL module contained code specific for the display adapter. Ironically, under OS/2 version 2.x and higher, no display-specific code actually exists in DISPLAY.DLL, and its purpose is to provide rasterization for the printer device. Under the WARP release of OS/2, the print rasterizer has been renamed to PMPRE.DLL, although the DISPLAY.DLL module that is the same code still exists for backward compatibility.

There is a third type of device context that is not associated with either a display or printer; it is called the *memory device context*. The memory DC is a powerful tool that can be used to greatly improve the performance of drawing within an application. The memory DC is designed to simulate a raster device in function, but since the device context is in memory, the manipulation of the image through the memory DC is much faster and totally transparent to the user so that the image can be redrawn and displayed to the user quickly. The graphics function **GpiBitBlt** is used to copy the individual bits to or from a presentation space that is associated with a memory device context.

Figure 15.8 shows the typical usage of the memory device context. The bitmap is first copied to a memory presentation space within a memory device context. The image can then be manipulated within the memory device context before finally being displayed within the display window. The SHOWOFF program uses the memory device context to draw the bitmap very quickly within the client window. This allows for smoother painting of the client window when sized or updated.

Understanding Presentation Spaces

There are three basic types of presentation spaces designed for drawing in the PM environment, and each type includes its own benefits and limitations. A well-written application makes the best use of different types of presentation spaces based on the requirements of the user. The three types of presentation spaces that can be used within the PM environment for drawing are the cached micro, the mirco, and the normal presentation spaces.

The *cached-micro* PS is the most basic of the presentation space types since it offers the ability to draw the image only on the screen, within a given

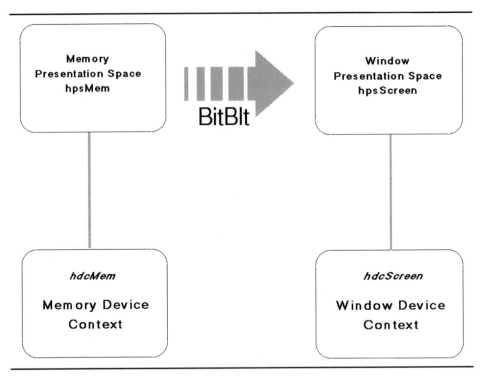

Figure 15.8 Understanding the memory device context.

window. Although it is the fastest of the presentation space types, it is also the one that provides the least flexibility and functionality. It is also the only one that offers window manager (WIN) APIs to create and destroy the presentation space.

The *micro* PS is more powerful than the cached-micro presentation space since it offers more of the functionality provided by the Gpi, combined with the ability to output to all different types of devices. The micro PS is typically slower than the cached-micro, but is faster than the normal presentation space and uses less memory.

The *normal* presentation space is the slowest, yet most powerful and complex of the presentation space types. It offers the complete functionality provided by the Gpi and, like the micro PS, allows the output to be directed to different types of devices.

Using a Cached-Micro PS within Regular Paint Processing

The cached-micro PS is very simple to use and very fast to implement. It can be created as part of the normal window painting functionality by calling the **WinBeginPaint** and **WinEndPaint** APIs. These two functions typically form

```
HPS   APIENTRY WinBeginPaint(HWND    hwnd,
                             HPS     hps,
                             PRECTL  prclPaint);
```

Figure 15.9   The WinBeginPaint API.

the nucleus of the painting operations within a PM program. The functions are called within the context of the window paint message WM_PAINT. The purpose of obtaining the presentation space within the paint message is to allow the application to simply paint the window every time it receives the WM_PAINT message. The presentation space is typically obtained each time the paint message is processed and released as the application returns from the message. If more complex painting is required by the window, this method of painting becomes tedious since the application will have to establish the attributes for the presentation space each time the paint message is processed. For applications that require the modification of presentation space attributes such as colors or fonts, using this method of painting becomes difficult to manage since the presentation space attributes also have to be created every time the presentation space is obtained within the WM_PAINT message.

The format of the **WinBeginPaint** API is given in Figure 15.9.

- The **hwnd** parameter specifies the handle of the window that is going to be painted.
- The **hps** parameter is set to NULLHANDLE to obtain a cached-micro PS. If another presentation space handle is specified, it effectively sets the clipping region to the update region of the window specified by the **hwnd** parameter.
- The **prclPaint** parameter specifies a pointer to a RECTL structure that will be used to return the surrounding rectangle of the paint region.

The function will return NULLHANDLE if an error occurs; otherwise, the function will return the handle of the newly created presentation space. The mouse pointer is hidden during the paint operation and is restored with **WinEndPaint** when the painting is complete.

Once the painting process is complete, the **WinEndPaint** function is used to conclude the painting of the window. Like the **WinBeginPaint** function, the **WinEndPaint** function is called within the context of the paint message, WM_PAINT. The format of the **WinEndPaint** function is shown in Figure 15.10.

```
BOOL   APIENTRY WinEndPaint(HPS hps);
```

Figure 15.10   The WinEndPaint API prototype.

```
HPS APIENTRY WinGetPS(HWND hwnd);
```

Figure 15.11   The WinGetPS API.

- The **hps** parameter specifies the handle of the presentation space that was used for the drawing. It is the same PS handle that was returned by the **WinBeginPaint** function.

The function will return TRUE if successful and FALSE if an error occured ending the paint operation. When this function is used to end a cached presentation space, the PS is once again returned to the cache. Also, all child windows that use the synchronous window painting style (CS_SYNCPAINT) with the window associated to the presentation space will be repainted if the update region contains valid coordinates.

Using a Cached-Micro PS outside Regular Paint Processing

The other method of creating and destroying a cached-micro PS is by using the built-in presentation space functions **WinGetPS** and **WinReleasePS**. Using this method is more effective for applications that will need to modify their window drawing process, because the application can explicitly modify elements of the presentation space that can be used throughout the duration of the program.
The format of the **WinGetPS API** is shown in Figure 15.11.

- The **hwnd** parameter specifies the handle of the window for which the cached-micro PS is to be created.

The function will return a valid cached-micro PS handle that can be used as the second parameter to **WinBeginPaint** every time the window updates its client area via a WM_PAINT message. This allows the visible region to be updated while leaving the presentation space attributes unaltered, so that every time the window receives a paint message it does not have to re-create the presentation space attributes along with the presentation space.

USING WINDRAWBITMAP

The PMWIN code provides a simple, yet powerful API to manipulate and display bitmaps within a specified presentation space. The **WinDrawBitmap** function provides an easy method of drawing bitmaps quickly and easily using the current image colors and mix modes. This function will resolve to the worker routine in the graphics engine for **GpiBitBlt**. The purpose of the function is to draw the contents of a bitmap into a specified rectangle within a presentation space.

The format of the **WinDrawBitmap** API is shown in Figure 15.12.

- The **hpsDst** parameter specifies the handle of the presentation space that the bitmap is to be drawn on.
- The **hbm** parameter is the handle of the bitmap that is to be drawn within the presentation space.
- The **prclSrc** parameter specifies a pointer to a rectangle structure. The rectangle is used to determine the part of the bitmap that will be drawn. If this value is NULL, then the entire bitmap specified by **hbm** is drawn within the presentation space. If this value is not NULL, thereby containing a valid rectangle, the part of the bitmap specified by the rectangle is the only part that is actually drawn. Each of the values in this structure must be within the range of a SHORT.
- The **pptlDst** parameter specifies the coordinates of the bitmap's destination in device coordinates.
- The **clrFore** parameter is simply the foreground color of the bitmap. This value is only used if the bitmap to be drawn is a monochome bitmap. All 0s in the bitmap are drawn using this color.
- The **clrBack** parameter is simply the background color of the bitmap. This value is only used if the bitmap to be drawn is a monochrome bitmap. All 1s in the bitmap are drawn using this color.
- The **fl** parameter specifies the flags that are used to determine how the bitmap will be drawn. These values correspond to the raster operations flags in **GpiBitBlt**. The valid flags include:

DBM_NORMAL	0x0000	specifies that the bitmap will be drawn normally. Corresponds to ROP_SRCCOPY.
DBM_INVERT	0x0001	specifies that the bitmap will be drawn inverted. Corresponds to ROP_NOTSRCCOPY.
DBM_HALFTONE	0x0002	specifies that the bitmap will be drawn halftoned. It can be used in conjunction with either the DBM_NORMAL or DBM_INVERT flags.
DBM_STRETCH	0x0004	specifies that the bitmap will be stretched within the rectangle specified by the two points in the POINTL structure passed in the **pptlDst** parameter.

```
BOOL  APIENTRY WinDrawBitmap(HPS      hpsDst,
                             HBITMAP  hbm,
                             PRECTL   prclSrc,
                             PPOINTL  pptlDst,
                             LONG     clrFore,
                             LONG     clrBack,
                             ULONG    fl);
```

Figure 15.12   The WinDrawBitmap prototype.

DBM_IMAGEATTRS   0x0008   specifies that the monochrome-to-color-bitmap conversion will use the image attributes. If this flag is used, the **clrFore** and **clrBack** parameters are ignored.

This function will return TRUE if the call is successful and FALSE if the call fails.

USING THE BIT BLOCK TRANSFER FUNCTION—GPIBITBLT

The graphics engine provides a powerful set of functions that are used to copy bitmaps within memory. The process of copying a bitmap within a given rectangle from one presentation space to another is known as the *bit-block transfer copy method* or *bitblt* (pronounced bitblit) for short. The PM graphics programming interface library (PMGPI) contains a function that allows the developer to access the bit block copy function. The function is called **GpiBitBlt** and its format is shown in Figure 15.13.

- The **hpsTarget** parameter contains the presentation space handle that the bitmap is being copied to.
- The **hpsSource** parameter contains the presentation space handle that the bitmap is being copied from.
- The **lCount** value is used to specify how many points will be contained in the point array specified by the **aptlPoints** parameter. If this value is 3, the source rectangle is the same size as the target rectangle. If the value is 4, then the bitmap will be stretched or compressed accordingly, based on the options specified by the **flOptions** parameter.
- The **aptlPoints** parameter is an array of values containing the coordinates of the target and source rectangles used in the bit block transfer. The values correspond to the following:

TX1, TY1   specifies the lower left corner of the target rectangle.
TX2, TY2   specifies the upper right corner of the target rectangle.
SX1, SY1   specifies the lower left corner of the source rectangle.

```
LONG APIENTRY GpiBitBlt(HPS       hpsTarget,
                        HPS       hpsSource,
                        LONG      lCount,
                        PPOINTL   aptlPoints,
                        LONG      lRop,
                        ULONG     flOptions);
```

Figure 15.13   The GpiBitBlt function prototype.

Sx2, SY2   specifies the upper right corner of the source rectangle. The SX2 and SY2 values are only valid if the value passed in **lCount** contained a 4, indicating that the bitmap is to be compressed or stretched.

- The **lRop** parameter is used to specify the raster operations. These are the valid ROP flags defined in PMGPI.H.

ROP_SRCCOPY	0x00CCL
ROP_SRCPAINT	0x00EEL
ROP_SRCAND	0x0088L
ROP_SRCINVERT	0x0066L
ROP_SRCERASE	0x0044L
ROP_NOTSRCCOPY	0x0033L
ROP_NOTSRCERASE	0x0011L
ROP_MERGECOPY	0x00C0L
ROP_MERGEPAINT	0x00BBL
ROP_PATCOPY	0x00F0L
ROP_PATPAINT	0x00FBL
ROP_PATINVERT	0x005AL
ROP_DSTINVERT	0x0055L
ROP_ZERO	0x0000L
ROP_ONE	0x00FFL

- The **flOptions** parameter contains flags that determine how the copied image is to be compressed. The remaining bits, 15-31, may be used to offer support for a private raster device. The predefined values are:

BBO_OR	0L	indicates that a logical OR operation will be performed on the eliminated rows or columns. This is typically used for white on black images, and this value is the default.
BBO_AND	1L	indicates that a logical AND operation will be performed on the eliminated rows or columns. This is typically used for black on white images.
BBO_IGNORE	2L	indicates that the eliminated rows or columns are ignored on compression so the alteration of the image when compressed is dependent on the colors of the bitmap itself.
BBO_PAL_COLORS	4L	indicates that a palette color table is used for the current palette, in replacement of actual colors.

The **GpiBitBlt** function will return GPI_OK, which is TRUE, if successful. The function will return FALSE, which is also GPI_ERROR, if an error occurred. The function can also return GPI_HITS, which is used to indicate the number of correlation hits.

The bit-block transfer is an effective method of copying bitmaps from one PS to another quickly and easily. The window manager code makes frequent use of the bitblt worker routines within the graphics engine to copy bitmaps across the screen.

CHANGING THE DESKTOP BITMAP

The workplace shell provides a wealth of functionality, including the ability to customize the background of the container window that is used represent the folder paradigm. Have you ever strolled by someone else's desk and admired their desktop bitmap? Through the use of the settings for the folder object, any user can "jazz up" the background of the folder by displaying a bitmap within the folder's background. Since the desktop window itself is represented by a folder, the user can customize the desktop container by adding a bitmap to its background.

Unfortunately, changing the desktop's bitmap via the Desktop settings is not exactly the most convenient way to view a bitmap, since it requires opening the settings notebook and turning to the background page every time you want to replace the desktop bitmap. Finding a programmatic solution to changing the desktop bitmap is probably one of the most frequently asked questions in IBM PM programming forums. Fortunately, changing the desktop bitmap is a relatively simple task, although it becomes somewhat perplexing if you actually read the documentation.

The Presentation Manager provides two APIs that can be used to query the desktop information and set the desktop background bitmap. The two APIs are **WinQueryDesktopBkgnd** and **WinSetDesktopBkgnd** respectively. The problem with these APIs is that they are designed to work outside the context of the container control, which means they do nothing for changing the workplace shell's background. In other words, the purpose of the **WinSetDesktopBkgnd** function is to allow an application that replaces the shell to set the appropriate background information. This function does not allow the caller to change the workplace shell's desktop background.

In order to change the workplace shell's desktop background bitmap, you have to actually update the contents of the folder by calling the **WinCreateObject** API. The code fragment in Figure 15.14 uses the standard file dialog to obtain a fully qualified path to a bitmap file and then dispatches a worker thread to update the workplace shell's desktop background. The **WinChangeDesktopBitmap** function is designed to change the background bitmap. The primary goal of this function is to build the required OBJECTID string needed for the call to **WinCreateObject**. The string that the function will build looks like this:

```
"OBJECTID=<WP_DESKTOP>;BACKGROUND=X:\\XXX\\XXX\\BITMAP.BMP",
```

```
BOOL WinChangeDesktopBitmap(HWND hwndFrame, PUCHAR szBitmap)
{
 static UCHAR szDesktopBuffer[CCHMAXPATH];
 UCHAR        szPathAndFilename[160];
 FILEDLG      filedlg;
 APIRET       rc;
 TID          tid;


 if (szBitmap)
  {
   strcpy (szPathAndFilename, szBitmap);
   strcpy (szDesktopBuffer, "\"OBJECTID=<WP_DESKTOP>;BACKGROUND=");
   strncat(szDesktopBuffer, szPathAndFilename, sizeof(szPathAndFilename));
  }

 else
  {
   memset(&filedlg, 0, sizeof(filedlg));
   filedlg.cbSize         = sizeof(filedlg);
   filedlg.fl             = FDS_CENTER | FDS_OPEN_DIALOG;
   filedlg.pszTitle       = "Change Desktop Background Bitmap";

   strcpy(filedlg.szFullFile,"*.BMP");   // File Filter = BMP Files

   if (WinFileDlg(HWND_DESKTOP, hwndFrame, &filedlg) && filedlg.lReturn == DID_OK)
    {
     strcpy (szPathAndFilename, filedlg.szFullFile);
     strcpy (szDesktopBuffer, "\"OBJECTID=<WP_DESKTOP>;BACKGROUND=");
     strncat(szDesktopBuffer, szPathAndFilename, sizeof(szPathAndFilename));
    }
  }

 rc = DosCreateThread(&tid,
                      (PFNTHREAD)DesktopBackgroundThread,
                      (ULONG)szDesktopBuffer,
                      0,
                      8192);

 if (rc != NULLHANDLE)
  {
   DisplayMessages(NULLHANDLE, "Error Dispatching Worker Thread", MSG_ERROR);
   return TRUE;
  }
return FALSE;
}
```

Figure 15.14   The WinChangeDesktopBitmap function.

where X:\\XXX\\XXX\\BITMAP.BMP is a valid path and file name to a bitmap file.

If the caller passed a valid path and file name to a bitmap in **szBitmap**, then the function will attempt to use that bitmap to set the desktop background. Otherwise, the function works by first obtaining the path and file name of the bitmap file from the user through the use of the standard file dialog. The path and file name returned in the *filedlg.szFullFile* element are stored in the **szPathAndFilename** string. From there, the first part of the OBJECTID string is copied into **szDesktopBuffer**.

Finally, the **szPathAndFilename** string is added to the end of **szDesktopBuffer**, which means that **szDesktopBuffer** contains the complete OBJECTID string required for **WinCreateObject**. The function then dispatches a separate worker thread by calling **DosCreateThread**, to complete the processing of the desktop bitmap change. The use of the separate thread is required to not tie up system input while the bitmap is being loaded. This handy little API is one that most developers really wish existed within PMWIN. Like any other PM API, the function will return FALSE on error, meaning it is unable to dispatch the worker thread, and will return TRUE if it was successful.

Figure 15.15 shows the code fragment for the worker thread.

This needs to be a PM-based thread to make the appropriate WIN calls; thus, the thread routine calls **WinInitialize** and **WinCreateMsgQueue**. The first real thing the routine does is to set the pointer to the WAIT pointer by calling the **WinQuerySysPointer** and **WinSetPointer** APIs. The WAIT pointer is required to indicate to the user that the application is busy doing something. The most important objective of the routine is to update the desktop folder by calling **WinCreateObject**.

```
static VOID EXPENTRY DesktopBackgroundThread(PUCHAR szDesktopBuffer)
{
  HAB    habThread;
  HMQ    hmqThread;

  habThread = WinInitialize(NULLHANDLE);
  hmqThread = WinCreateMsgQueue(habThread, NULLHANDLE);

  WinSetPointer(HWND_DESKTOP, WinQuerySysPointer(HWND_DESKTOP, SPTR_WAIT, FALSE));

  WinCreateObject("WPFolder",            // Workplace Object Class
                  "Change Desktop",      // Object Title
                  szDesktopBuffer,       // Setup String
                  "<WP_DESKTOP>",        // Location
                  CO_UPDATEIFEXISTS);    // Flags

  WinSetPointer(HWND_DESKTOP, WinQuerySysPointer(HWND_DESKTOP, SPTR_ARROW, FALSE));
  return;
}
```

Figure 15.15   The code for DesktopBackgroundThread.

OBTAINING THE SCREEN RESOLUTION

There may be times that an application may need to know the current video resolution; for instance, if a PM based installation program needs to install two different versions of a DLL based on the current screen resolution. The DLL's could contain information that is specific to the resolution, for example different bitmaps. It is important that the install program be able to know which files to correctly install based on the screen resolution. The code fragment shown in Figure 15.16 obtains the current screen resolution and displays it in a message box.

```
VOID QueryDeviceInfoStatus (HWND hwndFrame)
{
    LONG    lScreenHeight;
    LONG    lScreenWidth;
    LONG    lScreenColors;
    HDC     hdcTemp;
    LONG    lColorsArray[CAPS_COLORS];
    CHAR    szBuffer[150];
    APIRET  rc;

    // First get screen height and Width from PM using WinQuerySysValue
    lScreenHeight = WinQuerySysValue(HWND_DESKTOP, SV_CYSCREEN);
    lScreenWidth  = WinQuerySysValue(HWND_DESKTOP, SV_CXSCREEN);

    // Get a device context to obtain device capabilities
    hdcTemp = WinOpenWindowDC(hwndFrame);

    rc = DevQueryCaps(hdcTemp,
                      CAPS_COLORS,
                      CAPS_COLORS,
                      lColorsArray);

    if (rc != TRUE)
      {
       sprintf (szBuffer "DevQueryCaps failed with RC = %d", rc);
       DisplayMessages(NULLHANDLE, szBuffer, MSZG_INFO);
      }

    lScreenColors = lColorsArray[0];

    sprintf(szBuffer
            "The current screen resolution is: \n %ld x %ld x %ld colors",
            lScreenWidth, lScreenHeight, lScreenColors);

    DisplayMessages(NULLHANDLE, szBuffer, MSG_INFO);
    return;
}
```

Figure 15.16 Determining the screen resolution.

```
HDC APIENTRY WinOpenWindowDC (HWND hwnd);
```

Figure 15.17 **The WinOpenWindowDC prototype.**

The **QueryDeviceInfoStatus** function takes a single parameter, the frame window handle. The function works by first getting the height and width of the screen from the SV_CXSCREEN and SV_CYSCREEN system values and storing the values in the LONG variables *lScreenHeight* and *lScreenWidth*. The function then works by calling the **WinOpenWindowDC** API to easily obtain a device context for the frame window. This API will return a valid device context handle upon success. The *hdc* is needed to obtain the device capabilities from the device call, **DevQueryCaps**.

The **DevQueryCaps** call is used to obtain the **lColorsArray** which contains the number of colors supported at the screen resolution. The first element of the array is the second parameter to the function. In this case we used CAPS_COLORS constant, since we were looking for the screen colors. The third parameter to the call is the count of items to be returned in the array, **lColorsArray**. In this case, we also set it to CAPS_COLORS. The number of colors is therefore extracted from lColorsArray[0], and stored in the *lScreen-Colors* variable. Finally, the function will print the screen width, height, and colors as a single string in a message box using the **DisplayMessages** function.

DISPLAYING THE BITMAP

Ok, now that we reviewed the composition of bitmap we are finally ready to play. The routine **DisplayBitmap** is used to actually load the bitmap file from disk and display the bitmap file in the presentation space. The function takes four parameters; the actual filename obtained from the standard file dialog, a pointer to a memory device context, a pointer to a presentation space handle, and a pointer to a bitmap handle. The last three parameters will be filled in by this function. The function will return a ULONG error code that can be used by the caller to determine the cause of the failure. The error codes are defined in the header file SHERROR.H.

The function works by first opening the bitmap file passed in as **pszFilename** via a call to **DosOpen**, specifying the OPEN_ACTION_OPEN_IF_EXISTS open flag, indicating that the **DosOpen** API will open the file if the file exists on the disk and fail if it does not exist. If the call to **DosOpen** fails, the **DisplayBitmap** routine returns ERROR_OPENING_FILE immediately back to the caller.

The next step in the function is to allocate enough storage to store the bitmap in memory. The function **DosQueryFileInfo** is used to return the FILESTATUS3 structure which contains the *cbFile* element. The *cbFile* element represented by *fInfoBuf.cbFile* is the actual size of the bitmap file. The function uses the API **DosAllocMem** to allocate *fInfoBuf.cbFile* bytes of memory. The memory is committed by specifying the PAG_COMMIT flag. The pointer to the memory is returned in the *pvBuffer* variable and then the entire file is copied into the memory by using the **DosRead** API. If any of these three API's fail, the bitmap file is immediately closed and an error is returned.

The code fragment in Figure 15.18 is from the DisplayBitmap function, it is the code used to load the actual bitmapfile from disk.

```
habRet = WinQueryAnchorBlock(hwndFrame);

// Set the wait pointer to tell the user we are busy
WinSetPointer(HWND_DESKTOP, WinQuerySysPointer(HWND_DESKTOP, SPTR_WAIT, FALSE));

rc = DosOpen(pszFilename,                 // Valid Path and Filename
             &hBitmapFile,                // File handle
             &ulAction,                   // Action taken
             0,                           // Initial File Size
             0,                           // File Attributes
             OPEN_ACTION_OPEN_IF_EXITS,   // open, fail if file does not exist
             OPENMODE_FLAGS,              // open mode flags
             0);                          // Extended Attributes

if (rc != NULLHANDLE)
 {
  return ERROR_OPENING_FILE;
 }

rc = DosQueryFileInfo(hBitmapFile,        // File Handle
                      1,                  // Level Information
                      (PBYTE)&fInfoBuf,   // File Information Buffer
                      sizeof(fInfoBuf));  // File Information Buffer Size

if (rc != NULLHANDLE)
 {
  DosClose(hBitmapFile);
  return ERROR_OPENING_FILE;
 }

// Allocate enough storage to hold the file
rc = DosAllocMem(&pvBuffer,
                 fInfoBuf.cbFile,
                 PAG_READ | PAG_WRITE | PAG_COMMIT);

if (rc != NULLHANDLE)
 {
  DosClose(hBitmapFile);
  return ERROR_ALLOC_MEM;
 }
```

Figure 15.18   Processing the bitmap file.   continued

```
rc = DosRead(hBitmapFile,
             (PVOID)pvBuffer,
             fInfoBuf.cbFile,
             &ulAction);

if (rc != NULLHANDLE)
 {
  DosClose(hBitmapFile);
  return ERROR_READING_FILE;
 }
```

Figure 15.18   Processing the bitmap file.

The next few steps comprise the most critical parts of this routine.

The most critical part of the function is obtaining the graphical memory resources. The function obtains a memory device context by calling the device function **DevOpenDC** and specifying the OD_MEMORY parameter. The handle to the memory DC is stored in the pointer **phdcMem**. The normal presentation space is obtained through the call to the **GpiCreatePS** API. By specifying the GPIA_ASSOC flag the presentation space is immediately associated to the device context. Finally, the bit map is created by calling the **GpiCreateBitmap** API.

```
*phdcMem = DevOpenDC(habRet, OD_MEMORY, "*", 8L, (PDEVOPENDATA)pszDevData, hdcScreen);

*phpsMem = GpiCreatePS(habRet,
                       *phdcMem,
                       &sizel,
                       PU_PELS | GPIT_NORMAL | GPIA_ASSOC);

*phbmMem = GpiCreateBitmap(*phpsMem,                             // PS Handle
                           (PBITMAPINFOHEADER2)&pbmfh->bmp,      // BitmapInfoHeader2 ptr
                           CBM_INIT,                             // Options
                           pbmfh + pbmfh->offBits - ulArray,     // Buffer Init Data
                           (PBITMAPINFO2)&pbmfh->bmp);           // Pointer to BitmapInfo2
if (*phdcMem && *phpsMem && *phbmMem)
 {
 GpiSetBitmap(*phpsMem, *phbmMem);
 bmpinfohdr.cbFix = sizeof(bmpinfohdr);
 GpiQueryBitmapInfoHeader(*phbmMem, &bmpinfohdr);
 usBitCount = bmpinfohdr.cBitCount;
 }
else
 {
 FreeEngineResources(phdcMem, phpsMem, phbmMem);
 return ERROR_CREATING_BITMAP;
 }
```

Figure 15.19   Obtaining the resource handles.

The **GpiSetBitmap** function is used to set the bitmap into the presentation space. The **GpiSetBitmap** API will return an old bitmap handle if successful. The function will return HBM_ERROR if an error condition occurs. It is important to note that HBM_ERROR is defined to be -1, while GPI_ERROR is defined to be 0. It is a common mistake for application developers to check for the wrong return code. The **GpiQueryBitmapInfoHeader** function is used to obtain a BITMAPINFOHEADER2 structure from the bitmap. The painting of the client window is done by the **PaintBitmap** routine. This function uses the **GpiBitBlt** API to finally draw the bitmap in the window.

The purpose of the SHOWOFF program is to allow the user to create a presentation based on bitmap files. Through the use of the Create Presentation dialog, the user can enter all of bitmaps that they want in the presentation. The contents of the presentation can be saved to a text based profile. The File/Preview Presentation menuitem, will use a standard file dialog to allow the user to select the presentation file. Once a presentation file is selected, the SHOWOFF program will create a window that will display a miniature version of each bitmap in the presentation file. The **PreviewWndProc** window procedure contains the code that draws the miniature bitmaps. The code fragment is shown in Figure 15.20.

```
MRESULT APIENTRY PreviewWndProc(HWND hwnd, ULONG msg, MPARAM mp1, MPARAM mp2)
{
 HPS            hps;
 RECTL          rcl;
 RECTL          rclBmp;
 LONG           width;
 LONG           height;
 HDC            hdcMem;
 HPS            hpsMem;
 HBITMAP        hbmpMem;
 PSZ            pszTemp;
 LONG           index = 0;
 PPRESENTATION  pFirst;
 PPRESENTATION  pCurrent;

 // On the paint message - clear the window and setup to start drawing
 if (msg == WM_PAINT)
  {
    WinInvalidateRect(hwnd, NULL, FALSE);
    hps = WinBeginPaint(hwnd, NULLHANDLE, &rcl);

    if(hps != NULLHANDLE)
      {
      // Clear the window
      WinFillRect(hps, &rcl, CLR_PALEGRAY);
```

Figure 15.20   **The PreviewWndProc window procedure.**   **continued**

```
        // Set current node to first node
        pFirst = WinQueryWindowPtr(hwnd, 0);
        WinSetWindowPtr(hwnd, 4, pFirst);

        // Start index at first bitmap position
        WinSetWindowULong(hwnd, 8, 0);

        // Post message to draw a bitmap
        WinPostMsg(hwnd, WM_USER, MPFROMLONG(0L), MPFROMLONG(0L));
        WinEndPaint(hps);
      } // endif
    return FALSE;
  }

else if (msg == WM_USER)
  {
   // Get the presentation space
   hps = WinGetPS(hwnd);

   if (hps != NULLHANDLE)
     {
      // The first and current node - no drawing if current is NULL
      pFirst   = WinQueryWindowPtr(hwnd, 0);
      pCurrent = WinQueryWindowPtr(hwnd, 4);

      if (pCurrent)
        {
         // Must have a filename
         if (pCurrent && pCurrent->pszString[0] != '/')
           {
            // Get the position to draw the bitmap and compute the rectangle for drawing
            index = WinQueryWindowULong(hwnd, 8);

            WinQueryWindowRect(hwnd, &rcl);

            width         = (rcl.xRight - rcl.xLeft) / 4;
            height        = (rcl.yTop - rcl.yBottom) / 4;
            rclBmp.xLeft  = rcl.xLeft + (width * (index % 4));
            rclBmp.xRight = rclBmp.xLeft + width;
            rclBmp.yTop   = rcl.yTop - (height * (index/4));
            rclBmp.yBottom = rclBmp.yTop - height;

            // Blow off any options at the end of the filename
            pszTemp = strchr(pCurrent->pszString, ' ');

            if (pszTemp)
              {
               *pszTemp = '\0';
              }
```

Figure 15.20   The PreviewWndProc window procedure.   **continued**

```
        // Get the bitmap into memory
        DisplayBitmap(pCurrent->pszString, &hdcMem, &hpsMem, &hbmpMem);

        // Draw the bitmap
        WinDrawBitmap(hps,
                      hbmpMem,
                      NULL,
                      (PPOINTL)&rclBmp,
                      CLR_BLACK,
                      CLR_WHITE,
                      DBM_STRETCH | DBM_NORMAL );

        // Remove the bitmap from memory
        FreeEngineResources(&hdcMem, &hpsMem, &hbmpMem);

        // bump the position index
        index++;
       } // endif

     // update for the next node
     pCurrent = pCurrent->pNext;
     WinSetWindowPtr(hwnd, 4, pCurrent);
     WinSetWindowULong(hwnd, 8, index);

     // draw next - unless all drawn
     if (pCurrent != pFirst)
       {
       WinPostMsg(hwnd, WM_DRAWBITMAP, MPFROMLONG(0L), MPFROMLONG(0L));
       }
     } // endif pCurrent


   WinReleasePS(hps);
   } // if (hps != NULLHANDLE)
 return FALSE;
 }

else if (msg == WM_CLOSE)
 {
 WinDestroyWindow(WinQueryWindow(hwnd, QW_PARENT));
 return FALSE;
 }

// Clear the bitmap list when window destroyed
else if (msg == WM_DESTROY)
 {
 WinSetWindowPtr(hwnd, 0, NULL);
 WinSetWindowPtr(hwnd, 4, NULL);
 FreeMemory(WinQueryWindowPtr(hwnd, 0 ));
 return FALSE;
 }
```

Figure 15.20   **The PreviewWndProc window procedure.**   **continued**

```
// default is to call WinDefWindowProc
else
  {
   return WinDefWindowProc(hwnd, msg, mp1, mp2);
  } // end else
}
```

Figure 15.20   The PreviewWndProc window procedure.

SUMMARY

Most of the common PM performance problems that are reported and debugged are usually caused by slow painting of the window. This chapter provided a general review of the presentation space, device context and bitmap concepts and illustrated how an application can use the memory device context to speed the display of bitmap drawing within a given presentation space.

The sample program details several practical uses of the Graphical Programming Interface and uses both the **WinDrawBitmap** and **GpiBitBlt** functions. The SHOWOFF program is a fully functional presentation program that demonstrates how to programmatically use bitmaps. Programmers that make good use of drawing techniques and bitmaps can create quick and powerful programs that will dazzle any computer user. In today's demanding software market, it is not enough for an application to be well designed and well written, it must also be able to wow the user. Using the concepts discussed in this chapter and the corresponding sample program, you are well on your way to creating power programs.

CHAPTER 16

Getting It in Print: Mastering Fonts and Printing

Even though one of the popular trends in the world of computers is the concept of the paperless office, hard copy output still plays a very important role in most applications. Printed material is produced to transfer information (often in the form of correspondence), to present material, to provide off-line backup, and occasionally for such operations as writing this book. All of these functions can theoretically be performed without paper, provided the proper equipment is available; however, until this equipment is almost universally present, paper will still be important. This chapter discusses two very important aspects of PM programming related to producing hard copy output: font manipulation and printing.

FONTS

Drawing text to the display or a printer requires more than just a set of characters. Applications must also select the font used to draw the characters. A font is a set of instructions that tell the system how each character should be drawn. The application can choose to use the default font, select a font that exhibits a particular set of characteristics, select a specific font, or allow the user to choose a font from among those available on the system. In general, user selection of fonts is preferred, since this allows the user to modify the appearance of the displayed output as needed or desired. If necessary, the application can limit the user's choice of fonts to those that match the requirements of the application; for example, the simple editor in Chapter 3 only supported monospace fonts. Applications that provide hard copy output may also wish to limit the selection to the set of fonts supported by the printer. This section will describe the various types of fonts, user selection of fonts with the Font Dialog, and drawing text using the Win and Gpi APIs.

Font Terminology

When discussing fonts in connection with OS/2, you should be familiar with the terms used to describe fonts. The term *printer font* is used to describe a font that is specifically designed for a particular hard copy device, or printer. The font may be a permanent, resident font supplied with the printer, a font supplied on a cartridge or other device that may be physically attached to the printer, or a font that resides on the computer and is downloaded to the printer. The terms *bitmap font*, *raster font*, and *image font* all refer to a font defined as an array of pixels which are used to display characters on the system console. An *outline font* is described as a set of graphical strokes and may generally be used to draw characters on the console or a printer. OS/2 outline fonts are implemented using the Adobe font specifications and software. *System font* is a term used to describe the base fonts supplied with the operating system. These fonts have been specially tailored for increased performance. *ISO Font* describes a bitmap font that causes text to be displayed in accordance with the ISO Standards.

Knowing this terminology, we can now turn our attention to those fonts that are of most concern in application development—the bitmap and outline fonts. Typically, an application will allow the user to specify whichever font is desired; however, some applications may wish to restrict which set of fonts is used. For example, drawing with bitmap fonts is much faster than outline fonts. Thus, applications that are performance-sensitive may be designed to only use bitmap fonts. Applications that are more concerned with the quality of output typically use only outline fonts. If an application has a particular preference between speed and quality, then it should limit the users's font selection to the appropriate type.

USING FONTS

Many applications are not overly concerned about the font with which their text is drawn. In fact, many applications only display text inside of the various controls provided by the system and do not deal directly with fonts. However, some applications need to draw text into the client area of the window display, and will typically require at least some knowledge of the font in use, even if just the height of the font, in order to properly space between lines of text. As the application's use of text becomes more sophisticated, the application requires more knowledge of the font in use and may need to change the font to meet certain display criteria. When implementing these applications, remember that fonts are selected based on their characteristics, not a specific font or size.

WIN API

The Win API provides functions for basic text drawing and font manipulation. The **WinFontDlg** API allows user selection of fonts and character drawing attributes. The **WinSetPresParam** and **WinRemovePresParam** APIs provide a means for the application to change the font used for drawing characters, and the **WinQueryPresParam** API allows the application to determine the font currently in use. Characters are drawn using the current font with the **Win-DrawText** API. Applications that require more advanced capabilities should consider the functionality available within the Gpi API.

Determining the Currently Selected Font

When text is drawn using the **WinDrawText** API, the system selects the font based on the presentation parameter PP_FONTNAMESIZE. If this presentation parameter has not been set for the current window, a default system font is used, typically the SYSTEM PROPORTIONAL font. If a default font is not being used, an application can determine the current font by querying the presentation parameter using the **WinQueryPresParam** API. The syntax of this API is shown in Figure 16.1.

- Parameter **hwnd** is the handle of the window whose presentation parameters are to be queried.
- The **id1** parameter is the identity of the first presentation parameter to be queried.
- Parameter **id2** is the identity of the second presentation parameter to be queried.
- The **pulID** parameter is the identity of the actual presentation parameter found. PM searches the current window and its owners for a presentation

```
ULONG APIENTRY WinQueryPresParam(HWND    hwnd,
                                 ULONG   id1,
                                 ULONG   id2,
                                 PULONG  pulId,
                                 ULONG   cbBuf,
                                 PVOID   pbBuf,
                                 ULONG   fs);
```

Figure 16.1   The WinQueryPresParam API.

parameter of either **idAttrType1** or **idAttrType2**. The type of the actual presentation parameter found is stored in this location. If only one type is specified, this parameter may be set to NULL to prevent any value from being returned.

- The **cbBuf** parameter indicates the number of bytes available in **pbBuf**. This is the maximum size of the presentation parameter value, which will be stored in **pbPuf**.
- Parameter **pbBuf** is a buffer in which the value of the presentation parameter is stored.
- Parameter **fs** is a set of flags that modify the behavior of the query. The valid values are:

QPF_NOINHERIT	causes only the current window, not the windows along its owner chain, to be searched.
QPF_COLOR1INDEX	indicates that **id1** specifies a color index presentation parameter and that the color index should be converted to an RGB value for return.
QPF_COLOR2INDEX	indicates that **id2** specifies a color index presentation parameter and that the color index should be converted to an RGB value for return.
QPF_PURERGBCOLOR	indicates that either **id1** or **id2** contains an RGB reference and that the color must be pure. If necessary, the value is made pure, or undithered, after being translated to RGB.

WinQueryPresParam returns the length of the returned value in bytes, or zero if the presentation parameter was not found or an error occurred.

Figure 16.2 shows a sample routine, **GetCurrentFont**, which might be used to query the current font selected for the window. Unlike many of the APIs that query values, **WinQueryPresParam** does not provide a means of returning the length required to store the requested value, so **GetCurrentFont** uses a series of increasing size memory allocations to determine the required length and retrieve the value. The function begins by allocating a buffer the size of the defined maximum font face name string, FACESIZE. This buffer is then passed to **WinQueryPresParam** to retrieve the current value of the PP_FONTNAMESIZE parameter. If the length returned by **WinQueryPresParam** is equal to the length requested, then the program was either very lucky and specified precisely the correct length or the returned parameter value was truncated. Since the latter is the most likely scenario, the original buffer is freed and a new buffer of twice the previous size is allocated. **WinQueryPresParam** is then called again to retrieve more of the presentation parameter value. This sequence continues until the returned length is less than the size of the buffer, indicating that the entire value was retrieved. A pointer to the allocated string is then returned to the function's caller. Note that if the PP_FONTNAMESIZE parameter has not

```
static PSZ GetCurrentFont( HWND hwnd )
{
    PSZ     pszPresParam;
    ULONG   ulLength;
    ULONG   ulLengthReturned;

    ulLengthReturned = ulLength = FACESIZE;
    pszPresParam = malloc(ulLength);

    while( ulLengthReturned == ulLength ) {
        ulLengthReturned = WinQueryPresParam( hwnd, PP_FONTNAMESIZE, 0,
                                   NULL, ulLength, pszPresParam, 0 );
        if (ulLengthReturned == ulLength) {
            free(pszPresParam);
            ulLengthReturned = ulLength *= 2;
            pszPresParam = malloc(ulLength);
        } /* endif */
    } /* endwhile */

    return pszPresParam;
}
```

Figure 16.2   Obtaining presentation parameter fonts.

yet been set for **hwnd** or any of its owners, the initial length returned is zero, and a pointer to a zero-length string is returned to the caller.

The string returned by **WinQueryPresParam** for the PP_FONTNAMESIZE parameter is formatted as a series of fields separated by periods. The first field is one or more numeric characters that specify the point size of the font. The second field is the face name of the font and may include the bold and/or italic attributes. The remaining fields specify additional attributes of the font, which are generated by the system and are not part of the font itself. These attributes include strike-out, underscore, and outline, as well as bold and italic when the latter two are not included as part of the face name.

SELECTING A DIFFERENT FONT

While applications can internally select a particular font for text drawing, the normal course of action is to allow the user to select the font. If necessary, the application can limit the user's choices to those fonts whose characteristics match the application's requirements.

The easiest way of handling font selection from the application developer's standpoint is to merely allow the user to drag a font from the Font Palette. This functionality is supported without any intervention by the application; however, in order to observe the changes, the window must be repainted. This is easily accomplished by processing the WM_PRESPARAMCHANGED message and calling the **WinInvalidateRect** API whenever the message is received.

Most applications also provide an internal mechanism for selecting fonts. Many applications define their own method of listing the font choices available to the user; however, in some instances, an application can simply call the PM **WinFontDlg** API to perform this chore. This API displays a system-defined dialog box which allows the user to select a font, a point size, and various attributes of the font. The syntax of the API is given in Figure 16.3.

- **hwndP** is the window handle of the window that will be the parent of the font selection dialog box. This parameter is normally set to either the current application window or the desktop.
- **hwndO** is the window handle of the window that will be the owner of the font selection dialog box. This parameter is normally set to the current application window.
- **pfntd** is a pointer to a FONTDLG structure. This structure is used to pass information to the font dialog to determine the initial font selection to be displayed and any features of the dialog that are being customized by the application. After the font selection dialog is dismissed, this structure is updated to reflect the font selected by the user.

The return value from **WinFontDlg** depends on its modality. If the dialog is raised as a modeless dialog, the handle of the dialog window is returned if successfully created; otherwise, NULLHANDLE is returned. If the dialog is raised as modal, the function returns TRUE if the dialog was successfully created and FALSE if the dialog could not be created. In this case, the *lReturn* element of the FONTDLG structure contains the ID of the button used to dismiss the dialog, DID_OK if the OK button was clicked, and DID_CANCEL if the CANCEL button was pressed.

The FONTDLG structure passed to **WinFontDlg** consists of elements which allow the application to control the features and actions of the box, to specify the initial selections, and to retrieve the users selection from the dialog. This structure is relatively large and contains many elements which are not normally used by applications. Rather than list the entire structure here, we will discuss the pertinent elements in the text. One element which finds frequent use is *fl*, which contains style flags which can greatly influence the appearance and behavior of the dialog. The valid flags are:

```
HWND APIENTRY WinFontDlg( HWND hwndP,
                          HWND hwndO,
                          PFONTDLG pfntd);
```

Figure 16.3   The WinFontDlg API.

- FNTS_APPLYBUTTON (0x0010) adds an "Apply" button to the dialog. This button is used with modeless dialog boxes to allow the application to modify its display to match the current selection without dismissing the dialog.
- FNTS_BITMAPONLY (0x0100) specifies that the dialog should only list bitmap fonts for selection.
- FNTS_CENTER (0x0001) specifies that the dialog should be centered in its parent window.
- FNTS_FIXEDWIDTHONLY (0x0400) specifies that the dialog should only display monospaced fonts for selection.
- FNTS_CUSTOM (0x0001) specifies that the application is supplying a custom dialog template.
- FNTS_HELPBUTTON (0x0008) causes the dialog to display a "Help" button.
- FNTS_INITFROMFATTRS (0x0080) causes the dialog to initially select a font based on the attributes found in the *fAttrs* element.
- FNTS_MODELESS (0x0040) creates a modeless dialog which must be shown and destroyed by the application as it would a dialog created with the **WinLoadDlg** API.
- FNTS_NOSYNTHESIZEDFONTS (0x1000) prevents the dialog from synthesizing certain attributes of the fonts.
- FNTS_OWNERDRAWPREVIEW (0x0004) causes the dialog to send a WM_DRAWITEM message to the application to draw the preview string.
- FNTS_PROPORTIONALONLY (0x0800) limits the fonts available for selection to proportionally spaced fonts.
- FNTS_RESETBUTTON (0x0020) causes the dialog to display a reset button. When the reset button is clicked, the dialog returns its selections to their initial states.
- FNTS_VECTORONLY (0x0200) causes the dialog to only display outline fonts for selection.

Figure 16.4 presents routine **SelFont** as sample code for using **WinFontDlg**. This particular routine determines the currently selected font and initializes the dialog's selection to based on this font. When the dialog returns, the current font is changed to the font selected by the user.

The routine first obtains the presentation space handle for the current window by calling **WinGetPS**. The characteristics of the current font are then obtained by calling **GetCurrentFont** and **GpiQueryFontMetrics**. As discussed earlier, **GetCurrentFont** returns the presentation parameter string which identifies the size, name, and attributes of the font. **GpiQueryFontMetrics** retrieves the specific set of characteristics that define the font and that are used to select a font. The prototype for this API is shown in Figure 16.5.

```
static MRESULT selFont( HWND hwnd, ULONG msg, MPARAM mp1, MPARAM mp2 )
{
   HPS              hps;
   FONTDLG          fontdlg;
   FONTMETRICS      fm;
   PSZ              pszFullFaceName;

   hps = WinGetPS( hwnd );
   pszFullFaceName = GetCurrentFont( hwnd );
   GpiQueryFontMetrics( hps, sizeof(FONTMETRICS), &fm );
   memset( (PVOID)&fontdlg, 0, sizeof(FONTDLG));
   fontdlg.cbSize = sizeof(FONTDLG);
   fontdlg.hpsScreen = hps;
   fontdlg.pszFamilyname = fm.szFamilyname;
   fontdlg.usFamilyBufLen = FACESIZE;
   fontdlg.clrFore = CLR_BLACK;
   fontdlg.clrBack = CLR_WHITE;
   fontdlg.fl = FNTS_INITFROMFATTRS;
   fontdlg.fAttrs.usRecordLength = sizeof(FATTRS);
   fontdlg.fAttrs.lMatch = fm.lMatch;
   strcpy( fontdlg.fAttrs.szFacename, fm.szFacename );
   if( pszFullFaceName != NULL && strlen(pszFullFaceName) != 0 )  {
       ParseFaceName( hps, &fontdlg, pszFullFaceName );
   } /* endif */
   if( pszFullFaceName != NULL ) free( pszFullFaceName );
   if( WinFontDlg( HWND_DESKTOP, hwnd, &fontdlg ) &&
       fontdlg.lReturn == DID_OK ) {
       SetFontNameSize( hwnd, &fontdlg );
   } /* endif */
   WinReleasePS(hps);
   return (MRESULT)0L;
}
```

Figure 16.4   Using WinFontDlg.

- The **hps** parameter is the handle of the presentation space whose currently selected font is queried.
- Parameter **lMetricsLength** is the number of bytes of the font metric structure to be returned.
- Parameter **pfmMetrics** is a pointer to a FONTMETRICS structure in which the font characteristics of the currently selected font are returned.

```
BOOL APIENTRY GpiQueryFontMetrics( HPS hps,
                                   LONG lMetricsLength,
                                   PFONTMETRICS pfmMetrics);
```

Figure 16.5   The GpiQueryFontMetrics API.

GpiQueryFontMetrics returns TRUE if successful or FALSE if an error occurred.

With the font details in hand, the function clears the FONTDLG structure and begins the process of initializing the required fields. Element *cbsize* is set to the length of the structure. Element *hpsScreen* is set to the screen presentation space handle. The hps passed in this element is used by the dialog to obtain a list of the fonts which can be displayed in the presentation space. Though not used in this function, element *hpsPrinter* may be set to the handle of a presentation space associated with a printer device context to obtain a list of the fonts which may be displayed on the printer. Next, the elements which specify the family, or generic, name of the font are initialized; element *pszFamily name* is a pointer to the family name string which is contained in the FONTMETRICS structure. Since the dialog returns the family name of the selected font in this buffer, the size of the buffer must be specified in element *usFamilyBufLen* and is set to FACESIZE, the maximum length of the name and the size of the FONTMETRICS structure element. The colors of the preview string foreground, element *clrFore*, and background, element *clrBack*, are set to cause the preview text to be drawn with black characters on a white background. The *fl* style element is then set to FNTS_INITFROMFATTRS so that the dialog will initially select a font based on the characteristics contained in the *fAttrs* element which is initialized next.

The *fAttrs* element is a structure whose elements are the font characteristics which PM uses to select a font. In the sample function, elements of this structure which allow the font dialog to initially select the proper font are initialized from the characteristics of the current font contained in the FONTMETRICS structure and the attributes of the font found in the PP_FONTNAMESIZE presentation parameter string. Element *usRecordLength* is initialized to the size of the FATTRS structure. Element *lMatch* is a unique identifier for any given font on a specific system. The identifier is established when the font is loaded into the system and is not a part of the font itself. Applications should not assume that the lMatch value for a particular font on one system will select the same font on a different system. The *szFacename* element specifies the full face name of the font. The face name often includes some attributes of the font; for example, "Times Roman Bold Italic" would specify a font of the Times Roman family with bold and italic attributes. One other element of the FATTRS structure, the *fsSelection* element, is initialized in routine **ParseFullFaceName** which is discussed below. This element is used to specify additional attributes applied to the font. These attributes include the bold and italic attributes when they are not specified as part of the face name, and the outline, underline, and strike out attributes.

Before the font dialog is raised, **ParseFullFaceName** is called to analyze the presentation parameter string and fill in the *fxPointSize* element of the FONTDLG structure and the *fsSelection* element of the FATTRS structure. The *fxPointSize* element specifies the size of the current font and is used by the font dialog to select the proper size from those available for selection. The *fsSelection* element was discussed in the preceding paragraph. On return from **ParseFullFaceName**, the string obtained from **GetCurrentFont** is no longer needed and is freed.

The FONTDLG structure has now been initialized and the routine calls **WinFontDlg** to raise the dialog and obtain the user's selection. After a selection has been made, *selFont* calls routine **SetFontNameSize** to convert the FONTDLG data into a presentation parameter string for the selected font and to modify the PP_FONTNAMESIZE parameter for the window. When this function returns, the presentation space is released and *selFont* returns.

The code for routine **ParseFaceName** is shown in Figure 16.6. First, the point size of the font is extracted and stored in the *fxPointSize* element of the

```
void ParseFaceName( PSZ pszFullFaceName, PFONTDLG pfontdlg )
{
    PSZ     pszParse;
    int     i;

    pszParse = strtok( pszFullFaceName, "." );
    pfontdlg->fxPointSize = MAKEFIXED( atoi(pszParse), 0 );
    pszParse = strtok( NULL, "." );
    while( (pszParse = strtok(NULL, ".")) != NULL ) {
        for( i = 0;
                i <= ATTR_OUTLINE && strcmp(pszParse, &(pszfAttr[i][1]));
                i++ );
        switch (i) {
        case ATTR_BOLD:
            pfontdlg->fAttrs.fsSelection |= FATTR_SEL_BOLD;
            break;
        case ATTR_ITALIC:
            pfontdlg->fAttrs.fsSelection |= FATTR_SEL_ITALIC;
            break;
        case ATTR_UNDERSCORE:
            pfontdlg->fAttrs.fsSelection |= FATTR_SEL_UNDERSCORE;
            break;
        case ATTR_STRIKEOUT:
            pfontdlg->fAttrs.fsSelection |= FATTR_SEL_STRIKEOUT;
            break;
        case ATTR_OUTLINE:
            pfontdlg->fAttrs.fsSelection |= FATTR_SEL_OUTLINE;
            break;
        default:
            break;
        } /* endswitch */
    } /* endwhile */
    return;
}
```

Figure 16.6 Parsing the FACENAME string.

FONTDLG structure. This element is defined to be a fixed-point number, thus the **MAKEFIXED** macro is called to place the value in the proper format. Note that all screen fonts are an integral point size, thus the fractional portion of **fxPointSize** is always zero—printer fonts do not follow this convention as we will see later. Next the face name is extracted from the PP_FONTNAMESIZE string. Since this string was assigned from the FONTMETRICS structure, it is simply discarded here. The additional attributes are then extracted and matched with constant strings which contain the valid attribute names. For each attribute matched, the appropriate bit is set in the *fsSelection* element of the *fAttrs* element of the FONTDLG structure.

Routine **SetFontNameSize**, shown in Figure 16.7, extracts information from the returned FONTDLG structure to format the presentation parameter string and then calls **WinSetPresParam** to establish the new font. Formatting the PP_FONTNAMESIZE string is the opposite of the parsing operation seen in **ParseFullFaceName**. The function first determines the overall length of the string. The initial length of six reserves space for the size and following period. The length of the basic face name string is then added. Each attribute flag is then tested, and if set, an amount is added for the string naming the attribute. After the total number of characters is determined, space is allocated to hold the FACENAME string. The integer portion of **fxPointSize** and the **szFaceName** string from the FATTRS structure are then passed through *sprintf* to generate the base portion of the string. Next, an attribute name string is concatenated to the face name string for each requested attribute. When the full face name has been built, **WinSetPresParam** is called to change the presentation parameter. The syntax of this function is shown in Figure 16.8.

- **hwnd** is the handle of the window whose presentation parameter is to be modified.
- **idAttrType** is the presentation parameter to be set.
- **cbAttrVaueLen** is the number of bytes in the attribute value. NOTE: Include a byte for the terminating zero when determining the length of a parameter whose value is passed as a zero-terminated string, i.e. use strlen(string) + 1, not strlen(string).
- **pAttrValue** is a pointer to the value to be associated with the presentation parameter **idAttrType**.

The function returns TRUE if the presentation parameter was successfully modified or FALSE if an error occurred.

Though not used in this sample, an application can restore the font to its default value by calling the **WinRemovePresParam** API. The syntax for calling this function is shown in Figure 16.9.

- **hwnd** is the handle of the window whose presentation parameter is to be removed.

```
void SetFontNameSize( HWND hwnd, PFONTDLG pfontdlg )
{
    USHORT          ptSize;
    ULONG           ulLength;
    PSZ             pszFullFaceName;

    ptSize = FIXEDINT(pfontdlg->fxPointSize);
    ulLength = 6;
    ulLength += strlen(pfontdlg->fAttrs.szFacename);
    if (pfontdlg->flStyle & FATTR_SEL_BOLD)
        ulLength += strlen(pszfAttr[ATTR_BOLD]);
    if (pfontdlg->flStyle & FATTR_SEL_ITALIC)
        ulLength += strlen(pszfAttr[ATTR_ITALIC]);
    if (pfontdlg->flStyle & FATTR_SEL_UNDERSCORE)
        ulLength += strlen(pszfAttr[ATTR_UNDERSCORE]);
    if (pfontdlg->flStyle & FATTR_SEL_STRIKEOUT)
        ulLength += strlen(pszfAttr[ATTR_STRIKEOUT]);
    if (pfontdlg->flStyle & FATTR_SEL_OUTLINE)
        ulLength += strlen(pszfAttr[ATTR_OUTLINE]);
    ulLength++;
    pszFullFaceName = malloc(ulLength);
    if( pszFullFaceName != NULL ) {
        sprintf(pszFullFaceName, "%d.%s", ptSize, pfontdlg->fAttrs.szFacename);
        if (pfontdlg->flStyle & FATTR_SEL_BOLD)
            strcat(pszFullFaceName, pszfAttr[ATTR_BOLD]);
        if (pfontdlg->flStyle & FATTR_SEL_ITALIC)
            strcat(pszFullFaceName,pszfAttr[ATTR_ITALIC]);
        if (pfontdlg->flStyle & FATTR_SEL_UNDERSCORE)
            strcat(pszFullFaceName,pszfAttr[ATTR_UNDERSCORE]);
        if (pfontdlg->flStyle & FATTR_SEL_STRIKEOUT)
            strcat(pszFullFaceName,pszfAttr[ATTR_STRIKEOUT]);
        if (pfontdlg->flStyle & FATTR_SEL_OUTLINE)
            strcat(pszFullFaceName,pszfAttr[ATTR_OUTLINE]);
        WinSetPresParam( hwnd, PP_FONTNAMESIZE, strlen(pszFullFaceName) + 1,
                    pszFullFaceName );
        free(pszFullFaceName);
    } /* endif */
    return;
}
```

Figure 16.7   Building the FACENAME string.

```
BOOL APIENTRY WinSetPresParam( HWND hwnd,
                               ULONG id,
                               ULONG cbParam,
                               PVOID pbParam)
```

Figure 16.8   The WinSetPresParam API.

```
BOOL APIENTRY WinRemovePresParam( HWND hwnd,
                                  ULONG id);
```

Figure 16.9   The WinRemovePresParam API.

- **idAttrType** is the identifier for the presentation parameter to be removed. In the case of removing the font presentation parameter, PP_FONTNAMESIZE is used.

The function returns TRUE if successful and FALSE if an error occurs. If successful, the function removes the presentation parameter associated with a window resulting in a return to the default font if the PP_FONTNAMESIZE parameter is removed.

DRAWING TEXT

Now that a font has been selected, how is text actually drawn into a window? The **WinDrawText** API provides this functionality. The API also allows an application to query the area that a given string will occupy. The query functionality helps an application to determine the precise coordinates at which text should be drawn in order to be placed at a particular location within the window. For instance, the height of the font is important in order to provide proper spacing between lines when multiple lines of text are displayed. The prototype for the **WinDrawText** API is displayed in Figure 16.10.

- Parameter **hps** is the handle to the presentation space where the text is to be drawn.
- Parameter **cchText** is a 32-bit signed integer specifying the number of characters to be drawn. If this value is set to negative one (-1), parameter **lpchText** is assumed to point to a zero-terminated array of characters.
- The **lpchText** parameter is a pointer to the character or array of characters to be drawn.

```
LONG    APIENTRY WinDrawText(HPS hps,
                             LONG cchText,
                             PCH lpchText,
                             PRECTL prcl,
                             LONG clrFore,
                             LONG clrBack,
                             ULONG flCmd);
```

Figure 16.10   The WinDrawText API.

- Parameter **prcl** is a pointer to a RECTL structure containing the coordinates of the rectangle in which the text is to be drawn. If DT_QUERY-EXTENT of parameter flCmd is set, WinDrawText returns the coordinates of a rectangle that will just enclose the text to be drawn.
- The **clrFore** parameter is a signed, 32-bit integer that specifies the color index to be used for the drawing the actual characters. This value is ignored if **flCmd** flag DT_TEXTATTRS is specified.
- Parameter **clrBack** is a signed, 32-bit integer that specifies the color index to be used for the background of the characters. This value is ignored if **flCmd** flag DT_TEXTATTRS is specified.
- Parameter **flCmd** is an unsigned, 32-bit integer that is used as a set of flags indicating the actions which the API should take. The flags that may be specified are:

   DT_LEFT (0x0000) specifies that the text is to be left-justified, that is, the x coordinate of the origin of the text is the leftmost coordinate of the rectangle.

   DT_RIGHT (0x0200) specifies that the text is to be right-justified, that is, the x coordinate of the origin of the text is the rightmost coordinate of the rectangle.

   DT_CENTER (0x0100) specifies that the center of the text is located midway between the leftmost and rightmost coordinates of the rectangle.

   DT_TOP (0x0000) specifies that the top of the text is to be drawn at the topmost y coordinate of the rectangle.

   DT_VCENTER (0x0400) specifies that the vertical center of the text is located midway between the topmost and bottommost coordinates of the rectangle.

   DT_BOTTOM (0x0800) specifies that the bottom of the text is to be drawn at the bottommost y coordinate of the rectangle.

   DT_HALFTONE (0x1000) specifies that the text is to be drawn halftoned. Halftoning is a photographic process which exposes an image through a screen such that higher intensity areas of a picture have a higher dot density than lower-intensity areas. Halftone text appears to be "grayed" or lighter in intensity than normal text when drawn.

   DT_MNEMONIC (0x2000) specifies that when a mnemonic character is encountered, the mnemonic character is not drawn and the following character is drawn with mnemonic emphasis. In OS/2, this typically means that the tilde character (~) causes the following character to be underlined.

   DT_QUERYEXTENT (0x0002) specifies that, instead of actual drawing text, PM is to determine the rectangle that would surround the text and return its coordinates in the structure pointed to by **prcl**.

   DT_WORDBREAK (0x4000) specifies that only words which fit entirely within the given rectangle are drawn. At least one word is always drawn, whether it fits within the rectangle or not.

DT_EXTERNALLEADING (0x0080) specifies that the current font's external leading space is to be included in the rectangle returned by DT_QUERYEXTENT. This flag is ignored unless both DT_QUERYEXTENT and DT_TOP are also specified.

DT_TEXTATTRS (0x0040) specifies that the foreground and background colors of the presentation space are used rather than parameters **clrFore** and **clrBack**.

DT_ERASERECT (0x8000) specifies that the rectangle should be erased before drawing occurs. If not specified, the character background is drawn based on the background mix attribute of the presentation space.

DT_UNDERSCORE (0x0010) specifies that the characters are to be drawn underlined.

DT_STRIKEOUT (0x0020) specifies that the characters are to be drawn with overstrike, typically by drawing a line through the horizontal center of the characters.

Figure 16.11 provides an example of code which uses **WinDrawText** to vertically fill an application's client window with a constant string during

```
static MRESULT wmPaint( HWND hwnd, ULONG msg, MPARAM mp1, MPARAM mp2 )
{
    HPS     hps;
    RECTL   rectl;
    RECTL   rectlText;
    RECTL   rectlDraw;

    WinInvalidateRect( hwnd, NULL, TRUE );
    hps = WinBeginPaint( hwnd, NULLHANDLE, &rectl );
    if (hps != NULLHANDLE) {
        WinFillRect( hps, &rectl, CLR_WHITE );
        rectlText=rectl;
        WinDrawText( hps, strlen(szText),szText,&rectlText,
                    0, 0, DT_BOTTOM | DT_LEFT | DT_QUERYEXTENT );
        rectlDraw.yTop = rectl.yTop;
        rectlDraw.xLeft = rectl.xLeft;
        rectlDraw.xRight = rectlDraw.xLeft + rectlText.xRight;
        rectlDraw.yBottom = rectlDraw.yTop - rectlText.yTop;
        while( rectlDraw.yBottom >= 0 ) {
            WinDrawText( hps, strlen(szText),szText,&rectlDraw,0,0,
                        DT_BOTTOM | DT_LEFT | DT_TEXTATTRS );
            rectlDraw.yTop -= rectlText.yTop;
            rectlDraw.yBottom -= rectlText.yTop;
        }
        WinEndPaint( hps );
    } /* endif */
    return (MRESULT)01;
}
```

Figure 16.11   Drawing with WinDrawText.

processing of the WM_PAINT message. Since changing the size of the window can sometimes result in left over characters at the bottom of the window, this routine calls **WinInvalidateRect** to ensure that the entire client window area is included in the rectangle to be painted. **WinBeginPaint** is then called to initialize the drawing operation and obtain the portion of the window in which drawing will occur and **WinFillRect** is called to clear the client area in preparation for text drawing.

Next, the height and width of the text are calculated. Initially, the text rectangle is set to match the area to be painted and **WinDrawText** is called with the DT_QUERYEXTENT bit of **flCmd** set to obtain the rectangle that the text will occupy. Since the DT_BOTTOM and DT_LEFT bits are set, the bottom left coordinates of the rectangle are unchanged and the top right coordinates are adjusted to match the area required by the text. In general, the coordinates matching the justification flags will remain unchanged and the other pair of coordinates will be adjusted. Since the entire window is being painted, the bottom left corner of the rectangle is located at (0,0) and the returned top right coordinates provide the height and width of the text. The initial rectangle is then set such that the top of the rectangle matches the top of the window, the left of the rectangle matches the left of the window, the bottom of the rectangle is one character height below the top of the rectangle, and the right of the rectangle is the width of the text from the left of the rectangle.

A loop is now entered that fills the window with text. In a real application, code would probably be inserted at the top of the loop to pull the text from within a buffer before drawing; however, since this example uses a constant string, **WinDrawText** is called with a pointer to the constant text. The DT_TEXTATTRS **flCmd** bit tells PM to use the current foreground and background colors rather than those passed in the function call. After the text is drawn, the drawing rectangle is recalculated for the next line of text. Both the top and bottom coordinates of the rectangle are adjusted down by the height of a line of text. The left and right coordinates are left unchanged since all drawing in this example starts at the left edge of the window. If the bottom coordinate of the rectangle is now below the bottom of the window, the loop exits, preventing any partial lines of text from being displayed, **WinEndPaint** is called to release the presentation space, and the function returns.

WinDrawText uses the currently selected font for drawing. When a paint operation is started with **WinBeginPaint** and the PP_FONTNAMESIZE presentation parameter is present, the PP_FONTNAMESIZE font is selected into the presentation space as the current font.

GPI API

Programmers of applications that require additional text drawing capabilities such as justification or angular drawing will find that the **WinDrawText** API is too limited to be of practical value. Fortunately, the Graphics Programming Interface or Gpi, provides additional functionality to assist the programmer. The APIs provided by this interface allow an application to manage multiple fonts, to query the font definition details, to change the attributes with which text is drawn, to determine and/or set the exact position that each character in a line of text will occupy, and, of course, to draw the text to a presentation space. Unlike the **WinDrawText** API, the Gpi functions may be performed on any graphics device, not just the screen.

As an introduction to the Gpi functions, let's examine the program from the previous section modified to use a Gpi function instead of **WinDrawText**. The required changes are isolated to the function that processes the WM_PAINT message, which is shown in Figure 16.12. This routine follows the same logical flow as before. First, the entire window is invalidated and then the paint operation is started with a call to **WinBeginPaint**. Next, the height of the text is queried using the **GpiQueryCharBox** API in place of the preliminary call to **WinDrawText**. This API returns the size of the rectangle within which characters of the currently selected font, in this case, the default font, are drawn. The prototype of the API is shown in Figure 16.13.

```
static MRESULT wmPaint( HWND hwnd, ULONG msg, MPARAM mp1, MPARAM mp2 )
{
    HPS      hps;
    RECTL    rectl;
    POINTL   point;
    SIZEF    sizef;
    HDC      hdc;
    LONG     lCaps[2];

    WinInvalidateRect( hwnd, NULL, TRUE );
    hps = WinBeginPaint( hwnd, NULLHANDLE, &rectl );
    if (hps != NULLHANDLE) {
        GpiQueryCharBox( hps, &sizef );
        WinFillRect( hps, &rectl, CLR_WHITE );
        point.x = rectl.xLeft;
        point.y = rectl.yTop - FIXEDINT(sizef.cy);
        while( point.y >= rectl.yBottom ) {
            GpiCharStringAt( hps, &point, strlen(szText), szText );
            point.y -= FIXEDINT(sizef.cy);
        }
        WinEndPaint( hps );
    } /* endif */

    return (MRESULT)01;
}
```

Figure 16.12 Drawing text with GPI.

```
BOOL APIENTRY GpiQueryCharBox( HPS hps,
                               PSIZEF psizfxSize);
```

Figure 16.13   The GpiQueryCharBox API.

- Parameter **hps** is the handle of the presentation space whose character box size is to be returned.
- Parameter **psizfxSize** is a pointer to a SIZEF structure that is filled with the width and height of the character box when the function returns. This structure contains a **cx** value for the width and a **cy** value for the height, both in world coordinates in the form of a fixed point number.

The function returns TRUE if successful and FALSE if an error occurs.

After the font height is obtained, the location of the bottom, left corner of the first character is calculated. Since drawing begins at the top of the window, the y coordinate is computed as the top of the drawing rectangle less the height of the font. The x coordinate is set to the left edge of the window. This usage is valid if the text alignment has not been modified from the default, bottom left. Using the calculated point, the **GpiCharStringAt** API is called to draw text beginning at the calculated location. The prototype of this API is given in Figure 16.14.

- Parameter **hps** is the handle to the presentation space into which the characters will be drawn.
- Parameter **pptlPoint** is a pointer to a POINTL structure that contains an x and a y coordinate specified as long values in world coordinates.
- Parameter **lCount** is the number of characters to be drawn from the buffer pointed to by **pchString**.
- Parameter **pchString** is a pointer to a buffer containing the characters to be drawn. Note that the actual number of characters is determined by **lCount** so that no null-termination character is required.

The function returns GPI_ERROR if an error occurs and may return GPI_OK or GPI_HITS if successful. The GPI_HITS return code only occurs when correlation is enabled and the drawn string intersects a specified rectangle.

```
LONG APIENTRY GpiCharStringAt( HPS     hps,
                               PPOINTL pptlPoint,
                               LONG    lCount,
                               PCH     pchString);
```

Figure 16.14   The GpiCharStringAt API.

After the text is drawn, the starting point is adjusted to point to the start of the next line by subtracting the height of the text. The loop then continues until the screen is filled, at which time, the paint operation is terminated and the function returns.

This example, like that shown for **WinDrawText**, uses the default font established by **WinBeginPaint**. Unfortunately, most text processing applications require more sophistication than this method allows. For example, suppose the second word in the three-word string used in the previous examples were to be drawn using a boldface font. The WM_PAINT processing to select and use the boldface font is shown in Figure 16.15. This routine follows the same basic flow as the previous two WM_PAINT routines, but creates a logical font with the bold attribute before entering the text drawing loop. A logical font is PM's method of mapping a physical font along with any synthesized attributes into an application. Application routine **CreateAlternateFont** is called to create the

```
static MRESULT wmPaint( HWND hwnd, ULONG msg, MPARAM mp1, MPARAM mp2 )
{
    HPS      hps;
    RECTL    rectl;
    POINTL   point;
    SIZEF    sizef;
    BOOL     bBold;

    WinInvalidateRect( hwnd, NULL, TRUE );
    hps = WinBeginPaint( hwnd, NULLHANDLE, &rectl );
    if (hps != NULLHANDLE) {
        WinFillRect( hps, &rectl, CLR_WHITE );
        bBold = CreateAlternateFont( hwnd, hps, &sizef, 1 );
        GpiSetCharSet( hps, LCID_DEFAULT );
        point.x = rectl.xLeft;
        point.y = rectl.yTop - FIXEDINT(sizef.cy);
        while( point.y >= rectl.yBottom ) {
            GpiCharStringAt( hps, &point, strlen(szText1), szText1 );
            if( bBold ) {
                GpiSetCharSet( hps, 1 );
            }
            GpiCharString( hps, strlen(szText2), szText2 );
            if( bBold ) {
                GpiSetCharSet( hps, LCID_DEFAULT );
            }
            GpiCharString( hps, strlen(szText3), szText3 );
            point.y -= FIXEDINT(sizef.cy);
        }
        WinEndPaint( hps );
    } /* endif */

    return (MRESULT)01;
}
```

Figure 16.15 **Drawing with different attributes.**

logical font and then **GpiSetCharSet** is called to restore the current font to the default. Processing then continues as normal until the text drawing loop is entered. Inside the loop, **GpiCharStringAt** is called to draw the first word of the text. The application then selects the boldface logical font as the current font and then calls **GpiCharString** to draw the second word of the text. Note that this new API takes the same parameters as **GpiCharStringAt** without the start coordinates. GPI internally maintains a current location which is initialized by the coordinates passed to **GpiCharStringAt**. When the API finishes drawing the text, the current location is left at the point when the next character would be drawn. This location is then used as the starting point for the text drawn by **GpiCharString**. After the second word is drawn, the original, non-boldface font is again selected and **GpiCharString** is used to draw the remaining word. The loop then continues as normal to fill the window with text.

The code in the previous example was somewhat simplified by the inclusion of the font selection code into a subroutine. Since this can be a somewhat arduous task, we will examine this routine more closely. The code for CreateAlternateFont, which attempts to create a logical font with the bold attribute, is shown in Figure 16.16. After clearing a FATTRS structure, the routine obtains the presentation parameter string and the FONTMETRICS structure for the current font. If the presentation parameter existed, **ParseFaceAttrs** is called to extract the face name and font attributes and store them in the FATTRS structure. If no presentation parameter was available, the face name is copied from the FONTMETRICS structure. The remainder of the processing varies depending on the type of font, outline or bitmap.

If an outline font is encountered, routine **GpiQueryCharBox** is called to obtain the size of the characters in the font. Now if the current font is already bold face, there is no need to continue. Otherwise, the FATTRS structure is initialized to select a boldface, outline font. Note however, that outline fonts typically are packaged as four separate fonts, one for each combination of the boldface and italic attributes and that the system does not synthesize these fonts. Rather, the application must specify the proper face name containing the attributes in order for the font to be selected. To avoid naming convention problems, this routine calls a function, **GetBoldFont**, that enumerates all the fonts in the system and then checks each font for the proper family and combination of boldface and italic fonts. If the correct font is found, the lMatch value, a unique identifier, for the font is returned. Next, since the system does not synthesize the attributes, the boldface and italic flags are removed from the FATTRS fsSelection field. Function **GpiCreateLogFont** is then called to establish a logical font for the physical font with the lMatch value from **GetBoldFont**, or the font which most closely matches the required font. If a match is not found, the return value is set to FALSE to prevent the calling routine from attempting to use the requested font. The prototype for the **GpiCreateLogFont** API is shown in Figure 16.17.

```
BOOL CreateAlternateFont( HWND hwnd, HPS hps, PSIZEF psizef, ULONG lcid )
{
    FATTRS      fa;
    FONTMETRICS fm;
    PSZ         pszFullFaceName;
    BOOL        bBold = TRUE;

    memset( &fa, 0, sizeof( FATTRS ));
    fa.usRecordLength = sizeof( FATTRS );
    pszFullFaceName = GetCurrentFont( hwnd );
    GpiQueryFontMetrics( hps, sizeof(FONTMETRICS), &fm );
    if( pszFullFaceName != NULL && strlen(pszFullFaceName))
        ParseFaceAttrs( pszFullFaceName, &fa );
    else strcpy( fa.szFacename, fm.szFacename );
    if( fm.fsDefn & FM_DEFN_OUTLINE ) {
        GpiQueryCharBox( hps, psizef );
        if( fa.fsSelection & FATTR_SEL_BOLD ) bBold = FALSE;
        else {
            fa.fsFontUse = FATTR_FONTUSE_OUTLINE;
            fa.fsSelection |= FATTR_SEL_BOLD;
            fa.lMatch = GetBoldFont( hps, fa.fsSelection, fm.szFamilyname,
                                     fa.szFacename );
            fa.fsSelection &= ~(FATTR_SEL_BOLD | FATTR_SEL_ITALIC);
            if( GpiCreateLogFont(hps, NULL, lcid, &fa ) != FONT_MATCH )
                bBold = FALSE;
        }
    } else {
        psizef->cx = MAKEFIXED( fm.lAveCharWidth, 0 );
        psizef->cy = MAKEFIXED( fm.lMaxBaselineExt, 0 );
        if( fa.fsSelection & FATTR_SEL_BOLD ) bBold = FALSE;
        else {
            fa.fsSelection |= FATTR_SEL_BOLD;
            fa.lAveCharWidth = fm.lAveCharWidth;
            fa.lMaxBaselineExt = fm.lMaxBaselineExt;
            if( GpiCreateLogFont(hps, NULL, lcid, &fa ) != FONT_MATCH ) {
                fa.lMatch = GetBoldFont( hps, fa.fsSelection, fm.szFamilyname,
                                         fa.szFacename );
                if( fa.lMatch != 0 )
                    if( GpiCreateLogFont(hps, NULL, lcid, &fa ) != FONT_MATCH )
                        bBold = FALSE;
            }
        }
    }
    return bBold;
}
```

Figure 16.16   Creating a logical font.

```
LONG  APIENTRY GpiCreateLogFont(HPS hps,
                                PSTR8 pName,
                                LONG lLcid,
                                PFATTRS pfatAttrs);
```

Figure 16.17   The GpiCreateLogFont API.

- Parameter **hps** is the handle to the presentation space in which the logical font is to be created.
- Parameter **pName** is an application defined name for the font. This value is stored when a font is created in a metafile and may be useful to the application when files are transported between systems.
- Parameter **lLcid** is the logical font identifier the application wishes to create.
- The **pfatAttrs** parameter is a pointer to the FATTRS structure which contains the specifications for the desired font.

Routine **CreateAlternateFont's** processing for bitmap fonts is similar. Since bitmap fonts have specific sizes, **GpiQueryCharBox** cannot be used to obtain the size of the font. Instead the width and height of the font are set to the average character width and maximum character height from the FONTMETRICS for the font. Again, if the font is already bold, no further action is necessary. Otherwise, the FATTRS structure is initialized with the boldface attribute and the font size and **GpiCreateLogFont** is called to find a match for the requirements. If this call fails, **GetBoldFont** is called to determine if a specific font exists for the boldface attribute. This is basically the reverse of the procedure for the outline fonts since there is normally only one definition for a particular size bitmap font and the system synthesizes the boldface and italic attributes. If a match value is found by **GetBoldFont**, **GpiCreateLogFont** is again called to create a logical font which matches the lMatch value. If this also fails, the return value is set to FALSE to prevent the caller from attempting to use the font.

The **Gpi** API provides a number of other attributes that can be used to modify the appearance of drawn characters and functions for setting and querying these attributes either individually or as a group. The available attributes are all contained in the CHARBUNDLE structure and may be set in aggregate by calling the **GpiSetAttrs** API. The prototype of this API is shown in Figure 16.18.

- Parameter **hps** is the handle for the presentation space whose attributes are to be set.
- Parameter **lPrimType** specifies the graphic element type to which the attributes apply. Text attributes are set by specifying PRIM_CHAR (2).

```
BOOL  APIENTRY GpiSetAttrs(HPS hps,
                           LONG lPrimType,
                           ULONG flAttrMask,
                           ULONG flDefMask,
                           PBUNDLE ppbunAttrs);
```

Figure 16.18   The GpiSetAttrs API.

- Parameter **flAttrMask** contains a set of flags which indicate the attributes which are to be modified. See below for the appropriate flag for each attribute.
- Parameter **flDefMask** contains a set of flags which when set indicate that the corresponding attribute should be set to its default value.
- Parameter **ppbunAttrs** is a pointer to a structure containing the attributes. The type of the structure is interpreted based on the **lPrimType** parameter. For text attributes, the structure is the CHARBUNDLE structure defined below.

A similar function, **GpiQueryAttrs**, is used to obtain the setting of a group of attributes. The CHARBUNDLE structure used to set or query text drawing attributes with these functions is defined as follows in Figure 16.19.

- Element *lColor* is the foreground color used for drawing text. This may be either a color index or an RGB value depending on the mode of the presentation space. This attribute is set or queried when the CBB_COLOR (0x0001) mask flag is set. **GpiSetColor** and **GpiQueryColor** may be used to change or query this individual attribute.
- Element *lBackColor* is the background color used for drawing characters. This may be either a color index or an RGB value depending on the mode of the presentation space. This attribute is set or queried when the CBB_BACK_COLOR (0x0002) mask flag is set. **GpiSetBackColor** and **GpiQueryBackColor** may be used to change or query this individual attribute.
- Element *lMixMode* identifies the current mix mode for character drawing. The mix mode determines how the drawn characters interact with other text or graphics already drawn in the area of the text. This attribute is

```
typedef struct _CHARBUNDLE
{
    LONG     lColor;
    LONG     lBackColor;
    USHORT   lMixMode;
    USHORT   usBackMixMode;
    USHORT   usSet;
    USHORT   usPrecision;
    SIZEF    sizfxCell;
    POINTL   ptlAngle;
    POINTL   ptlShear;
    USHORT   usDirection;
    USHORT   usTextAlign;
    FIXED    fxExtra;
    FIXED    fxBreakExtra;
} CHARBUNDLE;
```

Figure 16.19   The CHARBUNDLE structure.

set or queried when the CBB_MIX_MODE (0x0004) mask flag is set. This value may be set or queried individually by calling the **GpiSetMix** and **GpiQueryMix** APIs.

- Element *usBackMixMode* identifies the current mix mode for the background of drawn characters. The mix mode determines how the background of the characters interacts with text or other graphics already drawn in the area occupied by the text. This attribute is set or queried when the CBB_BACK_MIX_MODE (0x0008) mask flag is set. This attribute may be set or queried individually with the **GpiSetBackMix** and **GpiQuery-BackMix** APIs.

- Element *usSet* is the LCID of the currently selected font. This attribute is set or queried when the CBB_SET (0x0010) mask flag is set. This attribute may be set or queried using the **GpiSetCharSet** and **GpiQueryCharSet** APIs.

- Element *usPrecision* specifies which attributes affect the drawing of bitmap fonts. Depending on this attribute, all attributes are used, only the direction attribute is used, or drawing with bitmap fonts is illegal and considered an error. This attribute is set or queried when the CBB_MODE (0x0020) mask flag is set. This attribute must be set or queried using the **GpiSetAttrs** and **GpiQueryAttrs** APIs as there are no APIs that deal with the individual attribute.

- Element *sizfxCell* specifies the width and height of the character box used for drawing outline fonts as FIXED values. This attribute is set or queried when the CBB_BOX (0x0040) mask flag is set. The **GpiSetCharBox** and **GpiQueryCharBox** APIs are used to set and query this attribute on an individual basis.

- Element *ptlAngle* specifies an x and y coordinate that are used to determine the angle at which a character string is drawn. The actual appearance of the characters depends on the character mode and the type of font. This attribute is set or queried when the CBB_ANGLE (0x0080) mask flag is set. This attribute is individually set or queried using the **GpiSetCharAngle** and **GpiQueryCharAngle** APIs.

- Element *ptlShear* specifies x and y coordinates that are used to determine an angle that is applied to the vertical component of character vectors in an outline font. Shear produces an effect similar in appearance to an italic font. This attribute is set or queried when the CBB_SHEAR (0x0100) mask flag is set. The character shear may be set and queried individually using the **GpiSetCharShear** and **GpiQueryCharShear** APIs.

- Element *usDirection* indicates the direction in which characters of a string are drawn within the rectangle defined by the string. Normally, characters are drawn with the first character at the left of the rectangle and the last character toward the right of the rectangle. Other options include the first character drawn at the right and the last character toward the left; the first character at the top and the last character at the bottom; and the first character at the bottom and the last character at the top of the rectangle. This attribute is set or queried when the CBB_DIRECTION (0x0200) mask flag is set. This attribute may be individually set and queried using the **GpiSetCharDirection** and **GpiQueryCharDirection** APIs.

- Element *usTextAlign* specifies the alignment of characters with respect to the current drawing location when the characters are drawn. This attribute contains a number of flags that indicate the horizontal and vertical alignment. Typical values might cause the text to be centered both vertically and horizontally with respect to the current drawing location. This attribute is set or queried when the CBB_TEXT_ALIGN (0x0400) mask flag is set. This attribute may be set or queried individually using the **GpiSetTextAlignment** and **GpiQueryTextAlignment** APIs.
- Element *fxExtra* specifies the amount of extra space to place between each character as a fixed point number. An example use of this attribute is adding additional space between characters to effect text justification. This attribute is set or queried when the CBB_EXTRA (0x0800) mask flag is set. This attribute may be set or queried individually using the **GpiSetCharExtra** and **GpiQueryCharExtra** APIs.
- Element *fxBreakExtra* specifies the amount of extra space to be given to the break character as a fixed point number. This character is defined by the font but would normally be the space character. This attribute is set or queried when the CBB_BREAK_EXTRA (0x1000) mask flag is set. This attribute may be set or queried individually using the **GpiSetCharBreakExtra** and **GpiQueryCharBreakExtra** APIs.

FONT SUMMARY

This section has discussed the various types of fonts, how fonts are selected, and both the **Win** and **Gpi** APIs for manipulating text attributes and drawing text. The knowledge should make working with fonts an easier task. In the next section, we will see that all of the information discussed so far applies not only to drawing text on the display, but also to sending text to the printer.

PRINTING

While PM programs can send data to printers in a device dependent manner using printer specific control codes, the OS/2 printing subsystem allows the program to generate output in a device independent manner by drawing to a presentation space through the **Gpi** APIs. This section describes the OS/2 printing subsystem and the programming required to perform output to devices other than the system console.

At the center of the printing subsystem is the spooler. Practically all hard copy output flows through the spooler. The spooler gathers all the data for a particular print job into a spool file. When the job is complete, the spooler routes the data to the printer or other output device. This allows multiple applications to simultaneously send information to the printer without interfering with each other. Note however, that applications can send output directly to the hard copy device, bypassing the spooler. When this happens, multiple jobs may be intermixed at the printer or one application may have to wait until all output from another application has been completed. This option should only be used in special circumstances such as when an application requires a dedicated printer, say for printing checks. This option should *never* be used for general printing.

Once the spooler has compiled the print job into a spool file, the file is passed to a queue driver. This driver determines the type of data in the file. If the file contains raw printer-specific data, it is transferred directly to the printer device driver. If the file contains PM graphic information in the form of a metafile, the queue driver uses PM to play the metafile to the printer driver. The printer driver then formats the data and sends the information to the low level OS/2 driver for the I/O port to which the printer is attached.

Preparing to Print

The actual drawing of output to a printer is often one of the easier parts of an application. The difficult part of the operation is bringing together all the information required to place the output on the correct device and in the desired format. A typical application allows the user to select the output device, the type and size of the paper, the area of the paper on which printing will occur, and in the case of textual output, the font to be used. The following sections describe the application coding necessary to perform these functions.

Selecting the Printer

In general, PM applications do not send output to physical printers but to printer queues. While there is usually a one-to-one correspondence between queues and printers, many system environments assign multiple physical printers to a single queue and others assign multiple queues to a single printer. If the user interface leads the user to believe that output is being directed to a particular physical printer, confusion and misunderstanding are sure to occur. PM applications should make the distinction between printers and queues patently clear and should always indicate to the user that a queue is being selected, not a printer.

With this in mind, the first application task in the printing process is to determine the queue to which output will be directed. This queue may be:

1. The default print queue as established by the user via a Workplace Shell printer object.
2. A saved queue from a previous invocation of the application.
3. A specific queue selected by the user from within the application.

The name of the Workplace Shell's default print queue is stored in the system's initialization files and may be queried using the **PrfQueryProfileString** API with application name PM_SPOOLER and key name QUEUE. This is the only queue/printer information that an application should directly query from the initialization files. While additional information about the available printer objects, queues, and printers is stored in the initialization files, the definition and usage of this information is not publically documented and is therefore subject to change and cannot be relied upon for future releases. Instead, the SPL API functions should be used to obtain any additional information required. Once the name of the default queue is known, the **SplQueryQueue** API may be called to obtain the pertinent information for the queue. This information is returned in a PRQINFO3 structure. Since this structure provides a large part of the data needed to create a print job, we have chosen to make it a part of our data structure. Figure 16.20 shows the code for obtaining the information for the default queue.

```
static BOOL QueryDefaultPrinter( PPRQINFO3 *pppqi )
{
    PSZ         pszValue;
    ULONG       cbValue;
    PSZ         pszSemi;
    ULONG       cbPqi;
    BOOL        bSuccess = FALSE;

    do {
        if (!PrfQueryProfileSize( HINI_PROFILE, DEFAULT_PRINTER_APP,
                            DEFAULT_PRINTER_KEY, &cbValue)) break;
        if (cbValue++ == 0) break;
        if ((pszValue = (PSZ)malloc( cbValue )) == NULL )break;
        if (!PrfQueryProfileString( HINI_PROFILE, DEFAULT_PRINTER_APP,
                            DEFAULT_PRINTER_KEY, "", pszValue,
                            cbValue)) break;
        if ((pszSemi = strchr( pszValue, ';' )) == NULL) break;
        *pszSemi = '\0';
        SplQueryQueue( NULL, pszValue, 3, NULL, 0, &cbPqi );
        if ((*pppqi = (PPRQINFO3)malloc( cbPqi )) == NULL) break;
        SplQueryQueue( NULL, pszValue, 3, *pppqi, cbPqi, &cbPqi );
        bSuccess = TRUE;
    } while ( false ); /* enddo */
}
```

Figure 16.20 Determining default queue information.

The first portion of this routine uses standard **Prf** API calls to obtain the size and content of the initialization file entry for the default queue. The function then removes the semi-colon which terminates the queue name and calls **SplQueryQueue** to obtain the setup information for the queue. The first call to **SplQueryQueue** passes a NULL pointer to the information pointer to obtain the length required to hold all of the information. Memory is then allocated for the buffer and **SplQueryQueue** is called again to actually obtain the information. The function then returns with a pointer to the data stored in the location supplied by the caller.

The **SplQueryQueue** API is prototyped as shown in Figure 16.21.

- Parameter **pszComputerName** is a pointer to the name of the computer whose queue is to be queried. This parameter is used in network environments and should be set to NULL to specify the local workstation or a standalone computer.
- Parameter **pszQueryName** is a pointer to the name of the queue to query.
- Parameter **ulLevel** specifies the level of information to be retrieved. Level 3 returns the basic queue definition information for local queues in a PRQINFO3 structure. Level 4 returns this information plus an array of PRJINFO2 structures which describe the print jobs currently waiting in the queue. Level 5 returns the queue name and level 6 returns the definition information in a PRQINFO6 structure which is the same as the PRQINFO3 structure plus information about the remote system where the queue resides in a network environment.
- Parameter **pBuf** is a pointer to the location in which the information is to be returned. If this parameter is NULL, the total number of bytes required is returned in **pcbNeeded**.
- Parameter **cbBuf** specifies the length of pBuf.
- Parameter **pcbNeeded** is a pointer to a location in which the API stores the number of bytes required to return the queue information.

SplQueryQueue returns NO_ERROR if successful.

The PRQINFO3 structure contains various information describing the definition and current status of the queue. Since some of this information is irrelevant to the current discussion, the structure will not be described in detail. The information in the structure that is relevant is used to open the

```
SPLERR APIENTRY  SplQueryQueue(PSZ    pszComputerName,
                               PSZ    pszQueueName,
                               ULONG  ulLevel,
                               PVOID  pBuf,
                               ULONG  cbBuf,
                               PULONG pcbNeeded);
```

Figure 16.21   The SplQueryQueue API.

display context in which the drawing for printing occurs and will be described as needed.

If the application saves the current printer selection between invocations—for example, in an initialization file—the application can restore the PRQINFO3 structure on startup (as an alternative, store the queue name in the initialization file and then call **SplQueryQueue** to obtain the queue information). The application should then use the **SplQueryQueue** API to ensure that the queue configuration has not changed since the last invocation. If the selected queue no longer exists, the application can select the default queue or request that the user select a queue. One element of the PRQINFO3 structure that is relevant at this juncture is the *pDriverData* element. This element contains driver specific information which specifies print job properties such as output orientation and quality which the application may wish to preserve across invocations. The application may wish to save this information before calling **SplQueryQueue** and then restore the information if the driver attached to the queue has not been changed.

The third option is to allow the user to select a queue. A typical printer selection dialog is provided in the sample code for this chapter. We will not indulge in what would be a rather long-winded discussion of the dialog, which basically obtains the user's choice and then calls **SplQueryQueue** as in the example above. However, the dialog initialization code shown in Figure 16.22 is of interest and shows how an application obtains a list of the print queues

```
static MRESULT wmInitDlg( HWND hwnd, ULONG msg, MPARAM mp1, MPARAM mp2 )
{
    PSELPRTDATA pspd = (PSELPRTDATA)mp2;
    ULONG       cPrinters;
    ULONG       cTotal;
    ULONG       cbNeeded;

    WinSetWindowULong( hwnd, QWL_USER, (LONG)pspd );
    SplEnumQueue( NULL, 3, NULL, 0, &cPrinters, &cTotal, &cbNeeded, NULL );
    pqi = (PPRQINFO3)malloc( cbNeeded );
    SplEnumQueue(NULL, 3, pqi, cbNeeded, &cPrinters, &cTotal,&cbNeeded, NULL);
    for (cPrinters = 0; cPrinters < cTotal; cPrinters++) {
        WinSendDlgItemMsg( hwnd, CID_PRINTERLB, LM_INSERTITEM,
                    (MPARAM)LIT_END, (MPARAM)(pqi[cPrinters].pszComment));
        if (!strcmp( pqi[cPrinters].pszName, pspd->ppqi->pszName)) {
            WinSendDlgItemMsg( hwnd, CID_PRINTERLB, LM_SELECTITEM,
                MPFROMLONG(cPrinters), MPFROMLONG(TRUE) );
            } /* endif */
        } /* endif */
    } /* endfor */
    return (MRESULT)TRUE;
}
```

Figure 16.22   Obtaining a list of available print queues.

defined on a system. This example uses the **SplEnumQueue** API to obtain the names of the print queues available.

The code makes two calls to **SplEnumQueue**. The first call determines the amount of space required to return the queue information. After sufficient memory is allocated to contain this information, the API is called the second time to retrieve the information into the buffer. In this instance, the information consists of an array of PRQINFO3 structures with an element for each printer queue defined in the system. A loop is then used to fill the contents of the dialog's selection listbox with the description of each queue found in the **pszComment** field of the PRQINFO3 structure. The content of this field is the name used as the printer object title by the Workplace Shell and is thus familiar to the user. A check is then made to determine if the queue name matches the name of the currently selected printer. If so, the listbox item is selected. The loop then continues until all available print queues have been added to the list. The prototype for the **SplEnumQueue** API is shown in Figure 16.23.

- Parameter **pszComputerName** is a pointer to the name of the computer whose queues are to be enumerated. Specify NULL to obtain information for the local workstation or a standalone computer.
- Parameter **ulLevel** indicates the level of information to retrieve. See **SplQueryQueue** for details on the values to which this parameter may be set.
- Parameter **pBuf** is a pointer to the location to store the retrieved information. Set this parameter to NULL to retrieve the required length.
- Parameter **cbBuf** specifies the length of **pBuf** and should be set to zero when retrieving the required length.
- Parameter **pcReturned** is a pointer to the location where the API stores the number of entries returned in the array at location **pBuf**.
- Parameter **pcTotal** is a pointer to the location where the API stores the total number of entries available.
- Parameter **pcbNeeded** is a pointer to the location in which the API stores the number of bytes required to return information on all queues.
- Parameter **pReserved** should be set to NULL.

SplEnumQueue returns NO_ERROR if successful.

```
SPLERR APIENTRY SplEnumQueue(PSZ     pszComputerName,
                             ULONG   ulLevel,
                             PVOID   pBuf,
                             ULONG   cbBuf,
                             PULONG  pcReturned,
                             PULONG  pcTotal,
                             PULONG  pcbNeeded,
                             PVOID   pReserved);
```

Figure 16.23   The SplEnumQueue API.

Selecting the FORM (paper size)

Next the user must be able to specify the form on which output is to be generated. By default, the form specifies the size of the paper and thus the overall area into which the application can draw. However, the user can define additional forms which are used to indicate paper which may contain pre-printed information. Printing to a specific form insures that the user has indicated that the form is in the printer before the spooler releases the job.

The simplest way of selecting a form is to display the Job Properties Dialog via the **DevPostDeviceModes** API. This API is an entry point into a routine supplied by the printer driver which allows the user to specify device specific information such as the form and other characteristics of the print job; page orientation, resolution, etc. Initial characteristics are passed in via the **pdrivDriverData** parameter which is updated with the new selections on output. If this parameter is set to the value of the *pDriverData* element of the PRQINFO3 structure obtained when the printer queue is queried, the new information is stored back into the application and is embedded into the print job when created. The prototype for **DevPostDeviceModes** is shown in Figure 16.24.

- The **hab** parameter is the anchor block handle for the calling thread.
- The **pdrivDriverData** parameter is a pointer to a device specific structure which contains the initial configuration for the device and in which the results of the call are returned. If this parameter is set to NULL, the required length of the structure is returned.
- Parameter **pszDriverName** points to the name of the printer driver whose characteristics are to be retrieved and/or changed.
- Parameter **pszDeviceName** is the pointer to the name of the device type for which information is to be changed and/or retrieved.
- Parameter **pszName** is the name of the specific printer for which current information is to be retrieved. If the information is being posted for user modification, this field can be set to NULL.
- The **flOptions** field indicates the type of operation to be performed. If set to DPDM_QUERYJOBPROP, the API returns the default information for the specified queue but does not interact with the user. If set to DPDM_POSTJOBPROP, the API uses the information in the **pdrivDriverData** parameter to initialize a dialog box in which the user can modify

```
LONG  APIENTRY DevPostDeviceModes(HAB hab,
                                  PDRIVDATA pdrivDriverData ,
                                  PSZ  pszDriverName,
                                  PSZ  pszDeviceName,
                                  PSZ  pszName,
                                  ULONG flOptions);
```

Figure 16.24 The DevPostDeviceModes API.

the device properties. When the dialog box is dismissed, the information pointed to by **pdrivDriverData** has been updated with the user's selections.

DevPostDeviceModes returns the number of bytes of information stored at location **pdrivDriverData**, or the number of bytes of information available if **pdrivDriverData** is NULL.

An alternative method is to call the **DevQueryHardcopyCaps** API to retrieve a list of the available forms. The user is then presented with this list and allowed to select a form. The application saves the name of the selected form and passes the information to the print job in the **DevOpenDC** call. A form name chosen in this fashion overrides the selection in the PDRIVDATA structure passed to **DevOpenDC**.

Establishing Margins

Applications typically provide a dialog or other means by which the user may modify the printable area of the selected form. In most cases, the user is allowed to specify the distance from the edge of the form within which no drawing will occur. This area is known as the margin.

Most printers also have hardware limitations which prevent the entire page from being printed. These hardware margins are available to the application in the HCINFO structure which may be retrieved using the **DevQueryHardcopy-Caps** API. The origin of presentation spaces created for the device is located at the lower left point defined by the hardware margins. Thus, when sending output to a printer, coordinate (0,0) is not at the corner of the paper but at the point defined by the hardware limitation. Be careful when computing the printable area based on user-defined margins that the calculations are from the edge of the paper, not the origin of the presentation space.

Selecting a Font

Text output to a hard copy device requires that some font be selected (even if it is the default font). Each device may have built-in or device fonts available, the use of which will increase performance and reduce the size of the spool file. System fonts may also be specified for the printer and will generate a series of graphic commands to actually draw the characters. The standard font dialog may be used to select the appropriate font by specifying a printer presentation space in element *hpsPrinter* of the FONTDLG structure.

Creating the Print Job

Now that all the setup data has been obtained, the application can actually generate output to the print queue. This operation can be divided into six convenient steps:

1. Opening the device context
2. Associating the presentation space
3. Starting the print job
4. Establishing job characteristics
5. Drawing the output
6. Ending the print job

Opening the Device Context

The first step in generating output is to open a device context. When output is drawn to the system display screen, the step is automatically performed by PM. When the output device is a printer, the application must explicitly open the device via a call to the **DevOpenDC** API. The prototype for this API is listed in Figure 16.25.

- Parameter **hab** is the anchor block handle for the current thread.
- Parameter **lType** is the type of context to open. For printing purposes, this parameter is normally set to OD_QUEUED to specify output via the spooler. OD_DIRECT may be specified to bypass the spooler and send output directly to the printer. OD_INFO is frequently used during setup and WYSIWYG operation to obtain information about the printer without creating a print job.
- Parameter **pszToken** is not used by OS/2. This parameter is a pointer to a string that identifies an initialization file token from which DEVOPEN-STRUC (discussed shortly) data may be obtained. For compatibility, specify a pointer to a null-terminated string containing a single asterisk (*) which indicates that this information should be obtained from the **pdopData** parameter.
- Parameter **lCount** is the number of elements of **pdopData** which are being passed. **pdopData** is treated as an array of pointers, and this parameter specifies how many elements are in the array. In most instances, this parameter should be set to the size of DEVOPENSTRUC, divided by the size of a pointer to void. This indicates that the entire structure is being passed and allows for future growth of the structure.

```
HDC APIENTRY DevOpenDC( HAB          hab,
                        LONG         lType,
                        PSZ          pszToken,
                        LONG         lCount,
                        PDEVOPENDATA pdopData,
                        HDC          hdcComp);
```

Figure 16.25   The DevOpenDC API.

- Parameter **pdopData** is a pointer to an array of pointers to strings. This parameter is typically passed by casting a pointer to a DEVOPENSTRUC structure, which specifies the appropriate pointers (see next for a definition of this structure). These pointers identify the device to be opened and its characteristics.
- Parameter **hdcComp** is used when **lType** is set to OD_MEMORY and specifies the handle to a device context from which the memory DC draws its characteristics. This allows bitmaps associated with the memory DC to be compatible with the device.

If successful, **DevOpenDC** returns a handle to the display context. If unsuccessful, the API returns NULLHANDLE.

The **pdopData** parameter is normally obtained by casting a pointer to a DEVOPENSTRUC structure. The elements of this structure, and thus the array elements of **pdopData**, are given in Figure 16.26.

- Element *pszLogAddress* is a pointer to a string that identifies the queue (for an OD_QUEUED DC) or device (for an OD_DIRECT DC), which the device context represents. For an OD_QUEUED device context, the queue name is specified. The name may be obtained from the *pszName* element of the PRQINFO3 structure. For an OD_DIRECT device context, the name of the logical device for the port to which the printer is attached is specified; for example, LPT1.
- Element *pszDriverName* is a pointer to a string that identifies the name of the printer driver to associate with the device context; for example, IBMNULL. This name may be obtained from the **pszDriverName** field of the PRQINFO3 structure, which contains the driver name and device type separated by a period. The driver name should be extracted and passed as **pszDriverName**.

```
typedef struct _DEVOPENSTRUC
{
    PSZ         pszLogAddress;
    PSZ         pszDriverName;
    PDRIVDATA   pdriv;
    PSZ         pszDataType;
    PSZ         pszComment;
    PSZ         pszQueueProcName;
    PSZ         pszQueueProcParams;
    PSZ         pszSpoolerParams;
    PSZ         pszNetworkParams;
} DEVOPENSTRUC;
```

Figure 16.26   The DEVOPENSTRUC structure.

- Element *pdriv* is a pointer to driver-specific data. This information may be obtained from element *pDriverData* of the PRQINFO3 structure or by calling the **DevPostDeviceModes** API.
- Element *pszDataType* specifies how the data will be stored in the spool file. Specifying PM_Q_RAW causes the data to be stored in printer specific format. Specifying PM_Q_STD causes the data to be stored as a metafile. PM_Q_STD should normally be used to reduce the size of the spool file and the time required to generate the spool file. In circumstances where the PM_Q_RAW format is required, the user can select this option through the printer object settings notebook which will override this parameter.
- Element *pszComment* is a pointer to a string that is stored in the spool file and displayed in the settings notebook for the print job. This element has no real effect on the printed output and is optional.
- Element *pszQueueProcName* is a pointer to a string that specifies the queue processor name, typically either PMPRINT or PMPLOT. The default name associated with the queue is typically used and may be obtained from element *pszPrProc* in the PRQINFO3 structure.
- Element *pszQueueProcParams* is a pointer to a string which specifies parameters to be passed to the queue processor. These parameters are specific to the actual queue processor; however, a common parameter which might be passed to the PMPRINT or PMPLOT processor is COP=nnn where nnn is 1 to 3 decimal digits that specify the number of copies of the job to be printed.
- Element *pszSpoolerParams* is a pointer to a string that specifies paramenters to be passed to the spooler. This string can be used to specify the form name for the job and the priority at which the spooler dispatches the job, higher priority jobs being dispatched first. Note: specification of a form name with the FORM= parameter overrides any form specification contained in element *pdriv*; so if **DevPostDeviceModes** is used, do not specify a form name here.
- Element *pszNetworkParams* is a pointer to a string which specifies various parameters for jobs direct across a network. The available parameters are dependent on the network.

Figure 16.27 shows a code fragment which fills in the DEVOPENSTRUC data from a PRQINFO3 structure and then opens the device context. The code first extracts the name of the printer driver from element *pszDriverName* of the PRQINFO3 structure. The number of characters before the period in the name is obtained and used to allocate a buffer for the driver name. The name is then copied from *pszDriverName*. The DEVOPENSTRUC is then initialized and **DevOpenDC** is called.

```
PPRQINFO3    ppqi;
DEVOPENSTRUC devopen;
PSZ          pszDriver;
ULONG        cbDriver;

cbDriver = strcspn( ppqi->pszDriverName, "." );
if (cbDriver == 0) cbDriver = strlen( ppqi->pszDriverName );
if ((pszDriver = (PSZ)malloc( cbDriver + 1 )) != NULL ) {
   strncpy( pszDriver, ppqi->pszDriverName, cbDriver );
   pszDriver[ cbDriver ] = '\0';
} /* endif */
devopen.pszLogAddress = ppqi->pszName;
devopen.pszDriverName = pszDriver;
devopen.pdriv = ppqi->pDriverData;
devopen.pszDataType = "PM_Q_STD";
devopen.pszComment = NULL;
devopen.pszQueueProcName = ppqi->pszPrProc;
devopen.pszQueueProcParams = NULL;
devopen.pszSpoolerParams = NULL;
devopen.pszNetworkParams = NULL;
hdc = DevOpenDC( hab, OD_QUEUED, "*",
                 sizeof( DEVOPENSTRUC )/sizeof(PVOID),
                 (PSZ *)&devopen, NULLHANDLE );
```

Figure 16.27   Opening the device context.

Associating the Presentation Space

Once the device context has been opened, a presentation space must be associated with the device before drawing can occur. This can be an existing presentation space or a new one can be created and associated specifically for the print job. Assuming the latter case, the presentation space is created with the **GpiCreatePS** API which is prototyped in Figure 16.28.

- The **hab** parameter is the anchor block handle for the thread.
- Parameter **hdc** is the device context handle returned by the **DevOpenDC** call discussed previously.
- Parameter **psizlSize** is a pointer to a SIZEL structure that specifies the width and height of the presentation space. Specify zero for either or both the width and height to set the presentation page to the default page size for the device.

```
HPS APIENTRY GpiCreatePS( HAB     hab,
                          HDC     hdc,
                          PSIZEL  psizlSize,
                          ULONG   flOptions);
```

Figure 16.28   The GpiCreatePS API.

```
sizel.cx = sizel.cy = 0L;
hps = GpiCreatePS( hab, hdc, &sizel,
                   PU_LOMETRIC | GPIT_NORMAL | GPIA_ASSOC );
```

Figure 16.29   Creating a presentation space.

- Parameter **flOptions** is a 32-bit value divided into bit fields that specify the units of measurement, the coordinate format, the presentation space type, and whether the presentation space is automatically associated with the device context. In the following example, the coordinate format is left at the default, the units of measurement are set to PU_LOMETRIC (.1 millimeter) for easy conversion of the values returned by **DevQueryHard-copyCaps**, a normal presentation space is used, and the presentation space is automatically associated with the device context.

GpiCreatePS returns a presentation space handle if successful, or NULLHAN-DLE if an error occurs.

Figure 16.29 shows a brief code fragment used to create a presentation space associated with the device context opened in Figure 16.27. The *cx* and *cy* elements of a SIZEL structure are initialized to zero to cause the presentation space to match the output device size. **GpiCreatePS** is then called, passing the anchor block handle and the device context handle. The **flOptions** parameter specifies that the presentation space coordinates are measured in one tenth millimeter units, that the presentation space will be a "normal" PS and space should be associated with the specified device context.

Starting the Job

The next step in creating the print job is to actually start the job by calling the **DevEscape** API with the DEVESC_STARTDOC escape code. This call opens the metafile for OD_QUEUED device contexts and must be called before any drawing occurs or before establishing any job characteristics such as fonts. Characteristics established before the DEVESC_STARTDOC code is sent will not be stored in the metafile and, therefore, will not be present when the job is actually sent to the printer. The parameters for the **DevEscape** call are in Figure 16.30.

```
LONG APIENTRY DevEscape( HDC   hdc,
                         LONG  lCode,
                         LONG  lInCount,
                         PBYTE pbInData,
                         PLONG plOutCount,
                         PBYTE pbOutData);
```

Figure 16.30   The DevEscape API.

- Parameter **hdc** is the handle of the device context obtained from the **DevOpenDC** call.
- Parameter **lCode** is the escape code; in this instance, DEVESC_STARTDOC.
- Parameter **lInCount** is the length of the input data; for DEVESC_STARTDOC, this is the length of the string passed in as the job name.
- Parameter **pbInData** is a pointer to the input data; for DEVESC_STARTDOC, a pointer to a string containing the name of the job.
- Parameter **lOutCount** is a pointer to a 32-bit integer specifying the length of the output buffer. Since no output is expected for DEVESC_STARTDOC, set this pointer to zero.
- Parameter **pbOutData** is a pointer to a buffer to store the output data. Since no output is expected for DEVESC_STARTDOC, set this pointer to NULL.

DevEscape returns DEV_OK if successful; otherwise an error code is returned.

Setting Characteristics

Once the metafile for the job has been opened, various characteristics for the output that must be stored in the metafile can be specified, such as scaling and rotation factors or the selection of the logical font to be used for the job. Figure 16.31 provides an example of establishing the font for a text printing job.

A logical font is created using the **GpiCreateLogFont** API. The FATTRS structure that was passed to the routine was saved when the user selected a font. The font is then selected as the current character set using the **GpiSetCharSet** API. Next, in case an outline font was selected, the point size is used to establish the character rectangle via the **GpiSetCharBox** API. Notice that the point size is first converted to presentation space units, .1 millimeter. Finally, the text alignment is set using the **GpiSetTextAlignment** API. The selected alignment is top-left since we want to start drawing from the top, left corner of the page. Other Gpi functions will tell us the height of the actual text so that the next line can be computed.

```
GpiCreateLogFont( hps, &"PRINTFN", LCID_PRINTER, &fattrs );
GpiSetCharSet( hps, LCID_PRINTER );
PointsToPUs( fixedPoints, &sizef, PU_LOMETRIC );
sizef.cy = sizef.cx;
GpiSetCharBox( hps, &sizef );
GpiSetTextAlignment( hps, TA_LEFT, TA_TOP );
```

Figure 16.31 Setting print job characteristics.

Drawing the Output

This phase of print job creation is no different than drawing output to the screen except that all drawing should occur using the Gpi API's since API's like **WinDrawText** only output to presentation spaces associated with display screen device contexts. Be careful when drawing not to exceed the space limitation imposed by user selected margins. Also, unlike drawing to the screen, when the bottom of the page is reached drawing does not stop. Instead, the application should call **DevEscape** with the DEVESC_NEWFRAME to eject the current page and begin a new page. Remember to reset any variables which track the current drawing location back to the start of the page.

Ending the Job

Once all the output is complete, **DevEscape** is called with escape code DEVESC_ENDDOC to close the metafile. Any resources—memory, presentation space, device context—allocated for the job should then be deallocated. If the job needs to be terminated without any output going to the printer, **DevEscape** may be called with escape code DEVESC_ABORTDOC. This will close the metafile and delete the spool file.

USING A NEW THREAD FOR PRINTING

Since generating print output is typically a relatively time-consuming operation, it should normally be performed in a separate thread. Basically, all the user-specified data needed to perform the print operation is gathered into a single structure and a pointer to this structure is passed as a parameter to the new thread. The new thread then performs the print operation while the application and user are free to perform other tasks. Make certain however, that the data needed by the print thread cannot be modified by the main application while printing is in progress. For example, if the data being printed is stored in a buffer, take care that the main application does not modify or destroy the buffer until the print operation is complete. Likewise, be sure that the print thread does not inadvertently modify data that the main application needs. Corruption caused by multiple threads accessing common resources is a frequent cause of malfunctions, including traps.

PRINTING SUMMARY

Drawing output to a printer is a relatively simple task; the hard part is getting everything set up to do the drawing. The programmer must first decide how the printing will take place, either directly to the printer or via a print queue.

Next, options exist that allow the programmer to print using printer control codes and sending a raw printer-specific data stream to the printer. Normally, the output is drawn in a device-independent fashion as a series of graphical primitives using the Gpi API set. Applications typically give the user the option of determining the print queue to which output will be directed and the characteristics of the printout, such as paper size, orientation on the page, etc. Optionally, the user may be given the opportunity to specify the margins at which the output will be drawn and, if text is to be presented, the font that will be used.

CHAPTER 17

Captain Hook Lives: Mastering PM Hooks

A *hook* is a method of capturing a user event or keystroke. The purpose of using a hook is to allow the developer the ability to display or modify the event before passing the event down to the user interface. Hooks provide a method of communication between the developer and the functionality of the Presentation Manager subsystem by allowing the developer to intercede on behalf of the application user. Essentially, hooks provide a powerful PM wide control over the user interface. Since hooks primarily involve message processing, they are exclusive to the PM screen group.

There are times that the default behavior of a particular message, function, or event does not achieve the effect that the developer is looking to accomplish. Since changing the default behavior for every request is unrealistic, the Presentation Management code within the operating system needs to make provisions for the developer to add or change functionality. Hooks give the developer the ability to provide this functionality. The worker routines for the API layer provide functions that will call the given hook procedure if a specific hook is installed.

For every hook type that is installed by an application, there is a prototype for the hook procedure. The *hook procedure* is simply the function that will execute when the event that is being hooked actually occurs. The intent of the hook process is to ensure that the hook procedure gets an opportunity to handle the event before PM passes the event on to the rest of the system for default processing.

One basic example of common hook usage is within a macro recorder. This functionality is common among several large spreadsheet or word processing applications. The macro recorder allows the user to record a sequence of keystrokes that can be played back at some other time. These macro utilities use a certain type of hook called the journal record hook to capture or record user keystrokes. Then at some later point, the recorded keystrokes are automatically executed when the user runs the macro. The hook that is used to play back the keystrokes is called the Journal Playback hook. The entire hook sequence is transparent to the user; all the user is responsible for is entering the keystrokes.

Understanding how hooks work requires understanding exactly how messages are processed. One of the most important structures with regard to hooks is the queue message structure or QMSG.

The format of the QMSG structure is defined in PMWIN.H shown in Figure 17.1.

- The **hwnd** parameter is the receiving window handle.
- The **msg** parameter is the message in the queue.
- The **mp1** parameter is the first message parameter.
- The **mp2** parameter is the second message parameter.
- The **time** parameter is the time the message was received.
- The **ptl** parameter is the pointer position at the time the message was generated.

The most common type of hook is known as the input hook. This hook can be used to filter keystrokes from the system message queue, so that if the user hits a certain key, the interpretation of the WM_CHAR message can be modified or thrown away entirely. For example, think of a simple screen capture utility. A screen capture utility must be able to run even when it does not have the keyboard input focus, so that it can allow the user to capture any window on the desktop by simply pressing a key. In general, screen capture utilities use the Print Screen key to initiate the capture since it makes logical sense. The default behavior of the Print Screen key is to send the output to a printer device not to a bitmap; therefore, it is up to the screen capture program to change the default behavior of the Print Screen key.

The purpose of a screen capture program is to allow the user to capture the contents of a particular window by translating the window into a graphical

```
typedef struct _QMSG      // qmsg
{
  HWND    hwnd;
  ULONG   msg;
  MPARAM  mp1;
  MPARAM  mp2;
  ULONG   time;
  POINTL  ptl;
  ULONG   reserved;
} QMSG;
typedef QMSG *PQMSG;
```

Figure 17.1   The QMSG structure.

image that the user can save in various graphical file formats, like bitmaps. From there, the user can copy the image into some other program like a word-processor or spreadsheet that supports the file format that the image was saved as. A well written screen capture program should provide an interface to the PM clipboard as well.

Given all of this, think about what it would take to code a screen capture program. There are two basic obstacles to programatically overcome:

- Changing the default behavior of the Print Screen key.
- The need for the application to work without input focus.

There are several shareware and commercial screen capture software programs available for OS/2. These applications make use of the input hook to capture the Print Screen keystroke, but rather than pass the key along to perform the default function, the key is changed to capture a given region of the screen to some other type of output, like a graphical image. The PMSCREEN sample program outlined in this chapter implements this use, by capturing a snapshot of the active window and storing the contents as a bitmap, when the Print Screen key is selected.

THE PURPOSE OF THE SAMPLE PROGRAM

The purpose of the sample program for Chapter 17 is to demonstrate the power of the Presentation Manager hooks. This chapter's sample program is called PMSCREEN. The sample source code provided on Wiley's FTP site (see Appendix A for details) builds two different modules. The first module is the actual executable, PMSCREEN which contains all of the regular PM application code. The second module is a dynamic link library called PMHOOKS, which actually contains the hook procedures that illustrate and perform most of the important hook concepts.

The PMSCREEN sample program is a simple screen capture utility that allows the user to capture the active window at the time the Print Screen key is depressed. The captured window is converted to a PM bitmap that can be copied to the PM clipboard; thereby allowing the bitmap to be pasted into another application. All of the graphics figures used throughout this book were captured using this program. The goal of the sample program is to illustrate how hooks can be implemented in a practical programming example. The chapter text and corresponding source code will also attempt to explain the usage of most of the defined PM hooks.

The PMSCREEN sample program uses several different types of hooks to illustrate the power that the PM developer has to alter messages on behalf of the user. Each hook used provides a different set of information or modifies a different event so that the behavior that the user sees is different.

The input hook is used to filter the Print Screen key allowing the program to capture the active window as a bitmap. The lockup hook is used to intercept the workplace shell's lockup utility so that we can use our own routines in place of the lockup code that displays a bitmap. This allows the PMSCREEN to display a customized version of lockup. Like the standard workplace lockup, all keyboard and mouse input is locked, and the reboot facility is disabled by issuing the correct device IOCTL.

The lockup code itself is essentially left intact, even with an installed lockup hook. All the lockup hook provides is the ability to alter the appearance of lockup. The code for locking the keyboard and mouse is still done by the workplace shell lockup code. The code basically works by issuing a category 4, function 56 device IOCTL. Consult the physical device driver reference for additional information. This IOCTL disables the Ctrl-Alt-Del reboot service to prevent the user from rebooting the machine while input is locked.

The lockup dialog box displayed by the workplace shell is made system modal by calling the **WinSetSysModalWindow** API. By making this dialog window system modal, all input is disabled except for the WM_CHAR character messages, that are received to unlock the keyboard and mouse. The system also restricts the Ctrl-Esc and Alt-Esc key sequences. In order to demonstrate how to write your own lockup code, the PMSCREEN program contains a similar routine that uses the specified IOCTL to restrict the Ctrl-Alt-Del reboot service. The routine is called what else, **DisableThreeFingerSalute**, and is shown in Figure 17.2.

```
VOID DisableThreeFingerSalute(VOID)
{
   HFILE     hfFile;
   USHORT    rc;
   USHORT    usCounter;
   ULONG     ulAction;
   ULONG     ulParmLength;
   ULONG     ulFileSize = 0;

   #define KBD             "KBD$"          // Open Keyboard Device
   #define KBDCATEGORY     0x04            // Device Category
   #define KBDFUNCTION     0x56            // Device Function
   #define TRY_AGAIN       1000            // Maximum Device Retry
   #define OPEN_FLAGS      OPEN_ACTION_CREATE_IF_NEW | OPEN_ACTION_OPEN_IF_EXISTS

   for (usCounter = 0; usCounter < TRY_AGAIN; usCounter++)
   {
    rc = DosOpen(KBD,                      // File Name - Keyboard Device
             &hfFile,                      // File Handle
             &ulAction,                    // Action Taken
```

Figure 17.2   The DisableThreeFingerSalute function.   **continued**

```
                ulFileSize,                 // File Size
                FILE_SYSTEM,                // File Attributes
                OPEN_FLAGS,                 // Open Flags
                OPEN_SHARE_DENYNONE,        // Open Mode
                NULL);                      // EA Buffer
    if (rc != 0)
     {
      DisplayMessages(NULLHANDLE, "DosOpen Failed", MSG_ERROR);
     }
    break;
    }

  for (usCounter = 0; usCounter < TRY_AGAIN; usCounter++)
  {
    Parm_Packet.KeyState   = 0;  // This is the structure we pass into DosDevIOCtl
    Parm_Packet.MakeCode   = 0;  // for changing the keyboard hotkeys.  See pmscreen.h
    Parm_Packet.BreakCode  = 0;  // for structure definition.  The keyID with a value
    Parm_Packet.KeyID      = -1; // of -1 acts as a toggle, setting and
                                 // removing the hotkeys.  See Category 4 Function 56H.

    ulParmLength = sizeof (Parm_Packet);

    rc = DosDevIOCtl  (hfFile,             // Device Handle
                       KBDCATEGORY,        // Device Category
                       KBDFUNCTION,        // Device Function
                       &Parm_Packet,       // Command Arguments List
                       ulParmLength,       // Command Arguments MAX Length
                       &ulParmLength,      // Command Arguments Length
                       NULL,               // Data Area
                       0,                  // Data Area MAX Length
                       0);                 // Data Area Length

    if (rc != 0)
     {
      DisplayMessages(NULLHANDLE, "DosDevIOCtl Failed", MSG_ERROR);
     }
    break;

    rc = DosClose(hfFile);

    if (rc != 0)
     {
      DisplayMessages(NULLHANDLE, "DosClose Failed", MSG_ERROR);
     }
  }
  return;
}
```

Figure 17.2   The DisableThreeFingerSalute function.

INSTALLING A HOOK

The process of installing a hook involves registering your hook with the Presentation Manager so that it can be added to the hook list. All hooks that are installed by an application are registered through the use of the **WinSetHook** API. The purpose of registering the hook is to provide the type of hook that is to be installed, along with the address of the hook procedure that is to be executed when the event occurs.

The prototype for the **WinSetHook** API is given in Figure 17.3.

- The **hab** parameter is the handle to the anchor block.
- The **hmq** parameter is the handle to the message queue that is to be hooked. If this parameter is set to NULLHANDLE, then the hook will be installed in the system hook chain to monitor the system message queue. If this parameter is set to the constant value HMQ_CURRENT, then the hook is installed in the application message queue for the current thread.
- The **lHookType** parameter is the type of hook that is to be installed. The hook type represents the purpose of the hook that the programmer wishes to use.
- The **pfnHookProc** parameter is the address of the hook function, which is the routine that is to be run when the hook is installed. The hook function will contain the code that can modify the message that the hook is intended to monitor or change.
- The **hMod** parameter is the module handle that contains the application hook function. The valid module handle can be returned from a call to the API's **DosLoadModule** or **DosGetModHandle**. An application that is installing a hook to monitor its own application message queue can set this value to NULLHANDLE. If an application intends to hook the system message queue, this value must contain a valid module handle.

If the **WinSetHook** API returns TRUE, then the attempt to install the hook succeeded. The function will return FALSE if an error occurred setting the hook. All hook routines that are installed to monitor the system message queue will be used by every application. The hook routines that are used to monitor the message queue of a particular thread are only available within that thread.

```
BOOL APIENTRY WinSetHook(HAB        hab,
                         HMQ        hmq,
                         LONG       lHookType,
                         PFN        pfnHookProc,
                         HMODULE    hmod);
```

Figure 17.3   The WinSetHook API.

In other words, if you set a hook to monitor a particular message, but the hook is only installed for the application message queue, only messages received by your application message queue are valid for the hook. Hooks that are intended to monitor the application message queue are called before hooks that are used to monitor the system message queue.

After the hook has been registered, it is added to an internal linked list maintained by PM. The **hook list** is used to reference the addresses of the hook functions. Typically, the addresses of the hook routines are linked together to form what is called the hook chain. Separate hook chains are maintained for the application message queue and system message queue.

The functionality of the **WinSetHook** API ensures that the hook is installed at the head node of the system message queue hook chain or application message queue hook chain on a most recently installed basis. Ultimately, this means that the most recently installed hook will be called first. In theory, the messages processed by the queue are passed down from one hook function to the next, until the chain is complete. Every hook routine has the capability to stop the message or modify its purpose, thereby altering the message before it reaches the window it was intended for and stopping the hook chain from completing its processing.

The hook procedures themselves should be declared with the EXPENTRY keyword. The EXPENTRY keyword is used to indicate that the *System* linkage convention should be used. The default linkage convention for the IBM CSET/2 compiler family is known as *Optlink*. The linkage convention affects how parameters are placed on the stack. Refer to the documentation provided with your compiler for additional information regarding linkage conventions.

TYPES OF HOOKS

There are several different types of hooks, each with its own purpose. Some hooks are designed to monitor either an application message queue or the system message queue. Some hooks are even designed to monitor both the system message queue and an application's message queue. The hook types, along with the function prototypes for the hook procedures, can be found in PMWIN.H. They are listed in Figure 17.4.

The numbers following the hook types shown in Figure 17.4 are the values of the hooks in decimal. You may have already noticed that there are several numbers missing from this list between 0 and 24. No, it's not another IBM numbering scheme that doesn't make sense. Most of the missing numbers correspond to hook types not defined publicly in PMWIN; therefore, these missing hook types are undocumented. However, as you can see from the list, there are many more public hooks available than are usually documented.

HK_SENDMSG	0	The Send Message Hook
HK_INPUT	1	The Input Hook
HK_MSGFILTER	2	The Message Filter Hook
HK_JOURNALRECORD	3	The Journal Record Hook
HK_JOURNALPLAYBACK	4	The Journal Playback Hook
HK_HELP	5	The Help Hook
HK_LOADER	6	The Loader Hook
HK_REGISTERUSERMSG	7	The Register User Hook
HK_MSGCONTROL	8	The Message Control Hook
HK_PLIST_ENTRY	9	The Program List Entry Hook
HK_PLIST_EXIT	10	The Program List Exit Hook
HK_FINDWORD	11	The Find Word Hook
HK_CODEPAGECHANGED	12	The Code Page Hook
HK_WINDOWDC	15	The Window Device Context Hook
HK_DESTROYWINDOW	16	The Destroy Window Hook
HK_CHECKMSGFILTER	20	The Check Message Filter Hook
HK_MSGINPUT	21	The Message Input Hook
HK_LOCKUP	23	The Lockup Hook
HK_FLUSHBUF	24	The Flush Buffer Hook

Figure 17.4   Publicly defined hook types.

There were several new hooks introduced with the release of the 2.1 version of OS/2. This chapter will attempt to provide an explanation for some of the most important of the documented PM hooks, along with the benefits of using the hook.

The Message Filter Hook—HK_MSGFILTER

As an OS/2 PM developer, you should already be familiar with the standard *while* loop that is used to get and dispatch messages. PM maintains its own message loop for processing modal messages. This loop is used for exclusive message processing for such events as drawing dialog or message boxes, processing the tracking rectangle, or performing a drag-and-drop operation. During the processing of these events, the system enters a modal message loop so that these important messages are dispatched as quickly as possible.

The purpose of the message filter hook is to allow an application to enter into this loop and thus gain access to the messages as they are processed. PM will call the hook function between the calls to get and dispatch the messages. Figure 17.5 shows a standard message loop.

The message filter hook gives any application the ability to filter a message between the time the message is retrieved from the queue and the time the

```
while(WinGetMsg(hab, &qmsg, (HWND)NULL, 0, 0 ))
  WinDispatchMsg(hab, &qmsg);
```

Figure 17.5   The message loop.

```
BOOL EXPENTRY MsgFilterHook (HAB      hab,
                             PQMSG    pqmsg,
                             ULONG    ulMsgFlag);
```

Figure 17.6   The message filter hook prototype.

message is actually dispatched, thereby allowing the application to process the message differently if desired.

The format of the message filter hook is given in Figure 17.6.

- The **hab** parameter is the handle to the anchor block.
- The **pqmsg** parameter is a pointer to a QMSG structure. The QMSG structure contains information regarding the message, and is shown in Figure 17.1.
- The **ulMsgFlag** parameter is a ULONG variable that contains the type of message that is to be filtered by the message filter hook.

Valid message filter hook flags, along with their decimal values, are listed in Figure 17.7.

The message filter hook function can return a value indicating whether the event should be passed down the hook chain to the next procedure or back to the application. If the function returns TRUE, then the message will not be passed to the next hook in the hook chain. If the function returns FALSE, then the message will be passed on. PM will even pass the WM_QUIT message to this hook if it happens to occur within one of the modal loops.

MSGF_DIALOGBOX	1	This flag is used to filter the dialog box message loop.
MSGF_MESSAGEBOX	2	This flag is used to filter the message box message loop.
MSGF_TRACK	8	This flag is used to filter messages out of the tracking rectangle message loop. The tracking rectangle is the term used to describe a window while it is being moved or sized. When this hook is used, the *fs* and *rclTrack* elements of the TRACKINFO structure are updated to provide the current position prior to the hook.
MSGF_DDEPOSTMSG	3	This flag is used to filter messages from the Dynamic Data Exchange message loop.
NOTE:		There is one additional flag that is not defined in PMWIN.H. This flag is also used for the message filter hook, but is defined in the header file PMSTDDLG.H:
MSGF_DRAG	10	This flag is defined for the standard file dialog to allow access to the drag-and-drop message loop.

Figure 17.7   The message filter hook flags.

The Input Hook—HK_INPUT

The most common type of hook is the input hook, which can be used to monitor either the system message queue or an application message queue. The input hook is provided to the developer to interpret all messages processed by the **WinGetMsg** or **WinPeekMsg** APIs. The input hook routine is called whenever either function is ready to return a message. The input hook is effective in monitoring virtually all input received from either the mouse or keyboard along with other messages posted to a message queue.

The input hook uses the prototype shown in Figure 17.8.

- The **hab** parameter is the handle to the anchor block.
- The **pqmsg** parameter is a pointer to a QMSG structure. The QMSG structure contains information regarding the message.
- The **fs** parameter is a ULONG variable that represents whether the message is to be removed from the message queue.

The **fs** parameter flags are actually the same constants defined for **WinPeekMsg**.

PM_REMOVE	0x0001	This flag is used to indicate that the message is being removed from the message queue.
PM_NOREMOVE	0x0000	This flag is used to indicate that the message is not being removed from the message queue.

The input hook allows an application to modify the message information by examining the contents of the QMSG structure and modifying the message information. For instance, an application can use the input hook to examine the message queue for WM_CHAR messages, allowing any particular character to be changed. If the hook function returns TRUE, the message will not be passed on to the next hook in the hook chain. If the hook function returns FALSE then the message will be passed on to the next hook in the hook chain.

Using the Input Hook

As discussed previously in this chapter, the input hook is used to filter messages from the system message queue. The PMSCREEN program uses the input hook to allow the capture to occur without the PMSCREEN window having input

```
BOOL EXPENTRY InputHook (HAB    hab,
                         PQMSG  pqmsg,
                         ULONG  fs);
```

Figure 17.8   The input hook.

focus. The window capture occurs as a result of the user pressing the Print Screen key. The process of changing the default functionality of the Print Screen key is actually accomplished in two steps. The first step is to actually disable the default behavior of the Print Screen key. The second step is to reassign the Print Screen key a new functionality to correspond to capturing the contents of a particular window as a bitmap.

The PMSCREEN sample program calls a routine within the PMHOOKS library called **SetInputHook** which is the routine responsible for setting the Input hook that will be used to trap the Print Screen key. This function is extremely simple; it does not take any parameters and will return the value of the **WinSetHook** API. All this code really does is attempt to set the hook. It is shown in Figure 17.9. All of the hook functions used in the PMHOOKS library are set by a worker function called **Set*Function*Hook**; where *Function* represents the type of hook that is to be registered with **WinSetHook**. Consequently, all of the hooks are released with a worker function called **Release*Function*Hook**. The release functions are responsible for freeing whatever resources were used by the hook function and for unloading the hook module via **DosFreeModule**. Finally, the last step in the **ReleaseFunctionHook** routines is to release the hook by calling the **WinReleaseHook** API. Figure 17.9 contains the routine used to set the input hook.

The second parameter being set to NULLHANDLE tells PM that this hook is being used to monitor the system message queue. Remember this is important since the goal of using the input hook within PMSCREEN is to trap all requests whenever the user hits the Print Screen key. The **pInputHook** parameter points to the address of the hook procedure that will execute when the input hook event occurs. The **hMod** parameter is the module handle where the hook procedure exists. Both of these values are obtained from the **DLLInitRoutine** function.

The actual hook procedure is called **InputHook**. This is the routine that will get executed every time the **WinGetMsg** or **WinPeekMsg** functions are about to

```
BOOL EXPENTRY SetInputHook(VOID)
{
BOOL rc;

rc = WinSetHook(hab,                        // Handle Anchor Block
                NULLHANDLE,                 // Hook System MsgQueue
                HK_INPUT,                   // Hook Type
                pfnInputHook,               // Hook Handler
                hMod);                      // DLL Needed for Hook

return rc;
}
```

Figure 17.9   Setting the Input hook.

return a message. Once we get a message, we are only interested in handling messages received from the keyboard, so we will check only WM_CHAR messages. Since we are only interested in processing the Print Screen key, we need only check for the virtual key VK_PRINTSCRN along with the KC_KEYUP and KC_VIRTUALKEY codes.

The code for the Input Hook is shown in Figure 17.10.

The first **if** conditional checks for all WM_CHAR messages in the QMSG structure and then checks to see if the virtual key VK_PRINTSCRN is contained within the *mp2* element of the structure. The macro CHAR3FROMMP is used to extract the message parameter containing the virtual key flag.

The next step is to actually disable the function of the Print Screen key. By default, PM contains an undocumented routine called **WinPrintScreen** which is the code responsible for creating the metafile that is sent to the printer everytime the user presses the Print Screen key. This code is not within the context of the hook, so it will be called regardless of whether or not we do anything with the VK_PRINTSCRN key. Therefore, the screen capture program needs to disable the functionality provided by pressing the Print Screen key. Disabling the Print Screen function requires modifying a system value called

```
BOOL EXPENTRY InputHook(HAB hab, PQMSG pqmsg, ULONG fs)
{
  CHAR  pEnabledState[2];
  HWND  hwndClient;
  BOOL  bValid;

  if ((pqmsg->msg == WM_CHAR) && (CHAR3FROMMP(pqmsg->mp2) == VK_PRINTSCRN) &&
    !(SHORT1FROMMP(pqmsg->mp1) & KC_KEYUP) && (SHORT1FROMMP(pqmsg->mp1) & KC_VIRTUALKEY))
    {
    DosBeep (500,500);

    PrfQueryProfileString(HINI_USER,
                          INI_APPNAME,
                          INI_KEYNAME,
                          INI_DEFAULT,
                          (PVOID) &pEnabledState,
                          2L);

    if (*pEnabledState == '1')      // If the Print Screen function is enabled,
      {                             // then we need to disable it by calling the
      DisablePrintScreenKey(TRUE);  // DisablePrintScreenKey function.
      }
      WinSendMsg(hwndGlobal, WM_UPDATEBITMAP, NULL, NULL);
    }
  return FALSE;
}
```

Figure 17.10   The Input Hook procedure.

```
#define INI_APPNAME   "PM_ControlPanel"
#define INI_KEYNAME   "PrintScreen"
#define INI_DEFAULT   "1"
```

Figure 17.11   The definitions for the INI file.

SV_PRINTSCREEN. It is good coding practice to ensure that you only disable the Print Screen function if it is currently enabled. The enable state is stored within the OS2.INI profile under the application name PM_ControlPanel and the keyname PrintScreen.

The PMHOOKS.H header file defines the values in Figure 17.11 which are used to check whether the default Print Screen function is currently enabled. The code that actually checks the current state of the key is shown in Figure 17.12.

The INI_DEFAULT value is used to take into consideration if the **pszApp** or **pszKey** information is missing from the OS2.INI, usually a result of a corrupt INI file. If the information is not available, assume that the Print Screen functionality has not been disabled.

The **if** conditional checks to see if the value of the enabled state stored in the **pEnabledState** pointer is set to a 1, which indicates that the Print Screen function is currently enabled. If the Print Screen function is enabled, then the **InputHook** procedure calls a routine named **DisablePrintScreenKey** with a value of TRUE. The code for the **DisablePrintScreenKey** will then set the appropriate system value to disable the default Print Screen functionality. The **DisablePrintScreenKey** function is shown in Figure 17.13.

The caller of this function passes a single BOOL parameter **bState**, which is used to indicate whether the default Print Screen functionality should be enabled or disabled. If the value is TRUE, the Print Screen functionality will be disabled by calling the **WinSetSysValue** API with a FALSE value indicating that the enable state of the Print Screen key will be disabled. Conversely,

```
PrfQueryProfileString(HINI_USER,              // Use the OS2.INI Profile
                   INI_APPNAME,               // pszApp "PM_ControlPanel"
                   INI_KEYNAME,               // pszKey "PrintScreen"
                   INI_DEFAULT,               // pszDefault "1"
                   (PVOID) &pEnabledState,    // The actual data string
                   sizeof(pEnabledState));    // The size of the data string

if (*pEnabledState == '1')     // If the Print Screen function is enabled
  {                            // then we need to disable it by calling the
   DisablePrintScreenKey(TRUE);  // DisablePrintScreenKey function.
  }
```

Figure 17.12   Checking if the Print Screen function is enabled.

```
BOOL DisablePrintScreenKey(bState)
{
 BOOL rc;

 // This conditional will disable the default
 // function of the Print Screen key.
 if (bState)
  {
   rc = WinSetSysValue(HWND_DESKTOP,      // Desktop window handle
                       SV_PRINTSCREEN,    // System value identifier
                       FALSE);            // System value - FALSE disables
  }

 // This conditional will enable the default
 // function of the Print Screen key.
 else
  {
   rc = WinSetSysValue(HWND_DESKTOP,      // Desktop window handle
                       SV_PRINTSCREEN,    // System value identifier
                       TRUE);             // System value - TRUE enables
  }

 // If either call to WinSetSysValue returns a TRUE, then the
 // enable state has changed, so we will broadcast a message
 // to tell others that the state has been changed by this call.
 if (rc)
  {
   WinBroadcastMsg(HWND_DESKTOP,
                   WM_SYSVALUECHANGED,
                   (MPARAM) SV_PRINTSCREEN,
                   (MPARAM) SV_PRINTSCREEN,
                   BMSG_POST | BMSG_FRAMEONLY);

   // If this function returns TRUE, then the enable state of the
   // Print Screen key has been toggled by this function.
   return TRUE;
  }

 else
  {
   // A FALSE return value tells the caller that the enable state
   // of the Print Screen key could not be modified by this function.
   // This is highly unlikely....
   return FALSE;
  }
}
```

Figure 17.13 Modifying the Print Screen enable state.

if the value is FALSE, the default Print Screen functionality is enabled by calling the **WinSetSysValue** API with a TRUE. In either case, if the Print Screen system value was successfully changed, the **WinSetSysValue** API will return TRUE. The API will return FALSE if an error occurred and the system value was not modified. If the system value was successfully modified by the **DisablePrintScreenKey** function, a WM_SYSVALUECHANGED message will be broadcast to all top level frame windows to alert them of the change. In the unlikely event that this function was unable to modify the Print Screen system value, the function will return FALSE, indicating no change in the system value occurred.

CAPTURING THE ACTIVE WINDOW

Obviously, the main purpose of a screen capture program is to capture a window that the user wants to incorporate into some other program. Therefore, the screen capture program must be able to render the window's image into some graphical format that the receiving application can understand and display. The source code for the PMHOOKS dynamic link library, contains a routine called **PrintScreenToBitmap** that performs the window capture for the program. The function works by capturing the contents of the active window and saving it as a PM bitmap.

The function does not take any parameters and is called from the context of the input hook procedure as a result of the WM_UPDATEBITMAP processing in PMSCREEN.C. The function will return a valid bitmap handle created by the **GpiCreateBitmap** API upon success. If an error occurs creating the bitmap from the active window, GPI_ERROR, which is also the equivalent of a NULLHANDLE will be returned.

The **PrintScreenToBitmap** function starts by creating a memory device context by calling the **DevOpenDC** device function. A memory presentation space is created by the subsequent call to the **GpiCreatePS** API. From there, the active window is queried and its handle is stored in the *hwndActive* variable. Based on this window, a cached micro presentation space is created, and is represented by the *hpsScreen* variable. The rectangle coordinates for the active window are stored in the rectangle structure represented by *rclActive*. The *xRight* and *yTop* coordinates of the rectangle structure are set as the bitmap size coordinates *bmp.cx* and *bmp.cy*. Ultimately, the bitmap is then created by calling the **GpiCreateBitmap** API. If the bitmap was successfully created, it is set into the memory presentation space, *hpsMemory* that is associated to the memory device context *hdcMemory*. Finally, the bitmap is ready to be displayed by calling the **GpiBitBlt** API and returning the bitmap handle to indicate that the bitmap can be painted in the client window.

The code fragment shown in Figure 17.14 creates the bitmap when the Print Screen key is hit.

```
HBITMAP PrintScreenToBitmap(VOID)
 {
  BITMAPINFOHEADER2 bmp;
  HBITMAP           hbmWindow;
  HDC               hdcMemory;
  HPS               hpsMemory;
  HPS               hpsScreen;
  LONG              alBitmapFormats[2];
  POINTL            aptl[3];
  SIZEL             sizl;
  HWND              hwndActive;
  RECTL             rclActive;

  // Get a memory device context
  hdcMemory = DevOpenDC (hab, OD_MEMORY, "*", 0L, NULL, NULLHANDLE);

  sizl.cx = sizl.cy = 0;

  // Get a memory presentation space
  hpsMemory = GpiCreatePS (hab,                       // anchor block handle
                           hdcMemory,                 // device context handle
                           &sizl,                     // PS page size
                           PU_PELS  | GPIF_DEFAULT |  // Options
                           GPIT_MICRO | GPIA_ASSOC);

  // Capture the active window, get its presentation space,
  // and rectangle coordinates
  hwndActive = WinQueryActiveWindow(HWND_DESKTOP);
  hpsScreen  = WinGetPS(hwndActive);
  WinQueryWindowRect(hwndActive, &rclActive);

  GpiQueryDeviceBitmapFormats (hpsMemory, 2L, alBitmapFormats);

  // Populate the bitmap info header structure
  // and create the bitmap by calling GpiCreateBitmap
  bmp.cbFix    = sizeof bmp;
  bmp.cPlanes  = alBitmapFormats[0];
  bmp.cBitCount = alBitmapFormats[1];
  bmp.cx       = rclActive.xRight;
  bmp.cy       = rclActive.yTop;

  hbmWindow = GpiCreateBitmap (hpsMemory, &bmp, 0L, NULL, NULL);

  if (hbmWindow != GPI_ERROR)
   {
    // Set Bitmap into memory PS
    GpiSetBitmap (hpsMemory, hbmWindow);
```

Figure 17.14 **Capturing the Active Window as a Bitmap.**   **continued**

```
    aptl[0].x = 0;
    aptl[0].y = 0;
    aptl[1].x = rclActive.xRight;
    aptl[1].y = rclActive.yTop;
    aptl[2].x = 0;
    aptl[2].y = 0;

    WinLockVisRegions (hwndActive, TRUE);
    GpiBitBlt (hpsMemory, hpsScreen, 3L, aptl, ROP_SRCCOPY, BBO_IGNORE);
    WinLockVisRegions (hwndActive, FALSE);

    WinReleasePS (hpsScreen);
    GpiDestroyPS (hpsMemory);
    DevCloseDC (hdcMemory);

    // If we have a valid bitmap, return it
    return hbmWindow;
  }

else
  {
    // If we got an error creating the bitmap, return GPI_ERROR
    return GPI_ERROR;
  }
}
```

Figure 17.14 Capturing the active window as a bitmap.

The Send Message Hook—HK_SENDMSG

The send message hook is designed to trap those messages that are sent rather than posted to a message queue. This hook can be used to obtain messages before the message is received by the window that the message was sent to, because the hook function is called from within the context of the **WinSendMsg** code. Any application that wishes to monitor all messages can use a combination of the send message hook along with the input hook. The format of the send message hook is similar to that of the input hook, except a send message structure is used instead of the QMSG structure. The send message hook function always calls the next hook in the chain, and the function does not return a value. The prototype of the function is given in Figure 17.15.

```
VOID EXPENTRY SendMsgHook (HAB           hab,
                           PSMHSTRUCT    psmh,
                           BOOL          fInterTask);
```

Figure 17.15 The send message hook prototype.

```
typedef struct _SMHSTRUCT  // smhs
 {
   MPARAM mp2;
   MPARAM mp1;
   ULONG  msg;
   HWND   hwnd;
   ULONG  model;
 } SMHSTRUCT;
```

Figure 17.16   The SMHSTRUCT structure.

- The **hab** parameter is the handle to the anchor block.
- The **psmh** parameter is a pointer to a SMHSTRUCT structure. The SMH-STRUCT structure contains information regarding the message.
- The **fInterTask** parameter is a BOOL variable that is used to determine whether the message is being sent within the same thread or two different threads. If this value is TRUE, then the message is being sent between two different threads (INTERTASK). If the value is FALSE, then the message is being sent within the same thread (INTRATASK).

The send message structure provides information about the message being sent, including all of the parameters that were passed to the call to **WinSendMsg**. The format of the SMHSTRUCT structure is as shown in Figure 17.16.

The Journal Record Hook—HK_JOURNALRECORD

This hook provides the developer the ability to monitor the system message queue with the purpose of recording the user's input. The purpose of the journal record hook is to allow the developer to capture a sequence of mouse and keyboard input. The events or keystrokes can be simulated again at some later point through the use of the commensurate hook, the journal playback hook. The hook is called after the input actually becomes a message. The prototype for the journal record hook is given in Figure 17.17.

- The **hab** parameter is the handle to the anchor block.
- The **pqmsg** parameter is a pointer to a QMSG structure. The QMSG structure contains information regarding the message.

```
VOID EXPENTRY JournalRecordHook (HAB    hab,
                                 PQMSG  pqmsg);
```

Figure 17.17   The JournalRecordHook prototype.

```
ULONG ulTime = JournalPlaybackHook (HAB     hab,
                                    BOOL    fSkip,
                                    PQMSG   pqmsg);
```

Figure 17.18 **The JournalPlaybackHook prototype.**

The journal record hook function always calls the next hook in the chain, and the function does not return a value. Along with the WM_CHAR message for keyboard input, several mouse input messages are passed to the journal record hook as well. The mouse messages include the WM_MOUSEMOVE, the WM_BUTTONnUP, and WM_BUTTONnDOWN* messages.

The Journal Playback Hook—HK_JOURNALPLAYBACK

The journal playback hook allows the developer to insert the input messages that were recorded by the journal record hook back into the system message queue. All standard mouse and keyboard input is disabled while the journal playback hook routine is running, because the messages are being inserted into the system message queue. It is extremely important that developers realize the consequences of suspending the regular message queue processing, and ensure that the journal playback hook is used carefully and only when required since overuse can cause system performance to degrade.

The prototype for the Journal Playback hook function is shown on Figure 17.18.

- The **hab** parameter is the handle to the anchor block.
- The **fSkip** parameter is a BOOL variable that is used to identify whether the next message is to be played back. If this parameter is TRUE, then the **PQMSG** parameter is NULL and the next hook in the hook chain is not called. If the parameter is FALSE, then the hook returns the next message repetitively until this parameter is TRUE.
- The **pqmsg** parameter is a pointer to a QMSG structure. The QMSG structure contains information regarding the message. The time element of the QMSG structure is a ULONG value that stores the current time prior to the journal playback hook actually being called. The hook function can use this value to monitor the the amount of time between messages or the delay time between the messages.

The journal playback hook returns a ULONG value that represents the amount of time in milliseconds that it will take before the current message is processed. The return value allows the hook to control the amount of time for the playback events.

*Where n represents the mouse button number.

```
BOOL EXPENTRY HelpHook(HAB     hab,
                       ULONG   usMode,
                       ULONG   idTopic,
                       ULONG   idSubTopic,
                       PRECTL  prcPosition);
```

Figure 17.19   The HelpHook.

The Help Hook—HK_HELP

The help hook is designed to allow application developers to provide additional help information in their applications. The Presentation Manager will call the help hook function during the default processing of the help message WM_HELP. The prototype for the help hook function is shown in Figure 17.19.

The WM_HELP message is typically generated when the user depresses the F1 key. The virtual key F1 generates a WM_CHAR message, which the default accelerator table translates via an ACCEL structure into a WM_HELP message. The WM_HELP message is then passed to the current focus window, which can either be the client window or a control window like a pushbutton or menu.

The WM_HELP message can also be generated when the developer includes the MIS_HELP menuitem style on an application menu item. In this case, the WM_HELP message is posted to the window that currently has input focus. A help message can also occur from a pushbutton window that is created with the BS_HELP button style. The resulting WM_HELP message is posted to the owner window of the button, which is typically the dialog box window if the button was created within a dialog template. Finally, a WM_HELP message can come as a result of the MB_HELP message box style, in which case the help message is posted to the message box.

The code for the default window procedure, **WinDefWindowProc**, passes the WM_HELP and WM_TRANSLATEACCEL messages to the parent window. If the messages get passed to the client window, they can be processed in the client window procedure; but if the message makes its way up to the default frame window procedure **WinFrameWndProc**, the help hook will be called if the parent's frame identifier is FID_CLIENT or if there is no parent. The help hook is also called if the help message originated while the user made a selection from the application menu.

The Lockup Hook—HK_LOCKUP

The lockup hook is relatively new to PM. It was introduced with the release of OS/2 2.1 based on requests from application developers. The lockup hook gives developers the opportunity to alter what users will see when they select the

```
BOOL EXPENTRY LockupHook(HAB hab, HWND hwndLockup)
{
  WinSetWindowPos(hwndGlobal, HWND_TOP, 0, 0, 0, 0,
                  SWP_MAXIMIZE | SWP_MOVE | SWP_SIZE | SWP_ZORDER);

  WinSetWindowPos(hwndLockup,
                  NULLHANDLE,
                  0,
                  0,
                  0,
                  0,
                  SWP_HIDE | SWP_MOVE | SWP_SIZE);

  WinInvalidateRect(hwndGlobal, NULL, FALSE);
  return TRUE;
}
```

Figure 17.20   The LockupHook.

workplace shell's lockup facility. This allows developers to either perform some alternate function or install another utility to block input from the keyboard and mouse. The code fragment shown in Figure 17.20 illustrates a simple LockupHook procedure.

The Message Input Hook—HK_MSGINPUT

The message input hook is another of the new hooks that was introduced with the release of OS/2 2.1. The purpose of this hook is similar to the journal playback hook in that, it will allow the application installing the hook to insert messages into the input queue, thereby simulating input from a user. The format of the input hook is given in Figure 17.21.

- The **hab** parameter is the handle to the anchor block.
- The **pqmsg** parameter is a pointer to a QMSG structure. The QMSG structure contains information regarding the message. The QMSG structure is to be filled in by the hook procedure with the mouse or keyboard message that is to be inserted into the message queue.

```
BOOL  bReturn = MsgInputHook(HAB    hab,
                             PQMSG  pqmsg,
                             BOOL   fSkip,
                             PBOOL  pfNoRecord);
```

Figure 17.21   The MsgInputHook prototype.

- The **fSkip** parameter is a BOOL variable that is used to identify whether to advance to the next message. If this parameter is set to TRUE, then the PQMSG structure is NULL and the hook will continue to advance to the next message. If the PQMSG structure is NULL, then there is obviously no message to process. In this case, the hook should be terminated using **WinReleaseHook**. If this parameter is FALSE then the hook returns the same message repetitively until this parameter is TRUE.
- The **pfNoRecord** parameter is a pointer to a BOOL variable. The developer can use this parameter to prevent the journal record hook from recording the message that was inserted into the message queue via the **msg** parameter of the QMSG structure. If this value is set to TRUE, then the message cannot be recorded by the journal record hook. If this value is set to FALSE, then the message can be recorded by the journal record hook.

If the **MsgInputHook** routine returns TRUE, then the QMSG structure will contain the current message information that is to be processed. If the function returns FALSE, then the QMSG structure is empty and no messages are to be processed by the hook.

The Find Word Hook—HK_FINDWORD

The title of this hook is probably a little deceiving. It might be more aptly termed the draw text hook since it is designed specifically to determine where the API **WinDrawText** will divide a character string that does not fit within the bounds of the drawing rectangle. This hook was developed for foreign language applications based on the National Language Support (NLS) requirements. It allows applications that use code page information with the double byte character set (DBCS) to control where the line of text will end to help avoid unsightly line-breaks. The hook will be called from within the context of the **WinDrawText** API if the DT_WORDBREAK flag is set. The prototype for the FindWordHook is shown in Figure 17.22.

- The **usCodepage** parameter represents the code page of the string that is to be drawn.

```
BOOL EXPENTRY FindWordHook(USHORT usCodepage,
                           PSZ     pszText,
                           ULONG   cb,
                           ULONG   ich,
                           PULONG  pichStart,
                           PULONG  pichEnd,
                           PULONG  pichNext);
```

Figure 17.22   The FindWordHook prototype.

- The **pszText** parameter represents a pointer to the string that is to be drawn.
- The **cb** parameter represents the number of bytes in the string.
- The **ich** parameter is used to represent a character index into the string that intersects the right boundary of the rectangle used for drawing the text.
- The **pichStart** parameter is the returned index of the first character of the word.
- The **pichEnd** parameter is the returned index of the last character of the word.
- The **pichNext** parameter is the returned index of the first character of the next word in the string.

If the hook procedure returns FALSE, the text will be drawn normally. Otherwise, if the hook procedure returns TRUE, the **WinDrawText** API will draw the string until the word break.

The Code Page Changed Hook—HK_CODEPAGECHANGED

The purpose of this hook is to provide an application with a notification whenever another application attempts to change the code page. The hook is designed for applications with multiple-language support to check whether another application is altering the code page information. The format of the code page changed hook is found in Figure 17.23.

- The **hmq** parameter is the handle to the message queue that is changing its code page information.
- The **ulOldCodePage** parameter is the number that represents the code page that is being changed.
- The **ulNewCodePage** parameter is the number that represents the code page that will replace the current code page.

The **CodePageChangedHook** function does not return a value, which means that all code page hooks represented by HK_CODEPAGECHANGE within the hook chain will get the notification of the code page change. The hook function is called after the new code page is set. The hook is called from within the context of the **WinSetCp** API.

```
VOID EXPENTRY CodePageChangedHook(HMQ     hmq,
                                  ULONG   ulOldCodePage,
                                  ULONG   ulNewCodePage);
```

Figure 17.23   The CodePageChangedHook prototype.

```
BOOL EXPENTRY FlushBufHook (HAB hab)
```

Figure 17.24   The FlushBufHook prototype.

The Flush Buffer Hook—HK_FLUSHBUF

The Flush buffer hook is used to filter the Ctrl-Alt-Del reboot sequence. The hook is designed to allow applications to receive notification that a reboot is about to occur and take an appropriate action, like saving critical data to the fixed disk instead of the data being lost as a result of a reboot. The hook is used internally by the workplace shell to flush the lazy write cache prior to rebooting. An application should not do too much within this hook procedure. The hook procedure should be used solely to save application critical data. Also, since the hook is called in the context of the reboot occurring, the PM API sub-systems may not be callable; therefore, an application should avoid calling **Win** and **Gpi** APIs. The prototype for the **FlushBufHook** procedure is shown in Figure 17.24. The flush buffer hook procedure takes only a single parameter, the anchor block handle.

The code fragment shown in Figure 17.25 from the PMSCREEN program demonstrates the use of the **FlushBufHook** function by creating a log file in the root directory of the user's boot drive. The log file contains the date and time that the machine was rebooted via Ctrl-Alt-Del. This allows a machine administrator to monitor when the last reboot occurred. This code will be executed if the user presses Ctrl-Alt-Del while the PMSCREEN program is running.

RELEASING THE HOOK

Once an application is finished using the hook, the resources used by the hook procedure should be released and the address of the hook procedure should be removed from the appropriate hook list. The **WinReleaseHook** API is designed to remove the hook once the purpose of the hook has completed. The **WinReleaseHook** code works by looping through the linked list of hooks and removing the specified hook from the list. The prototype for the **WinReleaseHook** API is shown in Figure 17.26. The parameters to this function are identical to **WinSetHook**.

- The **hab** parameter is the handle to the anchor block.
- The **hmq** parameter is the handle of the message queue from which the hook will be released. If this parameter contains the HMQ_CURRENT constant, then the hook will be released from the context of the current thread. A NULLHANDLE value is used to release the hook from the system hook chain.

```
BOOL EXPENTRY FlushBufHook (HAB hab)
{
 HFILE          hfFile;
 ULONG          ulAction;
 ULONG          ulWritten;
 Ulong          ulLength;
 CHAR           szDateTime[CCHMAXPATH];
 DATETIME       datetime;
 APIRET         rc;
 CHAR           *szLogFile[] = {"?:\\REBOOT.LOG"};
 PSZ            pszTemp;

 static CHAR    *szDayName [] = { "Sun", "Mon", "Tue", "Wed", "Thu", "Fri", "Sat"  };
 static CHAR    szFormat   [] = "The machine was rebooted on %s %d-%d-%d at %d:%d:%d %cM";

 DosGetDateTime (&datetime);
 datetime.year %= 100;

 pszLogFile = SubstituteBootDrive(szLogFile[0]);

 // Open our logfile in the root directory of the boot drive
 DosOpen (pszLogFile,         // File Name
          &hfFile,            // File Handle
          &ulAction,          // Action returned
          0L,                 // Initial FileSize
          FILE_ARCHIVED,      // File Attributes
          OPEN_FLAGS,         // Open Flags
          OPEN_MODE,          // Open Mode
          0L);                // Extended Attribute Info

 // Copy the date and time into our format string and write the
 // data to the logfile to indicate when the machine was rebooted.
 sprintf (szDateTime,
          szFormat,
          szDayName [datetime.weekday],
          datetime.month,
          datetime.day,
          datetime.year,
          (datetime.hours + 11) % 12 + 1,
          datetime.minutes,
          datetime.seconds,
          datetime.hours / 12 ? 'P' : 'A');

 DosWrite (hfFile, szDateTime, strlen(szDateTime), &ulWritten);
 DosWrite (hfFile,  "\r\n", 2, &ulWritten);
 DosClose (hfFile);

 // Beep so we know this worked!
 DosBeep(1000, 1000);
 return TRUE;
}
```

Figure 17.25   Using the flush buffer hook.

```
BOOL APIENTRY WinReleaseHook (HAB     hab,
                             HMQ     hmq,
                             LONG    lHookType,
                             PFN     pfnHookProc,
                             HMODULE hmod);
```

Figure 17.26   The WinReleaseHook prototype.

- The **lHookType** parameter is the type of hook that was installed and is about to be released.
- The **pfnHookProc** parameter is the address of the hook procedure to be removed.
- The **hmod** parameter is the module handle that contains the application hook function. A NULLHANDLE used in this parameter indicates that the hook procedure was stored in the application's executable rather than a separate dynamic link library.

The code fragment shown in Figure 17.27 is the wrapper function used in PMHOOKS to release the input hook. The wrapper function is called **ReleaseInputHook**. The function is very simple. It is responsible for releasing the input hook by calling **WinReleaseHook** and unloading the dynamic

```
BOOL EXPENTRY ReleaseInputHook(VOID)
{
  BOOL rc;

  rc = WinReleaseHook(hab                     // Handle Anchor Block
                      NULLHANDLE,             // Hook System MsgQueue
                      HK_INPUT,               // Hook Type
                      pfnInputHook,           // Hook Handler
                      hMod);                  // DLL Needed for Hook

  // If the input hook can be released, then we need
  // to re-enable the default Print Screen functionality
  //and unload the module.
  if (rc)
    {
    DisablePrintScreenKey(FALSE);             // Enable PrintScreen
    DosFreeModule(hMod);
    }

  // Return the returned value of WinReleaseHook back to the caller
  return rc;
}
```

Figure 17.27   Releasing the input hook.

link library via **DosFreeModule**. The function also ensures that the default Print Screen key functionality is restored by calling the **DisablePrintScreenKey** function with a value of FALSE.

SUMMARY

Hooks provide an extremely powerful, built-in mechanism for applications to modify the behavior of certain system defaults. In order to use a hook, an application defines a simple hook procedure that will be dispatched within the context of a particular system function; thereby, providing the application a defined interface to the API layer. The Presentation Manager sub-systems, offer a wide variety of hooks that can be used by applications. Unfortunately, most of the defined hooks have been poorly documented. This chapter, along with the sample programs provided on the Wiley FTP site attempt to document the usage of some of these hooks. The PMSCREEN sample program attempts to demonstrate the practicality of using some of these hooks in the context of an application.

Sample Programs on Wiley's FTP Site

This book comes with a set of sample programs that correspond to the chapter text. There are sixteen useful sample programs in all, that are designed to illustrate the various programming topics covered in each chapter.

Having the complete source code for the sample programs is essential to understanding the concepts discussed throughout the book. The companion programs, along with the complete and documented source code can be obtained via anonymous FTP from the John Wiley & Sons FTP site. The FTP address for this site is **ftp.wiley.com**. The directory for the software in this book is /public/computer_books/OS2.

The following sample programs are included in the package:

Chapter 2:   **BUTTONS**   A program launcher that makes use of the standard PM controls. This chapter focuses on basic control concepts and shows some of the enhancements made to the basic control classes in OS/2 Warp.

Chapter 3   **PMED**   A fully functional text editor designed to demonstrate how to handle keyboard input and scrolling within a PM program.

Chapter 4:   **CLKDRAW**   A graphical drawing program that demonstrates how to programmatically handle the pointing device, the PM clipboard and advanced GPI concepts.

Chapter 5:   **HELPME**   A template program that shows how to implement context sensitive help using the Information Presentation Facility.

Chapter 6:   **THREADS**   A program designed to demonstrate several effective multi-threading techniques.

537

Chapter 7:	**DRAGEM**	A workplace shell compliant drag and drop file manager.
Chapter 9:	**PMEDIT**	A simple text editor that uses a multi-line entryfield as its edit window. This program concentrates on teaching the effective use of dialog windows and menus and implements a button bar.
Chapter 10:	**SUBCLASS**	A program that demonstrates the power of subclassing a control.
Chapter 11:	**CARDFILE**	A handy little address book program designed to show the practical use of the advanced OS/2 controls including, the notebook, value set, and slider.
Chapter 12:	**CHKREG**	This applet makes use of the powerful container control to create a simple check register program.
Chapter 13:	**MATCH**	If you have the multimedia Presentation Manager that comes with OS/2 Warp installed, you'll appreciate this fun little game. MATCH is a simple match game that makes use of the animated buttons found in MMPM.
Chapter 14:	**TUTOR**	This sample program focuses on the principles involved in designing and developing your own control windows. The tutor program is a simple button control implementation using half text and half button to create a control that is ideal for creating tutorial presentations.
Chapter 15:	**SHOWOFF**	This utility allows the user to create presentations using bitmap files.
Chapter 16:	**PRINTIT**	A simple utility that allows the user to print a text file. This program demonstrates the various concepts involved in printing from a Presentation Manager application.
Chapter 17:	**PMSCREEN**	A screen capture utility that allows the user to capture the contents of the active window on the desktop to bitmap. The bitmap can be copied to another program via the PM clipboard. The code demonstrates how to use PM hooks, and makes use of several of the most powerful and least documented PM hooks; including, the Input hook, FlushBuf hook, and Lockup hook.

INDEX